James Franklin B

AN INTRODUCTION

TO THE

EARLY HISTORY OF
CHRISTIAN DOCTRINE

TO THE TIME OF THE
COUNCIL OF CHALCEDON

Elibron Classics
www.elibron.com

Elibron Classics series.

© 2005 Adamant Media Corporation.

ISBN 1-4021-5770-3 (paperback)
ISBN 1-4212-7935-5 (hardcover)

This Elibron Classics Replica Edition is an unabridged facsimile
of the edition published in 1903 by Methuen & Co.,
London.

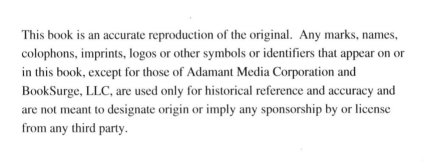

AN INTRODUCTION TO THE
EARLY HISTORY OF
CHRISTIAN DOCTRINE

AN INTRODUCTION
TO THE
EARLY HISTORY OF
CHRISTIAN DOCTRINE

TO THE TIME OF THE
COUNCIL OF CHALCEDON

J. F. BETHUNE-BAKER, B.D.
FELLOW AND DEAN OF PEMBROKE COLLEGE, CAMBRIDGE

36 ESSEX STREET W.C.
LONDON
1903

PREFACE

In the preparation of this volume the writer has been guided by the general purpose of the Series of Theological Handbooks of which it is a part. A continuous narrative is given in the text, with as much freedom from technical treatment as the subject allows; details and authorities are relegated to footnotes, and some special questions and difficulties are dealt with in notes appended to the several chapters.

The chief aim which has been kept in view throughout has been to offer to the student of the history of Christian Doctrine during the first four centuries of the life of the Church such information with regard to the facts and the sources as will enable him to prosecute his study for himself.

It is only a limited period with which the book deals, but a period in which the Christian theory of life—of the relations between God, the World, and Man—was worked out in its chief aspects, and all the doctrines to which the Church of Christ as a whole is pledged were framed. The 'authority' of these doctrines is only to be understood by study of their history. Their permanent value can only be appreciated by knowledge of the circumstances in which they came to be expressed, knowledge which must certainly precede any restatement of the doctrines, such as is from time to time demanded in the interests of a growing or a wider faith.

That Christian thinkers have been guided at various times, in later ages, towards fuller apprehension of various aspects of human life, and fuller knowledge of the divine economy, must be thankfully acknowledged. But whatever reason there is to hope for further elucidation from the growth of human knowledge in general, and the translation of old doctrines into the terms of the new knowledge, it seems certain that the work of the great leaders of Christian thought in the interpretation of the Gospel during the earlier ages can never be superseded. They were called upon, in turn, to meet and to consider in relation to the Gospel and to Jesus Christ nearly all the theories of the world and God which human speculation and experience have framed in explanation of the mystery of human life; and the conclusions which they reached must still be at least the starting-point for any further advance towards more complete solution of the problems with which they had to deal. Christians, whether conservative or progressive, will find in the study of the course through which doctrines were evolved their strongest stay and safeguard.

On the one hand, if defence of Christian doctrines be needed, it is found at its best in the bare history of the process by which they came into existence. On the other hand, in an age when other than the Catholic interpretations of the Gospel and of the Person of Christ are put forward and find favour in unexpected quarters, much heart-searching and laborious enquiry may be saved by the knowledge that similar or identical explanations were offered and ably advocated centuries ago; that they were tried, not only by intellectual but also by moral tests, and that the experience of life rejected them as inadequate or positively false. The semi-conscious Ebionism and the semi-conscious Docetism, for example, of much professedly Christian thought to-day may recognize itself in many an ancient 'heresy', and reconsider its position.

The mass of materials available for the study of even the limited part of the subject of Christian Doctrine which is dealt with in this book is so great that it has been necessary to exercise a strict economy in references to books and writers, ancient and modern, both English and German, from which much might be learned. I have only aimed at giving guidance to young students, leaving them to turn for fuller information to the larger well-known histories of Doctrine in general and the many special studies of particular doctrines. And as the book is designed to meet the needs of English students, I have seldom cited works that are not accessible to those who read no other language than their own.

I wish that every student of Christian Doctrine could have had the privilege of hearing the short course of lectures which Professor Westcott used to give in Cambridge. For my own part, I thankfully trace back to them the first intelligible conception of the subject which came before me. Some of these lectures were afterwards incorporated in the volume entitled *The Gospel of Life*.

Dr. Harnack's *History of Doctrines* occupies a position of eminence all its own, and will remain a monument of industry and learning, and an almost inexhaustible treasury of materials. To the English translation of this great work frequent references will be found in the following pages. But the student who is not able to examine the evidence and the conclusions, and to make allowances for Dr. Harnack's peculiar point of view, will still, in my judgement, find Hagenbach's *History of Doctrines* his best guide to his own work on the subject, although he will need sometimes to supplement the materials which were available when Hagenbach wrote.[1] He will learn a great deal also from Dorner's *Doctrine of the Person of Christ*, from Neander's *History of Christian Dogmas* and *Church History*, and from the works of the older English divines, such as Bull's *Defence of the Nicene Creed* and Pearson's *Exposition of the Creed*. Works such as these are in no way superseded by the many excellent books and treatises of later scholars, some of which are cited hereafter in regard to particular points.[2] Many of the articles in the *Dictionary of Christian Biography* (*ed.* Smith and Wace), the *Dictionary of Christian Antiquities* (*ed.* Smith and Cheetham), and Hastings' *Dictionary of the Bible* are of great value, while for the Creeds the collection of Hahn (*Bibliothek der Symbole und Glaubensregeln der alten Kirche*) is indispensable.

To two friends, who have special knowledge of different parts of the subject, I am much indebted for help in the revision of the proof-sheets—the Rev. A. E. Burn, rector of Kynnersley, and the Rev. J. H. Srawley, of Selwyn College, the latter in particular having generously devoted much time and care to the work. Their criticisms and suggestions have led in many cases to clearer statement of a point and to the insertion of notes and additional references which will make the book, I hope, in spite

---

[1] If he reads German he will do well to turn to Loofs' *Leitfaden zum Studium der Dogmengeschichte*[2] (Ritschlian), Seeberg's *Lehrbuch* (Protestant), and Schwane's *Dogmengeschichte*[2] (Roman Catholic). For introduction to the chief patristic writings he may consult Bardenhewer's *Patrologie*, or Swete's *Patristic Study* in the Series 'Handbooks for the Clergy'.

[2] Special attention may be directed to two volumes of this series—Mr. Ottley's *Doctrine of the Incarnation* and Mr. Burn's *Introduction to the History of the Creeds*, and to Dr. Swete's *The Apostles' Creed*.

of all the imperfections that remain, more useful for its purpose than it would otherwise have been.

In the earlier part of the book I had also the advantage of the criticism of Dr. Robertson, the Editor of this Series, who, even when the pressure of preparation for his removal from London to Exeter left him no leisure, most kindly made time for the purpose.

Finally, I have to thank the Syndics of the Cambridge University Press, and the Dean of Westminster, as Editor of the Series *Texts and Studies*, for permission to make use of various notes—and in some cases whole pages—from *The Meaning of Homoousios in the ' Constantinopolitan ' Creed*, which I contributed to that Series (vol. vii no. 1). I have not thought it necessary to include within inverted commas such passages as I have taken straight over, but when I have merely summarized conclusions, for which the evidence is more fully stated there, I have appended a reference to the volume.

The book, as I have indicated, makes no claim to originality. It only aims at being a sketch of the main lines of the historical developement of doctrine down to the time of the Council of Chalcedon.[1] But I am, of course, conscious that even history must be written from some ' point of view ', and I have expressed, as clearly as I can, the point of view from which I have approached the subject in the introduction which follows.

I believe that this point of view, from which Christian doctrines are seen as human attempts to interpret human experiences—the unique personality of Jesus of Nazareth supreme among those human experiences, is a more satisfying one than some standpoints from which the origin of Christian doctrines may appear to be invested with more commanding power of appeal. As such I have been accustomed to offer it to the attention of students at an age when the constraint is often felt for the first time to find some standpoint in these matters for oneself.

But any point of view—any kind of real personal conviction and appropriation—is better than none: and one which we

[1] Though much independent work over old ground has been bestowed upon it, and no previous writer has been followed without an attempt to form an independent judgement, yet the nature of the case precludes real independence, except to some extent in treatment.

cannot accept may serve to make clearer and more definite, or even to create, the point of view which is true for us. *Salvo jure communionis diversa sentire*—different opinions without loss of the rights of communion—opposite points of view without disloyalty to the Catholic Creeds and the Church— these words, which embody the conception of one of the earliest and keenest of Christian controversialists and staunchest of Catholics,[1] express a thought more widely honoured now than it was in Cyprian's day.

It is in the hope that this sketch of some parts of the early history of Christian doctrines may be useful in some such way that it is published now.

J. F. BETHUNE-BAKER.

PEMBROKE COLLEGE, CAMBRIDGE,
    1st May 1903.

[1] They are the words in which Augustine (*de Baptismo* 17—Migne *P.L.* xliii p. 202) describes the principles of Cyprian.

CONTENTS

CHAPTER I

INTRODUCTORY

CHAPTER II

THE BEGINNINGS OF DOCTRINES IN THE NEW TESTAMENT

CHAPTER III

THE DEVELOPEMENT OF DOCTRINE

CHAPTER IV

THE SOURCES OF DOCTRINE: ORAL TRADITION— HOLY SCRIPTURE

CHAPTER V

JEWISH ATTEMPTS AT INTERPRETATION. EBIONISM

CHAPTER VI

GENTILE ATTEMPTS AT INTERPRETATION. GNOSTICISM

CHAPTER VII

THE REACTION AGAINST GNOSTICISM.
MONARCHIANISM

CHAPTER VIII

THE CORRESPONDENCE BETWEEN DIONYSIUS OF ROME
AND DIONYSIUS OF ALEXANDRIA

b

CHAPTER IX

THE LOGOS DOCTRINE

CHAPTER X

TERTULLIAN'S DOCTRINE OF THE GODHEAD

CHAPTER XI

ORIGEN'S DOCTRINE OF THE GODHEAD

CHAPTER XIII

THE DOCTRINE OF THE HOLY SPIRIT AND THE TRINITY

CHAPTERS XIV–XVI—THE CHRISTOLOGICAL CONTROVERSIES OF THE FOURTH AND FIFTH CENTURIES

CHAPTER XIV

APOLLINARIANISM

CHAPTER XV

NESTORIANISM

CHAPTER XVI

EUTYCHIANISM

CHAPTER XVII

THE DOCTRINE OF MAN—SIN AND GRACE— PELAGIANISM

CHAPTER XVIII

THE DOCTRINE OF THE ATONEMENT

CHAPTER XIX

THE CHURCH

CHAPTER XX

THE SACRAMENTS—BAPTISM

CHAPTER XXI

THE SACRAMENTS—THE EUCHARIST

EARLY HISTORY OF
CHRISTIAN DOCTRINE

CHAPTER I

INTRODUCTORY

Christian Doctrines and Theology—Heresies

THE scope of this book is not the presentation of a system of
dogmatic theology, but only a sketch of the history of Christian
doctrine during the first four hundred years of its course. We
have not to attempt to gain a general view of Christian truth so
far as it has been realized at present in the Christian society,
but only to trace through some of its early stages the gradual
developement of doctrine.

Christianity—the student of Christian doctrine needs always
to remember—is not a system, but a life ; and Christian doctrine
is the interpretation of a life. Jesus taught few, if any, doctrines : his mission was not to propound a system of metaphysics
or of ethics. If the question be put, What is the Christian
revelation ? the answer comes at once. The Christian revelation
is Christ himself. And Christian doctrine is an attempt to
describe the person and life of Jesus, in relation to Man and the
World and God : an attempt to interpret that person and life
and make it intelligible to the heart and mind of men. Or,
from a slightly different point of view, it may be said that
Christian doctrines are an attempt to express in words of formal
statement the nature of God and Man and the World, and the
relations between them, as revealed in the person and life of
Jesus.

The history of Christian doctrine must therefore shew the

manner in which these statements were drawn up, the circumstances which called them forth: how the meaning of the earthly life and experiences of Jesus was more and more fully disclosed to the consciousness of the Church in virtue of her own enlarged experience.

The history of Christian doctrine is not concerned with the evidences of Christianity, internal or external; nor with the proof or the defence of the 'doctrines' thus formulated. That is the province of Apologetics. Nor does it deal with religious controversy, or Polemics, except so far as such controversy has actually contributed to the developement of doctrine and the elucidation of difficulties. Thus, while we have to follow up the history of many heresies, we have to do this only in so far as they constitute one of the most impressive instances of the great law of 'Progress through Conflict' which is written over the history of human life:—the law that the ultimate attainment of the many is rendered possible only by the failure of the few, that final success is conditioned by previous defeat.[1]

The supreme end to which Christian theology is directed is the full intellectual expression of the truth which was manifested to men, once for all, in the person and life of Jesus; and the history of Christian doctrine is the record of the steps which

---

[1] In this way 'heresies' have rendered no small service to theological science. The defence of the doctrines impugned and the discussion of the points at issue ed to a deeper and clearer view of the subject. Subtle objections when carefully weighed, and half-truths when exposed, became the occasion of more accurate statements. "A clear, coherent, and fundamental presentation is one of the strongest arguments. Power of statement is power of argument. It precludes misrepresentation; it corrects mis-statements" (Shedd). It is true the early Christian 'orthodox' writers seldom regard the influence of 'heretics' as anything but pernicious (*e.g.* Eusebius reflects the popular opinion that all heretics were agents of the devil, and applies to them such epithets as these—grievous wolves, a pestilent and scabby disease, incurable and dangerous poison, more abominable than all shame, double-mouthed and two-headed serpents. See *H.E.* i 1; ii 1, 13; iii 26–29; iv 7, 29, 30; v 13, 14, 16–20). Yet some of the greatest of the Fathers were able to recognize this aspect of the matter. See Origen *Hom. ix in Num.*: "Nam si doctrina ecclesiastica simplex esset et nullis intrinsecus haereticorum dogmatum assertionibus cingeretur, non poterat tam clara et tam examinata videri fides nostra. Sed idcirco doctrinam catholicam contradicentium obsidet oppugnatio, ut fides nostra non otio torpescat, sed exercitiis elimetur." And similarly (as Cyprian *de unit. eccles.* 10, before him), Augustine *Confess.* vii 19 (25), could write: "Truly the refutation of heretics brings into clearer relief the meaning of thy Church and the teaching of sound doctrine. For there needs must be heresies, in order that those who are approved may be made manifest among the weak." (Cf. Aug. *de Civ. Dei* xviii 51.)

were taken in order to reach the end in view—the record of the partial and progressive approximation to that end.[1] For several centuries men were but 'feeling after' satisfactory expressions of this truth. To many of them St Paul's words to the Athenians on the Areopagus still applied.[2] Even those who accepted Jesus and the Christian revelation with enthusiasm were still groping in the dark to find a systematic expression of the faith that filled their hearts. They experienced the difficulty of putting into words their feelings about the Good-News. Language was inadequate to pourtray the God and the Saviour whom they had found. Not even the great interpreters of the first generation were enabled to transmit to future ages the full significance of the life which they had witnessed. And as soon as ever men went beyond the simple phrases of the apostolic writers and, instead of merely repeating by rote the scriptural words and terms, tried to express in their own language the great facts of their faith, they naturally often used terms which were inadequate—which, if not positively misleading, erred by omission and defect. Such expressions, when the consequences flowing from them were more clearly seen, and when they were proved by experience to be inconsistent with some of the fundamental truths of Christianity, a later age regarded only as 'archaisms', if it was clear that those who used them intended no opposition to the teaching of the Church.[3] Often, it is evident, men were led into 'heresy' by the attempt to combine with the new religion ideas derived from other systems of thought. From all quarters converts pressed into the Church, bringing with them a different view of life, a different way of looking at such questions; and they did not easily make the new point of view their own. They embraced Christianity at one point

---

[1] Professor Westcott used to define Christian doctrine as 'a partial and progressive approximation to the full intellectual expression of the truth manifested to men once for all in the Incarnation'. Cf. *Gospel of Life*.

[2] Acts 17[27].

[3] Thus Augustine *de Praedestinatione* c. 14, says: "What is the good of scrutinizing the works of men who before the rise of that heresy had no need to busy themselves with this question, which is so hard to solve. Beyond doubt they would have done so, if they had been obliged to give an answer on the subject." So against the Pelagians he vindicates Cyprian, Ambrose, and Rufinus. Cf. *de dono Perseverantiae* c. 20, and the two volumes of his own *Retractations*. In like manner Athanasius defended Dionysius of Alexandria against the Arians (see *infra*), and Pelagius II (*Ep.* 5. 921) declared "Holy Church weigheth the hearts of her faithful ones with kindliness rather than their words with rigour".

or another, not at all points; and they tried to bring the expression of Christian doctrine into harmony with preconceived ideas. And not unfrequently it would seem that Christian thinkers and teachers, conscious of the force of objections from outside, or impressed by the conviction that beliefs which were widely current must contain some element of truth, were induced to go half-way to meet the views of those they wished to win. In the main, however, it would appear that 'heresies' arose from the wish to understand. The endowments of man include a mind and a reasoning faculty, and doctrine which is offered to him as an interpretation of the whole of his being—the whole of his life—he must needs try to grasp with the whole of his nature. He must try to make it his own and express it in his own words, or else it cannot be real to him, it cannot be living. In this process he is certain to make mistakes. And the remarkable fact about the history of Christian theology is that in almost every case the expression of Christian doctrine was drawn out—was indeed forced upon the Church as a whole—by the mistakes of early theologians. By their mistakes the general feeling of the faithful—the great common sense of the Catholic Church—was aroused, and set to work to find some phrase which would exclude the error and save the members of the Church in future from falling into a like mistake. So it was that the earliest creeds were of the scantiest dimensions, and slowly grew to their present form, step by step, in the process of excluding—on the part of the Church as a whole —the erroneous interpretations of individual members of the Church. Such individuals had drawn their inferences too hastily: fuller knowledge, longer deliberation, and consideration of all the consequences which would flow from their conclusions shewed them to be misleading, inadequate to account for all the facts. Those who persisted in the partial explanation, the incomplete and therefore misleading theory, after it had been shewn to be inadequate, the Church called heretics, factious subverters of truth. Clearly they could not be allowed to proclaim a mutilated gospel under the shelter of the Catholic Church. As members of that Church they had initiated discussion and stimulated interest, without which progress in knowledge, the developement of doctrine—the nearer approximation to a full interpretation—would have been impossible. But when they seized on a few facts as though they were all the facts, and from these few framed theories to explain and interpret all; when they put forward a meagre and immature conception as a full-grown representation of the Christian idea of life,—then the accredited teachers of Christianity were bound to protest against the one-sided partial developement, and to meet it by expansions of the creed which should exclude the error, and to frame formal statements of the mind of the Church to serve as guides to future generations—landmarks to prevent their straying from the line of ascertained truth. So creeds grew, and heresies were banished from the Church.

DOGMA

The word properly means that which has seemed good, been agreed or decided upon: so an opinion, and particularly, as having been determined by authority, a decree or an edict, or a precept. In this sense it is used by Plato, and Demosthenes, and in the Septuagint; and in the New Testament of (1) a particular edict of the emperor (Luke 2¹); (2) the body of such edicts (Acts 17⁷); (3) the ordinances of the Mosaic law (Eph. 2¹⁵, Col. 2¹⁴); (4) the decisions of the apostles and elders at the 'Council' at Jerusalem (Acts 16⁴, cf. 15²⁰), which dealt particularly with ritual questions. It is nowhere in the New Testament used of the contents or 'doctrines' of Christianity. The Stoics, however, employed the word to express the theoretical 'principles' of their philosophy (e.g. Marc. Aurel. *Medit.* 2. 3, ταῦτά σοι ἀρκείτω, ἀεὶ δόγματα ἔστω), and it bears a similar sense in the first Christian writers who used it: Ignatius *ad Magn.* 13, 'the dogmata of the Lord and the Apostles' (here perhaps 'rules of life'); *the Didache* 11. 3 (a similar sense), and Barnabas *Ep.* 1. 6, 9. 7, 10. 1, 9; and more precisely in the Greek Apologists, to whom Christianity was a philosophy of life, who apply the word to the doctrines in which that philosophy was formulated. And ˙though much later Basil *de Spiritu Sancto* 27 seems to contrast δόγματα, as rites and ceremonies with mystic meaning derived from tradition, with κηρύγματα, as the contents of the Gospel teaching and Scripture; yet generally the term in the plural denoted the whole substance of Christian doctrine (see e.g. Cyril of Jerusalem *Cat.* iv 2, where δόγμα as relating to faith is contrasted with πρᾶξις, which has to do with moral action: "The way of godliness is composed of these two things, pious doctrines and good actions,"—the former being the source of the latter; and Socrates *Hist.* ii 44, where δόγμα is similarly set in antithesis to ἡ ἠθικὴ διδασκαλία). Hence the general significance—a doctrine which in the eyes of the Church is essential in the true interpretation of the Christian faith, and therefore one the acceptance of which may be required of all Christians (*i.e.* not merely a subjective opinion or conception of a particular theologian). It is not the interpretation of any individual, or of any particular community, that can be trusted. Just as the œcumenicity of a council depends upon its acknowledgement by the Church as a whole, and a council at which the whole Church was not represented might attain the honour of œcumenicity by subsequent recognition and acceptance (*e.g.* the Council of Constantinople of 381); so no 'dogma' (though individuals may contribute to its expression) is authoritative till it has passed the test of the general feeling of the Church as a whole, the 'communis sensus fidelium', and by that been accepted.

Αἵρεσις—HERESY

Αἵρεσις, the verbal noun from αἱρέω, αἱρεῖσθαι, is commonly used both in the active sense of 'capture' and in the middle sense of 'choice'. It is the middle sense only with which we are concerned, and especially the limited sense of 'choice of an opinion'. Hence it is used of those who have chosen a particular opinion of their own, and follow it—a 'school of thought', a party, the followers of a particular teacher or principle.

In this usage the word is originally colourless and neutral, implying neither that the opinion chosen is true nor that it is false.

So it is used in the New Testament of the 'schools' of the Sadducees (Acts 5¹⁷) and Pharisees (Acts 15⁵), and of the Christians—'the αἵρεσις of the Nazaraeans' (Acts 24⁵. ¹⁴). It is true that in all these cases the word is used by those who are unfavourably disposed to the schools of thought which are referred to; but disparagement is not definitely associated with it. And Constantine uses it of the doctrine of the Catholic Church (ἡ αἵρεσις ἡ καθολική—Euseb. x 5. 21), just as Tertullian frequently uses 'secta'.

But though the Christian Society as a whole may be in this way designated a αἵρεσις, inside the Society there is no room for αἱρέσεις. There must not be 'parties' within the Church. It is Christ himself who is divided into parts, if there are (1 Cor. 1¹³). And so, as applied to diversities of opinion among Christians themselves, the word assumes a new colour (1 Cor. 11¹⁹), and is joined to terms of such evil significance as ἐριθεῖαι 'factions' and διχοστασίαι 'divisions' (Gal. 5²⁰).

The transition from the earlier to the later meaning of the word is well seen in the use of the adjective in Tit. 3¹⁰, where St Paul bids Titus have nothing to do with a man who is αἱρετικός if he is unaffected by repeated admonition. This is clearly the 'opinionated' man, who obstinately holds by his own individual choice of opinion ('obstinate', 'factious'). So the man who in matters of doctrine forms his own opinion, and, though it is opposed to the *communis sensus fidelium*, will not abandon it when his error is pointed out, is a 'heretic'.

To the question What is the cause of heresies? different answers were given. The cause was not God, and not the Scriptures. "Do not tell me the Scripture is the cause." It is not the Scripture that is the cause, but the foolish ignorance of men (*i.e.* of those who interpret amiss what has been well and rightly said)—so Chrysostom declares (*Hom.* 128 p. 829). The cause is rather to be sought in (1) the Devil—so 1 Tim. 4[1] was understood and Matt. 13[25]: Eusebius reflects this common opinion; (2) the careless reading of Holy Scripture—"It is from this source that countless evils have sprung up—from ignorance of the Scriptures: from this source the murrain of heresies has grown" (Chrys. *Præf. Ep. ad Rom.*); and (3) contentiousness, the spirit of pride and arrogance.

As to the nature of their influence and the reason why God permits their existence, see *supra* p. 2 note 1. On the latter point appeal was made to St Paul's words 1 Cor. 11[19], "for there must be 'heresies' among you, in order that those that are approved may become manifest among you." Heresies serve as a touchstone of truth; they test and try the genuineness of men's faith. So Chrysostom (*Hom.* 46 p. 867) says they make the truth shine out more clearly. "The same thing is seen in the case of the prophets. False prophets arose, and by comparison with them the true prophets shone out the more. So too disease makes health plain, and darkness light, and tempest calm." And again (*Hom.* 54 p. 363) he says: "It is one thing to take your stand on the true faith, when no one tries to trip you up and deceive you: it is another thing to remain unshaken when thousands of waves are breaking against you."

Θεολογία—θεολογεῖν

Four stages in the history of these words may be detected.

(1) They were originally used of the old Greek poets who told their tales of the gods, and gave their explanations of life and the universe in the form of such myths. Such are the 'theogonies' of Hesiod and Orpheus, and the 'cosmogonies' of Empedocles. These men were the θεολόγοι of what is called the prescientific age. It was in the actions of the gods—their loves and their hates—that they found the answer to the riddles of existence. So later writers (as Plutarch, Suetonius, and Philo) use the expression τὰ θεολογούμενα in the sense of 'inquiries into the divine nature' or 'discussions about the gods'.

(2) Still later the words are used to express the attribution of divine origin or causation to persons or things, which are thus regarded as divine or at least are referred to divine causes. So in the sense 'ascribe

divinity to', 'name as God', 'call God', 'assert the divinity of', the verb θεολογεῖν is used by Justin *Dial.* 56 (in conjunction with κυριολογεῖν), by the writer of the Little Labyrinth (θεολογῆσαι τὸν χριστόν, οὐκ ὄντα θεόν—'call Christ God, though he is not God'—Eusebius *H.E.* v 28), and by later writers of all the Persons of the Trinity and in other connexions.[1]

(3) The verb is found in a more general sense 'make religious investigations' in Justin *Dial.* 113; while in Athenagoras *Leg.* 10, 20, 22 the noun expresses the doctrine of God and of all beings to whom the predicate 'deity' belongs. (Cf. also the Latin 'theologia'—Tertullian *ad Nat.* II 2.)

(4) Aristotle describes θεολογία as ἡ πρώτη φιλοσοφία, and to the Stoics the word was equivalent to 'philosophy'—a system of philosophical principles or truths. For Hellenic Christians at least the transition from this usage to the sense familiar now was easy. Theology is the study or science that deals with God, the philosophy of life that finds in God the explanation of the existence of man and the world, and endeavours to work out theoretically this principle in all its relations; while Christian theology in a specific sense starts from the existence of Jesus, and from him and his experiences, his person, his life, his teaching, frames its theories of the Godhead, of man, and of the world. (See note on the words, Harnack *Dogmengeschichte* Eng. tr. vol. ii p. 202, Sophocles *Lexicon*, and Suicer *Thesaurus.*)

---

[1] In relation to the Son, in particular, θεολογία is used of all that relates to the divine and eternal nature and being of Christ, as contrasted with οἰκονομία, which has reference especially to the Incarnation and its consequences (so Lightfoot notes *Apost. Fathers* II ii p. 75). But this is only a particular usage of the term in a restricted sense.

CHAPTER II

The Beginnings of Doctrines in the New Testament

CHRISTIAN theology (using the word in the widest sense) is, as we have seen, the attempt to explain the mystery of the existence of the world and of man by the actual existence of Jesus. It is in him, in his experiences—in what he was, what he felt, what he thought, what he did—that Christian theology finds the solution of the problem. In the true interpretation of him and of his experiences we have, accordingly, the true interpretation of human life as a whole. In tracing the history of Christian doctrines, we have therefore to begin with the earliest attempts at such interpretation. These, at least the earliest which are accessible to us at all, are undoubtedly to be found in the collection of writings which form the New Testament. We are not here concerned with apologetic argument or history of the canon, with questions of exact date of writing or of reception of particular books. We are only concerned with the fact that, be the interpretation true or untrue, apostolic or sub-apostolic, or later still, the interpretations of the person of Jesus which are contained in these books are the earliest which are extant. In different books he is regarded from different points of view: even the writers who purpose to give a simple record of the facts of his life and teaching approach their task with different conceptions of its nature; in their selection of facts—the special prominence they give to some—they are unconsciously essaying the work of interpretation as well as that of mere narration. " The historian cannot but interpret the facts which he records." The student of the history of Christian doctrines is content that they should be accepted as interpreters: to shew that they are also trustworthy historians is no part of his business. From the pages of the New Testament there is to be drawn, beyond all question, the record of the actual experiences of the Christians nearest to the time of Jesus of whom we have any record at all. Their record of their own experiences, and their interpretations of them and of him who was the source of all, are the starting-point from which the developement of Christian doctrines proceeds. In this sense the authors of the Gospels and Epistles are the first writers on Christian theology.[1] No less certainly than later writers, if less professedly and with more security against error, they tried to convey to others the impression which Jesus, himself or through his earliest followers, had made upon them. In him they saw not only the medium of a revelation, but the revelation itself. What had before been doubtful about the purpose of the world and of human life—its origin and its destiny —all became clear and certain as they studied him, and from the observations which they could make of him, and of his relations to his environment, framed their inductions. Not only from his words, but from his acts and his whole life and conduct, they framed a new conception of God, a new conception of His relations to mankind, a new conception of the true relations of one man to another. They could measure the gulf that separates man as he is from man as he is meant to be, and they learnt how he might yet attain to the destiny which he had forfeited. Under the impulse of these conceptions—this revelation—the authors of the Gospels compiled their narratives, and the writers of the other books of the New Testament dealt with the matters which came in their way. Their method is not systematic:

---

[1] If it were necessary for our present purpose to attempt to discriminate nicely between the various ideas expressed in different writings of the New Testament, we might begin with the earliest and work from them to the later—on the chance of finding important developements. We might thus begin with the earlier epistles of St Paul, and shew what conceptions of the Godhead and of the person and work of Christ underlie, and are presupposed by, the teaching which he gives and the allusions which imply so full a background of belief on the part of those to whom he writes. And then we might go on to compare with these earliest conceptions what we could discover in the writings of later date that seemed different or of later developement. But this would be an elaborate task in itself, and without in any way doubting that further reflection and enlarged experience led to corresponding expansion and fulness and elucidation of the conceptions of the early teachers of the Gospel, it seems clear that some of the books of the New Testament which are later in time of composition (as we have them now) contain the expression of the earliest conceptions ; and therefore, for the purpose before us, we need not try to discriminate as to time and origin between the various points of view which the various writings of the New Testament reveal. We need only note the variety, and observe that the conceptions are complementary one to another.

it is in the one case narrative, and in the other occasional. But in no case are we left in doubt as to the interpretations which they had formed and accepted. It is, for example, absurd to suppose that the doctrine of the Person of Jesus which they held did not correspond to the teaching which they record that he gave of his own relation to God. And when an Apostle claims to have received his mission directly from Jesus himself, and not from men or through any human agency, it is obvious that he regards him as the source of divine authority. The writers of the New Testament have not formulated their interpretations in systematic or logical form perhaps; but they have framed them nevertheless, and the history of Christian doctrines must begin by an account of the doctrines expressed or implied in the earliest writings of Christians that are extant, and then proceed to trace through later times variations or developements from the interpretations which were then accepted as true.

The existence of God and of the world and of man is—needless to say—assumed throughout; and it is certain that the doctrine of creation by God (through whatever means) was accepted by all the writers before us, inherited as it would be from the Scriptures of the Jews. Of other doctrines all were not certainly held by all the writers, and in the short statement of them which can rightly have a place here it will only be necessary to indicate the main points. We shall take in order God (the Trinity), Man, the relations between God and Man (Atonement), the means by which the true relations are to be maintained (the Church, the Sacraments).

The doctrines are, as has been said, expressed in incidental or in narrative form, and so it is from incidental allusions and from the general tenour of the narrative that we infer them. They grow up before the reader.

The Doctrine of God in the New Testament

The doctrine of God, for example, is nowhere explicitly stated. It is easy, however, to see that there are three main conceptions which were before the writers of the New Testament. The three descriptions of God as Father, as Spirit, and as Love, express together a complete and comprehensive doctrine of the Godhead; and though the three descriptions are specially characteristic of different writers or groups of writings, respectively, yet it is easy to see that the thought of God as Spirit and as Love is present and natural to the minds of the writers who use more readily the description of him as Father, which indeed is the title regularly employed by all the writers of the New Testament.[1] It is the conception of God as Father that is most original. Not that the conception was entirely new.

The doctrine of God which is to be found in the pages of the New Testament has doubtless for its background the Jewish monotheistic belief, but the belief in the form in which it presented itself to the psalmists and the prophets rather than to the scribes and rabbis. To the latter the ancient faith of their fathers in one God, tenaciously maintained against the many gods of the nations round about them, had come to convey the idea of an abstract Unit far removed from all contact with the men and the world He had created, self-centred and self-absorbed, the object of a distant reverence and awe. The former, on the contrary, were above all else dominated by the sense of intimate personal relation between themselves and God; and it is this conviction—the certainty that such a close communion and fellowship exists—that the followers of Jesus discerned in him and learnt from his experience. But in his experience and in his teaching the conviction assumed a form so different from that in which the prophets realized it, that his conception of God seems to stand alone. Others had realized God as Father of the universe (the Creator and Sustainer of the physical world and of animate things), and by earlier teachers of the Jews He had been described as—in a moral and spiritual sense—Father of Israel and Israelites,[2] but their sense of 'fatherhood' had been limited and obscured by other conceptions.[3] In the experience and teaching of Jesus this one conception of God as Father controlled and determined everything. It is first of all a conviction personal and peculiar to

[1] The writer to the Hebrews is perhaps an exception, but see Heb. 1[2, 5] 12[9].

[2] See the references given by Dr. Sanday, Art. 'God' in Hastings' *D.B.* vol. ii p. 208 (*e.g.* Deut. 1[31] 8[5] 32[6], Ps. 103[13], Jer. 3[4,19], Isa. 63[16] 64[8]); and for the whole subject see, besides that article, G. F. Schmid *Biblical Theology of the New Testament.*

[3] In particular the image according to which Israel is depicted as Jehovah's bride, faithless to her marriage covenant, is incompatible with the thought expressed by the Fatherhood of God. One broad difference cannot be missed. In the one image the main thought is the jealous desire of God to receive man's undivided devotion, in the other it is His readiness to bestow His infinite love on man.

himself,—'My Father', he claimed Him.[1] But he also spoke of Him to his disciples as 'your Father',[2] and so the intimacy of relationship which they saw he realized they came to look upon as possible too for them,—and not only for them—the first disciples of Jesus—but also for all mankind. The Fatherhood of God extended to the good and the evil alike, the just and the unjust; and to all animate things—even the fowls of the air. God was Father in the highest and fullest sense of the word. So the earliest followers of Jesus understood his teaching and explained his life. That they also thought of God as essentially spiritual will not be disputed. The idea of God as 'Spirit' is in one sense co-ordinate with the idea of Him as 'Father', though definite expression is scarcely given to the idea except in the writings of St John.[3] This special description or conception brings into prominence certain characteristics which must not be passed over. The absolute elevation of God above the world and men is expressed when He is designated Spirit, just as the most intimate communion between men's life and His is expressed when He is styled their Father. As Spirit He is omnipresent, all pervading, eternal, and raised above all limitations.[4] He is the source of all life, so that apart from Him and knowledge of Him there can be no true life.[5]

When to the descriptions of God as Father and as Spirit St John adds the description that is—in words—all his own, and declares that the very essence of the being of God is Love;[6] when he thus sums up in a single word the revelation of the teaching and life of Jesus, he certainly makes a contribution to

[1] *E.g.* both as to natural and as to spiritual life, Matt. 11[27] 6[4, 6, 8], John 2[16] 5[17]. Cf. St Paul's frequent use of the phrase 'the Father of our Lord Jesus Christ', *e.g.* Col. 1[3], Eph. 1[3], 2 Cor. 1[3] 11[31], Rom. 15[6]; cf. 1 Pet. 1[3],—though he commonly writes 'God *the* Father', or 'our Father'.

[2] Matt. 6[8, 15] 10[20], Luke 6[36]. Cf. '*Our* Father', Matt. 6[9]; 'My Father and your Father', John 20[17]. The common addition of the designation 'heavenly', or 'that is in heaven', serves to mark the spiritual and transcendent character of the relation.

[3] *E.g.* John 4[24]. He alone has preserved the definite utterance of Jesus, 'God is Spirit', as he alone proclaims that 'God is Love'.

[4] *E.g.* Matt. 6[4, 6, 18], John 4[21].   [5] John 5[21, 26]; cf. 5[17] 17[3].

[6] John 4[8]. Though a triune personality in the Godhead is implied if God is essentially Love (cf. Augustine *de Trinitate* vi and viii), it does not appear that St John's statement was charged with this meaning to himself. It seems rather, from the context, to be used to express the spiritual and moral relation in which God stands to man (cf. John 3[16]), and not to be intended to have explicit reference to the distinctions within the Godhead.

Christian doctrine which is of the highest value. It is not too much to say that in the sentence 'God is Love' we have an interpretation of the Gospel which covers all the relations between God and man. And yet it is only the essential character of all true fatherhood that the words express. St John is only explaining by another term the meaning of Father, whatever fresh light he may throw upon the title by his explanation.

And all the other descriptions of God which are to be found in the New Testament add nothing to these three main thoughts; indeed, they only draw out in more detail the significance of the relationship expressed by the one word Father.[1]

But much more is implied as to the Godhead by St John's account of the sayings of Jesus in which he declared his own one-ness with the Father [2]—teaching which obviously lies at the back of the thought of St Paul [3] and of the writer to the Hebrews.[4] And more again is seen in the references to the Paraclete, the Spirit of truth, in the Gospel according to St John,[5] and to the Holy Spirit in the other books of the New Testament.[6] The Son and the Holy Spirit alike have divine functions to perform, and are in closest union with the Father. There are distinctions within the Godhead, but the distinctions are such as are compatible with unity of being. There is Father, there is Son, and there is Holy Spirit. Each is conceived as having a distinct existence and a distinct activity in a sphere of his own: but the being of each is divine, and there is only one Divine Being. Thus to say that the Godhead is one in essence, but contains within itself three relations, three modes of exist-

[1] As, for example, when God is described as holy and righteous, or as merciful and gracious; as judging justly, or as patient and long-suffering. In all aspects God is absolutely good, the standard and type of moral perfection, and His love is always actively working (Matt. 19[17], Luke 18[19], Mark 5[48] 7[11], John 3[16]).

[2] See John 1[18] 14[7-11]. Cf. John 10[38] 13[20] 14[9. 20] 15[24] 16[23], 1 John 1[1-3], Matt. 11[27].

[3] Cf. 2 Cor. 4[4], Col. 1[15], Phil. 2[6] (Christ the 'image' of God, and existent 'in the form' of God).

[4] Heb. 1[3] (the Son the 'effulgence of the glory' and the 'exact impress of the very being' of God). John 1[1-5], Phil. 2[6-8], Col. 1[15-18], and Heb. 1[1-3] should be carefully compared together.

[5] John 14[16-26] 15[26] 16[7-14].

[6] The baptismal commission, Matt. 28[19], which co-ordinates the Three would be the simplest and most decisive evidence, but if it be disallowed there remains in the New Testament ample evidence to the same effect (see the Pauline equivalent 2 Cor. 13[14], Rom. 8[26], 1 Cor. 12[11], Eph. 4[30]).

ence, is always at the same time actively existent in three distinct spheres of energy: this is only to say what is clearly implied in the language of the Gospels and Epistles, though the conception is not expressed in set terms, but is embodied in the record of actual experience. As from Jesus himself his disciples derived, in the first place, their consciousness of God as Father, so from him - they first learnt of God as Holy Spirit; but their realization of what was at first perhaps accepted on the evidence of his experience only, was soon quickened by experiences of their own which seemed to be obvious manifestations of the working of God as Holy Spirit.[1]

The doctrine of a triune God—Father, Son, and Spirit— is required and implied by the whole account of the revelation and the process of redemption; but the pages of the New Testament do not shew anything like an attempt to enter into detailed explanations of the inner being of God in the threefold relation.

It is to this fact that we must look for the explanation of the subsequent course of Christian thought, and the puzzling emergence of theories that seem to be so utterly at variance with the natural interpretation of the apostolic writings that we find it difficult to understand how they could ever have claimed the authority of Scripture. There are at least three points which must be noted. First, the New Testament leaves a clear impression of three agents, but the unity and equality of the three remains obscure and veiled. Secondly, the doctrine of the Incarnation is plainly asserted, but the exact relation and connexion between the human and the divine is not defined; there is no attempt to indicate how the pre-existing Christ is one with the man Jesus—how he is at the same time Son of God as before, and yet Son of Man too as he was not before; and how as Son of Man he can still continue to be equal with the Father. Thirdly, that the Spirit is divine is assumed, but that he is pre-existent and personal is an inference that might not seem to be inevitable. And so it was with these points that subsequent controversy dealt,—controversy that resulted in resolving ambiguities, and led to the clearer and fuller expression of the Christian conception of God.

[1] Such experiences are represented as beginning on the day of Pentecost, and as continuing all through the history recorded in the Acts of the Apostles; and they are also implied, if not actually expressed, in most of the Epistles.

The Doctrine of Man in the New Testament

In like manner, with regard to the conception which the writers of the New Testament, the first Christian theologians, had formed of man and his place in the universe, we find no full and systematic expression, but only a number of isolated—and for the most part incidental—indications of a doctrine.

The teaching of the Old Testament must be assumed as the background and as the starting-point, so far at least as regards, on the one side, the dignity of man—as made in the image of God [1] and destined to attain to the likeness of God; and, on the other side, his failure to fulfil his destiny, and his need of supernatural aid to effect his redemption.

At the outset it is clear that the doctrine of the Fatherhood of God in itself declares the dignity of human nature. Man is by his constitution the child of God, capable of intimate union and personal fellowship with God. It is on this relationship that the chief appeals of Jesus are based: it is to make men conscious of their position that most of his teaching was directed. It is to make them realize the sense of privilege, which it allows, that was the chief object of his life. It is because of this kinship that men are bidden to be perfect, even as their Father which is in heaven is perfect.[2] For this reason they are to look to heaven rather than to earth as the treasury of all that they value most.[3] Man is so constituted that he is capable of knowing the divine will and of desiring to fulfil it;[4] he has a faculty by virtue of which spiritual insight is possible,[5]—he can not only receive intimations of the truth, but also examine and test what he receives and form right judgements in regard to it.[6] Such, it is clear, is the sense in which the writers of the Gospels understood the teaching of Jesus, and the same theory of the high capacities of human nature is presupposed and implied by the general tenour of the teaching of St Paul.

At the same time the free play of this spiritual element in man is hindered by the faculties which bind him to earth—the elements represented by 'the flesh'; and the contrast between

---

[1] The phrase clearly refers to mental and moral faculties, such as the intellect, the will, the affections.

[2] Matt. 5⁴⁸.   [3] Matt. 6¹⁹ ff.

[4] *E.g.* John 5¹⁷.   [5] *E.g.* Matt. 6²²· ²³, Luke 11³⁴⁻³⁶.

[6] *E.g.* Matt. 11¹⁵ 13¹⁴, Mark 4²⁴, Luke 12⁵⁶· ⁵⁷, John 7²⁴.

them and the higher constituent is strongly expressed—'the spirit is willing, but the flesh is weak'.[1] And so at the same time there is declared the corruption of human nature in its present state, so that sin is a habitual presence in man, from which he can escape only by the aid of a power which is not his own, even though that power must work by arousing and quickening forces which are already latent in him.

As to the nature of sin the pages of the New Testament reflect the teaching of the Old. The account of the Fall of Adam shews the essence of sin to be the wilful departure on the part of man from the course of developement for which he was designed (the order determined by God, and therefore the order natural to him); and the assertion of his will against the will of God. The result of sin is thus a disordered world—a race of men not fulfilling the law of their nature and alienated from God, who is the source and the sustainer of their life. Exactly these conceptions are embodied in the treatment of the matter which is recorded, on the part of Jesus and the earliest Christian teachers, in the New Testament itself. The commonest words for sin denote definitely the missing of a mark or the breach of a law, the failure to attain an end in view or the neglect of principle.[2] And the other words which are used imply the same point of view: sin is a 'trespass' or 'transgression', that is, a departure from the right path which man is meant to tread; or it is 'debt', in the sense that there was an obligation laid upon man, a responsibility to live in a particular way, which he has not fulfilled and observed.[3] This manner of describing sin shews that it is by no means thought of as an act, or a series of acts, of wrong-doing. It is rather a state or condition, a particular way of living, which is described as sickness,[4] or even, by contrast with true life, as death. Those who are living under such conditions are 'dead'.[5] Of this state the opposite is life, or life eternal—a particular way of living now, characteristic of

---

[1] Matt. 26⁴¹, cf. John 3⁶: "That which is begotten of the flesh is flesh, and that which is begotten of the Spirit is spirit." Similarly 'flesh and blood' together Matt. 16¹⁷. ('Flesh' is the name by which mankind was commonly expressed in the Hebrew Scriptures, with particular reference to its weaker and more 'material' constituents.)

[2] The words ἁμαρτία and ἀνομία—the essence of sin (ἁμαρτία) being declared by St John to be lawlessness or the absence of law (ἀνομία) 1 John 3⁴.

[3] The words παράπτωμα, παράβασις, ὀφείλημα.

[4] *E.g.* Matt. 9¹². 　　　　　　　[5] *E.g.* John 5²¹⁻²⁵.

2

which is knowledge of God and love of the brethren.[1] It is to give this knowledge and to quicken this love that is declared to be the special object of the life and death of Jesus.[2] The condition of sin is one of estrangement from God and selfish disregard of what is due to others. It is a state which merits and involves punishment, and yet at the same time is its own punishment.[3]

[1] John 17³ 6⁶³· ⁴⁷ 3³⁶ 5⁴⁰ and 5²⁴.   [2] John 10¹⁰ 13³⁵ 15¹³, 1 John 4⁸.

[3] The conception of sin expressed in St Paul's epistles, though not essentially different from the conceptions which are reflected in other writings of the New Testament, is characteristic enough to call for special notice.

It was the common belief of the Jews at the time that the personal transgression of Adam was the origin of sin, and further that death came into the world as the penalty for sin.

St Paul assumes this belief. The keynote to his meaning in the chief passage in which he discusses the matter (Rom. 5¹²⁻²¹) is struck in the words 'through the one man's disobedience the many were made sinners' (ver. 19). Sin, then, entered the world by Adam's trespass, and death—which is the penalty of sin—followed. And, furthermore, death became universal, because all men sinned. Ἐφ' ᾧ πάντες ἥμαρτον can only mean 'because all sinned': but the question remains whether by these words St Paul means to assert the personal individual sin of every one since Adam, or whether he means that, in some sense, when Adam sinned, the whole race then and there became guilty of sin. It is also a question which of the two conceptions was familiar to Jewish (Rabbinic) thought. (See Sanday and Headlam on the passage, and the discussion by G. B. Stevens *The Pauline Theology* p. 127 ff. See also H. St J. Thackeray *The Relation of St Paul to Contemporary Jewish Thought* ch. ii 'Sin and Adam', and further 'Pelagianism' *infra* p. 309.) To determine the question we must look beyond the mere words to the argument of the context. Two things are clear—(1) the universality of sin is emphasized, and its connexion with Adam's sin; (2) the redemption from sin actually accomplished through the one man, Jesus Christ, is treated as parallel to the results of the sin of the one man, Adam.

In both cases alike there is implied an organic unity between the representative and the race (whether of all men, in the one case, or of those who are 'in Christ', in the other case). Cf. 2 Cor. 5¹⁵ "one died for all, therefore all died" (*i.e.* to sin, an ethical death to be followed by an ethical rising-again to life). The unity which exists between Christ (the head of the spiritual humanity) and Christians is parallel to that which exists between Adam (the head of the natural humanity) and all mankind. (Cf. 1 Cor. 15²² "as in Adam all died, even so in Christ shall all be made alive".) But in regard to Adam, at all events, St Paul does not attempt to define the way in which the connexion comes about. On this question the phrase ἥμεθα τέκκα φύσει ὀργῆς, Eph. 2³, must be considered. The doctrine of original or birth-sin has been found in it. But the context must determine the meaning, and three facts must be noted—(1) the order of the words shews that there is no stress on φύσει; (2) the expression 'children of wrath' is parallel to such Old Testament expressions as 'sons of death' and means 'worthy of God's reprobation'; (3) the reference is to individual personal sins actually committed; (4) so far as there is any emphasis on φύσει the intention is to mark the contrast between the natural powers of man, left to himself, and the power of the grace of God in effecting salvation. See the emphatic reiteration of χάριτι in the verses following. In this

The restoration of the true relations between God and man, from which will follow the establishment of the true relations between man and man, is thus the purpose which Christ was understood to have declared to be his purpose and his followers believed he had achieved.

The Doctrine of Atonement in the New Testament

Of the nature of the atonement which he effected there is no formal theory in the New Testament. It is certain that St John, at all events, understood his Master to have constantly taught that the knowledge of God and, with the knowledge of God, the increased knowledge of man's own position, was to play a large part in the work. And this mental and moral illumination was effected by the whole life and teaching of Jesus, while by his death in all its circumstances the true meaning of his life was brought to the consciousness of his disciples. So that the conception of redemption through knowledge can certainly claim to be among the earliest conceptions. At the same time, that the redemption was wrought in some special sense by this death of Christ—that the death in itself was one of the instruments by which the whole work of Christ became effective —is clearly implied by all the allusions to it.[1] But the

passage too, therefore, it is the actual prevalence of sin in the world, as a fact of general experience, that is in the Apostle's mind, rather than any theory as to the propagation of sin or a tendency to sin. Cf. Gal. 2⁵, where the Gentiles are regarded as sinners φύσει, i.e. belonging to the class of sinners—see Sanday and Headlam on Rom. 5¹⁹.

Furthermore, it is clear that St Paul speaks of the σάρξ, in antithesis to the πνεῦμα, as the seat and sphere of manifestation of this sin. He uses the expression in different senses: (1) literal or physical, of the body actually subjugated and ruled by sin, conceived as the sphere in which, or the medium through which, sin actually works; (2) ethical, of the element in man which is, in practical experience, opposed to the spiritual; (3) symbolic, of unregenerate human nature. The three senses tend to pass over into one another, and the first and second, and the second and third, respectively, cannot always be exactly distinguished.

But when he describes the sins of 'the flesh' he includes many forms of sin which have their origin in the mind or the will—see e.g. Gal. 5¹⁹ ff.; and the antithesis between the 'spirit' and the 'flesh' is not presented in the manner of Greek or Oriental dualism. (On Rom. 7⁷⁻²⁵, see Sanday and Headlam.)

[1] On the meaning of the 'blood' of Christ, see particularly Westcott *Epistles of St John*, where it is shewn that the 'blood' always includes the thought of the life, preserved and active beyond death, though at the same time it is only through the death that the blood can be made available. On the New Testament doctrine of the atonement in general, see Oxenham *Catholic Doctrine of the Atonement* p. 108 ff.; and R. W. Dale *The Atonement*, with the notes in the Appendix.

writers of the New Testament are content to treat the result as a fact and to emphasize some of its consequences. They do not attempt to explain the manner in which the result was obtained.

The work of the atonement is described under various images and metaphors, which may perhaps be grouped in four classes.

First, there is the idea of 'reconciliation' ($\kappa\alpha\tau\alpha\lambda\lambda\alpha\gamma\acute{\eta}$), expressed in some of the parables, as when the prodigal son is reconciled to his father, and in passages in which those who were once enemies and aliens are said to be reconciled to God by the death of His Son, and to have won 'peace' and union with God, or 'life' in union with Him, as the result.[1]

Under another image sin is regarded as personified: man is held in bondage to sin, and has to be purchased or bought with a price out of the slavery in which he is held; so a 'ransom' has to be paid for him.[2]

Again, corresponding to the notion of sin as a debt, there is

---

[1] The words $\kappa\alpha\tau\alpha\lambda\lambda\alpha\gamma\acute{\eta}$, $\kappa\alpha\tau\alpha\lambda\lambda\acute{\alpha}\sigma\sigma\epsilon\iota\nu$ in this sense are peculiarly Pauline (Rom. 5[10, 11] 11[15], 2 Cor. 5[18, 19, 20]), and $\dot{\alpha}\pi o\kappa\alpha\tau\alpha\lambda\lambda\acute{\alpha}\sigma\sigma\epsilon\iota\nu$ (Eph. 2[16], Col. 1[20, 21]), and it must be observed that the conception is of the world and man being reconciled to God (not God to man), just as it is always man who is represented as hostile to God and alienated from Him. The change of feeling has to take place on the side of man. The obstacle to union which must be removed is of his making. (But see Sanday and Headlam on Rom. 5[11].) For the result as peace, see John 14[27], Rom. 5[1], Eph. 2[14, 17], Col. 3[15]; as union with God or life in Christ, see esp. St John, e.g. John 3[15, 16] 20[31], 1 John 5[11, 12]; cf. Col. 3[3, 4], 2 Tim. 1[1], Rom. 5[10], Heb. 10[20].

[2] The chief words used to express this conception are $\dot{\alpha}\gamma o\rho\acute{\alpha}\zeta\omega$,1 Cor. 6[20] 7[23], Gal. 4[5]; $\dot{\epsilon}\xi\alpha\gamma o\rho\acute{\alpha}\zeta\omega$, Gal. 3[13]; $\lambda\upsilon\tau\rho\acute{o}\omega$, $\lambda\acute{\upsilon}\tau\rho\omega\sigma\iota\varsigma$, $\dot{\alpha}\pi o\lambda\acute{\upsilon}\tau\rho\omega\sigma\iota\varsigma$, Tit. 2[14], 1 Pet. 1[18], Eph. 1[7], Col. 1[14], Rom. 3[24], Heb. 9[12, 15]; and $\lambda\acute{\upsilon}\tau\rho o\nu$, $\dot{\alpha}\nu\tau\acute{\iota}\lambda\upsilon\tau\rho o\nu$, Matt. 20[28] || Mark 10[45], 1 Tim. 2[6]. It is only in connexion with this metaphor that Christ is said to have acted 'instead of' us ($\dot{\alpha}\nu\tau\acute{\iota}$), and even here the phrase in 1 Tim. 2[6] is $\dot{\alpha}\nu\tau\acute{\iota}\lambda\upsilon\tau\rho o\nu$ $\dot{\upsilon}\pi\grave{\epsilon}\rho$ $\dot{\eta}\mu\hat{\omega}\nu$. He paid a ransom 'instead of' or 'in exchange for' us. In all other cases his death or sufferings are described as for our sakes or on our behalf ($\dot{\upsilon}\pi\grave{\epsilon}\rho$ $\dot{\eta}\mu\hat{\omega}\nu$), and more simply still as 'concerning' us, or 'in the matter of' sin or our sins ($\pi\epsilon\rho\grave{\iota}$ $\dot{\eta}\mu\hat{\omega}\nu$ or $\pi\epsilon\rho\grave{\iota}$ $\dot{\alpha}\mu\alpha\rho\tau\acute{\iota}\alpha\varsigma$, $\pi\epsilon\rho\grave{\iota}$ $\dot{\alpha}\mu\alpha\rho\tau\iota\hat{\omega}\nu$ $\dot{\eta}\mu\hat{\omega}\nu$). That is to say, it is the idea of representation rather than of substitution that is expressed. The conception is clearly stated in the words, 'if one died on behalf of all, then all died' (2 Cor. 5[20]); that is, in Christ the representative of the race all die, and because they have died in him, all are made alive in him (cf. such passages as Rom. 6[3-11]). And, again, it must be observed that it is not said to whom the ransom is paid. It is indeed only when what is simply a metaphor is pressed as though it were a formal definition that the question could well arise. One thing, however, in this respect, is clearly implied—the person thus ransomed and freed from bondage belongs henceforward to his redeemer: it is only *in* him, by union with him, that he gets his freedom. See e.g. Rom. 6[15-7][6].

the metaphor of 'satisfaction'; as though a creditor as satisfied by the payment of the debt, or the debt was remitted. This is the thought when death is styled the wages of sin, when men are declared to be debtors to keep the law; when Christ is described as being made sin for us and bearing our sins on the tree, and when reference is made to the perfect 'obedience' of his life.[1] Yet again there is the conception, derived from the ceremonial system of the old dispensation, of the life and death of Christ, pure and free from blemish, as a sacrifice and expiation which cleanses from sin, as ceremonial impurities were removed by the offerings of animals of old. And so 'propitiation' is made.[2]

A complete theory of the atonement must, it is clear, take account of all these aspects of the work of Christ to which the various writers of the New Testament give expression. But it is not probable that all of them were present to the minds of each of the writers; rather, it is probable that each approached the matter from a different point of view, and that none of them would have wished the account which he gives—the metaphors which he uses—to have been regarded as exclusive of the other accounts and metaphors which others adopted.

The Christian theologians of later times in like manner put forward now one and now another aspect of the mystery, only erring when they wished to represent some one particular aspect as a sufficient interpretation in itself, or when, going behind the earlier writers, they tried to define too closely what had been left uncertain. But the Church as a whole has never been committed to any theory of the atonement. The belief that the atonement has been effected, and the right relations between man and God restored and made possible for all men, in and through Christ, has been enough.

---

[1] Rom. 6²³, Gal. 5³ 3¹³, 2 Cor. 5²¹, 1 Pet. 2²⁴, Phil. 2⁸, Heb. 5³ 10⁹; Ἄφεσις, 'remission' of sins, Matt. 26²⁸, Luke 24⁴⁷, Acts 2³⁸ et saepe, Eph. 1⁷, Col. 1¹⁴; cf. Heb. 9²².

[2] This conception is expressed especially in the Epistle to the Hebrews and by St John. See Heb. 2¹⁷ 9¹⁹⁻²³ 10¹⁰. ¹². ¹⁴. ²⁶, and 1 John 1⁷ 2² 4¹⁰; but cf. also Rom. 3²⁵, Eph. 5². Here too it must be noticed that the idea of propitiating God (as one who is angry with a personal feeling against the offender) is foreign to the New Testament. Propitiation takes place in the matter of sin and of the sinner, altering the character of that which occasions alienation from God. See Westcott *Epistles of St John*, note on ἱλάσκεσθαι, ἱλασμός, ἱλαστήριον, p. 85. But see also Sanday and Headlam, *l.c. supra*.

The Doctrine of the Church and of the Sacraments in the
New Testament

As to the means by which these true relations are to be
realized and maintained by individuals throughout their life
on earth, the teaching of Jesus and the practice of the first
Christians, as recorded in the New Testament, is clear, though
not detailed.

Membership of the society which gathered round him in his
lifetime upon earth was the first step to union with him. ' He
that is not with me is against me.' [1]   All who were sincere in
their acceptance of him and their faith in him must ' follow ' him,[2]
and thereby shew themselves his disciples.   The realization of
the ' kingdom ' was to be effected through the society which he
founded.[3]   And after his death, at any rate, admission to the
society was to be by baptism, baptism into himself ; and the life
of the society was to be sustained, and its sense of union with him
kept fresh, by the spiritual food which the sacrament of his body
and blood supplied.   The Church is thus primarily the company
or brotherhood of all who accepted Jesus as their Master and
Lord, and shared a common life and rites of worship, recog-

---

[1] Matt. 12[30], Luke 11[23].   The saying may have been intended only to give
emphatic expression to the truth that in the contest between Christ and Satan no
one can be neutral.   The side of Christ must be resolutely taken.   But the interpretation which was apparently put upon the saying by those who recorded it, and
by the Church from the first, was probably true for those days at all events.   There
might be here and there a secret adherent ; but, in the main, discipleship of Christ
and membership of the society were bound to go together, though there might be
some interval of time between the inward conviction and the outward act.   This
interpretation is not excluded by the other saying : ' He that is not against us (you),
is for us (you)' (Mark 9[40], Luke 9[50]), though that saying was elicited by an act which
was based on the principle that one who did not join the society could not be really
a follower of Jesus.   The chief purpose of this saying is to teach the apostles the lesson
of toleration.   One who was ready in those early days to publicly invoke the name of
Jesus was not far from the kingdom and should not be discouraged.   The half disciple
might be won to full membership of the society.   At least he should not be disowned.

[2] Note the frequency of this expression in the Gospels.

[3] The society was at first a society within the Jewish nation.   On the process by
which it outgrew its original limits, so far as it can be traced in the New Testament,
see Hort *The Christian Ecclesia.*   The kingdom was in one sense established when
the first disciples ' left all and followed him ' ; but they had to be trained for their
work of spreading the kingdom (see Latham *Pastor Pastorum*), and it would not be
realized till all nations of the world were made disciples (cf. the parables, Matt.
13[31, 32, 33], and the commission, Matt. 28[19]).   That the Church and the kingdom of
God are not convertible terms in the teaching of Jesus is certain.   See further
A. Robertson *Regnum Dei* p. 61 ff.

nizing their common responsibility and obligations; and this company or brotherhood was one and the same society or Church although existing in separate local organizations. There is no trace in the New Testament of any idea on the part of the first Christians that it was possible to be a member of the Church without being a member of one of these visible local societies, or to receive in any other way whatever benefits membership of the Church bestowed.[1]

This new society was to inherit the promises and succeed to all the privileges which had been granted to the special people of God—the Church is the 'Israel of God'. The natural descendants of Isaac, the 'Israel after the flesh', having proved for the most part unworthy of the destiny assigned to them, their privileges do not pass to the faithful remnant only, but room is found for all who by their spiritual character are rightly to be regarded as the true children of promise. These are all grafted in to the ancient stock, and take the place of the branches which are pruned away.[2]

From another point of view the whole of this new Church is the body of Christ, he himself being its head, the centre of union of all the different members, which have their different functions to fulfil, the source of the life which animates each separate part and stimulates its growth and progress, the guiding and controlling force to which the whole body is subject.[3] From this point of view, what Christ, while he was on earth, did through his human body, that he continues to do through the Church, which since his Ascension represents him in the world. It is his visible body: from him it draws its life and strength, and through it he acts.

And, in particular, he acts through the two great rites which he appointed—baptism and 'the breaking of the bread'. Neither of these rites has any meaning apart from membership of the Church. Except by baptism no one could enter the Christian society;[4] that no one could remain a member of it without par-

---

[1] If the idea finds any justification in such sayings of our Lord as 'He that is not against us is for us' (Luke 9[50], cf. Mark 9[40]); 'Other sheep I have which are not of this fold' (John 10[16]), at all events there is no evidence that they were so understood by his early followers.

[2] See Rom. 9[6], 1 Cor. 10[18], Gal. 6[16], Rom. 11[16-24]. So 1 Pet. 2[9. 10]. The titles of honour used of the people of God are applied to Christians.

[3] Eph. 4[11-16] 5[22-32] (Col. 1[18. 24] 2[19]); cf. 1 Cor. 12[12-27].

[4] Acts 2[41], 1 Cor. 12[13] 1[13].

taking in the one bread which was the outward mark of union and fellowship [1] seems certain.[2]

Baptism is thus primarily the rite by which admission to the Church, and to all the spiritual privileges which membership of the Church confers, is obtained. It is administered once for all.[3] It must be preceded by repentance of sins,[4] and it effects at once union with Christ—membership of his body and participation in his death and burial and resurrection.[5] It is thus the entrance into a new life, and so is styled a new birth, or a birth from above—that is, a spiritual birth or 'regeneration'.[6] As such it involves the washing away or remission of sins which had stained the former life,[7]—a real purification, by which the obstacle to man's true relationship to God is removed and he occupies actually the position of sonship which had always been ideally his.[8]

In the New Testament itself forgiveness of sins is always

[1] 1 Cor. 10[17]. It is because it is one bread of which all partake that the many are one body.

[2] Acts 2[42. 46], 1 Cor. 10[16. 21] 11[17-34].

[3] It is clear from all that is said in the New Testament, and from the very nature of the rite as it is there represented, that repetition could never have been thought of in those days. It is perhaps to baptism that the strong assertion in Heb. 6[4-6] of the impossibility of 'renewing again unto repentance those that have been once enlightened' refers.

[4] Acts 2[38] 8[36]. [5] Gal. 3[27]; cf. 1 Cor. 12[27], Rom. 6[3. 4].

[6] John 3[3. 5], Tit. 3[5]; cf. 1 Pet. 1[3] 3[21].

[7] 1 Cor. 6[11], Acts 22[16], Heb. 10[22]. So of the whole Church, Eph. 5[25. 26].

[8] This is implied in the phrases, 'born anew or from above', 'begotten of God', 1 John 3[9]; 'children of God', 1 John 3[1]; 'sons of God', Rom. 8[14], Gal. 3[26. 27]. The term υἱοθεσία, 'adoption as sons', is used (Rom. 8[14-16. 23], Gal. 4[5]) in specially close connexion with the action of the Spirit (more closely defined as 'the Spirit of God', or 'the Spirit of His Son'). So Tit. 3[5], 'the laver of regeneration and renewing of the Holy Spirit'. Whether the gift of the Holy Spirit was believed to be conveyed by baptism, or rather by the laying-on of hands as a subsequent rite, is not certain. The words of St Peter (Acts 2[38]) appear to imply that the gift was a result of baptism. The narrative in Acts 8[14-17] clearly records two distinct rites, separated by some interval of time,—the first, of baptism, unaccompanied by the gift of the Holy Spirit; the second, of 'laying-on of hands', which conferred the gift: the first performed by Philip, the second by the Apostles. From the narrative in Acts 19[1-6] a similar distinction is to be inferred, though the questions in verses 2 and 3 point to the closest connexion in time between the two rites. Cf. also 1 Cor. 12[13]. (See further A. J. Mason The Relation of Confirmation to Baptism, and note on 'Confirmation' infra p. 390.) The gift of the Holy Spirit, though actually conferred by a subsequent symbolic rite, was naturally to be expected as an immediate sequence to the washing away of sins which the baptism proper effected. Similarly, the writer to the Hebrews includes among the elementary fundamental truths familiar to all Christians 'the doctrine of baptisms and of laying-on of hands', at once distinguishing and yet most closely connecting the two parts of one and the same rite (Heb. 6[2]).

regarded as the accompaniment or result of baptism. It was to obtain remission of sins that Peter on the day of Pentecost bade the multitude be baptized[1] every one of them (Acts 2[37, 38]); and 'Be baptized and wash away thy sins, calling upon the name of the Lord', was the counsel Ananias gave to Saul of Tarsus (Acts 22[16]). St Paul's own references in his Epistles to the effects of baptism shew the same conception (e.g. 1 Cor. 6[11] and Eph. 5[25, 26]),[2] and the allusion in the first Epistle of St Peter to its 'saving' power is equally strong (1 Pet. 3[21]).

The fullest doctrine of baptism to be found in the writings of the apostles is given by St Paul (Rom. 6[3-11]). It is above all else union with Christ that baptism effects—in that union all else is included. Baptism into Christ Jesus is baptism into his death, and that involves real union with him. The believer in a true sense shares in the crucifixion and literally dies to sin, and in virtue of this true union he is buried with him and necessarily shares also in the resurrection—the new life to God. It is through baptism, which he also elsewhere (Tit. 3[5]) directly calls 'the bath of regeneration', that he reaches these results: and

---

[1] It is 'in the name of Jesus Christ' that they are bidden to be baptized in this —the first recorded—instance of Christian baptism, and all later instances of baptisms in the New Testament are described as in or into the single name of Jesus (or Jesus Christ, or Christ); see Acts 8[16] 19[5] 10[48], Gal. 3[27], Rom. 6[3]. It is possible that the baptism was actually so effected,—in which case its validity (from the later standpoint when baptism was required to be into the names of the Trinity) could be entirely defended on the ground that baptism into one of the 'persons' is baptism into the Trinity (cf. the doctrine of *circumincessio*). But in view of the Trinitarian formula given in Matt. 28[19] (which it is difficult to believe represents merely a later traditional expansion of the words which were uttered by Christ) it is possible that the actual formula used in the baptism did recite the three names, and that the writer is not professing to give the formula but rather to shew that the persons in question were received into the society which recognized Jesus as Saviour and Lord and made allegiance to him the law of its life. The former view had the support of Ambrose, and the practice was justified by him as above (*de Spir. Sanct.* i 4), and probably by Cyprian in like manner (*Ep.* 73. 17, though he is cited for the latter view). See Lightfoot on 1 Cor. 1[13], and Plummer, Art. 'Baptism' Hastings' *D.B.*

[2] There is, however, no trace of any idea that baptized Christians could be preserved from future lapses without effort. Though St John could declare— from the ideal standpoint—that any one who was truly born again was, as such, unable to sin (1 John 3[9]); though in aim and intention sin was impossible for any one who was 'in Christ': yet the constant moral and spiritual exhortations which the Apostles pressed upon the Churches, and such a confession as St Paul's, "the good which I would, I do not: but the evil which I would not, that I practise" (Rom. 7[19]), serve to shew that the Apostles did not consider that the hope of forgiveness was exhausted in baptism (cf. Jas. 5[16]).

there is no kind of unreality about them—death, burial, resurrection are all intensely real and practical. "As many of you as were baptized into Christ did put on Christ " (Gal. 3[26, 27]), and are become 'members of Christ' (1 Cor. 6[15]).

The main points in this conception of St Paul were seized upon and utilized by subsequent writers on baptism, and became the text on which sermons to catechumens were preached.[1] But it was still forgiveness of sins that was commonly regarded as the chief gift in baptism.

St Paul's conception of baptism was probably as original as any other part of his teaching; he applies to baptism his dominant thought of being 'in Christ', a 'new creature' in Christ: but from a slightly different point of view it is the same conception which St John expounds in his account of the conversation of Jesus with Nicodemus, the main principle of which was also seized and expressed by St Peter.

"Except a man be born from above (anew), he cannot see the kingdom of God. . . . Except a man be born of water and the Spirit, he cannot enter into the kingdom of God. That which is born of the flesh is flesh; and that which is born of the Spirit is Spirit. Marvel not that I said unto thee, Ye must be born from above." [2] Here St John reports his Master as explaining the birth from above to be a birth of water and the Spirit, and it is clear that he understood it to mean a real change of inward being or life. 'Becoming a child of God' and being 'begotten of God' are other expressions which St John frequently uses of the same experience.[3]

It is a new relation to God into which the baptized person enters. Becoming one with Christ, he also becomes in his measure a son of God: one of those to whom he gave "the right to become children of God, even to them that believe on his name: which were born, not of blood, nor of the will of the flesh, nor of the will of man, but of God ".[4]

So too St Peter speaks of God as begetting us again (regenerating us),[5] and of Christians as ' begotten again (regenerated), not from corruptible seed, but from incorruptible ',[6] and seems to

---

[1] See e.g. Cyril of Jerusalem Cat. xx 4–7. Cyril particularly insists on the truth of each aspect of the rite, shewing how much more is involved in it than mere forgiveness of sins.

[2] John 3[3-5].　　　[3] E.g. 1 John 3[1] 5[2] 3[9].　　　[4] John 1[12, 13].
[5] 1 Pet. 1[3].　　　[6] 1 Pet. 1[23].

have St Paul's teaching to the Romans in mind when he brings baptism and its effects into immediate connexion with the death of Christ in the flesh and the new life in the spirit.[1]

Seen then from slightly different points of view, but all consistent with each other, baptism is regarded by the writers of the New Testament as the manner of entrance into the Church, and so into the kingdom of God; or as conferring a new spiritual life and a closer relationship to God, as of a child to a father; or as effecting once for all union with Christ and all that such union has to give.

In like manner, as baptism, administered once for all, admits to union with Christ, and thus to membership of the Church, which is the body of Christ, so the Eucharist maintains the union of the members with Christ and with one another. Union with Christ necessarily involves the union with one another in him of all who are united with him, and it is as ensuring union with Christ that the Eucharist is treated in the only passages in the New Testament in which anything like a doctrine of the Eucharist is expressed.

In the first of these, the earliest in time of composition, St Paul is writing to the Corinthians, and trying to lay down principles by which to determine the difficult position of their relation to pagan clubs and social customs connected (directly or indirectly) with the recognition of the pagan gods (δαιμόνια, deities or demons). The reference to the Lord's Supper is introduced incidentally to illustrate the question under discussion. It is intended to point, by contrast, the real nature and effect of participation in a ritual meal of which the pagan god is the religious centre. It is impossible, the writer argues, to separate the meal from the god. Christians know quite well, he assumes, the significance of the Christian meal. What is true of it and its effect is true *mutatis mutandis* of the pagan meal.[2]

---

[1] 1 Pet. 3[18 ff.].

[2] It is clear that the Christian rite—assumed to be understood in this way—is the starting-point of St Paul's argument. But he might equally well, if his argument had so required, have reasoned from the pagan rite to the Christian; for recent studies have proved that the fundamental idea of sacrifice was that of communion between the god and his worshippers through the medium of the victim which was slain. Through participation in the flesh and blood of the victim a real union was effected between them, and so the divine life was communicated to the worshipper who offered the sacrifice. See especially Robertson Smith *Religion of the Semites*, and Art. 'Sacrifice' in *Encyl. Brit.*

In this connexion, accordingly, he describes the nature of the Christian rite [1] to which, in recording its institution, he gives the name 'the Lord's Supper'.[2] He insists that in it there is effected fellowship with the blood of Christ and with the body of Christ.[3] It is one bread which is broken, and therefore all who partake of it are one body. And so, in like manner, to eat of the things sacrificed to demons, to drink their cup and to partake of their table, is to become fellows (to enter into fellowship) with them. Such fellowship at one and the same time with demons and with the Lord is impossible. The two things are incompatible—union with demons and union with the Lord. This then is the main thought: the Lord's Supper means and effects the union with the Lord of those who partake in it. And it is in this sense that St Paul must be supposed to have understood the phrases used immediately afterwards in regard to the institution [4]—'This is my body which is (given) for your sakes', and 'This cup is the new covenant in my blood'. To eat of the bread and to drink the cup is to be incorporated with Christ. But though the act is thus so intimate and individual, it is also at the same time general and social. There is involved in it a binding together of the brotherhood of Christians one with another. In virtue of their sharing together in the one bread they are themselves one body. " Because it is one bread, we, who are many, are one body." [5]

Another aspect of the rite as it presented itself to St Paul [6]

[1] 1 Cor. 10[16 ff.]   [2] 1 Cor. 11[20 ff.]

[3] "The cup of blessing which we bless, is it not fellowship with the blood of Christ? The bread which we break, is it not fellowship with the body of Christ? Because it is one bread, we who are many are one body, for we all partake of the one bread " (1 Cor. 10[16, 17]).

[4] 1 Cor. 11[23 ff.]

[5] 1 Cor. 10[17]. This conception, which understands by the body not only Christ himself (and so a personal union with him), but also the society of Christians (and so membership of the Church), is easily detected in later times. Cf. *Didache* ix 4, Bp. Sarapion's Prayer-Book, p. 62, S.P.C.K. ed. ; Cyprian *Ep.* 73. 13 ; Aug. *Tract. in Joann.* xxv 13—in all of which passages the unity of the Church with its many members is associated with the idea of the loaf formed out of the many scattered grains of wheat collected into one.

[6] This conception of the Eucharist as a perpetual memorial, expressly ordained by Christ himself as a rite to be observed by his followers till his coming again, is only found in St Paul and, as an early addition to the original account of the institution (possibly made by the author himself in a second edition of his work), in the Gospel of St Luke. It is not necessary here to attempt to determine whether this conception was introduced by St Paul. We need only note that it certainly was St Paul's conception: that he claims for it the express authority of Christ's own

is shewn by the words, " Do this as a memorial of me ", and " As often as ye eat this bread and drink the cup, ye proclaim the death of the Lord ". It had not only union with Christ as its effect, but also the perpetuation of the memory of his death according to his own command. It was to be a memorial of him and of all that his death signified—the broken body and the shed blood ; and it was to continue till his coming again. Such a commemoration was in its very nature also an act of thanksgiving, and thanksgiving was always an essential part of the rite.[1] And if this memorial was to be observed with fitting dignity and solemnity, there was needed due preparation on the part of those who made the commemoration. They must be morally and spiritually worthy. So in this respect a subjective element in the rite must be observed.[2]

From yet another point of view, the incidental reference to the Manna and the Water from the Rock as spiritual food and spiritual drink (the Rock being interpreted as Christ),[3] shew that St Paul also thought of the bread and the wine (the body and the blood) as the means by which the spiritual life of those who partook of them was nourished and sustained.

It is this latter thought that is dominant in the only other passage in the New Testament which treats at any length of the doctrine of the Eucharist—St John's account of the discourse of Christ on the Bread of Life.[4] The doctrine is worked out step by step. The Lord is represented as beginning with the reproof of the people for the worldly expectations which the feeding of the five thousand had aroused in them, and then (as saying after saying causes deeper dissatisfaction and bewilderment in the

words delivered to him ; and that there is no trace of any opposition to the practice as indicated by St Paul's instructions to the Corinthian Christians, but on the contrary that all the evidence supports the assertion that Christ himself ordained the observance and that the idea of commemoration was present from the first. On the other hand, there is no evidence till later times that the words εἰς τὴν ἐμὴν ἀνάμνησιν were understood to mean a *sacrificial* memorial (*e.g.* Eusebius *Demonstr. I.* 13 seems to conceive it so).

[1] All the accounts of the institution give prominence to this aspect, and the early prevalence of the word (ἡ εὐχαριστία) as the name for the whole service shews how it was regarded.

[2] Cf. 1 Cor. 11[27 ff].   [3] 1 Cor. 10[1-5].

[4] John 6[26 ff]. Whatever opinion be held as to the time when the rite was instituted, and as to the freedom which the author of this Gospel permitted himself in interpreting the teaching which he apparently professes simply to record, it cannot well be doubted that when he wrote this account he had the Lord's Supper in mind, and that it expresses his doctrine about it.

minds of some) giving stronger and stronger expression to the doctrine, till many of his disciples were even driven away by the hardness of the saying.

First of all there is only the contrast between the ordinary bread, their daily food, and the food which he, the Son of man, will give. The earthly food has no permanence, it perishes ; the other is constant and continuous, and reaches on into life eternal.

Then, in reply to the demand for faith in him, they ask for a sign, and hint that greater things than he has done were done for their fathers of old : he has only given them ordinary bread, but Moses gave manna,—bread from heaven. He declares that it was not Moses who gave the bread from heaven, but that his Father gives the real bread from heaven, and that he himself is the bread of God (*or* the bread of life) which comes down from heaven and gives life to the world,—hunger and thirst are done away with for ever for all who come to him and believe on him.

' I am the bread which came down from heaven '—this the Jews find hard to understand, and against their murmuring the doctrine proceeds a step further in expression. The bread of life gives life eternal. Those that ate of the manna died in the desert all the same, but he that eateth of the living bread which came down from heaven shall not die but shall live for ever. And the bread which shall be given is the *flesh* of the speaker.

' How can he give us his flesh to eat ? ' The objection which is urged leads on to much more emphatic assertions. Not only does he who eats this bread have life eternal, but it is the only way by which true life at all can be obtained. And now the reporter records the words which shew beyond all question that he has the Eucharist in mind. The Christian must both eat the flesh and drink the blood of Christ (' Unless ye eat the flesh of the Son of man and drink his blood, ye have not life in your-selves '),—that is the only food (the only eating and drinking) on which reliance can be placed. It is the only sustenance provided.

And then the discourse carries the doctrine a stage further on, and as it were explains the inmost significance of the rite. It establishes union between the Christian and Christ. By its means the Christian becomes one with Christ and Christ one with him; and because of this union he will receive life just as Christ himself has life because of his union with the Father. It is Christ himself who is eaten, so he himself is received, and with him the life which is his.[1]

The comments which follow serve to complete the doctrine by precluding any material interpretation of the realistic language in which it is expressed. It is a real eating and drinking of the body and the blood of Christ, and a real union with him, and a real life that is obtained. But it is all spiritual. "The Spirit is that which maketh alive (*or* giveth life), the flesh doth not profit aught."[2]

The conception of the Eucharist as a sacrifice is not prominent in these early accounts, but the sacrificial aspect of the rite is sufficiently suggested. As the death of Christ was a sacrifice, to 'proclaim the death of the Lord' is to proclaim the sacrifice, or, in other words, to acknowledge it before men and to plead it before God. It was 'on behalf of' others that the body was given to be broken and the blood was poured out, and through the use of these words the Eucharist is unmistakeably

---

[1] "He that eateth my flesh and drinketh my blood *abideth in me and I in him*. Even as the living Father sent me and I live because of the Father, so he *that eateth me* shall himself too live because of me." It is not easy to determine what is the exact significance of the phrase 'the flesh and blood', but it seems that the *manhood* of Christ must be meant. The words 'eat the flesh of Christ' must mean something more than have faith in him. "This spiritual eating, this feeding upon Christ, is the best result of faith, the highest energy of faith, but it is not faith itself. To eat is to take that into ourselves which we can assimilate as the support of life. The phrase 'to eat the flesh of Christ' expresses therefore, as perhaps no other language could express, the great truth that Christians are made partakers of the human nature of their Lord, which is united in one person to the divine nature; that he imparts to us now, and that we can receive into our manhood, something of his manhood, which may be the seed, so to speak, of the glorified bodies in which we shall hereafter behold him. Faith, if I may so express it, in its more general sense, leaves us outside Christ trusting in him; but the crowning act of faith incorporates us in Christ." Westcott *Revelation of the Father* p. 40. Cf. Gore *The Body of Christ* p. 24: "He plainly means them to understand that, in some sense, his manhood is to be imparted to those who believe in Him, and fed upon as a principle of new and eternal life. There is to be an 'influence' in the original sense of the word—an inflowing of his manhood into ours." And he goes on to note that "it is only because of the vital unity in which the manhood stands with the divine nature that it can be 'spirit' and 'life'. It is the humanity of nothing less than the divine person which is to be, in some sense, communicated to us".

[2] On the patristic interpretation of this saying (sometimes as explaining, sometimes as explaining away, the previous discourse), see Gore *Dissertations* p. 303 ff.

the memorial of a sacrifice.[1]   It is, however, only in the Epistle to the Hebrews that this conception is clearly implied, the sacrament on earth being the analogue of the perpetual intercession offered by the High Priest on high.

The later statements of the doctrine during the four following centuries are for the most part, as will be seen, merely amplifications and restatements of the various aspects to which expression is given in the New Testament itself.

---

[1] Besides the four accounts of the institution, cf. Heb. 13[10]. The words τοῦτο ποιεῖτε naturally would have the meaning 'perform this action', though the sacrificial significance of ποιεῖν may possibly have been intended (viz. 'offer this'). But in any case, as is shewn above, the action to be performed is a commemoration of a sacrifice. [ποιεῖν is certainly used frequently in the LXX as the translation of asah in a sacrificial sense, but the meaning is determined by the context, and there is no certain instance of this use in the New Testament. Justin (Dial. c. Tryph. 41, 70) is apparently the only early Christian writer who recognizes this meaning in connexion with the institution of the Eucharist.]

CHAPTER III

DEVELOPEMENT OF DOCTRINE

WE have had occasion to speak of the growth or developement of doctrine. Exception is sometimes taken to the phrase, and the changes which have taken place have often been regarded as in need of justification. It is felt that a divine revelation must have been complete and have contained all doctrines that were true and necessary; yet it is undeniable that changes of momentous importance in the expression of their faith have been made by Christians and the Church. How are the differences between the earlier and the later ' doctrines' to be explained ?

To this question various answers have been given. Some have been unable to see in the later developements anything but what was bad—corruption of primitive truth and degeneration from a purer type. The simplicity of scriptural teaching has been, it is argued, from the apostolic age onwards, ever more and more contaminated. Men were not content with the divine revelation and sought to improve upon it by all kinds of human additions and superstitions. Above all, the Church and the priests, the guardians of the revelation, perverted it in every way they could to serve their own selfish interests, and so was built up the great system of ecclesiastical doctrines and ordinances under which the simplicity and purity of apostolic Christianity was altogether obscured and lost. Such a view as this was held and urged by the English Deists of the eighteenth century, when the wave of rationalism first began to sweep over the liberated thought of England. It is the dominant idea of a large part of Matthew Tindal's *Christianity as Old as the Creation*, and still inspires some of the less-educated attacks upon the Church. But for the present purpose this notion of universal apostasy may be dismissed.[1]

---

[1] It must, however, be said that it is practically the same pessimistic estimate of the course of the history of doctrine that underlies Harnack's great work on the subject. At all events, during the period with which we have to deal he does not

More consideration must be given to another explanation which was accepted at the Council of Trent, and is therefore still the authoritative answer to the question given by the Church of Rome. It affirms that there are two sources of divine knowledge: one, Holy Scripture; and the other, traditions handed down from the Apostles, to whom they had been dictated, as it were, orally by Christ or by the Holy Spirit, and preserved in the Catholic Church by unbroken succession since. According to this theory, the later doctrines were later only in the sense that they were published later than the others, having been secretly taught and handed down from the first in the inner circle of bishops, and made known to the Church at large when the need for further teaching arose. This is the theory of 'Secret Tradition' or *disciplina arcani*,—the latter term being one of post-Reformation controversy, which was applied to designate several modes of procedure in teaching the Christian faith. Between these modes we must discriminate, if we are to decide whether we have or have not in this practice the source of the developement of doctrine. In the first place it is obvious that some reserve would be practised by teachers in dealing with those who were young in the faith or in years. For babes there is milk; solid food is for adults.[1] 'Spiritual' hearers and 'carnal' hearers need different teaching.[2] Wisdom can only be spoken among the full-grown.[3] Knowledge must always be imparted by degrees, and methods must be adapted to the capacity of pupils. This is a simple educational expedient which was of

recognize (unless perhaps in the case of St Paul) any progressive developement of Christian truth, but rather a progressive veiling and corruption of the original Gospel through the spreading of Greek and other pagan influences in the Church. The disease, which he styles 'acute Hellenization' or 'secularizing' of the faith, wrought (he considers) deadly mischief, and obscured or even destroyed the original character and contents of early Christianity. It cannot, however, be claimed that any clear statement of the real constituents of this pure and uncorrupted early Christianity is given in the *History of Doctrine*, and till they are certainly determined without question we are left with no criterion by which to distinguish the later changes and accretions from the original teaching. This being so, we may adopt the words of a distinguished critic, who wrote that "where a definite conception, based on history, of the nature of Christianity is so wholly wanting, the question as to whether individual phenomena are truly Christian or a degeneration, corruption, and secularization of true Christianity, can only be answered according to personal taste" (Otto Pfleiderer *Developement of Theology* p. 299). Such a view remains subjective and defies scientific treatment. (We can now, however, refer to *What is Christianity?*)

[1] Heb. 5$^{12-14}$.   [2] 1 Cor. 3^1.   [3] 1 Cor. 2^6.

course always employed by Christian teachers. The deeper truths were not explained at first; catechumens were not taught the actual words of the Creed till baptism, and were not allowed to be present at the celebration of the Eucharist. The spiritual interpretation of the highest rites was not laid bare to them.[1] And the reticence observed toward catechumens was of course extended to all unbelievers. That which is holy must not be cast to dogs; pearls must not be thrown before swine. The mysteries of the faith must not be proclaimed indiscriminately or all at once to the uninitiated. Christian teachers had ever before them the parabolic method of their Lord. Rather than risk occasion of profanity by admitting catechumens or unbelievers to knowledge for which they were not prepared, they would incur the suspicion which was certain to fall upon a secret society with secret religious rites. But such a *disciplina arcani* as this could not be a source of fresh doctrines, even if it could be traced back to apostolic times. It was always a temporary educational device, not employed in relation to the initiated, the 'faithful' themselves, and always designed to lead up to fuller knowledge—to a plain statement of the whole truth as soon as the convert had reached the right stage. Of any reserve or œconomy of the truth among Christians, one with another, there is no trace: still less is any distinction between the bishops and others in such respects to be found.[2] The nearest approach to anything of the kind which we have is to be seen in the higher 'knowledge' to which some early Christian philosophers laid claim. It was said that Jesus had made distinctions, and had not revealed to the many the things which he knew were only adapted to the capacity of the few, who alone were able to receive them and be conformed to them. The mysteries (τὰ ἀπόρρητα) of the faith could not be committed to writing, but must be orally preserved. So Clement of Alexandria [3] believed that Christ on his resurrection had handed down the 'knowledge' to James the Just, and John

[1] The earliest reference to such reticence is perhaps Tertullian's "omnibus mysteriis silentii fides adhibetur" (*Apol.* 7); and his complaint that heretics threw open everything at once (*de Praescr.* 41). With regard to the secrecy of the Creed, see Cyprian *Testim.* III 50, Sozomen *H.E.* i 20, Augustine *Serm.* 212.

[2] See Additional Note οἰκονομία *infra* p. 39.

[3] See the passage from the *Hypotyposeis* bk. vii (not extant) quoted in Eusebius *Eccl. Hist.* ii 1. Cf. *Strom.* i 1, vi 7 *ad fin.*; cf. *Strom.* v 10 *ad fin.* on Rom. 15²⁵· ²⁶· ²⁹ and 1 Cor. 2⁶· ⁷; and i 12 on Matt. 7⁶, 1 Cor. 2¹⁴.

and Peter, and they to the other apostles, and they in turn to the Seventy. Of that sacred stream of secret unwritten knowledge or wisdom he had been permitted to drink. But this 'knowledge' of Clement was clearly not a distinct inner system of doctrine differing in contents from that which was taught to the many; it was rather a different mode of apprehending the same truths—from a more intellectual and spiritual standpoint—an esoteric theology concerned with a mystic exposition, a philosophical view of the popular faith.[1] There is no reason to suppose that it was more than a local growth at Alexandria, the home of the philosophy of religion, or that it was the source of later developements of doctrine.

A third explanation removes the chief difficulty in the way of the apologist, by recognizing the progressive character of revelation. The theory of developement which Cardinal Newman worked out is not concerned to claim finality for the doctrines of the apostolic age. In effect it asserts that under the continuous control of a divine power, acting through a supernatural organization—the Church, the Bishops, the Pope, there has been a perpetual revelation of new doctrines.[2] Under divine guidance the Church was enabled to reject false theories and explanations (heresy), and to evolve and confirm as established truth all the fresh teaching which the fresh needs of the ages required.

By this explanation those to whom the theory of perpetual revelations of new doctrines seems to accord but ill with the facts of the case, may be helped to a more satisfactory answer to the question. It is not new doctrines to which Christians are bidden to look forward, but new and growing apprehension of doctrine: not new revelations, but new power to understand the revelation once and finally made. The revelation is Christ himself: we approximate more nearly to full understanding of him, and to the expression of that fuller understanding. Such expression must vary, must be relative to the age, to the general state of knowledge of the time, to individual circumstances and needs. It is impossible to " believe what others believed under different circumstances by simply taking their words; if we are to hold their faith, we must interpret it in our own language ".[3]

---

[1] See *Strom.* vi 15.
[2] See the essay on the *Developement of Christian Doctrine*, 1845. Cf., however, C. Gore *Bampton Lectures* p. 253.
[3] Westcott *Contemp. Review* July 1868.

It is quite possible for the same theological language to be at one time accepted and at another rejected by the Church, according to the sense in which it is understood. The developement of doctrines, the restatement of doctrine, thus understood, is only an inevitable result of the progress of knowledge, of spiritual and moral experience. It might well be deemed a necessary indication of a healthy faith, adapting itself to the needs of each new age, so that if such a symptom were absent we might suspect disease, stagnation, and decay. If Christian doctrines are, as is maintained, formulated statements designed to describe the Person and Work of Christ in relation to God and Man and the World, they are interpretations of great facts of life. Nothing can alter those facts. It is only the mode in which they are expressed that varies. " It can never be said that the interpretation of the Gospel is final. For while it is absolute in its essence, so that nothing can be added to the revelation which it includes, it is relative so far as the human apprehension - of it at any time is concerned. The facts are unchangeable, but the interpretation of the facts is progressive. . . . There cannot be . . . any new revelation. All that we can need or know lies in the Incarnation. But the meaning of that revelation which has been made once for all can itself be revealed with greater completeness." [1]   Certainly the student of the history of Christian doctrines cannot discourage the attempt to re-state the facts in the light of a larger accumulation of experience of their workings. It is to such attempts that he owes the rich body of doctrine which is the Christian's heritage, and he at least will remember the condemnation passed on the Pharisees who resisted all reform or developement of the routine of faith and practice into which they had sunk. Their fathers had stoned the prophets—the men who dared to give new interpretations and to point to new developements; but what was then original and new had in a later age become conventional and old, and the same hatred and distrust of a new developement, which prompted their fathers to kill the innovators, led their children to laud them and to build their sepulchres.[2]

As a matter of fact, we can see that such developements have been due to many external causes, varying circumstances

[1] Westcott *Gospel of Life* preface p. xxiii. The revelation is in this sense continuous, present, and progressive.
[2] See *Ecce Homo* ch. xxi.

and conditions of personal life. Different nationalities, owing to
their different antecedents, apprehend very differently. The conception that as Christ came to save all men through himself,
so he passed through all the stages of human growth, sanctifying each in turn, was familiar in early days,[1] and doctrine
must correspond to the intellectual and moral and spiritual
growth of man. To the expression of doctrine every race in
turn makes its characteristic contribution, not to the contents
of the Revelation but to the interpretation and expression of
its significance. The influence of Hebrew, Greek, and Roman
modes of thought and of expression is obvious during the early
centuries with which we are concerned. It is indeed so obvious,
for example, that it was from Greek thought that the Church
borrowed much of the terminology in which in the fourth
century she expressed her Creed, that some have been led to
imagine she borrowed from Greek philosophy too the substance
of her teaching. In disregard of the highly metaphysical
teaching of St John and St Paul, and of the mystical conceptions underlying the records of the sayings of Christ himself,
it is argued that the Sermon on the Mount is the sum and
substance of genuine Christianity; that Christianity began as a
moral and spiritual 'way of life' with the promulgation of a
new law of conduct; and that it was simply under Hellenic
influences, and by incorporating the terms and ideas of late
Hellenic philosophy, that it developed its theology. An ethical
sermon stands in the forefront of the teaching of Jesus Christ:
a metaphysical creed in the forefront of the Christianity of the
fourth century.[2] What has been said already of doctrines and
their developement—of the finality of the revelation in Christ
and of the gradual process by which expression is found for the
true interpretation of it—recognizes the element of truth contained in these over-statements.[3] They seem to involve a con-

[1] Irenaeus ii 33. 2 (*ed.* Harvey vol. i p. 330).
[2] See Hatch *Hibbert Lectures*, and Gore *Bampton Lectures* iv. Cf. also
Lightfoot *Epistle to the Colossians* p. 125.
[3] It has been truly said that with the Incarnation of the Redeemer and the
introduction of Christianity into the world the materials of the history of doctrines
are already fully given *in germ*. The object of all further doctrinal statements
and definitions is, from the positive point of view, to unfold this germ; from the
negative, to guard it against all foreign additions and influences. This twofold
object must be kept in view. The spirit of Christianity had to work through the
forms which it found, attaching itself to what was already in existence and
appropriating prevalent modes of expression. Christ did not come to destroy but

fusion between conduct and the principles on which it is based; between the practical endeavour to realise in feeling and in act that harmony between ourselves, creation, and God, which is the end in view of all religion, and the intellectual endeavour to explain and interpret human life so as to frame a system of knowledge. It is with the early attempts to frame this system of knowledge that the student of Christian doctrines has to deal. They all rested primarily on the interpretations which were given by the first generation of Christians of the life and teaching and work of Christ.

οἰκονομία—RESERVE

Such an 'economy' or 'accommodation' of the truth as is described above is evidently legitimate and educationally necessary.[1] We must note, however, that among some leaders of Christian thought, through attempts at rationalising Christianity to meet the pagan philosophers and at allegorising interpretations of difficulties, the principle was some- times extended in more questionable ways. In controversy with opponents the truth might be stated in terms as acceptable as possible to them. It would always be right to point out as fully as possible how much of the truth was already implied, if not expressed, in the faith and religious opinions which were being combated. It would be right to shew that the new truth included all that was true in the old, and to state it as much as possible in the familiar phraseology: such *argumenta ad hominem* might be the truest and surest ways of en- lightening an opponent. But phrases of some of the Alexandrian Fathers are cited which sound like undue extensions of such fair 'economy'. Clement declared (*Strom.* vii 9) that the true Gnostic 'bears on his tongue whatever he has in his mind', but only 'to those who are worthy to hear', and adds that 'he both thinks and speaks the truth, unless at any time medicinally, as a physician dealing with those that are ill, for the safety of the sick he will lie or tell an untruth as the Sophists say' (οὔποτε ψεύδεται κἂν ψεῦδος λέγῃ). And Origen is quoted by Jerome (*adv. Rufin. Apol.* i 18; Migne *P.L.* xxiii p. 412) as enjoining on any one who is forced by circumstances to lie the need

---

to fulfil. All are God's revelations—πολυμέρως καὶ πολυτρόπως God spoke of old. The Son in whom He spoke to us in these latter days He made heir of all the partial and manifold revelations. The student of Christian doctrines has to study the process by which the inheritance was slowly assumed, and the riches of the Gentiles claimed for his service.

[1] See Newman *Arians* i 3, and his *Apologia*. See also his essay on *Developement of Christian Doctrine*.

of care to observe the rules of the art, and only use the lie as a condiment and medicine. To no one else can it be permitted. So his pupil, Gregory of Neo-Caesarea, used language about the Trinity confessedly erroneous,[1] and was defended by Basil (*Ep.* 210. 5 ; Migne *P.G.* xxxii p. 776) on the ground that he was not speaking δογματικῶς but ἀγωνιστικῶς (controversially), that is, not teaching doctrine but arguing with an unbeliever ; so that he was right to concede some things to the feelings of his opponent in order to win him over to the most important points.[2] And Jerome himself claimed to write in this manner γυμναστικῶς, and cited in support of the practice numbers of Greek and Latin Christian writers before him, and even the high authority of St Paul himself (*Ep.* 48. 13 ; Migne *P.L.* xxii p. 502). So Gregory of Nazianzus, in defence and in praise of Basil (see *Ep.* 58 ; cf. *Orat.* 43), insisted that true teaching wisdom required that the doctrine of the Spirit should be brought forward cautiously and gradually, and that he should not be described as God except in the presence of those who were well disposed to the doctrine. (See further Harnack *DG.* Eng. tr. vol. iv p. 116.)

Such expressions as these might easily lead to a perversion of the true pædagogic reticence. Yet language is, in any case, so inadequate to express the deepest thought and feeling on such questions, that it may well seem that if the true idea is secured it matters little in what precise language it is clothed. It is impossible to be certain that a particular term will convey the same idea to different people. The thing that matters is the idea. You want to convey your idea to your opponent—you may have to express it in his language. The limit would seem to be set only when feeling the ideas to be different you so express them as to make them seem the same. When reserve, economy, accommodation, gets beyond that limit, then and not till then does it become dangerous and dishonest. (See *D.C.A.* Art. "Disciplina Arcani".)

---

[1] When he said Father and Son were two ἐπινοίᾳ, but one ὑποστάσει (but really ὑπόστασις was then equivalent to οὐσία).

[2] Cf. also Basil *de Spir. Sancto* 66 on the value of the secret unwritten tradition. See Swete *Doctrine of the Holy Spirit* p. 64, and C. F. H. Johnstone *The Book of St Basil on the Holy Spirit.* On Reserve as taught by the later casuists see Scavini *Theolog. Mor.* ii 23, Pascal *Letters*, and Jeremy Taylor *Ductor Dubit.* iii 2 (Jackson 'Basil' *N. and P.-N. Fathers* vol. vii).

CHAPTER IV

THE SOURCES OF DOCTRINE: ORAL TRADITION—HOLY SCRIPTURE

THE original source of all Christian doctrines is Christ himself, in his human life on earth. The interpretations of him which were given by the apostles and earliest disciples are the earliest Christian doctrines. They were conscious that they had this work of interpretation of Christ to the world committed to them, and they believed they might look for the help of the Spirit which he had promised to send—the Spirit of truth—to guide them to the fulness of the truth.[1] Under his guiding inspiration many things would grow clear as the human power of apprehension expanded, as their experience was enlarged: when their capacity grew greater they would understand the things of which their Master had told them he had many to say to them, but they could not bear them yet.[2] For this function of witnesses and spokesmen—true 'prophets'—of Christ they would be more and more fitted by a living inspiration coming from him—a spiritual illumination and elevation which would intensify their natural powers and quicken their innate latent capacity into life and activity. Such was the earliest idea of Christian inspiration. It shewed itself in the earliest apostolic teaching, the oral record of which became at once the 'tradition' to which appeal was made. To this tradition, which naturally dealt both with doctrine and with practice, St Paul referred his converts in one of his earliest and in one of his latest Epistles. 'Hold fast the traditions which ye were taught'[3] he bids the Thessalonians, 'the tradition which ye received from us';[4] and again he urges Timothy to guard the deposit committed to him.[5]

By degrees this oral tradition was supplemented by the

---

[1] John 16[7, 13].   [2] John 16[12].   [3] 2 Thess. 2[15].
[4] 2 Thess. 3[6].   [5] 1 Tim. 6[20].

written tradition, so that already in his exhortation to the
Thessalonians St Paul was able to place side by side on a level
the traditions which they had heard from him, whether by word
or by letter, his teaching when with them and what he had
written since. But between the two traditions there was no
sense of discord, and we shall search in vain for any suggestion
that one possesses a greater measure of inspiration than the
other.[1] The one and only source of the teaching was Christ;
from him the stream flows, Scripture and 'tradition' are blended
in one great luminous river of truth, and do not separate into
divergent streams till later times. They were at first two forms
of the same thing. Both together constitute the Tradition, the
Canon or Rule of Faith.[2]

But that which is written has a permanent character which
oral tradition lacks. It is less capable of correction if error
or misunderstanding creep in. And as more and more of the
would-be interpreters wrote their comments and expansions, and
Christian literature of very various merit grew, and it became
important to exclude erroneous interpretations, a distinction was
made between the writings of apostles and those of a later age.
By the 'sensus fidelium'—by the general feeling of believers
rather than by any definite act—a selection was gradually
formed. In this process some have recognized a definite act
of Inspiration, the 'inspiration of Selection'.[3] The selection,
representative of so many types of interpretation, thus slowly
completed, was sanctioned by Councils, and the 'Canon' of
Scripture (the 'Canon' in a new sense) was formed. And so
in this way Holy Scripture came to be 'stereotyped' as a
source of doctrine, and regarded as distinct from the interpretations of the Church of post-apostolic times, whether contained
in oral or in written tradition, which henceforth constitute a
separate source of doctrine. So "the testimonies of primitive
and apostolic Christianity in collected form serve as an authoritative standard and present a barrier against the introduction of

---

[1] It might perhaps be inferred that in early times the oral tradition was regarded
as more trustworthy than the written account. Cf. the Preface to the Gospel
according to St Luke, and the Introduction to the work of Papias quoted by
Eusebius *H.E.* iii 39. Cyprian apparently styles Scripture *divinae traditionis
caput et origo* (*Ep.* 74.10), appealing to it as the ultimate criterion, but this conception
is unusual.

[2] The same terms κανών, regula (*sc.* fidei), παράδοσις, traditio, are applied to both.

[3] See Liddon's Sermon before the University of Oxford with this title.

all that was either of a heterogeneous nature or of more recent date which was trying to press into the Church" (Hagenbach).

It is no part of our work to study the process by which inspired Scriptures became an inspired book, invested with all the authority conceded to the Jewish collection, our Old Testament, which had been at first pre-eminently the Bible of the Christians. But in order to understand the growth of doctrine we must trace a little in detail the manner in which the early teachers of the Church viewed the authority of the Scriptures, their conception of Inspiration, their method of Exegesis, the place assigned to Tradition therein.

Inspiration of Scripture

Of Inspiration a formal definition was never framed. We can only point to personal conceptions and individual points of view, conditioned by various influences and differences of country and education as well as of temperament. Two broad lines of influence may be distinguished, Jewish and Gentile.

On the one hand there was the Jewish view of the verbal inspiration of their sacred writings, formed and fostered in connexion with the work of the scribes on the Law. After the Return from the Exile and the establishment of Judaism on a new basis, the religious interest of the nation was enlisted in the work of microscopic investigation of the letter of the Law. The leaders of Judaism desired to regulate every detail of the life of the nation. Immense reverence for the Law stimulated the aim of securing its sanction on the minutest points and working them out to their utmost consequences. And so arose the system of exposition of the Law to make it apply to the purpose in view, till every letter contained a lesson. And side by side with this view of the written revelation, by a process the reverse of that which took place in regard to the Christian revelation, there grew up the idea of the inspiration of the oral tradition as well. The network of scribe-law—the traditions of the scribes—entirely oral—was regarded as of equal authority with the written law. There even arose the notion of a *disciplina arcani* going back to the time of Moses, who it was said had handed down a mass of oral traditions, which were thus referred to divine authority.

On the other hand was the Ethnic idea of divination (ἡ μαντική), according to which the medium of the divine revelation, who was usually a woman, became the mechanical mouthpiece of the God, losing her own consciousness, so that she gave vent in agitated trance to the words she was inspired to utter.[1] Inspiration is thus an ecstatic condition, during which the natural powers of the individual who is inspired are suspended : it is ' an absolute possession which for the time holds the individuality of the prophetess entirely in abeyance '. A typical instance of this kind of inspiration is described in the lines of Virgil [2]—

> Struggling in vain, impatient of her load,
> And lab'ring underneath the pond'rous God,
> The more she strove to shake him from her breast,
> With more and far superior force he press'd ;
> Commands his entrance, and, without control,
> Usurps her organs, and inspires her soul.

If in later times under Platonic or Neo-Platonic influence a less external conception grew up, it probably did not establish itself or spread beyond the circle of philosophic thought.

The conception of Inspiration which was held by Christians was doubtless in some cases influenced by these Greek and Roman ideas, but it was probably in the main an inheritance from Judaism. This is a natural inference from the fact that the Jewish Scriptures were the first Christian Bible, and that the idea of verbal inspiration was at first associated much more definitely with them, and only indirectly and by transference with the selected Christian literature. The early Christian idea was, as we have seen, rather of inspired men than of an inspired book ; though the transition is an easy one, as the writings of inspired men would naturally also be inspired. When we come to definite statements on the subject we find now the one and now the other influence strongest.

In Philo [3] we might expect to find a transitional theory of inspiration, but he seems to combine the Jewish and the Ethnic views in their extremer forms. He applies the Ethnic conception of divination to the Hebrew prophets, and repeats with embellishments the fable of the miraculous translation of the Hebrew Scriptures by the Seventy. Even the grammatical errors of the Septuagint he regarded as inspired and rich in

[1] See F. W. H. Myers "Greek Oracles " in *Essays—Classical*.
[2] *Aen.* vi 77–80—Dryden.
[3] See William Lee *Inspiration of Holy Scripture*, Appendix F.

capacity for allegorical interpretation—a view of literal inspiration with which can be compared only the assertion by the Council of Trent of the sanctity and canonicity of the books of the Old Testament and the New Testament and the Apocryphal writings, 'entire with all their parts as they are accustomed to be read in the Catholic Church and in the old Latin Vulgate edition'. Philo's conceptions are shewn with equal clearness in his system of interpretation, examples of which will be cited in their place.

To the Apostolic Fathers the Scriptures are the books of the Old Testament, though if there is a reference to a written Gospel it is introduced by the same formula as is used in the other citations. Barnabas makes explicit allusions to the different parts of the Old Testament ('the Lord saith in the Prophet' or 'in the Law'), but it is clear that the whole collection is looked upon as one divinely inspired utterance— the voice of the Lord or of the Holy Spirit. There is of course no sign of a New Testament of definite books and of equal authority with the Old; but the Apostolic Fathers do separate the writings of Apostles from their own and disclaim apostolic authority.[1] Thus Clement, in writing to the Corinthians,[2] appeals to 'the Epistle of the blessed Paul the Apostle' to them as authority alike for him and for them. It was 'in the Spirit' that he had charged them against the sin of making parties, and Clement refers to his warnings as commanding the same attention which they would obviously give to the writings of the older 'ministers of the grace of God'.

A passage in the Muratorian Fragment throws light on the current conceptions of the authority of the written Gospels about the middle of the second century. "Though various principal ideas (*principia*) are taught in the different books of the Gospels, it makes no difference to the faith of believers, since in all of them all things are declared by one principal (*or* sovereign) Spirit (*uno ac principali spiritu*) concerning the Nativity, the Passion, the Resurrection, the manner of life (*conversatione*) [of our Lord] with his disciples, and his double Advent, first in lowliness and humiliation which has taken place, and afterwards in glory and royal power which is to come."

[1] Cf. Westcott *The Bible in the Church*, p. 86. (The citations are all anonymous. Clement has 'it is written', 'the Scripture saith', 'the Holy Spirit saith'; Ignatius, 'it is written'; Polycarp, no formula.)
[2] Cf. §§ 47, 8.

About the same time and later on we have some indications of the prevailing view of Inspiration in the writings of the Apologists and Irenaeus.

To Justin, for example, Scripture is the word of God, given by GOD through the Word, or through the Spirit. It is the Spirit of God who is the author of the whole of the Old Testament—the single author of one great drama with its many actors. The prophets were indeed inspired, but the words which they utter are not their own. We must not suppose, he says, "that the language proceeds from the men who are inspired, but from the Divine Word which moves them".[1] It is to prophecy, to Scripture, that he makes his appeal: on the fulfilment of prophecy he relies for proof of the truth of the claims of Christ.

In Athenagoras—Athenian philosopher though he was, and perhaps connected with the school of Alexandria—we find a description of the process of inspiration derived from purely pagan sources. The Spirit uses men as its instruments, playing upon them as a flute-player blows a flute. They are entranced and their natural powers suspended, and they simply utter under the influence of the Divine Spirit that which is wrought in them.[2]

Theophilus, however, recognises much more fully the quality of the human instrument. The inspired writers were not mere mechanical organs, but men who were fitted for their work by personal and moral excellence, and on account of their fitness were deemed worthy to be made the vehicles of the revelation of God and to receive the wisdom which comes from Him.[3]

Tertullian too lays stress on the character of the medium chosen. "From the very beginning God sent forth into the world men who by their justice and innocence were worthy to know God and to make Him known—filled full of the Divine Spirit to enable them to proclaim that there is one only God . . . " and so gave us a written testament that we might more fully know His will.[4] In the Scriptures we have the very 'letters' and 'words' of God. So much so indeed that, under the influence of Montanism, he argued that nothing could be safely permitted for which such a letter or word of God could not be cited in

---

[1] *Apol.* i 36 (cf. 33, and ii 10).
[2] *Legatio* 9.
[3] *Ad Autol.* ii 9 (cf. Euseb. *Hist. Eccl.* iv 20).
[4] *Apol.* 18.

evidence. The principle that nothing is required for salvation which cannot be proved by Scripture [1] was not enough for him: rather, Scripture denies that which it does not give instances of, and prohibits that which it does not expressly permit.[2]

To the Montanists the annihilation of all human elements was of the first importance. Prophecy must be ecstatic. Unconsciousness on the part of the person through whom the Spirit spoke was of the essence of Inspiration.

Irenaeus leaves us in no doubt about his view. The inspiration of the writers of the New Testament is plenary, and apparently regarded as different in degree from that of the prophets of old, whose writings—though inspired—were full of riddles and ambiguities to men before the coming of Christ: the accomplishment had to take place before their prophecies became intelligible. Those who live in the latter days are more happily placed. "To us . . . [the apostles] by the will of God have handed down in the Scriptures the Gospel, to be the foundation and pillar of our faith. . . . For after our Lord rose again from the dead the Holy Spirit came down upon them, and they were invested with power from on high and fully equipped concerning all things, and had perfect capacity for knowledge"[3] . . . and so they were exempt from all falsehood (*or* mistake)—the inspiration saving them from blunders—even from the use of words that might mislead; as when the Holy Spirit, foreseeing the corruptions of heretics, says by Matthew, 'the generation of Christ' (using the title that marked the divinity), whereas Matthew might have written 'the generation of Jesus' (using only the human name).[4] But this inspiration is not of such a character as to destroy the natural qualities of its recipients: each preserves his own individuality intact.

To the end of the second century or to the beginning of the third probably belongs the anonymous 'Exhortation to the Greeks', which used to be attributed to Justin.[5] It contains the following significant description of the manner in which inspiration worked. "Not naturally nor by human thought

---

[1] Cf. Article vi.   [2] *De Monog.* 4 ; *de Cor.* 2.
[3] See *adv. Haereses* iii 1 and 5—Harvey vol. ii pp. 2, 18.
[4] *Ibid.* iii 17—Harvey ii p. 83.
[5] Eusebius *Hist. Eccl.* iv 18 mentions two writings of Justin to the Greeks, but neither the extant *Oratio ad Gentiles* nor the *Cohortatio* which contains the above passage is believed to be the work of Justin.

can men get to know such great and divine things, but by the gift which came down from above at that time (*sc.* under the Jewish dispensation) upon the holy men, who had no need of skill or art of words, nor of any debating and contentious speech. They only needed to present themselves in purity to the influence of the divine Spirit, so that the divine power by itself coming down from heaven, acting on those just men, as the bow acts on an instrument—be it harp or lyre, might reveal to us the knowledge of divine and heavenly things. So it was that, as if with one mouth and tongue, they taught us in due gradation and concord one with another—and that too though they imparted their divine teaching to us in different places and at different times—concerning God and the creation of the world and the formation of man and the immortality of the human soul and the judgement which is to be after this life." Here it appears that moral fitness only is recognized as a necessary qualification for the medium of the revelation, and there is again the metaphor which seems to indicate a merely mechanical mode of inspiration. But the metaphor should not be strained, and the effect of the peculiar structure of the instrument in determining its tone must be taken into account.

Of the Alexandrines, whose special glory it was, in an age of wild anti-Christian speculation on the one side and fanatical literalism on the other, to lead men to the scholarly study of the Scriptures, Clement has little of special interest on the manner in which the inspiration worked. Recognizing as he did the action of God in the moral teaching of Greeks and barbarians, who had in philosophy a covenant of their own, he believed that the God of the Christians was also the giver of Greek philosophy to the Greeks, and that He raised up prophets among them no less than among the people of Israel. But it was by the chosen teachers of His peculiar people that He led men to the Messiah; the Word by the Holy Spirit reducing man, body and soul, to harmony, so as to use him—an instrument of many tones—to express God's melody.[1]

It is from Origen first that we get an express rejection of

---

[1] "But he that is of David and was before him, the Word of God, despising lyre and harp—mere lifeless instruments—took this cosmic order—yes, and the microcosm man, his body and soul, and attuned it to the Holy Spirit (*or* by the Holy Spirit), and so through this instrument of many notes he sings to God." *Protrept.* ch. i—Migne *P.G.* viii p. 60.

pagan conceptions in this respect. He assumes the doctrine of Inspiration to be acknowledged—it was the same Spirit who worked all along in the prophets of all ages : but it was to enlighten and strengthen them that His influence went—not to cloud or confuse their .natural powers like the Pythian deity. By the contact of the Holy Spirit with their souls the divine messengers became clearer in vision and brighter in intuition both in mind and in soul. The preface to the Gospel of St Luke is cited as shewing that this was so : what others attempted they—the inspired writers—moved by the Holy Spirit actually wrote. And St Paul's own words in his Epistles shew that he was conscious of speaking sometimes in his own person and sometimes with divine authority. None of the objections commonly alleged against the Scriptures in any way invalidated their claim to be received as containing a true revelation of God. What seemed to be unworthy of God, or beneath His dignity, should be understood as an accommodation to the intelligence of men, and things which we could not yet explain we should know hereafter.[1]

The method of interpretation adopted by Origen shews and illustrates his general conceptions. This method was partly his own, but largely an inheritance which he could not escape.

The Interpretation of Scripture

The ideas of inspiration, as applied to writings, and of exegesis, were formed, it has been said,[2] while the mystery of writing was still fresh. A kind of glamour hung over the written words. They were invested with an importance and impressiveness which did not attach to any spoken words, giving them an existence of their own. Their precise relation to the person who first uttered them and their literal meaning at the time of their utterance tended to be overlooked or obscured. Especially in regard to the writings of Homer is this process seen. Reverence for antiquity and belief in inspiration combined to lift him above the common limitations of time and place and circumstances. His verses were regarded as having a universal validity : they were the Bible of the Greek races, the

[1] See *de Princip.* bk. iv. Cf. Greg. Nyss. *de comm. Not.* p. 181 (Migne).
[2] Hatch *Hibbert Lectures*, 1888, from which (p. 50 ff.) the following paragraphs are taken.

voice of an undying wisdom. So when the unconscious imitation
of heroic ideals passed into conscious philosophy of life, it was
necessary that such philosophy should be shewn to be consonant with the old ideals and current standards. And when
'education' began it was inevitable that the ancient poets
should be the basis of education. So the professors of education, the philosophers and 'sophists', were obliged to base their
teaching on Homer, to preach their own sermons from his texts,
and to draw their own meanings from them; so that he became
a support to them instead of being a rival. "In the childhood
of the world, men, like children, had to be taught by tales"—
and Homer was regarded as telling tales with a moral purpose.
The developing forms of ethics, physics, metaphysics, all accordingly appeal to Homer; all claim to be the deductions from his
writings; and as the essential interval between them, between
the new and the old conceptions, grew wider, the reconciliation
was found in the exegetical method by which a meaning was
detected beneath the surface of a record or representation of
actions. In this way a narrative of actions, no less than the
actions themselves, might be symbolical and contain a hidden
meaning; and thus the break with current reverence for the old
authority and belief in its validity would be avoided.

It is not true that this method was never challenged; but it
had a very strong hold on the Greek mind. It underlay the
whole theology of the Stoical schools; it was largely current
among the scholars and critics of the early empire; and it survived as a literary habit long after its original purpose had failed.

The same difficulty which had been felt on a large scale in
the Greek world was equally felt by Jews who had become
students of Greek philosophy in regard to their own sacred
books. By adopting the method which was practised in the case
of the Homeric writings, they could reconcile their philosophy to
their religion and be in a position to give an account of their
faith to the educated Greeks among whom they dwelt. Of this
mode of interpretation far the most considerable monument is to
be found in the works of Philo, which are based throughout on
the supposition of a hidden meaning in the sacred scriptures,
metaphysical and spiritual. They are always patient of symbolical interpretation. Every passage has a double sense, the
literal and the deeper. In every narrative there is a moral.

As an instance of this method may be cited Philo's treatment of the narrative of Jacob's dream—" He took the stones of that place and put them under his head ", from which he extracts the moral, and also support for his own peculiar philosophical ideas. " The words ", he says,[1] " are wonderful, not only because of their allegorical and physical meaning, but also because of their literal teaching of trouble and endurance. The writer does not think that a student of virtue should have a delicate and luxurious life, imitating those who are called fortunate . . . men, who after spending their days in doing injuries to others return to their homes and· upset them (I mean not the houses they live in, but the body which is the home of the soul) by immoderate eating and drinking, and at night lie down in soft and costly beds. Such men are not disciples of the sacred Word. Its disciples are real men, lovers of temperance and sobriety and modesty, who make self-restraint and contentment and endurance the corner-stones, as it were, of their lives: who rise superior to money and pleasure and fame ; who are ready for the sake of acquiring virtue to endure hunger and thirst, heat and cold ; whose costly couch is a soft turf, whose bedding is grass and leaves, whose pillow is a heap of stones or a hillock rising a little above the ground. Of such men Jacob is an example: he put a stone for his pillow . . . he is the archetype of a soul that disciplines itself, who is at war with every kind of effeminacy. . . . But the passage has a further meaning, which is conveyed in symbol. You must know that the divine place and the holy ground is full of incorporeal Intelligences, who are immortal souls. It is one of these that Jacob takes and puts close to his mind, which is, as it were, the head of the combined person, body and soul. He does so under the pretext of going to sleep, but in reality to find repose in the Intelligence which he has chosen, and to place all the burden of his life upon it."

So when Christians came to the interpretation of their Scriptures, under this sense of their inspiration (whether articulated clearly or not), they had a twofold aim before them. Filled, on the one hand, with the conviction of the wealth of knowledge stored in them, they were bound, for practical as well as for speculative purposes, to explore as fully as possible the depths behind the obvious surface-meaning ; and, on the other hand, they were bound to explain away all that, when taken in its literal sense, was offensive to human reason or seemed unworthy of the Deity.

[1] Philo *de Somniis* i 20 on Gen. 28[11]—Hatch *l.c.*

Modern conceptions of careful scholarly interpretation and of the
need of investigation into the exact sense of words, in connexion
with the circumstances in which they were first used, were in
those days unknown. The inspired Scriptures were separated by
a wide chasm from all other books and writings—the heavenly
from the earthly; and so the superficial meaning was the furthest
from the real meaning. To the uninitiated Scripture was as a
hieroglyph which needed a key that few possessed to decipher its
enigmas. So from the first the method of typical and allegorical
interpretation was practised. It was the way which some at
least of the writers of the New Testament adopted in dealing
with the Old, and understood that Christ himself had sanctioned.[1]
And the author of the Epistle to Barnabas [2] carried on the same
method in an elaborate application to Christ and to men of the
imagery of the Day of Atonement.

It was never supposed that writings, because inspired, must
be easily understood by every one; but it was not till the time
of Origen that a definite theory was framed which excludes from
consideration the obvious literal sense of many passages.

Irenaeus was content to believe that there was nothing in
Scripture which did not serve some purpose of instruction and
yet to acquiesce in failure to explain all passages. There is
nothing undesigned, nothing which does not carry with it some
suggestion or some proof. But we are unable to understand all
mysteries; and " we need not wonder that this is our experience
in spiritual and heavenly matters and things which have to be
revealed to us, when many of the things which lie at our feet
. . . and are handled by our hands . . . elude our knowledge,
and even those we have to resign to God ".[3] And he cannot
see why it should be felt as a difficulty that when the Scriptures
in their entirety are spiritual some of the questions dealt with in
them we are able by the grace of God to solve, but others have
to be referred to God Himself: and so it is always God who is
teaching and man who is learning all through from God.[4] The
typical and allegorical method he condemns as used by the
Gnostics, but he does not shrink from adopting it at times himself.[5]

---

[1] *E.g.* as to Elias—Matt. 17[10] ff, Mark 9[11] ff; cf. *Epistle to the Hebrews* all through;
and St Paul, *e.g.* Gal. 4[22] ff.

[2] *Ep. Barn.* i 7.   [3] *Adv. Haer.* ii 41—Harvey vol. i p. 350.

[4] *Ibid.* p. 351. See further, Harnack *DG.* Eng. tr. vol. ii p. 251.

[5] The allegorical method was universally accepted, and it was only the extravagant
employment of it by the Gnostics in support of their wildest conceptions to which

In this he is at one with most of the early Fathers, of whom it has been said that since they knew nothing, thought of nothing, felt nothing but Christ, it is not surprising that they met him everywhere. Their great object was to shew the connexion between the Old and New Covenants—that the New was the spiritual fulfilment of the Old.

So Tertullian [1] could say that the form of prophetical utterance was "not always and not in all things" allegorical and figurative, and he refused to admit limitations of time in things connected with the revelation of God.[2] And Clement of Alexandria found rich meaning in the candlestick with its seven lights.[3]

It is in Clement that we first find a definite theory of a threefold sense of Scripture.[4] "The Saviour taught the Apostles", he says, "first of all in typical and mystic fashion, and then by parable and enigma, and thirdly when they were alone with him clearly without disguise", — the concealment which he practised leading men on to further enquiries.

Origen further developed this theory.[5] According to his teaching the Holy Scriptures are the only source from which knowledge of the truth can be obtained, and they convey a threefold sense which corresponds to the tripartite division of man into body, soul, and spirit. First, there is the grammatical or historical meaning, which corresponds to the body and may be called the bodily sense. And, secondly, there is the moral or anagogical meaning, which corresponds to the soul and may be called the psychic sense. And, thirdly, there is the mystical or allegorical meaning, which corresponds to the spirit and may be called the spiritual sense. "The individual ought", he writes,[6] "to pourtray the ideas of Holy Scripture in a threefold manner

exception could be taken. Far-fetched as the interpretations of some of the Fathers seem to a modern scholar, they were sane and commonplace in comparison with the meanings which Gnostic ingenuity discovered in plain and simple passages of Scripture.

[1] *De Resurrectione Carnis* 20 *ad fin.*

[2] Cf. 'Non habet tempus Aeternitas' *adv. Marc.* iii 5, i 8.

[3] Clem. Al. *Strom.* v 6.

[4] *Strom.* i 28 *q.v.* and fragment 66. "The sense of the law is to be taken in three ways—either as exhibiting a symbol or laying down a precept for right conduct, or as uttering a prophecy." Here is the triple sense of Scripture—mystic, moral, prophetic. Cf. *Strom.* vi 15.

[5] See esp. *de Princip.* iv §§ 1–27, esp. § 11.

[6] *De Princip.* iv § 11, Tr. A.-N.C. Library.

upon his soul : in order that the simple man may be edified by the
' flesh ', as it were, of the Scripture, for so we name the obvious
sense ; while he who has ascended a certain way [may be edified]
by the ' soul ', as it were.   The perfect man, again, and he who
resembles those spoken of by the apostle, when he says ' We
speak wisdom among them that are perfect . . .' [may receive
edification] from the spiritual law, which has a shadow of good
things to come.   For as man consists of body, soul, and spirit,
so in the same way does Scripture, which has been arranged to
be given by God for the salvation of men."   This method of
interpretation, Origen points out, is recognized in Holy Scripture
—Christ distinguished between the first and second in the
Sermon on the Mount and on other occasions ; and the allegorical
and mystical senses were utilized in the arguments of the Epistles
to the Galatians and to the Hebrews.[1]   The literal sense, however, was not always possible.[2]   Instances of things which have
no religious bearing (such as genealogies), or are repulsive to
morality, or unworthy of God, or opposed to the law of nature
or of reason, must be spiritualized by allegorical interpretation.
They do not instruct us if taken literally, and are designed to
call men to the spiritual explanation.   So with regard to contradictions in the narratives of the evangelists,[3] he argues that the
truth does not consist in the ' bodily characters ' (the literal
sense).   His treatment of such cases goes far to justify the
description of his method as ' biblical alchemy '.   It is applied by
him to the New Testament as well as to the Old.   The Temptation, for example, is not regarded as simple history, and precepts
such as Take no purse [4] and Turn the other cheek [5] are not to
have their literal sense attributed to them.   So too in respect
of the miracles, he finds their most precious significance in the
allegory which they include.   He lays great stress on the need
of study, which such a method obviously demands, and of attention
and purity and reverence.[6]

[1] Origen cites Gal. 4[24], 1 Cor. 10[6-11], Heb. 4[8, 9].
[2] *Ibid.* § 12 ; cf. *Hom.* ii in Gen. 6.   [3] Cf. *Hom.* x in Joh.
[4] Luke 10[4].   [5] Matt. 5[39], and so 1 Cor. 7[18].
[6] Cf. Athanasius *de Incarnatione Verbi, ad fin.*   "For the investigation and
true knowledge of the Scriptures there is need of a good life and a pure soul and
Christian virtue. . . . He who wishes to understand the mind of the divines must
previously wash and cleanse his soul by his life. . . ."

The same method of exegesis was followed, to a large extent at all events, by the later Eastern Fathers, especially by the Cappadocians. See *e.g.* Gregory of Nyssa *de comm. Not.* p. 181 Migne, *Or. Cat.* 32, *in Cant. Cant.* p. 756 Migne, *c. Eunom.* vii p. 744 Migne.

After Origen the first attempt at a formal statement of the principles of interpretation that calls for notice was that of Tyconius, an African Donatist (*c.* 370–420). He drew up seven rules of interpretation which Augustine a little later discussed and, with some reservations, recommended as useful though incomplete. (See the edition of F. C. Burkitt *Texts and Studies* vol. iii no. 1, and Augustine *de Doct. Christ.* iii chs. xxx–xxxvii. On Augustine as Interpreter, see W. Cunningham *Hulsean Lectures*—'St Austin'.) Methods very different from Origen's were followed by the chief leaders of the school of Antioch, but they were not systematized as his were. (See *e.g.* Theodore of Mopsuestia *ed.* Swete *Introd.* and Chrysostom—W. R. W. Stephens, p. 421 and ff.) In the West also, on the whole, a more literal and meagre method of interpretation prevailed, at least until the time of Ambrose, who brought back under the influence of the writings of Origen and Basil a richer and more varied treatment of the Scriptures.

The Place of Tradition in the Interpretation of Scripture

As long as such methods were accepted it is obvious that a great variety of interpretations was possible, and that Scripture by itself could hardly be considered a sufficient guide. It could be claimed by bòth sides on most questions. Hence in controversy, and particularly in controversy with the Gnostics, there originated the definite assertion that it can only be correctly understood in close connexion with the tradition of the Church. Such a claim was quite accordant with the primitive conception of tradition, not as an independent source of doctrine but as essentially hermeneutic, forming with the written words one river of knowledge.

Of the nature of this tradition somewhat different views were held, according as the security for its truth was found rather in the living personal voice of individuals (the continuous historical episcopate), passing on to one another from the earliest days the word of knowledge, or in the unbroken continuity of teaching which external descent of place guaranteed (the rule of faith). The latter offered, obviously, the easier test, and the highest importance was attached to it.

Irenaeus is the first to argue out the matter. He puts the

question — Supposing, as might have happened, that we had
no Scriptures, to what should we have to make our appeal?
"Should we not have to go back to the most ancient Churches,
in which the Apostles lived, and take from them . . . what
is fixed and ascertained? What else could we do? If the
Apostles themselves had not left us writings, should we not be
obliged to depend on the teaching of the tradition which they
bequeathed to those to whose care they left the Churches?"[1]
We must go back to the most ancient Churches—it is here, in
the consent of Churches, that Irenaeus sees the guarantee of truth.
He takes for granted that the Apostles are the ultimate authority,
and when the question of the meaning of the Christian revelation
is disputed it is to them that all men would agree to make
appeal. To the Apostles themselves, in person, appeal is no
longer possible; but their representatives and successors are
still to be found in every Church. The bishops, or the presbyters
(for Irenaeus uses either word for the heads or governing bodies
of Churches), were appointed at first and taught by them; and
they in turn, generation by generation, in unbroken succession,
have handed on to their successors the same tradition. Irenaeus
seems to have in mind the possibility that in a particular case
there might be some flaw in this traditional teaching—so he
appeals to the general consensus of many such Churches. That
in which you find the Churches of apostolic foundation agreeing,
scattered as they are over many regions of the world—that, at
all events, you may be sure is part of the genuine apostolic
tradition. As an instance he points to the one Church in the
West which was supposed to be able to claim apostolic foundation
—the Church of Rome. The prestige which attached to it, from
its central position in the world's metropolis, made it the most
convenient and conspicuous test.[2] Christians from all lands
were continually coming and going, and therefore any departure
from the tradition would be most easily detected. The Church
of Rome was, in this way, always before the eyes of the world
and under the judgement of other Churches, so that no innovation

[1] Iren. *adv. Haer.* iii 4. 1—Harvey vol. ii pp. 15, 16. It will be noted that though
priority is claimed for the tradition, yet it is appealed to not as an independent
source of doctrine but as a means of determining the true sense of the Scriptures.

[2] Such no doubt is the meaning of the phrase 'propter potentiorem principali-
tatem'—'on account of its more influential pre-eminence', *i.e.* its prominence and
influence (*ibid.* iii 3. 1—Harvey vol. ii pp. 8, 9). See also the note on 'principalis
ecclesia' in Abp. Benson's *Cyprian*, p. 537.

there had any chance of escaping notice and criticism. The tradition preserved at Rome might therefore be regarded as having the tacit sanction of all the other Churches, and by reference to it any one in doubt might easily convince himself of the oneness of the apostolic tradition of the whole Church. And so he could say that " the tradition of the Apostles, made manifest as it is through all the world, can be recognised in every Church by all who wish to know the truth ";[1] and to the pretended secret doctrine of heretics he opposes the public preaching of the faith of the apostolic Churches; against the mutability and endless varieties of their explanations he sets the unity of the teaching of the Church; against their novelty, her antiquity; against their countless subdivisions into schools and parties, the uniformity and universality of her traditional witness.[2] It is this which he regards as the chief instrument in the conversion of the nations, in conjunction with the Holy Spirit in their hearts.

A similar estimate of the authority of ecclesiastical tradition in the interpretation of Scripture was maintained by Tertullian, though he gives it different characteristic expression. In dealing with heretics he conceives them as arraigned before a tribunal as defendants in a suit which the Church as plaintiff brings against them. He does not take their many false interpretations one by one and proceed to prove them wrong, though he was ready to do this vigorously on occasion; but he exercises the right, allowed by Roman law to plaintiffs in an action, to limit the inquiry to a single point; and the point he chooses is the legitimacy of the heretics' appeal to Holy Scripture. He aims, that is, at shewing cause why the interpretations of any one outside the Church should be dismissed without examination, apart from any consideration of their intrinsic merit. If he establishes this point the heretics are at once ruled out of court, as having no *locus standi*; while, if he fails, it is still open to him, according to the principles of Roman law, to take fresh action on all the other points excluded from the suit. He insists,[3] accordingly, on this limitation of the question, and asks,

[1] Iren. *adv. Haer.* iii 3. 1.
[2] See further Lipsius, Art. "Irenaeus" in *D.C.B.*
[3] *De Praescriptione Haereticorum*—"Concerning the Limitation of the Suit against the Heretics", esp. §§ 15, 19, ed. T. H. Bindley, who rejects the common explanation of *praescriptio* as meaning the 'preliminary plea' or objection lodged at the commencement of a suit, which—if maintained—dispensed with the need of

" Whose are the Scriptures ?   By whom and through whose
means and when and to whom was the discipline (the teaching
or system) handed down which makes men Christians ?   Wherever you find the true Christian discipline and faith, there will
be the truth of the Christian Scriptures and expositions and all
traditions."   It is the Church which is the keeper and guardian
of all these possessions, and therefore it is the Church and the
Church only which can determine the truth.   Heretics have no
right to use Scripture in argument against the orthodox, who
alone are able to decide what is its meaning.

Clement of Alexandria goes so far as to say that he who
spurns the ecclesiastical tradition ceases to be a man of God.[1]

And Origen, for all his elaborate system of interpretation,
declares, in the Prologue to the work in which it is expressed,
the necessity of holding fast to the ecclesiastical preaching
which has been handed down by the Apostles in orderly succession from one to another, and has continued in the Churches
right down to the present time.   " That alone ought to be
believed to be truth which differs in no respect from the
ecclesiastical and apostolic tradition." [2]

It is still the consent of Churches that is the test of truth.
Athanasius seems to be the first to quote the 'Fathers' as
witnesses to the faith,[3] but more particularly as guaranteeing its
antiquity than as being themselves invested with personal
authority as interpreters.   So Cyril of Jerusalem, who strongly
asserts the importance of Scripture, recognizes the authority of
the Church at its back.   It is from the Church that the catechumen must learn what are the books to which he must go.[4]
And Augustine was only expressing the common sentiment
when he declared that he would not believe the Gospel if it
were not for the authority of the Catholic Church.[5]

---

entering into any discussion of the merits of a case. *Praescriptio* technically meant
a clause prefixed to the *intentio* of a *formula* for the purpose of limiting the scope of
an inquiry (excluding points which would otherwise have been left open for discussion before the *judex*), and at the time when Tertullian wrote it was used only of
the plaintiff. ' Demurrer' is thus technically wrong, and somewhat misleading as a
title of the treatise.

[1] *Strom.* vii 16.   [2] *De Princip.* Proem 1.

[3] See his letter on the Dated Creed in Socrates *H.E.* ii 37, and the *Ep.
Encycl.* 1.

[4] *Cat.* iv 33.

[5] 'Ego vero evangelio non crederem, nisi me catholicae ecclesiae commoveret
auctoritas' (*c. Ep. Manich.* 6).

The most elaborate, as the most famous, statement of the case for tradition was not drawn up till towards the middle of the fifth century, when Vincent of Lerinum was roused by the apparent novelty of Augustine's doctrines of Grace and Predestination to expound the principles by which the Faith of the Church might be determined.[1] The two foundations which he lays down are still the divine law (or Holy Scripture) and the tradition of the Catholic Church. The first is sufficient by itself, if it could be rightly understood, but it cannot be understood without the guidance of the tradition, which shews what has been believed everywhere, always, and by all. *Quod ubique, quod semper, quod ab omnibus*—this is the great principle on which Vincent takes his stand. But he recognizes that it is not always easy of application, and he has to support it by the testimony of majorities either of the Church as a whole or of teachers as against minorities, antiquity as against novelty, general Councils as against individual or local errors. If part of the Church separates itself from the common body, it is the larger society that must be followed; if a false doctrine arises and threatens the Church, the best test is antiquity, which can no longer be misled; if in antiquity itself particular teachers or localities have erred, the decision of a general Council is decisive, if a general Council has pronounced upon the matter; if not, the Christian must examine and compare the writings of the recognised teachers, and hold fast by what all alike in one and the same sense have clearly, frequently, and consistently upheld. All innovations are really wickedness and mental aberration: in them ignorance puts on the cloak of knowledge, weak-mindedness of 'educidation', darkness of light. Pure knowledge is given only in the universal, ancient, unanimous tradition. It is antiquity that is the really decisive criterion of truth.

Assertions such as these might seem to be prohibitive of any kind of growth or progress in Religion; but Vincent was much

---

[1] *Adversus profanas omnium novitates haereticorum Commonitorium*, written about 434, attention having been aroused in the West to the question of tradition by the Donatist and Pelagian controversies. Vincent seems to have adopted some of Augustine's rules, though he would use them against him. He was a member of the famous monastery on the island near Cannes, now known as L'île Saint Honorat, from Honoratus the founder. A good analysis of the *Commonitorium* will be found in Harnack *DG.* ii [3], pp. 106–108 (Eng. tr. vol. iii pp. 230–232); handy editions in vol. ix of Hurter's *S. Patrum Opuscula Selecta*, and in the *Sammlung Quellenschriften* ed. Krüger.

too scholarly and sound a thinker to commit himself to such a negation. When the argument brings him to the question, ' Is there in the Church of Christ a progress in Religion ? ' he answers, Yes ; there has been great progress. And he shews by the images of the increase of a child and of a plant the nature of the progress. It is an organic growth, which consists in deepening rather than in change. No innovation comes in, for a single innovation would destroy all. Religion is strengthened with years and widened with time, and built up more elegantly with age ; but all remains fundamentally the same. What the Church has always had in view has been the explanation and strengthening of doctrine already believed ; greater plainness, more exact precision of statement, finer discrimination of sense. Aroused by the novelties of heretics, she has, by decrees of Councils, confirmed for posterity the tradition received from her ancestors ; for the sake of enlightenment and better understanding she has embraced in a few letters a mass of things, and by a new term sealed the sense of the faith which was not new.

Yet in spite of this high estimate of the value of tradition, Vincent is obliged in some cases to fall back upon Scripture. Heresies which are already widely extended and deep-rooted cannot, he sees, be disproved by the appeal to the unanimity of teachers : so many of them could be cited in support of erroneous views. Old heresies, never quite destroyed, had had opportunity in the long course of time to steal away the truth, and their adherents to falsify the writings of the Fathers. In such cases we must depend on the authority of Scripture only.

It is hardly true to say that this admission involves the bankruptcy of tradition.[1] It may rather be taken as shewing the fair balance of the author's mind. He does not profess to give an easy road to truth. He lays down criteria, almost all of which demand for their use no little research and patience. He believes that the great majority of teachers have rightly interpreted the Christian revelation from the first, but where their consensus is not obvious he would decide the ambiguity by appeal to the Book which embodies the traditional interpretation of the earliest ages. He is really, in this, referring back to the standard tradition. And there never was in those days a time when the leaders of Christian opinion were not prepared to

[1] As Harnack *l.c.*

make a similar reference of disputed questions to that court, and to check by the authority of Holy Scripture too great freedom in reading into Christianity ideas that were foreign to its spirit. So staunch a champion of tradition as Cyprian could say that "custom without truth is the antiquity of error",[1] and that "we ought not to allow custom to determine, but reason to prevail";[2] even as Tertullian had insisted "Our Lord Christ called himself the truth, not the custom. . . . You may be sure that whatever savours not of truth is heresy, even though it be ancient custom".[3]

Such then were the principles which prevailed during the period with which we are concerned, in which the Creeds were framed and most of the great doctrines formulated. By such principles the partial and misleading explanations and theories were tested and banished from the Church as heresies, and the fuller and more adequate interpretations were worked out. It is the course of this progress that we have to trace.

It was, as we have seen, from Gentile quarters that the chief stimulus to the actual formulation of doctrines came, and it is with attempts at interpretation which spring from Gentile conceptions that we shall be most concerned. But first of all must be noted certain peculiar readings of the revelation in Christ, and of the relations in which the Gospel stands to the revelation given in Judaism, which are characteristic of Jewish rather than of Gentile thought.

[1] *Ep.* 74 § 9.   [2] *Ep.* 71 § 3.   [3] Tert. *de Virg. Vel.* § 1.

CHAPTER V

Characteristic Jewish Conceptions

ROOTED in Jewish thought were two ideas, from the obvious significance of which the dominant conceptions of the Christian revelation seemed to be drifting further and further. Characteristic of Judaism were its strong monotheism and its belief in the eternal validity of the Mosaic Law. There was one God and only one, a God of righteousness, far removed from the world; and the 'divinity' of Christ seemed to be a kind of idolatry, and to have more in common with the polytheistic notions of the heathen than with the truth revealed of old to the Israelites. And again, the Law was given by God: it was a divine revelation; and therefore it must have the characteristics of the divine, and be eternal, unchanging, and final. And therefore the mission of Jesus of Nazareth, if from God, was a mission to purify and revive the old revelation, and the Gospel does not supersede but only elucidates the Law.

For views such as these it is clear some support could be found in primitive Christian teaching before the full force of the revelation in Christ was widely felt. In the teaching of Christ himself, as recorded in the Gospels, there is no antagonism to the Law: the traditions of men which were a pernicious growth round it are brushed aside, but the Law is treated with reverence and its teaching developed rather than superseded. Disregard of the Law by Christians of Jewish birth, at any rate, might seem to lack all primitive authority; and we need not wonder if such Christians lagged behind the progress to a purely spiritual interpretation of the Jewish ordinances, which was so largely stimulated by the constantly increasing preponderance of Gentile over Jewish influence in the Church.[1] And the fear lest the

---

[1] It is clear from the Epistle of Clement that by the end of the first century all traces of the controversy between Pauline and Judaistic Christianity had vanished at Rome and at Corinth.

doctrine of the divinity of Christ might endanger the truth that God is one was, as a matter of fact, amply justified by the difficulty that was experienced in finding any satisfactory expression to account for all the facts.

Ebionism

These two ideas were the source of what are called the Judaizing heresies,[1] the representatives of which are known as Ebionites.[2] We have no record of their origin as a distinct and separate body.[3] It is as schools of thought within the Church that Justin, our earliest informant, seems to regard them.[4] He speaks of some Christians who still keep the Law, and maintain that it is necessary to salvation, and would enforce it on all members of the Church, and of others who only observe the ordinances of the Law themselves without desiring to impose them upon all. With the former he does not agree, and he thinks they ought to be excluded from Christian communion; with the latter he has no quarrel, they are still brothers, though some Christians refused communion to them.[5] He also speaks of some who regard Jesus as Christ, the Messiah, yet pronounce him a man born of men, but he does not shew whether these were identical with the intolerant observers of the Law or not. The one distinction which is clear is based on the attitude to the Law, milder or stricter.[6]

[1] 'Judaizing' may not be the most accurate designation for what perhaps is only in origin an archaic form of interpretation, but relatively to the Catholic interpretation of the Person and Gospel of Christ it expresses the facts sufficiently exactly.

[2] Heb. Ebionim, "poor men": *i.e.* men who taught a beggarly doctrine. Cf. the bad sense at first attaching to the name 'Christiani', 'Messiah-men'; and cf. Origen *de Princip.* iv 1. 22: Ἐβιωναῖοι, τῆς πτωχῆς διανοίας ἐπώνυμοι· Ἐβίων γὰρ ὁ πτωχὸς παρ' Ἑβραίοις ὀνομάζεται.

[3] Dr. Hort supposed they might have come into existence through the scattering of the old Jerusalem Church by Hadrian's edict. Some, like Hegesippus, who maintained the tradition of St James, when once detached from the Holy City would in a generation or two become merged in the greater Church without. Others would be driven into antagonism to the Gentile Church of Asia and become Judaistic in principle as well as in practice, being isolated and therefore less receptive of the influence of other Churches. (It should be noted that such Judaistic Christians are heard of only in the neighbourhood of Palestine, Syria, and Asia Minor.)

[4] Justin *Dial. c. Tryph.* 47 and 48.—See Hort *Judaistic Christianity* p. 196, on whose discussion the following statement of the facts is based.

[5] See Hort—the two lines, development and supersession of the Law, in the teaching of Christ himself (*ibid.* 'Christ and the Law', Lect. II).

[6] Before the time of Justin, Ignatius had had to denounce some Judaizing Chris-

On their teaching as to the person of Christ more stress is laid by Irenaeus,[1] who is the first to name them Ebionaeans, and describes them as holding a view like that of Cerinthus and Carpocrates, referring no doubt to denial of the divinity rather than to any 'Gnostic' conceptions. All such are condemned by him as heretics.

Origen[2] distinguishes two classes, and says that both rejected St Paul's Epistles (no doubt because of their views as to the Law).

And Eusebius[3] after him, more precisely, makes the difference to consist in higher and lower conceptions of the person of Christ, both classes insisting on the observance of the Law. One class held a natural birth and the superior virtue of a plain and ordinary man as a sufficient explanation : the others accepted the super- natural birth, but denied his pre-existence as the Word and Wisdom of God (did not, that is, accept the eternal Sonship and the doctrine of the Logos) ; they rejected the Pauline writings and used only the Gospel according to the Hebrews, while they still observed the Sabbath and other Jewish customs, but also the Lord's Day in memory of the Resurrection.

Later still Epiphanius[4] could assign different names to the two schools, regarding them as separate sects—Nazaraeans and Ebionaeans. But Epiphanius probably erred in this precision. There seems to be no evidence that there were two distinct com- munities with different designations. It is probable that 'Nazar- aeans' was the title used by the Jewish Christians of Syria as a description of themselves in the fourth century and before,[5] while 'Ebionaeans', an equally genuine popular term,[6] had become the traditional name in ecclesiastical literature.

That these schools of thought died hard is shewn by the judgement passed on them by Jerome,[7] who prefaces his reference by the words " What am I to say of the Ebionites who pretend to be Christians ? ", and then goes on to speak of some who in his own times were spread over the East, commonly known as

tians who were lagging behind the revelation of Christ, refusing credence to anything which could not be proved from the Old Testament and anxious still to maintain the old associations intact. See *Philad.* viii ; *Magn.* viii-xi, and *infra* Gnosticism p. 80 note 2.

[1] Iren. *adv. Haer.* i 22—Harvey vol. i p. 212, and iv 52. 1, v 1. 3—Harvey vol. ii pp. 259, 316.

[2] *Contra Cels.* v 61, 65.

[3] Euseb. *Hist. Eccl.* iii 27.

[4] Epiph. *adv. Haer.* xxix and xxx.

[5] Cf. Acts 24⁵.

[6] Cf. Matt. 5³.

[7] *Ep.* 112 § 13.

Nazaraeans, who believed in Christ, the Son of God, born of the Virgin Mary, and say that he suffered under Pontius Pilate and rose again, 'in whom', he says, 'we also believe'; but yet, he avers, they only pretend to be Christians, and while they want to be at one and the same time both Jews and Christians, they succeed in being neither Jews nor Christians.

These words of Jerome plainly shew that the belief in the eternal validity of the Law and in the need for observance of its ordinances survived as anachronisms in some circles, claiming the name of Christian, in which the 'orthodox' explanation of the nature and person of Christ was accepted.

Cerinthus and his School

Of all the Ebionites one individual only is known to fame, Cerinthus—and he had almost as much in common with the 'Gnostics' as with them. Really he stands with his followers as a separate school, distinct from both. The most trustworthy evidence as to the time at which he lived is furnished by the tale [1] of his meeting with St John in one of the public baths at Ephesus, when St John espying him rushed out, saying he was afraid the walls of the bath might fall and crush them, since Cerinthus the enemy of truth was there.

The province of Asia was probably the scene of his activity, though Hippolytus, without mentioning Asia, says he was trained in Egyptian lore. In his teaching, side by side with the 'Judaizing' elements, such as have been noticed (Jesus, the Son of Mary and Joseph, born as other men; circumcision and the observance of the Sabbath obligatory; rejection of the writings of St Paul, the Acts, and all the Gospels, except the Gospel of St Matthew in Hebrew, or more probably the 'Gospel according to the Hebrews'), there stand quite different and fresh ideas, which are akin to the conceptions of the 'Gnostics'. These have to do with the relations between the world and God, and between the human and the divine in the person and work of the Lord.

---

[1] Reported by Irenaeus iii 3, 4—Harvey vol. ii p. 13 ; and twice quoted by Eusebius (*Hist. Eccl.* iii 28, iv 14). Irenaeus also says (iii 11. 7—Harvey vol. ii p. 40) that the Gospel of St John was directed against Cerinthus (*e.g.* the doctrine of Creation by the Logos). Cf. Robert Browning *A Death in the Desert.* Epiphanius (*l.c.*) says he was the ringleader of St Paul's Judaizing antagonists at Jerusalem. Hegesippus does not seem to have mentioned him, nor does Justin, nor Clement, nor Tertullian.

5

The creation, he taught, was not effected by God Himself, but by angels—powers distinct from God—one of whom was the God of the Jews and the giver of the Law. As to the person of the Redeemer, he held that his Sonship to God could only be due to his ethical merits, which qualified him for a special gift of grace and spiritual power. God might not arbitrarily make a person holy. So the man Jesus was first tested in early life, and then at his baptism there descended upon him, in the form of a dove, the Spirit of God, the power from above, the Christ (regarded evidently as a pre-existent personality [1]), who revealed to him the Father, and enabled him to do his miraculous works, and before the Passion parted from him and returned to the place from whence he came.[2] Furthermore, he taught that the Resurrection of Jesus was still future. There was thus only a conjunction between the divine and the human in him, no real union of the Christ and Jesus. The principal object of the mission was educational rather than redemptive, fulfilling the prophetic office of Messiah; the sufferings were human only, and the revelation was of doctrine. Another object, corresponding to the kingly office of Messiah, was the introduction of the millennial reign, although its realization was still future. Of the millennium, the thousand years' reign of Christ upon earth, during which his followers would be rewarded for their loyalty, he held most sensual and material views;[3] but millenarianism was too widely accepted in the Church to be characteristic of any particular school of thought.[4]

The Clementines

Besides the Cerinthians we have knowledge of another set of Ebionites, who certainly worked out a peculiar system of doctrine and usage—the men of the 'Clementines'. Their teaching is embodied in the writings that have come down to us under the name of Clement, entitled *The Homilies* (extant in Greek), and *The Recognitions* (in the Latin translation of Rufinus and also partly in Syriac); which are probably independent abridgements of a voluminous book called the *Travels of Peter*, which was

---

[1] There is no evidence that he used the Gnostic term 'Aeon' of the Christ.

[2] Cf. the 'Gospel of Peter'. "My power, my power, thou hast deserted me!" This is the only docetic element in the teaching of Cerinthus.

[3] Eusebius, the determined opponent of 'Chiliasm', speaks specially of this (*l.c.*).

[4] See *infra* p. 68, Note on Chiliasm.

current early in the third century.[1] This book was of the nature
of a historical novel composed with a controversial purpose, professing to narrate the circumstances in which Clement became
the travelling companion of the Apostle Peter, and to give an
account of Peter's teaching.   It originated among the sect of
Elchasaites (Helxaites), who held the book Elchasai (Helxai)[2]
sacred.   These were probably Essenes of Eastern Palestine, who,
after the destruction of the Temple and the abolition of the
system of the Temple services and sacrifices, were brought to recognise Jesus as a true prophet, though regarding the idea of his
divinity as a delusion.   With this and other usual notes of
Ebionism they combined some Essene tenets as to sacrifice and
repeated purificatory washings and abstinence from the use of
flesh and ascetic practices, speculations about angels and a form
of 'emanation' theory; but they were free from Gnostic notions
of creation and docetism.[3]   Most characteristic, perhaps, is their
conception of the Christ (identical with the Son of God) as the
eternal Prophet of Truth, who appears from time to time incarnate in perfect men.   By virtue of their inward spirit men are
akin to the divine, the highest order of existence in the created
world; but they have also in them earthly desire, which tends
to lower them to earth; and so their state becomes one of
alienation from God, as the earth-spirit exerts its irresistible
attraction.   Therefore, to save men from utter deterioration,
must the Christ appear in successive incarnations.   Wherever
the idea of man appears perfectly in an individual, there is a
form of the appearance of Christ—the created idea of man. His
appearance shews God's image for the age in which it happens.
Such incarnations were recognized in Adam, Enoch, Noah,
Abraham, Isaac, Jacob, Moses, Jesus.   The manifestation in
Jesus is regarded as the last, after which the Christ has permanent repose.   To his death and resurrection no significance

[1] Hort *Judaistic Christianity* p. 201.   See also *D.C.B.* Art. 'Clementine
Literature', and Dorner.

[2] See Hippol. *Refut. Haer.* ix 13.   They professed to have obtained this book
from the Seres, a Parthian tribe (a mythical race like the Hyperboreans of Greek
legend), who were perfectly pure and therefore perfectly happy, the recipients of a
revelation which had been first made in the third year of Trajan (100 A.D.).   Helxai
(Elchasai)—an Aramaic word meaning 'the hidden power'—was both the name of
the divine messenger, who imparted the revelation, and the title of the book in
which it was recorded.   The book appears to have been a long time in secret
circulation before it became known to the orthodox teachers of the Church.

[3] See *infra* p. 75.

appears to be attached. His mission has an educational purpose only, to exhibit to men a kind of object-lesson.

Other details of the system represented in the 'Clementine' books (as well as the supposed attack on St Paul under the name of Simon Magus and the twisting of 'texts' of Scripture to support the views described) call for no further treatment here. It is enough to notice that it exhibits "the Judaizing principle, furnished with all the means of culture which the age supplied, gathering itself for its last stroke", and the failure of Judaism, reinforced by ascetic and other speculations selected from various philosophies, in its attempt to capture Christianity.

A similar endeavour from another quarter, doomed to like failure, comes before us next in Gnosticism.

CHILIASM

From the earliest times no doubt the Christian conception of salvation centred round two main ideas, one of which was the more intellectual or spiritual, and the other the more practical and material. The one was based on the conviction that in the person of the Christ there was given a full revelation of God—he was the Truth—and so salvation consisted essentially in the knowledge of God, as contrasted with the errors of heathendom and the defective conceptions of even the chosen people; a knowledge which included the gift of eternal life and all the privileges and joys of the highest spiritual illumination.[1] This is obviously an idea which requires for its full appreciation more cultivation of the mind and the spiritual faculties than the masses of men possess. More widely attractive was the other idea which saw in salvation membership of the glorious kingdom which Christ was about to establish on earth on his return, when a new order of things would be inaugurated, and for a thousand years his disciples would share the blessedness of human life under the happiest conditions. In this connexion the highest importance was attached to the doctrine of the resurrection of the body.[2] This conception of the reign upon earth of the Christ differed little from the common Jewish expectation, only the kingdom would be composed of Christians instead of the nation of Israel: and the Christian hopes in regard to it were largely derived from the Jewish apocalyptic writings, as were their conceptions of the fate of

---

[1] For this idea chief support was to be got from the Gospel according to St John.
[2] Probably the earliest indication of this is to be found in the case of the Thessalonians, some of whom feared that their relations and friends who had already died since they became Christians could have no share in the Messianic kingdom on earth.

the enemies of their Lord and all who rejected his claims.[1] The imagination pictured, and hopes were fixed on, a fairyland of ease and pleasure and delight. This was 'the great inheritance which the Gentile Christian communities received from Judaism, along with the monotheism assured by revelation and belief in providence', and though it was destined to be gradually dissipated—partly through the anti-judaistic spirit of the Greek and Roman communities, and partly through the growth of higher moral and spiritual conceptions—it was for a long time enjoyed and tenaciously held in wide and influential circles of Christian life. The second coming, in glory, involving the resurrection of the dead, judgement of living and dead, was probably deemed imminent by the great mass of early Christians, and the hope of it was their stay in persecution, and must have greatly aided them to bear their sufferings, whether associated with the further belief in the thousand years' reign upon earth or not. (It was equally foretold as the first coming in dishonour and suffering; cf. Justin *Apol.* i 52, and Iren. i 10, who distinguishes it as παρουσία from the first ἔλευσις.) This belief (so far as it was Christian rather than Jewish in origin) was based on sayings of Christ such as those in which he speaks of drinking with his disciples in his Father's kingdom (Matt. 26[29]), and promises that those who now hunger and thirst shall hereafter be satisfied (Matt. 5[6]), and that faithful service shall be rewarded by rule over many cities (Luke 19[17. 19]),—sayings which received a literal material interpretation.[2] And the definite assignment of a thousand years as the extent of the duration of the kingdom was made by the author of the Apocalypse (20[1-10]). For a thousand years the devil would be imprisoned, and martyrs and all who had not worshipped the beast and were free from his mark would come to life again and reign with Christ. This was 'the first resurrection', and only these—it appears—would have a share in the millennial kingdom, of which apparently Jerusalem 'the beloved city' was to be the centre. Among earlier writers[3] the belief was held by the authors of the Epistle of Barnabas,[4] the Shepherd, the second Epistle of Clement, by Papias, Justin, and by some of the Ebionites, and Cerinthus, according to the accounts of the Roman presbyter Caius in his treatise against the Montanists, quoted by Eusebius (*H.E.* iii 28). Of these Papias is one of the chief landmarks. Because of his belief in the millennium, Eusebius passed a disparaging criticism on his sense:[5] "I suppose he got those ideas through a misunderstanding of the apostolic

---

[1] *E.g.* the Apocalypses of Esra, Enoch, Baruch, Moses. Cf. the Apocalypse of Peter.

[2] Against this interpretation see Origen *de Princip.* ii 11 § 2.

[3] There is no reference to the millennial belief in Clement of Rome, Ignatius, Polycarp, Tatian, Athenagoras, Theophilus. But we are not justified in arguing from their silence that they did not hold it.

[4] *Ep. Barn.* 4, 15.　　　　　　　　　　[5] See Euseb. *H.E.* iii 39.

accounts, not perceiving that the things said by them were spoken mystically in figures. For he appears to have been of a very limited understanding, as one can see from his discourses." The materialistic character of their expectations is illustrated by the famous parable which he gives : "The days will come when vines shall grow, each having ten thousand branches, and in each branch ten thousand twigs, and in each twig ten thousand shoots, and in every one of the shoots ten thousand grapes, and every grape when pressed will give five-and-twenty measures of wine."

Justin shows the belief in exacter form. The Lord, Jesus Christ, was to return to Jerusalem, which was to be rebuilt, and there to eat and drink with his disciples,[1] and the Christian people were to be gathered together there and live in happiness with him and with the patriarchs and prophets.[2] This belief is not regarded by Justin as an essential part of the Christian faith (he acknowledges that many genuine Christians do not hold it), but he suggests that many who reject it reject also the resurrection of the dead (*i.e.* of the body), which is essential. For a thousand years the kingdom at Jerusalem would last for all believers in Christ, and then would take place the universal and eternal resurrection of all together and the judgement.[3] In support of the belief he cites the prophet Isaiah[4] and the apostle John,[5] and applies the imagery of the prophet Micah[6] to describe the happiness of the time when heaven and earth will be renewed,[7] but it will still be the same earth, and all who have faith set on Christ and know the truth expressed in his and his prophets' words will inherit in it eternal and imperishable blessings.[8]

These hopes were fully shared by Irenaeus (who derived them from Papias direct perhaps),[9] Melito,[10] Hippolytus,[11] Tertullian,[12] and Lactantius.[13]

---

[1] Justin *Dial. c. Tryph.* 51.

[2] *Ibid.* 80. This would be the first resurrection.

[3] *Ibid.* 81. Justin thus recognizes a twofold resurrection, as Irenaeus does. Apoc. xx was so understood. Tertullian seems to teach an immediate resurrection of those who are fitted for it, and a deferred resurrection of the more guilty, who must make amends by a longer course of purification in the under-world. See *de Anima* 58, where the suggestive thought is expressed that, as the soul must suffer, when disembodied, for the evil done in and by the flesh, so it may have refreshment on account of the pious and benevolent thoughts in which the flesh had no part. See also *de Res. Carn.* 42, and cf. Robert Browning *Rabbi Ben Ezra.*

[4] Isa. 65[17-25].   [5] Apoc. 20[4-6].   [6] Mic. 4[1-7] (*Dial.* 109, 110).

[7] *Dial.* 113.   [8] *Ibid.* 139.

[9] It is Irenaeus to whom we owe the parable of Papias quoted *supra* (see Iren. v 33–35). The letter from the Churches of Lugdunum and Vienna also shews Chiliastic ideas (Euseb. *H.E.* v 1 ff.).

[10] See Polycrates in Euseb. *H.E.* v 24.   [11] See *e.g. in Dan.* iv 23.

[12] See esp. *adv. Marc.* iii and *de Res. Carn.*

[13] *Inst. Div.* vii § 11 ff. (esp. § 24).

The Gnostics were the first to reject such conceptions (Marcion referred them to the prompting of the God of the Jews—the only resurrection possible was spiritual, partial here in this world, and in perfection hereafter).   The Gnostics were followed by 'Caius' and by Origen, who condemns the views as most absurd ;[1] but the most formidable assault upon Chiliastic teaching was made by Dionysius of Alexandria in his treatise *On the Promises*, rejecting the apostolic origin of the Apocalypse, which was the strongest support of all Chiliastic ideas.   To this work he was roused by one Nepos,[2] a bishop in the district of Arsinoe, who in the Chiliastic interest had written against the allegorical interpretation of the Apocalypse, insisting that it must be taken literally.[3]   The opposition of Dionysius seems to have been widely influential and effective in banishing all such materialistic expectations from the common faith of the Church.[4]   The Alexandrian theology made them impossible.   By the middle of the fourth century they had come to be considered heretical, and a final blow was struck by Augustine, who taught that the millennium was the present reign of Christ, beginning with the Resurrection,[5] and destined to last a thousand years.

---

[1] See *de Princip.* ii 11 § 2.   [2] See Euseb. *H.E.* vii 24.

[3] *The Refutation of Allegorists*—probably aimed at Origen.   (Euseb. *l.c.*)

[4] They died hard, however, among the monks of Egypt, as is shewn by the survival in Coptic and Ethiopic of materialistic Apocalypses which ceased to circulate elsewhere among Christians.   So Harnack *DG.* Eng. tr. vol. ii p. 30.

[5] See *e.g. de Civ. Dei* xx.   "Even now the Church is the kingdom of Christ . . . even now his saints reign with him."   At an earlier time Augustine had conceived of a corporeal 'first' resurrection of the saints, succeeded by a millennial rest upon earth, the delights of it being spiritual enjoyment of the presence of the Lord.

CHAPTER VI

Characteristics of Oriental Religious Thought

THOUGH it was to Jews that the earliest attempts at interpretation of the revelation in Christ were committed, and to Jews accordingly that the earliest explanations of the person and work of Jesus are due, it was not long before the Gentiles came in to take their share in the developement of Christian doctrine.

The first great movement which they originated came rather from the East than from the West; for the difference between the contemporary religious thought of the East and of the West was very marked.[1] The most fundamental feature of Oriental thought is probably 'the schism and unrest of the human mind, in view of the limitations of human nature, with uncontrolled longings after the infinite and absorption into God';[2] but Hellenism found in the world so much of beauty and of pleasure that its aspirations after the unseen were much less real. Both had in view, no doubt, the same end—the unity of the divine and the human; but Orientalism sought it by the annihilation of the human, while the method pursued by Hellenism certainly tended to annihilate the divine. The distinction between the two was not maintained. Characteristic of Oriental religions are frequent incarnations (or emanations) of God in the most perfect form available, to teach men knowledge of truth and conduct them to heaven; but all are transitory, there is no permanency about them and no true assumption of humanity: the human is to be absorbed in the divine. The Greeks, on the other hand, began from below; by virtue and valour men must for themselves mount up to the heights of Olympus and attain to the life divine, becoming as gods—the apotheosis of man. The divinity, such as it was, was dis-

---

[1] *E.g.* Indian and Persian compared with Greek.
[2] Neander *Hist. of Doct.* vol. i p. 6 (Bohn), cf. *Church Hist.* vol. ii.

tributed through the powers of nature, in many gods with limitations, Fate—a mysterious power—at the back of all (polytheism); or else it was regarded as the soul of the universe, diffused through all things, and not to be separated from the world, having no existence outside it (pantheism). In either case there is no God, as Jews and Christians conceived of God.

The Problem of Evil

The distinction between the religious thought of the East and of the West is readily seen in the different answers which were given to the question of the origin of evil, which was the great religious question. For the Jews no answer was provided in their sacred writings: they were only taught that the source of evil was not matter, that it was not inherent in the invisible material universe (which God, who made it, saw 'was very good'); they were taught that its essence was the assertion of the individual will against the will of God, or selfishness; and that God permitted its existence, being represented even in dramatic fashion sometimes as the cause of that which he permitted. By the writers of the New Testament no solution of the problem was attempted. But the Greek and Oriental philosophies had their answers ready.

The metaphysical schools of Greek philosophy hardly grappled with the problem.[1] It is the Stoics who represent the Greek solution, and their main object was to reconcile the fact of the existence of evil with the supposed perfection of the universe. The conclusions which they reached are expressed in the following theses. The imperfection of the part is necessary to the perfection of the whole: some things which appear evil are not really evil;[2] and again, on the other hand, evil is necessary to the existence of good, inasmuch as one of two contraries cannot exist without the other (so the existence of

[1] The Eleatics assert the dogma that the One alone exists, plurality and change have no real being (cf. the *Parmenides*). Plato did not elaborate any systematic treatment of the question, though apparently regarding matter as the source of evil—τὸ μὴ ὄν contrasted with τὸ ὄν (which is identified with τὸ ἀγαθόν, e.g. in the Timaeus). This conception was adopted by the Neoplatonists, e.g. Plotinus, and influenced Origen and other Christian thinkers. Aristotle deals with evil simply as a fact of experience. See further Mansel *The Gnostic Heresies* p. 23.

[2] This is illustrated by a saying of Seneca (*Ep.* 85. 30)—Grief (or pain) and poverty do not make a man worse; therefore they are not evils.

good connotes the existence of evil, the idea of the one being necessary to the idea of the other). These theses, it is rightly pointed out,[1] are not philosophical explanations of the origin of evil in the world, but examinations of the difficulties which its existence involves in relation to other facts or doctrines. The answer, such as it is, is negative rather than positive: evil is an unripe form of good, or the absence of good. It is the pantheistic solution, with the mark of somewhat flimsy optimism [2] on it: the unity of nature is preserved, but the reality of evil and of sin is sacrificed.[3] It was in keeping with the temper of the Greek, who worshipped nature 'naked and not ashamed', who was least of all men disposed to look on the gloomy side of the visible world, whose feelings opened out to all that was bright and beautiful and beneficial in nature.[4] The Hellenic mind was never much impressed by the sense of evil; and consequently Hellenic ethics had little influence in the earlier times on Christian doctrine. The influence of Hebraism was too strong.

The religious thought of the East, on the other hand, was much more deeply imbued with the sense of evil. Two principal theories characteristic of Persian and of Hindoo thought respectively stand out. The first is dualistic, based on the hypothesis of the existence of two eternal principles of good and of evil, between whom an original and perpetual struggle is maintained. The second supposes one original existence absolutely pure, the primitive source of good, from which by continuous descents (emanations) proceed successive degrees of lower and less perfect being, a gradual deterioration steadily taking place, till the final result is reached in evil, the form of being farthest removed from the primitive source of all existence.

Corresponding to these two theories of existence are two

---

[1] Mansel *l.c.*

[2] With it may be compared the position of Shaftesbury as represented by Pope, from which easily follows the complete subordination of the individual and the negation of personal religion, the natural transition to atheism—

    " Whatever wrong we call
    May, must be, right as relative to all.
    Discord is harmony not understood,
    All partial evil universal good."

[3] Hebraism, with one perfect God of righteousness outside the world, could realize sin. Hellenism, with no idea of perfection about its gods, had no place for sin in its thought: to break law, not to live in accordance with nature, was folly, not sin.

[4] Mansel *l.c.*

different views of evil.   The first is embodied in the Zoroastrian
system, according to which the material world was in the first
place created by the power of good (Ormuzd) in the space
between light and darkness,—first the heavens, then water, then
in succession the earth, the trees, cattle, men : and so far all
was good.   But the power of evil (Ahriman) obtained a footing
upon earth and attempted to counteract the work that had been
done by creating animals and plants of a contrary kind, and
inflicting upon men the evils of hunger, weariness that calls for
sleep, age, disease, and death, while leading them away from
their allegiance to the power of good.   And so the struggle
goes on, and man alone has the power of choosing on which
side he will fight, and so of partaking of good or evil.
According to this (the Persian or dualistic) theory of the universe, matter is the production of a beneficent being and not
essentially evil ; the source of evil is spiritual, and evil is a
terrible reality.

Quite different is the view which follows from the Hindoo
theory of existence.   The highest and truest mode of being is
pure spirit, and entirely good ; the lowest form of being is matter,
and entirely evil—it is indeed not properly to be called ' being '
at all : the only reality is spirit, and matter is—to speak accurately—a mere appearance and illusion, inasmuch as it lacks
true being.   Yet for practical purposes matter is synonymous
with evil, and the great aim of all religion is to free men from
its contamination, even at the cost of their annihilation.

Oriental Ideas applied to the Christian Revelation

Matter is essentially evil—this was the dominant principle
of Oriental religious thought to which its converts to Christianity clung most strenuously, though it was in flagrant opposition to the early Christian tradition.   If matter is evil, the
Supreme God (who is good) cannot have created the world, and
the Redeemer (who is divine) cannot have come in the flesh.
The creator of the world, the Demiurge, must be distinct from
the Supreme God—either an eternal power confronting him or a
rebellious servant.   And the body of Christ was not real, but
only seemed to be (Docetism) ; and so either the sufferings were
only apparent, or else the Redeemer who could not suffer was
separate from the man in whom he appeared.

The Gnostics—their Aims and Classification

The 'Gnostics' were thinkers who, starting from Oriental principles such as these, and feeling the need of redemption by a special divine revelation, believed that Jesus of Nazareth was the Redeemer sent to save sinners, and tried to work out this belief and these principles into a philosophical theory of the universe. It is this conviction of the need of Redemption, and the recognition of the person and work of Christ (in however perverted a form), which distinguish Gnosticism in all its schools as a real attempt at interpretation (*i.e.* a religious heresy) from a mere philosophical extravagance.[1] " The time is gone by ", wrote one of the soundest and soberest of modern scholars,[2] " when the Gnostic theories could be regarded as the mere ravings of religious lunatics. The problems which taxed the powers of a Basilides and a Valentinus are felt to be amongst the most profound and difficult which can occupy the human mind. . . . It is only by the study of Gnostic aberrations that the true import of the teaching of Catholic Christianity, in its moral as well as in its theological bearings, can be fully appreciated." They tried to find answers to such questions as, How can the absolute give birth to the relative ? unity to plurality ? good to evil ? There is no doubt that they made ' the first comprehensive attempt to construct a philosophy of Christianity ', and they have even been called the first Christian theologians.

They were schools of thought in the Church, esoteric philosophers, rather than sects, still looking to find in the Gospel the key to the enigmas of life, with no wish to withdraw from communion ; asking only for freedom of speculation, and finding no fault with the popular modes of presenting the Christian faith for the people.[3] But they drew a distinction between the popular simple faith, which was founded on authority and

---

[1] So Bigg (*Christian Platonists of Alexandria* p. 28) insists that "the interest, the meaning, of Gnosticism rests entirely upon its ethical motive. It was an attempt, a serious attempt, to fathom the dread mystery of sorrow and pain, to answer that spectral doubt which is mostly crushed down by force—Can the world as we know it have been made by God ? " He says "it is a mistake to approach the Gnostics on the metaphysical side ".

[2] Lightfoot—Preface to Mansel's *Gnostic Heresies.*

[3] Yet at least, when their teaching was repudiated by the official heads of the Church, they became rival Churches, and were obviously regarded as competitors by their 'orthodox' opponents (cf. Tert. *adv. Marc.* iv 5). They claimed to have all that the Church had, and more besides.

tradition, and the real knowledge—the Gnosis—which they themselves possessed. The former they regarded as merely the shell of the Christian theory of life, while they claimed a secret tradition of their own as the basis of the ' Gnosis ', and jealously guarded it as a mystery from all but the chosen few.[1]   No canons of interpretation, no theory of inspiration, had as yet been framed; and the open tradition and standards of the Church fell short of the aim they set before themselves—the apprehension of the spiritual contents of the Gospel in a spiritual manner in relation to aspects of life which seemed to be ignored.[2]   In this way they constituted themselves an intellectual aristocracy, for whom alone salvation in the full sense of the word was reserved; and they were therefore labelled ' Gnostics ' (knowing ones) by those who were not willing to admit the claim.   The label seems to have been affixed with little exact discrimination.   At all events it is used to cover very various forms of teaching, to some of which it scarcely applies at all; and no satisfactory classification of the Gnostics can be made.   A classification may be attempted based on two opposing views of the religion of the Jews.   By some it was regarded as an imperfect preparation for a Christian philosophy, which Christianity should complete and so supersede. By others it was regarded as a system fundamentally hostile to Christianity, which Christianity was to combat and overthrow. So Christ was differently regarded by different Gnostic schools as coming either to complete an imperfect revelation or to deliver the world from bondage to an evil creator and governour; and correspondingly diverse views of the Demiurge were held.   Another classification rests upon a broad distinction that was early

[1] From this point of view they have been called 'the first Freemasons' rather than the first theologians, though a closer analogy might be found in the practice of the Greek mysteries.

[2] Loofs (pp. 70, 73) distinguishes the chief variations of Gnosticism from (a) the Christian tradition (i.e. the popular creed) and (b) the Christian ecclesiastical philosophy.   He notes (a) the separation between the highest God and the Creator of the world (sometimes regarded as the God of the Jews in the Old Testament)—the emanations or series of aeons—docetic conception of the person of Christ—cosmical origin of evil and corresponding conception of Redemption—abandonment of early Christian eschatology ; and (b) salvation dependent on secret knowledge, or at least the Gnosis has promise of higher bliss than Faith alone can attain—a syncretic system in which the Christian elements are overpowered by foreign elements, Babylonian and Hellenic, which it continually took to itself in increasing volume—supersession of the genuine apostolic tradition through unlimited allegorical exegesis and its secret 'apostolic' tradition.

For fragments of Gnostic writings see especially Stieren's edition of *Irenaeus*.

noted—a moral difference; some of the Gnostics being ascetic, and some, it was said, licentious. The charge of immorality has always been brought against religious opponents in all ages and must never be received without examination; but in this case it appears to be justified, some of the Gnostics indeed making it a principle. If matter was essentially evil and antithetical to spirit, and yet man in his human life could not escape from it, two courses in regard to it were open to him. He might pursue a policy of rigorous abstinence, aiming at freeing his soul as much as possible from bondage to the material elements by which it was surrounded, and so of course refusing to marry and enthral new souls in the prison of the body: and thus he would win by ignoring, till he became unconscious of, the body. Or else he might adopt a 'superior' attitude to all that was material, and abandon all attempts to purify the hopelessly corrupt. Deeds of the body could not affect the soul—'to the pure all things are pure': it was even a duty to put the body to shame and set at nought the restrictions which had been imposed by commands of the malevolent being who shut up the souls of men in matter—' Give to the flesh the things of the flesh and to the spirit the things of the spirit '.[1] So they would keep the spirit pure, and triumph over the body by putting it to the most licentious uses.

But none of the classifications suggested [2] (Judaizing, anti-Judaistic, Hellenizing, ascetic, licentious) are more than partial descriptions of these chameleon forms of thought, of which neither the history nor the geography can be given,[3] older forms maintaining themselves side by side with later developements, and representative teachers and writers of the most diverse kinds

---

[1] Iren. i 1. 11, 12, τὰ σαρκικὰ τοῖς σαρκικοῖς καὶ τὰ πνευματικὰ τοῖς πνευματικοῖς ἀποδίδοσθαι λέγουσι. Cf. Clem. Al. Strom. iii 5.

[2] Westcott (Introduction to the Study of the Gospels ch. iv) points out the relation of the different Gnostic schools to the different modes of apprehension of Christian principles to which the New Testament bears witness. Cerinthus and the Ebionites exhibit an exaggeration of the Jewish sympathies of Matthew and James; the Docetae of the Petrine view represented by Mark (cf. Peter's refusal to face the possibility of the sufferings of Christ); Marcion of Pauline teaching if pushed to extreme consequences; while Valentinus shews the terminology of John if not the spirit.

[3] Loofs, p. 71. The greatest mixture of Eastern and Western religious and philosophical thought prevailed in Mesopotamia and Syria; and it is probable that Jewish and Christian conceptions working on this 'syncretic' soil produced in one direction the Judaizing heresies which have been already considered, and in the other these manifold forms of the Gnosis. Both have the same birthplace.

finding their way to the smaller communities as well as the greater centres of intercourse.

We must be content to take, as examples, particular teachers and schools, without examining too closely their origin and mutual relations, and to frame, from accounts which are often defective and inconsistent with one another, such a statement of the case as the evidence allows.

The Earlier Representatives of Gnostic Conceptions

The early Fathers almost unanimously trace the origin of Gnosticism to Simon Magus, the chief of the Powers (emanations) of God; [1] Hippolytus gives an account of a work attributed to him, called ' The Great Announcement ',[2] and Menander is named as his pupil and successor. So too the Nicolaitans of the Apocalypse were usually considered Gnostics,[3] and the Gospel of St John was supposed to have been written to oppose the Gnostic views. Irenaeus cites the saying of St Paul, ' knowledge (Gnosis) puffeth up but love edifieth ',[4] as a condemnation of the Gnosis ; but it is extremely improbable that the word has any such associations here or elsewhere in the New Testament, nor does the term ' aeon ' occur in the Gnostic sense of ' emanation '.[5] In the false teaching opposed in the Epistle to the Colossians, and perhaps in the Epistles to Timothy, the seeds of something like the Gnostic conceptions may be detected,[6] but they are probably of Jewish rather than ' Gnostic ' origin.

The docetic view of the person of Christ, however, is certainly under consideration in the reference in the First Epistle of St. John [7] to " Jesus Christ come in flesh " and the condemnation of those who do not ' confess Jesus '. Such as do not recognize the humanity of the divine Redeemer—this is what the expression means—are not ' of God '; nay, they are Antichrist. It is

---

[1] Acts 8[9. 10].   [2] Ἡ Ἀπόφασις μεγάλη—Hippol. *Refut. Haer.* vi 9 ff.

[3] Iren. iii 11. 7, says they were forerunners of Cerinthus.

[4] 1 Cor. 8[1]. Cf. 13[8], and contrast 2 Cor. 11[5].

[5] Probably not till its use by Valentinus. Similarly πλήρωμα (Eph. 1[23] 4[13]) has no technical sense, though its use in Col. 1[19] 2[9] of the totality of the divine attributes approximates towards the Gnostic conception.

[6] *E.g.* the higher knowledge, Col. 2[8. 18], 1 Tim. 6[20]; the idea of the Demiurge, Col. 1[16. 17]; angel-worship, Col. 2[18]; asceticism, Col. 2[20-23] 3[3-5]; incipient Docetism, Col. 2[9] ('bodily'); and the evil of matter, 2 Tim. 2[16-18] (matter being evil could not be eternal, so the resurrection would be spiritual only).

[7] 1 John 4[2. 3]. Cf. 2 John 7.

not enough to acknowledge his divinity ; that he was also 'very Man' is of the essence of the faith. He who tries to distinguish the man Jesus from the Christ is far from the truth.[1]

And it is a similar docetic view, which made the human nature and the sufferings of the Lord unreal, that roused the strenuous opposition of Ignatius.[2] "He verily suffered, as also he verily raised himself again : not as some unbelievers say, who talk of his seeming to suffer, while it is they themselves who are the 'seemers'; and as they think, so it shall happen to them, bodyless and spectral as they are."[3] They who would make of Christ's humanity nothing but a spectre are themselves but spectral men. And again—with a personal appeal to his own experiences on his way to martyrdom, which were in vain if Christ had not by a real Passion won for men a real salvation —he insists "He was really crucified and died. . . . Why, if it were as some godless ones (that is, unbelievers) assert, who say that he only seemed to suffer, while it is they who are the 'seemers'—Why am I in chains?"[4] It was indeed as man he was made manifest, though he was God.[5] He must be recognised as one person, though having the twofold experiences of the human and the divine natures. "There is one Physician in flesh and in spirit (*i.e.* human and divine), generate and ingenerate (*or* originate and unoriginate), God in man (*i.e.* in human form) . . . first capable of suffering and then incapable of suffering."[6]

To docetic thinkers the divinity of Christ presented no

[1] 1 John 2[22].

[2] The 'Judaistic' and the 'docetic' heresies, which are combated by Ignatius, seem to be distinct. In the letter here cited there is no reference to any Judaistic form of error. There are only two cases in which there is even apparent conjunction of Judaistic and docetic conceptions, and in both it is only apparent, namely, the Epistles to the Magnesians and to the Philadelphians. In both cases he passes at once from argument against the Judaizers to the supreme argument which the facts of the Gospel history furnish, and in this connexion lays stress on the reality of those facts. [*Philad.* viii to those who said "unless I find it foretold in the Old Testament (the 'archives') I do not believe it", he replies "my archives are the actual facts"; and *Magn.* viii-xi in warning against μυθεύματα τὰ παλαιά (we cannot go back, that would be to confess that we had not got grace under our present system,—with which compare St Paul's argument that if salvation can be got in the Law, then the death of Christ was gratuitous) he turns them to the present. Look at the actual facts, from which our present grace is derived.] If there had been docetic teaching in these two Churches it is inconceivable that he would not have expressed himself plainly and strongly in regard to it. As it is, it is not the reality of the humanity of the Lord to which he refers, but the reality of the Gospel itself—the very facts which speak for themselves.

[3] *Smyrn.* 2.   [4] *Trall.* 9, 10.   [5] *Eph.* 18.   [6] *Eph.* 7.

difficulties. It was the humanity (with its close relation to matter) that they could not acknowledge. It was only the channel by which he came into the world. " Jesus ", they said, " passed through Mary as water through a tube." [1] He was ' through ' or ' by means of ' but not ' of ' Mary; that is to say, he derived from her no part of his being. " For just as water passes through a pipe without receiving any addition from the pipe, so too the Word passed through Mary but was not derived from Mary." [2] The humanity was only the organ of revelation, the momentary vehicle for the introduction into the world of the eternal truth, and when the end was attained it was allowed to perish. Such denial of the fundamental idea of the Incarnation naturally aroused the most vigorous opposition wherever it was found.

The first of the heads of schools whose names have come down to us is Saturninus (or Saturnilus), a Syrian (of Antioch), in the reign of Hadrian (117–138 A.D.). He seems to have believed in the malignity of matter and in the existence of an active principle of evil. God the Father was unknowable, he held; without origin, body, or form; and He had never appeared to men. He created the angels, and seven of the angels created the world and man. The God of the Jews was only one of the angels, who kept men under his control; and Christ came to abolish his power and lead men back to the truth.

Cerdo, also a Syrian, who came to Rome a little later, carried out further still the distinction between the God of the Old Testament and the God of the New Testament: the former was ' just ' and could be known, the latter was ' good ' and unknowable. [3] It was perhaps from Cerdo that Marcion derived his leading thought.

Marcion and his Followers

Marcion [4] is perhaps hardly to be classed with other Gnostics. He had no emanation theories and no such extravagant alle-

[1] Iren. iii 11. 8.

[2] [Origen] *Dial. adv. Gnosticos* iv p. 121 (Rufinus v 9). Cf. Tert. *de Carne Christi* 20 (Hahn [3] p. 10); Theodoret *Ep.* 145 (Migne *P.G.* lxxxiii 1380B).

[3] Views similar to those of Saturninus and Cerdo seem to have been adopted late in life by Tatian. Bardesanes, another Syrian, at the end of the second century (whose hymns were in use by the Syrian Christians till the time of Ephraem two centuries later), had more in common with Valentinus.

[4] The son of a bishop of Sinope in Pontus (said to have been expelled from the

6

gorizing as they indulged in ; and while all the rest regard the
redemptive work of Christ as consisting in his doctrine, whether
treated mainly from the theoretic or from the ethical point of
view, he laid due stress on the Passion and Death, as shewing
the highest proof of love, and on faith rather than on knowledge.
In this respect, at least, he was immeasureably nearer the
Catholic standpoint than they: his interest was predominantly
soteriological.   But he and his followers were commonly reckoned
Gnostics by their opponents, and the instinct of such men as
Irenaeus and Tertullian was probably not much in error.   It is
at any rate certain that the dualism of the Gnostics, which was
always felt to be destructive of all true interpretation of the
Gospel, was carried out in some respects more thoroughly by
Marcion than by any others.   Starting from the conviction of
the antagonism between the Law and the Gospel, he could not
believe them both to have been given by one God : the teaching
of the God of the Jews and the teaching of Christ were too
different for both to have come from the same source ; and he
wrote a book to point out the contradictions between the Old
Testament and the Gospel.   So the practical antagonism to the
Jewish law, which some of the writings of St Paul exhibited,
became with him theological too ; and he conceived two Gods.
One was the God of the Jews, who made this world ; the author
of evil works, bloodthirsty, changeable—far from perfect, and
ignorant of the highest things, concerned with his own peculiar
people only, and keeping them in subjection by means of the Law
and the terror of breaking it.   The other was the God of love
and of Christ, the creator of the immaterial universe above our
world.   The God of the Jews might be said to be just, inasmuch
as he carried out scrupulously all the provisions of the Law :
' An eye for an eye, and a tooth for a tooth '—' Thou shalt
love him that loveth thee, and hate thine enemy.'   This might
be just, but it was not good.   Goodness was the attribute of
the God who bade men, if smitten on one cheek, to turn the
other also, to love their enemies and to pray for their perse-
cutors ; and this conception of God was new and peculiar to
the Gospel of Christ.   Things in which evil is found could not
proceed from the good God, and the Christian dispensation
could have nothing in common with the Jewish.   Most charac-

Church by his own father, but this is probably a libel—Epiph. *adv. Haer.* xlii 1),
who came to Rome in the first half, towards the middle, of the second century.

teristic of Marcion was this idea of the absolute newness and grandeur of Christianity as separate from all that had gone before; and his absolute rejection of Judaism and of all the historical circumstances and setting of Christianity. Of evolution or developement in religion, of a progress in the self-revelation of God adapted to the age, he had no notion. So, naturally, his conception of Jesus corresponded to his other theories. Jesus appears suddenly on the earth with no preliminary preparation, sent down by the Supreme God the Father from the higher regions where he dwelt.[1] With a material body he could have nothing to do, nor with a birth;[2] but a body in some sense capable of suffering he had, assumed for the special purpose of his mission—to reveal to men the God of Love and to abrogate the law and the prophets[3] and all the works of the God who had created and ruled their world. This God—the Demiurge —he conquered and cast into hell, but his influence remained, and it is against him that the struggle for men still lies. For victory in this conflict he urged the need of an ascetic and celibate life, that the kingdom of the Demiurge might not be increased. The earthly body and its desires must be kept in check; it was doomed in any case to perish; the soul only could attain to blessedness, and the way to it lay through virtue.

The practical character of the Marcionite school no doubt contributed largely to its growth. In this and in its opposition to Judaism[4] its strength undoubtedly lay. It could not have been on moral grounds that Polycarp professed to recognize in Marcion "Satan's firstborn".[5] It is recorded of one of

[1] It is not clear in what relation he held Christ to stand to the Supreme God: perhaps he made no distinction between Father and Son—the Supreme God Himself appearing without any mediator in the world. (So a kind of Modalism, see *infra* p. 97).

[2] The birth and infancy and the genealogy he excised from the only Gospel which he admitted (viz. our Gospel according to St Luke amended to harmonize with his views). Against this 'docetic' conception of Marcion see Tertullian *de Carne Christi*, who maintains that Christ was as regards his flesh and body altogether one with us (*concarnatio* and *conviscaratio*).

[3] Christ was not the Messiah of whom the prophets conceived. Their Christ was a warrior king come to save Israel, ours was crucified to save the world.

[4] They regarded the Church as still in the chains of the Law—'sunk in Judaism'. See Tert. *adv. Marc.* i 20—"They say that Marcion by his separation between the Law and the Gospel did not so much introduce a new rule of faith as restore the old rule when it had been falsified."

[5] The tale is told by Irenaeus (iii 3. 4). Marcion had known Polycarp in the

Marcion's most distinguished followers [1] that he maintained that
those who had their hope set on the Crucified would be saved,
only if they were found doers of good works. His teaching
proved extraordinarily attractive. Justin declared it was
diffused through every race of men.[2] Tertullian compared the
Marcionites, who had "churches" with bishops and presbyters
and songs and martyrs of their own, to swarms of wasps
building combs in imitation of the bees.[3] As well as their
own churches and organization, they had their own Canon of
Scripture, based on the conviction that Paul alone had understood the teaching of Jesus;[4] and some of their alterations and
corrections exerted a disturbing influence on the text which
was current outside the Marcionite communities.[5] The popul-
arity and permanence of the movement (there were Marcionite
churches in existence till the seventh century) is of great
significance in the history of the interpretation of the Christian
revelation, although the interpretation which was championed
at the time by Justin and Irenaeus and Tertullian prevailed.[6]

Carpocrates and his Followers

Another of the ' Gnostics ' who really stands in some
respects alone is Carpocrates,[7] a Platonic philosopher at Alex-

East ; but Polycarp passed him when they met at Rome. " Do you not know me ? "
cried Marcion. " I know [you to be] Satan's firstborn " was Polycarp's uncompromising answer.

[1] Apelles (with his companion Philumene, a 'prophetess') — opposed by
Rhodon (see Euseb. *Hist. Eccl.* v 13), Hippolytus, and Tertullian (*de Carne Christi*
6, 8).

[2] *Ap.* i 26.

[3] *I.e.* the Catholics (Tert. *adv. Marc.* iv 5).

[4] Their Bible had no Old Testament, and only a mutilated edition of the Gospel
according to St Luke and of the ten Epistles of St Paul (Gal. 1, 2, Rom. 1, 2, Thess.,
Eph., Col., Phm., Phil.), the Pastoral Epistles being rejected. Marcion's own book,
the 'Αντιθέσεις, was also standard.

[5] See Rendel Harris *Codex Bezae*, p. 232.

[6] The writings of Irenaeus and Tertullian only are extant, though Justin
Dialogue 80 describes the Gnostic schools. Eusebius mentions also works by
Theophilus of Antioch, Philip of Gortyna, Dionysius of Corinth, Bardesanes,
Rhodon, and Hippolytus.

[7] Mentioned in the list of Hegesippus (Euseb. *H.E.* iv 22). Our chief authority is
Irenaeus i 20 ; ii 48—*H.* vol. i pp. 204 ff., 369 f.; cf. Clem. Al. *Strom.* iii 2. Dorner
calls him 'a religious genius'. Apart from the usual Gnostic notions of a special
secret doctrine and of emanations of angels and powers, the lowest of whom had
created the world, the theory of Carpocrates derived its special character from an

andria, early in the second century: the sect which he founded being still active at Rome in the time of Irenaeus, who took elaborate pains in his refutation of their teaching. In common with Marcion he held the view that redemption was only possible for him who had the sense to despise Judaism, and that it was to be found in escape from the control of the powers who ruled the material world. Not through any obedience to their laws, but through faith and love would man be saved. Works were 'indifferent'—having no moral value—good or bad in human opinion only; that is to say, the human standard is untrustworthy.

This antinomianism seems with Carpocrates to have remained theoretic, and he inculcated a life of perfect purity (the reproach of licentiousness is not supported by the oldest sources of information). But his followers carried out the principle into practice, and became proverbial for deliberate immorality, indulged in without scruple.[1] Indeed it was the Gnostic's duty to enlarge his experiences of every kind of life to the utmost. So taught his son Epiphanes, and the Cainites, who got their name from taking the murderer of Abel as their hero. They and the Ophites [2] absolutely inverted the commonly accepted notions of good and evil, and of the Old Testament all through. The creator of the world being regarded

adaptation of the Platonic conception of Recollection ('Ανάμνησις) expressed in the great Phaedrus myth (Plato *Phaedrus* 246 ff.). The souls of men had been carried round the immaterial heavens, and in their course had been granted vision of the suprasensual Ideas (Truth, Beauty, Virtue, and the like, as they really, *i.e.* spiritually, exist). To their recollection of what they then saw, the souls, when joined to bodies, owe all their knowledge of higher than mundane things. Those that are able to reach the Ideas receive from above a spiritual 'Power' which renders them superior to the powers of the world. Such a power was received by Homer and Pythagoras, and Plato and Aristotle, and Peter and Paul, as well as pre-eminently by Jesus—the perfect man; and every soul which like Jesus was able to despise the powers of the world would receive the same power. With this conception went also that of Transmigration of souls:—he who has lived in perfect purity goes on death to God; but all other souls must expiate their faults by passing successively into various bodies, till at last they are saved and reach communion with God.

[1] See p. 78 *supra.*

[2] Ophiani (Clem., Orig.), Ophitai (Hippol., Epiph.)—*i.e.* worshippers of the serpent; or Naassenes (the Hebrew form of the same word) (see Iren. i 28. 3—*H.* vol. i p. 232). Hippolytus says they were the first to assume the name 'Gnostics', asserting that they alone knew the deep things (v 6). No names of individuals are recorded. The use of the serpent as a religious emblem (a relic of Totemism) was common in countries which were specially receptive of Gnosticism (*e.g.* among the Phoenicians and Egyptians). The serpent represented the vital principle of nature; and the figure of a circle with a snake in the middle (like the Greek letter Θ) symbolized the world. It was said that the Ophites allowed tame snakes to

as an evil power, acting in hostility to the Supreme God, the
Fall became the emancipation of man from the authority of a
malevolent being: the serpent was the symbol of true wisdom
and freedom, wishing to be man's friend against the jealous
Jehovah; and so the usual reading of the Old Testament was
reversed—the bad characters becoming good, oppressed by the
servants of Jehovah.

Of sects with these general principles there were many
varieties and degrees. In principle probably, and in practice
certainly, they are the furthest removed of all the Gnostic
schools from the Catholic view of the purport of the Christian
revelation, and exhibit the greatest admixture of foreign elements.[1]

The School of Basilides

For the finest representatives of the Gnostic philosophy of
life we must turn to very different men—Basilides and Valentinus.

Basilides was probably of Syrian origin, but taught at
Alexandria in the second quarter of the second century. Of
his system very different accounts are given:[2] for the present
the following may be taken as a general description.

The Supreme God, the unbegotten Father, could only be
described by negations. To reach to knowledge of Him it was
necessary to ascend through a long series of grades of spiritual
being which had emanated from Him. Of these the highest
—the first emanations from Him—were a group of eight (the
first Ogdoad), comprising in descending order Mind (or Reason

crawl about and 'sanctify' the Eucharistic bread; and their teaching and actions
no doubt encouraged the belief of the heathen in the tales of debauchery practised
at the Christian love-feasts.

[1] One of the chief Gnostic works that is extant seems to belong to this Ophite
school (though there are in it no signs of its immoral practices). It is entitled
Pistis Sophia, *i.e.* Sophia penitent and believing, and is extant in a Coptic version,
though incomplete. It is thought to have been written originally in Greek
c. 200 A.D. The work is composed in the form of a dialogue in which the
disciples, male and female, put questions to Jesus and elicit answers giving expression to Gnostic conceptions. There is a Latin translation by Schwartze, and
an English translation published by the Theosophical Publishing Society.

[2] The Basilides of Irenaeus is described as an emanationist and dualist; the
Basilides of Hippolytus as an evolutionist and pantheist (Stoic and monistic). So
Bigg (p. 27) says the aeons have no place at all in his system, following the
account of Hippolytus *Refut. Haer.* His teaching was probably understood, or
developed by his followers, in different ways.

in itself), Reason or Word or Speech (the expression of Mind), Understanding (or practical Wisdom), Wisdom, Power, Virtues, Chiefs, and Angels.[1] These made or comprised the first heaven, the highest region or grade in the spiritual world; and from them as source proceeded, in succession, each in turn from the one immediately preceding it, a series of emanations and heavens, till there were in all no fewer than three hundred and sixty-five gradations of spiritual being.[2] The lowest of these heavens is the one which is seen by us. Its angels made and rule the terrestrial world we know. Their chief is the God of the Jews (the Ruler), who wished to make all nations subject to his, but the other heavenly powers arrayed themselves against him, as the other nations arrayed themselves against his nation. But for the redemption of man there was needed the entrance of some superior power from the higher worlds into the lower terrestrial world; and the Father, seized with compassion, sent forth his first-born 'Mind' (the first of the emanations), who is Christ, to deliver all who believe in him from the powers that rule the world. He appeared in human form, uniting himself with the man Jesus at his baptism: the man Jesus not being the Redeemer, but merely the instrument selected by the redeeming God for the purpose of revealing himself to men. It was only in appearance that he was subjected to death upon the Cross, and those who believe in the Crucified One are still under the dominion of the rulers of the world. The body must needs perish, the soul only is immortal; and for this reason Christ suffered his bodily nature to perish and be resolved into formlessness, while the constituents of the higher nature ascended to their own region.[3] So all who are capable of redemption are gradually illuminated by the divine light of knowledge, and purified, and enabled to ascend on high: and when all who are capable are redeemed the rest will be involved in utter ignorance of all that is above them, so that they have no sense of deficiency or of unsatisfied desire, and thus the restoration of all things will be effected. The ethical

---

[1] Νοῦς, Λόγος, Φρόνησις, Σοφία, Δύναμις, Ἀρεταί.

[2] The whole spiritual world, the totality of spiritual existence, is thus expressed by the mystical watchword often found on Gnostic gems, 'Abraxas' (the Sun-God), which stands for 365 according to the Greek reckoning by letters of the alphabet ($a=1$, $\beta=2$, $\rho=100$, $\xi=60$, $s=200$).

[3] It was also said that he did not suffer himself to be crucified, but substituted Simon of Cyrene in his stead.

work of man is the extirpation of all traces of the low grade of life which cling to him, as appendages which must be torn away.[1]

The strength and the weakness of the system of Basilides has been well appraised when it is said that of all the Gnostic systems it "least recognizes any break or distinction between the Christian revelation and the other religions of the world. His leading thought is the continuity of the world's development—its gradual purification and enlightenment by a progressive series of movements succeeding one another by a fixed law of evolution. But while the system thus gains in philosophical unity, it loses in moral and religious significance. No place is left for the special providence of God, nor for the freewill of man : there is almost a Stoical pantheism, quite a Stoical fatalism. . . . The Supreme God is impersonal, capable of no religious relation to man, introduced . . . to give the first impulse to the mechanical movement of the world's self-developement. . . . As he is elevated to the position of an absolute first principle, he is stripped of the attributes which alone can make him the object of moral obedience or religious worship." [2]

The Valentinians

Similar to the teaching of Basilides, at least in many of its chief conceptions, was the system of Valentinus,[3] who lived at Alexandria and in Cyprus till towards the middle of the second century he came to Rome, and only late in his life, it is said, seceded from the Church. His system seems to have been the most comprehensive and the most eclectic of all, but three leading ideas may be detected. From Plato comes the conception that the higher existences of the terrestrial world have their superior and real counterparts in the celestial world, the earthly shadows only imperfectly reflecting the ideal substances. From the pantheistic philosophy of India

---

[1] So Isidorus, the son of Basilides, if not Basilides himself.

[2] Mansel *Gnostic Heresies* p. 165.

[3] Of the Valentinian school there are some literary remains. His disciple Heracleon is the earliest commentator on the gospels,—fragments of his work on St John's Gospel are extant (see the edition of A. E. Brooke *Texts and Studies* vol. i no. 4). A letter by Ptolemaeus, another disciple, who roused the opposition of Irenaeus, is given by Epiphanius (*adv. Haer.* xxxiii 3-7) ; and also an extract from an anonymous work (*ibid.* xxxi 5, 6). Fragments from Valentinus are in Clem. *Strom.* ii 8, 20 ; iii 7, 13 ; vi 6 ; and Hippolytus vi 29-37. Irenaeus gives a detailed account of the system (i 1-21) and a criticism of it (ii).

he derived the thought that the origin of material existence was due to an error or fall or degradation of some higher mode of being—a transient blot on the perfection of the absolute. This thought he nevertheless combined with the belief derived from Judaism that the creation of the world was to be attributed to the wisdom of God, regarded nearly as a separate personality as in the later writings of the Jews.

The term ' aeons ' seems to have been used first by Valentinus to denote the personifications of the divine attributes,[1] which all together formed the whole spiritual world to which the name Plerôma was given (the totality of spiritual functions and life— ideal being). Of these aeons, thirty in all, there were three orders; the first of eight, the second of ten, the third of twelve. They proceeded always in pairs,[2] male and female; the first pair in each successive order from the lowest pair in the order above it. The first order, the Ogdoad, represent the original existence of the Divine Being, in his absolute nature, inscrutable and unspeakable, and in his relative nature, manifesting himself in operation. The second order, the Decad, represent the action of the Deity through his attributes in the formation of a world—ideal, primary, and immaterial. The third order, the Dodecad, represent the divine operations in nature or grace. All these are of course supra-sensual, immaterial, ideal: the spiritual types and patterns and realities,[3] as it were, of anything that afterwards came within the range of human experience. In this way all existence is conceived as having its

---

[1] Αἰῶνες, probably from Plato's use of the singular ' aeon ' to express the ever-present form of the divine existence prior to time,—so applied by Valentinus to the manifestations of this existence.

[2] Each of these pairs is the consort (σύζυγος) of the other. Their names are as follows. The Ogdoad—Ἄρρητος (or Βυθός or Πατὴρ ἀγέννητος) and Σιγή (or Ἔννοια or Χάρις); Νοῦς (or Πατὴρ or Μονογενής) and Ἀλήθεια (forming together the highest tetrad, from which proceeds a second tetrad); Λόγος and Ζωή; Ἄνθρωπος and Ἐκκλησία [the ideal man, the most perfect expression of the divine thought, is the Gnostic spiritual man, separated from the rest as the Church (the ideal society) is from the world]. The Decad—Βύθιος and Μίξις; Ἀγήρατος and Ἕνωσις; Αὐτο-φυής and Ἡδονή; Ἀκίνητος and Σύγκρασις; Μονογενὴς and Μακαρία. The Do-decad—Παράκλητος and Πίστις; Πατρικὸς and Ἐλπίς; Μητρικὸς and Ἀγάπη; Αἰώνιος and Σύνεσις; Ἐκκλησιαστικὸς and Μακαριότης, Θελητὸς and Σοφία. The term Βυθός (the abyss) for the first great cause, expresses the infinite fulness of life, the ideal, where the spirit is lost in contemplation. See Irenaeus, i 1. 1 (Epiph. adv. Haer. xxxi); cf. Tert. adv. Valcnt.

[3] It is in connexion with this conception, with special reference to the idea that the crucifixion under Pontius Pilato was only of the animal and fleshly Christ—a delineation of what the higher Christ had experienced in the higher,

origin in the self-limitation of the Infinite, and it is of supreme importance that each form of being should remain within the limits of its own individuality, keeping its proper place in the evolution of life. This principle is personified in Horos (Boundary), the genius of limitation, who fixes the bounds of individual existence and carefully guards them against disturbance. Even in the spiritual world this function had to be exercised, for there too there was in idea an archetype of the fall and redemption of the world. Of all the aeons one only was, by the will of the Supreme, cognisant of his nature —Mind, the first of the pair which proceeded immediately from him. In the others arose a desire for the knowledge which Mind alone enjoyed, and in the youngest of all the aeons, Sophia (Wisdom), this desire became a passion. Then Horos came, to fulfil his function, and convinced her that the Father was incomprehensible by her; and so she recognized her limitations and abandoned her design. And in order to prevent any recurrence of the kind a new pair of aeons issued from Mind, Christus and the Holy Spirit, who conveyed the same truth to all the aeons, and they then combined to produce a new aeon-Christ, ' the most perfect beauty and constellation of the Plerôma '. This is the prototype of the process of redemption in the world.

The design which Sophia abandoned was itself personified and banished to the region outside the Plerôma (or spiritual world), which is styled the Kenôma (the region void of spiritual being). As the result of this fall of the lower Sophia (or Achamoth) in some way or other [1] life is imparted to matter, and the Demiurge (Jaldabaoth) who creates the lower world we know is formed, and the first man Adam. In man is deposited, through the agency of Achamoth, a spiritual seed, and it is to redeem this spiritual element and draw it back to its proper spiritual home that the last emanation from the aeons, the Christ, by his own wish and with their consent, assumes a spiritual body [2] and descends from the Plerôma. As Saviour he

the real, world—that Tertullian styles them Christians in imagination rather than in reality. "Ita omnia in imagines urgent, plane et ipsi imaginarii Christiani" (adv. Valent. 27 ; cf. Ignatius loc. cit. supra).

[1] The accounts differ in details. All that is clear is that ἡ κάτω σοφία, as having been in the Plerôma, has in her something of the spiritual or real existence, and therefore imparts to the matter into which she falls the seed of life.

[2] This is what was visible in Jesus. According to Irenaeus (i 1. 13—H. vol. i p.

awakes the soul of men out of sleep and fans into flame the spiritual spark within them by virtue of the perfect knowledge he communicates; and, as the consort of Achamoth, by the sign of the cross leads back the souls that he rescues out of the power of the Demiurge into the region of spiritual life. And so there is a restoration of the heavenly element in the human frame struggling to return to its native place, and the material part is dissolved. But it is not all men who are capable of such redemption. By Valentinus the nature of man was conceived as threefold: the bodily part (itself twofold, one subtle, hylic, and one gross, earthy), the soul derived from the Demiurge, and the spirit derived from Achamoth. And men themselves fell into three classes according as one or other of these elements prevailed. The spiritual were only a select few from among men, and they were certain of salvation; the bodily were incapable of salvation; the others, forming an intermediate class between the two extremes, might either rise to the higher or sink to the lower lot. By the introduction of this middle class Valentinus intended no doubt to soften the hardness of the line of demarcation between the Gnostic and all other men. But the principle remained the same, and the general feeling in regard to it was fairly expressed by Irenaeus[1] when he declared that it was " better and more expedient for men to be ignorant and of little learning, and to draw near to God through love, than to think themselves very learned and experienced and be found blasphemers against their Lord ".[2]

The Influence of Gnosticism on the Developement of Christian Doctrine

It is not easy to compute exactly the influence of Gnosticism on the developement of Christian doctrine. It is certain that its

61) the nature of Christ, as conceived by Valentinus, was fourfold : (1) a πνεῦμα or spiritual principle (such as was derived from Achamoth); (2) a ψυχή or animal soul derived from the Demiurge ; (3) a 'heavenly' body, formed by a special dispensation, visible, tangible, passible, not of the substance of the Virgin—who was only the channel by which it came into the world ; (4) the pre-existent Saviour who descended in the form of a dove at the Baptism and withdrew with the spiritual principle before the Crucifixion. (There was thus no real humanity or body ; it was only apparent, docetic.)

[1] Iren. ii 39—*H.* vol. i p. 345.

[2] Of the school of Valentinus was Theodotus, whose writings were well known to Clement. See the *Excerpta ex Scriptis Theodoti* (extracts made perhaps

triumph would have meant the overthrow of Christianity as a historical religion and the disruption and ruin of the Church. It is said that its influence was almost entirely negative—in that it discredited Dualism and the negation of the human free will and Old Testament criticism, and by its appeal to apostolic writings and tradition which were not genuine occasioned the formal establishment of genuine apostolic standards in the Church.[1] If, however, it is difficult to point to any definite positive influence of Gnostic thought on the developement of the doctrine of the Church (which had, of course, begun and went on independently); it seems probable that it played an important part in rousing or stimulating interest in Christianity, as not only the practical way of salvation but also the truth and the way of knowledge in its widest sense; and that it did much to introduce studies, literature, and art into the Christian Church,[2] and to force the great teachers to shew that in Christianity was contained the essence of all the truth there was in the pre-Christian religions.[3]

To this end, at any rate, some of the greatest devoted their energy, and in the working out of the doctrine of the Divine Logos,[4] and of his Incarnation in Jesus Christ, there was found—as a substitute for the wild conceptions of the Gnostics—the expression which seemed to the more philosophical and cultured Christians to satisfy the unique conditions of the Gospel revelation.[5]

But there were other difficulties in the way of the acceptance of the Logos doctrine, and strong currents of thought and

by Clement for his own use); Migne *P.G.* ix pp. 653-698.   An account of his system in Bigg *l.c.* p. 31 ff.

[1] *E.g.* Loofs, p. 73.

[2] See King *Gnostic Gems*. So Dorner *Person of Christ* Eng. tr. vol. i p. 254 writes "hardly any one could wish that the Church might have escaped the Gnostic storms".

[3] See Harnack's account of the results—*DG.* Eng. tr. vol. ii p. 317.

[4] Before Gnosticism the term Logos (cf. St John's Gospel) seems to have been little used and taken rather in the sense of Reason.   Christ was more commonly spoken of in this connexion as the Wisdom (cf. 1 Cor. 1[24], Col. 2[3], Matt. 14[19], Luke 1[35] 11[49]).

[5] Dorner (i p. 252) points out the witness both of Ebionism and of Gnosticism to the Christological conceptions of the early Church.   Ebionism asserted that the genuine Church truth held only the humanity of Christ.   This clearly shews that the humanity was universally acknowledged—otherwise Ebionism could not, in laying stress on this, have claimed a Christian character.   Gnosticism, on the other hand, proposed to find the deeper meaning of Christianity by emphasizing the higher element in Christ.   This presupposes that the Church recognized this element, but did not give it adequate expression from attaching weight also to the humanity.

feeling to be stemmed before the haven of agreement could be reached.

MANICHEISM

Manicheism was a school of thought in some of its chief features closely akin to Gnosticism, aiming at similar ends ; but it is not easy to give in short compass a satisfactory account of it.   A few notes on its connexion with the history of Christian doctrine must suffice.

(1) The source of nearly all Christian accounts is the *Acta Archelai*, which professes to report dialogues between Manes and Archelaus (a Bishop of Carchar in Mesopotamia) in the reign of Probus (supposed to have been composed in Syriac and translated into Greek, but probably spurious and composed in Greek in the fourth century—now extant in a Latin translation from the Greek, long fragments of which are quoted by Epiphanius *adv. Haer.* lxvi 6, 25–31 ; cf. Cyril *Cat.* vi 27 ff.).   More is to be learnt from Titus, Bishop of Bostra, in Arabia (*c.* 362–370), who wrote four books against the Manichaeans (the first two of which are extant in Greek, and all in a Syriac translation).   He derived his information from a book of a follower of Manes, but softened down the doctrines so as not to give offence, and thereby opened the way to misunderstanding.   But most trustworthy is the testimony of Mohammedan historians of later times (ninth to twelfth centuries), who had better opportunities of information about the literature (Babylon having been the birthplace and remaining the centre of the movement till the tenth century, the head of the sect residing there), while they had no polemical purpose, being led to their investigations by a genuine scientific curiosity.   For the form which Manicheism assumed in the West the works of Augustine on the system are the chief authority.

(2) Manes was born about 215 at Ctesiphon, whither his father had moved from Ecbatana.   Originally an idolater, he had joined the sect of 'Ablutioners' (who also laid special stress on vegetarianism and abstinence from wine), and Manes was brought up in this sect, and its essentially ascetic character was the chief mark of the hybrid type of religion which he conceived.   He first came forward as a teacher at a great festival in March 242, and preached for years in the East of Babylonia, and in India and China, obtaining favour in high quarters —from officers of state and the king himself.   But between 273 and 276, through the hostility of the Magi, he was put to death as a heretic, and flayed, and his head was set up over a gate still known by his name in the eleventh century.

(3) The religion was essentially dualistic, based on the contrast between light and darkness, good and evil, conceived in poetical form (as was usual in the East) as a struggle between personal agents, and elaborated in a manner somewhat similar to that of the Gnostic

cosmologies. No distinction was drawn between the physical and the ethical, and thus "religious knowledge could be nothing but the knowledge of nature and its elements, and redemption consisted exclusively in a physical deliverance of the fractions of light from darkness. . . . Ethics became a doctrine of abstinence from all elements arising from the realm of darkness" (Harnack). The powers of darkness or evil sought to bind men (who always had some share of light) to themselves through sensuous attractions, error, and false religions (especially that of Moses and the prophets); while the spirits of light were always trying to recall to its source the light which was in men, by giving them the true gnosis as to nature—through prophets and preachers of the truth, such as Adam, Noah, Abraham, Zoroaster, Buddha, Jesus (in some form), and Manes himself—who was held to be the last and greatest prophet, the guide, the ambassador of light, the Paraclete, by whose instrumentality the separation of light from darkness is accomplished. Practical religion thus became a rigorous asceticism, abstaining from all sensuous enjoyment (the three seals, the *signaculum oris, manus, et sinus*—the mouth, the hand, the breast—symbolized the complete abstinence from everything containing elements of darkness), practising constant fasts (in all about a quarter of the year) and ablutions and prayers four times a day. Such an asceticism, however, was only possible for comparatively few, and a twofold moral standard was permitted, only the 'perfect' Manichaeans—the elect—fulfilling these strict rules, while the lower class of secular Manichaeans, catechumens or hearers (*auditores*), were only required to avoid idolatry, witchcraft, and sensual vices, and to kill no living creature. Worship consisted exclusively of prayers and hymns; they had no temples, altars, or images.

(4) To the difficult question why Manicheism spread so far and wide, Harnack gives the answer that its strength was due to the combination of ancient mythology and a vivid materialistic dualism with an extremely simple spiritual cultus and a strict morality—supplemented by the personality of the founder. It retained the mythologies of the Semitic nature-religions, but substituted a spiritual worship and a strict morality. It offered revelation, redemption, moral virtue, and immortality and spiritual blessings, on the ground of nature-religion; while the learned and the ignorant, the enthusiast and the man of the world, could all find a welcome. And it presented a simple—apparently profound and yet easy—solution of the pressing problem of good and evil.

(5) Why it should have gained recruits among Christians is a further question. To Western Christians there were great obstacles in the foreign language and the secret script in which the books were written, and they must have derived their knowledge from oral sources. Manes himself seems to have been very little influenced by Christianity;

as presented by the Church he must have regarded it as full of errors, but he probably drew from the forms it had assumed among the followers of Basilides and Marcion. His system had points of contact with the ancient Babylonian religion—the original source of all the gnosis of Western Asia, transformed by Christian and Persian elements into a philosophy of the world and of life (Buddhism seems to have made no contributions). The doctrine of the Incarnation was rejected; yet the Western Manichaeans succeeded in giving the system a kind of Christian colour, while retaining its rigid physical Dualism, its rationalizing character, and its repudiation of the Old Testament. At its first appearance in the Roman Empire it was probably as a sect originating in Persia, an inveterate enemy and object of fear to the Roman government, that it was denounced by an edict of Diocletian, c. 287 or 308. Eusebius knew little about them, but by the middle of the fourth century they had spread widely in the empire, particularly among the monks and clergy of Egypt and North Africa. Owing to their principle of mystical acceptance and interpretation of orthodox language, they could hold the position of Christian bishops or conform outwardly to Mohammedan rites. Besides the distinction between *Electi* and *Auditores* there was a carefully graduated hierarchy of travelling missionaries, deacons, presbyters, seventy-two bishops, and twelve apostles—with a thirteenth (or one of the twelve) representing Manes as head of all. Severe laws against them were promulgated by Valentinian (372) and Theodosius (381), but they were very active in the time of Augustine, who was for nine years an *auditor*. They also reached Spain and Gaul, through Dacia, along the highroad to North Italy (they were feared and denounced as *pseudo-ecclesia* by Niceta of Remesiana + c. 414—see his 'Sermon on the Creed' Migne *P.L.* lii. p. 871); and at Rome itself their doctrines had a large following. Active measures against them were taken by Leo, supported by the civil power, and edicts of Valentinian III and Justinian made banishment, and even death, the penalty. Yet Manicheism lasted till far on into the Middle Ages in East and West. [See *D.C.B.* Art. 'Manichaeans', and Harnack *DG*. Eng. tr. vol. iii p. 316 ff. I am also indebted to a lecture by Prof. Bevan.]

CHAPTER VII

MONARCHIANISM

IT was in conflict with Monarchianism that the doctrine of the Logos (and of the Trinity) was developed. Against Gnosticism, with its number of 'aeons' intermediate between God and Creation, the champions of the primitive Christian faith in the second century were driven to insist on the sole and independent and absolute existence and being and rule of God. "On the Monarchy of God" was the title of a treatise written at this time, it is said, by Irenaeus to a presbyter of Rome, Florinus, who had been led to Gnostic views. One God there was, and one God only, who made and rules the world, and Christians could recognize none other gods but Him: and it was possible to hold this belief without believing that this one God was the maker of evil.[1]

So, in origin, Monarchianism was an 'orthodox' reaction to an earlier tradition. But it was soon turned against the orthodox themselves.[2]

The doctrine of the divinity of Christ, accepted at first without precision of statement by the consciousness of Christians, when subjected to closer logical examination, seemed to be irreconcileable with the belief in the unity of God, and so to endanger the dominant principle that God is One. Many who

---

[1] The full title of the treatise is given by Eusebius *H.E.* v 20, 'Concerning Monarchia, or that God is not the Author of Evil Things'. It is clear (though Eusebius misunderstood the difficulty of Florinus) that Irenaeus wrote to shew that the belief in a single first principle did not necessarily lead to the conclusion that evil was His work.

[2] So Tertullian *adv. Prax.* 1 says that the Devil, who vies with the truth in various ways, makes himself the champion of the doctrine that God is One, in order to manufacture heresy out of the word 'one'.

differed in other ways agreed in their dread of undermining this belief. Tertullian describes them as "simple folk (not to call them shortsighted and ignorant) of whom the majority of believers is always composed", who "since the very Creed itself brings them over from the many gods of the world to the one true God, not understanding that He is to be believed as one, but in connexion with His own 'economy', are afraid of the divine 'economy'.[1] And so they keep saying that two—yea, three—gods are preached by us, while they themselves profess to be worshippers of the one God. We hold fast, they say, to the Monarchy". So Hippolytus described Zephyrinus, on account of similar fears, as "an ignorant man inexperienced in the definitions of the Church"; and Origen wrote of the matter as one " which disturbed many who, while they boasted of their devotion to God, were anxious to guard against the confession of two gods".[2] Such men accordingly were called 'Monarchians', and during the third century the Church had to devote itself to the attempt to attain a true conception of God, consistent with the unity of His being, and yet with the divinity of Christ.

To Monarchians two alternatives were open. They might defend the monarchy by denying the full divinity of Christ, or reducing it to a quality or force: or else they might maintain the divinity to the full, but deny it any individual existence apart from God the Father. So we find two classes of Monarchians, akin respectively to the Ebionites and to the Gnostics. The one class (rationalist or dynamic Monarchians[3]) resolved the divinity of Christ into a mere power bestowed on him by God, while admitting his supernatural generation by the Holy Spirit, and regarded Jesus as attaining the status of Son of God rather than by essential nature being divine. Of such were the Alogi, Theodotus, Artemon, and Paul of Samosata. The other class, merging the divinity of Christ into the essence of the Father, recognized no independent personality of Christ, regarding the Incarnation as a mode of the existence or manifestation of the Father. To this class belong Praxeas, Noetus, Callistus, Beryllus, and Sabellius. They are known as 'Patripassians' (see *infra*

---

[1] οἰκονομία—the providential ordering and government of the world, so the plan or system of revelation, so especially the Incarnation. Tert. *adv. Prax.* 3.

[2] Origen on John 2².

[3] Harnack labels them 'Adoptionist', but the title does not seem to be specially appropriate to them, and it belongs peculiarly and by common consent to a mode of thought of later date.

7

p. 103 n. 2), or Sabellians (from the chief exponent of the system in its most developed form), or 'modalistic' Monarchians.

THE ALOGI

The earliest representatives of these Monarchians seem to have been the 'Alogi', so called because they rejected not the Logos doctrine altogether, but the Gospel of St John, which was its strongest apostolic witness.   They believed Cerinthus to have been the author of it, and based their doctrine on the Synoptic Gospels only, accepting the supernatural birth, and in some sense the divinity, but not the developed Logos doctrine, nor the doctrine of the Holy Spirit.   They did not, probably, admit distinctions within the Godhead; such deity as resided in Christ being the deity of the Father, pre-existent therefore, and brought into peculiar union with the man Jesus, but whether in that union remaining personal or being a mere force seems not to be determined.   And so the Alogi were possibly the point of departure for both forms of Monarchian thought; but very little is known about them, and it is not clear that they ever existed as a definite sect at all.[1]

(a) 'DYNAMIC' MONARCHIANISM

The Theodotians

Theodotus, the first representative of the dynamic Monarchians whose name is recorded, was described by Epiphanius as an 'offshoot of the heresy of the Alogi', and by the author of the Little Labyrinth as 'the captain and father of this God-denying heresy'.   In common with the Alogi he laid most stress on the reality of the human nature and life of Christ and the Synoptists' record, and while refusing the title God to him believed he was at baptism endowed with superhuman power.[2]   He was a

---

[1] 'Alogi' is a nickname coined by Epiphanius *adv. Haer.* li.   It is uncertain from what source he derived his information about this school of thinkers, and it is possible that, with his love for rigid classification, he is mistaken in representing them as a definite sect.   But Irenaeus *adv. Haer.* iii 11, *H.* ii p. 51 (misunderstood by Harvey of the Montanists) seems to justify his account in this respect.

[2] He is said by Tertullian *de Praescr.* 53 to have regarded Christ as a mere man, though born of the Virgin.   But neither he nor any of the school really held Christ to be an ordinary man.   Their creed was probably: Jesus miraculously born,

leather-seller of Byzantium who came to Rome, and was excommunicated by the Bishop Victor (c. 195), himself a 'modalist'.

The same views were held by a second Theodotus, a banker at Rome, a student of the Peripatetic philosophy and a critic and interpreter of Scripture[1] in the time of Zephyrinus (199–217).

The Theodotians regarded the Logos as identical with the Father, having no personal existence of his own, but only the 'circumscription'[2] of the Father attaching to him from eternity in which alone we are enabled to know God. That is to say, the Logos is a 'limitation' of the Father—the infinitude of God brought, as it were, within bounds. In effect, the Logos is God in the aspect of revelation to man. It was the image of the Logos that Christ bore. In becoming incarnate in him the Logos took not only flesh but personality from man, and used it for the purpose of his mission. The person of Christ is thus entirely human, with the Logos as controlling Spirit. Similar incarnations had taken place in the prophets.

Artemon

Artemon (al. Artemas), a later member of the school at Rome, asserted that it was an innovation to designate Christ 'God', appealed to Scripture and the Apostles' preaching, and tried to prove that all the Roman bishops down to Victor had been of his opinion. This attempt to claim the authority of Scripture and tradition for such views was vigorously contested

equipped by baptism, and prepared for exaltation by the resurrection (so that the title God might be given him when risen); stress being laid on his moral developement ($\pi\rho\sigma\kappa\sigma\pi\eta$) and the moral proof of his sonship—by growth in character he grew to be divine.

[1] On the biblical criticism and textual 'corrections' and dialectic method of the Theodotians, see Euseb. *H.E.* v 28. 13, quoting the Little Labyrinth. The author of this refutation of their teaching charged them with falsifying and corrupting the Scriptures, and with preferring Euclid and Aristotle and Galen to the sacred writers. The charge may be true; but it is at least possible that they were genuine biblical critics making *bonâ fide* attempts to secure the true text in an uncritical age, and to apply scientific methods of interpretation. So Harnack is disposed to hail them as better scholars than their opponents (*DG.* Eng. tr. vol. iii p. 25). They themselves, in turn, after the time of Zephyrinus, brought a counter-charge against the Roman Church, accusing it of having recoined the truth, like forgers, by omitting the word 'One' with 'God' in the primitive Creed (so Zahn *Apostles' Creed* Eng. tr. p. 35).

[2] $\pi\epsilon\rho\iota\gamma\rho\alpha\phi\eta$ is the word used, see *infra* p. 110 n. 1.

by the author of the Little Labyrinth,[1] who aimed at shewing that from the earliest times Christians had regarded Christ as God, and he succeeded so far at least that this form of Monarchianism soon passed into obscurity in Rome.   The explanation that Christ was supernaturally born, superior in sinlessness and virtue to the prophets, and so attaining to unique dignity, but yet a man, not God—this was felt to be no adequate interpretation of the power he wielded in his lifetime and ever since over the minds and hearts of men.   Yet in the West it lingered ; and the hold which it had is shewn by the fact that Augustine, a little time before his conversion, actually thought it was the Catholic doctrine.   " A man of excellent wisdom, to whom none other could be compared " he thought a true description of Christ, " especially because he was miraculously born of a virgin, to set us an example of despising worldly things for the attainment of immortality ". . . . And he held that he merited the highest authority as a teacher, " not because he was the Person of Truth, but by some great excellence and perfection of this human nature, due to the participation of wisdom ".[2]

Paul of Samosata

Of this dynamic or rationalist Monarchianism the most influential teacher was a Syrian ; Paul of Samosata,—a man of affairs as well as a theologian, for some years Bishop of Antioch and chancellor to Zenobia, Queen of Palmyra, to whose kingdom Antioch at this time belonged.[3]   Following Artemon, and laying all stress on the unity of God as a single person, he denied any ' hypostasis ' of the wisdom or Logos of God—regarding the intelligence or reason in the human heart as analogous.   The

---

[1] Anonymous, perhaps by Hippolytus (c. 230 or 240) ; extracts in Euseb. *H.E.* v 28.

[2] Augustine *Confessions*, vii 19 [25], *ed.* Bigg.

[3] See Euseb. *H.E.* vii 30.   He was appointed bishop in 260, and deposed on account of his heretical views by the Council held at Antioch in 268 or 269, two previous synods having proved ineffective.   He refused, however, to submit to the decree of deposition, and would not vacate the episcopal residence, and so became the cause of the first appeal by the Church to the civil power, technically on a question of property.   After the fall of his protectress Zenobia in 272 Aurelian decided against him ; the ecclesiastical fabrics were to belong to the bishop who was recognized as such by the Bishops of Italy and Rome.   Political motives, as well as ecclesiastical, probably contributed to this decision.   Paul's fall was one of the early victories of Rome.

Logos therefore could not ever come into personal existence; even though he might be called the Son of God, such a title was only a description of the high nature of the power of the divine Logos. A real incarnation of the Logos was thus impossible; He existed in Jesus not essentially or personally, but only as a quality.[1] The personality of Jesus was entirely human;[2] it was not that the Son of God came down from heaven, but that the Son of man ascended up on high. The divine power within him grew greater and greater as the course of his human developement proceeded, till at last through its medium he reached divinity.[3] Whether this goal was attained after the Baptism or not till after the Resurrection is not decided; but the union, such as it is, between God the Supreme and Christ the Son of God is one of disposition and of will— the only union possible, in the thought of Paul, between two persons.

He was thus represented as teaching that Jesus Christ was 'from below', and that the Son was non-existent before the Nativity; and the synods which considered his conceptions were at pains to maintain the distinct individual existence of the Logos as Son of God before all time, who had himself taken active personal part in the work of Creation, and was himself incarnate in Jesus Christ.[4]

His condemnation by no means disposed of his views.[5] If we cannot say with certainty that he is the direct ancestor of Arianism, we know that Arius and the chief members of the Arian party had been pupils of Lucian (a native of the same city of Samosata), who, while Paul was bishop, was head of the theological school of Antioch, and seems to have combined the Monarchian adoptionism of Paul with conceptions of the person of Christ derived from Origen[6]; while in the great theologians of Antioch, a century later still, a portion of the spirit of Paul of

---

[1] οὐκ οὐσιωδῶς ἀλλὰ κατὰ ποιότητα.

[2] So Eusebius says "he was caught describing Christ as a man, deemed worthy in surpassing measure of divine grace".

[3] Cf. Athanasius *de Synodis* 26, 45, quoting the *Macrostich*, ἐκ προκοπῆς τεθεοποιῆσθαι—ἐξ ἀνθρώπου γέγονε θεός. See Hahn[3] § 159.

[4] See Hahn[3] § 151. See note on Paul's use of ὁμοούσιος *infra* p. 111.

[5] Harnack points to the *Acta Archelai* §§ 49, 50, as shewing the prevalence of similar conceptions in the East at the beginning of the fourth century. The Council of Nicaea, by ordering the rebaptism of followers of Paul, treated them as not being Christians at all.

[6] See Additional Note on Lucian *infra* p. 110.

Samosata lived again, and in the persons of a Theodore and a Nestorius [1] was again condemned.

(b) 'MODALISTIC' MONARCHIANISM

The rationalist or 'dynamic' form of Monarchian teaching was so obviously destructive of the real divinity of Jesus that it can scarcely have been a serious danger to the faith in the Incarnation. Much more likely to attract devout and earnest thinkers was the 'modalistic' doctrine. While maintaining the full divinity of Christ it was safe from the reproach of ditheism, and free from all connexion with emanation theories and subordination. The doctrine of an essential or immanent Trinity (the conception of three eternal hypostases) had not as yet been realized in full consciousness. The chief concern of the exponents of Christian doctrine had been to establish the personal pre-existence of Christ and his essential unity with the Father (against Ebionism), and so the distinction between him and the Father might be somewhat blurred; and though, of course, opposition to Ebionism was never carried so far as to ignore the real humanity of Christ, still it would tend to relegate to the background the evidence for the distinction between the Father and the Son which is implied in the incarnation. And to all who felt the infinite value of the atonement effected by Christ—the power of the death upon the Cross—the theory which seemed to represent the Father Himself as suffering would appear to furnish a more adequate explanation of the facts than Ebionism had to offer.[2] So it is easy to understand the great impression which was made by the earliest representatives of the 'modalistic' school of thought, Noetus and Praxeas,[3] both of whom came from Asia Minor (the home of Monarchian views) to Rome towards the end of the second century.

[1] Paul seems to be differentiated from Nestorius chiefly by the denial of the personality of the Logos.

[2] The 'unreflecting faith' of the Church and the vagueness of its doctrine at this time is shewn in the phrases used by Irenaeus (e.g. 'mensura Patris filius') and Clement of Alexandria (e.g. 'the Son is the countenance of the Father') and Melito (θεὸς πέπονθεν ὑπὸ δεξιᾶς ἰσραηλίτιδος).

[3] Our knowledge of Noetus comes from Hippolytus (Ref. Haer. ix ad init., x 23 (72), and the special treatise c. Noet.). Hippolytus does not mention Praxeas, against whom Tertullian wrote as the originator of the heresy, without mentioning Noetus. Probably Praxeas had founded no school at Rome, and Hippolytus had no knowledge of him.

Praxeas and Noetus

Praxeas, already a 'confessor' for the faith, was welcomed in Rome, and with the information he was able to give of the excesses of the Montanists in the East proved to be a strong opponent of the new movement which was then threatening the order of the Church. The 'modalism' which he represented was for some time prevalent and popular at Rome, and it appears that the erroneous character of his teaching was not discovered till after his departure to Carthage. Early in the third century [1] Tertullian wrote against him (using his name as a label for the heresy), and in epigrammatic style described him as having done 'two jobs for the Devil at Rome',—"He drove out prophecy and introduced heresy: he put to flight the Paraclete and crucified the Father". In this rhetorical phrase he expressed the inference which was promptly drawn from the teaching of Praxeas and Noetus. If it was the case that the one God existed in two 'modes', and the Son was identical with the Father, then the Father Himself had been born, and had suffered and died. Hence the nickname Patripassians,[2] which was generally applied in the West to this school of Monarchians. In word, at all events, it was unfair. While denying the existence of any real distinction in the being of God Himself (which would amount, they thought, to 'duality', however disguised), they seem to have admitted a distinction (dating at least from the Creation) between the invisible God and God revealed in the universe, in the theophanies of the Old Testament, and finally in the human body in Christ; and the name Father was restricted to the invisible God, who in revelation only could be called the Logos of the Son.

A compromise perhaps was found [3] in the theory that the

---

[1] The exact date is uncertain—c. 210, Harnack.

[2] Origen explains *Patripassiani* as those who identify the Father and the Son, and represent them as one person under two different names. They did not themselves accept the inference ; e.g. Zephyrinus avowed, "I know one God Christ Jesus, and besides him no other originate and passible",—but also, "It was not the Father who died, but the Son". In two cases only that are known to us was the Creed expanded (to exclude the idea that the Father suffered) by the addition of the words 'invisibile' and 'impassibile' to the first article : viz. in the Creed of the Church of Aquileia (Hahn [3] p. 42), and in the Creed of Auxentius, the semi-Arian predecessor of Ambrose as bishop of Milan, whose Creed may be the baptismal Creed of Cappadocia (Hahn [3] p. 148).

[3] Possibly by Callistus, whose modified 'Praxeanism' Tertullian is thought to be

Father, unborn, invisible (though as Spirit, as invisible God, He could not suffer), somehow participated in the sufferings of Christ, the Son who was born—"The Son suffers, the Father however shares in the suffering"; though really in such a compromise the essential principle of Modalism would be lost.[1]

Noetus, however, when brought face to face with the logical issue, seems to have scorned all compromise. There was one God, the Father, invisible or manifesting Himself as He pleased, but whether visible or invisible, begotten or unbegotten, always the same. The Logos is only a designation of God when He reveals Himself to the world and to men. The Father, so far as He deigns to be born, is the Son. He is called Son for a certain time, and in reference to His experiences on earth; the Son, or Christ, is therefore the Father veiled in flesh, and it was the Father Himself who became man and suffered. The distinction seems accordingly to be not merely nominal, but is connected with the history and process of redemption, though it leaves the Incarnation dependent on an act of will. The two great aims of these Monarchians—to safeguard the unity of God (against what they regarded as the ditheistic tendencies of their opponents), and to uphold the divinity of Christ—are curiously shewn in the two different versions which have come to us of the answer which Noetus made to his assailants. "Why! what have I˙done? I believe in one God"—so Epiphanius reports him; or "Why! what harm am I doing in glorifying Christ?"—as Hippolytus gives his words.[2]

Sabellius and his Followers

For these two aims so much support could naturally be obtained, that in spite of excommunication the teaching of Noetus was carried on by his pupil Epigonus and later by Cleomenes and Sabellius as heads of the party at Rome. What

attacking under the name of Praxeas. "Filius patitur, pater vero compatitur." "Compassus est pater filio."

[1] It involves a distinction in the person of the Lord between Christ the divine and Jesus the human—the latter suffering actually, the former indirectly; the latter being the Son (the flesh) and the former the Father (the spirit). Cf. Irenaeus, Hahn³ p. 7. Cf. the Arian conception—the Logos *compatitur* with the human which *patitur* in the person of Christ. See Hahn³ § 161 (the Synod of Sirmium 357), and *infra* pp. 180, 181 *notes.*

[2] τί οὖν κακὸν πεποίηκα; ἕνα θεὸν δοξάζω—Epiphanius. τί οὖν κακὸν ποιῶ, δοξάζων τὸν Χριστόν—Hippolytus.

exactly each contributed we cannot tell: even of Sabellius the full accounts belong to the fourth century.[1] To him the developed form of the teaching—embracing the whole Trinity—seems to be due,[2] and it is by his name that the champions of the theory were best known throughout the East ('Patripassians' or 'Monarchians' being the usual designation in the West).

God is, according to his teaching, essentially one, and the Trinity which he recognizes is a Trinity not of essence but of revelation; not in the essential relations of the Deity within itself, but in relation to the world outside and to mankind. The relations expressed by the three names are co-ordinate, forming together a complete description of the relations of the one self-evolving God to all outside Him. Father, Son, and Holy Spirit are simply designations of three different phases under which the one divine essence reveals itself—three names of one and the same being.[3] He seems to have adopted the language of the Church so far as to speak of three 'persons', using the term πρόσωπα, but in so different a sense (meaning parts or rôles of manifestation rather than 'persons') that the word was altogether discredited in the East. These different parts or functions were assumed to meet the varying needs of the occasion; one and the same God appearing now as Father, now as Son, and now as Holy Spirit. The account that Basil gives implies a merely temporary assumption of each part, but it is possible that Sabellius taught [4] that God had, rather, put forth His activity in separate stages: first, in the 'person' of the Father as Creator and Lawgiver; secondly, in the 'person' of the Son as Redeemer (in the work of the Incarnation up to the Ascension); and thirdly, after the redemption was effected, in the 'person' of the Spirit as giver and preserver of life. In any case it is clear

---

[1] He was by birth a Libyan of Pentapolis in Africa, active at Rome in the early part of the third century (c. 198–217). Of his writings, if he wrote anything, phrases may be extant in Hippolytus (*Ref. Haer.* ix) and in Athanasius (*c. g. Or. c. Ar.* iv)—the earliest accounts of him. Cf. Basil *Epp.* 210, 214, 235 ; Epiph. *adv. Haer.* 62. It is probable that ideas of which Marcellus was the originator have been erroneously attributed to him, but Athanasius (*l.c.* esp. §§ 13, 14, 25) certainly says that conceptions of expansion and contraction were taught by Sabellius, and not, as some have argued, that their natural consequences were Sabellian.

[2] It is possible that he went beyond Noetus only in including the Holy Spirit in his theory.

[3] He even coined a word υἱοπάτωρ (Son-Father) to exclude the thought of two beings.

[4] As Harnack understands Epiphanius and Athanasius.

that there is no permanence about such 'personalities'. There is no real incarnation; no personal indissoluble union of the Godhead with the Manhood took place in Christ. God only manifested Himself in Christ, and when the part was played and the curtain fell upon that act in the great drama there ceased to be a Christ or Son of God. This conception of a merely transitory personality of Christ[1] (which seems to involve the negation of an eternal personal life for any one) is essentially pantheistic. All the Monarchian theories really strike in this way at the root of the Christian interpretation of life. If God Himself, as final being, as a whole, so to speak, comes forth in revelation and nothing is left behind, then God passes over into the world and becomes the world, and nothing but the world is left. It is clearly impossible, on any Christian theory of the world and of the divine economy, that God should exist even for a moment only in a single mode, or that the Incarnation should be only a temporary and transient manifestation.

And, further, Sabellianism, in recognizing only a Trinity in human experience, disregards the fact that such a Trinity of revelation is only possible if the very being of the Godhead, which is thus revealed, is itself a Trinity.

Partial Sympathy with Sabellianism at Rome

In Rome, though the fierce opposition of Hippolytus[2] got little support, and Callistus[3] at first was favourable to the modalistic conceptions, Sabellius was condemned and excommunicated, and the Monarchians soon found few followers in the West,[4] though, as Harnack points out, the hold which they had had for twenty or thirty years on the Roman Church left a permanent mark. It was Rome that condemned Origen, the ally of Hippolytus. Rome was invoked against Dionysius of Alex-

---

[1] Contrast with it the Catholic interpretation according to which Christ is the eternal centre of regenerated humanity.

[2] See esp. *Ref. Haer.* bk. ix, and see Additional Note on Hippolytus *infra* p. 108.

[3] Callistus was bitterly attacked by Hippolytus for his protection of the school of which Epigonus and Cleomenes, and later on Sabellius, had been head. It is probable that Callistus, as Zephyrinus before him, simply wished to secure as much toleration and comprehension as possible, to protect the Church from the *rabies theologorum* (as Harnack phrases it). The compromise which he attempted has been alluded to above. He was ultimately driven to excommunicate the leaders on either side, both Sabellius and Hippolytus.

[4] Cyprian could class *Patripassiani* with ' ceterae haereticorum pestes ' (*Ep.* 73. 4).

andria. Rome and the West were chiefly responsible for the ὁμοούσιον formula of Nicaea (so long opposed as Sabellian). Rome received Marcellus, who carried out the Sabellian principles, and rejected τρεῖς ὑποστάσεις and supported the Eustathians at Antioch. And finally, it was with Rome that Athanasius was most at one. Indeed, Sabellianism no doubt prepared the way for the Nicene theology—the full recognition of the truth underlying the principles of modalism being a necessary step in that direction; though it also led immediately, on the other hand, to the developement of the Origenistic Christology in the direction of Arianism. One of the intermediate stages—the prelude to the Arian struggle—was the controversy between Dionysius of Alexandria and Dionysius of Rome.

NOVATIAN

That the Sabellian view did not prevail at Rome is seen from the treatise *On the Trinity* by Novatian, the most learned of the presbyters of Rome in the middle of the third century. It is the theology of Africa—an 'epitome of Tertullian's work', as Jerome styled it. It professes to be an exposition of the Rule of Faith, and as such includes "a doctrine of God in the sense of the popular philosophy, a doctrine of the Trinity like Tertullian's (though without all his technical terms), and the recognition of the true manhood of Christ along with his true Godhead" (Loofs). His doctrine of the Trinity can, however, still be described as 'economic' rather than essential. Though he regards the existence (*or* generation) of the Son as eternal in the past, he speaks of the future consummation as though the distinction of persons (Father and Son) would cease. The idea of *communio substantiae* (ὁμο-ουσία) is combined with that of subordination. It is clear that he makes it his special concern to oppose Sabellianism, and to maintain the personality of the Son. So he keeps the *personarum distinctio*, speaks of Christ as *secunda persona post patrem* and of the *proprietas personae suae*, and regards the union in its moral aspect as concord. He even speaks of the Son as proceeding from the Father *when the Father willed*. But at the same time he insists on the *substantiae communio*. In respect of the person of Christ he is concerned to maintain both the true deity and the true humanity—the *filius dei* and the *filius hominis*. The union is emphasized—the *filius hominis* is made by it the *filius dei*—but the nature of the union is not discussed. The doctrine of the Logos falls into the background. [The authority of Jerome *de Vir Ill.* c. 70, who names the treatise as Novatian's, while he notes that many "who did not know" thought it was Cyprian's (or Tertullian's) may be accepted, in spite of more modern doubts; cf. Harnack *Gesch. der altchristl. Litteratur* i 652–656. The treatise is printed in Migne *P.L.* iii 885–952. With it may be compared the *Tractatus Origenis* discovered by Battifol and ascribed by Weyman to Novatian, though Dom Butler with greater probability assigns it to an anonymous writer of the fifth or sixth century. See *J.T.S.* vol. ii pp. 113 ff. and 254 ff.]

This work of Novatian is described by Harnack as creating for the West a dogmatic *vade mecum*.

THE THEOLOGY OF HIPPOLYTUS

It is worth while over against the theories of the Noetians and Sabellians to set the theory of their uncompromising opponent, Hippolytus—whose own theology gave almost equal offence and was charged with ditheism. It is to be found in his *Refutatio Haeresium* and in his sermon against Noetus (which was earlier and less definite, but expresses the same views, often in the same words). For his Christology, see especially *Ref. Haer.* x 33, and *c. Noet.* 10–15. The following is a summary of Döllinger's account in his *Hippolytus and Callistus.*

God—one and only—originally was alone, nothing contemporary with him. All existed potentially in him and he himself was all.

From the first he contained the Logos in himself as his still unsounding voice, his not yet spoken word, and together with him the yet unexpressed idea of the universe which dwelt in him.

This Logos—the intelligence, the wisdom of God—without which he never was, went out from him according to the counsels of God—*i.e.* ὅτε ἠθέλησεν, καθὼς ἠθέλησεν—in the times determined beforehand by him, as his first begotten—prince and lord of the creation that was to be. He had within him as a voice the ideas conceived in the Father's being, and in response to the Father's bidding thereby created the world in its unity ἀρέσκων θεῷ.

The whole is thus the Father, but the Logos is a power proceeding from the whole—the intelligence of the Father, and therefore his οὐσία, whereas the world was created out of nothing.

There was thus another God by the side of the first, not as if there were two Gods, but as a light from the Light, water from the Fountain, the beam from the Sun. He was the perfect, only-begotten Logos of the Father, but *not yet perfect Son : that he first became when he became man.* Nevertheless God already called him Son because he was to be born (*c. Noet.* 15).

Hippolytus thus distinguishes three stages or periods of developement in the second hypostasis—the Logos :—

(1) He is still impersonal—in indistinguishable union with God as the divine intelligence : potentially as the future personal

Logos—and inherently as the holder of the divine ideas (patterns after which the universe was to be created).

(2) God becomes Father, by act of will operating upon his being— *i.e.* he calls his own intelligence to a separate hypostatic existence, placing him as ἕτερος over against himself: yet only in such wise as a part of a whole which has acquired an existence of its own—the whole remaining undiminished: as the beam and the Sun. The Logos has thus become hypostatic for the purpose of the manifestation of God in creation: and the third moment ensues.

(3) The Incarnation—in which he first completes himself as the true and perfect Son; so that it is also through the Incarnation that the idea of the divine Fatherhood is first completely realized.

Objectionable or doubtful points in this view are—(1) the existence of the Logos as a person is προαιώνιος before all time, but not from eternity ἀΐδιος; (2) strict subordination: the Son is merely a force to carry out the Father's commands; (3) the Trinitarian relation is not original in the very being of God, but comes into existence through successive acts of the divine *will*; (4) his representation of the Logos as the κόσμος νοητός— the centre of the ideas of the universe or the universe conceived ideally, —which is foreign to primitive Christian tradition, being borrowed from Philo,—is not really balanced by his maintenance of the substantial equality of Father and Son.

Specially objectionable is (3) (an idea which was later a main prop of Arianism), as it leaves open the possibility for the Logos to have remained in his original impersonal condition, and so for the Son never to have come to any real hypostatic existence, *i.e.* for God to have remained without a Son. Hence arose later the fierce contest for or against the proposition that the Father brought forth the Son by an act of his own free-will: on which see *infra* p. 194.

And thus Hippolytus was viewed with suspicion, although the Church was wont then to be very tolerant of attempts made by Christians of philosophic culture to explain the mystery of the Trinity by the help of Platonic speculations.

BERYLLUS

A kind of midway position seems to have been occupied by thinkers of whom we have a representative in Beryllus, Bishop of Bostra in Arabia, a learned writer and administrator of high repute. Almost all that we know of his teaching is expressed in a sentence of Eusebius (*H.E.* vi 33; cf vi 20) recording that "he dared to assert that our

Saviour and Lord did not pre-exist in an individual existence of his own[1] before his coming to reside among men, and that he did not possess a divinity of his own, but only that of the Father dwelling in him ". This seems to indicate a semi-Monarchian or conciliatory tendency, rejecting the doctrine of the hypostatical existence of the Logos, but repelled by the hypothesis of an incarnation of God the Father Himself, and so seeking a solution in the recognition of (1) a distinct personality after—though not before—the Incarnation, and (2) an efflux from the divine essence of the Father rather than whole deity in Christ. Thus a divine power was, as it were, sunk into the limitations of human nature and so became a person. Dorner regards Beryllus as a connecting link between the Patripassians, who allowed no πρόσωπον side by side with the πατρικὴ θεότης, and Sabellius, with his recognition of a distinct πρόσωπον or περιγραφή both of the Logos and of the Spirit. Origen is said to have convinced him of his error at a synod held c. 244.

MONARCHIAN EXEGESIS

The Monarchians claimed, of course, to have the authority of Scripture on their side. Praxeas seems to have depended chiefly on the texts :—" I am the Lord, and there is none else : beside me there is no God " (Isa. 45[5]) ; " I and the Father are one " (John 10[30]) ; " Shew us the Father . . . Have I been so long with you . . . and dost thou not know me ? I am in the Father, and the Father in me " (John 14[9.10]). Against his interpretation of such passages, see Tertullian chs. xxi–xxiv. Other texts which Noetus used were Ex. 3[6] 20[2], Isa. 44[6] 45[14], Bar. 3[36], Rom. 9[5] (Christ—God over all)—see Hippolytus contra Noetum.

LUCIAN

Lucian appears, after the deposition of Paul, to have been in a state of suspended communion for some time, but to have been ultimately reconciled to the bishop. He was a man of deep learning and ascetic life, held in the highest honour by his pupils, and his death (7th January 312), as one of the last victims in the persecution begun by Diocletian, won for his memory universal esteem. For our knowledge of his teaching we have little first-hand evidence. On two vital points he seems to have been much nearer the Catholic doctrine than was Paul, recognizing the personality of the Logos and his incarnation

---

[1] κατ' ἰδίαν οὐσίας περιγραφήν—περιγραφή primarily 'limit-line', 'circumscription', so used of personal individual existence, regarded as a 'limitation' of absolute existence.

in the historical Christ (in whom he was as soul, having taken to himself a human body). But none the less he did not regard the Christ as essentially one with the eternal God, clinging to the conception of a perfect human developement (προκοπή) as the means by which he reached divinity ; and he seems to have distinguished between the Word or Son in Christ (the offspring of the Father's will) and the immanent Logos— the reason of God. So it is said to have been counted a departure from Lucian's principles to acknowledge the Son as 'the perfect image of the Father's essence', though this phrase is used in the Creed of the Council of Antioch (341), which was believed to have been based on Lucian's teaching, if not his very composition. (See Sozomen *H.E.* iii 5 and vi 12 ; but possibly it was the fourth Creed, in which there is no such clause, that was Lucian's, and not the second. So Kattenbusch, see Hahn [3] p. 187.)

He is probably fairly described as 'the Arius before Arius' (Harnack *DG.* ii p. 182), and among his pupils were, besides Arius himself, Asterius, the first Arian writer, Eusebius of Nicomedia, Theognis of Nicaea, Maris of Chalcedon, and Athanasius of Anazarba. His activity in textual criticism and exegesis is certain, whether there was actually produced in his famous academy a revision of the text of the New Testament (the 'Syrian' Text) or not (see Westcott and Hort *Introduction to the New Testament* pp. 138, 182).

PAUL OF SAMOSATA AND THE TERM ὁμοούσιος

The Council which condemned Paul condemned also the use of the word Homoousios to express the relation between Christ and God the Father. But whether it was that Paul had used the word himself, or that he was able to produce ingenious arguments against it, must remain uncertain. The accounts of Athanasius, Hilary, and Basil are at variance.

Athanasius (*de Syn.* § 45), having said that he has not himself seen the bishops' letter, accepts the statement of the Semi-Arians that it was rejected because it was taken in a material sense, and Paul used the sophistical reasoning that "if Christ did not become God after starting as man, he is Homoousios with the Father, and there must be three Ousiai, one principal and the two derived from it", so that to guard against such a piece of sophistry they said that Christ was not Homoousios — the Son not being related to the Father as Paul imagined.

Hilary (*de Syn.* §§ 81, 86) implies that the word was used by Paul himself to express the idea that the Father and Son were of one single and solitary being. (But this seems to be more like the teaching of Sabellius than the teaching of Paul.)

It seems possible that objection was taken to Paul's reasoning that the Logos was one person with God as the reason is one with man, on the ground that the doctrine of the Church required one God but more than one πρόσωπον, and that to meet this objection he declared that he recognized such πρόσωπα—God and Christ standing over against each other as Homoousioi—meaning alike personal (οὐσία being taken in the sense of particular, individual being); (τόδε τι). This would be, in the opinion of his opponents, to introduce a human personality into the Godhead, and so the word would be rejected. (It is of course quite clear that if οὐσία were taken in the sense of substance or essence, Paul could not have accepted the term.)

Basil (Ep. 52 [30])—so far agreeing with the account that Athanasius gives—regards Paul as bringing an argument against the word which was certainly familiar in later times, viz.—that if Christ was not made God out of (after being) man, but was Homoousios, then there must have been some common substance (Ousia) of which they both partook, distinct from and prior to the divine persons themselves, and that out of it two beings—the Father and the Son—were produced as two coins are struck out of the same metal.

The term may therefore have been withdrawn as being likely to perplex weak minds. So Bull Def. N. C. ii 1 and Newman Arians ch. i suggest. In any case, as Athanasius insists, caring, as always, little for the words and much for the sense, it was capable of being understood in different ways, and it was rejected in one sense by those who condemned the Samosatene and championed in another sense by those who resisted the Arian heresy. "It is unbecoming to make the one conflict with the others, for all are fathers; nor is it pious to determine that the one spoke well and the others ill, for all of them fell asleep in Christ" (de Syn. § 43). "Yes, surely each Council has a sufficient reason for its own language."

[The tradition that the use of the term ὁμοούσιος was considered and disapproved by the Council of Antioch has recently been questioned by Dr. Strong in the Journal of Theological Studies vol. iii p. 292. There does not seem, however, to be sufficient reason to doubt what Athanasius, Hilary, and Basil accepted as an awkward fact which they had to explain as best they could, though the Acts of the Council contain no reference to the matter, and the positive evidence for it comes to us from Arian sources.]

CHAPTER VIII

THE CORRESPONDENCE BETWEEN THE DIONYSII

THE result of the struggle with the Monarchian tendency, which emphasized unduly the unity of the Trinity, was to mark more precisely the distinctions and gradations, so that in some cases a pronounced system of subordination ensued. In the West, as we have seen, the conviction of the unity of essence was too strong for other elements to overpower it; but in the East the fear of Sabellianism and the loss of the personal distinctions which it involved led to the use of phrases which were hardly consistent with the equality of the persons and unity of essence.

A conspicuous example of this tendency we have in Dionysius 'the Great', Bishop of Alexandria (247–265 A.D.), who was equally distinguished as a ruler and as a theologian.[1] In controverting Sabellianism he used expressions which later on became the watchwords of the Arian party. In his anxiety to maintain the personality of the Son and his distinction from the Father, he said the Son did not exist before he was begotten (or came into being); that there was a time when he did not exist; and he styled him with reference to the Father a thing made (or work), and different (or foreign) in being ($ο\mathring{v}σία$), and so not of the same being with the Father (homoousion). Jesus himself had said " I am the vine, my Father is the husbandman ", and so it was right to describe the relation between him and the Father as analogous to that of the vine to the

[1] He took a leading part in all the controversies of the time, concerning the lapsed, re-baptism, Easter, Paul of Samosata, Sabellianism, and the authorship of the Apocalypse. Many of his letters, festal ($ἐπιστολαὶ ἑορταστικαί$) and others, are mentioned by Eusebius and Jerome (the sixth and seventh books of the history of Eusebius are mainly based on them), but nearly all are lost. Only fragments are extant, e.g. of a treatise $περὶ φύσεως$—a refutation of materialism and the theory of atoms, of the $περὶ ἐπαγγελιῶν$—a thorough rejection of millennial expectations and a vindication of the allegorical interpretation of the prophetic descriptions of the Messianic kingdom (and incidental denial of the Johannine authorship of the Apocalypse).

husbandman, or that of the boat to the shipbuilder. He insisted on the fact that there were three distinct hypostases in the Godhead, and for these and other similar expressions he was charged with error by some members of the Alexandrian Church, and the judgement of the Bishop of Rome, his namesake (Bp. 259–268), was invoked. A synod, accordingly, was held at Rome,[1] which condemned the views reported to it, proclaiming the verbally simple creed that the Father, Son, and Spirit exist, and that the three are at the same time one ; and a letter was written by the bishop[2] expressing the sentiments of the synod, exposing the erroneous nature of the arguments on which other views depended, and asking for an explanation of the charges. In reply Dionysius of Alexandria composed four books of 'Refutation and Defence' against the accusation made by his assailants and in justification of the doctrine he had taught. He carefully explained that the phrases used by him, to which objection had been taken, were only illustrations, to be interpreted in close connexion with their context. He gave them, he says, as examples cursorily, and then dwelt on more apposite and suitable comparisons. "For I gave the example of human birth,

---

[1] So Athanasius implies, *de Syn.* 43 ; but cf Art. 'Dionysius of Alexandria' *D.C.B.*

[2] Athanasius *de Decr. Nic.* 26 gives an extract from it. What more there was can only be inferred from the reply of Dionysius of Alexandria, of which considerable quotations of the most important passages are preserved in Athanasius *de Sententia Dionysii* (cf. *de Synodis* 44 and *de Decr. Nic.* 25), who was at pains to prove the orthodoxy of the great bishop whose authority the Arians claimed. The teachers condemned by the Bishop of Rome are "those who divide and cut in pieces and destroy the most sacred doctrine of the Church of God, the Monarchy, dividing it into three powers (as it were) and partitive 'hypostases' and three godheads, . . . and preach in some sense three gods, dividing the holy Monad into three hypostases foreign to each other and utterly separated". The faith which he maintains is " in God the Father all-sovereign, and in Christ Jesus His Son, and in the Holy Spirit, and that the Logos is united with the God of the universe ; . . . for it must needs be that the divine Logos is united with the God of the universe, and the Holy Spirit must be contained (repose) and dwell in God ; and further, it is absolutely necessary that the divine Triad be summed up and gathered together into one, as into a summit, I mean the all-sovereign God of the universe" (Ath. *de Decr.* 26). It should be noted that Dionysius of Alexandria in the passage quoted uses the words ὁμογενής (and συγγενής) and ὁμοφυής as though they were near equivalents to ὁμοούσιος. This usage is significant). It shews, at least when regarded in connexion with the whole discussion of the question at issue, that he had not fully grasped the conception, which was traditional in the West, of the one *substantia* of Godhead existing in three *personae*. He thought more naturally of the three *personae* of the same genus and nature ; that is to say, he was more ready to acknowledge the *generic* than the *essential* oneness of the Godhead. See further *infra* p. 236, Note on ὑπόστασις.

evidently as being homogeneous, saying that the parents were only other than their children in that they were not themselves the children, . . . and I said that a plant sprung from a seed or root was other than that from which it sprang, and at the same time entirely of one nature with it; and that a stream flowing from a well receives another form and name—for the well is not called a river, nor the river a well—and that both existed, and the well was as it were a father, while the river was water from the well. But they pretend not to see these and the like written statements, . . . and try to pelt me with two unconnected expressions like stones from a distance, not knowing that in matters unknown and needing preparation for their apprehension, frequently not only foreign but even contrary proofs serve to make the subjects of investigation plain." [1] The word 'homoousios' he could not find in the Scriptures, but the sense, as expounded by the Bishop of Rome, he could find and accepted. The word 'made' he insisted was applicable to some relations between the Father and the Son, but when he said the Father created all things he did not reduce the Son to the rank of a creature, for the word Father was to be understood to be of significance in relation to the divine nature itself: that is to say, it includes the Son in the creative power; and when he has said Father he has already implied the Son even before he names him—the idea of Father connotes the idea of Son. He also shews his meaning by speaking of the generation of the Son as 'life from life', and uses, to express the relation between the Son and the Father, the image of a bright light kindled from an unquenchable light. The life, the light, is one and the same. To the charge of tritheism, and of dividing the divine 'substance' into three portions, he answers that "if, because there are three hypostases, any say that they are partitive (divided into portions), three there are though they like it not, or they must utterly destroy the divine Trinity". [2] So, he concludes, "we extend the Monad indivisibly into the Triad, and conversely gather together the Triad without diminution into the Monad".

It is obvious that the difference between the two bishops was a difference in the use of terms rather than in doctrine. [3]

---

[1] Ath. _de Sent. Dion._ 18.　　　　　　　　[2] Basil _de Spiritu S._ 72.

[3] Dionysius of Rome contented himself with shewing the false consequences of the teaching attributed to Dionysius of Alexandria. Athanasius at a later date,

The fact that the one was accustomed to speak and think in Greek and the other in Latin is almost enough in itself to account for the misunderstanding.

Οὐσία—Being, Existence, Essence—was used in two senses, particular and general. In the first sense it meant a particular being or existence or essence, and so in such connexions as this was almost equivalent to our word individual or 'person'. To say that the Son was of the same *οὐσία* as the Father would, in this sense of the word, be saying that they were one person,—and so plunging straightway into all the errors of Sabellius; and these were the very errors against which the Alexandrine was contending. But *οὐσία* was also used in the more general sense of the being or essence which several particular things or persons might share in common. This was the sense in which the Roman understood *substantia*, the Latin equivalent of the term, and in this sense Dionysius of Alexandria (though much more willing to declare unity of *nature*, *i.e.* much less than *substantia* meant) was induced to agree to proclaim the Son of one *οὐσία* with the Father.

Again, the word *ὑπόστασις*—hypostasis—could bear two different meanings. Primarily it was that which underlay a thing, which gave it reality and made it what it was. It was generally used by Greeks as almost equivalent to *οὐσία* in the general sense of underlying principle or essence or being, and the two words are interchangeable as synonyms long after the time at which the Dionysii discussed the matter. But 'hypostasis' (as *οὐσία*) could also be used of the underlying character of a particular thing—of a particular essence or being—of individual rather than of general attributes and properties, and so it might bear the sense of 'person'. In the general sense the Trinity was of course one hypostasis—one God ; there could be only one existence or essence that could be called divine. But in the more limited and particular significance of the term the Christian faith required that three 'hypostases' should be confessed, three modes of the one being, three 'persons' making up the one divine existence—a Trinity within the Unity.

The matter was still further complicated as regards the terminology of East and West by the unfortunate translation of the Greek terms into Latin. Abstract terms (as abstract

with fuller knowledge, vindicates the perfect orthodoxy of his predecessor, whether his language might be misunderstood or not.

thought) found little favour with the concrete practical Roman. The proper rendering of οὐσία was 'essentia' ('being', 'existence' in the general sense), but though a philosopher here or there (as Cicero) might use the word, it never got acclimatized at Rome,[1] and the more concrete term 'substantia' (substance) —with some suggestion of material existence—usurped its place. But this was the very word that was the natural equivalent of the Greek 'hypostasis'. When Dionysius of Rome was told that his brother-bishop spoke of 'three hypostases', he could not fail to think he meant three 'substances', so dividing up the essence of the Godhead and making three separate Gods, whereas he only meant to express the triune personality. A Latin would of course have said three 'personae' (persons), but the Greek πρόσωπον had (as we have seen) too bad a history, —the Sabellian use of it suggesting merely temporary rôles assumed and played by one and the same person, as he pleased.

It was long before Greek-writing theologians themselves came to agreement to use the word 'hypostasis' always of the special characteristics and individual existence of each 'person' in the Trinity, and to keep οὐσία to express the very being (or the essence of the nature) of the Godhead. Till this was done, and the Latins realized that by 'hypostasis' the Greeks meant what they meant by 'persona', and by οὐσία what they meant by 'substantia', there remained a constant danger of misunderstanding and suspicion between the East and the West.

The correspondence between the Dionysii rather exposed this danger than removed it. It was only a few years later, in spite of it, as we have seen, that a council of bishops at Antioch withdrew the word ὁμοούσιος from use. The great influence of Origen in the East supported the tendency to emphasize the distinction of persons even at the cost of their unity, so that at Alexandria itself Pierius, his successor, taught that the Father and the Logos were two οὐσίαι and two natures, and that the Holy Spirit was a third, subordinate to the Son; and Theognostus, in the time of Diocletian, worked out still further the subordination-elements in his theory. Pierius was the teacher of Pamphilus,

---

[1] Seneca (*Ep.* 58. 6) apologizes for using the word and shields himself under Cicero's name, who also used *indoloria*, saying, "licet enim novis rebus nova nomina imponere" (see Forcellini) ; and Quintilian (ii 14. 1, 2) speaks of it and *entia* together with *oratoria* (to represent ῥητορική) as equally harsh translations, but defensible on the ground of the poverty of language resulting from the banishment of terms formed from the Greek.

the presbyter of Caesarea, whose great collection of books and devotion to the memory of Origen were inherited by Eusebius, —the spokesman and leader of the great majority of Eastern bishops in the controversy which, during the following century, seemed to threaten the very foundations of the Christian faith. That they did not more quickly appreciate the issues—the inevitable results of Arianism and the necessity of a precise and definite terminology to exclude it—was due to their theological lineage: men of whose orthodoxy they had no doubt, whose teaching they revered, whose children they were, had used some of the very terms in which Arius clothed his explanation of the person of Christ.

Before, however, we pass on to the Arian controversy we must retrace our steps in order to review the course of the developement of the doctrine of the Logos which had been in progress all through the Monarchian teaching.

CHAPTER IX

THE LOGOS DOCTRINE

IN tracing the developement of the Logos doctrine we are at once confronted by the statements in the preface to the Gospel according to St John,[1] which in untechnical and simple language seem to cover—and if their authority be accepted to decide— all the vexed questions which Monarchianism raised. The eternal pre-existence, the personality, the deity—all are stated in the first three clauses which describe the Logos in his divine relations in eternity before Creation. The second stage, if we may say so, is then set before us—the Logos in relation to Creation and to man, before the Incarnation: in which he is declared the universal life, the light of mankind—in continuous process coming into the world, though unrecognised by men. And thirdly, the same personal, eternal, and divine being is proclaimed as having become flesh and thereby in his Incarnation revealed himself and God to men. In this connexion the derivative character of his being and deity is first suggested:—it is the highest form of derived being, that of an only Son of his Father—whose being is at once derivative and yet the very same as that from which it is derived, equal in deity, on a level with its source.

Wherever the Gospel according to St John was current, there was witness borne that should have precluded all notions of imperfect deity or separate nature or external being of the Logos in relation to the Father, while at the same time his individual personality was clearly marked. The language used to express the eternity of the personal distinction is perhaps less obviously decisive, and misunderstanding might more easily arise in this than in other respects.

That the doctrine was not fully realized, even by well-instructed leaders of Christian thought, is obvious; and its full application to the interpretation of the person of Jesus was not easily made. Now to one aspect and now to another pro-

---

[1] See Westcott *Gospel according to St John*.

minence is given.   Now one relation, now another, is emphasized
by different writers.   The limitations of human thought and
experience are such that we are perhaps justified in saying in
such cases that only the particular aspect, the particular relation,
was grasped by the writer or thinker in question.   But such an
inference—in view of the scanty character of the material available for our consideration—is at least always precarious ; and it
is often far too readily assumed (in the case of early Christian
writers) that the particular aspect of the question which is
presented was the only one with which the writer was familiar.
It would probably be nearer the truth, as it would certainly be
more scientific in method, to regard as typical and complementary, rather than as mutually exclusive, the following few
representative points of view of the doctrine of the Logos.

In every case the historical Jesus Christ is identified with the
Logos.   The chief induction is this : Jesus was the Logos, or at
least the Logos was in Jesus.   That is the primary explanation
of his person which is implied, whatever else is said.   But
inasmuch as the title Logos readily suggested the idea of reason
ruling in the universe, when it was treated as the chief expression for the person of Christ there was great risk of too close
or exclusive connexion with the universe, and so of the divine
power of life in Christ being regarded as a cosmic force.[1]   This,
and failure to distinguish precisely the individual personality of
the Logos, were the chief difficulties in the way of the application
of the induction.   But it is surely going astray to reproach the
writers of this period—or at least the apologists—with transform-
ing the genuine gospel of Christ into natural theology.   They
were anxious, of course, to find what common ground they could
with the Greeks or Romans whose hostility they desired to dis-
arm, and so they naturally presented the doctrine of the Logos
to them in the form in which they would most readily receive
it.   And, broadly speaking, the doctrines which are common to
' natural theology ' and to Christianity were those which it was
most necessary for them to set forward, pointing as they did to
Christ as the centre of all, and to the confirmation of these
doctrines, and the new sanctions in support of them, which the
coming of Christ into the world supplied.[2]

[1] To this effect Harnack *DG*. Eng. tr. vol. i p. 330.
[2] See further on this point J. Orr *The Progress of Dogma* pp. 24, 48, 49 ff.,
against Harnack's view (*DG*. Eng. tr. vol. ii pp. 169-230).

The Ignatian Epistles

In the epistles of Ignatius references to the doctrine are only incidental. Jesus Christ is the Logos "who came forth from silence"[1]—the only utterance of God; "the unlying mouth by which the Father spake truly";[2] he is "God made manifest in human wise".[3] The one God "manifested Himself through Jesus Christ His Son".[4] It cannot be said that these phrases, which Ignatius has used in the few hastily written letters which are all we have, give evidence of any clear conception of distinct personal relations between the eternal Son and the Father.[5] The central idea of Ignatius is the conquest of sin and Satan and of death, the renovation of man, in Christ, by virtue of his divinity in union with his manhood—the beginner of a new humanity: but he is content to insist on both divinity and humanity without attempting to distinguish the relation of the divine to the human. In the chief passage in which he makes reference to this relation he uses language which in a later age would have been judged heretical, as it might be understood to mean that the distinct personality dated from the Incarnation only.

"There is", he writes,[6] "one Physician, fleshly and spiritual, begotten and unbegotten, God in man, true life in death, both of Mary and of God, first passible and then impassible, Jesus Christ our Lord." And "Our God Jesus the Christ was borne in the womb by Mary according to the dispensation of God, of the seed of David, yet of the Holy Spirit: who was begotten and was baptized."[7] It seems that these sentences could not have been written by one who had clearly formed in his mind the conception of the eternal generation of the Son, or even perhaps of his pre-existence in the personal relation of sonship to the Father (n.b., first passible, and then impassible). Unbegotten the Logos, the Son, never was in his relation to God the Father—which is the relation of which the word is used. Yet Ignatius was obviously not really of opinion that the Logos first became a person at the Incarnation. He speaks of Jesus Christ "who was before the ages with the Father and in the end appeared".[8] And the explanation is to be found

---

[1] *Magn.* 8.   [2] *Rom.* 8.   [3] *Eph.* 19.   [4] *Magn.* 8.
[5] There is some justification for the description of his theology as 'modalistic.'
[6] *Eph.* 7.   [7] *Ibid.* 18.   [8] *Magn.* 6.

partly in a laxity in the use of terms due to some indistinctness (rather than inaccuracy) of theological conception; and partly also in the close similarity in the Greek of the words ingenerate or unbegotten and unoriginate or without origin. The doubling of a single letter changes the latter into the former, which Ignatius wrote, though he really meant the latter. By classical writers the distinction was always observed, but in Christian writings the one word used by Ignatius seems to have sometimes done duty for both.[1]   We may feel sure that Ignatius did not intend to deny the existence of the Son in eternity, although the generation of which he speaks is that in time of the Virgin.

The chief effect of his mission is to bring to men knowledge of God, but that knowledge gives incorruptibility to those who become "imitators of the Lord", and "in all chastity and temperance abide in Jesus Christ both in the flesh and in the spirit",[2] breaking the one bread "which is a medicine that gives immortality—a remedy against death—giving life in Jesus Christ for ever".

[1] Cf. Justin *Dial. c. Tryph.* 5 and 8.   The words in question are ἀγένητος and ἀγέννητος.   Against the argument that the interchange of the words is due to clerical error in the manuscripts—the ν being wrongly repeated or omitted, see Lightfoot *Ignatius* vol. ii p. 90.   Lightfoot points to the discussion by Athanasius in 359 (*de Syn.* 46, 47 on the meaning of ὁμοούσιος) of the twofold sense of ἀγέννητος—(1) that which exists but was not generated and has no originating cause, and (2) that which is uncreate.   In the latter sense the word is applicable to the Son, in the former it is not ; and so he says both uses are found in the Fathers, and therefore apparently contradictory language may be orthodox, a different sense of the word being intended.   [In the other passages referred to by Lightfoot, *de Decr.* 28 and *Or. c. Ar.* i 30 (written earlier *c.* 350–355 and *c.* 357–358), it seems certain, as he implies, that the word under discussion is ἀγένητον.   So Robertson insists that in the later passage (*de Syn.* 46, written in 359) Athanasius wrote ἀγένητος, not ἀγέννητος.   See his note 'Athanasius' *N. and P.-N.F.* p. 475.]   Properly ἀγένητος denies origin, and so maintains eternal existence ; while ἀγέννητος denies generation or parentage and thereby the ontological relation of Father and Son in the Godhead, whether in time or in eternity.   The Arian controversy cleared up any uncertainty there was ; and the Son was declared to be γεννητός, but not γενητός ("begotten, not having come into being") ; and when the Arians tried to confuse the issue, saying the two words were the same, they were told that this was so only in the case of creatures, not in regard to God (Epiph. *adv. Haer.* lxiv 8).   In this way the Father only was ἀγέννητος, but the orthodox had no liking for the phrase and were disposed to retort upon the Arians that it was unscriptural (Epiph. *adv. Haer.* lxxii 19).   When, however, the fear of Arianism had passed, it became a convenient term by which to express the relation between the Father (ἀγέννητος) and the Son (γεννητός, but not γενητός)—Lightfoot *l.c.*

[2] *Eph.* 10, 20.

The Letter to Diognetus

The writer of the letter to Diognetus [1] declares the Logos to be no servant or angel or prince, but the Artificer and Creator Himself to whom all things are placed in subjection, sent by the Almighty in consideration and gentle compassion, as a king sends his son, himself a king—so God sent him as God and as man to men, with a view to his saving them, yet by persuasion not by constraint. The purpose of his mission was to reveal God to men, since till he came no man had really known God. It was His own only Son that He sent in His great mercy and loving-kindness and long-suffering, the incorruptible, the immortal, the Saviour able to save. That he distinguished the Logos as a person seems obvious from such expressions, though in almost the same breath he says that God (the Father) " Himself revealed Himself ", and " Himself in His mercy took upon Himself our sins "—phrases which shew at least how close, in his thought, was the union between the Father and the Son. And the function of the Logos previously to the Incarnation seems to be conceived particularly in relation to the world— it was the very Lord and Ruler of the universe who was sent, " by whom He created the heavens, by whom He enclosed the sea in its own bounds, whose secrets all the elements faithfully keep, from whom the sun received the measure of the courses of the day to keep, whose bidding to give light by night the moon obeys, whom the stars obey as they follow the course of the moon, from whom all things received their order and limits and laws (to whom they are subject), the heavens and the things in the heavens, the earth and the things in the earth, the sea and the things in the sea, fire, air, the void, the things in the heights, the things in the depths, the things in the space between. Him it was He despatched to them."

We probably ought, however, to recognize in such a passage as this, addressed to a heathen, a Stoic philosopher, an eloquent amplification of the majesty of the messenger and of his intimate connexion with the eternal universe rather than evidence that the writer was not familiar with the conception of the immanent relations of the Logos and the Father in the inner being of the Godhead.

[1] *Ep. ad Diognetum* vii–x.

Justin Martyr

A much more systematic treatment of the doctrine is found in the writings of the Greek Apologists. Justin Martyr, in the *Dialogue with Trypho*,[1] gives deliberate expression to the chief conceptions in clear view of the objections to them from the monotheistic standpoint.

He insists that Christians really hold monotheism inviolate and yet recognize true deity in Christ. Some of his phrases imply that the Logos existed with God before the creation potentially only, coming to actuality when the world was made; but he also speaks of him in relation to God before creation as "numerically other" (or distinct), and as "being with the Father",[2]—*i.e.* as an individual person. All his highest titles, Glory of the Lord, Son, Wisdom, Messenger, God, Lord, Word, are his by virtue of his serving the Father's purpose and being born[3] by the Father's will. Yet he is not the absolute God, who is unoriginate.[3] The Logos has come into being. It might thus appear that there was a time when he was not, that his coming into being depended on the Father's will, and that the being of God was in some way impaired by the separate (or distinct) existence of the Son. To exclude this inference the analogy of human experience is cited. When we put forth Logos (reason or speech) we generate Logos, not, however, by a process of curtailment in such a way that the Logos within us is impaired or diminished when we put it forth. And again, in the instance of fire being kindled from fire, the original fire remains the same unimpaired, and the fire which is kindled from it is self-existent, without diminishing that from which it was kindled. No argument, accordingly, can be brought against this interpretation of the person of Jesus—that he is indeed the Logos who was with God from the beginning and was His vehicle of creation and of revelation through the old dispensation—on the ground that such a conception detracts from the unity and fulness of being of the Godhead.

[1] See esp. ch. 61—Otto's edition.
[2] This when arguing that it was to him personally that the words "Let us make man" were addressed.
[3] It is uncertain here and frequently throughout the Dialogue whether Justin wrote the word meaning 'come into being' or the word 'be born' (*i.e.* γενητός or γεννητός), even if he discriminated between them at all, though in some cases the context is decisive as to the particular sense intended. See *supra* on Ignatius p. 122 n. 1.

But though Justin, with the other Greek Apologists, may be said to start from the cosmological aspect of the problem, yet the ethical interest—the soteriological aspect of the question— is really very strong with him. The one chief mission of the Logos in all ages has been to interpret the Father to men. He it was who appeared in all the instances recorded in the history of the Jews. In him every race of men has had a share;[1] he was present among them from the first, disseminated as seed scattered among them,[2] and those who, before his birth as the Christ in the time of Cyrenius and his teaching in the time of Pontius Pilate, lived in accordance with his promptings (*i.e.* with Logos) were Christians, even though they were deemed godless;[3] and those who lived otherwise (without Logos) were hostile to Christ and to God. It is because they all partook of the Logos that they are all responsible. It was because through disobedience to his guiding they had received corruption so deeply into their nature as to be unable to recover that the Logos at length assumed flesh.[4] The essential life was united with that which was liable to corruption, in order that the corruption might be overpowered and cast out and man elevated to immortality.[5] In Christ, and in Christ only, the whole Logos appeared, and fully revealed the Father so that all might know Him. It is in this fact that the newness and the greatness of the revelation in Christ are seen. And so Christ, the first-born of all creation, has become also the beginning (the principle) of

[1] See *Apol.* i 46. The Logos (Reason) is the divine element in all men—the Reason within them (almost the conscience).

[2] Cf. *Apol.* ii 13: ὁ σπερματικὸς θεῖος λόγος. It was the seed of the implanted word that enabled them to see clearly realities (cf. ii 8).

[3] He names among others Socrates and Heracleitus and Abraham and Elijah.

[4] That Justin fully recognized the humanity of Christ, and asserted it strongly against Docetic tendencies, is patent. The Logos was made *man* (*Dial. c. Tryph.* 102, λόγος ἀνδρωθείς). The question has, however, been raised—Did he recognize a human soul in Christ? There is no doubt he speaks of σῶμα, λόγος, and ψυχή (body, Logos, soul) as the constituents of his person, and he uses ψυχή in the sense of ψυχή ἄλογος, the animal principle,—so that it might be inferred from this phrase that he regarded the Logos as taking the place of the human (rational) soul or spirit or mind. But he may have used the popular division of man into 'body and soul' rather than the more precise and technical threefold division into σῶμα, ψυχή, πνεῦμα. There is, however, nothing to shew that the question had ever presented itself to Justin's thought. All that can certainly be maintained is that he regarded the manhood of Christ as complete and would not have consciously used expressions which were inconsistent therewith.

[5] Fragment—Otto vol. ii p. 550 (*Corp. Apol.* iii p. 256). The genuineness of the fragment is, however, disputed.

another race,—the race which is born again by him through water and faith and wood (the tree), which possesses the secret of the cross.[1] Those who are thus prepared beforehand and repent for their sins will escape (be acquitted in) the judgement of God which is to come.

Tatian

Tatian was, both as his pupil and in thought, closely connected with Justin. In his defence of Christian doctrine *To the Greeks*[2] he is at pains to try to express the relation of the Logos to the Divine Being (the inner nature and existence of the Deity) and the manner in which he has a personal distinct existence without impairing the unity of the divine existence. He states the matter as follows:—"God was in the beginning (at the first); and the beginning (the first principle),[3] we have been instructed, is the potentiality[4] of the Logos. For the Lord of the universe, who is himself the essence[5] of the whole, in so far as the creation had not yet come to be, was alone: but inasmuch as he was all potentiality,[4] and himself the essence of things seen and things unseen, in company with him were all things. In company with him, through the potentiality of the Logos, the Logos too, who was in him, himself essentially was (ὑπέστησεν, subsisted). By the simple will of God the Logos springs forth, and the Logos, proceeding not without cause, becomes (*or* comes into being as) the first-born work of the Father. Him (*i.e.* the Logos) we know to be the first principle (beginning) of the world. He came into being by a process of impartation, not of abscission: for that which is cut off is separated from that from which it is cut; but that which has imparted being, receiving as its function one of administration,[6] has not made him whence he was taken defective. For just as from one torch there are

[1] *c. Tryph.* 138.

[2] *Oratio* ch. v (*al.* vii and viii). His own title was simply Τατιανοῦ πρὸς Ἕλληνας. The text of Otto is followed (but see *ed.* Schwartz).

[3] ἡ ἀρχή—'beginning', and also first cause or guiding governing principle.

[4] δύναμις. The conception is that the Logos was not actually, but only potentially, existent (δυνάμει not ἐνεργείᾳ).

[5] ἡ ὑπόστασις—"that which makes things what they are and gives being or reality to them." See on the *Correspondence of the Dionysii* p. 116. All things were potentially in Him.

[6] "The part of οἰκονομία", administration of the world, revelation.

kindled fires many, and the light of the first torch is not lessened on account of the kindling from it of the many torches; so too the Logos, by coming forth from the potentiality of the Father, has not made Him who has begotten him destitute of Logos. For I myself speak and you hear, and I who converse with you certainly do not become void of speech (Logos) [1] through the passage of my speech from me to you."

The Logos is here regarded mainly in relation to the world, as the principle on which it was made, and the vehicle of revelation. Personal existence seems to attach to the Logos in this connexion only. The hypostatic distinction in the being of God before Creation—and essentially—is not expressed. The pre-existence is only potential (the only distinction is that of the Father from His own reason)—God is all in all; the Logos is in him, but so are all things, and it is only when God wills that the Logos proceeds to personal being for the work which is assigned him.

Theophilus

A very similar view to that of Tatian appears to have been held by Theophilus a little later.[2] He was probably the first to use the actual term Triad (Trinity) [3] and to apply Philo's terms 'indwelling' (or 'immanent') and 'proceeding' (or 'projected' or 'transient') [4] to the Logos. Till God willed to create the world the Logos dwelt in Him, in His inner being, as counsellor—His mind and intelligence—this is the only kind of pre-existence which appears to be recognized, and it is not clear in what way the Logos could be distinguished from the Father. Before Creation He begat him 'vomiting him forth':—He begat him as " proceeding, first-born of all creation; not himself being made empty of the Logos, but

[1] The twofold sense of λόγος, reason and the expression of it in speech, must be borne in mind; but the dominant thought in this passage is of the outward expression.

[2] His Defence of Christianity ad Autolycum, see esp. ii 10 and 22.

[3] The Triad named is "God and his Word and his Wisdom", of which the three days which passed before the lights in the firmament of heaven were created are said to be types.

[4] ἐνδιάθετος and προφορικός. The use of these terms is of Stoic origin, marking the two senses of λόγος (reason and word), so mental and uttered or pronounced. As representing two aspects of the same truth the use is recognized, but neither term isolated from the other would be accurate.

begetting Logos and continually consorting with his Logos ".[1]
The Logos is clearly regarded as the medium for the Father's
work in the world and among men.   Always with God, he is
the principle of all things.   The Father Himself cannot be
contained in space—but the Logos can ; and so he assumed in
the world the part [2] of the Father—the Lord of all.

The Distinction of the Logos from the Father cosmic rather than hypostatic

Neither Justin nor Tatian nor Theophilus, accordingly,
would seem to have clearly conceived a hypostatic distinction
in the being of God Himself:—the distinction is found ex-
ternally in relation to the world, and there is danger, on the
one hand, of the Logos being identified with God.   His essence
($o\dot{v}\sigma\iota a$), as it were, rests eternally in God—immanent : his
hypostasis is conceived only in the work of revelation.   And so,
on the other hand, as a personal existence it may be argued
that the Logos is not really God, but only a manifestation of
Him, and the Christology of the Apologists has thus been said
to fall short of the genuine Christian appreciation of Christ—
inasmuch as "it is not God who reveals Himself in Christ, but
the Logos, the depotentiated God, a God who as God is subordinate to the highest God " (Loofs).   The limits within which
this criticism of the Apologists may fairly be accepted have
been already noted at the outset.[3]

Athenagoras : his fuller recognition of the conditions to be accounted for

In Athenagoras is found a clearer view of the personal
existence of the Logos (or the Son) before Creation, and a fuller
perception of the problem how to secure the unity and yet
assign its due place to the distinction.

It is the chief concern of Christians, he writes, " to know
God and the Logos who comes from Him : to see what is the
unity of the Son in relation to the Father, what the communion
of the Father with the Son, what the Spirit ; what is the union
($\dot{\epsilon}\nu\omega\sigma\iota\varsigma$) of all these and the distinction ($\delta\iota a\acute{\iota}\rho\epsilon\sigma\iota\varsigma$) of the

---

[1] This idea of continuous generation has something in common with Origen's
doctrine of the eternal generation.
[2] The word used is $\pi\rho\acute{o}\sigma\omega\pi\sigma\nu$.   [3] See *supra* p. 120.

united—the Spirit, the Son, the Father:[1]—"proclaiming at the same time their power in unity and a distinction in their order".[2] This distinction is more clearly conceived of as independent of the creation of the world than by the other Greek Apologists. He speaks of the whole divine sphere as itself a 'perfect world' (κόσμος), and God as being in Himself all to Himself, so that there was no necessity for the world we know to be created. The distinctions in the being of God are thus conceived as self-existent, and the part which the Logos afterwards plays in the work of creation he only plays because he is already in idea all that was required for the exercise of the special work of creation. The term 'generated' ('a thing begotten'), and the epithet 'first' in connexion with it, are applied to him, yet "not as having come into being (for from the beginning God, since He is eternal Mind, had in Himself the Logos (reason), since He is eternally possessed of Logos (rational)); but as having proceeded forth as idea and energy (i.e. in exercise of the idea)".[3] "God's Son is the Logos of the Father in idea and in operation." He has thus a previous relation to the Father, as has the Holy Spirit—and the three names represent eternally existing distinctions within the being of the Divine itself. It is in this clear repudiation of the conception that the Logos first acquired a personal existence in connexion with the creation of the universe (while he fully recognizes his operation therein), that Athenagoras seems to furnish a link between the earlier less precise and the later more exact expressions of the Christian consciousness. Precision of terminology is first to be found in Tertullian, but his contemporary Clement, and Irenaeus before him, make important contributions to the developement of the doctrine.

Irenaeus

Irenaeus is one of the most conspicuous figures in the history

---

[1] *Leg.* 12 (for Son he writes παῖς). The best edition of Athenagoras is that of E. Schwartz, Leipzig 1891 (*Texte und Untersuchungen* iv Bd. 2 Heft).

[2] *Leg.* 10. So "who would not be perplexed", he writes, "to hear described as 'atheists' men who believe in God the Father and God the Son and the Holy Spirit, and declare their power in unity and their distinction in order"; and again, "the Son is in the Father and the Father in the Son by unity and power of the Spirit" (the conception expressed by the later term περιχώρησις, see *infra* p. 226 n. 2).

[3] *Ibid.* The terms are ἰδέα and ἐνέργεια—the latter being the actualization of the former.

9

of the early Church. It is unnecessary here to enlarge on the importance of the various parts he played. His thought was no doubt mainly moulded by his Eastern origin and built up on a foundation of early traditions and modes of thought current in Asia Minor,[1] though largely developed and determined in opposition to Gnostic theories.[2]

It was Gnosticism that led him to lay such stress on the eternal coexistence of the Logos with the Father, to repel the idea that he was ever 'made', and to discriminate creation from generation, rejecting anything of the nature of an emanation as a true expression of the relation between the Logos and the Father. Nor does he ever tend to identify the divine in Christ with the world-idea or the creating Word or Reason of God. He is familiar with the conception of a twofold generation,[3] and uses the terms Son and Logos alike—interchangeably (the Logos being always Son). He conceives of the Logos as the one great and absolute organ of all divine revelations from all time (so that in them it was not God Himself but the Logos who appeared), and apparently of some kind of subordination of the Logos,—but he is prevented by his religious feeling and his consciousness of the limitations of the human understanding from carrying far his investigations into the nature of the relations between Father and Son. They are a mystery. The Father is God revealing Himself; the Son is God revealed. The Father is the invisible of the Son, while the Son is the

---

[1] E.g. he held to the early millennial expectations (adv. Haer. v 5 and 25 ff., ed. Harvey).

[2] See Loofs Leitfaden³ p. 91 ff. He points to Asia Minor as the scene of the greatest spiritual activity in the Church in the second half of the second century (cf. the Apologists: Melito of Sardis, Apollinarius of Hierapolis, Rhodon—a pupil of Tatian in Rome, Miltiades, Apollonius, and other Montanist writers, whose names are unknown), and as the home of a special theology, of which he notes the following characteristics:—(a) The clear recognition of the distinction between the Old and the New Testaments. (b) The concern to make Christ the centre to which the whole history of the divine οἰκονομία converges. (c) The appearance of modalism which resulted from the close connexion of its Christology with the popular conception that Christ had brought perfect knowledge of God (the revelation of Christ —the revelation of God), and (as he styles it) the paradoxical contrasting of the real death and real humanity of Christ with his immortality and deity. (d) The connexion of the knowledge of God with the assurance of immortality, based on the saying, 'This is eternal life, that they should know Thee' (John 17³); yet an essentially physical expression of the means of salvation.

[3] The generation from eternity, whereby the Godhead exists both as Father and as Son in itself; and afterwards the generation in time, when the Son became man, being born into the world.

visible of the Father. But the personal distinction is strictly maintained: and he insists that it is one and the same person —Jesus Christ—the Logos—the Son of God—who created the world, was born as man, and suffered and ascended into heaven, still man as well as God.

The deepest interest of Irenaeus (however) does not seem to be centred in speculations of this kind, but in the Incarnation as the fulfilment of the eternal purpose of God which was manifested when He created man in His image after His likeness. Irenaeus marks the distinction between the image, which connotes reason and freedom, in which man was made, and the likeness, which is the capacity for immortality, to which he was destined to attain. A course of developement was thus set before men by the Creator, following which they would become in very truth as He Himself was: but man in the exercise of his freedom, using the power which the 'image' gave him, departed from the course assigned him, and by his transgression (in the Fall) became subject to death and could no longer reach the goal of immortality. To restore to him the power of which he had been deprived was the purpose of the Incarnation, so that what had been lost in Adam might be recovered in Christ Jesus. In him the final predestined developement was realized,—it had been interrupted, but he resumed and completed it. It is Irenaeus who first expresses the thought which others after him delighted to emphasize— " On account of his infinite love he became what we are, in order that he might make us what he himself is." He summed up in himself the whole race and the whole course of developement, completing thereby the whole revelation of God to man, and by passing through all stages of human life consecrated each and all. In this way in the person of Christ Jesus— the Person of the Logos become man—the whole race is again united to God, and becomes capable of attaining to incorruptibility. The possessor of immortality actually united himself with human nature, so that by adoption he might deify it and guarantee it the inheritance of life. He thus brought about the condition which God had ordained from the beginning— the realisation of which the entrance of sin had checked. So it is that Jesus Christ—he who is God and man—is the real centre of all history. He is the person who, as man, first attained the destination set before the race. Special means of

reaching this consummation are offered to individuals in the
institution of the Sacraments of Baptism (which gives forgiveness of sins) and the Lord's Supper (partaking of the
Eucharist our bodies no longer are corruptible but have the
hope of the resurrection),—but there is also the mystic presentation which is summed up in the pregnant saying, "the
vision of God is the life of man".[1]   The real life is the
knowledge, the vision, of God.   This knowledge, this vision,
the Incarnation of the Word gave to men, and not only to those
who actually saw him in his incarnate life upon earth, but also
to all who afterwards should see him with the eye of faith—
"They who see God will partake of life.   It was for this reason
that the infinite and incomprehensible and invisible offered himself to be seen and comprehended and contained by the faithful,
so that he might give life to those that contain and see him by
faith."[2]   For them too the invisible is made visible, the incomprehensible comprehensible, and the impassible passible.   But
faith—believing in him—involves the doing of his will;[3] and it
is, in turn, by the fulfilment of his commands, by obedience to
him, that we learn to know him more completely.   For the
knowledge which is possible for man is essentially moral,[4] the
affinity between man and God is based on character.   "Exactly
in proportion as God is in need of nothing, man is in need of
communion with God; for this is man's glory—to preserve and
continue in the service of God."[5]

It is his strong hold on the conception of the unity and
continuity of God's purpose and revelations of Himself thus
manifested in the Incarnation as the natural sequence and
culmination of the design of creation, not necessarily conditioned
by the fall of man, that is most characteristic of the thought of
Irenaeus.   He was apparently the first of the great church
teachers to follow up the clues which St Paul had given[6] in
this respect.

---

[1] Irenaeus *adv. Haer.* iv 34. 7 (*ed.* Harvey).   [2] *Ibid.* iv 34. 6.

[3] Credere autem ei est facere ejus voluntatem (*ibid.* iv 11. 3).

[4] *Ibid. l.c.* and iv 34.

[5] *Ibid.* iv 25. 1 (*ed.* Harvey).   Harnack finds in Irenaeus two main ideas—
(1) The conviction that the Creator of the world and the Supreme God are one and
the same ; (2) the conviction that Christianity is real redemption, and that this
redemption was only effected by the appearance of Christ.   But these two ideas are
part of the stock—the very root—of all Christian thought.

[6] *E.g.* in the Epistle to the Ephesians 1[10] 3[11].

The thought and teaching of Clement of Alexandria is in several ways closely akin to his, and comparison of the one with the other is instructive. Clement's travels before he went to Alexandria had taken him to ground familiar to Irenaeus in his earlier life before he settled down at Lyons, and there was much in common between the two contemporary teachers of the Egyptian and the Gallican Churches.

The characteristics of the Alexandrine school are clearly marked in Clement, one of its chief representatives. Its love of learning, its sympathy with intellectual activities, its enthusiasm for knowledge of every kind as the only avenue that would lead to true interpretation of the Gospel; its no less sincere recognition of the need of faith and of love in the search after truth, its desire to bring the whole of human life consciously under the rule of Christ, and to apply to every domain of thought and conduct the principles embodied in his life and teaching: these characteristics shew themselves in the work of all members of the school, and the result is an interpretation of the Gospel which is at once inclusive of the best Greek philosophical thought and genuinely Christian.

Clement of Alexandria

It was Clement who elevated "the idea of the Logos, who is Christ, into the highest principle in the religious explanation of the world and in the exposition of Christianity".[1] "Christianity is the doctrine of the creation, training, and redemption of mankind by the Logos, whose work culminates in the perfect Gnostic." But the perfect Gnosticism with Clement is the true knowledge of God, which is to be reached by disciplined reason. His 'Gnostic' is no visionary, no mystic. "Though the father of all mystics, he is no mystic himself."[1]

The doctrine of the Logos is the centre and mainspring of the whole system of Clement.

He was eternally with the Father, who never was without him as Son. The being which he has is the same as the being of God the Father.[2] He is the ultimate beginning (cause or

[1] C. Bigg *The Christian Platonists of Alexandria* ch. iii p. 98 f.

[2] "One must assume", says Harnack, "that the word [Homoousios] was really familiar to Clement as a designation of the community of nature both with God and with men, possessed by the Logos." He certainly wrote (*Strom.* iv 13) with

principle) of all things that are, himself without beginning (or origination). He is author of the world, the source of light and life, in a sense himself at the head of the series of created beings, but, by reason of his divine being, specifically different from them. He is the interpreter of the Father's attributes, the manifestation of the truth in person, the educator of the human race,[1] who at last became man to make men partakers of his own divine nature.

That Clement thus held clearly a distinction between the Logos and the Father need not be argued. The real question which calls for consideration is whether he did not also so far distinguish between the Logos as originally existent and the Logos who was Son of God as to conceive two persons,[2]—the Logos proper who remains unalterably in God (the Logos immanent), and the Son-Logos who is an emanation of the immanent reason of God (the Logos proceeding forth in operation).

He is said to have written,[3] " The Son-Logos is spoken of by the same name as the Father's Logos, but it is not he who became flesh, nor yet the Father's Logos, but a certain power of God, as it were an effluence from the Logos himself, who became mind and visited continually the hearts of men." This, however, is the only passage in which such a distinction is obviously drawn,[4] and its real meaning is so obscure that apart from the context (which is not extant) it is impossible to use it in support of a view which is really contradicted by the whole conception of

reference to the Valentinian doctrine of a peculiar race sent to abolish death, who were themselves saved by nature, that if this doctrine were true then Christ had not abolished death unless he too was homoousios with them, and in another place (*Strom.* ii 16) that men are not ' part of God and homoousioi with God ' (implying that the Son was homoousios with God).

[1] Of the Greeks through philosophy, of the Jews through the Law, and afterwards, in Christ, of all who accept his teaching through faith leading up to knowledge, through knowledge to love, and through love to ' the inheritance '. See *e.g.* *Strom.* vii 2 and vii 10. "The Greek philosophy, as it were, purges the soul and prepares it beforehand for the reception of faith " (*Strom.* vii 3 ; cf. i 13).

[2] So Harnack (*DG.* Eng. tr. vol. ii p. 352) says that in many passages he "expresses himself in such a way that one can scarcely fail to notice a distinction between the Logos of the Father and that of the Son ". See also Loofs *Leitfaden* p. 107.

[3] In the *Hypotyposcis* (Harnack *DG.* Eng. tr. vol. ii p. 352).

[4] In *Strom.* v 1 Clement seems to me to be certainly objecting to the term λόγος προφορικός as applied to the Son, on the ground that it depreciates his dignity, and not (as Harnack and Zahn take it) himself sanctioning a distinction between the higher λόγος ἐνδιάθετος and the lower λόγος προφορικός.

Clement's great trilogy—the conception of the Logos, one and the same, from the beginning to the end of things, drawing men to faith, training them, and at last bringing them to the full knowledge of God.

Here, as in all similar cases, the only safe canon of criticism is that which bids us interpret the less known in a sense in keeping with the more known; and we must assume that the doubtful expression was less well said rather than let it subvert the whole purpose and aim of the mass of its author's work. The general conception of Clement was certainly that the Logos —eternally equal with, but distinct from the Father, as His Son —was manifested all through the world's history, and at last was incarnate in the person of Jesus Christ. He cannot have intended, by any phrase that the exigencies of any particular line of argument may have brought to him, to evacuate that main idea of its proper force and consequences.[1]

[1] The prologue to the *Exhortation to the Greeks* is really quite decisive—

The Word is the harmonious, melodious, holy instrument of God (*Exhortation to the Greeks* i).

Inasmuch as the Word was from the first, He was and is the divine source of all things.

He has now assumed the name of Christ . . . the cause of both our being at first and of our well-being.

This very Word has appeared as man, He alone being both, both God and man.

The Saviour, who existed before, has in recent days appeared—He who is in Him that truly is—the Word—has appeared . . . as our teacher . . .

He pitied us from the beginning . . . but now he accomplished our salvation.

Our ally and helper is one and the same—the Lord, who from the beginning gave revelations . . . but now plainly calls to salvation.

The teacher from whom all instruction comes (*ibid.* xi).

And Clement puts these words into the mouth of Jesus, the one great High Priest of the one God his Father—an appeal to men, "Come to Me, that you may be put . . . under the one God and the one Word of God . . . I confer on you both the Word and the Knowledge of God, my complete self. . . . This am I . . . this is the Son, this is Christ, this the Word of God . . . I will give you rest" (*ibid.* xii *ad fin.*).

Our Instructor is like His Father God . . . God in the form of man . . . the Word who is God, who is in the Father (*Paed.* i 2).

"The good Instructor . . . the Word of the Father, who made man . . . the Saviour . . . 'Rise up' he said to the paralytic" (*ibid.*).

"One alone, true, good, just, in the image and likeness of the Father, His Son Jesus, the Word of God, is our Instructor" (*ibid.* xi).

"The Word Himself is the manifest mystery: God in man and the man God. And the Mediator executes his Father's will: for the Mediator is the Word, who is common to both—the Son of God, the Saviour of men: His Servant, our Teacher" (*ibid.* iii 1).

There are frequent references to the Son being what he is and exercising the functions he exercises ' by the will ' and ' according to the will ' of the Father, but they are obviously intended rather to safeguard the authority of the Father than to limit the power of the Son. Such phrases do not imply any non-Catholic conception of the subordination or ' inferiority ' of the Son to the Father. They express the complete moral harmony between the Father and the Son ; they exclude anything like dualism, anything that would mar the unity of the divine being; they certainly do not support any notion of temporal origin of the Son or of his derivation from any other source than the very essence of the divine.[1]

The influence of Clement on the developement of doctrine was, however, not exercised so much directly as through his more famous pupil Origen, whose greater ability and untiring labours, continued over fifty years, made him the chief representative of the Alexandrian school.

Before, however, we pass to him, we must turn our attention to the great representative of the Church of Africa—in geographical position situated between Gaul and Egypt, but separated from each by sea and desert, and no less isolated by antecedents and character. The differences between the Churches of Africa on the one hand and Gaul and Egypt on the other is reflected in the thought and teaching of Tertullian on the one hand, and Irenaeus and Clement on the other. In passing from Clement to Tertullian we pass from sentiment and imagination to practical precision and legal reasoning, from poetry to prose. Instead of picturesque description we have attempts at accurate definition. We leave the mystic atmosphere of the Logos doctrine, with its blended beauties and obscurities, its lights and its shadows, and come into the region in which it is overpowered by the doctrine of the Sonship—the doctrine which is much more obviously in harmony with human analogies and experience, and by its greater simplicity was found to be much more easily grasped by the practical Western mind.

---

[1] In the *Stromateis* (vii 2) he definitely calls him the paternal Word, declares him to be always everywhere, being detained nowhere ; the complete paternal light . . . before the foundation of the world the counsellor of the Father . . . the power of God as being the Father's most ancient Word before the production of all things and His wisdom. "The Son is ", he says, "so to speak an energy of the Father", but this is said to shew that "being the Father's power, he easily prevails in what he wishes ".

From this time forward the explanation of the person of Christ and of his relation to the Godhead as a whole, which was furnished by the Logos doctrine, tended more and more to recede into the background of theological thought. The main ideas had no doubt in large measure passed into the common stock, but the name was less and less used, and attention was concentrated rather on the group of ideas which the title Son suggests. The more philosophical conception gives way to the one which can best be brought to the test of conditions with which every one is familiar.

So the conception of the Sonship occupies the chief place in the thought and exposition of an Origen no less than in that of less speculative and more prosaic theologians like Tertullian.

CHAPTER X

TERTULLIAN

IT is in Tertullian that we first find the accurate definition and technical terms that passed over into Catholic theology, winning prompt acceptance in the West and securing—when the time came—the grudging but certain approval of the East.[1] With his legal rhetorical training and ready application of forensic analogies to the expression of doctrine, and his genius for terse and pregnant description, he effectively moulded the Latin language to the service of ecclesiastical needs, and fashioned the formulas of the later orthodoxy. The terms seem to come to him so readily that one would suppose them already familiar, were it not that no earlier traces are found.

It will be remembered that he was a chief opponent of the modalistic form of Monarchianism, which he understood to mean that the Father Himself suffered; and it was under the provocation of this Monarchian teaching that his own conceptions were expressed and probably worked out.

Tertullian was perhaps less a philosopher than a jurist, and we are helped to understand his theory—his expression of the Christian doctrine of God and of the Person of Christ—by the legal use of the terms he employs.[2] 'Substance' (*substantia*) meant 'property'—the sense in which we use the word when we speak of 'a man of substance'—a man's possessions, estates, fortune, the owner's rights in which were carefully protected by Roman law from invasion or infringement. 'Person' (*persona*)

---

[1] See *infra* p. 166 n. 1, on the influence of the West (through Hosius) in framing the Nicene formula. It is an 'epitome' of Tertullian that was made by Novatian, whose treatise *On the Trinity* was a dominant influence in the West. So it was Tertullian's doctrine that Dionysius of Rome pressed on his namesake of Alexandria.

[2] See Harnack *DG*. ii³ p. 285 ff.(Eng. tr. vol. iv pp. 122, 123). But the passages cited *infra* shew that the conceptions and expressions of Tertullian were by no means entirely controlled by legal usage, and the philosophical sense of the terms must also be borne in mind.

meant a being with legal rights, a 'party', an 'individual', whose being as such was recognized by law as one of the facts of which it took cognizance, a real existence (*res*) within its own limitations. Such a person's position or circumstances would be his status, or condition (*status, condicio*),—perhaps even his nature (*natura* or *proprietas*), when looked at from a more inward point of view,—and obviously a number of persons might occupy the same status, or be in the same condition, or have the same nature. So too there might be various kinds of 'substance', each marked by special characteristics or 'properties' (in the sense of that which is proper or peculiar to each) or 'nature' (*proprietas, natura*).

Thus, if these human analogies be applied to the interpretation of the Christian revelation, one substance is divinity—all that belongs to the divine existence. This is, as it were, one piece of property; but, following still the human analogy, there is nothing to hinder its being held in joint ownership by three individuals with the same rights in it on equal terms. And so the description of the divine existence would be one substance shared by three persons in one condition (*una substantia, tres personae, in uno statu*). But there is also another substance—all that belongs to human existence, all that is owned by men *qua* men. This is another piece of property, and, still from the point of view of Roman law, there is nothing to hinder one and the same person from holding at the same time two quite different pieces of property. So the two substances, divinity and humanity, might be owned, and all the rights and privileges attaching to each exercised and enjoyed, at one and the same time, by one and the same person, Jesus Christ.[1] Thus there is no contradiction or confusion of thought in speaking as regards the being of God of one substance and three persons,[2] and as

---

[1] Melito (*de Incarn. Christi* (Routh *Rel.* i p. 121)) uses οὐσία as Tertullian uses *substantia* in this connexion, and speaks in regard to Christ of τὰς δύο αὐτοῦ οὐσίας—the two realities, Godhead and manhood, which were his.

[2] Tertullian seems, however, to avoid the use of the word *personae* in this connexion, using *tres* alone to express 'the three', without adding 'persons' in the case of the Trinity; just as later Augustine, while feeling compelled to speak of three 'persons', apologized for the term and threw the responsibility for it on to the poverty of the language (*de Trinitate* v 10, vii 7–10; see *infra*). Tertullian has the definite expression only when it cannot well be omitted—*e.g.* when supporting the doctrine of the Trinity from the baptismal commission, he writes "nam nec semel, sed ter, ad singula nomina in personas singulas tinguimur" (*adv. Prax.* 26).

On the other hand, he has no scruple about using the term *persona* of Jesus Christ, both man and God—combining in himself the two *substantiae*, but one

regards the constitution of the person of Christ of two substances and one person, he being at once God and man (*Deus et
homo*).

In this way the unity of the Godhead is strongly marked;
it is one and the same divinity which all three share alike.
This is "the mystery of the providential order which arranges
the unity in a trinity, setting in their order three—Father,
Son, and Holy Spirit—three, however, not in condition (*status*)
but in relation (*gradus*), and not in substance but in mode of
existence (*forma*), and not in power but in special characteristics
(*species*); yes, rather of one substance and of one status and
power, inasmuch as it is one God from whom these relations and
modes and special characteristics are reckoned in the name of
Father and of Son and of Holy Spirit".[1]

When Tertullian passes from this juristic sense of substance
to the wider philosophical use of the term, and declares that he
always maintains in regard to the Godhead " the substance in
three (persons) who together form the whole ",[2] yet it is always
with him something concrete—a particular form of existence.
It has of course a particular character or nature of its own;
but *it* is not its nature—rather its nature exists in *it*, and, in
part at least, in other similar substances. " Substance and
the nature of substance ", he writes,[3] " are different things.
Substance is peculiar to each particular thing; nature, however,
can be shared by others. Take an example : stone and iron are
substances ; the hardness of stone and of iron is the nature of
the two substances. Hardness brings them together, makes them

person. Cf. *adv. Prax.* 27 " Videmus duplicem statum, non confusum, sed con-
iunctum in una persona, deum et hominem Jesum."

[1] *Adv. Prax.* 2. *Tres autem non statu sed gradu, nec substantia sed forma, nec
potestate sed specie.* Apparently by *gradus* (relation or degree) is meant " the order
whereby the Father exists of Himself, the Son goes forth immediately from the
Father, and the Holy Spirit proceeds from the Father through the Son ; so that
the Father is rightly designated the first, the Son the second, and the Holy Spirit
the third Person of the Godhead. And by the expressions *formae* and *species*
(forms and aspects) he seems to have meant to indicate the different modes of
subsistence (τρόπους ὑπάρξεως), whereby the Father, the Son, and the Holy Spirit
subsist in the same divine nature" (Bp. Bull *Def. N.C.* ii, vii).

Between 'species' and 'forma' there is no perceptible difference, at least
Cicero (*Op.* 7, cited by Forcellini) says the same thing is signified by *species* as
by *forma*, which in Greek is ἰδέα.

[2] Unam substantiam in tribus cohaerentibus (*adv. Prax.* 12).

[3] *De Anima* 32. Similarly (*adv. Prax.* 26) he distinguishes between *substantia*
and the *accidentia* or *proprietates uniuscuiusque substantiae.*

partners; substance sets them apart (that is to say, hardness—
their 'nature'—is what they have in common; substance is
what is peculiar to each). . . . You mark the likeness of nature
first when you observe the unlikeness of substance,"—that is
to say, that you must first recognize that they are two things
(as to substance) before you can compare them (as to nature).
'Substance' can, accordingly, never have to Tertullian the
meaning 'nature',[1]—the thing itself cannot be its properties.
And so, in working out the doctrine of the Person of Christ, by
the expression 'two substances' he does not mean simply two
natures in any indefinite sense, but that the one person is both
God and man, enjoying the two distinct possessions of deity and
humanity.

It is in describing the nature of the relation between the
Son and the Father that he most loses sight of the legal sense
of the term 'substance', and employs it to express a particular
form of existence; which is, however, still regarded as concrete.
" The Son I derive ", he says, " from no other source but from the
substance of the Father ",[2] where the substance of the Father is
only an exegetical periphrasis for the Father Himself—His own
being: so that he can use the single word, " We say that the
Son is produced (projected) from the Father, but not separated
from Him ".[3] He who is emitted from the substance of the
Father must of course be of that substance,[4] and there is no
separation between the two. The Word is " always in the
Father . . . and always with God . . . and never separated
from the Father or different from the Father ". He speaks, it
is true, of the Father as being 'the whole substance', while
the Son is 'a derivation from, and portion of, the whole', and
so 'made less' than the Father;[5] but his only purpose is to
mark the distinction between them as real, and not as involving diversity between them or division of the one substance.
The relation between them may be illustrated by human
analogies. The root produces (emits) the shrub, the spring the
stream, and the sun the ray. The former is in each case, as
it were, the parent, and the latter the offspring: they are two
things, but they are inseparably connected. The being of both
is one and the same. That which proceeds, moreover, is second
to that from which it proceeds, and when you say 'second'

---

[1] See further *Journal of Theological Studies* vol. iii p. 292 and vol. iv p. 440.
[2] *Adv. Prax.* 4.   [3] *Ibid.* 8.   [4] *Ibid.* 7.   [5] *Ibid.* 9.

you say that there are two. It is in order to mark clearly
the distinct personality of the Son that he calls him ' second '.
There is no suggestion or thought of subordination, in any
other sense than in regard to origin, and even that is merged
in the unity of substance. In the case under consideration
there is a third. " The Spirit is third from God and the Son,
just as the fruit which comes from the shrub is third from the
root, and the river which flows from the stream is third from
the spring, and the ' peak ' of the ray third from the sun." [1]
There is, moreover, a sense in which the Father is one, and
the Son other, and the Spirit yet other ; as he who generates is
other than he who is generated, and he who sends than he who
is sent. Yet there is no division of the one substance, though
there are three in it, and each of the three is a substantive
(substantial) existence out of the substance of God Himself.[2]

Seizing the Monarchian watchword, he turns it against
themselves, and insists that no rule or government is so much
the rule of a single person, so much a ' monarchy ', that it
cannot be administered through others appointed to fulfil their
functions by the monarch. The monarchy is not divided, and
does not cease to be a monarchy, if the monarch's son is
associated with him in the rule. The kingdom is still the
king's ; its unity is not impaired.[3]

That God was never really alone (since there was always
with Him the Logos as His reason and word) is shewn by the
analogy of the operation of human thought and consciousness,[4]
and by His very name of Father—which implies the existence
of the Son ; He had a Son, but He was not Himself His Son—
as well as by numerous passages of the Scriptures. But
between Him and the Son there was no division, though they
were two (and though it would be better to have two divided
gods than the one ' change-coat ' God the Monarchians preached).

The treatise against Praxeas is more technical in phraseology
and definitely theological in purpose than the *Apology*,[5] which
was intended for more general reading ; but in the *Apology* he

[1] *Adv. Prax.* 8. Yet it is a '*trinitas unius divinitatis*'. See *de Pudicitia* § 21.
[2] *Adv. Prax.* 26, and cf. *ibid.* 25. " So the connexion of the Father in the Son
and of the Son in the Paraclete produces three coherent one to the other. And
these three are one thing (*unum*), not one person (*unus*) ; as it was said, ' I and the
Father are One (*unum*) ', in regard to unity of substance, not in regard to singularity
of number."
[3] *Adv. Prax.* 3.   [4] *Ibid.* 5.   [5] See *Apol.* 21.

expresses the same thoughts in somewhat different language. God made the world by His word and reason and power (*virtus*). This is what Zeno and Cleanthes also said, using the word Logos —that is, word and reason—of the artificer of the universe. The proper substance of the Logos is spirit. He was produced from God, and by being produced was generated, and is called Son of God, and God, because his substance is one and the same as God's. For God too is spirit. As in the case of a ray being shot forth from the sun, the ray is a portion of the whole sun; but the sun is really in the ray, because it is a ray of the sun; and the substance of the ray is not separated from the sun; but the substance of the sun is extended into the ray: so that which is produced from spirit is spirit, and from God God, just as from light is kindled light. So the Logos is God and God's Son, and both are one. It was, as it were, a ray of God which glided down into a certain virgin, and in her womb was fashioned as flesh, and was born man and God blended together.[1] The flesh was built up by the spirit, was nourished, grew to manhood, spoke, taught, worked, and was Christ.

The relation between the spirit and the flesh in the constitution of the person of Jesus Christ he discusses in the treatise against Praxeas.[2]

It was not that the spirit was transformed (*transfiguratus*) when he became flesh, but that he 'put on' flesh. God, as being eternal, is unchangeable and incapable of being transformed. To have been transformed would have been to have ceased to be God; but the Logos never ceased to be what he was to begin with. If the Logos had really become flesh by any process of transfiguration and change of substance, then Jesus would have been a new substance formed out of the two substances flesh and spirit, a kind of mixture, a *tertium quid*. But there was no kind of mixture; each substance remained distinct in its own characteristics—the Word was never any-

[1] 'Homo deo mixtus.' Tertullian did not mean that the two together made a third thing. He expressly repudiates the conception, using the illustration of electrum, a compound of gold and silver, neither one nor the other (see *adv. Prax.* 27); and he emphasizes the distinct parts played by the divinity and the humanity respectively as clearly as Leo himself (*Ep. ad Flav.*) more than two hundred years later. But had he lived in Leo's time he probably would not have used this phrase. See *infra* p. 243 n. 3 and p. 247.

[2] *Adv. Prax.* 27. Cf. also *de Carne Christi*, esp. § 18, where he insists on the distinct origin of the spirit and the flesh and discusses the interpretation of John 3⁶ as spoken by Christ of himself, shewing that each remains what it was.

thing but God, the flesh was never anything but man. He who was Son of God as regards the spirit was man and son of man. " We see ", he says, " the double status, the two not confused but conjoined in one person, God and man (Jesus). . . ." This is Christ. " And the peculiar properties of each substance are preserved intact, so that in him the spirit conducted its own affairs, that is, the deeds of power and works and signs, . . . and the flesh underwent its sufferings, hungering in the instance of the Devil (the Temptation), thirsting in the instance of the Samaritan woman, weeping for Lazarus, sorrowful unto death; and finally it died." It is clear, he insists, that both substances exercised their functions each by itself. *Qua* flesh and man and son of man, he died; *qua* Spirit and Word and Son of God, he was immortal. " It is not in respect of the divine substance, but in respect of the human, that we say he died." [1]

It may thus be fairly said that the later developed orthodox doctrine of the Trinity and of the Person of Christ—even in details—is to be found in Tertullian. Certain crudities of thought may perhaps be detected,[2] but as having developed and created a series of most important doctrinal formulae which became part of the general doctrinal system of the Catholic Church, his importance cannot be overestimated.[3]

[1] *Adv. Prax.* 29, where he argues against the conception that the Father 'suffered with' the Son, on the main ground that in the divine substance (which was all the Father and the Son had in common) the Son himself did not suffer. On the parts played by the two *substances* see also *de Carne Christi* (§ 5), where the doctrine of the *communicatio idiomatum* is expressed for the first time.

[2] Harnack (*DG.* Eng. tr. vol. iv p. 121) notes as obvious the following : (1) Son and Spirit proceed from the Father solely in view of the work of creation and revelation ; (2) Son and Spirit do not possess the entire substance of the Godhead, but are 'portiones' ; (3) they are subordinate to the Father ; (4) they are transitory manifestations—the Son at last gives back everything to the Father ; the Father alone is absolutely invisible, the Son can become visible and can do things which would be simply unworthy of the Father. But this criticism seems to emphasize unduly particular expressions in relation to others, and to be corrected by the excellent summary of the treatise *adv. Prax.* which follows it (Harnack *DG.* Eng. tr. vol. iv p. 122).

[3] Cf. Harnack *DG.* Eng. tr. vol. ii p. 235. So Bull could write (*Def. N.C.* bk. ii ch. vii, Ox. tr.), "Read only his single work against Praxeas, in which he treats fully and professedly of the most holy Trinity ; he there asserts the consubstantiality of the Son so frequently and so plainly, that you would suppose the author had written after the time of the Nicene Council."

CHAPTER XI

ORIGEN is one of the great landmarks in the history of doctrine.[1] He was the first of the theologians whose work is really known to us to attempt the scientific systematic[2] exposition of the Christian interpretation of life. And however much the knowledge of previous controversies may have stimulated his own thought and aided to determine his exposition, he has the great advantage over previous theologians that his work was not immediately called forth by apologetic motives and the exigencies of controversy. He was able to face the problems with the scholar's and the teacher's aim of clear and simple exposition only. There is no sign of haste or of heat about his work. He had not got to 'score' a victory over dangerous enemies, within or without the Church: he had not to use *argumenta ad hominem*; he had perhaps some *obiter dicta* to recall,[3] but his opinions were quietly formed, and there is little reason to doubt that even those which were not accepted by his own or later generations represented his deliberate and reasoned convictions. His system was built up on Tradition—as embodied in the Scriptures and the custom of the Church—but he put his own mark upon it all and aimed at giving it his own expression.

---

[1] Harnack says we can clearly distinguish in the history of dogma three styles of building, and names as the masters of these styles, Origen, Augustine, and the Reformers (*DG*. i p. 10).

[2] This seems to be the fact, although it is true that "his writings represent an aspiration rather than a system, principles of research and hope rather than determined formulas" (Westcott 'Origenes' *D.C.B.*, an article of the highest value. Cf. his Essay on Origen in *Religious Thought in the West*). See also particularly C. Bigg *The Christian Platonists of Alexandria* (Bampton Lectures, 1886), esp. pp. 152–192; but for the study of the conceptions of Origen the most helpful book is still perhaps that of Redepenning, with its rich quotations from his writings.

[3] Cf. the saying of Jerome, that in some of his earlier treatises, written in the immaturity of youth, Origen was 'like a boy playing at dice'.

It is in his great writing περὶ ἀρχῶν (*de Principiis*) that this expression is chiefly to be found.[1]

Basing the whole of his work on " the teaching of the Church transmitted in orderly succession from the Apostles, and remaining in the Churches to the present day ", he first lays down a summary of the rule of faith as expressed in the Scriptures, and declares that every one must make use of elements and foundations of that kind if he desires to form a connected series and body of doctrine, following up each point by means of illustrations and arguments, whether found in holy Scripture or discovered by a correct method of deduction. He then proceeds, not without digressions and repetitions, to set out in three successive books the doctrine of God, of creation and providence, of man and redemption; and in conclusion, in the fourth book, he examines the questions of the inspiration and the interpretation of the Bible. The book was obviously not written for the simple believer, but for scholars who were familiar with the speculations of the Gnostics and of other—non-Christian—philosophers.

In his interpretation of the Christian revelation, accordingly, Origen started from the philosophical conception, to which Plato and the Neo-Platonists had given currency, of the One and the Many. The One represents the only real existence, the Source of all being: the Many represents the Universe with all its varying forms of apparent being, none of which have any real existence apart from the One from which they are derived. They do, however, in various ways pourtray the One, and in them alone can He be understood: for the One, the self-existent, the source of all that really is, is a living Person. In His absolute nature and being He is unknowable by man (or any of the Many), but He is relatively knowable so far as He is revealed through the medium of the universe which derives its existence from Him and in some measure reflects His nature and attributes. Such relative knowledge as is in this way attainable shews Him to be not only one, without origin, the cause of all that is, but also spiritual and eternal, and above all else absolutely good. His very essence is love. From this ethical conception, which is at the back of all his theology, Origen argues that He must

---

[1] Besides the *de Principiis* (228–231), the most important works in which his theological teaching is set forth are the *Commentaries on St John* (228–238), the *Contra Celsum* (249), and the *de Oratione*.

impart Himself. Love cannot be thought of, except as giving. Goodness desires that all shall share in the highest knowledge. And so there must be some medium, some channel, by which He effects the revelation of Himself. As the required organ He chose the Logos.[1] It is for the very purpose of revealing God that the Logos exists,[2] and for this reason he has a personal subsistence side by side with the Father,[3] and must be (if he is to reveal Him truly), as regards his being, of one essence with God. He must be in his own being God, and not only as sharing in the being of God.[4] He is thus, as being the perfect image of God, the reason and wisdom of God, himself too really God.

His generation as Son is effected as the will proceeds from the mind, as the brilliance from the light, eternal and everlasting. It cannot be said that there was any time when the Son was not. No beginning of this generation can be conceived—it is a continuous eternal process.[5] It is this conception of a con-

---

[1] It is only in connexion with the revelation of God that Origen conceives, or at least expounds, the Trinity. God is goodness—the αὐτὸ ἀγαθόν : He must therefore reveal Himself. Origen does not, as later on Augustine did, derive the essential Trinity from this conception of Love as the very being of the Godhead, so that a plurality of Persons was a necessary inference from this main characteristic. It is only the Trinity of revelation (God in relation to the world) that he sets forth. See *infra* pp. 204, 228.

[2] See *e.g. de Princ.* i 2. 6.

[3] *Ibid.* i 2. 2. "Let no one imagine that we mean anything impersonal. . . . The only-begotten Son of God is His wisdom existing as a hypostasis."

[4] Pamphilus (*Apology for Origen* c. 5 tr. Rufinus) quotes him as using, in his *Commentary on the Epistle to the Hebrews*, the very word ὁμοούσιος to express the identity of being of the Father and the Son, "And these similitudes . . . shew most clearly that the Son has communion of essence (substance) with the Father ; for an effluence (aporrhoea) is evidently homoousios, that is, of one essence (substance) with the body of which it is an effluence or vapour." Cf. also *de Princ.* i 2. 5, "the only one who is by nature a Son, and is therefore termed the Only-begotten" ; *ibid.* i 2. 10, "in all respects incapable of change or alteration, and every good quality in him being essential and such as cannot be changed and converted" ; *ibid.* i 2. 12, "there is no dissimilarity whatever between the Son and the Father". Cf. the similitude of the iron heated by the fire (*ibid.*.ii 6. 6), and of the statue (*ibid.* i 2. 8).

[5] "Who . . . can suppose or believe that God the Father ever existed even for a moment without having generated this Wisdom (which is His only-begotten Son)" (i 2. 2). "His generation is as eternal and everlasting as the brilliance which is produced from the sun " (i 2. 4 ; cf. i 2. 9) ; and "No one can be a father without having a son" (i 2. 10 ; cf. iv 28). And *in Jerem.* Hom. ix 4, "The Father did not beget the Son and let him go from the Source of his generation (ἀπὸ τῆς γενέσεως αὐτοῦ, *i.e.* Himself the Father,—or perhaps 'after, or in consequence of, his generation '), but He is always begetting him (ἀεὶ γεννᾷ αὐτόν)."

tinuous timeless process that brings the idea of the generation of the Son, which earlier thinkers had expressed, into the sphere of living reality. It ceases to be an act in time, and becomes an action outside time—living and moving and real. It is Origen's chief permanent contribution to the doctrine of the Person of Christ.

The Son is indeed said to be begotten of or by the will of the Father [1]—but within the being of the Father no contradiction could be thought of—His will is of His very essence. And so, though there should be an act of will, there would be also an inner necessity for it, and the Son would be equally truly said to be begotten of the essence of the Father.[2]

The function of revelation is also exercised by the Holy Spirit,[3] who is the most exalted of all the beings that have come into existence through the Logos.[4]

These three existences together constitute the Trinity, which

[1] *E.g. de Princ.* i 2. 6, "who is born of Him, like an act of His will proceeding from the mind ".

[2] Loofs (*Leitfaden³* p. 125) sets in antithesis various phrases, extracted from different contexts, to shew the subordinate rank of the Son in relation to the Father. The Father alone is ἀγέννητος (*de Princ.* i 2. 6 ; *in Joh.* 2⁶), the Son in relation to Him a κτίσμα. [Justinian is the only authority for the assertion that Origen styled the Son a κτίσμα. Origen certainly never meant it in any Arian sense.]

The Father is αὐτόθεος and ἀληθινὸς θεός (*in Joh.* 2³), the Son is δεύτερος θεός (*c. Cels.* 5. 39) and ἄξιος τῆς δευτερευούσης μετὰ τὸν θεὸν τῶν ὅλων τιμῆς (*ibid.* 7. 57).

The Father is ἀπαραλλάκτως ἀγαθός, the Son is εἰκὼν ἀγαθότητος τοῦ θεοῦ, ἀλλ' οὐκ αὐτοαγαθός (*de Princ.* i 13). [But this antithesis must be corrected by reference to *de Princ.* i 2. 10 and ii 6. 5, 6.]

The Father is ὁ θεός, the Son is θεός (*in Joh.* 2²), and prayer should be made to the Father only (*de Orat.* 15). [But nevertheless the Son is equally with the Father an object of worship, Father and Son being two actualities τῇ ὑποστάσει, but one in unanimity and harmony and sameness of purpose (*c. Cels.* 8. 12). So worship is offered to Christ as he is in—as he is one with—the Father. And it is really only the highest form of petition which Origen says is to be addressed to the Father only in the Son's name. (See Bigg *l.c.* p. 185.)]

In the case of such a writer as Origen it is peculiarly dangerous to isolate particular phrases :—it is of course just the error into which the Arians fell. They must be studied always in their context and in their connexion with contemporary thought, if their general scope and proportion is not to be misconceived. (Cf. Westcott *l.c.* p. 133.) Any summary statement of his teaching must therefore be peculiarly precarious.

[3] *De Princ.* i 3. 4, "All knowledge of the Father is obtained by revelation of the Son through the Holy Spirit", but "we are not to suppose that the Spirit derives his knowledge through revelation from the Son". He has the same knowledge and, just like the Son, reveals it to whom he will.

[4] See *Comm. in Joh.* i 3 and *infra* p. 202.

in its real inner being transcends all thought—essentially of one Godhead, eternal and co-equal.[1]

But in manifestation to the created universe a difference between the Persons may be seen, at least as to the extent of their action. " God the Father, holding all things together, reaches to each of the things that are, imparting being to each from His own; for He is absolutely. Compared with the Father the Son is less, reaching to rational things only, for he is second to the Father. And the Holy Spirit again is inferior, extending to the saints only. So that in this respect the power of the Father is greater, in comparison with the Son and the Holy Spirit; and the power of the Son more, in comparison with the Holy Spirit; and again the power of the Holy Spirit more exceeding, in comparison with all other holy beings." [2]

As regards the Son, in particular, it is clear that Origen maintained his distinct personality,[3] his essential Godhead (κατ' οὐσίαν ἐστὶ θεός), and his co-eternity with the Father (ἀεὶ γεννᾶται ὁ σωτὴρ ὑπὸ τοῦ πατρός): though he placed him as an intermediary between God and the universe, and spoke of the unity of the Father and the Son as moral, and insisted on the Father's pre-eminence (ὑπεροχή) as the one source and fountain of Godhead, in such terms as to lead many, who believed themselves his followers and accepted his authority, to emphasize unduly the subordination of the Son.[4]

[1] See de Princ. i 3. 7, nihil in trinitate majus minusve (though Loofs, op. c. p. 126, regards Rufinus as responsible for this clause, it seems certainly to express the conviction of Origen with regard to the mutual relations of the three Persons in their inner being). See further infra p. 201, on the Holy Spirit; and on the impossibility for men of understanding anything but the Trinity in its manifestations (revelation), see the strong assertions de Princ. i 34 and iv 28.

[2] De Princ. i 3. 5, Gk. fr. Cf. Athanasius ad Serap. iv 10, and Origen de Princ. iv 27 f.

[3] This (namely, that the Son is not the Father) is certainly the meaning of the passage de Oratione 15 : ἕτερος κατ' οὐσίαν καὶ ὑποκείμενον τοῦ πατρός—οὐσία being used in its primary sense of particular or individual existence.

[4] Bigg (op. c. p. 181) insists that to derive the Subordinationism which is a note of Origen's conceptions from metaphysical considerations is to wrong him. " It is purely scriptural, and rests wholly and entirely upon the words of Jesus, ' My Father is greater than I ', ' that they may know Thee the only true God ', ' None is Good save One '. The dominant text in Origen's mind was the last. Hence he limits the relativity to the attribute to which it is limited by Christ himself. The Son is Very Wisdom, Very Righteousness, Very Truth, perhaps even Very King ; but not Very Goodness. He is Perfect Image of the Father's Goodness, but not the Absolute Good, though in regard to us he is the Absolute Good. . . . Where he pronounces his real thought, the difference between the Persons is conceived not as

The special affinity in which the Son stands to rational beings establishes the fitness of the Incarnation, and through the human soul [1] the divine Logos was united with the man Christ Jesus—perfect manhood, subject to the conditions of natural growth, and perfect divinity becoming one in him, while each nature still remains distinct. To describe this unity he was the first to use the compound word God-Man ($\Theta\epsilon\acute{a}\nu\theta\rho\omega\pi\sigma$), and the relation between the two natures was expressed by the image of the fire and the iron, when the fire heats and penetrates the iron so that it becomes a glowing mass, and yet its character is not altered—the fire and the metal are one, but the iron is not changed into something else.[2]

So, through the union of the divine and the human nature effected in the Incarnation, all human nature was made capable of being glorified, without the violation of its proper characteristics. The work of Christ was for all men. It was so revealed that it could be apprehended according to the several powers and wants of men—he was ' all things to all men '. His manifestation to men is present and continuous. He is ever being born, and is seen as each believer has the faculty of seeing— and as each reflects him he becomes himself a Christ—an anointed one. For the union of man and God accomplished

quantitative nor as qualitative, but as modal simply. The Son *qua* Son is inferior to the Father *qua* Father. . . . He could not, he dared not, shrink back where the Word of God led him on. He could not think that a truth three times at least pressed upon the Church by Christ himself might safely be ignored. To his dauntless spirit these words of the Master seemed to be not a scandal but a flash of light."

[1] See *de Princ.* ii 6. 3. It is "impossible for the nature of God to intermingle with a body without an intermediate instrument", and the soul is "intermediate between God and the flesh ". The human soul with which the Logos was united was, according to Origen's conception of the creation of all souls before all worlds at the beginning of creation, the only soul which had remained absolutely pure, by the exercise of free choice in its pre-existent state. Irrespective of Origen's peculiar theory of the origin of the soul, it is to be noted that he was one of the first Christian thinkers to see the importance of the recognition of the human soul in Christ. See *de Princ.* ii 6. 3, 5, where he explains how the nature of his rational soul was the same as that of all other souls (which can choose between good and evil), and yet clung to righteousness so unchangeably and inseparably that it had no susceptibility for alteration and change. See further on this point *infra* Apollinarianism p. 242, and Note p. 247.

[2] See *de Princ.* ii 6. 6. The human soul is the iron, the Word is the fire which is constant. The soul placed perpetually in the Word, perpetually in God, is God in all that it does, feels, and understands . . . and so possesses immutability. Yet the two natures remain distinct (*ibid.* i 2. 1 ; ii 6. 3).

absolutely in Christ is to be fulfilled in due measure in each
Christian as Christ had made it possible. His work is efficacious for the consummation of humanity and of the individual—both as a victory over every power of evil and also as
a vicarious sacrifice for sin; for the whole world, and for
heavenly beings (to whom it may bring advancement in blessedness), and for other orders of being in a manner corresponding
to their nature.[1]

Origen's doctrine of the Logos and the Sonship was an
attempt to recognize and give due weight to all the conditions
of the problem, so far as a human mind could realize them.
Origen himself might see at once the many sides and aspects of
the problem and succeed in maintaining the due proportion;
but he was obliged to express himself in antithetical statements,
and his followers were not always successful in combining them.
They tended to separate more and more into two parties, a right
wing and a left wing—the former laying more stress on the
assertion of the unity of being of the Trinity (as Gregory Thaumaturgus), the latter on the distinctness of personality and the
subordination of the persons in regard at least to office.

It appears to have been the 'subordination' element in the
Christology of Origen—with its safeguard against Sabellianism
and its zeal for personal distinctions in the Godhead—that was
most readily appropriated by his admirers in the East. And many
of his phrases lent themselves at first sight more readily to the
Arian conceptions of a separate essence and a secondary god,
than to the Nicene teaching of identity of essence and eternal
generation from the very being of the Father. Yet it cannot be
doubted that Origen is really explicitly against the chief Arian
theories, and at least implicitly in harmony with the Nicene
doctrine of the Person of the Son.[2] Nevertheless the sympathies
of his followers in the East—in the great controversy which

---

[1] Westcott (*l.c.*), who refers (for the statements in this paragraph) to *c. Cels.*
iv 3 f., 15; vi 68; iii 79; ii 64; iv 15; vi 77; iii 28; iii 17. On his theory of
the atonement see *infra* p. 337.

[2] The matter cannot be better put than it was by Bp. Bull *Def. N.C.* ii, ix § 22
(Oxford translation): "In respect of the article of the divinity of the Son and
even of the Holy Trinity, [Origen] was yet really catholic; although in his mode of
explaining this article he sometimes expressed himself otherwise than Catholics of the
present day are wont to do; but this is common to him with nearly all the Fathers
who lived before the Council of Nice." Cf. also Harnack *DG.* Eng. tr. vol. ii p. 374 :
"To Origen the highest value of Christ's person lies in the fact that the Deity has
here condescended to reveal to us *the whole fulness of his essence.* . . ."

broke out early in the following century—were rather with the Arians than with their opponents.

ORIGENISTIC THEOLOGY AND CONTROVERSIES

Among the special conceptions and theories of Origen, which led at a later time to his condemnation as heretical (apart from misconception of his doctrine of the Trinity), are these. Moral evil is negative, a state from which good is absent, rather than a positive active force. All punishment is disciplinary, designed to effect the reformation of the sinner. Christ made atonement for the sins of all, and all will in the end be saved—all created beings, even Satan. There is no break in the moral continuity of being. All souls were created—each by a distinct fiat—at the beginning of Creation as angelic spirits: the souls of men sinned in their first condition and for their apostasy were transferred into material bodies, and their mundane existence is a disciplinary process (pre-existence and fall of the soul). There are more worlds than ours—the heavenly bodies are inhabited. The resurrection will be purely spiritual. God is Spirit, and all representation of Him under human form or attributes is untrue to His real nature.

Conceptions and theories such as these may have contributed to bring about the condemnation of Origen at Alexandria in his lifetime, though ecclesiastical irregularities were the pretext.

Some of them were certainly attacked very soon by theologians who had no prejudice against a philosophic Christianity (as Methodius, Bishop of Olympus in Lycia, a martyr in the persecution under Maximin), and abandoned or corrected by 'Origenistic' bishops themselves. (Socrates (*H.E.* vi 13) quite unfairly speaks of them as 'cheap' critics, who were unable to attain distinction on their own merits and so endeavoured to attract attention by carping at their betters. He names Methodius first, and then Eustathius of Antioch, and Apollinarius, and Theophilus.)

The attack of course produced defenders. Chief among the champions, who included his successors Pierius and Theognostus, were Pamphilus and Eusebius of Caesarea, who together composed an elaborate Defence of Origen (of which one book only is extant, in the Latin translation of Rufinus), based on the distinction between speculation and doctrine. They shewed that on the essential points, on which the teaching of the Church was certain, Origen was 'orthodox'; and that his freedom of speculation was exercised only in relation to subsidiary questions.

In the Arian controversy many 'Origenistic' bishops, who were in great force in Palestine, were to be found on the side of the supporters of Arianism (Marcellus pointed to him as the originator of the mischievous mixture of philosophical speculations with the doctrines of the faith—see Zahn *Marcellus* p. 55 ff.); and after a time (though not, it seems, in the early stages of the struggle) the authority of his great name was definitely claimed by them; and Athanasius, accordingly, argued against their inferences, and cited passages from his writings to prove that he was 'Nicene' rather than Arian, insisting that much that he had written was only speculative and experimental, and that only what he definitely declares ought to be taken as the real sentiment of the 'labour-loving' man (*de Decr.* 27 ; cf. *ad Serap.* iv 9 ff.), and highly approving his doctrine of the Trinity. What Basil and Gregory of Nazianzus thought of him is shewn by their selection from his works, the *Philocalia*, which included passages from the *de Principiis*; while Gregory of Nyssa adopted many of his speculations, and at least some of the Commentaries were translated into Latin—even by Jerome, who in his earlier days was full of admiration for him.

On the other hand, Epiphanius numbered him among the heretics and developed and emphasized the charges which Methodius had brought against him. (See esp. *Ancoratus* 13, 54, 55, 62, 63, and *adv. Haer.* lxiv.) But it must be remembered that Epiphanius was in sympathy with the Egyptian monks represented by Pachomius, who were specially repelled by Origen's repudiation of all anthropomorphic conceptions.

It was Epiphanius who, going to Palestine in 394, convinced Jerome, in spite of his previous admiration for Origen, of the unorthodox character of his writings, and stirred up the bitter strife which followed between him and his former friend Rufinus, and led to the condemnation of Origen by Anastasius, Bishop of Rome (though probably not at a formal synod), after Rufinus had translated into Latin the *Apology of Pamphilus* and the *de Principiis*. After much wrangling, and a change of sides by Theophilus, Bishop of Alexandria, who had supported the Origenists but was terrorized by the anthropomorphist monks, various synods condemned Origen and his writings (at Alexandria in 400, in Cyprus a little later, and at Chalcedon *c.* 403 in effect—in the person of Chrysostom, who was attacked because of his sympathies with Origenists). Still more distrust and suspicion were engendered by the supposed connexion between Origenism and the teaching of the Pelagians (Jerome regarded the two as closely allied), and his name was bandied about in the course of the christological controversies of the following years. Augustine was always opposed to anything that savoured of his teaching, and Leo the Great regarded him as justly condemned, at least for his doctrine of the pre-existence of the soul. But admiration for him was not crushed out, and early in the sixth century a revival of enthusiasm for his teaching led to disturbances among the monks of Palestine, and about the years 541–543 he was again condemned by a synod of bishops held at Constantinople (the 'Home' Synod), in obedience to the rescript of the Emperor Justinian, who had drawn up an elaborate statement of his errors, a refutation of them, and anathemas on all his followers (Hahn[3] p. 227). Whether this condemnation was or was not renewed at the Fifth General Council which met in 553 cannot be determined. The belief that it was has prevailed from an early date, and he is included among other heretics in the eleventh of the anathemas ascribed to the Council (Hahn[3] p. 168), but there is some reason to think that the name is a later insertion, and no direct evidence that his opinions were considered on that occasion. In any case, though the ideas of Origen have found supporters in all ages, Origenists as a party were effectually stamped out. [See A. W. W. Dale 'Origenistic Controversies' *D.C.B.*, and C. Bigg *op. c.* pp. 273–280.]

CHAPTER XII

Introductory

BY the beginning of the fourth century it seemed that, though fixity of theological terminology had not yet been secured, the lines of interpretation of the person of Jesus Christ had been safely and firmly laid, and so the developement of doctrine might quietly proceed, keeping pace with enlarged experience and able to meet new conditions as they arose. The old religions and the old philosophies of the world had contributed to the process of interpretation what they could. The minds which had been trained in the old schools of thought had been brought to bear upon the Gospel and its claims. Sometimes they had, as it were, laid siege to it and tried to capture it, and so to lead it in their train. But assaults of this kind had all been repelled. The Church as a whole, while welcoming, from whatever sources it came, the light that could be thrown on the meaning of the revelation in Jesus in its fullest scope, had preserved tenaciously the traditional explanation and accounts of his life and of the Gospel history. So it was able to test all newer explanations by the earliest tradition, and though erroneous ones—faulty or partial—might win adherents for a time, the *communis sensus fidelium* had rejected in the end any that— when tested by fuller experience of their significance—were seen to be inconsistent with the principles which were involved in the ancient faith and institutions of the Church.

But when, at the beginning of the fourth century, persecution ceased, and the Church won peace and protection from the State, the ordinary course of developement was interrupted. The influence of pagan conceptions was felt with fresh force within the Church, and victories which seemed to have been already achieved had to be fought for and secured again. No sooner had outward peace from persecution been won than the inward peace of the Church was shattered by the outbreak of the Arian controversy.   It was in and round this controversy that all the forces of the old religions and philosophies of the world were massed in the effort to dictate an interpretation of the Christian revelation which would have nullified the work of the Church during previous centuries.   The long continuance of the controversy was also due in part to the ambiguities and uncertainties of much of the teaching which had been prevalent in the East, which made men doubtful whether the Arian conceptions were really such innovations on the traditional faith as they seemed to the few who led the opposition to them.   Thanks to the clear and simple teaching of Tertullian, the Western Church was never in such doubt, and Arianism never gained such hold in the West as it did in the East.   That the leaders of the Church of Alexandria, where it originated, were able to detect its real nature at the outset was probably due in no small measure to the memories of the discussion in the time of Dionysius and the influence of the Western tradition which was then asserted.

The controversy was so important and the questions raised are of such permanent significance that we must trace its course at length, at least in regard to its chief features and the main turning-points of the history.[1]

Arius and his Teaching

Arius, like all the great heresiarchs, whatever defects of character he may have had, undoubtedly wished to carry to greater perfection the work of interpretation of the Christian revelation.   He aimed, with sincerity and all the ability at his command, at framing a theory of the Person of Christ, which would be free from the difficulties presented to many minds by current conceptions, and capable of providing a solution of some of the problems by which they were met.

He tried to interpret the Christian revelation in such a way as to render it acceptable to men whose whole conception of God and of life was heathen.   In doing this he shewed himself to be lacking in real grip of the first principles of the Christian con-

---

[1] On the history of Arianism the works of Professor Gwatkin are invaluable— *Studies of Arianism*, 1st ed. 1882, 2nd ed. 1900, and *The Arian Controversy* in the series 'Epochs of Church History'.

ception, and in sound judgement and insight; but the long continuance of the controversy, and the wide acceptance which his theories won, prove clearly how great a need there was for further thought and teaching on the points at issue.[1]

Before tracing the history of the controversy we must note what were the principles on which Arius based his thought.[2]

[1] An excellent sketch of the developement of the doctrine of the Person of Christ up to the time of Arius is given by Professor Gwatkin (*Studies of Arianism* p. 4 ff.). Inherited from Judaism and the Old Testament was the fundamental principle, with which Christians started, of the existence of God, His unity and distinction from the world. As a second fundamental doctrine of their own they had the revelation of this God in Jesus Christ—the Incarnation and the Resurrection. They had an instinctive conviction that the fulness of the Lord was more than human, the life that flowed from him more than human life, the atonement through him an atonement with the Supreme Himself, the Person of the Lord the infinite and final revelation of the Father. So his divinity became as fixed an axiom as God's unity—and of his humanity there was of course no doubt. The problem was how to reconcile this view of Christ's person with the fundamental principle of the unity of God. At first bare assertions were enough; but, when the question of interpretation was raised, new theories had to be tested by Scripture; and the two great tendencies, which are innate in human thought, emerge: the rationalist, which questions the divinity and so the incarnation; and the mystic, which, recognising full divinity in Christ, regards it as a mere appearance or modification of the One, and so endangers the distinction between him and the Father. By the fourth century it was becoming clear that the only solution of the problem was to be found in a distinction inside the divine unity. Neither Arianism with its external Trinity, nor Sabellianism with its oeconomic Trinity, satisfied the conditions of the problem. So it was necessary to revise the idea of divine personality and to acknowledge not three individuals but three eternal aspects of the Divine, in its inward relations as well as in its outward relations to the world (that is, three eternal modes of the divine being, God existing always in three spheres). But this was just what the heathen could least do. Here was experienced the greatest difficulty in the pre-Christian conception of God which prevailed in the world, and which converts brought with them—namely, the essential simplicity—singleness—of His being (cf. the Sabellian Trinity of temporal aspects (πρόσωπα) of the One; and the Arian Trinity of One increate and two created beings). Insistence on the Lord's divinity was leading back to polytheism. The fundamental idea of God at the back of all must be rectified before the position was secure.

[2] The extant writings of Arius are few—a letter to Eusebius of Nicomedia (Theodoret *H.E.* i 4 or 5), a letter to his bishop, Alexander (Epiph. *adv. Haer.* lxix, and Ath. *de Syn.* 16), extracts from the *Thalia* (Ath. *Or. c. Ar.* i, ii, and *de Syn.* 15), and a Creed (Socr. *H.E.* i 26, and Soz. *H.E.* ii 27). Asterius seems to be regarded by Athanasius (see *Or. c. Ar.* i 30–33, ii 37, iii 2, 60, and *de Decr. Syn. Nic.* 8, 28–31) as the chief literary representative of Arianism (for his history see Gwatkin, p. 72, note), but we have only quotations from his writings in the works of Athanasius and in Eusebius Caes. *contra Marcellum* (who had written against Asterius). Philostorgius, a Eunomian, of Cappadocia (*c.* 368–430), wrote a history in twelve books of the time from the appearance of Arius to the year 423, in which he defended Arianism as being the original form of Christianity. Of this there are extant many short pieces and one long passage (see Migne *P.G.* lxv 459–638). The letter of Eusebius of Nicomedia to Paulinus (Theodoret *H.E.* i 5) is of importance.

To be included in his theory there was God, and the Son of God, and the Son had to be accounted for in such a manner as not to endanger the unity of God. For his strongest interest was the maintenance of Monotheism; and a first principle with him was the 'simplicity'—the singleness—of God, as being absolutely One and transcendent, far-off, unknown, inaccessible, and incommunicable, hidden in eternal mystery and separated by an infinite chasm from men. God willed to create the world; but in virtue of His nature he could not directly create the material universe, and so He created the Logos for the purpose as His Son. (This was the reason for his existence.) The Son of God is therefore before time and the world, independently of the Incarnation, and distinct from the Father—a middle being between Him and the world.

Two lines of reasoning by which Arius came to his results must be remarked. In the first place, accepting as true the Catholic teaching that Christ was the Son of God, he argued by the analogy of human experience that what was true of human fatherhood was true of the relation between God and His Son. In the case of human fatherhood there is priority of existence of the Father; therefore in regard to the Father and the Son there is such priority of existence of the Father.   Therefore once there was no Son.   Therefore he must at some time, however remote, have been brought into being.

For the refutation of Arianism proper the writings of Athanasius are of peculiar importance (a useful summary of the teaching of Arius in the letter of Alexander on the Synod of 321 in the tract—probably composed by Athanasius—called the *Depositio Arii*; see also the letter of Alexander in Theodoret *H.E.* i 3). Basil's *Epp.* 8, 9 are full of interest, and besides there are the writings of Hilary, Gregory of Nazianzus, and Phoebadius. For the tenets of the Anomoeans see Basil's five (? three) books against Eunomius, and Gregory of Nyssa's twelve, written after Basil's death in reply to the answer of Eunomius. Other champions of orthodoxy are represented to us only by fragments.

For a short statement of what Arius himself said of his own conceptions, see his letter to Eusebius of Nicomedia, his 'fellow-Lucianist', the 'truly pious' (εὐσεβής), given by Theodoret *H.E.* i 4 (5). "We say and believe, and have taught and do teach, that the Son is not unbegotten, nor in any way part of the unbegotten; and that he does not derive his subsistence from any matter; but that by his own wish and counsel he has subsisted before time and before ages as perfect God, only begotten and unchangeable, and that before he was begotten or created or purposed or established he was not. For he was not unbegotten. We are persecuted because we say that the Son has a beginning, but that God is without beginning, . . . and likewise, because we say that he is of the non-existent. And this we say because he is neither part of God, nor of any essential being." In this phrase there is no doubt reference to the notion supposed to be contained in the term ὁμοούσιος of some οὐσία prior to Father and Son—a *tertium quid*—in which they both alike had part.

And in the second place, as to the nature and manner of this divine Sonship, Arius held that the isolation and spirituality of the Father was a truth to be safeguarded above all else. But the idea of generation was inconsistent with this primary principle; for generation not only ascribes to the Father corporeity and passion (feelings) (which are human attributes) and involves some kind of change (whereas the divine must be thought of as absolutely immutable), but also it would imply unity of nature between the Father who generates and the Son who is generated, and so the singularity of God would be destroyed. Ingenerateness must accordingly be of the very essence of divinity, and the Son could not have come into being from or out of the essence (or being) [1] of the Father, but only by a definite external process or act of the Father's will. But *ex hypothesi* there was then nothing in existence but the Father, and therefore the Son was called into being out of nothing. This exercise of the Father's will was equivalent to a creative act, and the Son therefore was created by the Father.[2]

By these lines of reasoning the Arians were convinced that the Son was not eternal and was a creature,[3] though coming

---

[1] For other objections to this expression, see *infra* p. 171 n. 1.

[2] To say that the Son was begotten or born 'of the will' or 'by the will' of the Father seems to have been a common way of speaking before this time, and the expression is in itself quite free from objection. So, for example, Justin wrote κατὰ τὴν τοῦ πατρὸς πάντων καὶ δεσπότου θεοῦ βουλὴν διὰ παρθένου ἄνθρωπος ἀπεκυήθη (*Apol.* i 46), and used similar expressions (*Dial. c. Tryph.* 63, 85); Origen, see *supra* p. 148; and Novatian (less accurately) 'ex quo (*sc.* the Father), quando ipse voluit, sermo filius natus est'. Cf. the Creed in the *Apostolic Constitutions* vii 41— τὸν πρὸ αἰώνων εὐδοκίᾳ τοῦ πατρὸς γεννηθέντα. It was only when the 'will' was unnaturally placed outside of the 'being' of the Father, and the expression 'of the will' was employed in opposition to 'of the being' of the Father, to denote a later and external origin, that it ceased to be used by careful writers as a true and proper description. See further additional note p. 194.

[3] A typical instance of Arian logic seems to be furnished by Asterius in this connexion. He wrote a tract (see Ath. *Or. c. Ar.* i 30–33) of which the main thesis apparently was that there could not be two ἀγένητα. He then defined ἀγένητον as τὸ μὴ ποιηθὲν ἀλλ' ἀεὶ ὄν, and proceeded to argue that as the Father alone was ἀγένητον it was to Him alone that the description οὐ ποιηθὲν ἀλλ' ἀεὶ ὄν applied. That description was thus not true of the Son; and therefore as it was not true to say of him 'not made but always (eternally) existent', he must have been made and have come into existence at some remote period.

The formula ἀγένητον, as sounding more philosophical and having traditional sanction, became a plausible substitute for the original phrases of the Arians when they were driven from 'out of nothing' and 'once he was not'.. See Ath. *de Decr.* 28, and *Or. c. Ar.* i 32. And so objection was taken on the part of their opponents to any such use of the words ἀγένητον and γένητον—*e.g.* by Athanasius *de Decr.* 31:

into existence before time [1] and before all other creatures, and not like other creatures (inasmuch as they were all created mediately through him, while he was created immediately by the Father's will). Yet since he was a creature, and in this sense external to the being of the Father, he must be subject to the vicissitudes of created beings, and so he must be limited in power and wisdom and knowledge. With free-will and a nature capable of change and morally liable to sin he must depend on the help of grace and be kept sinless by his own virtue and the constant exercise of his own will.

Yet, nevertheless, though in all these ways inferior to the Father, he was really Son of God and an object of worship. And he it was—the Logos—who, taking upon him a human body with an animal soul, having been the medium by which the whole universe was originally created, was afterwards incarnate in the person of Jesus Christ.[2]

Such was the theory by which Arius sought to conciliate the pagan and the Christian conceptions of God and the universe.[3] It seems to us quite clear that the Jesus to whom such a theory could apply would be neither really human nor really divine, and this was obvious at the time to some of the ablest and

"Nowhere is [the Son] found calling the Father Unoriginated ; but when teaching us to pray, he said not, 'When ye pray, say, O God Unoriginated', but rather when ye pray, say, 'Our Father, which art in heaven'." And "He bade us be baptized, not into the name of Unoriginate and Originate, not into the name of Uncreate and Creature, but into the name of Father, Son, and Holy Spirit"—though at the same time it is of course allowed that the term Unoriginate does admit of a religious use (*ibid.* 32).

[1] For this reason they were careful to say only 'there was once when he was not' ($\mathring{\eta}\nu$ $\pi \text{o} \tau \epsilon$ $\mathring{\text{o}} \tau \epsilon$ $\text{o} \mathring{\text{v}} \kappa$ $\mathring{\eta}\nu$), and not 'there was a *time* when he was not'. Cf. their phrase $\mathring{\alpha} \chi \rho \acute{\text{o}} \nu \omega \varsigma$ $\pi \rho \grave{\text{o}}$ $\pi \acute{\alpha} \nu \tau \omega \nu$ $\gamma \epsilon \nu \nu \eta \theta \epsilon \acute{\iota} \varsigma$ (Ath. *de Synod.* 16).

[2] The Logos took the place of the human rational soul, the mind, or spirit. See *infra* on the Human Soul of Christ p. 247.

[3] Arius seems, in part at least, to have been misled by a wrong use of analogy, and by mistaking description for definition. All attempts to explain the nature and relations of the Deity must largely depend on metaphor, and no one metaphor can exhaust those relations. Each metaphor can only describe one aspect of the nature or being of the Deity, and the inferences which can be drawn from it have their limits when they conflict with the inferences which can be truly drawn from other metaphors describing other aspects. From one point of view Sonship is a true description of the inner relations of the Godhead : from another point of view the title Logos describes them best. Each metaphor must be limited by the other.

The title Son may obviously imply later origin and a distinction amounting to ditheism. It is balanced by the other title Logos, which implies co-eternity and inseparable union. Neither title exhausts the relations. Neither may be pressed so far as to exclude the other.

most far-seeing and intelligent of the leaders of Christian thought. But the doctrine of the Church had not yet been defined with exactitude: if it was not really confused, it was at any rate lacking in precision of terms; and to many it seemed that reason and Scripture alike gave strong support to the Arian conclusions.

All passages of Scripture which imply in any way that Christ was in the category of creatures; which ascribe to him, in his incarnate state, lack of knowledge or growth in knowledge, weariness, or sorrow, or other affections and states of mind; which teach some kind of subordination of the Son to the Father—the Arians pressed into the service of their theory.[1]

Athanasius in particular is at pains to refute their exegesis, or to cite other passages which balance those to which alone they give attention. We may take three crucial cases in which to test the Arian arguments.

(1) Prov. 8[22-25] (LXX, which was regarded as authoritative by nearly all on both sides), *The Lord created me a beginning of his ways for his works, before time (the age) he founded me in the beginning . . . before all hills he begets me.* On this passage we have the comments of Eusebius of Nicomedia in his letter to Paulinus (Theodoret *H.E.* i 5 (6)). The manner of his beginning, he says, is incomprehensible; but "if he had been of Him, that is, from Him, as a portion of Him, or by an emanation of His substance ($o\dot{v}\sigma\acute{\iota}a$), it could not be said that he was created or established . . . But if the fact of his being called the begotten gives any ground for the belief that, having come into being of the Father's substance (essence), he has also in consequence sameness of nature, we take note that it is not of him alone that the Scripture uses the term begotten, but that it also thus speaks of those who are entirely unlike him by nature. For of men it says, 'I begat and exalted sons, and they set me at nought' (Isa. 1[2]), and 'Thou hast forsaken the God who begat thee' (Deut. 32[18]); and in other

---

[1] Among the chief passages to which they appealed were these:—For the unity of God, Deut. 6[4], Luke 18[19], John 17[3]; for the nature of the Sonship, Ps. 45[8], Matt. 12[28], 1 Cor. 1[24]; for the creation of the Logos, Prov. 8[22] (LXX), Acts 2[36], Col. 1[15], Heb. 3[2]; for his moral growth and developement ($\pi\rho o\kappa o\pi\acute{\eta}$), Luke 2[52], Matt. 26[39ff.], Heb. 5[8-9], Phil. 2[6ff.], Heb. 1[4]; for the possibility of change ($\tau\grave{o} \tau\rho\epsilon\pi\tau\acute{o}\nu$) and imperfection of knowledge, Mark 13[32], John 11[34] 13[31]; for his inferiority to the Father, John 14[28], Matt. 27[46]. (Cf. Matt. 11[27] 26[39] 28[18], John 12[27], 1 Cor. 15[28].)

II

places it says, 'Who is he that begat the drops of dew?'
(Job 38²⁸), not implying that the nature of the dew is derived
from the nature of God, but simply in regard to each of the
things that have come into being, that its origination was according to His will. There is indeed nothing which is of His substance (essence), yet everything has come into being by His will,
and exists even as it came into being. He is God ; and all things
were made in His likeness, and in the future likeness of His
Word, having come into being of His free-will.—All things have
come into being by his means by God. All things are of God."
The combination of apparent reasonableness and slippery argument in this exegesis speaks for itself.

(2) Col. 1¹⁵, *Who is the image of the invisible (unseen) God*
πρωτότοκος πάσης κτίσεως. If the last three words were isolated,
their meaning might be doubtful, and it might be supposed
that the πρωτότοκος (first-born) was included in the πᾶσα κτίσις
(all creation). The Arians took the passage so, and explained
it as teaching that the Son was a creature, though created
before all other creatures and superior to them. But the context shews plainly that though the intention is clearly to
describe the relation in which Christ stands to the created
universe, yet the πρωτότοκος does not himself belong to the
κτίσις. Such an attribution would be inconsistent with the
universal agency in creation ascribed to him in the words immediately following—'in (*or* by) him were created all things',
and with the absolute pre-existence and self-existence claimed
for him in the same breath, 'he is before all things' (αὐτὸς ἔστιν
πρὸ πάντων). It would also be inconsistent with many other
passages in St Paul.[1]

[1] See Lightfoot's note *ad loc.* He argues that the word is doubtless used with
reference to the title πρωτόγονος given to the λόγος by Philo, meaning the arche-
typal idea of creation, afterwards realized in the material world ; and with reference
to its use as a title of the Messiah in the Old Testament (Ps. 89²⁸), implying that
he was the natural ruler of God's household with all the (Hebrew) rights of primo-
geniture. Priority to all creation and sovereignty over all creation are thus the
two ideas involved in the phrase, and patristic exegesis was on these lines until
the Arian innovations. In opposition to them the Catholic Fathers sometimes put a
strained sense on the phrase, and would apply it to the Incarnate Christ rather
than to the Eternal Word, so being obliged to understand the 'creation' of the new
spiritual creation,—against which view see Lightfoot. Cf. also Athanasius *de
Decr.* 20, and Basil on the text *adv. Eunom.* iv ; and against the secondary
meaning of sovereignty over creation, see Abbott *International Critical Commentary ad loc.* All that the phrase can be said with certainty to mean is 'born
before all creation (*or* every creature)'.

(3) John 14²⁸, *My Father is greater than I.* . . . This saying of Jesus seemed to the Arians conclusive proof of his inferiority to the Father and of the secondary character of his divinity. To Athanasius and those like-minded with him it had exclusive reference to the state of humiliation of the Incarnate Logos, voluntarily undergone and accepted when he 'emptied himself'; and the fact that he could use such a phrase was proof of his divinity. In the mouth of a created demi-god (such as the Arians conceived) it would be unmeaning and absurd. So Basil (*Ep.* 8) argues that the saying proves the oneness in essence—"For I know that comparisons may properly be made between things which are of the same nature. . . . If, then, comparisons are made between things of the same species, and the Father by comparison is said to be greater than the Son, then the Son is of the same essence as the Father."

The Outbreak of the Controversy and its History up to the Council of Nicaea

The immediate cause of the outbreak of the controversy is not known.¹ Arius was a presbyter of the Church of Alexandria, highly esteemed for his learning and gravity of life. He had been a pupil in the famous school of Lucian of Antioch, who seems to have combined in his theology the subordination element in Origen's doctrine of the Person of Christ with a leaning to the Monarchianism of Paul of Samosata.² About the year 317 his teaching excited attention, and exception was taken

¹ Professional jealousy has been assigned as the cause. Theodoret (*H.E.* i 2) says Arius was disappointed in his expectation of succeeding to the bishopric. He was certainly not free from intellectual vanity. He probably thought the teaching of Alexander unsound and Sabellian, and perhaps attacked it as such. But it may have been his own teaching that aroused opposition. (Controversy in the fourth century was not trammelled by rules of courtesy to opponents, and Athanasius himself describes the Arians as madmen, or fanatics, and enemies of God and of Christ, and—frequently in allusion to scriptural similes—as dogs, lions, wolves, chameleons, cuttlefish, leeches, gnats, hydras. See also the *Historia Arianorum* of Athanasius.) Many of the same ideas, and the same terms and texts, are found current and matter of controversy in the middle of the third century. See the Correspondence between the Dionysii *supra* p. 113, and the extracts in Ath. *de Decr.* 25–27.

² "It is not clear that Lucian of Antioch was heretical"—Gwatkin *Studies of Arianism* ² p. 17. It will be borne in mind that the style of exegesis at Antioch was literal, and that the Lucianists thought that logic could settle everything.

to its character.   The bishop, Alexander, seems to have been at first conciliatory; but Arius was convinced that he was right and would not yield.   Persuasion and argument having failed, a synod was summoned in 321, and Arius was deposed from his office.   He enlisted support, however, both in Egypt and farther afield—especially from fellow-pupils in the school of Lucian, many of whom occupied positions of power and influence.   In particular, he won the sympathy of Eusebius,[1] bishop of the capital, Nicomedia, and high in the emperor's favour, who called a Council at Nicomedia, and issued letters to the bishops in support of Arius.   Many of the bishops, following the lead of Eusebius, thought Arius had been unjustly treated, and the deposition of the presbyter assumed more serious proportions. The rulers of the Church of Alexandria were put on their defence.   They had to justify their actions.   Accordingly, Athanasius, a deacon of the same Church, drew up at once a note of the proceedings at the synod of 321, with the signatures of the bishops present appended, and Alexander sent it out to place the facts before the bishops of the Church at large.[2] Meanwhile the emperor, whose one wish was for peace and the unity of the Church, was induced to intervene, and sent in 324 a letter to Alexandria exhorting the bishop to restore peace to the Church; that was, to readmit Arius to his office.   But the bearer of his letter, Hosius, the Bishop of Cordova, one of his chief advisers, had to return to him with a report which put a different complexion on the matter, and Constantine sent a rebuke to Arius.   But feeling was too much roused by that time for any one's intervention to be decisive, and, probably on the suggestion of Hosius, a Council of the whole Church was summoned by the emperor to meet in the following year (325) at Nicaea, in Bithynia.[3]   In this way it was hoped that the mind of the Church on the points at issue might be expressed.

[1] Cf. the letter of Arius to him (Theodoret *H.E.* i 4), and his letter to Paulinus of Tyre (*ibid.* i 5—*or* 5 and 6).

[2] This is the treatise known as the *Depositio Arii* among the writings of Athanasius.   It is described by Robertson ('Athanasius' *Nicene and Post-Nicene Fathers* vol. iv) as the germ of all the anti-Arian writings of Athanasius.

[3] The bishops assembled numbered three hundred and eighteen, about one-sixth of the whole body of bishops.   The Council lasted about three months.

The Council of Nicaea and its Creed

But the mind of the Church was not made up. The actual form of the question at issue was new and technical—a question for experts; and all the bishops were not experts. The Arians called Christ God, and Son of God, and offered him worship; and they professed entire allegiance to the teaching of Scripture. It might well seem to the mass of the bishops assembled in council that the Arians were sound at heart, and that technical details should not be pressed against them. This was the attitude of the great majority, composed of the bishops of Syria and Asia Minor. Largely influenced by as much of the teaching of Origen as they understood; dreading above all else Monarchianism and any Sabellian confusion of the Persons, and seeing something of the kind in the opponents of Arius, they simply did not realize the gravity of the crisis. They were very unwilling to go beyond the Scriptures, or to impose a new test, or to add to definitions; and they wished to be lenient to Arius and his friends. They wished to maintain the *status quo*, and they did not see that Arianism was utterly inconsistent with the traditional interpretation.[1] With them, however, so far as voting power went, the decision lay; and in the person of Eusebius, the great Bishop of Caesarea, they found a spokesman and leader, whose historical learning and research and literary talents could not but command universal respect.[2]

[1] To this 'middle' party the name 'Conservatives' has been given. The label is a useful one, and true in the sense explained above; but it is capable of misleading, and if we use it we must guard ourselves against the inference that the opponents of Arius were in any sense innovators. The real innovation was Arianism, and its uncompromising adversaries were the true Conservatives. This became quite clear in the course of the controversy, while many of the 'middle' party at Nicaea leant more and more towards the Arian side. It is therefore only in this limited sense, and with this temporary application, that the description holds.

[2] Eusebius, c. 260–340, a native of Palestine, probably of Caesarea, spent his early life at Caesarea, where he was fortunate in the friendship of the presbyter Pamphilus, who left to him his great collection of books. At the time of the Council he was beyond question the most learned man and most famous living writer in the Church (Lightfoot, Art. *D.C.B.*, *q.v.*). His teaching may fairly be taken as representing the prevailing doctrine of the Trinity and the Person of Christ, which made it possible for many to vacillate between Subordinationism and Sabellianism, and shewed the need for more precise definitions. Dorner describes his doctrinal system as a chameleon-hued thing—a mirror of the unsolved problems of the Church of that age. It was the Arian controversy which compelled men to enter for the first time on a deeper investigation of the questions (see Dorner *Person of Christ* Eng. tr. div. i vol. ii pp. 218–227). But on the main points he is explicit

Prominent in support of Arius were two Egyptian bishops, Secundus of Ptolemais and Theonas of Marmarica, unfaltering in their opinions to the end; and with them at heart three other bishops, pupils of Lucian—Eusebius of Nicomedia, Theognis of Nicaea, and Maris of Chalcedon, and a few more.

Of the resolute opponents of Arianism, Alexander, the Bishop of Alexandria, was of course the centre, with Athanasius as his 'chaplain' and right-hand.   But the most decisive part in the opposition seems to have been played rather by Hosius[1] of Cordova, as representative of the Western bishops, and Eustathius of Antioch, and Marcellus of Ancyra, with a few other Eastern bishops.   The test which was at last agreed upon emanated apparently from this small group.

Agreement was not easy.   That the Arians proper were in a minority was evident at once.   The heart of the Church repudiated the terms they freely used about their Lord and Saviour. But, as the question had been raised and the matter had gone so far, it was necessary to do more than simply negative the conclusions which they drew.   Arian logic forced some closer definition on the Church.   A positive statement of what the Church believed was required, as well as a negation of Arian teaching.

against Arianism, namely—(1) that the Logos was *not* a κτίσμα like other creatures, and (2) that there was not a time when he was not; though he speaks of the Father as pre-existent before the Son, and of the Son as a second existence and second cause. His alliance with the Arian party—so far as it went—was probably largely due to personal friendships, and to his deep-rooted aversion to the 'Sabellianism' of Marcellus and others on the opposite side.   And he followed what seemed at the time to be the policy of 'comprehension'.   (Cf. Socrates *H.E.* ii 21, where passages are cited to prove his orthodoxy against those who charged him with Arianizing.)

[1] The Western bishops present were few, but thoroughly representative.   Africa was represented by Caecilian of Carthage, Spain by Hosius of Cordova (the capital of the southern province, Baetica), Gaul by Nicasius of Dijon, Italy by the two Roman presbyters and the Bishop Mark, metropolitan of Calabria, Pannonia by Domnus of Stridon.

Hosius had been for years the best known and most respected bishop in the West (born in 256, he had already presided at the Synod of Elvira in *c.* 306), and as such had been singled out by Constantine as his adviser in ecclesiastical affairs. It is probable that after the emperor had opened the Council with the speech recorded by Eusebius (*Vit. Const.* iii 12), Hosius presided, and the term ὁμοούσιος is only the Greek equivalent of the Latin *unius substantiae*, with which all Latin Christians were familiar from the days of Tertullian and Novatian.   On Hosius, see P. B. Gams *Kirchengeschichte von Spanien* vol. ii div. i, esp. p. 148 ff.   It was more by word and by deed than by writings that he fought for the faith of the Church, but Athanasius has preserved a letter which late in life he wrote to the Emperor Constantius, urging him to abandon his policy of protection of the Arians and persecution of their opponents (*Hist. Arian.* § 44).

It was in drawing up this that the difficulty was felt. The majority of the bishops assembled in council were very unwilling to employ new terms not sanctioned by tradition, not hallowed by apostolic use. But all the familiar scriptural phrases which were suggested in succession were accepted by the Arians. They could put their own interpretation on them. The historian of the Council draws a vivid picture of the scene—their nods and their winks and their whispers, and all the evasions by which they endeavoured to maintain their cause and elude condemnation. Little progress was made till the friends of Arius produced a creed in writing which was really Arian, and proposed that the Council should endorse it. It was torn in shreds amid the angry cries of the bishops.[1] At all events the Council was not Arian.

At last Eusebius of Caesarea read out what was probably the Baptismal Creed of his Church,[2] in the hope that it might be sufficient and that all would accept it. The Creed was received with general approval, but it was not precise enough to exclude the possibility of Arian interpretation, and the emperor — no doubt prompted by one of the Alexandrine group (probably Hosius) — proposed the addition of the single word 'Homoousios' (of one 'substance'). Its insertion led to a few other

[1] See Theodoret *H.E.* i 7.

[2] The Creed is given by Socrates *H.E.* i. 8 (Hahn³ p. 257), in the letter which Eusebius wrote to his Church explaining the proceedings at Nicaea. He describes the Creed as in accordance with the tradition which he had received from his predecessors in the see, both when under instruction and at the time of his baptism, with his own knowledge learnt from the sacred Scriptures, and with his belief and teaching as presbyter and as bishop. The natural inference from his letter is that it was the very Baptismal Creed of the Church of Caesarea (and probably of all Palestine) that he recited, but it is possible that he gave a free adaptation of it, expanding some and omitting or curtailing other clauses (see Hahn³ pp. 131, 132). The words as to the Son are, "And in one Lord Jesus Christ, the Logos of God, God from God, light from light, life from life, only [begotten] Son (υἱὸν μονογενῆ), first born before all creation (πρωτότοκον πάσης κτίσεως), begotten from the Father before all the ages, by means of whom too all things came into being, who on account of our salvation was incarnate (σαρκωθέντα) and lived as a man among men (ἐν ἀνθρώποις πολιτευσάμενον—the metaphor of citizenship in a state had faded, and the word means simply 'lived', or at most 'lived as one of them'), and suffered and rose again on the third day, and went up to the Father, and will come again in glory to judge living and dead." To the Creed Eusebius added an assertion of the individual existence of each person in the Trinity (the Father truly Father, the Son truly Son, and the Holy Spirit truly Holy Spirit), with an appeal to the baptismal commission (Matt. 28¹⁹), which was no doubt intended to be taken to heart by any who, in opposing Arianism, might tend to slide unawares into 'Sabellian' error. For this anti-Sabellian declaration, however, in the Creed of the Council there was substituted an anti-Arian anathema.

168 CHRISTIAN DOCTRINE

small alterations; and at the end was added an express repudiation of the chief expressions of the Arians.[1]

The Creed thus modified was in its final form as follows:[2]

"We believe in one God the Father all-sovereign,[3] maker of all things both visible and invisible. And in one Lord Jesus Christ the Son of God, begotten from the Father as only-begotten God[4] from God, that is from the [very] being of the Father[5] [or 'begotten from the Father as only

---

[1] In drawing up the Creed of Nicaea from the Creed of Eusebius the following phrases were struck out: (1) λόγον—which represented the vague Eusebian Christology, instead of which the *Sonship* was to be brought prominently forward ; (2) πρωτότοκον πάσης κτίσεως and πρὸ πάντων τῶν αἰώνων ἐκ τοῦ πατρὸς γεγεννημένον, because susceptible of Arian interpretation ; (3) ἐν ἀνθρώποις πολιτευσάμενον, because too vague, not expressing explicitly the real manhood. Modifications of phrases, in effect new, were the following : τὸν υἱὸν τοῦ θεοῦ, and γεννηθέντα ἐκ τοῦ πατρὸς μονογενῆ (instead of λόγον and later on in the Creed υἱὸν μονογενῆ), and ἐνανθρωπήσαντα. Three phrases only were quite new additions : τουτέστιν ἐκ τῆς οὐσίας τοῦ πατρός, γεννηθέντα οὐ ποιηθέντα, and ὁμοούσιον τῷ πατρί.

[2] The Creed agreed to by the Council must not be regarded as a full and complete statement in symbolic form of the faith of the Church at the time. The express purpose for which the Council was summoned was to examine the Arian doctrines, and to declare the authoritative teaching of the Church on the matters in dispute—not to frame a new Baptismal Creed for all. The Creed may be said to have been limited by the 'terms of reference', and therefore it deals at length with the doctrine of the Person of Christ and with nothing else : and there is even no statement on the birth from the Virgin, nor on the suffering under Pontius Pilate, which were certainly part of the common tradition, and contained in the Baptismal Creed of Eusebius, though omitted by him too, as immaterial to his purpose, in his letter to his people. Cf. also the First Creed of Antioch, 341, at the end of which are the words "and if it is necessary to add it, we believe also concerning the resurrection of the flesh and life eternal ".

[3] παντοκράτωρ, the termination signifies the active exercise of rule—'all-ruler', 'all-ruling'. In the New Testament it is used in the Apocalypse (ὁ θεὸς ὁ π., nine times) and in 2 Cor. 6[18] (quotation of LXX, Amos 4[13] = Lord of Hosts). All-mighty—simply possessing all power, apart from any notion of its employment—is παντοδύναμος. Both words are represented by the Latin *omnipotens*.

[4] That this is the construction intended is strongly maintained by Hort *Two Dissertations* p. 61 ff., as also that the clause 'that is, of the essence of the Father' explains 'only-begotten', being designed to exclude the Arian interpretation of it as expressing only a unique degree of a common relationship. See Additional Note p. 195. Athanasius, however, never dwells on μονογενῆ and always treats the clause ἐκ τῆς οὐσίας τοῦ πατρός as a mere exegetical expansion of ἐκ τοῦ πατρός or ἐκ θεοῦ (see next note), and the order of the clauses is extremely awkward if Dr. Hort's interpretation be right. However familiar the collocation μονογενῆ θεόν was at the time, I am not confident that it was intended here, and the more generally accepted rendering, which is given in the text as an alternative, may be accepted with less misgiving.

[5] ἐκ τῆς οὐσίας τοῦ πατρός. Οὐσία here certainly means the inmost being of the Father, his very self. The translation 'substance' which comes to us through the Latin (substantia = essentia) is not satisfactory. 'Essence' hardly conveys to English

(Son), that is from the being of the Father, God from God '],
light from light,[1] very God from very God,[2] begotten, not
made,[3] sharing one being with the Father,[4] by means of
whom all things came into being, both the things that are
in heaven and the things that are on earth : who on account
of us men and on account of our salvation came down and
was incarnate, became man,[5] suffered, and rose again on the
third day, went up into heaven, and is coming to judge living
and dead. And in the Holy Spirit.

ears the real meaning, and 'nature' too is strictly quite inadequate. The phrase
is intended to mark the essential unity of the Son with the Father, declaring that
he has his existence from no source external to the Father, but is of the very being of
the Father—so that the Father Himself *is* not, does not exist, is not conceived of as
having being, apart from the Son. So it is that Athanasius (*de Decr.* 19) says
the Council wrote 'from the *essence* of God' rather than simply 'from God', expressly to mark the unique unoriginate relation in which the Son stands to the
Father, in view of the sense in which it is true that all things are '*from God*'. Of
nothing originate could it be said that it was 'from the *essence* of God'. The
essence of the Father is the sphere of being of the Son. He is inseparable from the
essence of the Father (*ibid.* 20). To say 'of the essence of God' is the same thing
as to say 'of God' in more explicit language (*ibid.* 22).

[1] In this phrase there is taken into the service of the formal Creed of the Church
a familiar analogy—the sun and the rays that stream from it—to shew that, though
in one way they are distinct, there is no kind of separation between the Father and
the Son. The being, the life, that is in the Son is one and the same as the being
that is in the Father ; just as there is no break between the ray of light which we
see and the source of all our light in the sky. The ray is not the sun—but the
light is the same, continuous, from the sun to the ray. The simile illustrates
equally both 'of the essence' and 'one in essence' (Ath. *de Decr.* 23 and 24).

[2] In these words the analogy is dropped. It is no mere reflection of the divine
being that is in the Son. Father and Son alike are *really* God—each and individually.

[3] It is generation, and not creation, by which the Son exists : as it is asserted
later that he was himself the agent through whom Creation was effected.

[4] ὁμοούσιον τῷ πατρί. The οὐσία of the Son is the οὐσία of the Father : as far as
οὐσία goes, no distinction can be made between them. Yet it is a distinct existence
which the Son has in relation to the Father. So, as ἐκ τῆς οὐσίας τοῦ πατρός expresses
the one idea, ὁμοούσιον τῷ πατρί safeguards the other ; and Basil was able to insist
that the latter phrase, so far from agreeing with the Sabellian heresy, is plainly
repugnant to it. "This expression", he says, "corrects the evil of Sabellius : for
it does away with the sameness of the hypostasis (*i.e.* the oneness of person—τὴν
ταυτότητα τῆς ὑποστάσεως—according to Basil's limited use of ὑπόστασις), and introduces the conception of the persons in perfection. For a thing is not itself of one
essence with itself, but one thing with another."—Basil *Ep.* 52 (and see Bull *op. c.*
p. 70).

[5] ἐνανθρωπήσαντα. The preceding phrase σαρκωθέντα, 'was incarnate', 'became
flesh', was not enough in view of the Arian Christology (see *supra* p. 160). So
this term was added. The Son, whose οὐσία is the same as the Father's, became
man. Whatever is necessary to human nature—all that makes man man, all the
constituents of a normal human existence—he took upon himself.

"And those that say there was once when he was not, and before he was begotten he was not,[1] and that he came into being out of nothing, or assert that the Son of God is of a different essence (subsistence) or being,[2] or created, or capable of change or alteration[3]—the Catholic Church anathematizes."

This Creed was signed by all the bishops present except Secundus and Theonas;[4] and when shortly afterwards an imperial decree was issued banishing Arius and those who did not accept the decision of the Council, it seemed that Arianism was disposed of.   But this result was far from being effected.

[1] It seems certain that the thesis here anathematized ' he was not before he was begotten ' is the Arian thesis equivalent to the denial of the eternity of the Sonship (*i.e.* which negatives the Catholic doctrine of the eternal generation—the existence from eternity of the Son as Son—and upholds the Arian conception expressed in the previous clause 'there was once when he was not'). The anathema is thus intended to maintain simply the eternity of the existence of the Son—though he is Son yet he never had a beginning (contrasted with the Arian 'because he is Son, therefore he must have had a beginning'). [Some early writers, however, including Hippolytus (*c. Noet.* 10) and Theophilus (*ad Autol.* ii 10–22, and *supra* p. 127) seem to conceive of the existence of the Lord (as Word) before he became Son—as though he was only *generated* Son at a later stage, at the beginning of all things: and Bull (*Def. F.N.* iii 5–8) argues that the generation thus spoken of was only metaphorical, and that in harmony with such a mode of representation the Nicene anathema has not reference to the Arian thesis stated above, but expressly maintains (in this sense) that "the Son *was* (though not yet, strictly speaking, generated) before his *generation*"—this generation being only one of a succession of events in time by which the real and eternal truth was shadowed out. See Robertson *Athanasius* pp. 343–347.]

The anathemas are of considerable value for the elucidation of the Creed, shewing precisely at what misinterpretation particular phrases of the Creed were directed. Statements and denials thus go together ; and any uncertainty as to the meaning of the positive definitions is removed by the negative pronouncements that follow.

[2] ἐξ ἑτέρας ὑποστάσεως ἢ οὐσίας. The words are certainly used as synonyms, as they were by Athanasius till the Council at Alexandria in 362. In repeating the anathema (*de Decr.* 20) he has only ἐξ ἑτέρας οὐσίας, shewing that to him at least no new conception was added by the alternative ὑποστάσεως. It was perhaps intended for the West (=*substantia*). See Additional Note on ὑπόστασις *infra* p. 235.

[3] τρεπτὸν ἢ ἀλλοιωτόν. In these words we pass from metaphysics to ethics,—and the chief ethical inference of the Arians from their metaphysical theory is rejected. See *supra* p. 160.   In virtue of the divine being which was his, Jesus Christ (although man as well as God) was sinless and incapable of moral change or alteration of character.   How he could be at one and the same time both man and God, the Creed does not attempt to explain.   It is content to repudiate the Arian teaching, which was inconsistent with his being God.   See *infra* p. 250.

[4] So Theodoret. Socrates, however, says all except five.

The Reaction after Nicaea—personal and doctrinal

The victory over Arianism achieved at the Council was really a victory snatched by the superior energy and decision of a small minority with the aid of half-hearted allies. The majority did not like the business at all, and strongly disapproved of the introduction into the Creed of the Church of new and untraditional and unscriptural terms.[1] They might be convinced that the results to which Arianism led were wrong; but probably few of them saw their way to a satisfactory logical defence against the Arian arguments. A test of this kind was a new thing, and sympathy for Arius and its other victims grew. A reaction followed in his favour. This was the motive of the first stage in the complicated movements of the time between the two first General Councils of the Church. Sympathy with Arius connoted dislike of the chief agents of the party which procured his condemnation, and Athanasius and Marcellus [2] were singled out as most obnoxious. They had to bear the brunt of the attack.

---

[1] The objections to the new terms ἐκ τῆς οὐσίας and ὁμοούσιος were numerous.

(1) There was the scriptural (positive) objection which every one could appreciate. The words were not to be found in the inspired writings of the evangelists and Apostles. Every Creed hitherto had been composed of scriptural words, and men had not been pinned down to a particular and technical interpretation. (This objection Athanasius meets in *de Decretis* 18, where he turns the tables on the objectors, asking from what Scriptures the Arians got their phrases ἐξ οὐκ ὄντων, ἦν ποτε ὅτε οὐκ ἦν and the like, and shewing that scriptural expressions offered no means of defence against such novel terms. The bishops had to 'collect the sense of the Scriptures'—*ibid.* 20.)

(2) There was the 'traditional' or ecclesiastical (negative) objection. The use of the word ὁμοούσιος had been condemned at the Council of Antioch in 269 (see *supra* p. 111). (Athanasius, however, claims 'tradition' for it—see *de Decr.* 25; and insists that it is used in a different sense from that in which Paul used it, and that it is a true interpretation of Scripture.)

(3) There was the doctrinal objection. To all who held to the conception of the singleness—the simplexity—of the divine existence, to all who took οὐσία in the primary sense of particular or individual existence, it was difficult to see any but a 'Sabellian' meaning in the word which implied common possession of the divine οὐσία. Ditheism (and Tritheism) all were agreed in repudiating, but this word seemed to imply that the persons were only temporary manifestations of the one οὐσία.

(4) There was the philosophical objection. The words implied either that there was some οὐσία prior both to Father and to Son, which they shared in common (and then this οὐσία would be the first principle and they would be alike derived from it); or else they connoted a materialistic conception, Father and Son being as it were parts or pieces of one οὐσία. (This objection being based on the identification of οὐσία with εἶδος or ὕλη.) See Ath. *Or. c. Ar.* i 14, *De Syn. Arim. et Sel.* 51; Hilary *de Fide Orient.* 68.

[2] See Additional Note on Marcellus, p. 190.

After years of intrigue and misrepresentation Arius was recalled and would have been reinstated but for his sudden death, and Athanasius and Marcellus were exiled (336 A.D.). Allowed to return on the death of the emperor, they were again within two years sent into exile, and the way was cleared for an attempt to get rid of the obnoxious Creed—the terms of which so relentlessly excluded Arian conceptions. The reaction ceases to be so personal, and becomes more openly doctrinal—a formal attack upon the definition ὁμοούσιος under cover of the pretexts to which reference has been made.

Attempts to supersede the Nicene Creed—Council of Antioch 341

The opportunity was found at the Council of Antioch in 341, when some ninety bishops assembled for the dedication of Constantine's 'golden church'. The personal question only came up for a moment, when a letter from Julius, Bishop of Rome, urging the restoration of Athanasius and Marcellus, was read; but the Council resented his interposition and proceeded to consider forms of Creed which might be substituted for the Nicene. Four such Creeds were produced,[1] all of them carefully avoiding the terms by which Arianism was excluded. The first of the four, though prefaced by a specious repudiation of Arian influence (how should bishops follow the lead of one who was only a presbyter?), was 'Arianizing' not only in its avoidance of any expressions which Arians could not have accepted, but also in its explanation of 'only begotten', and its marked attribution of the work of the Incarnate Son to the good pleasure and purpose of the Father. The majority of the Council, however, were not prepared to offer this as a substitute for the Creed of Nicaea, and a second Creed more acceptable to the 'moderates' was adopted by the Council in its stead. Its shews exactly how far the average 'orthodox' bishop of the time was prepared to go in condemnation of Arian theories and in positive statement of doctrine. It is as follows:—

"In accordance with the evangelical and apostolic tradition [2] we believe in one God, Father all-sovereign, the framer and

---

[1] They are given in Ath. *de Synod.* 22 ff., and Socr. *H.E.* ii 10 (Hahn[3] p. 183 ff.).

[2] The appeal which is made throughout to Scripture and Tradition (though the authors are forced to admit some non-scriptural words) carries with it the tacit condemnation of the new Nicene terms.

maker and providential ruler of the universe. And in one Lord Jesus Christ His Son, the only-begotten [1] God, by means of whom [were] all things, who was begotten before the ages (worlds) from the Father, God from God, whole from whole,[2] sole from sole,[3] complete from complete, king from king, lord from lord, living Logos, living wisdom, true light, way, truth, resurrection, shepherd, door, unchangeable and unalterable, invariable image of the deity—both being (essence) and purpose and power and glory—of the Father,[4] the first-born before every creature [5] (or the first-born of all creation), who was in the beginning by the side of (with) God, God the Logos, according to the saying in the Gospel: And the Logos was God—by means of whom all things came into being, and In whom all things consist: who in the last days came down from above and was begotten from a virgin, according to the Scriptures, and became man, a mediator between God and men, apostle of our faith and captain of life, as he says: I have come down from heaven, not to do my own will, but the will of Him who sent me.[6] Who suffered on behalf of us and rose again on the third day, and went up into heaven and took his seat on the right hand of the Father, and is coming again with glory and power to judge living and dead. And in the Holy Spirit, who is given for comfort and hallowing and perfecting to those that believe, even as our Lord Jesus Christ commissioned his disciples, saying: Go ye forth and make disciples of all the nations, baptizing them into the name of the Father and of the Son and

---

[1] 'Only-begotten' must in this case certainly be joined with 'God', which otherwise would stand in an impossible position. See *supra* p. 168 n. 4.

[2] These words are directed against any notion of partition of the Godhead, as though a portion only of the divine were in the Son and the entirety of the Godhead were thereby impaired. God is entire and the Son is entire.

[3] *I.e.* the son alone was begotten by the Father alone, all else being created by the Father not alone, but through the Son whom He had first begotten alone. See Ath. *de Decr.* 7. This phrase is in accord with the Arian explanation of μονογενής, and became a favourite formula of the Anomoeans.

[4] This is the nearest equivalent to the discarded ὁμοούσιον. The passage should perhaps be punctuated with a colon after 'unalterable', but the four words which are bracketed are clearly explanatory of the 'deity' of the Father, of which the Son is said to be the unvarying image. εἰκών means the complete representation, and εἰκὼν τῆς οὐσίας τοῦ πατρός, if fairly interpreted, might suffice to exclude Arianism ; but Arians could accept it as being practically true.

[5] There is nothing in the Creed to exclude the Arian interpretation of this phrase. See *supra* p. 162.

[6] This emphatic reference to the Father's will would be agreeable to Arians.

of the Holy Spirit—clearly meaning¹ of a Father who is truly
Father, and of a Son who is truly Son, and of the Holy Spirit
who is truly Holy Spirit, the names not being applied in a
general sense (vaguely) or unmeaningly, but indicating accurately
the peculiar existence² (? individuality) and rank and glory belonging to each of the [three] named—namely, that they are three
in existence (? individuality), but one in harmony.³

"Inasmuch therefore as this is the faith we hold, and hold
from the beginning and to the end, before God and Christ we
anathematise every heretical evil opinion.   And if any one,
teaches contrary to the sound right faith of the Scriptures,
saying⁴ that there was or has been a time or season or age
before the Son was begotten, let him be anathema.   And if any
one says that the Son is a creature as one of the creatures, or a
thing begotten as one of the things begotten, or a thing made as
one of the things made, and not as the divine Scriptures have
handed down the aforesaid articles one after another—or if any
one teaches or preaches differently from the tradition we
received, let him be anathema.   For we truly and reverently
believe and follow all the things drawn from the divine
Scriptures which have been handed down by the prophets and
apostles."⁵

This Creed seems a clumsy and cumbersome substitute for the
clean-cut clauses of the Creed of Nicaea.   Vague and verbose
accumulations of scriptural phrases are no compensation for the

---

¹ Anti-Sabellian.   The names correspond to permanent numerical distinctions
within the Godhead.

² ὑπόστασιν.   The word here probably comes close to the meaning 'personal
existence'.   See the history of its use p. 235.

³ This expression, which really makes the unity of the three persons moral rather
than essential, has been described (Robertson *Athanasius* p. xliv) as an artfully
chosen point of contact between Origen, on the one side, and Asterius, Lucian, and
Paul of Samosata, on the other side.   It was protested against at Sardica 343 (see
Hahn³ p. 189) as implying a blasphemous and corrupt interpretation of the saying
'I and the Father are one'.

⁴ None of the assertions here anathematized was made by the leaders of the
Arians.   The expressions used represent just those subtle distinctions which seemed
to Athanasius to be merely slippery evasions of direct issues.

⁵ On the authority of Sozomen (*H.E.* iii 5, vi 12) this Creed is supposed to
have been composed by Lucian, and to have won acceptance under cover of his
distinguished name.   If it was so, the anathemas at the end and (probably) a few
phrases in the body of the Creed must have been added by those who produced it at
Antioch.   The Lucianic origin of the Creed has, however, been called in question in
recent times, and the latest suggestion is that Sozomen was mistaken, and confused
this (the Second) with the Fourth Creed assigned to this Council, which might be

loss of its well-balanced terse expressions. The spirit of its framers is shewn by their constant appeal to the Scriptures, and by the weakening down of the anti-Arian definitions. In effect such a Creed as this is powerless against Arianism, and takes things back to the indeterminate state in which they were before the outbreak of the controversy. In the Creed itself there is probably not a single phrase which Arians could not have accepted. The strongly worded rejection of a merely 'nominal' Trinity reflects the fear of Sabellianism by which the framers of the Creed were haunted, while their explanation of the nature of the Unity of the Godhead is compatible with different grades of deity. And the anathemas of the Creed of Nicaea, while apparently retained in the main, are so modified that, though they seem to put Arian teaching under the ban, they condemn positions which nobody, of any party, wished to maintain. Such as it is, however, it was approved by the Council as its official statement, and is known as the Creed of the Dedication.

A third formula, which was signed by all, is notable only for its condemnation of Marcellus, both by name and by the addition of clauses emphasizing the personal and permanent existence of the Son. But it was the personal profession of faith of a single bishop, and not intended apparently as a complete creed.

Yet a fourth Creed was drawn up by a few bishops a little later, after the Council had really separated, and sent—as if from the synod—to the Emperor Constans in Gaul. It is much shorter than the Second, the scriptural phrases and appeals being curtailed or omitted. The eternity of the kingdom of the Son is strongly maintained against Marcellus (though he is not named), and the Nicene anathema against those who say ' out of nothing or out of a different essence ($\dot{\upsilon}\pi\acute{o}\sigma\tau\alpha\sigma\iota\varsigma$) ' is qualified by the further definition ' and not out of God ', so that though intended to be more acceptable to Nicenes it became the basis of the subsequent Arianizing confessions of the East.

Lucianic. [The argument is that the Creed in the *Apostolic Constitutions* vii 41 (Hahn[2] p. 139) is Lucian's, and that the Fourth Creed of Antioch more closely resembles this Creed than the Second does. But the resemblance is not in any case at all close, and the attribution of the Creed in the *Apostolic Constitutions* to Lucian is quite hypothetical (though its basis may well have been the old Baptismal Creed of Antioch).] The assumption of a mistake seems unnecessary. The bishops' statement that they had found it in the writings of Lucian (see Sozomen) would not be inconsistent with its having been touched up here and there before the Council approved it. (See Hahn[3] pp. 139 and 184.)

Opposition of the West to any New Creed—Council of Sardica 343

Constans refused to receive the deputation. The Western bishops were averse to any tinkering with the Creed, and, in the hope of putting a stop to it, Constans, with the assent of Constantius, summoned a general Council to meet at Sardica.[1] The Council met in 343, but the division between East and West revealed itself at once. The Western bishops refused to ratify the decisions against Athanasius, and the Eastern bishops thereupon withdrew and held a Council of their own at Philippopolis, at which they reaffirmed the condemnation of Athanasius and approved a Creed which was substantially the same as the Fourth of Antioch with the addition of new anathemas.[2]

The Westerns, left to themselves, declared Athanasius and Marcellus innocent of offence and protested against the wickedness of their accusers. An explanation of the Nicene Creed was proposed but not adopted (though it is included in the circular letter announcing the proceedings of the Council).[3] In its stead a denunciation of any one who proposed a new Creed was agreed to. The Faith had been declared once for all and no change was to be considered—this was the attitude of the Western bishops throughout the whole period of the controversy from the Council of Nicaea onwards.

Renewed Attempts to secure a non-Nicene Creed

But in the following year (344–345) another synod that met at Antioch to deal with the case of the Bishop Stephen put out a fresh edition of the Fourth Creed of 341 (actually drawn up early in 342), with such expansions of the anathemas and such elaborate explanations intended to conciliate the West that it reached unprecedented dimensions and was known as the long-lined or 'prolix' Creed (the Macrostich).[4] The positive senti-

[1] In Dacia, in the dominions of Constans, between Constantinople and Servia—the modern Sophia in Bulgaria. According to Theodoret *H.E.* ii 6, two hundred and fifty bishops met; according to Socrates and Sozomen, following Athanasius, about three hundred: but see Gwatkin's note as to the real number present (*Studies of Arianism* [2] p. 125). Hosius, Athanasius, and Marcellus were among them.

[2] Hahn [3] p. 190 (a Latin version).

[3] See Theodoret *H.E.* ii 6–8, and Hahn [3] p. 188.

[4] μακρόστιχος ἔκθεσις—so Sozomen (*H.E.* iii 11) says it was called. The Creed is given by Socrates *H.E.* ii 19, and Hahn [3] pp. 192–196.

ments contained in it are for the most part unexceptionable : as when the eternal Sonship is maintained and the Arian phrases are rejected as unscriptural and dangerous and intruding on the incomprehensible mystery of divine processes, and the subordination of the Son is asserted but balanced by words declaring him to be by nature true and perfect God and like the Father in all things; [1] or when the expression 'not begotten by the will of the Father' is denounced in the sense that it imposes necessity on God, whereas He is independent and free and unfettered in His action ; or when the mutual inseparable union of Father and Son in a single deity is proclaimed. Yet the Nicene position is being covertly turned all through, and the real sympathies of the authors of this Creed are shewn in the incidental use of the phrase 'like the Father in all things ' (which was soon to become the watchword of the ' Semi-Arian ' party), and in the peculiarly strong expressions which are used in condemnation of Marcellus and Photinus [2] and all who thought as they thought.

In 346 Athanasius was recalled from exile and for the next ten years enjoyed a hard-won period of peace. This suspension of hostilities was mainly due to the political troubles of the time, which absorbed the energies of those friends without whose help the enemies of the Nicenes could do little against them. During this time, however, two events of the first importance occurred.

Pacification of the ' Conservatives' by Condemnation of Photinus

In 351 a synod was held at Sirmium at which Photinus, the chief follower of Marcellus, was condemned and deposed.[3] This meant the final overthrow of the ideas attributed to Marcellus. In future the ' Conservatives' had nothing to fear from that quarter. They could breathe freely again so far as Sabellianism was concerned. And so they were at liberty to reconsider their position in relation to their Arian allies, with whom the dread of ' confusion of the persons ' had united them, and to reflect whether

---

[1] The use of this phrase $\tau\hat{\omega}$ $\pi\alpha\tau\rho\grave{\iota}$ $\kappa\alpha\tau\grave{\alpha}$ $\pi\acute{\alpha}\nu\tau\alpha$ $\check{\delta}\mu o\iota o\nu$ is notable, but it does not occur conspicuously till 359 (see *infra* p. 182).

[2] $\Sigma\kappa o\tau\epsilon\iota\nu\acute{o}s$, ' Son of Darkness' rather than ' of Light'—his opponents' perversion of his name, it seems—is the form which Athanasius gives.

[3] For the Creed of this synod (the Fourth of Antioch with new anathemas) see Hahn [3] p. 196.

12

after all Arianism was compatible with the doctrine of the Lord's divinity.

Developement of Extreme Form of Arianism

By the death of Constans in 350 Constantius was left sole emperor, without the restraining influence of any colleague of Nicene convictions; and, as soon as he had secured his position against revolt, he was free to indulge to the full his own fanatical Arian sympathies. And so, under these favourable conditions, there was fostered an extremer developement of Arianism (winning adherents in the West as well as in the East) than might otherwise have found expression, the leaders of the new party being Aetius,[1] Eunomius,[2] and Eudoxius.[3]

At Councils held by Constantius in 353 at Arles, after the defeat and death of Magnentius, and in 355 at Milan,[4] the condemnation of Athanasius was voted; and in 356 took place a

---

[1] Aetius actively attacked the teaching of the semi-Arian bishops Basil of Ancyra and Eustathius of Sebaste. Gallus, who was at the time in charge of the Government at Antioch, ordered him to be put to death by ' crurifragium ', but he was rescued by the intercession of friends. A short treatise in forty-seven theses, and a preface written by him defending his use of the watchword ἀνόμοιος against misrepresentation of his opponents, are preserved in Epiph. adv. Haer. lxxvi, and letters to Constantius in Socr. H.E. ii 35. He was condemned at Ancyra in 358 and at Constantinople in 360; recalled by Julian and made a bishop; but he had chequered fortunes till his death in 367 (see Socr. H.E. ii 35, and Dict. Christian Biog. 'Aetius').

[2] Eunomius, the pupil and secretary of Aetius, was the chief exponent of Anomoeanism. His writings were numerous, but were regarded as so blasphemous that successive imperial edicts (from the time of Arcadius in 398, four years after his death) ordered them to be burnt, and made the possession of them a capital crime. Against him in particular Basil and Gregory wrote. (See Art. D.C.B.)

[3] Eudoxius, described by Gwatkin (op. cit. p. 175 n.) as 'perhaps the worst of the whole gang ', a disciple of Aetius and friend of Eunomius, and after him the leader of the Anomoean party, was ordained and made Bishop of Germanica (on the confines of Syria, Cilicia, and Cappadocia) after the deposition of Eustathius (331), who had refused him orders as unsound in doctrine. Having improperly procured his election to the see of Antioch (347-348), he managed to hold his position till 359, when the Council of Seleuceia deposed him; but by court influence he was appointed patriarch of Constantinople in 360 in succession to Macedonius, and by the favour of Constantius and Valens was able to resist opposition till his death in 370. He seems to have been entirely lacking in reverence, and incredibly self-confident (see Art. D.C.B.).

[4] See Soz. H.E. iv 9. Only some half-dozen bishops opposed and protested, and were exiled by imperial decree. Socrates, however (H.E. ii 36), represents the protest as effectual. It was on this occasion, when the orthodox bishops refused to sign the condemnation of Athanasius as being against the canon of the Church, that Constantius made his famous utterance "Let my will be deemed the Canon". Gwatkin (p. 149) says "the Council . . . only yielded at last to open violence ". Three bishops, including Lucifer of Calaris, were exiled.

savage assault on his Church at Alexandria, his narrow escape
and retirement into exile in the desert, and the apparently complete overthrow of the Nicene party in the East. This third
exile of Athanasius lasted till 362, and during this time the fate
of Arianism was really settled, though twenty years more elapsed
before the victory was finally won.

The ultimate issue was made clear by the effect of the
[Second] Council of Sirmium in 357. Under the leadership of
Valens,[1] Ursacius,[1] and Germinius,[2] the bishops agreed to a Creed
which hints that the Son is not really God, declares with emphasis the superiority of the Father and the subjection of the
Son along with all other things, and forbids the use of the term
'substance' or 'essence' (being) in any form, whether 'of one
substance' or 'of like substance (or being)', on account of the
difficulties to which such terms have given rise, and because they
are not to be found in the Scriptures and transcend human
knowledge.[3] Such a declaration was of course a strongly Arian
manifesto; 'Anomoean' even in effect, since it condemns 'of
like essence' no less than the Nicene 'of one essence'. And
as such it was at once denounced, and by the name which
Hilary, the great champion of the Nicene Faith in the West,[4]

---

[1] Valens and Ursacius had been personal disciples of Arius, probably during his
exile into Illyricum after Nicaea. Later on they found it politic to profess 'conservative principles' (see Socr. *H.E.* ii 37), and seem to have held a very confused
doctrine. In 347, at a Council at Milan, they confessed the falsehood of the
charges against Athanasius, but that there was no genuine recantation of Arian
views is proved by their part in the Sirmium 'blasphemy'. After that, they
formed the Homoean party in the West (Acacius in the East), on what seemed to
be the line of least resistance, and accepted the 'Dated Creed' at the Sirmium
conference in 359, where Valens distinguished himself by trying to omit the words
κατὰ πάντα. They were at Ariminum and Nice, and Valens by artful dissembling
and jugglery with words succeeded in getting Arianizing phrases adopted. Valens
was Bishop of Mursa in Pannonia and Ursacius of Singidunum (Belgrade).

[2] Germinius was Bishop of Sirmium.

[3] The Creed is in Hahn[3] p. 199 (Latin), and (Greek) Ath. *de Syn.* 28; Socr.
E.H. ii 30. Ὁμοιούσιον occurs here for the first time.

[4] Though the West never felt the stress of the Arian controversy to the same extent
as the East, and was fortunate in having—for some time—emperors who favoured the
Nicene rather than the Arian cause, yet the work of Hilary, a religious layman elected
Bishop of Poictiers in 353 ('the Athanasius of the West'), and Ambrose in establishing the Homoousian doctrine must not be passed by in any account of its history.
Arianism was strongly (and at times violently) championed in Gaul by such men
as Ursacius, Valens, and Saturninus; and after the Council of Milan in 355, at
which the condemnation of Athanasius was pronounced, Hilary and a number of
other bishops withdrew from communion with the three, who thereupon, by representations (probably false) to the emperor, secured an edict banishing Hilary to

suggested—'the blasphemy of Sirmium'[1]—it has since been

Phrygia (356). The exile lasted three years, and during it Hilary carried on the war against Arianism by his writings, *de Synodis* (conciliatory as Athanasius was towards semi-Arians, who seemed really to accept the Nicene teaching but to stumble at the Nicene terms) and *de Trinitate*. And on his return, till his death in 360, by zeal tempered by tact and mutual explanations of uncertain terms, he effectively won over the waverers and reduced the Arian party to the smallest dimensions. (See J. G. Cazenove 'Hilarius Pictav.', *D.C.B.* ; and for his doctrinal teaching especially Dorner *Doctrine of the Person of Christ* Eng. tr. div. i vol. ii p. 399 ff.)

Hardly less important was the work of Ambrose later—like Hilary, a layman suddenly elevated to the episcopate to be a pillar of the Faith (Bishop of Milan 374–397). The successor of the Arian bishop Auxentius, and unflinching in his resistance by word and by deed to Arianism, however supported in imperial circles, he steadily maintained the Catholic teaching against all heresy. As a diligent student and warm admirer of the Greek theologians, especially Basil, he exerted all his great influence to secure the complete victory of the Nicene doctrine in the West. (See especially *De fide ad Gratianum* (ed. Hurter, vol. 30) and *De Spiritu S.*)

[1] The blasphemy of Sirmium runs as follows : "Since there was thought to be some dispute concerning the faith, all the questions were carefully dealt with and examined at Sirmium, in the presence of our brothers and fellow-bishops Valens, Ursacius, and Germinius. It is certain that there is one God, all-ruling and Father, as is believed through the whole world, and His only Son Jesus Christ, the Lord, our Saviour, begotten from (the Father) Himself before the ages : but that two gods cannot and ought not to be preached, for the Lord himself said 'I shall go to my Father and to your Father, to my God and to your God' (John 20[17]). Therefore there is one God of all, as the Apostle taught : 'Is God God of the Jews only ? is He not also of the Gentiles ? Yea, of the Gentiles also. Since there is one God, who justifies the circumcision from faith and the uncircumcision through faith' (Rom. 3[29, 30]). And everything else too was concordant and could not be at all discrepant. But as regards the disturbance caused to some or many with regard to substance, which is called in Greek *usia*, that is—to make it more clearly understood—*homousion*, or the term *homoeusion*, no mention at all of it ought to be made and no one ought to preach it—for this cause and reason, that it is not contained in the divine Scriptures and that it is beyond human knowledge, and no one can declare the nativity of the Son, concerning whom it is written 'Who shall declare his generation ?' (Isa. 53[8]). For it is plain that only the Father knows how he begat His Son, and the Son how he was begotten by the Father. There is no uncertainty that the Father is greater : it cannot be doubtful to any one that the Father is greater than the Son in honour and dignity and renown and majesty, and in the very name of Father, since he himself testifies—'He who sent me is greater than I am' (John 14[28]). And no one is ignorant that this is Catholic—that there are two persons of Father and Son, that the Father is greater, the Son subject along with all the things which the Father subjected to Himself ; that the Father has not a beginning, is invisible, is immortal, is impassible ; that the Son, however, has been born from the Father, God from God, light from light—the Son whose generation, as has been said before, no one knows except his Father ; that the Son of God, our Lord and God, himself, as is read, took upon him flesh or body, that is, man (humanity), from the womb of the Virgin Mary, even as the angel proclaimed. And as all the Scriptures teach, and particularly the Apostle himself the master (teacher) of the Gentiles, (we know) that from the Virgin Mary he took man (humanity), by means of which he shared in suffering. Futhermore, the chief thing and the confirmation of the whole faith is that a Trinity should always be maintained, as we read in the Gospel, 'Go ye and

known.[1] It was much too late in the day to seek to make peace by snatching the bone of contention away. A coalition formed with such an idea was bound to fail; but it did much worse—it played into the hands of Arianism, and, whatever the East was, it was not really Arian. And so the coalition fell to pieces. Its Arian members had gone too far, and in the moment of victory they lost their half-unconscious allies. At a synod held at Antioch early in the following year, it is true, the flagrant blasphemies of Aetius and Eunomius were allowed by the president, Eudoxius, to pass; but the moderates ('Conservatives') were the more stimulated to take immediate action.

Protests of the Moderates in the East

They held a counter meeting at Ancyra under Basil, the bishop, at which they anathematized in general every one who did not faithfully confess the essential likeness of the Son to the Father, and in particular (with reference to numerous passages in the Gospel according to St John) all who so misinterpreted the sayings of Jesus as to conceive him to be 'unlike' the Father.[2] The anathemas covered all the extreme

baptize all nations in the name of the Father and of the Son and of the Holy Spirit' (Matt. 28[19]). Entire and complete is the number of the Trinity. And the Paraclete the Spirit is through the Son, and he was sent and came according to the promise to build up, to teach, to sanctify the Apostles and all believers."

[It will be noted that the Father is here stated to be invisible and incapable of suffering, and the Son in contrast to Him is regarded as passible, joining in the suffering of his human nature. The Son as a divine being is contrasted with the human nature which he assumed. A reference in the explanation of the Creed which was offered at Sardica in 343 in order to repudiate Arian conceptions (Hahn[3] p. 189), "This (sc. the Spirit) did not suffer, but the human nature ($\mathring{\alpha}\nu\theta\rho\omega\pi\sigma\varsigma$) which he put on suffered—which he assumed from Mary the Virgin, the human nature which is capable of suffering", shews that Arians taught that the divine nature itself in the Incarnate Christ shared the suffering. That is, no doubt, the view intended here. Such teaching obviously makes the divine nature of the Son (passible) different from the divine nature of the Father (impassible), and as such it was repudiated by the opponents of Arianism. The later exact teaching of Cyril of Alexandria and Leo on the subject (see infra pp. 268, 290) was already in some connexions expressed by Athanasius (Or. c. Ar. iii 31–33), as it had been previously by Tertullian (see supra p. 144).]

[1] See Hilary de Synodis 11 and adv. Constantium 23. Hosius, Bishop of Cordova —to whose suggestion the term Homoousios at Nicaea was probably due—was present at this synod, and was compelled by violence to sign the Creed (see Soz. H.E. iv 6). So Hilary could call it also 'the ravings of Hosius', a singularly uncharitable obiter dictum in view of all the facts and the great services of Hosius.

[2] See Hahn[3] p. 201.

Arian theses, and the emphatic declaration that the Son was like the Father even in essence (*i.e.* in his very being) was at this juncture just the bridge which was needed to lead wanderers back to the Nicene faith in its fulness. But now the 'moderates' went too far for the temper of the time. The good effects of their action were largely undone when they procured a sentence of exile against Aetius, Eudoxius, and a large number of the Anomoean party, whom Constantius obliged them to recall after an Arian deputation had put their case before him. And so there was a deadlock, and a compromise had to be found.

The Homoean Compromise

A new party was formed—the party of compromise—intended to be the rallying-point of all moderates, with the watchword 'like in all respects', and the prohibition of technical terms. This compromise, promoted by Acacius, Bishop of Caesarea, was accepted by Basil of Ancyra (the president of the last Council) and the Emperor Constantius. To draw up a Creed embodying it, and to prepare the business for a great ecumenical Council to accept it, a conference was held at Sirmium, under the presidency of the emperor, in the month of May 359.[1] The Creed which was approved is 'moderate' in tone, and unusually strong in its declarations as to the eternal generation of the Son ('before all the ages, and before all beginning, and before all conceivable time, and before all comprehensible being (or substance)'). But it only says, 'like the Father who begat him, according to the Scriptures', and 'like the Father in all things, as the holy Scriptures say and teach'; and it forbids all mention of the term 'substance' (or essence or being) in reference to God, on the ground that though it was used in a simple or innocent sense by the Fathers, yet it was not understood by the people and caused difficulties, and was

[1] This was the third assembly at Sirmium within the decade, and the Creed is commonly counted the 'third' of Sirmium (there was, however, one drawn up at Sirmium against Photinus in 347, which, strictly speaking, is the first of Sirmium—see Hefele *Councils* ii 192). It was probably composed by Mark, Bishop of Arethusa, perhaps in Latin, but this cannot be proved (see Hahn[3] p. 204, and Burn *Introd. Hist. Creeds* p. 92). The framers of the Creed prefixed a clause giving the date of its publication ('the eleventh day before the Calends of June'—May 22). To their opponents (see Ath. *de Syn.* 8) it seemed ridiculous to date the Catholic faith, and as 'the Dated Creed' it is commonly known. The Greek of it is given in Ath. *de Syn.* 8; Socr. *H.E.* ii 37; Hahn[3] p. 204.

not contained in the Scriptures. Such was the Creed [1] by which it was hoped to unite all parties and bring back harmony to the Church. But though the ' Cabinet-meeting ' of Sirmium could agree, the new party of ' Homoeans ' (or ' Acacians ', or ' semi-Arians ') did not really unite the Church. Honestly interpreted, the formula ' like in all things ' would cover ' like in substance (essence, being) ' and exclude all difference ; [2] yet the very word ' like ' seems to connote some difference, and the divine οὐσία of Father and Son was one and the same. But the emperor meant this formula to be accepted, and with a view to greater ease of manipulation the bishops were summoned to meet in two synods—one for the Westerns at Ariminum and another for the Easterns at Seleuceia.

The Western synod met,[3] Ursacius and Valens representing the Homoean cause. But the bishops were so far from accepting the Dated Creed that they reaffirmed the Creed of Nicaea, with a declaration in defence of οὐσία, anathematized Arianism, and condemned the Homoean leaders (who at once went off to the emperor to secure his support), and sent a deputation to Con-

---

[1] The Creed is of further interest as being the first which contained the clause on the Descent into Hades—"and went down into the nether world and set in order things there (τὰ ἐκεῖσε οἰκονομήσαντα), and when the door-keeeprs of Hades saw him they were affrighted " (Job 38[17] LXX)—a clause which probably shews the influence of Cyril of Jerusalem, who refers to the Descent several times, and in his list of ten *dogmata* includes it as explanatory of the burial (*e.g. Cat.* iv 11, 12).

[2] Basil of Ancyra, one of the ' cabinet ', felt it necessary to draw up a statement that the formula ὅμοιον κατὰ πάντα really embraces everything, and is enough to exclude any difference between Father and Son. He shews at length that though the bare term οὐσία is not contained in either the old or the new Scriptures, yet its sense is everywhere. The Son is not called the Word of God as a mere force of expression (ἐνέργεια λεκτική) of God, but he is Son (a definite hypostasis) and therefore οὐσία, and so the Fathers called him. He then goes on to describe and to argue against Arian and semi-Arian tenets, and, referring to the attempt to proscribe οὐσία, says they wished to do away with the name οὐσία in order that if it were no longer uttered by the mouth their heresy might grow in the hearts of men. He suspects they will be caught writing ' like in will and purpose ', but ' unlike in οὐσία '. But if they *bonâ fide* accept ' like in all things ', then they gain nothing by getting rid of the term. For it makes the Son like the Father not only in regard to purpose and ' energy ', as they define it, but also in regard to his original being and his personal existence, and in regard to his very being as Son. In a word, he declares the formula ' in all things ' embraces absolutely everything and admits of no difference. See Epiphanius *Haer.* lxx iii 12–22 (esp. 15). [It is the theology of Basil of Ancyra expressed in this treatise that Harnack regards as ultimately adopted, with developements, by the Cappadocians Basil and the Gregories. See *infra* p. 193.] See Additional Note on ὁμοιούσιος and the Homoeans *infra* p. 192.

[3] See Socr. *H.E.* ii 37.

stantius to explain affairs and urge that no change ought to be
allowed. The emperor shewed all honour to Ursacius and
Valens, and sent back the other deputation with a dilatory
reply, so that at last the bishops of the Council, without being
formally dissolved, returned to their cities. And then somehow or other at Nice in Thrace, near Hadrianople, a few
bishops (whether the original deputies, or the partisans of
Ursacius[1] only, is uncertain) published as the work of the
Council of Ariminum a revised translation of the Dated Creed,[2]
in which the expression 'likeness' is weakened by the omission
of 'in all things'.

Meanwhile the Eastern synod met at Seleuceia. The majority
were 'moderate' and wished simply to reaffirm the Creed
of the Dedication of 341. But the leading spirit was Acacius,
and in view of the present distress caused by the difficulties
with regard to Homo-ousion and Homoi-ousion and the new term
Anomoion (un-like), a declaration was put forward [3] rejecting all
three terms and anathematizing all who used them, and simply
declaring the likeness of the Son to the Father, in the sense
intended by the Apostle when he said (Col. 1[15]), "who is the
image of the unseen God". And the Creed concludes with an
assertion that it is equivalent to the one put forward at
Sirmium earlier in the year. The leaders of the extreme Arian
party were thus conjoined with the upholders of the Nicene faith,
and all alike were put under the ban.   It was of the proceedings
of this year that Jerome said, "The whole world groaned and
wondered to find itself Arian".[4]

A Council held immediately afterwards at Constantinople
(Dec. 359) completed the work, and early in the year 360 the
modified form of the Dated Creed, which had been signed at

---

[1] Cf. Socr. l.c. with Ath. de Syn. 30.

[2] Hahn[3] p. 205. The phrases now run, 'like the Father according to the
Scriptures' and 'even as the holy Scriptures say and teach', and the expression μία
ὑπόστασις also is forbidden.

[3] Hahn[3] p. 206. This declaration was not really accepted by the synod, which
the Quaestor Leonas dissolved, as agreement seemed impossible; but the principle
of it was assented to by the deputies sent to Constantius from the synod. (A
majority of the Council even deposed Acacius, Eudoxius, and others; but their
sentence was disregarded.)

[4] Jerome Dial. adv. Lucif. 19 (Migne P.L. xxiii p. 172). On the Councils of
Ariminum and Seleucia (and the whole question), see the great work of Athanasius
de Synodis, written while he was in exile (359), before he heard of the subsequent
proceedings, references to which were afterwards inserted. Its real aim was to

Nice (with 'in all things' omitted), was issued as the faith of the Church [1]—and the victory of Arianism in the Homoean form was apparently complete. As representative and scapegoat of the Anomoeans, Aetius was abandoned—excommunicated and deposed; but Eudoxius and Acacius triumphed. 'Comprehension' was secured on these conditions. The Homoean formula allowed the freedom which was desired, and admitted all who repudiated the unlikeness of the Father and the Son. It was the 'authorized' Creed for the next twenty years, though all the time the way back to the full acceptance of Homoousion was being prepared.

Gradual Conversion of Semi-Arians and Convergence of Parties to the Nicene Definition

The first turning-point was the death of Constantius in 361. In the early part of the following year Athanasius returned to his see and held a synod at Alexandria, at which the Creed of Nicaea was of course presupposed. The synod decided that all that should be required of Arians who wished to be readmitted to communion [2] was that they should accept this test, and anathematize Arianism and the view which spoke of the Holy Spirit as a creature.[3] The Arian teaching as to the constituents of the person of Christ came under consideration, and the integrity of his human nature and its perfect union with the Word was asserted.[4] Furthermore, in connexion with the

convince the genuine semi-Arians that nothing but ὁμοούσιον would suffice, and that it really was what they meant (§§ 41–54).

[1] Hahn [3] p. 208. It was at this Council that Macedonius, Bishop of Alexandria, ordained by Arian bishops in opposition to Paul and Athanasius, was deposed. See *infra* 'Doctrine of the Holy Spirit' p. 212.

[2] Lucifer of Calaris, who had been exiled to Egypt, was present at the Council. He could not agree to the Arians obtaining *veniam ex poenitentia*. Hence his schism. He too who had consecrated Paulinus in opposition to Meletius at Antioch.

[3] The Arian thesis with regard to the Son was being extended to the Holy Spirit, and apparently some, who were now willing to accept the Nicene teaching as to the Son, still wished to be free from any similar definition as to the Holy Spirit, and to distinguish between them in regard to deity. See *infra* pp. 206, 209.

[4] This was in opposition to the christological conceptions already noted (*supra* p. 160), which were destined to excite greater attention |when championed in another interest by Apollinarius. "They confessed", writes Athanasius, "that the Saviour had not a body without a soul, nor without sense or intelligence; for it was not possible, when the Lord had become man for us, that his body should be without intelligence; nor was the salvation effected in the Word himself a salvation of body only, but of soul also" (*Tom. ad Ant.* 7).

most 'practical' problem before the Council—the position of affairs at Antioch, the dissensions between the Nicene party (Eustathians) and the Homoiousian party (Meletians)—the meaning of the word ' hypostasis ' in relation to the Godhead was discussed. It was recognized that two usages were current, and that questions of words ought not to be allowed to divide those who really agreed in idea. Both ' one hypostasis' and ' three hypostases' could be said in a pious sense. The former was in accordance with the usage of the Creed of Nicaea, in which the word is an equivalent for οὐσία; the latter was equally accurate when the phrase was used to signify not three divine ' substances ' (three gods), but three eternal modes of the existence of the one divine substance (three ' persons '). In the East there had been some disposition to use the word ' hypostasis ' in this latter sense—the usage which finally prevailed; but since the time of the Dionysii the question had not arisen; and to get behind the terms to the sense in which they were used, and so to reveal to the disputants the merely verbal nature of their apparent difference, was a conspicuous success achieved by Athanasius.[1]

But hardly was the Council over when Athanasius was again expelled by Julian from his diocese—to return a little more than a year later by the new emperor's consent.

In 363 a Council at Antioch too reaffirmed the Creed of Nicaea,[2] but with a significant explanation of the keyword of the Creed. Homoousion, suspected by some, has received from the Fathers a safe interpretation—to signify ' that the Son was begotten from the οὐσία of the Father ' and ' that he is like the Father in οὐσία '; and they add that it is not taken in any sense in which it is used by the Greeks, but simply to repudiate the impious Arian assertion in regard to Christ that he was ' from nothing '.

A short-lived revival of Arianism marked the year 364, and some renewal of persecution by the ' Augustus ' Valens in

---

[1] See the account of the Council in the Letter which he wrote to the Church of Antioch (the *Tomus ad Antiochenos*)—' calm and conciliatory, the crown of his career '—urging them to peace. Both sides are represented as agreeing to give up the use of the terms in dispute and to be content with the expression of the faith contained in the Creed of Nicaea.

[2] This was the work of the Acacians, to gain the support of Meletius, who was in high estimation with the Emperor Jovian. Their acceptance of the Nicene Creed may therefore have been to some extent opportunist. See Socr. *H.E.* iii 25.

the following year drove Athanasius again into banishment for the winter, but the revolt of Procopius and the indignation of the people of Alexandria led to his speedy recall early in 366, and the remaining seven years of his life were free from any such disturbance.

A Council was held at Lampsacus in the autumn of 364, at which the formula 'like in essence' was accepted, but its supporters were powerless to take decisive action against opponents who were favoured by Valens. Imperial influence effectually barred the way to the complete establishment of the Nicene faith.

In 375 Valentinian was succeeded by Gratian, who was entirely led by Ambrose; but it was not till Valens was killed in 378, and Theodosius—a strong Nicene—was appointed by Gratian in his place, that the unanimity of the emperors made possible for the Church as a whole the restoration of the Creed for which the struggle had been so long maintained.

Final Victory of the Nicene Interpretation at the Council of Constantinople

The Council which met at last in 381 [1] at the capital, Constantinople, solemnly ratified the faith of the Council of Nicaea

[1] Only Eastern bishops were present, and Meletius of Antioch, who was held in universal estimation (though he had been so much distrusted in the West), was appointed to preside. Gregory of Nazianzus had already been some time in Constantinople, hard at work building up the Nicene faith in his Church of the Anastasia, since Gratian's edict of toleration in 379 had made it possible again to give the Catholics of Constantinople a diocesan administrator. But as bishop only of the insignificant Sasima, he had hardly ecclesiastical rank enough to preside. The first act of the Council was to appoint him, much against his will, Bishop of Constantinople; and on the death of Meletius, shortly after the beginning of the synod, he naturally took the place of president. When, however, the synod insisted on electing a successor to Meletius, and so continuing the schism at Antioch (in violation of the agreement that when either of the two bishops Meletius and Paul died, the survivor should be acknowledged by both parties); and when the Egyptian bishops (who probably desired the recognition of Maximus, an Alexandrine, who had been previously secretly consecrated Bishop of Constantinople) protested against Gregory's appointment as a violation of the Nicene canon which forbade the removal of a bishop from one see to another; Gregory insisted on resigning and was succeeded by Nectarius. See Hefele *Councils* vol. ii p. 340 ff.

The West had no part in the Council, and it was not till 451 that it took rank as ecumenical—the Second General Council—and then only in respect of its decrees on faith (the canons as to the *status* of the Bishop of Constantinople not being accepted at Rome).

In preparing the way for the acceptance of the Nicene definitions the work of Gregory and Basil and Gregory of Nyssa —the Cappadocian Fathers—had been of highest value. See further in regard to them Chapter XIII.

in its original shape,[1] and condemned all forms of Arian teaching; and edicts of Theodosius were issued—in accordance with

---

[1] No new Creed was framed (see Socr. *H.E.* v 8, and Soz. *H.E.* vii 9). An enlarged Creed, afterwards known as the Creed of the Council of Constantinople, was
apparently entered in the Acts of the Council (which are not extant), as it was read
out from them at the Council of Chalcedon. Possibly it was the Creed professed
by Nectarius on his baptism and consecration as Bishop of Constantinople during
the progress of the Council. See Kunze *Das nicänisch-konstantinopolitanische
Symbol*, and A. E. Burn *Guardian*, March 13, 1901. Possibly Cyril of Jerusalem,
whose 'orthodoxy' had been more than doubtful (he certainly disliked the test-
word homoousios), and who on this occasion publicly proclaimed his adherence
to the homoousian formula (see Socr. *l.c.*), recited in evidence of his opinions the
form of Creed which was in use in his Church—a form based upon the old Baptismal
Creed of Jerusalem (which can be gathered from his catechetical lectures on it in
348–350)—revised and augmented from the Creed of Nicaea about 362, after he
was reinstated in his bishopric. And this Creed, being approved by the Council,
was entered in the Acts—though not intended for publication and general use;
and then, inasmuch as it was manifestly useful in view of later developements of
teaching as to the Holy Spirit, it passed into wider currency, and came at length
to be regarded as a Creed drawn up on this occasion by the authority of the
Council itself. (As early as the very year following the Council a synod of
bishops who met at Constantinople, in a letter to Damasus, Bishop of Rome,
referred to 'a more expanded confession of the faith' recently set forth in Constantinople.) It is certain that a Creed almost identical with that which tradition
came to attribute to the Council was in existence seven years before the Council
met, when it was appended to an exposition of the Faith (styled ὁ Ἀγκυρωτός—
Ancoratus—the Anchored One), composed by Epiphanius, Bishop of Salamis (Con-
stantia), in Cyprus. The connexion of Salamis with Jerusalem (its metropolis) would
lead to the use of the same form of Creed in both places. Epiphanius seems to
regard it as the faith of the 318 bishops who met at Nicaea; but it is scarcely
possible that such an error could have been made at the Council itself, and there
is no evidence that the enlarged Creed was adopted by this Council except the
unsupported statement of the deacon Aetius at the Council of Chalcedon seventy
years later. At this Council of Chalcedon the genuine Nicene Creed was received
with enthusiasm as the baptismal confession of all (it had apparently been adopted
as such in the first half of the fifth century), but the so-called Constantinopolitan
only as the true faith. It is obviously not based on the Nicene Creed, though
in close agreement with its teaching as to the Person of Christ. Thus it does not
contain the clause ἐκ τῆς οὐσίας τοῦ πατρός, one of the most contested of Nicene
phrases, nor 'God from God' (though this was afterwards inserted in the Western
versions of the Creed); nor 'things in heaven and things in earth', in the clause
attributing creation to Christ. The first of these clauses could be dispensed with
more easily when there was no longer danger of Sabellian ideas threatening the
personality of the Son; and though it is true that no words so effectually preclude the possibility of the Homoean interpretation of the Creed, yet Athanasius
always insisted that they were only an explanation of ἐκ τοῦ πατρός (see Additional Note). To sum up—(1) All the historians of the Council say that it was
(only) the Nicene Creed that was affirmed. (2) There is no evidence during the
seventy years after the Council that anybody thought there had been an enlarged
Creed drawn up then. At Ephesus in 431 no mention was made of any but the
Creed of Nicaea. (3) The enlarged Creed in question was in existence seven years
before the Council, and was probably drawn up still earlier (perhaps *c.* 362). (4) It

the decisions of the Council—forbidding Arians to occupy the existing churches or to build new ones for themselves. Attempts were made to bring Arians over and unite them to the Church ; but, when they proved unsuccessful, the heresy was rigorously suppressed by force and expelled from the greater part of the empire.[1]

has as its basis not the Nicene Creed, but the Baptismal Creed of Jerusalem (being an enlarged edition of the latter with Nicene corrections and amendments). See Hort *Two Dissertations*. It is possible that before the time of the Council of Chalcedon it had been taken into use as the baptismal Creed of the Church of Constantinople (so Kunze argues *op. cit.*). The traditional view of the origin of the 'Constantinopolitan' Creed has recently been again championed by a Russian scholar, Professor Lebedeff, of Moscow (see *Journal of Theological Studies* vol. iv p. 285), who considers that the Creed given in the *Ancoratus* was really the Nicene Creed, as Epiphanius describes it, and that the form in which it now stands in the texts is due to the work of a copyist who interpolated into the original Nicene form additions from the (genuine) Constantinopolitan Creed. His argument will need careful examination ; but meanwhile at all events the view stated above holds the field. See also *infra* pp. 214–217.

[1] Though Arianism was thus banished from the Church of the Roman Empire it became the faith of the barbarian invaders of the empire and of the Gothic soldiers in the armies of the empire. The whole Gothic nation (with their successive rulers, Alaric, Genseric, Theodoric) were Arians from the days of the great work among them of the Arian bishop Ulphilas. The Lombards were Arian till the time of Queen Theodelinda, at the end of the sixth century. So were the Visigoths in Spain till the time of King Reccared (the Council of Toledo in 589 was intended to emphasize the national renunciation of Arianism ; and the unconscious addition, on this occasion, of the words *et a Filio* to the clause on the procession of the Spirit well illustrates the intention). The Franks alone of Teutons were free from Arianism.

The familiar form of the *Gloria* in all Western liturgies in which the three Persons are co-ordinated—instead of other variable forms—also witnesses to the struggle. And the Creed which contains the Homoousion was first ordered to be used before the Eucharist to guard against Arian intruders.

Of the causes of the failure of Arianism, Prof. Gwatkin writes (*op. cit.* p. 265) : "It was an illogical compromise. It went too far for heathenism, not far enough for Christianity. It conceded Christian worship to the Lord, though it made him no better than a heathen demi-god. As a scheme of Christianity it was overmatched at every point by the Nicene doctrine, as a concession to heathenism it was outbid by the growing worship of saints and relics. Debasing as was the error of turning saints into demi-gods, it seems to have shocked Christian feeling less than the Arian audacity which degraded the Lord of Saints to the level of his creatures." In breadth of view and grasp of doctrine Athanasius was beyond comparison superior to the Arians. Arianism was indeed "a mass of presumptuous theorising, supported by scraps of obsolete traditionalism and uncritical text-mongering—and, besides, a lifeless system of unspiritual pride and hard unlovingness ".

The victory of ὁμοούσιος was clearly a victory of reason. It was, further, the triumph of the conviction that in Jesus of Nazareth had actually been revealed a Saviour in whom the union of humanity and deity was realized.

And there is no doubt that "Arian successes began and ended with Arian command of the palace". "Arianism worked throughout by Court intrigue and military outrage."

MARCELLUS

The chief authorities for the teaching of Marcellus, the chief representative of the supposed Sabellian tendencies of the Nicene Christology, are two treaties of Eusebius of Caesarea (*contra Marcellum* and *de Ecclesiastica Theologia*), which contain extracts from his own work *On the Subjection of the Son*; a letter to Julius in Epiphanius *Haer.* lxxii; fragments of a writing of Acacius against him, and a Creed of the Marcellians, also in Epiphanius, *l.c.* (Migne *P.G.* xlii 383–388, 395–400). In Athanasius *Or. c. Ar.* iv (as Newman thinks, and Zahn insists) the system of Marcellus is probably attacked (without his name). See Th. Zahn *Marcellus von Ancyra*, Gotha, 1867.

He was Bishop of Ancyra in Galatia (perhaps as early as 315), and at Nicaea was one of the minority whose persistence secured the insertion of the test-word ὁμοούσιος; and after the Council he wrote his treatise περὶ τῆς τοῦ υἱοῦ ὑποταγῆς against Asterius the literary representative of the Arians. His own interpretation, however, was by no means to the mind of the dominant (Eusebian) party, and was called in question at successive synods at Tyre and Jerusalem, and at Constantinople in 335, when he was deposed from his office on the charge of teaching false doctrine. Eusebius of Caesarea took in hand the refutation of his theories, and from his treatises it appears that Marcellus agreed with the Arians that the conceptions of Sonship and of generation implied the subordination of the Son, who was thus generated—he must have had a beginning and be inferior to the Father; he could be neither co-equal nor co-eternal. The notion of Sonship was accordingly improperly applied to the divine in Christ; it referred only to the person incarnate, as the use of the term in Scripture shewed. Of the eternal—the divine—element in Christ there was one term only used: not Son, but Logos. The Logos is the eternally immanent power of God, dwelling in him from eternity, manifested in operation in the creation of the world, and for the purpose of the redemption of mankind taking up a dwelling in Christ, and so becoming for the first time in some sense personal. The God-man thus coming into being is called, and is, the Son of God; but it is not accurate to say the Logos was begotten, nor was there any Son of God till the Incarnation. The title Logos is the title which must dominate all others, expressing as it does the primary relation. The relations expressed by other titles (*e.g.* πρωτότοκος) are only temporary and transient. When the work which they indicate has been effected the relations will cease to exist. The relation of Sonship will disappear: it is limited to the Incarnation and the purposes for which the Logos became incarnate, and the Logos will again become what he was from eternity, immanent in the Father.

For theories such as these little support could be expected; they had too much in common with Sabellianism—the bugbear of the East. Marcellus was regarded as teaching that the Son had no real personality, but was merely the external manifestation of the Father.

[Harnack names four contemporary objections to his system :—(1) That he called only the Incarnate Person the Son of God; (2) that he taught no real pre-existence; (3) that he assumed an end of the kingdom of Christ; (4) that he talked of an extension of the indivisible Monad.]

Basil describes his teaching as a "heresy diametrically opposite to that of Arius", and says he attacked the very existence of the only-begotten Godhead and erroneously understood the term 'Word' (implying that he taught no permanent existence of the Only-begotten, but only a temporary 'hypostasis'). See *Epp.* 69, 125, 263.

It is impossible to determine how far the picture of Marcellus, which Eusebius gives, is coloured by the widespread fear of Sabellian views in the East. Either Marcellus was an arch-intriguer and trimmer, as some do not hesitate to style him, or he was much misrepresented.

It must be borne in mind that opinion had scarcely yet been definitely formulated as to the eternity of the Son's separate existence in the future. St Paul's words (1 Cor 15[28]) 'then shall the Son himself too be subjected to him that subjected all things to him, in order that God may be all in all' might be understood to point to an ultimate absorption of the Son in the Father. Tertullian, at any rate, and Novatian after him, had taught that the Son, when his work was accomplished, would again become mingled with the Father—ceasing to have independent existence (see Novatian *de Trin.* 31). And probably the West was more influenced by Novatian's work than by any other systematic work on doctrine. So that on this point too support might be expected, in general, from the West.

In any case it is clear he could boast, as Jerome (*de Vir. ill.* 86) asserts that he boasted, that he was fortified by communion with Julius and Athanasius, the chief bishops of the cities of Rome and Alexandria; and Athanasius could never be induced to condemn him by name at all events, and late in life when an inquisitive friend questioned him about Marcellus he would only meet an appeal with a quiet smile (Epiphanius, who tells the tale, *adv. Haer.* lxxii 4). In 340 a synod at Rome, under Julius, pronounced him orthodox; and it is also certain that the Council of Sardica in 343, when the Eastern bishops had withdrawn, declared him orthodox. "The writings of our fellow-minister, Marcellus", they wrote, "were also read, and plainly evinced the duplicity of the adherents of Eusebius; for what Marcellus had simply suggested as a point of enquiry, they accused him of professing as a point of faith. The statements which he had made, both before and after the enquiry, were read, and his faith was proved to be orthodox. He did not affirm, as they represented, that the beginning of the Word of God was dated from his conception by the holy Mary, or that his kingdom would have an end. On the contrary, he wrote that his kingdom had had no beginning and would have no end" (Theodoret *Hist. Eccl.* ii 6—*N. and P-N.F.*).

Hilary indeed declares that at a later time, by some rash utterances, and by his evident sympathy with Photinus, he came to be suspected by all men of heretical leanings; but in face of the evidence it is difficult to suppose him heretical at the earlier time, however strong the extracts in Eusebius (who was clearly biassed) may seem.

What the followers of Marcellus said for themselves may be seen from a statement of belief which was presented on behalf of an 'innumerable multitude' by a deputation from Ancyra, sent to Athanasius, in or about the year 371 (shortly before the death of Marcellus), under the leadership of the deacon Eugenius (see Hahn[3] p. 262). They expressly anathematize Sabellius and those who say that the Father Himself is the Son, and when the Son comes into being then the Father does not exist, and when the Father comes into being then the Son does not exist: and they proclaim belief in the eternal personal existence of the Son, as of the Father and the Holy Spirit; adding a further anathema on any who blasphemously taught that the Son had his origin in the Incarnation in his birth from Mary. They thus clearly maintain the eternal Sonship and the reality of the three ὑποστάσεις of the Deity.

HOMOIOUSIOS AND THE HOMOEANS

To say that the Son is 'like' the Father is not at first sight open to objection. The expression had been widely current without protest. Athanasius in his earlier treatises against the Arians was content to speak of the Son as being like the Father (see *e.g.* the *Depositio Arii*, c. 323, and the *Expositio Fidei*, ? 328 A.D., Hahn[3] p. 264), and in argument with Arians he does not disallow the term even later (*Or. c. Ar.* ii 34, c. 356–360; cf. *ad. Afros* 7, c. 369). But at this later time he used it himself in general only with qualification (*e.g. Or. c. Ar.* ii 22, κατὰ πάντα, and i 40, iii 20; but alone ii 17).

So Cyril of Jerusalem in his Catechetical Lectures (c. 348–350), while insisting on the necessity of scriptural language, and contradicting the doctrines of Arius (without mentioning his name), protests against terms of human contrivance (*Cat.* v 12) and uses 'like the Father' *either* 'according to the Scriptures' *or* 'in all things'.

But as early as *de Decr.* 20 (c. 351–355) Athanasius had written that by saying the Son was "one in οὐσία" with the Father the

Council meant "that the Son was from the Father, and not merely like, but the same in likeness . . ." his likeness being different from such as is ascribed to us: and he proceeded to shew (§ 23) that mere likeness implies something of difference. "Nor is he like only outwardly, lest he seem in some respect or wholly to be other in οὐσία, as brass shines like gold or silver or tin. For these are foreign and of other nature, are separated off from each other in nature and virtues, nor does brass belong to gold . . . but though they are considered like, they differ in essence." And later, de Syn. 53 (c. 359–361), he argued altogether against the use of the term 'like' in connexion with οὐσία on the ground that 'like' applies to qualities rather than to 'essence'.

So Basil after him in Ep. 8 (perhaps dependent on de Syn.), c. 360. "We in accordance with the true doctrine speak of the Son as neither like nor unlike the Father. Each of these terms is equally impossible, for like and unlike are predicated in relation to quality, and the divine is free from quality. . . . We, on the contrary, confess identity of nature and accept the one-ness of essence. . . . For he who is essentially God is of one essence with Him who is essentially God." So it was that when the partial truth of 'likeness' was put forward as the whole truth, the expression had to be abandoned. No form of likeness will really do. It would apply to some qualities and attributes perhaps; but in being God (that is, in their οὐσία) Father and Son were not like but the same—of one οὐσία: in their special attributes and individual characteristics they were not like—they were distinct ὑποστάσεις.

THE MEANING OF HOMOOUSIOS IN THE 'CONSTANTINOPOLITAN' CREED

Dr. Harnack (following Dr. Zahn and Prof. Gwatkin to some extent) maintains that though Homoousios triumphed at the Council of Constantinople and finally won its place in the Creed of the universal Church, yet it was accepted in the sense of Homoiousios. He speaks accordingly of the 'old' and the 'new' orthodoxy, the 'old' and the 'new' Nicenes—the 'old' being represented by the champions of ὁμοούσιος at Nicaea, and by the West and Alexandria, the 'new' by the Antiochenes, the Cappadocians, and the Asiatics.

Of old, he argues, it had been the unity of the Godhead that had stood out plain and clear: the plurality had been a mystery. But after 362 it was permitted to make the unity the mystery—to start from the plurality and to reduce the unity to a matter of likeness, that is, to interpret Homoousios as Homoiousios, thus changing the 'substantial' unity of being into a mere likeness of being.

This is, in effect, to say that it was permitted to believe in three beings with natures like each other, οὐσία receiving a sense nearer to 'nature' than to 'being'. Instead of one Godhead, existing permanently in three distinct forms or spheres of existence, there are three forms of existence of like nature with one another, which together make up the Godhead.

It would indeed be strange if expert theologians, after so long a controversy, at last agreeing to reject homoiousios in favour of the Nicene homoousios, strained out the term and swallowed the sense. It would indeed be a scathing satire on the work of councils and theologians. It would be proof of strange incompetence and blindness on the part of the historians of doctrine that such a conclusion of the Arian controversy should only have been discovered in the nineteenth century.

But this new reading of the history is a paradox. It is not really supported by the evidence cited in its favour. The facts when patiently reviewed confirm the old historical tradition and do not justify the new hypothesis, according to which the Church has all these centuries been committed to an essentially tritheistic interpretation of the Person of her Lord. [See further "The Meaning of Homoousios in the 'Constantinopolitan' Creed" *Texts and Studies* vol. vii no. 1.]

"BY THE WILL OF THE FATHER"

The teaching that God called the Logos into personal existence by a decree, by the free action of His will, involves ideas that are inconsistent with the Catholic interpretation of the Gospel. It conceives God as already existent as a Person by Himself alone, so destroying the Trinitarian idea of the personality of the Godhead; and declares that God, who had been thus alone, after a time brought forth the Logos, which he had hitherto borne within himself as one of his attributes (his intelligence), and endowed it with a hypostatic existence, and the Logos thus became a Being distinct from God Himself. The generation of the Logos is thus represented not as necessary, founded in the very being of God; nor as eternal, although it is prior to all time : but as accidental, inasmuch as the Logos might have been left, as originally, impersonal. So the Son might never have come to a real hypostatic existence, and there might not have been the relation of Father and Son in the Godhead. That is to say, the Christian conception of God would be only *de facto* true, and would not be grounded in the very essence or being of the Godhead.

If it were the case, as the Arians taught, that the Son was created 'by the will of the Father', then the counsel and will preceded the creation; and thus the Son is not from all eternity, but has come into being. There was a time (though not 'time' as we know it) when he was not. Therefore he is not God as the Father is. "It was an Arian dialectical artifice (see Epiphanius *Ancor.* 51) to place before the Catholics this alternative:—God produced his Son either of free will or not of free will. If you say 'not of free will', then you subject the Godhead to compulsion. If you say 'of free will', then you must allow that the will was there before the Logos. Ambrose (*de Fide* iv 9) answered that neither expression was admissible, for the matter concerned neither a decision of the divine will nor a compulsion of God, but an act of the divine nature, which as such falls under the idea neither of compulsion nor of freedom. To the same effect Athanasius (*Or. c. Ar.* iii and *de decr. Nic. Syn.*) argued that the generation, as an act 'of the divine nature, goes far beyond an act of the will (cf. Greg. Naz. *Theol. Or.* iii 3 ff.). And Cyril of Alexandria makes a distinction between the concomitant and the antecedent will of the Father; maintaining that the former, but not the latter, is concerned with the generation of the Son (σύνδρομος θέλησις, not προηγουμένη—see *de Trin.* ii p. 56)."

So Döllinger writes, but he goes on (*Hippolytus and Callistus* Eng. tr. p. 198) to shew that, though the Catholics contended vigorously against the Arian teaching on this point, the Trinitarian self-determination of God must not, of course, be represented as a merely natural and necessary process; that is to say, as a process in any sense unconditioned by His will. "In God, in whom is found nothing passive—no mere material *substratum*, who is all movement and pure energy, we can conceive of no activity, not even directed towards Himself, in which the will also does not share. The eternal generation of the Son is at once necessary (grounded in the divine nature itself, and therefore without beginning), and also at the same time an act of volition (*voluntaria*). That is, the divine will is one of the factors in the act of begetting. Not without volition does the divine essence become the Father and beget the Son. But this volition is not a single decree of God; not something which must be first thought or determined, and then carried into effect: but it is the first, essential, eternal movement of the divine will operating on itself, and the condition of all external, that is, creative, acts."

Μονογενής—UNIGENITUS, UNICUS

The word μονογενής, according to the original and dominant use of it in Greek literature, and by the prevailing consent of the Greek Fathers, was applied properly to an only child or offspring. So Basil *adv. Eunom.* ii 20 explains it as meaning ὁ μόνος γεννηθείς, and repudiates the meaning ὁ μόνος παρὰ μόνου γενόμενος (or γεννηθείς) which was arbitrarily put upon it by Eunomius. The special kind of unicity which belongs to an only child is latent in the word in the few usages in which it is not apparent, as when it is used of the Phœnix, or by Plato *Tim.* 31B with οὐρανός (as made by the Father of all, *ib.* 28c), and by later writers of the κόσμος. In a few cases only the word is loosely applied to inanimate objects that are merely alone in their kind, as if it were connected with γένος.

The paraphrase μόνος γεννηθείς, which Basil gives, is essentially true to the sense, but the passive form goes beyond μονογενής. So probably does *unigenitus*; and ' only-begotten ' is still narrower in meaning. If it is connected with υἱός, ' only Son ', as in the Apostles' Creed, would be the nearest equivalent in English. If it is connected with θεός, ' only ' would not, of course, be a possible translation : ' sole-born ' might express the meaning more exactly.

Unicus was the rendering of μονογενής throughout the Bible in the earliest Old Latin versions, but it was supplanted by *unigenitus* in some forms of the Latin before the time of Jerome in the five passages in the New Testament in which it has reference to our Lord (namely John 1[14, 18] 3[16, 18], 1 John 4[9]). Nearly all the native Latin Creeds have *filium unicum eius*, though *unigenitus* is used in translations of comparatively late Greek creeds. Even Augustine uses *unicus* more readily, and when he has *unigenitus* he explains it as equivalent to *unicus*. But in the course of time the more explicit word prevailed, except in the Apostles' Creed. So we have *filium unicum* in the Apostles' Creed (English ' only '), but *filium unigenitum* in the Latin translations of the ' Constantinopolitan ' Creed (English ' only begotten '). See Hort *Two Dissertations*.

CHAPTER XIII

The Doctrine of the Holy Spirit and the Trinity

The Course through which the Doctrine went

In tracing out the history of the doctrine of the Holy Spirit we
are confronted by a course of developement similar to that which
is seen in the history of the other great Christian doctrines.
The experiences of Christ himself, and such teaching in regard
to them as he gave his disciples, were sufficiently understood to
secure recognition of the most important principles. It is clear
that the earliest teaching and some at least of the earliest writings of the Apostles were conditioned by belief in the personality
and divinity and manifold operations of the Holy Spirit.[1] And
this faith has beyond all question always remained implicit in
the life of the Church; and whenever the Church as a body has
been called on to give expression to the Christian theory of life
—to interpret the Christian revelation—she has never been for
a moment in doubt as to her mind upon this point. She has
had no hesitation in declaring that in the Christian conception
of the existence of the One God there are included three persons
—that Father, Son, and Holy Spirit are alike and equally essential to the idea of the one Godhead. As to the exact relations
existing between them, the exact mode of existence, she has not
wished to lay down definitions, and she may perhaps have been in
doubt. In regard to the Holy Spirit, as in regard to the Son, she
was ultimately forced to some measure of definition. Meanwhile
individual thinkers without exact guidance sometimes strayed a
little aimlessly and missed the path, in spite of the indications
afforded by earlier teaching and existing traditions and institu-

---

[1] Whatever opinion may be held as to the date of the Johannine writings, the
Acts of the Apostles and the Epistles of St Paul seem to give decisive evidence
in regard to belief in the Holy Spirit which was daily acted on in the practice and
life of earliest Christian communities.

tions. In seeking unguardedly for closer definition they sometimes reached results inconsistent with main principles, or in
devoting attention to particular lines of reasoning they ignored
others.

Tracing out the history of the doctrine, therefore, means
tracing out the teaching of some of the few individual thinkers
or teachers whose writings happen to bear upon the subject;
until, quite late in the day, there arose a school of teachers that
consciously questioned the main principles of the faith of the
Church, and educed the unmistakeable expression of what had
often hitherto been only half-consciously held.

The Doctrine of the Spirit in the Bible

As to the teaching of the Bible with regard to the essential
nature of the Holy Spirit there can be no doubt. It is explicit
and unanimous in its witness that he is divine.[1] " But to the
further enquiry, whether this Divine Spirit is a person, the reply,
if on the whole decisive, does not come with equal clearness
from the earlier and the later books. The Old Testament
attributes personality to the Spirit only in so far as it identifies
the Spirit of God with God Himself, present and operative in the
world or in men. But the teaching of Christ and of the Apostles,
whilst accentuating the personal attributes of the Spirit, distinguishes the Spirit from the Father and the Son." [1]

" The Spirit of God as revealed in the Old Testament is God
exerting power. On this account it is invested with personal
qualities, and personal acts are ascribed to it. . . . The Spirit
. . . is personal, inasmuch as the Spirit is God. There is,
besides, a quasi-independence ascribed to the Spirit, which
approaches to a recognition of distinct personality, especially in
passages where the Spirit and the Word are contrasted. But
the distinction applies only to the external activities of these
two divine forces; the concept of a distinction of Persons within
the Being of God belongs to a later revelation." [2]

Functions of the Holy Spirit are recognized in the Old Testament in nature, in creation and conservation; in man, in the

---

[1] See Swete 'Holy Spirit' in Hastings' *D.B.* for a full statement of the biblical
presentation of the doctrine which is here only summarily and partially sketched
in relation to the later expressions of the doctrine. Cf. also *supra* pp. 11-15.

[2] *Ibid.* ; cf. Ps. 43³ 57³ 139⁷, Isa. 48¹⁶ 63⁹·¹⁰.

bestowal of intellectual life and prophetic inspiration and moral and religious elevation—while all his gifts are to be bestowed upon the Messiah.

In the New Testament his work is recognized in the Conception, Baptism, and Ministry of the Lord; and in all the χαρίσματα which he bestows on individuals and the Church.

Some ambiguity in the expression of the doctrine may be observed when St Paul calls him also the 'Spirit of Christ' (Rom. 8⁷) (a phrase which he also uses of Christ's human spirit, Rom. 14; of his pre-existent nature, 2 Cor. 3¹⁷; and of his risen life, 1 Cor. 15⁴⁵); while in some cases the Holy Spirit is apparently identified with Christ (Rom. 8⁹·¹⁰), since through the Spirit the ascended Lord dwells in the Church and operates in believers.

The Doctrine in the Early Church

Incidental references in the writings of the Apostolic Fathers[1] shew the same teaching; but in *The Shepherd* of Hermas, which contains many allusions to the Holy Spirit, language is used which identifies the Spirit with the Son.[2]

Some of the Apologists were so much concerned to expound the doctrine of the Logos[3] that they not only fail to dwell on the Holy Spirit, but even refer to Christ himself much that would have been more accurately attributed to the Holy Spirit; and in some cases they shew a disposition to rank the Spirit lower than the Son.[4]

---

[1] *E.g.* Clement 1 *Ep.* 2. 48, 58, and frequently of his inspiration of Scripture, as also Barnabas constantly (*e.g.* 9, 10). So Ignatius recognizes his distinct personality, his procession from God, his mission by the Son, his operations in the Incarnation, and in members of the Church (*Magn.* 13; *Philad.* 7; *Eph.* 17, 18, 9; *Smyrn.* 13). He is included in the doxologies in *Mart. Polyc.* 14, 22, and *Mart. Ign.* 7. See Swete 'Holy Ghost' *D.C.B.*, an article which so thoroughly covers the field that a subsequent worker over the ground can probably reach no true results that are not already carefully stated there. Here, for the most part, a short summary of them is all that is possible.

[2] See Swete *ibid.*

[3] See *supra* p. 124. This is true perhaps especially of the teaching of Justin Martyr in regard to the λόγος σπερματικός. He also says that the Word himself wrought the miraculous conception (*Apol.* i 33). Similarly Theophilus speaks of 'the Word, being God's Spirit' coming down on the prophets (*ad Autol.* ii 33), and the writer to Diognetus used similar expressions.

[4] *E.g.* Justin, "We place the Spirit of prophecy in the third order", but in the same breath "for we honour him with the Word" (μετὰ λόγου τιμῶμεν—*Apol.* i 13; cf. 60; see also *Apol.* i 6); and Tatian describes the Spirit as the minister of the Son (*Oratio ad. Graec.* 13).

Conspicuous among those of these early writers who are known to us stand Theophilus, who is the first to use the term Triad (Trinity) in reference to the Godhead (though it must be noted that he does not actually name the Holy Spirit),[1] and Athenagoras, who sees in the Spirit the bond of union by which the Father and Son coinhere, and implies the doctrine of his essential procession by the image in which he describes him as an effluence from God, emanating from Him and returning to Him as a ray of the sun or as light from fire.[2]

Gnostic thought upon the subject shews points of contact both with Catholic doctrine and with the heretical theories which were rife in the fourth century. The excesses of the Montanists, champions as they were of the present reign of the Spirit in the world, led no doubt to some unwillingness to fully recognize the place of the Spirit in the divine economy, but the movement was probably still more influential in stimulating interest on the matter and arousing thought.

The Montanist conception of a special age in which the Holy Spirit ruled implied at least a full sense of his personality and divinity, and it was not inconsistent with a belief in his eternal existence. But neither eternity nor personal existence, in any true sense, was assigned to the Spirit by any of the Monarchians. As Spirit, he was merely a temporary mode of existence of the one eternal God, in his relation to the world.[3]

Meanwhile Irenaeus had vigorously repudiated Gnostic misconceptions, and by the aid of various images had partly pourtrayed the relation of the Spirit to the Father [4] and to the Son,[5] and had described his work as Inspirer and Enlightener, in the Church and in the Sacraments. And Tertullian at the end of the second century had expressed in all its essential elements the

[1] As the Triad he names 'God and his Word and his Wisdom' (ad Autol. ii 15).
[2] "The Son being in the Father and the Father in the Son by the unity and power of the Spirit" (Leg. 10 and 24).
[3] This is true, of course, particularly of the school of Sabellius. The earlier Monarchians, so far as we know, paid little attention to the doctrine of the Spirit. See further supra p. 105.
[4] The Son and the Spirit are the two hands of God. The Son is the Offspring, the Spirit is the Image of the Father: the Son is His Word, the Spirit His Wisdom. Together they minister to the Father, as the hands and intellect minister to man, not as though created or external to the Life of God, but eternal as God Himself. See adv. Haer. esp. iv praef. and chh. 14 and 34 cd. Harvey.
[5] This particularly in relation to men, since the Incarnation, of which the gift of the Spirit is a fruit (ibid. iii 38, v 36). See further Harvey's Index 'Spirit'.

full Catholic doctrine of the relations between the Three Persons in the one Trinity, linked together in the one divine life.[1]   This is the first attempt at a scientific treatment of the doctrine.

The deity, personality, and distinct mission of the Holy Spirit were certainly recognized (if with some individualities of conception or expression) by Cyprian, Hippolytus,[2] Novatian, and Dionysius of Rome.

Whether Clement of Alexandria formally investigated the doctrine or not we do not know; but he certainly conjoins the Holy Spirit with the Father and the Son in worship and praise, and so implicitly recognizes Him as a divine person, and regards Him (though sometimes not clearly distinguishing him in this respect from the Word) as the source of inspiration and illumination and as imparted in the Sacrament of Baptism.[3]

Origen's Expression of the Doctrine

A more systematic exposition of the doctrine was undertaken by Origen; and in treating of some of the problems it suggests he was led into language (as in regard to the Son) which the Arians afterwards pressed to conclusions destructive of the conception of the Trinity. His standpoint in the matter is shewn in his great work *On first Principles*, which he prefaces by a statement of the points clearly delivered in the teaching of the Apostles.[4]   Third among these points he says: "The Apostles related that the Holy Spirit was associated in honour and dignity with the Father and the Son. But in his case it is not clearly distinguished whether he is to be regarded as generate or ingenerate,[5] or also as a Son of God or not; for these are points

---

[1] See *supra* p. 140.   This doctrine is expressed particularly in his tract against Praxeas.   See §§ 2, 4, 8, 25, 30.

[2] See *supra* p. 108.

[3] See esp. *Paed.* iii 12, i 6 ; *Strom.* v 13, 24.

[4] He says they delivered themselves with the utmost clearness on points which they believed to be necessary to every one, leaving, however, the grounds of their statements to be examined into by those who should receive the special aid of the Holy Spirit ; while on other subjects they merely stated the fact that things were so, keeping silence as to the manner or origin of their existence, in order to leave to their successors, who should be lovers of wisdom, a subject of exercise on which to display the fruit of their talents.   *De Princ.* Preface 3—Ante-Nicene Christian Library.

[5] The Greek of this passage is not extant.   Rufinus translates 'natus an innatus', which represents γεννητὸς ἢ ἀγέννητος.   Jerome, however, has 'factus an infectus',

which have to be enquired into out of sacred Scripture according to the best of our ability, and which demand careful investigation. And that this Spirit inspired each one of the saints, whether prophets or apostles; and that there was not one Spirit in the men of the old dispensation and another in those who were inspired at the advent of Christ, is most clearly taught throughout the Churches." This passage is highly instructive; but it is uncertain whether Origen intended to say 'generate or ingenerate (begotten or unbegotten)', or 'originate or unoriginate'. The former expression might only imply some uncertainty as to the exact phraseology which should be used to describe the relation of the Spirit, as one of the persons of the Trinity, to the others. But the latter expression would at least cover the conception that the Holy Spirit, as belonging to the class of things that had come into being (been made or created), was not truly God. For further elucidation of Origen's meaning we must look elsewhere. In his commentary on the *Gospel according to St John* he discusses at length the passage in the prologue, " All things came into being (were made) through him", and asks, Did then the Holy Spirit too come into being through him?[1] To this question he says there are three possible answers—The first: Yes, if the Holy Spirit belongs to the class of things that have come into being, since the Logos is older than the Spirit. The second: for anyone who accepts this Gospel as true, but is unwilling to say the Spirit came into being through the Son—that the Holy Spirit is ingenerate.[2] The third: that the Holy Spirit has no being of his own (personality) other than that of the Father and the Son.[3] The third and the second answer Origen rules out, on the ground that there are three distinct 'hypostases', and that the Father alone is ingenerate.[2] It remains therefore that the Spirit has come into being through the Logos, though he is higher in honour and rank than all the things that have come into being (by the agency of the Father) through the Logos. And Origen goes on to suggest that this

which points to the Greek γενητὸς ἢ ἀγένητος (originate or unoriginate). The frequent confusion of the words would justify Rufinus if, as some suppose, he found the latter in his text and interpreted it as the former. See *supra* p. 122 n. 1.

[1] Origen *Comm. in Joh.* i 3, ed. Brooke vol. i p. 70 f.

[2] ἀγέννητον, but the argument requires rather ἀγένητον, unoriginate, the opposite of γενητόν, to exclude Him from the class of γενητά.

[3] μηδὲ οὐσίαν τινὰ ἰδίαν ὑφεστάναι τοῦ ἁγίου πνεύματος ἑτέραν παρὰ τὸν πατέρα καὶ τὸν υἱόν.

perhaps is why he is not also called 'Son' of God; since the Only-begotten alone is from the beginning Son by nature, and his ministry is necessary for the personal existence of the Holy Spirit, not only for his very being but also for his special characteristics which he had by participation in Christ (his wisdom, for example, and rationality, and justice). It is also the Holy Spirit who provides what may be called the material for the charismata (the various gifts and endowments) which are given by God to those who, on account of the Spirit and of their participation in him, are called 'holy' (saints)—this 'material' being actualized by God and ministered by the agency of Christ and having its subsistence in accordance with the Holy Spirit.[1]

It is thus clear that Origen regarded the Fourth Gospel as teaching that the Spirit owes his origin to the medium of the Son, and that therefore he is in the order of the divine life inferior to the Son; and indeed this is the inference which he explicitly draws from the consideration of passages of Scripture which seem at first sight to give to the Spirit precedence in honour above the Son [2]—"He is to be thought of as being one of the 'all things' which are inferior to him by means of whom they came into being, even though some phrases seem to draw us to the contrary conclusion." It is, however, no less clear that at the same time he regarded the Spirit as a divine hypostasis, removed high above the category of creatures; and he carefully guards (for instance) against the idea that the Holy Spirit in any way owes his knowledge and power of revelation to the Son, implying that he has it in virtue of his very being. "As the Son, who alone knows the Father, reveals Him to whom he will, so the Holy Spirit, who alone searches the deep things of God, reveals God to whom he will." [3] The Son alone has his being direct from the Father, but he is not therefore—in Origen's thought—a creature. Nor is it necessary that all things that have come into being through the Son should be creatures.[4]

---

[1] To this thought Origen is led by the passage in 1 Cor. 12[4 ff.]: "There are differences of charismata, but the same Spirit: and there are differences of ministrations, and the same Lord: and there are differences of workings (modes of bringing to actuality), and it is the same God who works all things in all."

[2] Passages examined are Isa. 48[16], and the Sin against the Holy Spirit (Matt. 12[32]).

[3] *De Princ.* i 34.

[4] Cf. *de Princ.* i 33: "We have been able to find no statement in Holy Scrip-

The special idea of creation does not seem to be present to Origen's mind in this connexion. It is rather origination simply that he is dealing with. This is the primary meaning of the word he uses—the word on which he is commenting; and it is really the origination of the Spirit through the Logos, and consequently his inferiority in order to the Logos, that he is concerned to maintain.

He does indeed definitely extend to the Spirit[1] the conception of eternity of derivation which he realized of the Son; and it seems clear that, wherever he speaks of the Spirit as in any way inferior in rank or order, he has under consideration only human experience of the Trinity (God as manifested in revelation), and is not attempting to deal with the inner being and relations of the Godhead.[2] But though, as is probable, he was not in this respect far removed from the ' orthodox ' Catholic faith, it is certain that his language lent itself to misconception and may be said to anticipate Arius; and some of his pupils are said to have represented the Spirit as inferior in glory to the Father and the Son.[3]

Gregory Thaumaturgus

One of the most famous of them, however, Gregory of Neo-Caesarea,[4] strongly asserted the unity and eternity of the Three—"a complete Trinity, in glory and eternity and reign not divided nor estranged. There is therefore in the Trinity nothing created or serving, and nothing imported—in the sense that it did not exist to start with, but at a later time made its way in; for never was there wanting Son to Father nor Spirit to Son, but there was always the same Trinity unchangeable and unalterable." Here too the Spirit seems to be associated es-

ture in which the Holy Spirit could be said to be a thing made or a creature. . . . The Spirit of God which moved (was borne) upon the waters is no other than the Holy Spirit.

[1] See *de Princ.* i 34 : "The Holy Spirit would never be reckoned in the unity of the Trinity, *i.e.* along with the unchangeable Father and His Son, unless he had always been the Holy Spirit."

[2] See *e.g.* such strong assertions as *de Princ.* i 37 : "Nothing in the Trinity can be called greater or less. . . . There is no difference in the Trinity, but that which is called the gift of the Spirit is made known through the Son and operated (actualised) by God the Father."

[3] See Swete *l.c.*

[4] Known as Thaumaturgus, the evangelist of Pontus and Cappadocia. See his Creed (Hahn[3] p. 253), composed probably soon after 260.

pecially closely with the Son, as he is in the preceding clauses of the Creed which describe him as "having his existence from God and appearing through the Son, the Image of the Son, perfect (image) of perfect (Son); Life—the first cause of all that live; Holiness—the provider of hallowing, in whom is made manifest God the Father who is over all and in all, and God the Son who is through all". The derivation of the Spirit is thus referred to God through the Son as medium, but the thought that such derivation implies any inferiority of divine attributes is absolutely excluded.

Dionysius of Alexandria

And Dionysius of Alexandria was equally emphatic in regard to the co-eternity of the three hypostases. Each of the names is inseparable and indivisible from the next. As he had insisted that the names Father and Son connoted each other, so that he could not say 'Father' without implying the existence of the Son, so he says :[1] "I added the Holy Spirit, but at the same time I further added both whence and through whom he proceeded. Neither is the Father, *qua* Father, estranged (ἀπηλλο-τρίωται) from the Son, nor is the Son banished (ἀπῴκισται) from the Father ; for the title Father denotes the common bond. And in their hands is the Spirit, who cannot be parted either from him that sends or from him that conveys him. . . . Thus then we extend the Monad indivisibly into the Triad, and conversely gather together the Triad without diminution into the Monad."

Eusebius of Caesarea

Eusebius of Caesarea shews in his references to the Holy Spirit the same unconscious Arian tendency that marked his action in the controversy as to the person of the Son. The Spirit is third in dignity as well as in order—the moon in the divine firmament, receiving all that he has from the Word ; his very being is through the Son. "He is neither God nor Son, since he did not receive his genesis from the Father in like manner as the Son received his ; but he is one of the things which came into being through the Son." Yet he transcends the whole class of things that have come into being. Eusebius

---

[1] See Ath. *de Sent. Dionys.* 17, and *supra* p. 115.

seems not to discriminate between the procession and the mission of the Holy Spirit, and uses the same term both of him and of the Son.[1]

The Arian Theories expressed but not emphasized, and for a time ignored

At the Council of Nicaea the battle raged round the doctrine of the Godhead of the Word—the doctrine of the Holy Spirit was not under direct consideration. "The opinion on this subject in the hearts of the faithful was exposed to no attack";[2] so the simplest expression of belief was enough,[3] and little more found place in any of the many Creeds (Arian and Semi-Arian) which were drawn up in the following thirty years. But by degrees, as individuals began to question the deity of the Spirit, the Arians extended to him the phrases they applied to the Son—a 'creature', 'divided from the being (essence) of Christ'; as indeed in *The Thalia* Arius had already declared that the essences of Father, Son, and Holy Spirit were of their very nature distinct, alien, and separate. "Assuredly there is a Trinity with glories not alike. . . . One is more glorious than the other with glories to infinitude."[4]

But though Arius expressed himself in this way, all attention was for many years concentrated on the doctrine of the Son; and teaching went quietly on in the Church on the lines on which it had proceeded before the time of Arius.

The Church Teaching in the Middle of the Fourth Century— Cyril of Jerusalem

An excellent specimen of such instruction is furnished by the Catechetical Lectures of Cyril of Jerusalem shortly before the year 350.[5]

At the very outset he makes his appeal to Scripture. In view of the danger of the sin against the Holy Spirit, and of the

---

[1] Swete *l.c.* The passages referred to are *Praep. Evang.* vii 16; *de Eccl. Theol.* iii 6.

[2] Basil *Ep.* 125, in explanation of the absence of any detailed profession of faith.

[3] See *supra* p. 4, on the willingness of the Church to acquiesce in simple 'Creeds' till forced to exclude erroneous interpretations by closer definition.

[4] See Ath. *de Syn.* 15.

[5] These lectures to catechumens (*Cat.* xvi and xvii) are really the first systematic attempt to present the doctrine of the Spirit that we have.

fact that the Holy Spirit spoke the Scriptures, and said about himself all that he wished or all that we could receive, we may well limit ourselves to the teaching of Scripture (§§ 1, 2).

He disclaims the attempt to accurately describe his being (hypostasis), and will only mention misleading ideas of others so that his pupils may not be seduced from the right path and all together may journey along the king's highway (§ 5).

It is really sufficient for salvation for us to know that there is "one God the Father, one Lord his only Son, one Holy Spirit the Comforter". We need not busy ourselves about his nature or being ($\phi\acute{\upsilon}\sigma\iota\nu$ $\mathring{\eta}$ $\acute{\upsilon}\pi\acute{o}\sigma\tau\alpha\sigma\iota\nu$),—as it has not been written we had better not essay it (§ 24).

Accordingly Cyril devotes himself for the most part to enumerating various beneficent operations of the Spirit before the Incarnation, in and during the life of Christ on earth, and in the Apostles and the faithful ever since.[1] All through he appeals to present experience of the wonderful power with which he works, and is at pains to point the lesson that, varied as are the modes in which his energy is manifested, it is one and the same Spirit who spoke through the prophets of old of the coming of Christ; who, when he had come, descended upon him and made him known; who was with and in the Apostles; who illuminates the souls of the just, and supplies the force which purifies or strengthens according to the need; who bestows all the varied graces and virtues of Christian life,[2] directly and through the appointed channels of the ordinances and sacraments of the Church,[3] the 'good Sanctifier and Ally and Teacher of the Church', the true Enlightener.

At the outset he warned his hearers that it was of 'a mighty power divine and mysterious' that he was about to speak, and his whole treatment of his subject is conditioned by his recognition of the full divinity of the Spirit. Only in one connexion, however, does he at all elaborate this point, and that

---

[1] In *Cat.* xvi he cites instances chiefly from the Old Testament; in *Cat.* xvii from the New, especially the Gospels and the Acts (time failing him for more).

[2] See particularly *Cat.* xvi §§ 16, 19, 20, 30, xvii 36, and the fine passage xvi 12, in which, applying the words of Joh. 7³⁸ and 4¹⁴ to the Spirit, he declares the Spirit the source of all that is beautiful in moral and spiritual life, as it is on water that the varied charm and loveliness of the life of nature depends.

[3] He is himself given to us in Baptism when he seals the soul (*Cat.* xvi 24), and in the Chrism (*Cat. Myst.* iii 2, 3), and effects the consecration of the elements in the Eucharist, so that the very body and blood of Christ is received (*ibid.* iii 3, iv 3, v 7); and he is the giver of various gifts and graces for ministry.

by way of negation, when he declares that none of the things that have come into being is equal in honour with him. None of the order of the angels has equality with him. He has no peer among them; they are contrasted with him as recipients of a mission of service: whereas he is 'the divinely appointed ruler and teacher and sanctifier' of all angelic orders.[1] But he also insists that the gracious gifts which he gives are all the gifts of the one God—"there are not some gifts of the Father and some of the Son and some of the Holy Spirit . . . the Father freely bestows them all through the Son together with the Holy Spirit";[2] the Holy Spirit is honoured along with Father and Son; and comprehended in the Holy Trinity, and all three together are one God. "Undivided is our faith, inseparable our reverence. We neither separate the Holy Trinity, nor do we make confusion as Sabellius does."[3]

Over against Sabellian 'confusion' he expresses repeatedly the distinct personality of the Spirit. He states with emphasis that it was by his own initiative that he descended upon Christ. He draws attention to the directly personal action attributed to him in many instances.[4]—"He who speaks and sends is living and subsisting (personal) and operating." And once he drives home the teaching of such incidental comments in the words: "It is established that there are various appellations, but one and the same Spirit—the Holy Spirit, living and personally subsisting and always present together with the Father and the Son; not as being spoken or breathed forth from the mouth and lips of the Father and the Son, or diffused into the air; but as a personally existing being, himself speaking and operating and exercising his dispensation and hallowing, since it is certain that the dispensation of salvation in regard to us which proceeds from Father and Son and Holy Spirit is indivisible and concordant and one."[5]

With regard to the procession, he quotes the report of the discourse of the Lord contained in the Fourth Gospel, bidding his pupils attend to it rather than to the words of men;[6] and in another passage he brings together two sayings of Christ to shew that the Son himself derives from the Father that which he

---

[1] See esp. xvi 23 and viii 5, excluding the idea that the Spirit was among the δοῦλα of the Son.

[2] xvi 24.   [3] xvi 4; cf. iv 16.   [4] *E.g.* xvii 9, 28, 83, 34.

[5] xvii 5.   [6] xvii 11.

gives in turn to the Spirit.[1] More than this he did not think fit to say to catechumens, even if he was prepared at all to define more closely the mystery of the relation between the Holy Spirit and the Father and the Son.

The Need for Authoritative Guidance on the Doctrine

The first clear indication that the question was becoming ripe for synodical consideration is seen in the anathemas appended to the Creed of the Synod of Sirmium in 351 [2] against any one who styled the Father, Son, and Holy Ghost 'one person' ($\pi\rho\acute{o}\sigma\omega\pi\sigma\nu$), or spoke of the Holy Spirit as the 'unbegotten God', or as not other than the Son, or as a 'part' ($\mu\acute{e}\rho\sigma\varsigma$) of the Father or of the Son, or described the Father, Son, and Holy Spirit as 'three Gods'.

The Teaching of Athanasius

Some years later the growth of the doctrine that the Spirit was merely a creature, and one of the 'ministering spirits', superior to the angels only in degree, was reported by Sarapion, Bishop of Thmuis, in the Delta, to Athanasius, who was then in exile in the desert. Athanasius in reply drew up a statement of the doctrine of the deity of the Spirit.[3]

The particular assailants of the doctrine of whom Sarapion told him professed to regard the Son as divine, and this furnishes Athanasius with his chief argument all through. The relation of the Son to the Father is admitted in the sense of the Creed of Nicaea, and the relation of the Spirit to the Son in the sense of the Scriptures. These are the two premises. Athanasius sets himself in various ways to shew that the Homoousia

---

[1] xvi 24: "All things were committed to me by the Father ", and "he receives of mine and shall declare it to you ".

[2] Hahn [3] p. 198.

[3] He sent four letters in all (*ad Sarapionem Orationes* iv)—the first a long one, the second and third intended to be simpler (the second really deals with the Godhead of the Son, while the third summarizes the first), and the fourth in reply to objections (particularly with regard to the blasphemy against the Holy Spirit). [A convenient edition of the letters in *Bibliotheca Patr. Graec. dogmatica*, ed. Thilo, vol. i.]

The opponents of the doctrine against whom he argues he calls Tropici (Metaphoricals), because they would interpret as tropes or metaphors the passages of Scripture in which the doctrine was expressed.

14

of the Spirit is a necessary inference from them. On this theme he rings the changes. It recurs with each fresh argument, in answer to each objection. The Spirit is the Spirit of the Son and has the same unity with him as the Son has with the Father. If therefore the Son is not a creature, it is impossible that his Spirit can be. And further, as it is impossible to separate the Spirit from the Son, their doctrine would introduce into the Trinity a foreign and alien nature, so that they really destroy the Trinity and really come to a Duality instead. Their error as to the Spirit involves necessarily error also as to the Son, and error as to the Son involves error as to the Father (i 2; cf. i 9 and 21). The Trinity as a whole is 'one God' (i 17) indivisible and homogeneous. The term 'Spirit' is used in various senses in the Scriptures; but, when the Holy Spirit is meant, the article or some further designation (such as 'Holy', 'of the Father', 'of the Son') is always added to the mere term Spirit; and it is only passages in which the word occurs by itself that even seem to lend themselves to their interpretation (i 3, 4). To prove this he cites a great number of instances from Old and New Testaments alike.[1] And later on he argues that the giver of life, and of all the endowments which the Spirit confers, can be no creature, but must be divine (§§ 22, 23).

Nor is there any more support in Scripture for the view that he is an angel[2] (i 10–14).

But driven from Scripture, as they could find nothing to their purpose there, they go on, out of the overflowing of their own heart, to produce a new argument:—if not a creature and not an angel, if he proceeds from the Father, he must be called a Son; and so the Word would not be 'Only-begotten', and there will be two brothers in the Trinity. Or yet again, if he is said to be the Spirit of the Son, then the Father is grandfather of the Holy Spirit (§ 15). It is against these inferences that Athanasius works out the doctrine of the procession of the Spirit, though he protests against being compelled to enter upon such questions at all. He begins by shewing that human

[1] The passage which he starts from as typical of the passages in which they supposed he was represented as a creature (but which, Athanasius says, do not refer to him) is Amos 4¹³.

[2] The chief passage on which they depended was 1 Tim. 5²¹, "I charge thee before God and the Lord Jesus Christ and the elect angels" (arguing that, as the Spirit is not expressly mentioned, he must be included among the angels).

analogies will not apply—a human 'father' is always the 'son' of another (he has been son before he in turn became father); but in the Trinity this is not so, there have been always both Father and Son, each always remaining the same (§ 16).[1]

It is on Scripture that we must depend, and Scripture describes the Father as the Fountain, and the Son as the River, and we drink of the Spirit or the Father as the Light, and the Son as the radiance, and with the Spirit we are illumined.

The Father alone is wise, the Son is his Wisdom, and we receive the Spirit of wisdom. In no case can one be separated from another. When we receive life in the Spirit, Christ himself dwells in us, and the works which he does in us are also the works of the Father (§ 19). All things which are the Father's are also the Son's ; therefore the things which are given us by the Son in the Spirit are the Father's gifts. They are given from the Father, through the Son, in the Holy Spirit (§ 30). All come from one God (cf. iii 5).

The Spirit is the Son's own image, and he is said to proceed from the Father,[2] because he shines forth and is sent and given by the Logos (παρὰ τοῦ λόγου) who is from the Father (§ 20). He is the Son's very own (ἴδιον τοῦ υἱοῦ) and not foreign to God (ξένον τοῦ θεοῦ) (§ 25).

He is said to be in God Himself and from God Himself. Now since, in the case of the Son, "because he is from the Father, he is (admittedly) proper to the essence of the Father (ἴδιος τῆς οὐσίας αὐτοῦ) ; it follows in the case of the Spirit, that, since he is admitted to be from God, he is proper to the Son in essence (ἴδιον κατ' οὐσίαν τοῦ υἱοῦ). . . . He is proper to the deity of the Father.[3] . . . In him the Trinity is complete [4] (§ 25). Of the Trinity, which is like itself and indivisible in nature, and of which the actions and operations are one (§ 28), the holiness also is one, the eternity one, the immutable nature one (§ 30).

This is the ancient tradition and teaching and faith of the Catholic Church, received from the Lord, preached by Apostles,

---

[1] Cf. iv 6. The Father is always Father, and the Son always Son, and the Holy Spirit is and is called always Holy Spirit.

[2] The terms are παρὰ (or ἐκ) τοῦ πατρὸς διὰ τοῦ υἱοῦ.

[3] He is also in Him (iv 4).

[4] The Scriptures further prove his divinity by shewing him to be immutable and invariable and ubiquitous (§ 26 ; cf. iii 4). So too his functions prove his difference from men—the principle of sanctification cannot be like that which it sanctifies : the source of life for creatures cannot itself be a creature.

and preserved by the Fathers,—it is the very foundation of the Church—and no one who falls away from it can be, or can be said to be, any longer a Christian. This was the foundation which the Lord himself bade the Apostles lay for the Church when he said to them ' Go ye and make disciples of all nations, baptizing them into the name of the Father and of the Son and of the Holy Spirit ' (§ 28).

Those who dare to separate the Trinity and reckon the Holy Spirit among created things are as audacious as the Pharisees of old who attributed to Beelzebub the works of the Holy Spirit —let them take heed lest along with them they incur punishment without hope of forgiveness here or hereafter (§ 33).

Hilary of Poictiers

At the same time as Athanasius was expounding the doctrine in the East, Hilary of Poictiers, a representative of the Nicene faith in the West, was maintaining similar teaching in more systematic form [1] in his treatise *On the Trinity*, written during his exile in Phrygia. Particularly noteworthy is what he says of the procession. The Father and the Son are his authors. He is through (*per*) him through whom are all things (*i.e.* the Son), and from (*ex*) him from whom are all things (*i.e.* the Father). . . . The Spirit receives from the Son and so from the Father also, so that he may be said to receive from each ; but Hilary does not decide whether receiving connotes proceeding, nor does he venture to speak of a procession of the Spirit from the Father and the Son. His own phrase is *ex Patre per filium*.[2]

The Theories of Macedonius

The chief representative known to us of the Arian teaching with regard to the Holy Spirit is Macedonius, who had been appointed Bishop of Constantinople after the deposition and subsequent murder of Paul (a Nicene), but was himself in turn

---

[1] The importance of the great dogmatic work of Hilary (358 or 359)—at a time when comparatively few Christians in the West could read such treatises as those of Athanasius in Greek—can hardly be exaggerated, whatever blemishes in the execution of the work there may have been, and though Augustine was destined to overshadow and supersede Hilary. (Aug. *De Trinitate* was published more than fifty years later, c. 416.) See Cazenove 'Hilarius Pictaviensis' *D.C.B.*

[2] See Swete 'Holy Ghost' *D.C.B.*

deposed by the Synod of Constantinople in 360.[1] In his retirement he is said to have elaborated the theories connected with his name; teaching that whereas the Son was God, in all things and in essence like the Father, yet the Holy Spirit was without part in the same dignities, and rightly designated a servant and a minister similar to the angels.[2] If not true God he must be a creature. The favourite argument seems to have been a *reductio ad absurdum* : the Holy Spirit is either begotten or not begotten; if not begotten, then there are two unoriginated beings—Father and Spirit; if begotten, he must be begotten either of the Father or of the Son—if of the Father then there are two Sons in the Trinity (and therefore Brothers); if of the Son, then there is a Grandson of God, a θεὸς υἱωνός.[3]

The Doctrine declared at the Council of Alexandria 362, and subsequent Synods in the East and in the West

The question came before a synod for the first time at Alexandria in 362, on the return of Athanasius from his third exile.[4] The view that the Holy Spirit is a creature and separate from the essence of Christ was there declared anathema, " for those who, while pretending to cite the faith confessed at Nicaea, venture to blaspheme the Holy Spirit, do nothing more than in words deny the Arian heresy while they retain it in thought ". And all present agreed in the faith in " a Holy Trinity, not a Trinity in name only, but really existing and subsisting, both a Father really existing and subsisting, and a Son really and essentially existing and subsisting, and a Holy Spirit subsisting and himself existing: a Holy Trinity, but one Godhead, and one Beginning (*or* principle); and that the Son is co-essential with the Father, as the

---

[1] The synod dominated by Acacius at which, in the Arian interest, the strict Homoean formula ('like' only) was agreed to, and Semi-Arians and Anomoeans alike were suppressed. Macedonius and others (*e.g.* Basil of Ancyra and Cyril of Jerusalem) were deposed really because they were Semi-Arians, to whom the strict Homoean formula seemed 'Arian', but nominally on various charges of irregularity. See Hefele *Councils* vol. ii p. 273, and *supra* p. 185.

[2] So Soz. *H.E.* iv 27. His followers were known as Macedonians or Pneumatomachi (contenders against the Spirit) or Marathonians, from Marathonius, Bishop of Nicomedia, a chief supporter of the teaching.

[3] See *e.g.* Greg. Naz. *Or. Theol.* v 7, and Athanasius *supra* p. 210.

[4] See *supra* p. 185, and Ath. *ad Antiochenos*, esp. §§ 5, 6. Note the claim to hold the Nicene faith along with the 'Macedonian' doctrine of the Holy Spirit. Cf. Theodoret *H.E.* iv 3.

fathers said; while the Holy Spirit is not a creature, nor foreign, but proper to, and inseparable from, the essence of the Father and the Son. . . . For we believe that there is one Godhead, and that its nature is one, and not that there is one nature of the Father, to which that of the Son and of the Holy Spirit are foreign."

From this statement it seems clear that a more ample profession of faith in the Holy Spirit than the Creed of Nicaea supplied was at this time required as a condition of the restoration of Arians to communion. Special circumstances were in view and were provided for in this particular way. But there is no proof that any fresh definition was pressed upon others. There is, on the contrary, evidence to shew that Athanasius approved of the policy of non-intervention which Basil followed in the matter.[1]

About this time the same faith was embodied in a letter to the Emperor Jovian,[2] declaring that the Holy Spirit must not be separated from the Father and the Son, but rather glorified together with the Father and the Son in the one faith of the Holy Trinity, because there is only one Godhead in the Holy Trinity.

A few years later (366 ff.), synods at Rome under Damasus condemned the Arian or Macedonian conceptions, and maintained the Trinity of one Godhead, power, majesty, and essence; and the profession of faith addressed to the Eastern bishops, which was published by one of these synods in 369,[3] was in 378 (*or* 379) subscribed by a hundred and forty-six Eastern bishops at Antioch.

The Epiphanian Creed

The heresy, however, gained ground, and the need for an expansion of the Creed to cover this fresh subject grew urgent. A short expression of the general traditional belief was already in existence in the Creed contained in the *Ancoratus*[4] of Epi-

---

[1] Basil was suspected and attacked by the monks because of his reserve in speaking of the doctrine of the Holy Spirit. Athanasius wrote in his support and defence, urging his children to obey him as their father, and to consider his intention and purpose (his οἰκονομία)—"to the weak he becomes weak to gain the weak". He is utterly astonished at the boldness of those who venture to speak against him (Ath. *Epp.* 62 and 63; Basil *Ep.* 204).

[2] Theodoret *H.E.* iv 3. Dr. Robertson 'Athanasius' lxxxiv *n* has shewn that Theodoret is mistaken as to a synod being held in 363; but the letter remains.

[3] This is known as the 'Tome of Damasus'. The anathemas repudiate in detail all false ideas about the Spirit and maintain the divine attributes of each person of the Trinity (see Hahn[3] p. 271). They shew what teaching was current.

[4] Hahn[3] p. 134. But as to the origin of this Creed see *supra* p. 188 n. 1.

phanius, Bishop of Salamis in Cyprus, which was published in 374. It declares in simple untechnical phrase the divine personality of the Spirit, as one to be worshipped and glorified together with the Father and the Son; his procession from the Father; his pre-existence as the source or power of life and the Inspirer of the prophets; and his operation in the Incarnation of the Son.

Simple and unsystematic as the language of this Creed is, it clearly recognises the personality, the eternity, and the divinity of the Holy Spirit; and his chief functions.

(a) The Personality. He is co-ordinated with the Father and the Son, the same form of words being used—εἰς ἕνα θεὸν πατέρα —καὶ εἰς ἕνα κύριον . . . τὸν υἱόν—καὶ εἰς τὸ πνεῦμα τὸ ἅγιον. He too is κύριον as the Son, and he proceeds ἐκ τοῦ πατρός (i.e. ἐκ τῆς οὐσίας τοῦ πατρός, he was therefore in the Father). He is worshipped and glorified together with (σύν) . . . as a person.

(b) The Eternity. This is implied in the phrases which shew the personality, particularly by the present ἐκπορευόμενον, which connotes neither beginning nor end; also, to some extent, by the operations attributed to him, especially the title ζωοποιόν.

(c) The Divinity. He is placed on a level with the Father and the Son, styled Lord, said to be in the Father, and to be worshipped as only one who is God can be—along with the Father and the Son.

(d) His Operations. He is the source of all real life (making alive—Giver of Life), the source of inspiration of the prophets, the agent in the Incarnation of the Son; and by collocation he is the source of the graces which the 'holy' Church administers.

(e) His relation to the Godhead is simply described in the words 'proceeding from the Father'.[1]

---

[1] The 'procession' is stated to be from the Father, and the Eastern theologians generally laid stress on the derivation of the Spirit from the Father (without denying it from the Son also, but preferring the expression 'through the Son' as medium—as Tertullian in the West had said a Patre per filium). So Epiphanius never uses the word 'procession' to express the relation of the Spirit to the Son. He only says that he receives of him 'proceeding from (ἐκ or ἀπὸ) the Father and receiving of the Son' (τοῦ Υἱοῦ λάμβανον; cf. John 15²⁶ and 16¹⁴). But he does not hesitate to say that the Spirit is 'from the Father and the Son' and 'from the same essence' or Godhead (always using the prepositions ἐκ or παρά; see Ancor. 8, 9, 67, 73, 69-70; adv. Haer. lxii 4).

It will thus be seen that though, in common with the Greek Fathers, he does not express the procession from the Son, he comes nearer in his language than others to putting the Father and the Son together as the joint source of derivation of the Spirit.

In the West, Ambrose, writing a little later (381) (see de Sp. S. i 11) makes the derivation of the Spirit dependent on the Son; and the declaration of Cyril of

Compared with the Creed of Nicaea (which, however, was only intended to deal with the doctrine of the Person of Christ, see *supra* p. 168 n. 2) all these clauses are new, except the one bare statement of faith ' in the Holy Spirit '.[1] But they only amount

Alexandria that the Spirit is the Son's very own (Anathema ix against Nestorius —Hahn [3] p. 315) was approved by the Council of Ephesus in 431.

The first definite denial that the Holy Spirit receives his essence from the Son (as well as from the Father) was expressed by Theodoret in answer to Cyril's anathema. If, by the Spirit being the Son's very own, Cyril only meant to describe him as of the same nature and proceeding from the Father, he would agree and accept the phrase as pious ; but if he meant that the Spirit derived his being from the Son or through the Son, then he must reject it as blasphemous and impious. Cyril in reply justified his expression (without going into Theodoret's charge), on the ground that the Spirit proceeds from God the Father but is not alien from the Son, who has all 'things along with the Father according to his own declaration, "All things that the Father hath are mine—therefore said I to you that He shall take of mine and shall declare it to you". And the Council of Ephesus, at which his anathemas were approved, condemned a Creed of Theodore of Mopsuestia (Hahn [3] p. 302), which incidentally denied that the Spirit had received his being through the Son. But the question was not further examined or discussed for some time in the East. [On Theodore's peculiar conceptions of the Spirit see Swete *l.c.* p. 127.]

Augustine (see *infra*), and Leo after him (*Ep.* xciii 1), taught 'from the Father and the Son', and this became the conception so thoroughly accepted in the West that the additional words expressing it appear to have been inserted in the Creed in its Latin version without the insertion attracting attention. At a Council held at Toledo in 589 (summoned by Reccared, king of the Visigoths), to emphasize the national renunciation of Arianism, the Creed was quoted with the words 'et Filio' added. There is no evidence to shew that the addition was intentional ; the Creed was little known in the West at the time, and the Council no doubt supposed that the Latin version recited was a true translation of the original Greek. It was further ordered that the Creed should henceforward be recited before the *Pater noster* in the Eucharist. As a defence against Arianism the addition was eminently useful, and the doctrine it taught was emphasized by several subsequent synods. It was contained in a local creed put forth by a synod at Hatfield in 680. But it was not till after the middle of the eighth century that the doctrine of the procession was formally debated at a Council: first in 767 at Gentilly, near Paris, when some Eastern bishops were present, and the question was not regarded as urgent: then in 787 at Nicaea, when the doctrine of the procession 'from the Father through the Son' was approved : then in 794, at a great assembly of Western bishops at Frankfort, when the cultus of images approved at Nicaea was disallowed and the doctrine of the procession from the Son was reasserted and supported by the influence of the Emperor Charles the Great: and again in 809, at a Council at Aix, at which both the doctrine and the interpolation in the Creed were vindicated. The Pope, Leo III., however, while agreeing in the doctrine, refused to sanction the addition of the words *et Filio* to the ancient Creed of the Church, authorized by a General Council and universally received ; and, though the use continued elsewhere in the West, it was not till two centuries later that it found its way into the Church of Rome. Meanwhile it had been one of the matters of controversy that led to the breach of communion between the Church of the East and the Church of the West. [On the form of the Creed at Toledo see Burn *Introd. to Creeds* p. 115.]

[1] The Creed contains all the chief Nicene clauses and anathemas.

to a scanty summary of the teaching which, as is shewn above, an ordinary presbyter gave his catechumens before any controversy as to the Holy Spirit arose. (The words τὸν παρά-κλητον which are in Cyril's own Creed have dropped out.)

And, indeed, Epiphanius himself declares that this was the faith which was handed 'down' by all the holy bishops, together above three hundred and ten in number'—that is, by those who composed the Council of Nicaea : a statement which is literally inaccurate, but no doubt conveys the truth as regards the convictions of the bishops in question.

This Creed, no doubt, was the Baptismal Creed in use in Salamis (and probably throughout Palestine), but Epiphanius also gives a longer one [1] (probably composed by himself), more a paraphrase than a creed, which was required of candidates for baptism who had been or were suspected of still being connected with any of the heresies then rife. With regard to the Holy Spirit its terms are these : "And we believe in (εἰς τὸ . . .) the Holy Spirit, who spake in the law and preached in the persons of the prophets and came down upon the Jordan, speaking in the apostles, dwelling in the saints ; thus we believe in him (ἐν αὐτῷ), that he is the Holy Spirit, the Spirit of God, the perfect Spirit, the Spirit Paraclete, uncreated, proceeding from the Father and received [2] from the Son and an object of faith ", — and in the anathema appended to the Creed the catechumen is required to repudiate, in regard to the Holy Spirit also, all the Arian phrases which the Nicene Council anathematized in regard to the Son.

There was thus, it is clear, abundant teaching being given in the Church to counteract the effects of the theories of the Macedonians, and the way was prepared for the full assertion of the doctrine of the Trinity by a General Council.

Basil's Treatise on the Holy Spirit

About the same time, in reponse to the prompting of his friend Amphilochius, Bishop of Iconium, Basil wrote his treatise on the Holy Spirit (374–375).

He begins by explaining that he had been criticized because

---

[1] Hahn [3] p. 135.

[2] A variant reading gives the active sense 'receiving'; cf. John 16[14]. The phrase is first found here.

he had used two forms of the doxology, " to God the Father *through* the Son *in* the Holy Spirit ", and " *with* the Son *together with* the Holy Spirit ";[1] that the two forms were regarded as mutually inconsistent, and the latter as an innovation. Aetius had framed a rule by which the use of the prepositions in Scripture was governed, and argued that the difference of use corresponded to, and clearly indicated, a difference of nature (§ 2); and according to this rule the first form of doxology only was legitimate—God being widely differentiated from the Son, and both from the Spirit.

In the first place, therefore, Basil argues that the rule is imaginary, and that no such distinction holds in the use of the sacred writers; and, having established this point, he infers that the use of identical terms should shame his opponents into admitting that no difference of essence either exists (§ 11).

He insists that the Church knows both uses and does not deprecate either as destructive of the other. Sometimes *with* (μετά), sometimes *through* (διά), is the more appropriate; according as, for example, praise or thanksgiving for blessings received through the Son is the more immediate purpose (§ 16).

Then, after an enquiry into the real meaning of the expression ' *through* the Son ', he passes on (§ 22) to his chief subject —the doctrine of the Spirit, in the Scriptures, and in the unwritten tradition received from the Fathers. After a glowing description of the nature of the Spirit and the manifold forms of his gracious influence and varied gifts (the crown of all of which is said to be ' abiding in God, likeness to God, and the supreme desire of the heart—becoming God '), he meets in succession objections urged against his being ranked with God in nature and glory.[2] In the course of the review of the evidence of Scripture and tradition he is led to conclusions such as the following :—

" He who does not believe in the Spirit does not believe in the Son, and he who does not believe in the Son does not believe in the Father." " In every operation the Spirit is conjoined with and inseparable from the Father and the Son."[3] In every dis-

---

[1] διὰ τοῦ υἱοῦ ἐν τῷ ἁγίῳ πνεύματι and μετὰ τοῦ υἱοῦ σὺν τῷ πνεύματι τῷ ἁγίῳ.

[2] Among other interesting points in the course of the discussion are the description of the effects of Baptism (§ 26 ; cf. § 35), the references to baptism into Christ only (§ 28), the value of the secret unwritten tradition (§ 66).

[3] To express with some show of ' worldly wisdom ' the idea that the Spirit was not co-ordinate with Father and Son but subordinate to them, the opponents of the

tribution of gifts the Holy Spirit is present with the Father and the Son, of his own authority (in his own right), dispensing in proportion to the deserts of each. And in our own experience, in the reception of the gifts, it is with the Holy Spirit—the distributer—that we first meet; and then we are put in mind of the Sender (that is, the Son); and then we carry up our thoughts to the fountain and author of the blessings (§ 37). It is through the Spirit that all the dispensations are carried out—Creation, the Old Covenant, the Incarnation in all its circumstances, the ministry of the Church, the future Advent (§ 39; cf. 49).

The Spirit's relation to the Father is thus essential and eternal. There is no doubt about the distinction of the three persons and the unity of essence. The one Spirit, conjoined through the one Son with the one Father Himself, completes the adorable and blessed Trinity (§ 45).

The Spirit is from God . . . he comes forth from God: yet not by generation as the Son, but as the spirit of his mouth. But he is also called the Spirit of Christ, as being in respect of nature made his own (ᾠκειωμένον κατὰ τὴν φύσιν αὐτῷ § 46); he is as it were an 'intimate' of the Son. He is thus in some sense through the Son; but Basil indicates rather than expresses this conception.

After shewing at length that the prepositions in question have been and may be used indifferently, he points to the advantages of 'with' (σύν § 59). It is as effectual as 'and' in refuting the mischief of Sabellius and establishing the distinction of persons, and it also bears conspicuous witness to the eternal communion and perpetual conjunction which exists between them. 'With' exhibits the mutual conjunction of those who are associated together in some action, while 'in' shews their relation to the sphere in which they are operating (§ 60).

Other reasons are then given for glorifying the Spirit, and the treatise concludes with a sombre picture of the state of the times, in which self-appointed place-hunters first get rid of the dispensation of the Holy Spirit, and then allot to one another the chief offices in all the Churches.

doctrine adopted a curious verbal subtlety and argued that he was not 'numbered with' them, but was 'numbered under' them, and that co-numeration suits things equal in honour, but sub-numeration things relatively inferior (§§ 13, 41, 42). Basil says this doctrine of sub-numeration introduces polytheism into Christian theology (§ 47). Number has not really any place in the sphere of the Divine. Cf. also Greg. Naz. Or. Theol. v 17 ff.

Gregory of Nyssa—Quod non sint tres Dei

The same teaching was being given by Gregory of Nyssa too about the same time. The devoted younger brother of Basil, of whom he constantly speaks as his ' master ', while not intending to depart in any way from his brother's teaching, he certainly gave it somewhat more formal expression in some connexions, and contributed largely to win currency for the ' Cappadocian ' theological distinctions.

As in his treatise on *Common Notions* (Migne *P.G.* xlv pp. 175–186), so in his letter to Ablabius, *That there are not three Gods* (*ibid.* pp. 115–136),[1] written about 375, he works out the position that ' God ' is a term indicative of *essence* (being), not declarative of *persons* (not προσώπων δηλωτικόν but οὐσίας σημαντικόν); and therefore it is, and must be, always used in the singular with each of the names of the persons.   So we say ' God the Father, God the Son, and God the Holy Spirit ', and if we insert the conjunction ' and ' between the clauses it is only to conjoin the terms which declare the persons, not the term which indicates the singularity of the essence.   The three terms express the three modes of being, the three relations ; but the being remains one and the same, and the term expressing it must therefore always be used in the singular.

The analogy of human nature and the common use in the plural of the term ' man ', which expresses it, no doubt presents a difficulty.   (This was the question Ablabius had put to Gregory.) But strictly, it is an abuse of language to speak of so many ' men ' ; it would be more accurate to describe each individual (Peter, James, John) as a ' hypostasis ' of ' man '.   Only in this case we tolerate the inaccuracy, because there is no danger of our thinking that there are many human natures, while in respect to the Deity we might be thought to have some community of doctrine with the polytheism of the heathen.   This is a solution of the difficulty sufficient for most men.   Yet the difference of use may be justified by a deeper reason.   The term ' Godhead ' is really significant of operation (ἐνέργεια) rather than of nature. And the operations of men (even of those who are engaged in the same spheres of work) are separate and individual, whereas the operations of the Godhead are always effected by the Three together " without mark of time or distinction—since there is no

[1] An English translation in ' Gregory of Nyssa' *N. and P-N. F.*

delay, existent or conceived, in the motion of the divine will from the Father, through the Son, to the Spirit ". " In the case of the divine nature we do not learn that the Father does anything by Himself in which the Son does not work conjointly, or again, that the Son has any special operation apart from the Holy Spirit; but every operation which extends from God to the creation, and is named according to our variable conceptions of it, has its origin from the Father, and proceeds through the Son, and is perfected in the Holy Spirit."

An objection which Gregory foresees might be brought against this argument—that by not admitting the difference of nature there was danger of a mixture and confusion of the persons—leads him to his most characteristic statement of the distinction between the persons as based on a constant causal relation. " While we confess the invariable character of the nature, we do not deny the difference in regard to that which causes and that which is caused ($\tau\grave{\eta}\nu$ $\kappa\alpha\tau\grave{\alpha}$ $\tau\grave{o}$ $\alpha\H{\iota}\tau\iota\iota\nu$ $\kappa\alpha\grave{\iota}$ $\alpha\H{\iota}\tau\iota\alpha\tau\grave{o}\nu$ $\delta\iota\alpha\phi\rho\rho\acute{\alpha}\nu$), wherein alone we conceive that the one is distinguished from the other—namely, by our belief that the one is that which causes, and the other of or from that which causes. And we apprehend yet another difference in that which is of or from the cause: for one (part) is directly from the first, and another (part) is through that which is directly from the first . . . so that in the case of the Son the fact that he is Only-begotten remains undoubted and does not throw doubt on the fact that the Spirit is from the Father, inasmuch as the mediation (or intermediate position sc. between Father and Spirit) of the Son guards for him the fact that he is Only-begotten, and does not exclude the Spirit from his relation of nature to the Father." At the same time, the difference in respect to causation denotes no difference of nature, but only a difference in the mode of existence (e.g. that the Father does not exist by generation, and that the Son does not exist without generation). It does not touch the question of existence—of nature. That he exists we believe first—viz. what God is: then we consider how He is. " The divine nature itself is apprehended through every conception as invariable and undivided; and therefore one Godhead and one God, and all the other names which relate to God, are rightly proclaimed in the singular."

In this argument it is clear that the absolute co-eternity and co-equality of the Three Persons is recognized. The idea of causation serves only to distinguish the three modes of existence. God is one (ὁ Θεός); but within His being there is Cause (τὸ αἴτιον), to which the name 'Father' corresponds, and there is caused (τὸ αἰτιατόν), which includes the immediately caused (τὸ προσεχῶς ἐκ τοῦ πρώτου) to which the name 'Son' corresponds, and the mediately caused (τὸ διὰ τοῦ προσεχῶς ἐκ τοῦ πρώτου) to which the name 'Holy Spirit' corresponds. The Holy Spirit is thus in such wise '*from* the Father', that he is also '*through* the Son'. And this connexion of the Spirit with the Son and the Father is Gregory's teaching also in his other writings, though not always in the same terms.[1]

A year later, in 376, a synod at Iconium, presided over by the bishop to whom Basil had written, decided that the Nicene Creed was enough, but that in doxologies the Spirit should be glorified together with the Father and the Son; and the doctrine of the Spirit was laid down as Basil had taught it. And his treatise itself was at this time formally sanctioned and confirmed by a synod in Cappadocia.[2]

The prevailing uncertainty reflected in the Sermons of Gregory of Nazianzus

The uncertainty, however, which still prevailed is clearly reflected in one of the sermons which Gregory of Nazianzus

---

[1] Cf. the *Oratio Catechetica* ii, "an essential power existing in its own proper person, but incapable of being separated from God, in whom it is, or from the Word of God, whom it accompanies"; On the Holy Spirit (Migne xlv p. 1304), ἐκ τοῦ θεοῦ ἐστι, καὶ τοῦ χριστοῦ ἐστι, καθὼς γέγραπται; "not to be confounded with the Father in being unoriginate, nor with the Son in being only-begotten"; the image of a separate flame burning on three torches—the third flame caused by that of the first being transmitted to the middle and then kindling the end torch; "proceeding from the Father, receiving from the Son"; "The Father is always Father, and in Him the Son, and with the Son the Holy Spirit"; and On the Holy Trinity (cf. Basil *Ep.* 189 *or* 80), in which the main argument is that the identity of operation seen in regard to Father and Son and Holy Spirit proves identity of nature or essence.

He also touches the line of argument which Augustine afterwards worked out so fully (see *infra* p. 228)—the analogy of our own nature, in which certain shadows and resemblances may be detected that go to prove the existence of a Trinity in the Deity. (See *e.g. Oratio Cat.* i–iii.)

It is to be noted that Gregory of Nyssa does not claim that the οὐσία of the Godhead in itself can be known, but only its ἰδιώματα or γνωρίσματα. See *de Communibus Notionibus* (Migne xlv p. 177), *Refut. alt. lib. Eunomii* (*ibid.* p. 945), *Quod non sint tres dii* (*ibid.* p. 121). So, among others, Augustine *in Joh. Tract.* xxxviii 8, "ego sum qui sum, *quae mens potest capere?*"

[2] Hefele *Councils* vol. ii p. 290.

preached at Constantinople about the year 380, while engaged
in his noble task of building up again a 'Catholic' congregation
in the city which had so long been given over to the Arians.
"Of the wise among us", he says, "some have held the
Holy Spirit to be an Energy, others a Creature, others God.
Others again have not decided which of these he is—out of
reverence, as they say, for the Scriptures, because they lay down
nothing precise upon the point.   On this account they neither
concede to him divine veneration, nor do they refuse him honour;
thus keeping in their disposition concerning him to some sort of
middle way, which, however, is in effect a very wretched way.
Of those, however, who have held him to be God, some keep this
as a pious opinion to themselves (are pious so far as opinion
goes), while others have the courage to be pious in expression of
it also.   Others I have heard in some kind of way mete out the
Deity, more wise in that they conceive and acknowledge the
Three as we do, but maintain a great distinction between them,
to the effect that the One is infinite both in respect of being and
of power, the second in respect of power, but not of being, the third
circumscribed in both of these relations." [1]   And while for himself he insists as strongly as possible on his essential eternity
and equality with the other persons of the Godhead—which
cannot be complete, and therefore cannot be Godhead without
him (§ 4)—he is certainly God, and if God necessarily co-essential
with the Father (§ 10); and while he sweeps away all inquisitive and petty reasonings about his generation and origin by
appeal to the Lord's own words as to procession, and refuses to
enquire into its nature or to attempt to invade the mysteries of
the divine existence—it is enough to know that he is not begotten but proceeds: yet he seems to regard the uncertainty of
former times with no little sympathy, as in harmony with the
appointed order of developement in the revelation of truth—
"the Old Testament proclaimed the Father clearly, but the Son
more darkly; the New Testament plainly revealed the Son, but
only indicated the deity of the Spirit.[2]   Now the Holy Spirit
lives among us and makes the manifestation of himself more
certain to us; for it was not safe, so long as the divinity of the
Father was still unrecognized, to proclaim openly that of the

[1] Greg. Naz. *Or.* 31 § 5 (*Or. Theol.* v § 5).
[2] Language of this kind might have seemed to the Montanists of earlier times to
support their main conceptions.

Son ; and, so long as this was still not accepted, to impose the burden of the Spirit, if so bold a phrase may be allowed." [1]

From the point of view of Gregory the Macedonians would be lagging behind the necessary—the divinely appointed—course of developement of revelation of the nature of the Godhead. And before, and at the time of, the Council of Constantinople in 381 every effort was made to win them over to the recognition of the truth and the unity of the Church—unfortunately in vain.

The Council of Constantinople

Amongst the bishops who were present there appears to have been no uncertainty as to the doctrine of the Church ; [2] they reaffirmed the Nicene Creed with an explanation [3] of various points of doctrine, among which the Godhead of the Spirit was affirmed, and every heresy was declared anathema ; [4] and the emperor gave authoritative expression to their conviction and decision when he issued the command—at the close of the Council—that " all the churches were at once to be surrendered to the bishops who believed in the Oneness of the Godhead of the Father, the Son, and the Holy Spirit ". [5]

And so the faith in the triune personality of God was proclaimed against the last attempt of Arianism, and the Catholic interpretation established—one God existing permanently and eternally in three spheres of consciousness and activity, three

[1] *Ibid.* § 26 ff. See the whole of this Sermon, esp. §§ 9, 10 and 28 for the testimony of Scripture to the Holy Spirit.

[2] They included (besides those mentioned) Cyril of Jerusalem, Helladius the successor of Basil at Caesarea, Gregory of Nyssa, and Amphilochius of Iconium—all well versed no doubt in the Catholic doctrine.

[3] This is not extant, but the synod which met at Constantinople in the following year states that the Council had put forth a tome, and at Chalcedon they were said to have communicated their decisions to the Westerns (Hefele ii p. 348). It is not certain to which of the Councils—in 381 or in 382—some of the canons attributed to the Council of 381 belong. The synodical letter of the Council of 382 (to Damasus and other Western bishops), excusing themselves from attending a Council at Rome, is given in Theodoret *H.E.* v 9, and again declares the faith that there is " one godhead, power, and essence of the Father and of the Son and of the Holy Spirit ; the dignity being equal in three perfect hypostases (ὑποστάσεσιν) and three perfect persons (προσώποις) ".

[4] The heresies specified are those of the Eunomians or Anomoeans, the Arians or Eudoxians, the Semi-Arians or Pneumatomachians, the Sabellians, Marcellians, Photinians, and Apollinarians.

[5] "One and the same Godhead in the hypostasis of three Persons of equal honour and of equal power ; namely, the Father, the Son, and the Holy Spirit."— Soz. *H.E.* vii 9. On July 30, 381.

modes, three forms, three persons : in the inner relations of the divine life as well as in the outer relations of the Godhead to the world and to men.

From this time forward it was only in connexion with the procession of the Spirit that any fresh developement of the doctrine is to be noted.   But it was so lucidly summed up, and in some of its aspects so appealingly presented by Augustine, that a short statement of his summary of it may be given in conclusion.[1]

Augustine's Statement of the Doctrine

The aim of his treatise is to shew that " the one and only and true God is a Trinity, and that the Father, Son, and Holy Spirit are rightly said and believed to be of one and the same substance or essence " (i 4).   First of all the proof from Scripture is detailed, and passages which are alleged against the equality of the Son are examined (14 ff).   By the way, the puzzle how the Trinity is said to operate in everything which God operates, and yet particular actions are attributed exclusively to particular Persons is noted. With regard to the Holy Spirit, special stress is laid on the use in connexion with him of the verb λατρεύειν (which is used of divine service) : and interesting distinctions are drawn with regard to the Incarnate Son between the *forma Dei* and the *forma servi*, in explanation of passages in Scripture in which he is spoken of as less than the Father—some things being said according to ' the form of God ', and some according to ' the form of a servant '.

To elucidate the relations to the Trinity of the Son and the Holy Spirit in their operations, he examines the appearances recorded in the Old Testament, whether they were of the Trinity or of individual Persons, and decides that though some corporeal or outward means were adopted we cannot rashly affirm which Person it was that appeared.[2]

[1] The first Latin treatise devoted to the subject was by Ambrose, the spiritual father of Augustine, in the year of the Council of Constantinople. He answers objections and sets forward such arguments as have already been noticed. He teaches procession from the Son as well as from the Father, but not expressly an eternal procession from the Son. Augustine completed the presentation of the doctrine for the West. He had stated it shortly in the sermon he preached before a Council at Hippo in 393 (see *de Fide et Symbolo*, 16 ff.), and again a few years later in a Sermon to catechumens (§ 13), and also in his sermons on the Gospel of St John (see *Tract.* xcix esp. 6 ff.) ; but it was not till after the year 415 that he published the treatise *On the Trinity*, at which he had been working at intervals for many years, and in which he gave to the doctrine the fullest expression.

[2] Bk. ii ; the means being further considered in bk. iii.

Just as the Son, though said to be sent by the Father, is equal and consubstantial and co-eternal with the Father—the difference between the sender and the sent being only that the Son is from the Father, not the Father from the Son—so too the Holy Spirit is one with them, since these three are one, and he proceeds not only from the Father but also from the Son.[1] The Lord himself says of the Spirit 'whom I will send unto you from the Father' to shew that the Father is the beginning of the whole divinity or Deity: and though this sending of the Holy Spirit is eternal, yet there was a special sending such as had never been before after the glorification of Christ—a sending which was made plain by visible signs. In the case of such sensible manifestations, it is true that the working of the Trinity cannot be seen as indivisible; just as it is impossible for men to name the Three without separation by the intervals of time which each name, Father—Son—Holy Spirit, occupies; yet the Three work indivisibly (§ 30).[2] It is possible to predicate of God

[1] Bk. iv § 27 ff.

[2] To the thought of the inseparable operation and intercommunion of the Three Persons, which Augustine expressed here and again in bk. viii *ad init.*, later theologians applied the term περιχώρησις. Both senses of the verb χωρεῖν, 'move' and 'contain', are included in its meaning. The persons interpenetrate each other, and each contains the other. "The Father, the Son, and the Holy Ghost, while they are in very deed three Persons, still do not by any means exist as three men separately and apart from each other, but they intimately cohere together and are conjoined One with Another, and thus exist One in the Other, and so to speak mutually run into and penetrate each other" (Bull *Def. N.C.* bk. ii ch. ix),—and so the numerical unity of substance is maintained. Latin equivalents of the term are thus either *circumincessio* (the three mutually pervade each other) or *circuminsessio* (the three mutually contain or rest in each other). 'Interpenetration' or 'coinherence' are perhaps the nearest English representatives of the term. The whole Trinity is present in each of the Persons—each is full and complete, and each includes the others: a notion of personality which is so different from ordinary human experience that Augustine shrinks from the use of the term at all (*infra* v 10). The scriptural basis of the doctrine is to be found in the Gospel according to St John 1[18] 10[30] and 14[10, 11] ("the only-begotten Son which is in the bosom of the Father", and "I am in the Father and the Father in me . . . the Father that dwelleth in me"): and Athanasius used it against the Arians (see *Or. c. Ar.* ii 33, 41, and especially iii 1-6), and quoted Dionysius of Rome as expressing the same thought (in language very near to the later technical term), "For it must needs be that with the God of the universe the divine word is united, and the Holy Ghost must repose and habitate in God" (ἐμφιλοχωρεῖν τῷ θεῷ καὶ ἐνδιαιτᾶσθαι—*in Deo manere et habitare*), and supporting it by the same passages of Scripture (*de Decretis* § 26). Similar expression is given to the doctrine in the Macrostichos (Antioch, 345) § ix. "For we have believed that they (the Father and the Son) are conjoined with one another without medium or interval and exist inseparably from one another, the Father entire embosoming the Son, and the Son

'according to substance'—that is in respect to Himself (as good, great), or 'relatively'—that is, in respect to something not Himself (as Father in respect to the Son, and Lord in respect to the Creature). Whatever is spoken of God 'according to substance' is spoken of each person severally and together of the Trinity itself—which is rightly described as one essence, three hypostases or persons; though the term 'persons' is only used for want of a better way of expressing the facts (bk. v, § 10). "For, indeed, since Father is not Son, and Son is not Father, and the Holy Spirit, who is also called the gift of God, is neither Father nor Son, they are certainly three. And so it is said in the plural, 'I and the Father are one'—for he did not say 'is one' as the Sabellians say, but 'are one'. Yet when it is asked what the three are (*quid tres*), human utterance is weighed down by deep poverty of speech. All the same, we say three 'persons', not that we wish to say it, but that we may not be reduced to silence." It is simply, as he says further on in his essay,[1] recurring to the same subject, "for the sake of speaking of things that are ineffable, that we may be able in some way to say what we can in no way say fully"—especially against the devices of errors of heretics—that the terms 'one essence and three persons' are permissible. The persons are not the Trinity, but the Trinity can be called also (the) Holy Spirit, because all three are God, and Spirit, and Holy. He is the gift of both the Father and the Son, the communion of them both, called specially what they are called in common (§ 12).[2] This communion or unity or holiness, which links each to the other, is properly called love (vi 7), for it is written 'God is Love'. And herein may be seen how the Persons in the Deity are three and not more than three: One who loves Him who is from Himself; and One who loves Him from whom He is; and Love itself. And in this Trinity is the supreme source of all things, and the most perfect beauty and the most blessed delight (§ 12).

After a further consideration of some of the aspects of the question already reviewed (bk. vii), and a short recapitulation

entire depending upon and adhering to the Father and alone perpetually (continu-ally) resting in the Father's lap." Hahn[3] p. 195.

[1] *De Trin.* vii §§ 7-10.

[2] They are together the only beginning (*principium*) of the Holy Spirit (§ 15). He is a gift, given in time, but also eternally existent (as a gift may exist before it is given) (§ 16).

of the argument (bk. viii), in which he emphasizes the perfect
equality of all the 'Persons' and the completeness of each in
respect of Deity (no one in the Trinity, nor two together,
nor even all three together, being greater than each one
severally); Augustine passes on to the most characteristic
argument of his essay. On the ground that man is the image
of God, he is led to look for indications of a Trinity in his
constitution—since Scripture also points to this method of
attaining to knowledge of God, the "invisible things of Him
being understood ever since the creation by the things He has
made ".[1]

At the outset he argues that it is by love that we really
arrive at knowledge of the Trinity, and love really implies three
things and is in itself—as it were—a trace of the Trinity.
" Love is of some one that loves, and with love something is
loved. So here are three things: he who loves, and that which
is loved, and love.[2] What else then is love but as it were a
life that links together or seeks to link together some two
things—him that loves, to wit, and that which is loved." This,
then, he says, is where we must look for what we are seeking—
we have not found it, but we have found where it is to be
sought (viii 14).

So in the creature, step by step, he seeks through certain
trinities—each of their own appropriate kind, until he comes at
last to the mind of man—traces of that highest Trinity which
we seek when we seek God. And first (bk. ix 3, 4–8) he finds
a trinity in the mind of man, the knowledge with which it
knows itself, and the love with which it loves itself and its own
knowledge.[3] These three are one and equal and inseparable;
they exist substantially and are predicated relatively; they are
several in themselves, and mutually all in all. The knowledge
of the mind is as it were its offspring and its word concerning
itself, and the offspring is not less than the parent mind, since
the mind knows itself just to the extent of its own being; and
the love is not less since it loves itself just to the extent of
its knowledge and of its being.[4]

---

[1] Rom. 1[20]. Cf. Wisd. 13[1-5] (bk. xv § 3).

[2] Amans, et quod amatur, et amor.

[3] Mens, notitia qua se novit, amor quo se notitiamque suam diligit.

[4] Nec minor proles, dum tantam se novit mens quanta est: nec minor amor dum
tantum se diligit quantum novit et quanta est (ix 18).

Other trinities may be seen in the mind—in memory, understanding, will [1]; in sight—the object, the act of seeing or vision, the attention of the mind or the will which combines the two (though these are not equal nor of one essence, and belong to the sphere of the outer man which is not an image of God [2]); and in connexion with sight, in the mind itself—the image of the object seen which is in the memory, the impression formed from it when the mind's eye is turned to it, the purpose of the will combining both (but this trinity also—though in the mind —is really of the outer man, because introduced from bodily objects which are perceived from without [3]). Later on in the treatise [4] this instance is applied in a somewhat different form, the example of the Faith or Creed when learnt orally being taken, and the trinity found in memory (of the sounds of the words), recollection (when we think thereon), and the will (when we remember and think) combining both.

Yet another peculiar kind of trinity is found in knowledge [5] —of which there is the higher (wisdom), dealing with things eternal; and the lower, of things temporal, in which the wholesome knowledge of things human is contained, enabling us to so act in this temporal life as to attain in the end to that which is eternal. In considering first the lower knowledge, he describes how man is made in the image of God, and how he turns away from that image and by gradual steps sinks lower and lower, sinking often in thought and imagination, even when not intending to carry the sin out into act. And so, starting from the incidental premiss that all men desire blessedness, he goes on to shew how it may be attained by faith in Christ, and so is led to expound the reasons for the Incarnation and the Passion.[6] Then, reverting [7] to the discussion of the trinity in memory, intelligence, and will, he declares that it is in the noblest part of the mind that the Trinity, which is the image of God, is to be sought—that part of the mind which is the sphere of the higher knowledge. It is here that he finds the surest indication of the Holy Trinity—in the inmost being of the mind which remembers and understands and loves itself, but above all God, and so is brought into most intimate relation to Him. So it is that the constitution of man himself, made in the

[1] Memoria, intelligentia, voluntas suimetipsius (x).
[2] xi 2-10. [3] xi 11 ff. [4] Bk. xiii.
[5] Bk. xii. [6] Bk. xiii. [7] Bk. xiv.

image of God, bears witness to the truth of the doctrine of the Trinity.

The main thesis of the treatise is thus apparently concluded; but it is of the Trinity itself, not only of evidence for its existence, that Augustine writes; and in the last book he adds largely to what he has before said in regard to the Holy Spirit, particularly as to his relation to the Father and the Son.

The Holy Spirit, he says,[1] according to the holy Scriptures, is neither of the Father alone nor of the Son alone, but of both; and so he intimates to us a mutual love wherewith the Father and the Son reciprocally love one another. The love is, indeed, proper to each individually and to all collectively; yet the Holy Spirit may be specially called love, as the Son only is called the Word, and the Holy Spirit alone the gift of God, and God the Father alone He from whom the Word is born and from whom the Holy Spirit principally proceeds. He adds 'principally' (i.e. as beginning or principle), because we find that the Holy Spirit proceeds from the Son also. This was the Father's purpose and design—he gave this to the Son (namely, that the Spirit should proceed from him too), not subsequently to his generation, but by begetting him: He so begat him as that the common gift should proceed from him also, and the Holy Spirit be the Spirit of both (that is, the Spirit proceeds from the Son by virtue of the Father's gift to the Son in his generation—both alike eternal). The Holy Spirit may thus be specially called love; as similarly the Word of God was specially called also the Wisdom of God, although both Father and Holy Spirit also are Wisdom. No gift of God is more excellent than love.

And it must not be supposed that the Holy Spirit is less than the Father and the Son, because they give and he is given. Even though he were given to no one, he is himself God and was God, co-eternal with the Father and the Son, before he was given to any one. And when he is given as a gift of God, it is in such a way that he himself, as being God, also gives himself.

It is certain that the procession of the Holy Spirit is from both Father and Son apart from time. We neither say the Holy Spirit is begotten nor do we say he is unbegotten (for the latter term, though not found in the Scriptures, is conveniently applied to the Father alone); and we abhor the idea

[1] Bk. xv § 27 ff.

that he is begotten of both Father and Son. What we say is, that he proceeds eternally from both, without any kind of interval of time between the generation of the Son from the Father and the procession of the Spirit from the Father and the Son. This the Son and the Spirit each has from the Father.[1]

This is certain, but we must be on our guard against too much reasoning. We must not press too far the analogy between the image of the Trinity in us and the Trinity itself. Many questions can only be understood when we are in bliss, and no longer reason but contemplate. It is in love, he implies, rather than in reason, that the solution of difficulties is to be found.

So in the prayer with which he closes the treatise he asks for increase of remembrance, understanding, love.[2]

Mr. Burn draws my attention to the fresh and vigorous treatment of the doctrine by Niceta of Remesiana in Dacia (near Palanka in Servia), a great admirer of Basil. His treatise was written, Mr. Burn thinks, soon after 381, as part of the third book of his *Libelli instructionis*. (It is printed in Migne vol. lii p. 853, under Mai's mistaken title *de Spiritus sancti potentia*.) He begins by reference to the puzzles put forward by some as to whether the Spirit was 'born or not born', and directs his argument against those who style him a creature. He appeals to the words of Scripture to decide all such questions, and makes some interesting applications and interpretations of texts (*e.g.* Col 1[26], Rom 8[15], John 20[22] 16[13], 1 John 2[1], 1 Cor 14[24]). Scripture and all his operations, whether benignant or awe-inspiring, shew his full Godhead. He is to be worshipped and glorified with the Father and the Son with one and the same worship. When we worship one, we worship all; and by so doing we do not add to the glory of the divine majesty, but thereby we acquire glory for ourselves. To this faith we must hold fast, and be true to our profession in the Mysteries 'Holy, holy, holy is the Lord God of Hosts'.

SUBSTANTIA

Substantia, the verbal noun from *substo*, means 'that which underlies a thing', 'that by which anything subsists or exists', 'the essence or underlying principle by which each *res* is what it is'. So things which

---

[1] Here he refers to his Sermon on St John's Gospel—*in Joh. Tract.* xcix 6 ff., where he insists that the saying "proceeds from the Father" does not exclude procession also from the Son.

[2] With Augustine's statement of the doctrine may be compared the statement of Hilary *de Trinitate* esp. ii 29–35, viii 25, ix 73, xii 55.

have *substantia* are contrasted with those which only have an imaginary existence, being fashioned by illusory or unreal thought, like Centaurs or giants (Seneca *Ep.* 58):—a contrast which shews the meaning of *substantia* to be 'real existence'. And again, it is said that before you can enquire about a man, Who he is, you must have before you his *substantia* (*sc.* his real existence, the fact that he *is*) : so that you cannot make the question of his *being* a subject of examination (Quintilian vii 2. 5). That is to say, *substantia* denotes real existence, as to the particular form or character of which enquiry may be made. So, too, *substantia* and *qualitas* are distinguished as subjects of investigation (*ib.* 3. 6) ; and in this way it comes about that the *substantia* of a thing is an easy periphrasis for the thing itself.

A secondary sense of the term—'property', 'patrimony', 'fortune'— has been sufficiently referred to in the text in connexion with Tertullian's usage (see *supra* p. 138).

It is in its primary sense that it was adopted for doctrinal purposes in connexion with the attempt to describe the Godhead. It had to do duty, as we have seen (*supra* p. 117), for both οὐσία and ὑπόστασις. Both words alike are rendered *substantia* by the Latin translator of Irenaeus, the sense expressed being the *substratum* of a thing or being, having of course particular qualities or form, but conceived of as apart from its qualities or form.

The regular philosophical sense on which the doctrinal use of the term is really based is seen, for example, in Tertullian *de Anima* 11, where he distinguishes between the soul as *substantia* and its acts or operations ; and in the adjectival forms which he employs, for instance, *de Res. Carn.* 45 and *adv. Prax.* 7, 26. [He discusses the relation between the 'old man' and the 'new man' and argues that the difference is *moral* not *substantial* ; that is to say, the *substantia* man is the same. And commenting on the Monarchian wish to avoid recognition of the Son as a distinct entity (*substantivus*), he declares that he is a *substantiva res*, whereas 'the power of the Most High' and the like are not, but only *accidentia substantiae*. Or again 'faith' and 'love' are not *substantiva animae* but *conceptiva*,—that is not the *substantia* but the concepts of the *substantia*.]

This difference which Tertullian defines between *substantia* and the *nature* of *substantia* (see also *supra* p. 140, and cf. p. 235) practically held its ground through the later developements of Latin theology. *Substantia* is the term regularly employed to express the being of God— the Godhead in itself, as a distinct entity. The *substantia* has its own *natura* which is inseparable from it, but the *substantia* is not the *natura*. The retention of the distinction is plainly perceptible in the expression of the doctrine of the Person of Christ—the union of the Godhead and the manhood. Latin theologians shrink from speaking of the union of the two 'natures' merely. If they do not actually employ the term *substantia* (speaking of the *substantia* of Godhead and the *substantia* of manhood as united in the Person of the Son), they use some other phrase to represent it rather than *natura*. Thus *forma Dei* and *forma servi* are preferred by Hilary, as *filius Dei* and *filius hominis* by Novatian and Augustine; and Leo, though he freely uses *utraque natura*, is careful to mark his full meaning by adding *et substantia* to *natura*, and by interchanging with it the expression *utraque forma* (*forma* conveying a more definite conception of an actual entity—a substantial existence—than *natura*). Vincent, too (*Commonit.* xii, xiii), owing to this clearness of Latin usage, was able to put the case in regard to the Christological controversies which Leo had in view without the ambiguities with which it was confused for Greeks. He describes the error of Apollinarius as the refusal to recognize in Christ two substances (*duas substantias*), the one divine and the other human; whereas Nestorius, pretending to discriminate the two *substances* in Christ, really introduces two *persons*: and he sets out as the Catholic faith 'in God one substance, but three persons; in Christ two substances, but one person'. Using *substantia* throughout, defined either as *divina* or as *humana*, and retaining Tertullian's distinction, he can also speak with perfect lucidity of the *natura* of the substance.

So too in the Chalcedonian definition of the doctrine, in terms entirely consonant with the teaching and discrimination of Latin theologians from Tertullian to Leo, first there is recognized in the person of Jesus Christ the two *substantiae* of Godhead and manhood (he is *unius substantiae* with the Father *secundum deitatem*, and also *unius substantiae* with us *secundum humanitatem*), and then it is declared that the one person exists in the two *natures*. (See further *Texts and Studies* vol. vii no. 1 pp. 65–70.)

PERSONA—πρόσωπον

The history of the word *persona* outside ecclesiastical use is clear. First, it is an actor's mask; then, by an easy transition, the part the actor plays, which is represented by his mask; then, any part or rôle assumed by any one without regard to its duration. Secondly, it is the *condicio, status, munus* which any one has among men in general, and in particular in civil life. And so it is the man himself so far as he has this or that *persona*. Thus slaves, as not possessing any rights of citizenship, were regarded by Roman law as not having *persona*: they were ἀπρόσωποι or *persona carentes*. (Cf. the phrase *personam amittere* 'to lose rank or status' and the Vulgate rendering of πρόσωπον λαμβάνειν— viz. *respicere* or *aspicere personam*.) It is this second sense of the word by which ecclesiastical usage is controlled; and the most important fact to notice is that it never means what 'person' means in modern popular usage, even when it seems to be used very nearly in the sense of 'person', and when it has no other representative in English. It always designates status, or character, or part, or function: not, of course, that it is conceived as separate from some living subject or agent, but that attention is fixed on the character or function rather than on the subject or agent. It is always a person looked at from some distinctive point of view, a person in particular circumstances; that is, it conveys the notion much more of the environment than of the subject. It expresses in its ecclesiastical usage in a single word precisely what Basil's τρόπος ὑπάρξεως denoted, and what ὑπόστασις was ultimately narrowed down to mean.

The history of πρόσωπον is similar, as to its primary uses, to that of *persona*. In the New Testament the regular sense of the word is 'face': either literally (of living beings or *trop.* of *e.g.* the face of the earth), or as equivalent to 'presence'. It is also found in the phrase πρόσωπον λαμβάνειν and cognate expressions, which have been referred to above; while it is used in some special senses by St Paul—*e.g.* (1) the outward contrasted with the inward, as in 1 Thess 2[17] where it means nearly 'presence', and 2 Cor 5[12] where it denotes 'outward show' or 'demeanour' as contrasted with real feeling; (2) the phrase ἐν προσώπῳ Χριστοῦ, 2 Cor 2[10] 4[6], where it stands for 'character' or 'part'; (3) 2 Cor 1[11] where it is almost exactly like Tertullian's *persona*. But it is probably as a translation of the Latin term that it is first found in connexion with Christian doctrine, and there seems to be no reason in the nature of things why it should not have served Greek theology as *persona* ultimately served the Latins. Only, it was entirely spoiled for doctrinal purposes by the use which Sabellius and his followers made of it and its derivatives (see *supra* p. 105).

When it had once been definitely employed to express the conception of distinctions in the Godhead which were merely temporal and external, different parts played in the process of self-revelation to the world and to men by one and the same Person, it was almost impossible that it should ever be adopted to denote distinctions which were eternal and rooted in the very being of the Godhead, entirely apart from any relation to the created universe and the human race. Like the Latin *persona*, it was just the word that was wanted to express the thought of the three relations in which the one God always exists, the three distinct spheres of being—each representing special functions—which together make up the divine life. There was no reason why it should not have connoted all the notion of permanent 'personality' which properly attaches to the names of Father, Son, and Holy Spirit. It could easily have been safeguarded in use from limitation to merely temporary rôles (or parts or characters or functions) assumed simply for particular purposes. But

Sabellius stole the word away ; and Greek theologians were left without any suitable way of expressing the conception, till they could agree among themselves to use another term which properly meant something quite different, and could win general acceptance for the artificial sense which they put upon the term they used. (See further *Texts and Studies* vol. vii no. 1 pp. 70–74.)

Οὐσία—Ὑπόστασις

The word οὐσία expresses primarily real existence, actual being—that which actually is. As used by Plato it was the special characteristic of the Ideas—the realities (τὰ ὄντα) as contrasted with the appearances on earth (τὰ φαινόμενα) : the Ideas by imitation of which, or participation in which, things as we know them are what they are. And each class of things has its own particular οὐσία, namely, the Idea—so far, that is to say, as anything but the Idea can be regarded as existent at all.

But it was Aristotle, rather than Plato, who fixed for later times the usage of the word. To him (besides having commonly the meaning 'possessions', 'property', as *substantia* in Latin) it is equivalent to τὸ εἶναι; but particularly he uses it to express real concrete existence—τὸ ὄν, τὸ ἁπλῶς ὄν. It is the first in the series of categories, 'substance': and to it attach, and from it are distinguished, all conceptions of quantity or quality, all attributes or properties (συμβεβηκότα). And thus, in accordance with Aristotle's inductive method, it is primarily and properly descriptive of individual particular existence—each particular entity (the τόδε τι) : and this primary sense is distinguished as πρώτη οὐσία. But inasmuch as there may be many examples of one particular οὐσία, it may signify that which is common to them all—to whole species or classes : and this secondary sense of the word is distinguished as δευτέρα οὐσία.

These are the two main usages of the word. It always expresses substantial existence. It may be used of the whole entity, or of the 'matter' or the 'form' of which every perceptible substance is conceived by Aristotle as consisting. Or it may be used where for the immediate purpose it seems that the sense required might be conveyed by φύσις or 'nature'—the sum total of the attributes or properties (συμβεβηκότα). But it is never employed as a mere synonym for φύσις. It always means much more, including φύσις perhaps, but logically to be discriminated from it.

Ὑπόστασις, as a philosophical term, is a later and much more rarer word. Aristotle only uses it in its literal meaning of 'a standing beneath' or 'that which stands beneath' (*i.e.* either of the action of subsiding, or of that which remains as a result of such action, viz. 'sediment'). But the philosophical usage of the term is derived directly and naturally from an earlier and not uncommon use of the verb of which it is the noun. The οὐσία was said to exist at the outset, to be the underlying existence (ὑφεστάναι); and so the noun ὑπόστασις was a possible equivalent for οὐσία, expressing the essential *substratum*, the 'foundation' of a thing, the vehicle of all qualities. The earliest examples of its use are found in Stoic writers, and thenceforward both words, οὐσία and ὑπόστασις, were current without any clear distinction being drawn between them. But οὐσία was by far the commoner term, ὑπόστασις being comparatively rarely found. So Socrates (*H.E.* iii 7) could say 'the ancient philosophical writers scarcely noticed this word', though 'the more modern ones have frequently used it instead of οὐσία'. It was, however, as has been stated *supra* p. 117, the equivalent of ὑπόστασις (viz. *substantia*) which was acclimatized in the Latin language more readily than the equivalent of οὐσία (viz. *essentia*), and therefore *substantia* was all through the normal term by which Latin theologians expressed the conceptions for which οὐσία stood.

The LXX translators of the Old Testament employed the word to express the '*ground* or *foundation* of hope'; and it was introduced into Christian theology by the writer of the Epistle to the Hebrews. In his phrase χαρακτὴρ τῆς ὑποστάσεως αὐτοῦ (Heb. 1³), ὑπόστασις is exactly the equivalent of οὐσία ('being', 'essence', 'substance', as in the μία οὐσία or *una substantia* of later technical theology); and so it was expounded by the later Greek theologians, who would themselves have used οὐσία there instead and have kept ὑπόστασις to express the characteristics of the existence of the 'persons' of the Trinity. The same metaphysical conception is seen in the definition of 'faith' as ἐλπιζομένων ὑπόστασις (Heb. 11¹)—viz. that which gives reality to things hoped for, the faculty by which we are able to treat as realities things which are as yet only objects of hope—and probably in the other passages in the New Testament in which ὑπόστασις occurs (Heb. 3¹⁴, 2 Cor. 9⁴ 11¹⁷—in which at least the meaning 'subject-matter', 'the matter of' is possible ; cf. the Vulgate and Tyndale's versions).

So οὐσία and ὑπόστασις remain in use side by side. Origen was the first to attempt to discriminate between them ; but the use of ὑπόστασις as the equivalent of οὐσία was too firmly rooted to be much shaken. The supposition that Dionysius of Alexandria was familiar with a different usage, and that τρεῖς ὑποστάσεις meant to him exactly what it meant to the Cappadocian fathers, is no doubt extremely attractive; but the temptation to antedate in this way the developement of precision of terminology in this connexion must be resisted. The fragments of the correspondence between him and Dionysius of Rome that are extant shew that he had not arrived at the conception of such a clear distinction. He realized three forms of existence more vividly than one substantial entity of Deity (see *supra* p. 114 n. 2). So great was his reputation, that if the discrimination had been in any way due to him, it is impossible that it could have died out in the great theological school of his see; and the whole history of the subsequent century proves conclusively that no more at Alexandria than anywhere else in the East had the implied precision of terms been attained.

So the framers of the Creed of Nicaea and its anathemas still used οὐσία and ὑπόστασις as synonyms, and as synonyms still the Arianizing parties in the Church in subsequent years put both words alike under the ban. (So Athanasius de Decr. 20, repeating the Nicene anathema, has only ἐξ ἑτέρας οὐσίας; and in one of his latest writings ad Afros 4, refuting the objections brought against the words as non-scriptural, he says " ὑπόστασις is οὐσία and means nothing else but simply being." And, though most of the creeds devised as substitutes for the Creed of Nicaea are content to forbid the use of οὐσία without mention of ὑπόστασις, the Synod of Constantinople in 360 declared against ὑπόστασις too, evidently regarding the words as synonymous—see the Creed in Hahn [3] p. 209.)

It was at the Synod of Alexandria in 362 (see *supra* p. 186), presided over by Athanasius, that formal recognition was first conceded to the usage of the word ὑπόστασις which made it possible to speak of the Trinity as τρεῖς ὑποστάσεις, while still being faithful to the definitions of the doctrine at Nicaea; though at the same time the older and original usage, according to which μία ὑπόστασις only could be said, received like recognition (see Ath. *ad Antiochenos* 5, 6, and Socr. *H.E.* iii 7). By this time many 'orthodox' theologians were becoming accustomed to the usage of the two terms οὐσία and ὑπόστασις, whereby οὐσία expresses the existence or essence or substantial entity of the Trinity as God, and ὑπόστασις expresses the existence in a particular mode, the manner of being of each of the 'Persons'. The Cappadocian fathers, more than any others, contributed to securing currency for this distinction. Basil of Caesarea, in particular, clearly defines the sense of ὑπόστασις as τὸ ἰδίως λεγόμενον—a special and particular sense of οὐσία. It denotes a limitation, a separation of certain circumscribed conceptions from the general idea. " Not the indefinite conception of οὐσία, which, because what is signified is common to all, finds no fixity, but that which by means of the special characteristics (or properties) which are made apparent gives fixity and circumscription to that which is common and uncircumscribed (*Ep.* 38)." And again (*Ep.* 214): " Οὐσία has the same relation to ὑπόστασις as the common has to the particular. Every one of us both shares in existence by the common term of οὐσία and by his own properties is such or such an one. In the same manner, in the matter in question, the term οὐσία is common, like goodness or Godhead or any similar attribute (*i.e.* it is not 'goodness' or any attribute); while ὑπόστασις is contemplated in the special

property of Fatherhood, Sonship, or the power to sanctify." That is
to say, ὑπόστασις expresses the particular mode of existence or special
function.

So the two terms passed together into Catholic use to express
respectively the one Godhead and the forms of its existence.   There is
μία οὐσία and τρεῖς ὑποστάσεις, or μία οὐσία ἐν τρισὶν ὑποστάσεσιν—one
substance or essence or entity, in three subsistencies or forms or modes or
spheres of existence or consciousness : one God permanently existing in
three eternal modes.   The οὐσία of Father and Son and Holy Spirit is
one and the same.   Both Father and Son together with the Holy Spirit
are the Godhead.   The one Being exists in three forms, or spheres, or
functions. The one God is tri-personal. (See further *Texts and Studies*
vol. vii no. 1 pp. 74–81.)

CHAPTER XIV

The Results of the previous Developements

As a result of all the controversies on which the Church pronounced at the Council of Constantinople, it may be said that the Christian conception of God was clearly enough defined. From the observed facts of human experience—the experiences of the people of Israel recorded in their sacred books, the experiences of the life on earth of Jesus of Nazareth, observed and interpreted by his immediate followers and their successors, the experiences of those same disciples and subsequent generations, the experiences of the continuous life of the Christian society through more than three hundred years—the deduction had been drawn. As an interpretation of human life, and of experiences which were felt to connote the workings of God in the world, the experience of the whole Christian revelation, the doctrine of the Trinity was framed.

The facts of human experience, thus marshalled and examined, pointed to the existence of one Supreme Being, at once outside the world and in the world, eternally existing and manifesting Himself in three modes of existence—three spheres of being—represented by the three names, Father, Son, and Holy Spirit: the three names representing three eternal relations existing within the Godhead, and manifested in operation in the universe and in the world of human experience.

The three eternal relations or modes in which the One God simultaneously exists and operates are distinct, and are capable of being distinguished in human thought and experience, and are to be attributed respectively to Father, Son, and Holy Spirit. These three 'Persons' together form the One Godhead.

So much of definition of experience and description the Church had reached. But it cannot be said there was yet any precise and clear conception of personality. And this difficulty, not even yet surmounted, was at the root of the next great controversy to which the Church was led.

At the outset of the sketch of the controversies up to this time, it was stated that the Catholic doctrine of the Person of Christ, as ultimately framed, took note of four main factors—his full and perfect divinity, his full and perfect humanity, the union of the two in one person, the relations existing between the two when united in the one person.

By the time the Arian controversy ended, the first two explicitly and the third implicitly of these four factors had been fully recognized in the doctrine of the Trinity; but the attempt to examine the relations existing between the two natures in the incarnate Son was attended by no less serious troubles. The uncertainty as to what constituted a 'nature' was as great as the uncertainty in regard to a 'person'.

This uncertainty is the keynote to the debates of the fifth century, in the prelude to which Apollinarius played the leading part.

The Points of Departure of Apollinarius and His Theories

Apollinarius [1] had been a chief champion of the Nicene doctrine against the Arians, and it was in opposition to them

---

[1] Apollinarius, Bishop of Laodicea, in the latter half of the fourth century, was son of the *grammatista* (schoolmaster) of Berytus, and afterwards presbyter of Laodicea, who undertook the composition of Christian works, in imitation of the old classics, when Julian's educational laws precluded Christians from studying and teaching the ancient Greek and Latin literature. In this work the son helped his father, and also wrote in defence of Christianity against Julian and Porphyry, and against heretics, such as the Arians and Marcellus, besides commentaries on Scripture and other works, of which only fragments are extant in the answers of Gregory Naz. *Epp.* ci, cii (to Cledonius), Gregory of Nyssa *Antirrheticus adv. Apoll.* and *Ep. ad Theophilum adv. Apoll.*, and Theodoret. Cf. also Epiphanius *adv. Haer.* lxxvii, 'Athanasius' *Contra Apoll.* (Eng. tr. Bright *Later Treatises of St Athanasius*, probably not the work of Athanasius—see Dräseke *Zeitschrift f. wiss.-schaft. Theologie* 1895 pp. 254 ff.—but written while the controversy was at its height), Theodoret *Fabulae Haer.* iv 7, v 9, 11, and Basil *Ep.* 265 (very vague). Jerome was among his pupils in 374, and he was at first on terms of warm friendship with Athanasius and Basil, on account of his learning and support of the Nicene party in the Arian controversy. His, or a similar, doctrine was condemned by a synod at Alexandria in 362, but the doctrine does not seem to have been widely known till about 371, and he did not secede from the Church till 375. The condemnation was renewed by synods at Rome, under Damasus, in 377–378, and by the Second General Council in 381; and imperial decrees were issued prohibiting the public worship of Apollinarians 388–428, till they became absorbed in the Church or the Monophysites. He died in *c.* 392. See P. Schaff Art. 'Apollinarius' *D.C.B.*

that he was led to devise his peculiar theory. Two motives in particular determined him.

First, the Arian teaching of the possibility of moral change in Christ, by which the Logos was subjected to the course of growth and developement of character, and the decision for good was in every case the free act of a will that might have chosen evil. From such a theory of free will and freedom of choice it seemed to follow that the redemption effected by Christ was only the work of a finite being, making himself redeemer by his own free act, and therefore not really effective for the human race, except as shewing how such redemption might be won. And no human soul could be entirely free from the taint of human weakness. Zeal for the full true deity and perfect sinlessness of Christ by very nature was thus a foremost motive to Apollinarius.

A second motive was conditioned by the ambiguity of ter-

It is also probable that some writings of Apollinarius were intentionally attributed by his followers to various 'orthodox' fathers, in order to gain currency for them. One of the earliest essays in literary criticism deals with this matter. Under the name of Leontius of Byzantium (485–543), a contemporary of Justinian, there is extant (Migne lxxxvi 2 p. 1948) a critical study of the authorship of writings attributed to Gregory Thaumaturgus, Julius, Athanasius, which contain teaching other than that of the Chalcedonian Definition. The writer decides (chiefly on the ground that they contain sentences which his disciples quoted as from his works) that three of them were by Apollinarius—(1) The κατὰ μέρος πίστις Hahn[3] p. 278, an exposition of the faith, ascribed to Gregory Thaumaturgus ; (2) some letters ascribed to Julius of Rome ; (3) a Creed on the Incarnation Hahn[3] p. 266—ascribed to Athanasius, accepted as Athanasian, and followed as such by Cyril of Alexandria —containing the formula μία φύσις τοῦ θεοῦ λόγου σεσαρκωμένη (one incarnate nature of the Divine Word), but quoted from by writers against Monophysites as a composition of Apollinarius. In the judgement of the writer of this study (who seems not to have been Leontius, but perhaps John of Scythopolis, c. 500, who did investigate genuine remains of Apollinarius) the fraud passed because the Church was ready to welcome teaching as to the one nature of the incarnate Son. This example of early literary criticism has recently been followed by a modern scholar, who argues that whole treatises have been so dealt with, and assigns to Apollinarius, as well as the Creed above named and fragments of a work on the Incarnation, the correspondence with Basil (Epp. 361–364 in Basil's Works), the last two books of Basil's Treatise against Eunomius (written c. 360, thoroughly orthodox, especially in regard to the Holy Spirit), Dialogues on the Holy Trinity (assigned variously to Athanasius, Theodoret, and others), and the περὶ τριάδος under the name of Justin (which clearly cannot be earlier than this time, while Gregory Naz. refers to a treatise of Apollinarius on the Trinity). None of these writings, however, shew any of the peculiar theories known as Apollinarian. See further 'Apollinarius von Laodicaea' J. Dräseke, Texte und Untersuchungen (Gebhardt und Harnack) 1892 ; and article in Church Quarterly October 1893. And on the date and authorship of the work adversus fraudes Apollinistarum see Loofs Texte u. Unt. iii 1, 2. On the correspondence with Basil see Texts and Studies vii 1 p. 38 ff.

16

minology already noted. To Apollinarius it seemed that a complete 'nature' was the same thing as a 'person'. A complete divine nature and a complete human nature joined together meant two persons joined together. If, therefore, Christ had all the constituents of humanity, the two complete natures thus supposed would make two persons, for there could not be a composition of his person out of two. (The current teaching of the union of full divinity and full humanity in one person— two wholes in one whole—he regarded as an absurdity.)

It was this fear of a double personality, and of a human freedom of choice in Christ, that dominated the thought of Apollinarius.

Now, the freedom of choice resided in the mind or spirit, or rational human 'soul', in the higher sense of the term.[1] This was the determining and ruling element in human nature, necessarily instinct with capacities for evil—in virtue of which developement—good or evil—was possible. Furthermore, it was this that differentiated one man from another—the seat or centre of the power of self-determination, and therefore of all real personal distinction—and constituted independent personality.

If Christ possessed no human soul there would be in his person no sphere in which freedom of choice could be exercised, and there would be no human personality to be combined with the divine. There would be only the divine Logos himself, as the sole determining power, in the person of the incarnate Christ.

This, therefore, was the interpretation which commended itself to Apollinarius as a way of escape from all the difficulties. Christ was actually God become man. A real union of the Logos with a rational human soul there could not be, because either the human being thus united would preserve his own will distinct (and so there would be no true union of the divine and the human), or the human soul would lose its liberty and be,

---

[1] He followed the threefold division of man, to which Plato gave currency, into body, soul (irrational or animal—the principle of life), and spirit (or rational soul, the controlling and determining principle). Cf. 1 Thess. 5²³, Gal. 5¹⁷. But some of his opponents ('Athanasius' and Gregory of Nyssa) expressly disallowed this three-fold division, maintaining that Scripture recognized only a 'dichotomy' into body and soul. (They refer to the account of the Creation of man in *Genesis* and to the Gospel narrative of the death of the Lord—while his body lay in the grave, he went with his soul into Hades.) See *Adv. Apoll.* i 14, and *Antirrhet.* 8, 35.

as it were, absorbed.[1] The Logos therefore occupies the place of
the human rational soul, taking to himself a human body and
an animal soul, becoming himself the controlling power and
principle thereof, and completely filling and animating the human
elements with the higher life of God. In this way the unity
of the person was preserved,[2] though the person was "neither
wholly man nor wholly God, but a blending of God and man";[3]
and the Scriptural teaching was maintained—"the Word became
flesh" (not spirit), and God was "manifest in the flesh".[4]

Objections to his Theories and his Defence of them

To this theory the obvious objection was soon taken, that
the 'soul' was the most important element in human nature,
and that, in denying to the person of the Christ a human soul,
Apollinarius was emptying the Incarnation of its meaning and

[1] See Note 'The Human Will in Christ' *infra* p. 249.

[2] It will be noticed that in two particulars Apollinarius was in harmony with
the ultimate verdict of the Church—(1) In rejecting the personality of the human
nature; (2) in finding the centre of personality in the Logos (see *infra* p. 294).
It must further be observed that the formula μία φύσις τοῦ θεοῦ λόγου σεσαρκωμένη, "one incarnate nature of the God-Word", attributed to Apollinarius and
adopted by Cyril (see *infra* p. 274), is widely different from the formula, "one nature
of the Word incarnate" (μία φύσις τοῦ θεοῦ λόγου σεσαρκωμένου). The former
phrase includes the 'flesh' in the nature which is defined as one, and so it was
used by Cyril without implying a new nature neither divine nor human (for he
said, ἐκ δύο φύσεων). But to Apollinarius it probably did connote the idea of a
fresh and uniquely constituted nature. Cyril believed the phrase to have been
used by Athanasius in a treatise *on the Incarnation*, which was, however, probably
written by Apollinarius, and ascribed to Athanasius by his followers (*see* Note
on p. 241 *supra*).

[3] οὔτε ἄνθρωπος ὅλος, οὔτε θεός, ἀλλὰ θεοῦ καὶ ἀνθρώπου μίξις. This mode of
expression, 'mixture' or 'blending', had been used in all good faith in earlier
times, *e.g.* by Tertullian *Apol.* 21 *homo deo mixtus*, Cyprian *de idol. vanit.* 11, and
Deus cum homine miscetur, Lactantius *Inst.* iv 13 *Deus est et homo, ex utroque genere
permixtus*. Origen speaks of the union of the two natures as an interweaving
(συνυφαίνεσθαι) and a κρᾶσις or ἀνάκρασις (*Contra Cels.* iii 41, cf. *de Princip.* ii 6.3).
So Irenaeus *adv. Haer.* iii 19.1, and others, down to the two Gregories, who both
use the terms σύγκρασις and ἀνάκρασις, and nearly approach the idea of a transmu-
tation of the human nature into the divine (as Origen *l.c.*), though they express
definitely the duality of the natures (φύσεις μὲν δύο, θεὸς καὶ ἄνθρωπος). Even
Augustine says, "Man was linked and in some small way commingled with
(*commixtus*) the Word of God, to effect the unity of person" (*de Trin.* v 30).
None of the opponents of Apollinarius express the *manner* of the union satisfactorily; though they do maintain the entirety both of the Godhead and of the
manhood.

[4] To this Gregory of Nazianzus replied *Ep.* ci that 'flesh' was here used for
human nature, the part for the whole—ἐνσάρκωσις really meant ἐνανθρώπησις.

making it unreal.[1] If his theory were true, the highest faith and deepest convictions of Christians were delusions. God had not become man : He had only, as it were, put on a garment of flesh.[2] And, further, the spirit or soul, which, as he argued, was the seat of sin, needs redemption as well as the lower soul and body of man. That which transgressed was that which stood most in need of salvation.[3]

Yet Apollinarius undoubtedly held the person so composed to be human as well as divine, and maintained that since the Logos was himself the archetype of all human souls the objection to his theory could not be upheld. The Logos occupied no external or foreign position in relation to man, but was the very truth of human nature. All human souls were in a way adumbrations of the Logos, and therefore when the Logos himself was present in a human body, the very highest and truest form of human existence was realized.

This extremely interesting and subtle argument met with less acceptance than might, perhaps, have been expected. The recognition of the natural affinity existing between the human soul and God might have smoothed the way to a really satisfactory doctrine of the Person of Christ. But the particular expression which was given to the thought was certainly open to the gravest suspicions. Apollinarius denied to Christ a human soul. That was clear ; and the consequences of the denial were readily appreciated. Against such a mutilated humanity in Christ the faith of the Church revolted. The Incarnation was the assumption of the entire human nature—sin only excluded, as being no part of a perfect human nature ;[4] and the argument of Apollinarius was ingenious rather than convincing.

[1] See Additional Note to this chapter on 'The Human Soul in Christ' p. 247.

[2] Christ was only θεὸς σαρκοφόρος—God clad in flesh (just as later on, by contrast, Nestorianism was said to teach an ἄνθρωπος θεοφόρος—a man bearing with him God—but on this latter phrase see infra p. 276). Ignatius had used the word σαρκοφόρος of Christ (ad Smyrn 5).

[3] See e.g. 'Ath.' contra Apoll. i 19 ; and the retort of Gregory Naz. Ep. ci 'If only half Adam fell, then that which Christ assumes and saves may be half also', and that if Christ could not have had a human soul, because the soul is 'under condemnation' (through sin), still less could he have assumed a human body : what he did not assume remains unredeemed. Cf. note following. "Those who do away with the humanity and the image within cleanse only our outside by means of their new spectral person" Ep. cii.

[4] The question how entire manhood could be compatible with entire sinlessness in Christ is dealt with at length in 'Ath.' contra Apoll. bk. ii—the answer being that the human nature assumed was all that God had made, and this excluded sin,

He was indeed accused by Gregory of Nazianzus and Gregory of Nyssa[1] of actually teaching that the flesh of the Lord was pre-existent, that his body was accordingly of a celestial substance, not formed from the Virgin, but a portion of the divine essence clothed in matter. The saying, "No one has ascended into heaven but he that came down from heaven, the Son of Man who is in heaven", he was said to have interpreted as if he was the Son of Man before he came down, and came down bringing with him his own flesh which he had had in heaven, being, as it were, itself eternal and made co-essential with him. Such teaching would be, of course, in effect the old Docetism, and the prospect would be nothing short of a revival of Oriental mysticism, which would virtually deny Jesus Christ as come in flesh.[2]

But in his own words to the Emperor Jovian, he emphatically condemns as 'insane' the teaching that the flesh of Christ is consubstantial (co-essential) with God, and "came down from heaven", and therefore was not really derived from the Virgin.

The wild theory attributed to him, therefore, must have been an unauthorized inference from his real teaching, possibly made by his own adherents, going farther than their master, and applying to the whole human nature what he said of the spirit

which was the work of the Devil. Cf. Greg. Nyss. *Ep. adv. Apoll.* "Though he was made sin and a curse on account of us . . . and took our weaknesses upon him, . . . yet he did not leave the sin and the curse and the weakness encircling him unhealed. . . . Whatever is weak in our nature, and subject to death, was mingled with the Godhead and became what the Godhead is." See *infra* pp. 246, 247.

[1] A Creed, still in use among the Armenian Christians, is remarkable for the clear and copious language in which it precludes Apollinarianism: "Came down from heaven and was incarnate, was made man, was born of the holy Virgin Mary through the Holy Spirit completely—so as to take a body and soul and mind, and everything that there is in man (*or* all that goes to make a man) really, and not in seeming . . . went up into heaven in the very body, and sat on the right hand of the Father, will come in the very body." The Creed is given in Greek in Hahn[3] p. 151 ff., cf. p. 137, and is regarded by Hort (*Two Dissertations* p. 116 ff.) as the 'Cappadocian' Creed at the end of the fourth century, composed perhaps about 366–369, at Tarsus (where Apollinarian teaching at Laodicea might well be known earlier than elsewhere) by Silvanus (the teacher of Basil and of Diodorus), and introduced by Basil into the churches of Cappadocia, and thence into the Church of Armenia (whose patriarchs were consecrated at Caesarea, the Cappadocian capital, till the end of the fourth century, the Church owing its origin at the beginning of the century to Cappadocia). For other views of the origin of this Creed see Hahn[3] *Appendix* p. 154.

[2] See Greg. Naz. *Ep.* ci, ccii, and Bright *St Leo on the Incarnation* p. 518.

only.[1] This was indeed an inference that might be easily, if carelessly, drawn from his own assertion, that the flesh of Christ—while really derived from the Virgin—might be called co-essential with the Word, because of its close union with him; from the close connexion, on which he insisted, between all human nature and the Logos who was the means by which it was originally made; and from his use of phrases such as ' God is born ', ' God died ', ' our God is crucified '.[2]

It was the Apollinarian use of phrases such as these that was peculiarly abhorrent to Diodorus of Tarsus and Theodore of Mopsuestia, the leaders of the thought of the school of Antioch at the end of the fourth century and the beginning of the fifth; and the opposition which they roused was followed by the years of controversy on which the Church at last pronounced at the Council of Chalcedon.

It has been stated[3] that the manner of the union of the two natures in Christ was not satisfactorily expressed by the opponents of Apollinarian theories. Gregory of Nyssa, in particular, frequently uses expressions which imply the absorption of the human into the divine, so that the special characteristics

---

[1] It should, however, be noted that Hilary of Poitiers, in his treatise *de Trinitate* (written c. 356–359 in Asia Minor, to expound the teaching of the Church against Arianism), does not hesitate to use the expression ' heavenly body ' (corpus cœleste) of the body of Christ, and to say that his flesh was from heaven (caro illa de cœlis est), c 15 ; x 73. The creation of the human soul of Christ was really a work of the Logos (Hilary held ' creationism ' as to the origin of souls), and it was only the material of the body that he derived from his mother. But the material is at first a formless mass, and only becomes a body by the operation of the animating form-giving soul : and this soul was really of his own creation, so that he was himself the fashioner (conditor) of his body (ipse corporis sui origo est, c 18), and therefore it had a heavenly origin. (He is, however, quite clear that from the Virgin was derived the earthly material of the body).—See further Dorner *D.P.C.* Eng. tr. I ii p. 402 ff.

[2] It was in view of such expressions that the theological principle known as *communicatio idiomatum* (ἀντίδοσις ἰδιωμάτων) was finally worked out (see *infra* p. 293), though the conception was already fully expressed by Athanasius *Or. c. Ar.* iii 31, and by Tertullian before him. The opponents of Apollinarius refused to associate the sufferings of the Christ with his divine nature. The Apollinarians therefore argued that their opponents held that he who was crucified had nothing divine in his own nature, and that their refusal to associate the sufferings with the divine nature involved the recognition of two persons—one human and one divine, one a Man who suffered and one a God who could not suffer. This inference was, of course, repudiated at once, and the doctrine was laid down, as clearly as at a later time, that there was one Person and that he underwent the different experiences in virtue of his two different natures. See especially ' Ath.' *adv. Apoll.* and Greg. Nyss. *Antirrhet.* 27, 52, 54.

[3] See p. 243 n. 3, p. 244 n. 4.

of the human nature disappear. He says[1] "The firstfruits of the human nature assumed by the almighty Godhead, as one might say—using a simile—like some drop of vinegar commingled with the infinite ocean, are in the Godhead, but not in their own peculiar properties. For if it were so, then it would follow that a duality of Sons might be conceived—if, that is, in the ineffable Godhead of the Son some nature of another kind existing in its own special characteristics were recognized—in such wise that one part was weak or little or corruptible or temporary, and the other powerful and great and incorruptible and eternal." This is to say that the human nature is so overpowered by the divine, that it no longer remains in any effective sense an element in the being of the Person of the Incarnate Son. It is a full and complete human nature that is assumed; but the effect of the union is represented here in a manner inconsistent with any real human probation and developement. Where can real human experiences come in, if the manhood, which is the sphere of them, is so transformed?

Such a presentation of the matter by so distinguished a theologian shews how much had yet to be done before a satisfactory doctrine of the Person of Christ could be framed. Other passages in Gregory no doubt go far to correct the expressions which he uses here, as, for example, when he ridicules Apollinarius for attributing all the experiences of the Incarnate Person to the Godhead;[2] and[3] where he defines μίξις (as used by Apollinarius) to mean 'the union of things which are separated in nature'. But if this passage were taken by itself it would be Eutychianism before Eutyches. It as little recognizes for practical purposes a true human nature in Christ as did the teaching of Apollinarius. Such conceptions could not be allowed to pass without protest: there was need for a Nestorius to play his part in the developement of doctrine and secure once again—even at his own cost —the faith of the Church in the manhood as well as the Godhead of the Saviour of men.

THE HUMAN SOUL IN CHRIST

If the doctrine of the Incarnation is not to be emptied of its true significance, if the full humanity as well as the full divinity of Jesus is

---

[1] *Ep. adv. Apoll.* (Migne xlv p. 1276).
[2] *Antirrhet.* 24.   [3] *Antirrhet.* 51.

to be maintained, it seems to be obvious that he must have had a human
soul as well as a human body: if the term soul be used to mean, as
it is in this connexion, without more modern precision of definition,
the higher element in human nature that controls and determines
thought and action—the mind, the reason, the spirit, the will.   A
human nature robbed of this constituent would be merely animal.   It
is inconceivable that any of the contemporaries of Jesus and first
preachers of the Christian revelation should have been in any doubt
about the matter.   But the thinkers of later generations, under stress
of their sense of the essential evil of matter and all things connected
with the body, formed theories of the person of Christ which excluded
the human nature altogether; and then the defenders of the doctrine of
the Incarnation were naturally led to lay chief emphasis on the reality
of the human body and its visible experiences.   Had the question been
raised, it seems possible, indeed, that their opponents, the 'Gnostics',
might have accepted the theory of a human soul while still denying
the reality of the human body.   But the distinction between soul and
body seems not to have been thought of in this connexion.   (Yet see
Tert. *de Carne Christi* § 10.)   "The Word became flesh" was the
simplest expression to hand, and this antithesis offered the readiest
distinction.   The Word—his essential divinity: the Flesh—from which
all human characteristics came.   So it seems to have been the 'flesh'
which was regarded as the source of all human feelings and experiences
by those who insisted most strongly on the human nature: and the
antithesis 'fleshly and spiritual' stands for 'human and divine.'   To
Ignatius, for example, this contrast comes naturally (see the passages
cited *supra* p. 121).   It was the reality of the body or the flesh that
was denied, and it is in terms of the body and the flesh that he
maintains the human nature.   And Irenæus (*adv. Haer.* iii 22. 2),
in speaking of his experiences of fatigue and grief and pain, says that
they were signs or tokens of "the flesh, assumed from earth, which he
recapitulated in himself, saving that which he himself had formed".
So, too, Justin Martyr, anxious to maintain the truth of Christ's
humanity, like that of other men, made use of phrases which expressed his possession of body or flesh, and of the animal soul (ψυχή);
and it seems certain that he intended to assert his full entire manhood.
But he speaks of him as being constituted out of body, the Logos, and
soul—whence it might be inferred that he regarded the Logos as taking
the place of the rational soul or spirit.   [It is, perhaps, possible that he
may have meant body and soul to express the whole human nature,
though he commonly accepts the threefold division of man, in which
'soul' is used to express the animal principle.]
    Tertullian is the first to give unmistakeable expression to the
Catholic conception.   It was easier for him to avoid mistakes, as he

adopted the twofold division of human nature into body and thinking soul, as animating principle (see *de Anima e.g.* 27, 51). But he also maintained the soul to be the real essence of man, and explicitly argued that if Christ was to be the redeemer of men he must have united to himself a soul of the same kind as that which belongs peculiarly to men (cf. *de Carne Christi* 11 ff.).

Origen, as we have seen (*supra* p. 150), had a definite theory in regard to the human soul with which the Logos was united.

The Arians were the first to frame an explanation of the person of Christ which, while admitting as constituents a human body and an animal soul (ψυχὴ ἄλογος), expressly excluded the rational soul (νοῦς, πνεῦμα) and supposed its place to be taken by the Logos, thus and so far anticipating Apollinarius. It was in accordance with this theory that they preferred the description in the Creed 'made flesh' 'incarnate' (σαρκωθέντα) to the term 'made man' (ἐνανθρωπήσαντα) which their opponents were constrained to introduce : the 'flesh' they fully admitted, but they knew that the latter term would pin them down to the human soul as well, as they could not exclude from 'man' the very constituent which raises him above all other created things.

It was reserved for Apollinarius to take up their theory in this particular, and to try to turn it against their teaching in other respects, while professedly maintaining the full humanity of Christ by the ingenious argument noted above.

THE HUMAN WILL IN CHRIST

Probably the most important result of the Apollinarian controversy, as regards the developement of doctrine, was the strengthening of the conviction that the manhood of the Lord was complete, including a human soul. This conviction, at least when consciously realized, involved the recognition of a human will and of the possibility of a real moral probation and developement, as regards his human nature, in Christ. Such a recognition of a human will seemed to Apollinarians to be an obstacle to the personal unity of the Logos (see *supra* p. 242)— two whole wills could not coexist together. This was one difficulty which their opponents had to meet.

They dealt with it sometimes by arguing that the denial of the human free will led to still greater difficulties. Thus Gregory of Nyssa (*Antirrhet.* 45) declared that if the human soul of the Lord did not possess free will (the power of choice and self-determination), his life could neither be a real example and a moral pattern for us, nor could it effect any gain for the human race. But sometimes a different line of reasoning was adopted, as by Gregory of Nazianzus (*Ep.* ci 9), who admits some incompleteness of the human mind relatively to the divine mind. Our mind, he says, is a complete whole (τέλειον) and possessed of sovereign power (ἡγεμονικόν); that is to say, it has sovereign power over the animal soul and body. Relatively to the rest of us, it is sovereign and complete. But absolutely it is not so; it is God's slave and subject. In relation to His rule and honour, it is inferior and incomplete. (So a hill, while complete in itself, is incomplete in comparison with a mountain; and a grain of mustard seed in comparison with a bean, although it may be larger than any other seed of the same kind.) So a relative incompleteness of the human mind (soul) is recognized, in relation to the Godhead of Christ, in virtue of which the problem of the coexistence in his person of two complete wholes (the human mind and the divine) is set aside. Viewed absolutely, it is not a case of one whole crowding out another whole. So the two wills may be acknowledged without fear that the one must yield place to the other. (But see also *Or. Theol.* iv 2.)

But the question had also to be considered, not only in regard to the unity of person, but also in regard to the freedom of the person from sin. It was an ethical question as well as a metaphysical problem. Could the Lord have a human soul (and the human will which it implied) and yet be sinless (χωρὶς ἁμαρτίας)?

HOW CAN CHRIST BE 'COMPLETE MAN' AND 'WITHOUT SIN'?

The fullest consideration of this question is to be found in 'Athanasius' *adv. Apoll.* ii 6 ff. (cf. i 17), in reply to the Apollinarian objection "If He assumed human nature entire, then assuredly He had human thoughts. But it is impossible that in human thoughts there should not be sin. How then will Christ be 'without sin'?" The answer given on the 'orthodox' side is first—that God is not the maker of thoughts which lead to sin, and that Christ attached to himself only what he himself had made. Adam was created rational by nature, free in thought, without experience of evil, knowing only what was good. He was capable of falling into sin, but was endowed with power to withstand it, and in fact had been free from it. It was the Devil who sowed in the rational and intellectual nature of man thoughts leading to sin, and so established in man's nature both a law of sin and death as reigning through sinful action. Thus it became impossible for that nature, having sinned voluntarily and incurred condemnation to death, to recall itself to freedom. Therefore the Son of God assumed this inward nature of man, not a part of it only, but the whole of it (for sin was not a part of it—but only a disposition infused by the Devil), and by his own absolute sinlessness emancipated man's nature henceforward from sin.

The Apollinarians, however, were not to be silenced so easily. They declared that the nature which had become accustomed to sin, and had received the transmission of sin, could not possibly be without sin. That is to say, they argued that human nature had become tainted by sin—the intellectual nature of man was incapable of escaping sin: and therefore there was no human nature free from sin for Christ to assume (such seems to be the meaning of their objection § 8). Its natural bias was to sin, and the human nature of Christ could only have escaped sin through the overpowering constraint of his Godhead — a constraint which would in effect destroy the freedom of will. The writer insists, on the contrary, that sin is not of the essence of manhood, and that the victory was won through the human nature which had once been defeated: Jesus went completely through every form of temptation, because he assumed all those things that had had experience of temptation; and it was not with the Godhead, which he knew not, but with man, whom he had long ago seduced and against whom he had ever since directed his operations, that the Devil engaged in warfare, and, finding in him no token of the old seed sown in man, was defeated. It was the form of man as at first created, flesh without carnal desires and human thoughts, that the Word restored or renewed in himself. The will belonged to the Godhead only. (This passage was adduced at a later time by the Monothelites, but the context shews clearly that the writer fully recognized a human will in Christ, and only intended to maintain that all the volitions of the human nature in him were in harmony with the will of the divine nature.)

Apollinarians have no right whatever to say 'it is impossible that human nature which has once been made captive should be set free from captivity'. In so doing they ascribe impotence to God and power to the Devil.

Such in brief is the answer which was given. It may, perhaps, be said to fairly meet the Apollinarian objection. But this writer does not seem to have faced the question "If the human nature which was assumed was not a nature so far fallen as to be capable of sinning, although remaining free from sin, how can the Incarnation and the perfect obedience of the Incarnate Son have effected the redemption of fallen man? What more did it do than exhibit an example of man as he was before the Fall, as he might have been if there had been no Fall? How could a mere example of sinless humanity, preserved all through from sin through union with the Godhead, avail to save men whose nature was already sinful?"

Gregory of Nyssa, however, does seem to regard the human nature assumed by Christ as fallen (sinful) human nature. So he writes (*Antirrhet.* 26 Migne xlv p. 1180) "For we say that God who is essentially free from matter and invisible and incorporeal, when the time of the consummation of all things was drawing near, by a special dispensation of love toward men; when wickedness had grown to its greatest; then, with a view to the destruction of sin, was blended with human nature, like a Sun as it were making his dwelling in a murky cave and by his presence dissipating the darkness by means of his light. For though he took our filth upon himself, yet he is not himself defiled by the pollution: but in his own self he purifies the filth. For, it says, the light shone in the darkness, but the darkness did not over-power it.[1] It is just what happens in the case of medicine. When curative medicine is brought to bear upon the disease, the ailment yields and vanishes, but it is not changed into the art of medicine."

And he recognizes progress of the human nature (Jesus) under the influence of the divine wisdom (Christ) with which it was united (*ibid.* 28). So again he maintains with reference to Lk. 22^{42} 'Not my will, but Thine be done', that there was in him the human will which shrank from pain as well as the divine will (though the latter always prevailed), the human weakness as well as the divine strength. The Lord made his own 'the lowly things of human fearfulness', and gave proof of his possession of our nature by sharing in its affections (*ibid.* 32). (Cf. 'Ath.' *de Incarn. et c. Arian.* 21.) And again (*ibid.* 53) "In his great long suffering he endured not to repel from communion with himself our nature, fallen though it was as the result of sin, but to receive it to himself to give it life again."

That is to say, the human will, though fallen, is able by union with the divine will to realize its true power. In this conception the solution of the problem may be found.

'THE ATHANASIAN CREED'[2]

Recent investigation has firmly re-established the traditional view of the unity of the *Quicumque vult* as against the theory advocated by Prof. Swainson and others, that the Creed was composite, formed out of separate parts—expositions of the doctrine of the Trinity and of the Incarnation. There are no indications of such patchwork about it: early commentaries on the Creed as a whole are in existence; and the 'two-portion' theory depends on the evidence of mere fragments of texts and assumptions which are quite inadequate to prove it.

There is also general agreement that it is to the south of Gaul that we must look for its origin, and great probability that its birthplace and early home was the famous monastery of Lerinum, founded by Honoratus, of which Faustus and Vincent and Hilary of Arles were members.

---

[1] This seems certainly to be the sense in which Gregory understood the passage John 1^5—οὐ κατέλαβεν contrasted with ἀναλαβών above.

[2] See Hahn^3 p. 174.

It is further recognized that the Creed is prior to Eutychianism, though some of its phrases are clearly applicable to a similar form of thought; but there is still dispute as to whether it is really directed against Nestorian or against Apollinarian conceptions.

It must suffice here to indicate reasons for the conviction that it is Apollinarianism that is opposed, and to cite the chief christological passage from the Creed for examination, as bringing into focus the different points in dispute throughout the controversy which has just been reviewed. It is as follows:—

". . . Dominus noster Jesus, Dei filius, Deus pariter et homo est. Deus est ex substantia Patris ante secula genitus, homo ex substantia matris in seculo natus: perfectus Deus, perfectus homo, ex anima rationali et humana carne subsistens, aequalis Patri secundum divinitatem, minor Patre secundum humanitatem. Qui licet Deus sit et homo, non duo tamen, sed unus est Christus: unus autem non conversione divinitatis in carnem, sed assumptione humanitatis in Deum; unus omnino non confusione substantiae, sed unitate personae. Nam sicut anima rationalis et caro unus est homo, ita et Deus et homo unus est Christus."

Let us see (1) what is opposed, (2) what is maintained.

(1) Opposed is conversion of divinity into flesh, and confusion of substance (which means 'confusion of God and man' as passages in Vincent and Augustine clearly shew). To these charges Nestorians were certainly not open. Apollinarians as certainly were, in their desire to avoid the risk of a double personality.

(2) Maintained is the completeness of the Godhead and of the manhood (the former being in substance the same as the Father's, the latter in substance the same as his Mother's), and the assumption of humanity into God, in such a way that there are not two persons, but one; that one being both God and man.

That is to say, we may recognize to the full the two natures (though it is the inclusive term *substantia* that is used), without fear that by so doing we shall be involved in recognition of a double personality.

There is nothing here that would hit Nestorians. The completeness of the humanity (as well as of the divinity) was a cardinal tenet with them, and they at any rate did not raise the difficulty of the union of the two substances in a single person.

The real aim of the Creed is to uphold (1) two complete substances, (2) united in one person. This is exactly what we should expect from an opponent of Apollinarianism (see *e.g.* Vincent *Commonit.* xii, and cf. Note on 'Substantia' *supra* p. 233); and the incidental phrases *ex substantia matris, in seculo natus, ex anima rationali et humana carne,* and the reference later on in the Creed to the Descent into Hell (on which much stress is laid by writers against Apollinarius), favour the conclusion that the composition of the Creed may be assigned with the greatest probability to the period during which Apollinarianism was rife, preceding the outbreak of Nestorianism in 428 A.D.

(The best collection of materials for the study of the problems connected with the Creed is to be found in G. D. W. Ommanney *A Critical Dissertation on the Athanasian Creed* 1897, side by side with which should be read A. E. Burn *The Athanasian Creed* Texts and Studies vol. iv no. 1, where a lucid statement of the history of criticism of the Creed is given in the Introduction. Waterland's *Critical History* is still valuable.)

CHAPTER XV

The Theological Schools of Alexandria and Antioch

IN these controversies, as in others, considerations which were really outside the main questions came in to complicate and embitter the relations between the two parties. Personal and ecclesiastical rivalries played their usual disconcerting part, and permanent differences in the mental constitution of men were reflected in the two great schools of thought which were engaged. The Alexandrian school had lost much of the scholarly instinct and interests which had characterized its representatives in earlier days, and the inheritance had passed to Antioch. The mystic tendency was to be found at Alexandria, the rational at Antioch. The theologians of Alexandria fixed their attention almost entirely on the divine element in the person of Christ, and so asserted in the strongest terms the unity of the divine and the human in him. While confessing the duality, they emphasised the unity. The human nature was taken into organic union almost as if it were absorbed with the divine : though the union was a mystery, incomprehensible. By the teachers of the school of Antioch, on the other hand, attention was concentrated in the first place on the human element. The completeness of the human nature of the Lord was certain, even if its separate personality was thereby implied. The tendency at Antioch was thus to separate the natures and explain the separation—to confess the unity but emphasise the duality.

Cyril, if himself untainted by the extreme conclusions, was at least an exponent of conceptions that easily led to the view of Christ as a composite being—a confusion of God and man— the Logos having absorbed humanity—one person and one nature. Nestorius, in his teaching, was only carrying on the traditions of the school of Antioch, which tended to see in

Christ a man who bore the divine nature, or the Logos joined
to human nature—two persons and two natures.

Diodorus and Theodore

These traditions had been formed and maintained by the
great teacher Diodorus of Tarsus († 394) and his more
famous pupil Theodore, the teacher in turn of Nestorius, and
probably the real originator of 'Nestorianism'. He seems to
reflect both in his life and teaching the best spirit of the
school of Antioch. For ten years after his ordination[1] to the
priesthood by Flavian, Bishop of Antioch, he devoted himself
to the pastoral work of the office, and to assiduous teaching and
writing, first at Antioch and afterwards at Tarsus (c. 383–393).
During this time he established so high a reputation that he
was chosen as Bishop of Mopsuestia in Cilicia, and until his
death, thirty-six years later (c. 428), his fame as a scholar and
bishop continually grew. He died "in the peace of the Church
and in the height of a great reputation"; retaining to the last
the warmest affection of Chrysostom and the highest regard of
the emperor. An excellent scholar, far-famed in his day as a
pillar of the truth and a commentator on the Scriptures,[2] and
honoured as a bishop and administrator, he may thus be taken

[1] Theodore was born at Antioch, of distinguished parentage, about 350. He
was a pupil also of the famous sophist Libanius (also a native of Antioch), in
whose school he began his lifelong friendship with that other pupil of Libanius,
whose eloquence won for him the name of Chrysostom (the 'John' who should
have succeeded his master 'if the Christians had not stolen him'). In early youth
he was caught by the prevailing enthusiasm for monasticism, and went from the
feet of Libanius to the ascetic and studious life of the cloister; but his ardour
soon cooled, and he returned to the prospect of office and honours in public life,
and even wished for marriage. Chrysostom succeeded in dissuading him from such
a change of purpose, and at the age of thirty-three his ordination took place
(c. 383).

[2] He is said to have composed Commentaries on the Psalms (noticeable for their
free investigations into questions of authorship and date), and on other books of the
Old Testament, as well as on the New Testament—some of which are still extant in
Syriac or Latin translations, if not in their original Greek, though of many there are
only fragments left. (He became to the Nestorian—East Syrian—Church the great
exponent and critic of the Scriptures, and his works were at once translated into
Syriac.) But besides these commentaries he wrote a large number of dogmatic and
controversial treatises, and, in particular, one *On the Incarnation*, of which fragments are extant ('Against the Incarnation' an opponent a century later styled it).
See Migne *P.G.* lxvi and lxxxvi; Leontius *c. Nest. et Eutych.* iii 43; and H. B.
Swete *Theodore of Mopsuestia on the Minor Epistles of St Paul* Appendix A vol. ii
pp. 293 ff.

as a good representative of the theological thought of the Eastern Church at the end of the fourth century. The views to which he gave expression—though some took exception to them — commended themselves to the Christian scholars of his time, and shew us the stage in the developement of the doctrine of the Person of Christ which had then been reached. It was left for a general council after his death to condemn his teaching (though not himself[1]) and to hunt to death his pupil Nestorius—who was elected Patriarch of Constantinople in the very year in which Theodore died—when he gave expression to the same or similar thoughts. Not till a hundred years after his death was the anathema pronounced which marked him as a heretic, outside the Catholic Church.[2]

His characteristic conceptions can be clearly seen in the fragments, which are still extant, of his work *On the Incarnation*.

In one of the longest of these[3] he discusses the nature of the indwelling of God in Christ. It is clear, he argues, that God does not dwell in all men, for it is promised as a special privilege to those that are holy (the saints) (Lev. 26[12]). Some have supposed that the indwelling spoken of is the indwelling of the 'being' of God. If this were so, the being of God would have to be limited to those in whom he is said to dwell, if the indwelling is to have any special significance : in which case he would be outside all else. This, however, is absurd, since He is infinite, everywhere present, and cannot be locally circumscribed. Or if we admit that He is everywhere, then by using the expression 'being' in this way, we should have to concede to everything a share in his indwelling too :—to everything, not only to men, but even to irrational things and those that have no soul

---

[1] A confession of faith drawn up by him was laid before the Council of Ephesus (431), and attacked by Charisius, a presbyter of Philadelphia. It had, he said, been sent by the Nestorians in Constantinople to some Quartodeciman heretics in Lydia, who wished to return to the Catholic Church, and had misled them into still greater errors than those from which they were to be brought. See Hahn[3] pp. 302–308. This creed was regarded by Cyril (*Quod unus est Christus* § 728) and by Marius Mercator (Migne *P.L.* xlviii p. 877) as the recognized statement of the Nestorian position.

[2] At the Fifth General Council, at Constantinople, in 553 :—a contrast to the earlier verdict which was voiced in the cry often heard in the churches, "We believe as Theodore believed ; long live the faith of Theodore !" (Cyril Al. *Ep.* 69).

[3] The extant fragments were collected and edited by O. F. Fritzsch, 1847, and again by H. B. Swete *l.c.* This passage is from the seventh book of the work *On the Incarnation*, quoted by Leontius (485–543) *c. Nest. et Eutych.* iii 43 (Migne *P.G.* lxxxvi 1 pp. 1267–1396).

17

(*or* life). So both alternatives are equally absurd, and it is clear that we must not speak of the indwelling as of the 'being' of God. Others have described the indwelling as the indwelling of the energy (force, activity, operative power) of God. But this supposition brings us face to face with precisely the same difficulties—the same alternatives. The only way in which the truth can be expressed is by the use of the term complacency (or good pleasure or approval).[1] The indwelling of God is the indwelling of the divine approval. With the disposition of some God is well-pleased; and in or by His pleasure in them, His approval, He dwells in them. By nature, as has been said, He cannot be limited or circumscribed; He is omnipresent: 'near' and 'far' are words that cannot be applied to Him. But in this moral relation He is near some and far from others. There is a divine aloofness and separation from those who have not affinity to the divine nature. A divine indwelling is established in those who are by character, by moral disposition, worthy of it. Of this 'indwelling' there are grades: in some it is closer than in others, according as they have a closer or less close affinity to him. It is the same indwelling in the apostles and the just as in Christ. But Theodore repudiates, as the height of madness, the idea that the indwelling in Christ was comparable in degree to the indwelling in the saints. For, in the first place, the fact of his sonship to God, he declares, removes him to another plane. It means that God united with Himself entirely the man that was assumed, and prepared him to partake with Him of all the honour which he who dwelt in Him—who is son by nature—shares. The sonship thus brings Christ into a uniquely close relation to God, who dwells in him in a unique degree. This indwelling furthermore, in the second place, began, in accordance with the divine foreknowledge, with the very first formation of the manhood in the Virgin's womb (in the case of the 'saints' the idea seems to be that they must prove their worthiness first), and shewed itself in his quick discernment of good and evil and his constant and easy choice of good and hatred of evil[2]—in all of which

---

[1] The terms used are οὐσία, ἐνέργεια, and εὐδοκία. Cf. the earlier use of the terms θελήματι, βουλῇ, and the like, in connexion with the generation of the Son. So εὐδοκία . . . γεννηθέντα in the Creed of the Apostolical Constitutions, Hahn[3] p. 140.

[2] Thus, though contending against Apollinarian denial of moral freedom in Christ, Theodore does not allow the idea of liberty to result in liberty of choice,

he received the co-operation of the divine Word, proportioned to his own natural disposition. Thus he advanced to the most perfect virtue, the pattern of which he afforded us, being appointed as it were for us a way to that end. And, thirdly, the union which he enjoys with God is indissoluble.

Such is the general account which Theodore gives of the relation between the two natures in Christ [1]—the human and the divine. He does not shrink from the term unification—union (ἕνωσις), though he often uses a word which means 'conjunction' (συνάφεια) rather than 'union.' It was his use of this term rather than the other to which exception was taken by his opponents. An extract which we owe to them enables us to understand his drift. It would be quite unfitting, he says, to speak of 'mixture' of the natures, for each retains indissolubly its own characteristics. 'Union' is the proper term, through which the natures concur to form one person, so that

but rather conceives the idea of the higher liberty, which consists in the unchangeable harmony of the human will with the divine—a kind of liberty which practically excluded all sin (Hefele *Councils* vol. iii p. 5). Comp. Augustine's conception of free will, as freedom to do always that which is right—see *infra* p. 310.

[1] Dr. Swete sums up the teaching of Theodore upon this point, as exhibited in his commentaries on the Pauline epistles, in the following sentences :—

"In Jesus of Nazareth the invisible Word, the Only-Begotten of the Father, manifested Himself, dwelling in the Man, and inseparably united to Him. The Man Christ . . . is thus the visible image of the invisible Godhead; and on account of his union with the true Son of God, he possesses the privileges of a unique adoption, so that to him also the title Son of God belongs. . . . But if it be asked, in what sense God dwelt in this Man, we must reply that it was by a special disposition towards him, a disposition of entire complacency. God, in His uncircumscribed nature and essence, fills the universe, nay, is all in all; in Christ He dwells in the person of the Word by a moral union, so unexampled and complete, that the divine Word and the humanity which He assumed are constantly regarded as being one person. The Man who thus became the habitation of God the Word received at his baptism the further indwelling of God the Holy Ghost, by whose power he wrought miracles, attained to moral perfection, and accomplished all that was necessary for the salvation of mankind" (*Theodore of Mopsuestia on the Minor Epistles of St Paul* vol. i pp. lxxxi ff.).

And, pointing out the source of Theodore's doctrinal errors, he says: "With the true estimate of the evil of sin, the necessity for an actual Incarnation of the Eternal Word disappears; a man indissolubly united to God through the permanent indwelling of the Word suffices for the work of vanquishing death" (*ibid.* p. lxxxvii).

In connexion with Theodore's "defective estimate of sin", it is to be noted that Marius Mercator charged him with being one of the originators of Pelagianism, and that he received Julian of Eclanum and other Italian bishops, when they were banished from their sees by Zosimus in 418 for refusing to accept the condemnation of Pelagius and Coelestius (see *infra* p. 320 n. 2). Theodore, however, afterwards concurred in the condemnation of Julian.

what the Lord says in the case of husband and wife, " They are no longer two, but one flesh ", we too might reasonably say of the conception of union, " they are no more two persons but one "—the natures of course being distinguished. For just as in the case of marriage, the fact that they are said to be one flesh does not prevent their being numerically two (the sense in which they are styled ' one ' is evident); so in the case before us the unity of the person does not preclude the difference of the natures (the fact that the person is one does not prevent the natures being different). This is how the matter stands—When we consider the natures separately, we say that the nature of the divine Word is complete, and the person is complete, for we cannot speak of a distinct existence ($\dot{\nu}\pi\acute{o}\sigma\tau\alpha\sigma\iota\varsigma$) as impersonal; and we say that the human nature and person likewise is complete: when, however, we have regard to the conjunction of the two, then we say that there is one person.

The conception of personality may not be very precise— the difference between ' nature ' and ' person ' not exact or definitive—but Theodore certainly means to recognize (and other passages have the same effect) the divine and the human nature in Christ, and the unity of his person. The one person has for its constituents the divine Word (the God-Word) and the humanity—each in its entirety; the person resulting from the union of the two is one.[1]

When his exposition was represented as implying that there were two sons (the human element in Christ was son in one sense, and the divine element—the God-Word—in the fullest sense), he expressly repudiated this inference from his teaching. His main desire had been to provide for a free moral developement in the Saviour's manhood, and to preclude the errors of Apollinarian theories.

The Outbreak of the Controversy—Nestorius at Constantinople

Such were the literary and theological traditions in which Nestorius was trained. This was the environment in which, as

---

[1] Dorner's view is that "Theodore never really arrived at the conception of volitions and thoughts, which were at once divine and human (divine-human): for he supposed the two natures (represented by him, at the same time, also as two persons), as to their inmost essence, to continue separate and distinct . . . Strictly speaking, the two persons were one only in outward appearance, as the image of marriage shews ! " (*Doct. of the Person of Christ* Eng. tr. Div. ii vol. i p. 47).

a member of the monastery of Euprepius near Antioch, he won so great a reputation for eloquence and austerity that he was elected Patriarch of Constantinople ; and thither he went in 428 with his chaplain Anastasius, a presbyter of Antioch, and an adherent of Theodore's views. At Constantinople he at once began an active campaign against heresies, which was sure to rouse up animosities; but it was apparently [1] his chaplain who actually kindled the flame, by preaching against the use of the title 'Theotokos'[2] applied to the Virgin Mary. The title had been in use for many years,[3] but now apparently, as a result of the increasing tendency to pay her homage, it was being brought into new prominence; and when Anastasius declaimed against it, "Let no one call Mary 'Theotokos'; for Mary was but a woman, and it is impossible that God should be born of a woman", the fanatical feelings of the crowd were stirred, and the title became at once the watchword of a party.

Nestorius followed up his chaplain's attack.[4] 'Theotokos' was held to savour of heathenism and to be opposed to the scriptural phrases which could be applied.[5] Mary was mother of the human nature only. God alone was Theotokos. All that could be properly be said of Mary was that she was the receptacle of God and gave birth to Christ.[6] The divine and human natures were distinctly separated. There was only a 'conjunction' of them—an 'indwelling' of the Godhead in the

[1] So Socrates *H.E.* vii 32 relates. The exact circumstances are not quite certain.

[2] Θεοτόκος (Lat. *deipara, dei genetrix*)—'Mother of God' is the common English translation, but the word means more precisely 'who gave birth to God'—Godbearer. Cf. German 'Gottesgebärerin'. It is not really equivalent to μήτηρ Θεοῦ which was used at a later time. As Dr. Robertson writes—"In the Greek word Θεοτόκος the component Θεός is logically a *predicate*, and as such is absolutely justified and covered by the Catholic doctrine. On the other hand, in the English phrase *Mother of God*, 'God' is practically a subject rather than a predicate, and therefore includes logically the person of the Father." See also *infra* p. 262.

[3] It had been used by Origen, Alexander of Alexandria, Eusebius (*V.C.* iii), Athanasius (*c.g. Or. c. Ar.* iii 33), Cyril (*Cat.* x 19), and others.

[4] The sermons of Nestorius (five *adv. dei genetricem Mariam* and four *adv. haeresim Pelagianam*) are extant in a Latin translation in the works of Marius Mercator, an African orthodox layman, who was in Constantinople at the time and took great interest in the controversy. His other works were diligently destroyed, and only fragments are extant as quotations in the writings of opponents, *e.g.* in the Acts of the Council of Ephesus, and in Cyril Al., especially his five books against the blasphemy of Nestorius. The twelve anathemas in answer to Cyril's are only extant in the translation of Marius.

[5] *e.g.* the ἀπάτωρ ἀμήτωρ of Heb. 7³.

[6] The terms that could be used were Θεοδόχος and χριστοτόκος.

man, resulting in a moral and sympathetic union. "I separate the natures, but the reverence I pay them is joint", are the words in which Nestorius defended his teaching.[1]

Such a union is rightly described as 'mechanical' and as due to the arbitrary exertion of the divine power, by which natures incongruous and incompatible in their essence had been brought together in an artificial alliance rather than a living union.

The Title Θεοτόκος

To refuse to the Mother of the Lord the title 'Theotokos' was doubtless to deny her a title of honour that was rightly hers; but it was much more than this. The English translation 'Mother of God' brings into undue prominence the thought of the glory of her motherhood; the Greek term fixes attention rather on the Godhead of him who was born. To deny that she was Theotokos was really to deny that he who was born of her was God[2] as well as man. The abruptness of the English phrase does not attach to the Greek, which effectually guards the interpretation of the revelation in Christ that sees in him Very God made man, and teaches that the Son of God in assuming manhood from the Virgin lost nothing of the Godhead which was eternally his. At the same time it is worthy of note that it guards equally well against an opposite error from that which is now before us—he who was born of Mary must have been man as well as God.

Cyril of Alexandria—Denunciation of the Nestorian Teaching

The natural deduction from the denial of the title was indeed speedily made. Cyril[3] of Alexandria declared that some of his monks refused to call Christ God, styling him only the instrument of divinity; and later on he charged Nestorius with denying the divinity of Christ. At Easter 429 he issued an elaborate exposition of the doctrine, and stirred up the

---

[1] Separo naturas, sed conjungo reverentiam. Cf. the reply of Noetus *supra* p. 104.

[2] See on this point and for the whole question the admirable notes to Bright's *Sermons of Leo on the Incarnation* (note 3 pp. 127, 128), and his *Waymarks in Church History*, pp. 180, 181.

[3] For the history and character of Cyril see the Church Histories and W. Bright's article in *D.C.B.* He was certainly the best theologian of all who were engaged in this controversy.

Egyptian monks and clergy in Constantinople and the ladies of the court, and engaged in a heated correspondence with Nestorius. Throughout the controversy, though Cyril had no doubt the better case, his methods of conducting it were most unamiable; and he cannot be acquitted of the suspicion of being prompted by worldly motives, and jealousy of the rising see of Constantinople, as well as by the desire for theological truth. To Nestorius Apollinarianism was a 'red rag', and he was less dignified in manner than his chief assailant; but impetuous as he was, he would have accepted, instead of 'Theotokos', a term that perhaps sufficiently defined the theory,[1] had the controversy been less à outrance. As it was, Cyril secured from Celestine, the Bishop of Rome, the formal condemnation of Nestorius, by a Council held in August 430; and, having ratified the sentence at a Council of his own at Alexandria, he sent it to Constantinople in November, with a long expository letter and a dozen anathemas, which constituted an attack upon the whole school of Antioch.[2] The letter, though couched in somewhat arrogant and dictatorial terms, is of high importance as a statement of the doctrine which is the basis of the anathemas. Nestorius responded to it by twelve counter-anathemas.[3]

Cyril's Anathemas and the Answers of Nestorius

These two sets of anathemas reveal sufficiently clearly the points at issue.

i. Cyril maintains that Emmanuel[4] (the Incarnate Son) is truly God, and that therefore the Holy Virgin is 'Theotokos'— for she has generated (in fleshly wise) the Word of God who has become flesh. Nestorius replies that he who is Emmanuel is not to be called God the Word, but rather 'God with us', in the sense that, by the fact of his union with our constituents received from the Virgin, he dwelt in the nature which is like ours; and the Holy Virgin is not to be called Mother 'of God

---

[1] Viz. Χριστοτόκος or Θεοδόχος.

[2] The letter is given in Heurtley *de Fide et Symbolo* as the 'third letter' to Nestorius pp. 182 ff. It is also known as the *Epistola Synodica*. The anathemas are given in Hahn [3] pp. 312–316 with the Latin translation of Marius Mercator. (The English is in Hefele *Councils* iii p. 31 ff. who, however, follows a different text.)

[3] These are only extant in the Latin translation of Marius Mercator—Hahn [3] pp. 316–318.

[4] 'God with us'—*i.e.* the Incarnate Person, both God and man.

the Word', but 'of him who is Emmanuel'. Nor is God the Word himself to be said to be changed into flesh, which he received for the purpose of manifesting the deity, so that he might be found in bearing as a man.

ii. Cyril maintains that the Word of God the Father was hypostatically united with flesh, and with His own flesh is one Christ—one and the same God and man together. Nestorius replies by an anathema on any one who, "in the conjunction of the Word of God which was made with the flesh, says that a change from place to place of the divine essence was made, and that the flesh was able to contain the divine nature, and that it was partially united to the flesh; or again ascribes to the flesh an infinite extension, so that it could contain (or receive) God, though the divine nature cannot be contained within the limits of the flesh",[1] and says that the same nature is both God and man.

iii. Cyril condemns the view of those who in the case of the one Christ divide the *hypostases* (? persons or substances) after the union, conjoining them only by a conjunction of dignity, or by an arbitrary act of authority or power, and not rather by a concurrence or combination of them such as effects a 'natural' union. Nestorius insists that Christ, who is Emmanuel, is not to be called one in regard to nature, but in regard to the conjunction (of the natures); and that out of both 'substances' (that of the God-Word and that of the man assumed by him) there is one combination—the Son, and that the substances still preserve this combination without being 'confused'. [Nestorius probably used both οὐσία and *hypostasis*.[2] He understood Cyril to mean a union into one nature, though he really meant a real union into one being, one *hypostasis*, as opposed to a moral or external union. Nestorius was anxious to uphold the permanent distinction between the divine and the human, and to repudiate any mixture or merging of one in the other, and to him there were still two *hypostases* in the one

---

[1] The Latin is very obscure "in infinitum incircumscriptam divinae naturae cooxtenderit carnem ad capiendum Deum". Perhaps the Greek was ἀπερίγραφον τῆς θείας φύσεως.

[2] In the corresponding anathema of Cyril, Marius M. translates ὑπόστασις by *substantia*, though in others he has *subsistentia*. If Nestorius wrote ὑπόστασις (and not οὐσία), it was probably in the sense of οὐσία, according to the older usage; and so it was rightly rendered by *substantia*. (Marius M. has *essentia* once—Anath. ii.)

Christ. Cyril meant nearly what we mean by *person*, Nestorius meant what Latins meant by *substantia*.]

iv. The Scriptures contain sayings about Christ by himself, and by others of him, some of which seem to apply to him as man, some as the Word. Cyril condemns the method of interpretation which would separate these sayings into two classes, and apply them respectively to the two persons or hypostases (the man and the Word) conceived of separately from each other.[1] Nestorius replies that Christ is of both natures, and that to apply these sayings, as though they were written of one nature, is to attribute to the very Word of God human affections and passions.

v, vi, vii, viii. Cyril protests against calling Christ 'a God-bearing man'[2] (rather than truly God and the one Son by nature), or calling the Word the God or Lord of Christ; or saying that in Jesus as man the Divine Word operated, and that the glory of the Only-begotten was attached to him as something foreign. Nor may we say that the man who was assumed is to be worshipped and glorified together *with* the Divine Word, and together *with* him be called God, as distinct from him (different from that in which he is); but one worship and one doxology is to be offered to 'Emmanuel'. Nestorius, on the other hand, declares it anathema to say that after the assumption of man the Son of God is naturally (by nature) one; or after the Incarnation to name as God the Word anyone but Christ, and to say that the 'form of a servant' which was with God the Word did not have a beginning but was uncreated as He is, instead of acknowledging it to have been created by him as its natural lord and creator and God. Again, we must not say that the man who was created of the Virgin is the Only-begotten who was born from the womb of his Father before the Day-star; whereas he is acknowledged by the title of Only-begotten by reason of his union with him who is by nature the Only-begotten of the Father. And, on the question of worship, Nestorius replies that it cannot be offered to the 'form of a servant' itself, which is reverenced only in virtue of the fellowship by which it is conjoined and linked together with the blessed and naturally sovereign nature of the Only-begotten.

ix. Cyril repudiates the teaching that the one Lord Jesus Christ received glory from the Spirit, and used the power which he

---

[1] Cf. on this point Leo's *Letter to Flavian* § 5, *infra* p. 290.
[2] See note on Θεοφόρος ἄνθρωπος *infra* p. 276.

had through him as other than his own (external), and received
from him the power of action against unclean spirits, and of
performing his miracles on men; and declares that the spirit
through which he wrought these signs was 'his very own'.
(This is against the Antiochene teaching with regard to the Holy
Spirit, especially Theodore's—see *supra* p. 216 n.)   The anathema
of Nestorius, on the other hand, is directed against those who say
that the Holy Spirit is consubstantial with the 'form of a
servant,' and do not rather explain the miracles of healing and
the power of driving out spirits by the connexion and conjunction which exist between the Spirit and God the Word from
his very conception.

x. Cyril condemns the view that it was not the Word of
God himself who became our high-priest and apostle, but the
'man born of a woman', regarded separately as distinct from the
Word; and also the view that he offered the sacrifice for himself
as well as for us.   Nestorius declares that the high-priesthood
and apostleship are Emmanuel's rather than the Word's, and
that the parts of the oblation ought to be separately attributed to
him who united and to him who was united, assigning to God
what is God's and to man what is man's.[1]

xi, xii. In conclusion, Cyril requires the confession that the
Lord's flesh is life-giving and belongs to the Word of God the
Father.   It must not be regarded as belonging to some other,
who is merely conjoined to Him or enjoys a divine indwelling:
it is life-giving in that it has become the Word's own—the
Word's who has power to bring all things to life.   And we must
confess that the Word of God suffered in the flesh, and was
crucified in the flesh, and tasted death in the flesh, and became
first-born from the dead.   Nestorius, on the other hand, insists
that the flesh which was united to the Word of God is not life-
giving by any property of its own nature; that God the Word
was not made flesh as touching his 'substance'; and that the
sufferings of the flesh must not be attributed to the Word of
God and the flesh in which he was made *together*, without
discriminating between the degrees of honour which belong to
the different natures.

---

[1] This means apparently that the Logos, who unites, offers the sacrifice of the
manhood, which is united.   But Hefele seems to understand the anathema
differently, and certainly in an earlier sermon Nestorius had protested against the
idea that God could act as High Priest.

The Significance of these Anathemas—the Reception given to them

It is clear that, in regard to nearly all the points involved, each of the disputants was setting in the most unfavourable light what he regarded as the natural premises or conclusions of his opponent's teaching. Scarcely ever does Nestorius meet the anathema by a direct negative. He suspects that there is at the back of it an idea which he regarded as false, and it is this latent error that he denounces. In the same way the anathemas of Cyril seem to deal more with possible inferences · from Nestorian teaching than with the actual tenets of Nestorius. These anathemas of Cyril were indeed by no means universally acceptable.[1] They were read and approved, it is true, with the letter to which they were appended, at the Council of Ephesus; but a request that the same approval should be given at Chalcedon was passed over.

Cyril's Dogmatic Letter

Greater authority attaches to an earlier letter (the 'Second' or 'Dogmatic' Letter, written in the first months of the year 430),[2] which was formally sanctioned by both Councils. Cyril sets himself the task of expounding what the Creed really means by the 'Word of God' being 'incarnate and made man', and what it does not mean.

It does not mean that there was any alteration in the nature of the Word, or that it was changed into man as a whole (body and soul); but rather that " the Word united hypostatically to himself flesh ensouled (animate) with a reasonable soul, and in a manner indescribable and inconceivable, became man, and was called 'Son of man', not simply by an act of volition or complacence, nor yet in the sense that he had merely adopted a rôle; but that while the natures which are brought together to form the true unity are different, out of both is one Christ and Son. Not that the difference of the natures is destroyed by reason of the union; but rather that the Godhead and the manhood, by

---

[1] At the time itself they were supposed to be 'Apollinarian' (esp. the third and the twelfth), and as such were opposed by the Antiochene school in general, and particularly by John of Antioch and Theodoret of Cyrrhus (on whom see *infra* pp. 284, 285).

[2] The letter is given in full in Heurtley *de Fide et Symbolo* p. 182 ff., and the greater part in Hahn[3] p. 310.

means of their inexpressible and mysterious concurrence to form a union, have produced for us the one Lord and Son Jesus Christ." It is in this sense that, though existing before the ages and having an eternal generation from the Father, he is said to have had also a generation of the flesh, since for our sakes and on account of our salvation he united human nature with himself as a *hypostasis* and came forth from a woman. This does not mean "that in the first place an ordinary man was generated of the holy Virgin, and that afterwards the Word came down upon him"; but it means that, "since a union was effected in the womb itself, he is said to have undergone a fleshly generation, inasmuch as he made his own the generation of his own flesh".

The sense in which he suffered and rose again is similarly explained. The divinity, inasmuch as it is also incorporeal, cannot suffer, and it was not in regard to his own nature that the divine Word suffered blows, or piercings of nails, or the other wounds. "But since it was the body which had become his own that suffered these things, he himself is said to have suffered on our behalf. For he who cannot suffer was in the body that was suffering." In like manner the Word of God is by nature immortal and incorruptible, and life and life-giving. "But inasmuch as it was his own body which by the grace of God tasted death on behalf of everyone, he himself is said to have suffered that death on behalf of us—not, of course, that he experienced death as regards his own nature—it were madness to say or think such a thing—but that . . . *his* flesh tasted death." Similarly it was his body that was raised again, and so the resurrection is called his.

The Logos with the flesh and body which are his own is absolutely one, and so it is one Christ and Lord that we confess; and as one and the same we worship him (*i.e.* not as though we worshipped a man *together with* the Logos)—not making any distinction in this respect between the Logos and the manhood. Indeed, if any one takes objection to the hypostatic union, either as incomprehensible or as unseemly, he cannot escape the error of speaking of 'two sons'; but the one Lord Jesus Christ must not be divided into two sons. Nothing is gained either by speaking ominously of a union of *persons*—"for Scripture has not said that the Logos united to himself the person of man, but that he became flesh; and to say that the Logos became flesh is precisely to say that he partook of blood and of flesh just as we do." That is to say, the manhood which he assumed was impersonal, but the mode and the result of the union was personal.[1] Furthermore, he remained God all through, and the human generation in time did not in any way detract from the divine generation in eternity. "He made our body his own and came forth from a woman as man, not having lost his being God and having been born of God his Father, but even in the assumption of flesh remaining (continuing to be) what he was."[2]

Such, Cyril declares, has always been the accurate account of the faith of the Church, and, in conclusion, he adds an explanation of the use of the term 'Theotokos' as meaning what he has expressed. "It was in this sense that the holy fathers have been bold to speak of the Holy Virgin as 'Theotokos': not in the sense that the nature of the Logos, or his deity, received from the Holy Virgin the beginning of its being; but in the sense that the holy body was born of her and rationally ensouled (received a rational soul); and therefore the Logos, being hypostatically united to this body, is said to have been born as regards the flesh." That is to say, the Virgin is the Bearer of God, because she bore him who is God as well as man, though she is the Mother of the Saviour in regard to his humanity only.

Earlier Teaching in the Church on the Subject. Tertullian, Origen, Athanasius

With regard to the main issue there can be no doubt that Cyril was right in claiming for this teaching the support of the fathers of the Church. He was indeed using almost the very words of Tertullian[3] of old, and of the greatest of the teachers of Alexandria before his own time.

Origen, without any sense of saying anything that was not universally allowed, declared that the Logos "while made man remained the God which he was"[4]—and again, "the Son of

---

[1] See Note on 'The Impersonality of the Human Nature of The Lord' p. 294.

[2] See Note on 'The Κένωσις' p. 294.

[3] Tertullian (as we have already seen *supra* p. 144) had been the first to give expression to the doctrine. Leo, at a later time, is simply restating his teaching almost in his very words. See esp. *c.g. adv. Prax.* 27, "Deus autem neque desinit esse, neque aliud potest esse. Sermo autem deus, et sermo domini manet in aevum, perseverando scilicet in sua forma." Cf. also Greg. Naz. *Theol. Or.* iv. esp. 20 ff.

[4] Origen *de Princip.* preface, § 4.

God, through whom all things were created, is named Jesus Christ and the Son of man. For the Son of God is said to have died—in respect, namely, of that nature which could admit of death; and he who is announced to be about to come in the glory of God the Father with the holy angels is called the Son of man. And for this reason, all through the Scriptures, not only are human predicates applied to the divine nature, but the human nature is adorned by appellations of divine dignity."[1]

And, with regard to the sufferings and other experiences of the human nature, Athanasius wrote:[2] "For this reason the special properties of the flesh, such as to hunger, to thirst, to be weary, and the like of which the flesh is capable, are predicated of him (or are described as his)—because he was in it; while, on the other hand, the works which are proper to the Logos himself, such as to raise the dead, to restore sight to the blind, and to cure the woman with an issue of blood, he did through his own body. The Logos endured the infirmities of the flesh as his own, for the flesh was his; and the flesh ministered to the works of the Godhead, because the Godhead was in it, for the body was God's. . . . When the flesh suffered the Logos was not external to it, and therefore the passion is said to be his; and when he wrought divinely the works of his Father, the flesh was not external to him, but in the body itself the Lord did them." And he proceeds to give instances—just the same as those which Leo afterwards adduced—to shew how, though the different experiences and works were accomplished by one and the same divine and human person, it was in virtue now of the manhood and now of the Godhead.[3]

The Council of Ephesus, 431, and the Victory of Cyril

The emperor, Theodosius, was under the influence of Nestorius, and accused Cyril of disturbing the peace and trying to sow

---

[1] Origen de Princip. ii 6 3. Hefele (Councils vol. iii p. 8) cites from the Commentary on the Epistle to the Romans the note, "Through the indissoluble unity of the Word and the flesh, everything which is proper to the flesh is ascribed also to the Word, and what is proper to the Word is predicated of the flesh."

[2] Ath. Or. c. Ar. iii 31–33; cf. iv 6, 7; and incidentally, de Sent. Dionys. 26 "For he himself permits the special properties of the flesh to be predicated of him, that it may be shewn that the body was not another's but his very own."

[3] Cf. also Epiphanius Ancorat. 36 and 95; adv. Haer. lxix 24, 42, lxxii 23.

sedition; but by general consent a council was summoned to deal
with the questions at issue, to meet at Ephesus at Pentecost in
the following year.

Nestorius with his bishops, and Cyril attended by as many
as fifty of his, arrived at Ephesus before the time appointed, and
within a few days of Pentecost there were gathered together
most of those who had been summoned. But there were still
some very important absentees. John, the Metropolitan of
Antioch, and the bishops of his province, had been delayed on the
journey, and sent word that they were coming as quickly as
they could. When, however, the days went by and they did
not arrive,[1] Cyril and his friends determined to open the Synod;
and in spite of the protests of the imperial commissioner and
some seventy bishops (including Theodoret of Cyrrhus), and the
refusal of Nestorius to appear, a session was held (on June 22nd)
from early morning into the night, and the excommunication of
Nestorius was decreed by a unanimous vote of two hundred.
Some acts of violence against Nestorius and his friends were
committed by the people of Ephesus, but they were provided
with a guard by the imperial commissioner. A few days later,
John of Antioch arrived with forty Syrian bishops, and at once
held a council and deposed Cyril and Memnon of Ephesus for
their disorderly proceedings. Cyril's party continued to hold
sessions, and both sides endeavoured to secure the emperor's
support, the Antiochenes, in particular, charging Cyril with
Apollinarianism and violence and injustice. The emperor decided
to confirm the depositions on both sides, and early in August
Cyril and Memnon, as well as Nestorius, were arrested at Ephesus
and imprisoned. The majority and their friends at once made
fresh representations to the emperor; and at last, after receiving
deputies from both sides at Chalcedon, he ordered the release
and restoration of Cyril and of Memnon; while Nestorius was
to remain at his old monastery of Euprepius, whither he
had already been sent, and a new bishop was appointed in his
place.

Cyril had thus, partly by the inherent merits of his cause,

[1] It is reported (see Hefele *Councils* vol. iii p. 45) that two bishops of the
province of Antioch said that John had bidden them tell Cyril not to wait for
him, and it has been inferred that John wished not to be present at the condemnation of his former priest and friend. But, as the same two bishops signed
the protest against the subsequent proceedings of Cyril, the account must be
received with suspicion.

but partly also by the aid of bribes or customary presents[1] to some of the great officials of the Court, secured his own position in the East, while he had been strong all through in the support of the West, through the Bishop of Rome.

Terms of Agreement between Cyril and the Antiochenes. The Union Creed

But the Antiochenes were by no means satisfied, and Cyril saw that it was necessary to divide them if possible, and to win over the Metropolitan—the natural leader of the Syrian opposition. He and those who were most anxious for peace and concord were steadfastly determined not to recognize Cyril till he had given satisfactory explanations, and with this end in view, after much discussion, an envoy (Paul of Emesa) was despatched to Alexandria in 433, bearing with him a form of creed to serve as a test, which Cyril was to be required to accept. This creed[2]—intended to unite the Antiochenes and to be an *Eirenicon* to their opponents—contains the following declarations on the points at issue: " We confess therefore our Lord Jesus Christ the Son of God, the only begotten, complete God and complete man, of a rational soul and body: begotten of his Father as touching his Godhead before the ages, but all the same in the last days, on account of us and on account of our salvation, of Mary the Virgin as touching his manhood: co-essential with the Father as touching his Godhead and all the same co-essential with us as touching his manhood: for there has been effected a union of two natures—therefore we confess one Christ, one Son, one Lord. In accordance with this conception of the unconfused union we confess the Holy Virgin to be the bearer of God (Theotokos), because God the Word was incarnate and made man, and from the very conception united to himself the temple which was received from her. And of the expressions of evangelists and apostles concerning the Lord, we know that theologians apply some generally as referring to one person, and discriminate others as referring to two natures; and those which

---

[1] So his apologists (*e.g.* Hefele) prefer to style them. The abbot Eutyches first comes before us as Cyril's agent in this matter. The monks of Constantinople, under Dalmatius the Archimandrite, were also strong and even violent allies.

[2] See Hahn[3] p. 215. In the main it was the same as one previously sent to the emperor, probably composed by Theodoret.

are of a divine character they refer to the Godhead of Christ, and those that are lowly to his manhood."

This statement certainly seems to favour the Antiochene rather than the Alexandrian point of view—but the title Theotokos is expressly admitted, and 'union' is used instead of 'conjunction'; and Cyril accepted the Creed and embodied it in his reply, John on his part agreeing to the judgement pronounced against Nestorius, and anathematizing his 'infamous doctrines'. Cyril further defended himself in his letter [1] against misrepresentations, and particularly requested John to join in checking the senseless ideas of a mixture or blending of the Logos with the flesh, or of any change at all in the divine nature, "for that remains ever what it is and never can be changed".

Dissatisfaction with the Definitions on both sides. Cyril's Vindication of them

The 'union' which was thus brought about failed to satisfy many on both sides. Of Cyril's former adherents there were some who thought that he was now accepting Nestorian errors; some merely misunderstood the terms which were used; while others—the forerunners of Monophysite conceptions—consciously disapproved of the teaching which Cyril represents. Accordingly, in a series of letters,[2] he defended the 'union', insisting that there were two natures, and yet there was a complete but unconfused union of the two, and that the doctrinal statement agreed upon simply excluded misapprehensions of the doctrine which he himself had constantly repudiated. The Nestorians were right in teaching two natures; their error lay in their not acknowledging a real union of the two. So, now that the Orientals agreed in allowing no separation of the natures, only teaching a distinction between them in thought, they were really accepting what he himself meant by the phrase " one incarnate nature of the Logos ". So, too, with regard to the predications in Scripture, they did not say " one class refer only to the Logos of God, the other only to the Son of man"; but they said "the one refer only to the Godhead, the other to the manhood "—and in saying

---

[1] The letter known as *Laetentur Coeli* (Heurtley *de Fide et Symbolo* p. 199 ff.).

[2] To Acacius *Ep.* 40, Eulogius *Ep.* 44, Valerian *Ep.* 50, and Successus *Ep* 45 (Migne lxxvii p. 181 ff.). See Hefele *Councils* vol. iii p. 140 ff.

so they were right, ascribing both alike to the one Son (who is both Son of God and Son of man).

Inasmuch as Cyril thus clearly recognizes the distinction between the natures, and insists that there is no kind of mixture of one with the other (though holding the union to be so complete that in the incarnate Christ the distinction is apprehended rather in our own thought than in his person), it seems to be certain that the expression "one incarnate nature of the Word" is intended to denote the unity of the person. The centre of this personality was the Logos who "remained always what he was" before the Incarnation.

And this was the teaching for which a large number of the 'Nestorian' bishops were not prepared. It seemed to them to endanger the full recognition of the manhood of Christ. They would not anathematize Nestorius; they would not accept the compromise in which apparently some were able to acquiesce without giving up their old ideas; and they would not recognize Cyril as orthodox.

The Strength and the Weakness of Nestorianism

The real strength of Nestorianism lay in its clear perception of the reality of the human nature of the Lord. The Saviour of men really went through the normal experiences of the life which man must live. At a time in the developement of doctrine —in the work of interpretation of the Person of Christ—when there was once again danger lest the full and complete humanity of the Redeemer should fail to win theoretic recognition, and an interpretation of his Person should be accepted which would practically be a denial of the Incarnation in its true significance, Nestorianism rendered service to the Church. It insisted that the human experiences of the Lord were really human. But what it gave with one hand it took away with the other. Its theory failed to cover the deepest conviction of the Christian consciousness that in Jesus God and man had really been brought together in a vital and permanent union, never henceforward to be dissolved: that the chasm between God and man had been bridged over, so that all who were united with Jesus were united with God Himself. The Nestorian theory only provided for an external union, which was understood to be an alliance of two distinct beings. And so the Incarnation was as much emptied of its meaning as it was by any theory which failed to provide recognition either for the complete manhood or for the complete Godhead of the Saviour. But though Nestorianism was inevitably condemned, the Church had still to seek for a clearer conception of the relation between the Godhead and the manhood and of their union in one Person.

Nestorians were at all events convinced that Jesus Christ was both God and man; that in him the experiences of both natures were fully represented. Nor can they be accused of exaggerating the distinction between the divine and the human natures and functions. They did not realize that distinction too vividly; but they failed to realize the idea of God becoming man—one who was eternally God entering upon the sphere of human life. In this respect at all events a fundamental issue was made clear by Cyril. The Catholic interpretation of the Gospel is based on the idea of God condescending to be born as man; a divine Person stoops to assume human nature and live a human life, without ceasing to be divine. About this conception there is a unity which is never for a moment in danger of dissolution. But the very starting-point of Nestorian thought excluded the possibility of unity. Indeed, Nestorians started not from one point, but from two, and the lines of their thought ran always parallel, side by side. There was Man, and there was God. Both were persons, and the conjunction in which the two were brought together was only one of relation ($\sigma\chi\epsilon\tau\iota\kappa\dot{\eta}$ $\sigma\upsilon\nu\dot{\alpha}\phi\epsilon\iota\alpha$). And so they never reached a clear conception of a Person living in two spheres of consciousness and experience.[1] To this conception Cyril seems really to have attained, though there were some difficulties of terminology which he did not altogether overcome.

As a theory of the Person of Christ, Nestorianism is weak and inadequate, so far as it fails to realize the union of manhood and Godhead as actually effected in a single Person who lived the life of men. But as against any theory which in any way in effect, if not intentionally, tends to annul the entirety of the manhood of Jesus, Nestorianism is strong, and makes its appeal direct to the heart of men. It is a mistake to regard it as merely 'rationalistic'.

---

[1] They 'could not see that the distinction between the two spheres of existence might be maintained without abandoning or denying the unity of their subject' (W. Bright *The Age of the Fathers* vol. ii p. 281).

And so it won and retained its hold over great numbers of men.

Suppression of Nestorianism within the limits of the Empire

Against those who were not to be won over by explanations and negotiations, the Patriarch of Antioch at last appealed for the aid of the civil power. Nestorius in 435 was turned out of his monastery and banished to Petra in Arabia, and a little later to Ptolemais, a kind of Siberia, to which the worst criminals were sent.[1] The emperor ordered all his writings to be burnt, and his adherents all the more eagerly disseminated those of Diodorus and Theodore, and translated them into other languages (Syriac, Armenian, and Persian). Many bishops were deposed and expelled from their sees, and, in consequence of the stringent measures adopted, the Nestorian heresy was soon suppressed throughout the whole of the Roman Empire. For a time it found a refuge in the school of Edessa, but, when this famous centre of theological learning was closed by the Emperor Zeno in the year 489, Nestorianism lost its last hold in the Empire.[2]

By these means the controversy was silenced for the time. But the theological tendencies which prompted it were too opposed to admit of easy combination, and on the death of Cyril the extreme champions of the oneness of the natures, whom he had been able to keep in check, broke loose; and, when the controversy which resulted was closed, the Church had lost another band of enthusiastic, if mistaken, Christians.

Θεοφόρος ἄνθρωπος

In a note on the use of the title θεοφόρος by Ignatius, as a second name for himself (ὁ καὶ θεοφόρος) Lightfoot writes (*Apostolic Fathers, Ignatius* vol. ii p. 21) "This word would be equally appropriate to the true Christian, whether taken in its active sense (θεοφόρος *bearing God, clad with God*) or in its passive sense (θεόφορος *borne along by God, inspired by God*)"; citing in support of his comment the words of Clement Al. (*Strom.* vii 13) θεῖος ἄρα ὁ γνωστικὸς καὶ ἤδη ἅγιος, θεοφορῶν καὶ θεοφορούμενος.

But he proceeds to shew that Ignatius certainly used the word in

---

[1] He was still alive in 439 when Socrates wrote his history, and a Coptic MS. of the life of Dioscorus says he was summoned to the Council of Chalcedon in 451. It seems unlikely that he lived so long, but when and where he died is unknown.

[2] See Additional Note—"The Nestorian Church" p. 279.

the active sense (as other similar compounds such as ναοφόρος, χριστο-φόρος, σαρκοφόρος, νεκροφόρος); and that it was so interpreted universally till a very late date, when the legend grew up that Ignatius was the very child whom our Lord took up in his arms (Mark 9³⁶ and ||s). He also cites passages proving that the metaphor of 'bearing God' or 'bearing Christ' was familiar to early Christian writers, and that it is this sense rather than that of 'wearing God' as a robe that is intended, though the Syriac translator rendered it 'God-clad' and St Paul's metaphor of 'putting on Christ' might suggest that image.

The word has also commonly, if not universally, been understood in the active sense in the phrase ἄνθρωπός θεοφορος as used in the Christo-logical controversies of the fourth and fifth centuries, and so it has been taken in the foregoing account to mean 'a man who bears God with him', implying that the man, so to say, was prior in time, and was favoured with the special choice of God, who is pleased to dwell in him —a man in whom God dwells.

But Dr Robertson writes that he holds that this is a mistake, and that the word is here passive in sense, 'God-borne' i.e. inspired.[1]

There is only room here for a brief statement of the question.

The phrase seems to be first used by Apollinarians as a taunt which they cast at the doctrine of their opponents, charging them with worshipping an ἄνθρωπος θεοφόρος, and maintaining that the true object of worship was rather a θεὸς σαρκοφόρος. (See Greg. Naz. Ep. 102 where the allusion is brought in incidentally to shew the absurdity of the Apollinarian position by an interchange of σάρξ and ἄνθρωπος in one of their own expressions.) The antithesis shews that the word is used in the active sense.

It is again as a taunt that we meet it next, though in a sense the tables are turned. Apollinarians said that the Christ of the 'orthodox' was a 'God-bearing man'; but now it is Nestorians against whom the charge is brought that they preach a θεοφορος ἄνθρωπος, and this by Cyril who was himself suspected—not without reason as far as his language went—of Apollinarian tendencies. The historical antecedents of the phrase suggest, accordingly, that it is the active sense that is still intended—'a man bearing with him God'. It was certainly understood and used in this sense by later writers (see passages cited in Suicer's *Thesaurus*); and thus interpreted it expresses concisely the objections which are constantly reiterated against Nestorians—viz. that they made the manhood (the man) the starting-point, so to say, of their doctrine, and conceived of Christ as a man, with whom God was joined in some

---

[1] It must be noted that, whether the compound is active or passive, the general sense 'inspired' would hold. If active, the idea is that of a man who bears within him God, and so has with him a divine guide. If passive, the idea is that of a man who is upheld and sustained by the divine light and strength.

other way than in that of a real union (συνάφεια, not ἕνωσις); so that his Person was composed, as it were, of a man and a God—the Son of Man and the Son of God. So their opponents argued that the sense in which they applied the term 'God' to the individual human person whom they called Christ could not exclude the notion of two Sons. The idea of the indwelling of God κατ᾽ εὐδοκίαν in a human being was the source of their doctrine of the Person of Jesus Christ.[1] And so their Christ was fairly described by the nickname ἄνθρωπος θεοφόρος.

If the word be passive—θεόφορος—it would not convey this sense. In the term 'a God-borne man' God is put first. There is God, and he takes up and bears with him a man. The objection that the doctrine implied two persons might still hold good, but the point of view would not be the same as that from which opponents of Nestorianism set out.

But, nevertheless, it seems to have been in the passive sense that Cyril applied it to the Nestorian teaching. Dr Robertson points out that the anathemas must be interpreted by the 'covering' letter to which they were appended. That letter is the *substratum* of the anathemas. And, in the passage in the letter which corresponds in positive exposition to the statements which are negatived in the anathemas, Cyril quotes two sayings which are apparently the sayings of Nestorius—(1) διὰ τὸν φοροῦντα τὸν φορούμενον σέβω, διὰ τὸν ἀόρατον προσκυνῶ τὸν ὁρώμενον, (2) ὁ ληφθεὶς τῷ λαβόντι συγχρηματίζει θεός. (That is, 'On account of him that bears I reverence him that is borne; on account of him that is unseen I worship him that is seen', and 'He that is taken up is called God (shares in the name of God) along with him that took him up'.) In these sayings there is no doubt that the active agency is ascribed to God throughout. It is God that bears, man that is borne. It is God that took up, man that was taken up. The name God, which properly belongs only to him that takes, is extended by virtue of the new association to him that is taken. The συστοιχία of ideas is unmistakeable. The 'man' is, as it were, passive throughout. And the phrases in the anathemas, which repudiate such ideas, are at least patient of the same interpretation (viz. θεόφορος ἄνθρωπος—ὡς ἄνθρωπον ἐνηργῆσθαι παρὰ τοῦ θεοῦ λόγου τὸν Ἰησοῦν—τὸν ἀναληφθέντα ἄνθρωπον συμπροσκυνεῖσθαι δεῖν τῷ θεῷ λόγῳ . . . καὶ συγχρηματίζειν θεὸν ὡς ἕτερον ἐν ἑτέρῳ).[2]

We must therefore recognize that Cyril meant θεόφορος, in the

---

[1] See *supra* Theodore's exposition of the doctrine.

[2] Dr. Robertson also points out that in the instance from the *Excerpta Theodoti* 27 (τὸ θεοφόρον γίνεσθαι τὸν ἄνθρωπον προσεχῶς ἐνεργούμενον ὑπὸ τοῦ κυρίου καὶ καθάπερ σῶμα αὐτοῦ γινόμενον) which Lightfoot quotes in support of the active sense, he has overlooked the drift of the passage, and that the word is there passive (θεόφορον), being explained by ἐνεργούμενον ὑπὸ τοῦ Κυρίου.

passive sense. As applied to Nestorian teaching the phrase θεόφορος ἄνθρωπος is probably his own coinage. It is not probable that Nestorius or his followers would have chosen it as their own expression of their doctrine, though the saying of Nestorius—if it be his, which Cyril quotes, would seem to give him justification for the phrase.

But in the active sense, θεοφόρος ἄνθρωπος, the phrase was so convenient and concise an expression of the Nestorian doctrine, as commonly understood, that it was seized upon and regularly used in later times as a label for the famous heresy. And therefore, though— as Dr Robertson has convinced me—with some sacrifice of historical accuracy, I have given the phrase the sense which it has universally been believed to bear, from the days of Marius Mercator (see *supra* p. 261 n. 4), who slips in the gloss *id est, Deum ferentem*, down to the present time.

THE NESTORIAN (EAST-SYRIAN) CHURCH

The expelled bishops laid the foundation of the great East-Syrian Church. A temporary refuge was found by Nestorians in the great school of Edessa, which had been famous for generations as the literary centre of Christianity for Armenia, Syria, Chaldaea, and Persia. At the time of the Council of Ephesus (431) its head was a Persian, Ibas, an ardent disciple of Theodore of Mopsuestia. After the Council he was expelled by the bishop Rabulas (who had himself been Nestorian at first), and spread translations of Theodore's works among the Christians in Persia. In 435 he was elected Bishop of Edessa, in succession to Rabulas, and a great stimulus was given to Nestorianism. The school was finally dissolved by the Emperor Zeno in 489, but it was transferred (to flourish more freely than ever) to Nisibis, where already, under Barsumas, a Nestorian school had been founded, and the support of the Persian king was secured for Nestorian Christians only. In spite of occasional persecution, Nestorian schools and missionaries rapidly spread in Persia and India, and even far into China (where a bilingual inscription in Chinese and Syriac, found by the Jesuits at Singanfu, relates that a Nestorian missionary laboured as far back as the year 636). The Nestorian Church, strongly established in this way by the end of the fifth century, and always famous for its educational and missionary enthusiasm, had become in the eleventh and twelfth centuries the largest Christian body in the world—the Christian Church of the far East. The Patriarch (or Catholicos) resided at Seleucia-Ctesiphon, and later at Bagdad, and was acknowledged by twenty-five metropolitans (or archbishops) as their spiritual head. The Khalifs of Bagdad protected their Christian subjects, and important offices of state were often filled by them; but when a Tartar race of sovereigns succeeded, bitter persecution broke out, and at last the invasion of Tamerlane in the fourteenth century spread universal devastation, and almost blotted out the Church. Only a fragment—a nation as well as a Church—survived; and, in spite of almost incredible persecution and suffering, still survives in the mountains and plains of Kurdistan (partly in Turkey and partly in Persia). The Euphrates valley expedition of 1835 first brought their existence to the knowledge of the West, and, in response to repeated appeals from the Catholicos for help, Archbishop Benson founded an educational mission to restore and build up, if possible, free from Nestorian error, something of their ancient state. [See "Archbishop's Mission to the Assyrian Christians" *Annual Report*, published by the S.P.C.K.]

CHAPTER XVI

EUTYCHIANISM

THE difficulty of finding a suitable expression of the union of the two natures in the person of Jesus Christ, which should recognize fully the earliest conviction, that, though one person, he was yet both God and man, was shewn again within a few years of the condemnation of Nestorian teaching. This time it was teaching of an opposite kind that called for correction.

Cyril died in 444, and was succeeded by Dioscorus, who had, in an exaggerated form, all the bad qualities which have been attributed to Cyril, without his undoubted learning.[1] The Archbishop of Constantinople was Flavian, a moderate man, averse from controversy, desiring peace and quiet for the Church. But peace was not to be had when followers of Cyril were not content to use his language and abide by the qualifications which explained it. On the contrary, there were some who seem to have made it their business to scent out traces of Nestorianism in men who were reputed orthodox, and so to wound their good name.

The Teaching of Eutyches—his Condemnation

It was one of these who caused the renewal of the strife—Eutyches, who had been an enthusiastic follower of Cyril, and was archimandrite of a monastery outside Constantinople, and high in the imperial favour. He had fallen under suspicion of Apollinarian tendencies already, and at an ordinary synod of thirty-two bishops, held at Constantinople in November 448, a charge was brought against him by Eusebius, Bishop of Dorylaeum—a former friend and ally in the contest against

---

[1] He seems to have been violent, rapacious, and scandalously immoral (see the evidence adduced at the Council of Chalcedon—Hefele *Councils* vol. iii 323 ff.). He brought all kinds of charges against Cyril, and confiscated his money and property on the ground that he had impoverished the Church.

Nestorianism—that he confounded the natures, and scandalized
many of the faithful by his teaching.   Eutyches was invited to
attend before the synod and offer explanations.   Again and
again he refused to appear, and sent evasive answers to the
messengers who were despatched to summon him; but at last
he came.   The question was put to him : " Dost thou confess the
existence of two natures even after the incarnation, and that
Christ is of one essence (ὁμοούσιον) with us after the flesh ? "
After trying to evade a direct answer, Eutyches declared that he
had never hitherto used the latter phrase (though the Virgin from
whom the flesh was received was of one essence with us), but
that he would do so, if required by the synod.   (He had really
held the human nature to be assimilated, deified, by the Logos ;
so that the body was no longer of the same essence as ours, but
a divine body [1]—so the human nature was as it were transmuted
into the divine.)   And at last he was obliged to admit that he
confessed that the Lord was of two natures before the union,
but after the union he confessed one nature.   When required to
anathematize all views opposed to the one declared by the
synod (that Christ was of one essence with us as regards the
flesh, and of two natures), he answered that though he would
accept the manner of speech required, he found it neither in
Holy Scriptures nor in the Fathers, and that therefore he could
not pronounce the anathema which would condemn the Fathers.
And he appealed to the writings of Athanasius and Cyril
in support of his own teaching,[2] saying, ' before the union they
speak of two natures, but after the union only of one '—though
all the same he repudiated all change and conversion of one
into the other.   As it was only in so equivocal a fashion that
Eutyches would accept the test, the synod decided that he did
not really hold the orthodox faith and pronounced his deposition
and excommunication.

Appeal to the West and Counter-Attack on Flavian

Eutyches maintained his ground and offered a stubborn
resistance.   Enjoying already the emperor's sympathy, he

---

[1] This view was represented as if he said that the Logos had brought his body
from heaven (ἄνωθεν).   This he denied that he held.

[2] Some of the writings on which he depended were really Apollinarian, fraudu-
lently ascribed to others.   See *supra* p. 241 *note.*

wrote to Leo, the Bishop of Rome, in ingratiating terms, and tried to secure his support. Leo, however, waited till he had heard the other side, and then wrote briefly to Flavian, condemning Eutyches, and promising full and complete directions in the matter. Feeling ran high in Constantinople. The emperor supported Eutyches and required of Flavian a profession of belief, in answer to the charges of Eutcyhes. Flavian in reply drew up a statement,[1] in which he declared his faith in the twofold generation of him who was " perfect God and perfect man, . . . of one essence with the Father as regards his Godhead, and of one essence with his mother as regards his manhood. For while we confess Christ in two natures after the incarnation from the Holy Virgin and the being made man, we confess one Christ, one Son, one Lord, in one subsistence and in one person ; and we do not refuse to speak of one nature of God the Word, if it be understood to be one nature incarnate and made man, inasmuch as our Lord Jesus Christ is one and the same (person) out of both (natures)." Flavian here was careful to use the phrase ' one nature ' with the qualification which Cyril too had added, ' one *incarnate* nature '. Eutyches, on the contrary, did not shrink from acknowledging ' one nature of the incarnate God made man '.

The Council of Ephesus

Against the wish of Leo and of Flavian, Theodosius II summoned a Council to meet at Ephesus, and, with the hope of determining the judgment of this Council, Leo wrote to Flavian the letter he had promised before.[2] The letter was written on June 13, and the Council met in August, with Dioscorus as president. Dioscorus was attended by a strong body of Egyptian bishops and monks, who all behaved with scandalous violence. They cried out against Eusebius for dividing Christ —' Bury him alive ; as he divides Christ, let him be divided himself ! ' Flavian was ' mobbed ' by the monks of Barsumas ; Dioscorus refused to have the letter of Leo read ; the statements of Eutyches were received with applause. The Council

[1] Hahn [3] p. 320. The letter containing it was sent to the emperor in the spring of 449.
[2] Hahn [3] p. 321 ff. An English translation in Bright *St. Leo on the Incarnation,* and in the English translation of Hefele (*Councils* vol. iii 225 ff.). See *infra* p. 288.

asserted that after the incarnation the distinction between the two natures no longer existed. Eutyches was declared orthodox and restored, and all his opponents were deposed. Flavian appealed against the decision, supported by the Roman legates, who protested and retired in haste. The signatures of many of the bishops were extorted by threats and physical force. It seems certain from the evidence, even when allowance is made for some exaggeration, that the result was only reached by insolent intimidation which proceeded to personal violence; and when the news reached Leo, he at once denounced the action of Dioscorus, and later on declared that a Council characterized by such ‘ brigandage ’[1] was no true Council at all.

Victory of the Eutychians through the Emperor's Support

Theodosius, however, supported Dioscorus and his party, and applauded the decision of the Council. He denounced Flavian, Eusebius, and the others as Nestorians, and deposed and exiled them.[2] Theodoret, who had not been at the Council, was included in this sentence, and his writings were forbidden to be read.

The result of the stringent edict which was issued was hopeless dissension in the East. Egypt, Thrace, and Palestine, on the one side, held with Dioscorus and the emperor ; on the other side, Syria, Pontus, and Asia protested against the treatment of Flavian and the acquittal of Eutyches. With them was Rome ; and Leo, excommunicated by Dioscorus, excommunicated him in turn and demanded a new Council. As long as Theodosius lived nothing could be done, though the sympathies of Pulcheria were on the other side. His death in July of the year following the Robber Synod (450) opened the way to the end of the wretched wrangle.

The Council of Chalcedon

Pulcheria and her husband, Marcian, favoured the cause which Leo represented, and the exiled bishops were recalled.

---

[1] ‘Latrocinium’ *Ep.* 95 (to Pulcheria), dated July 20, 451 :—hence the name by which the Council is known to history, ‘the Robber Synod’ (σύνοδος λῃστρική).

[2] Some accounts declare that Flavian died three days after the Council from the results of the violence of which he was the victim, and at Chalcedon Barsumas was denounced as his murderer. Other accounts say he was exiled and died at Epipa, a city of Lydia, perhaps by a violent death.

A synod was held at Constantinople, at which the bishop, Anatolius, signed Leo's letter to Flavian—by this time widely known and warmly welcomed by such men as Theodoret and other leaders of the Antiochenes; and a General Council was summoned to be held at Nicaea.[1] Thither in the summer of 451 the bishops and the papal legates journeyed; but to suit the convenience of the emperor (whose presence was required at the capital) the Council was transferred to Chalcedon. A number of sessions were held between the 8th October and the 1st of November, about six hundred bishops and others being present.[2]

At the outset the papal legates protested against the presence of Dioscorus, and the commissioners (who were in charge of the business arrangements) directed him to sit apart from the others, as not entitled to vote. All the documents relating to the case were read. While this was proceeding, the introduction of Theodoret, by command of the emperor, caused a violent outbreak of angry protests from the party of Dioscorus (who taunted him as 'the Jew, the enemy of God') and counter-accusations from his friends.[3] Quiet was with difficulty restored by the commissioners, who declared " such vulgar shouts were not becoming in bishops, and could do no good ". Over the proceedings at Ephesus a heated debate took place, and many of the bishops who had been present disavowed their share in the decisions, declaring that they had been induced, through fear of the violence of Dioscorus and his monks, to act in violation of their real belief and judgement. Dioscorus declared that Flavian had been justly condemned, because he maintained that there were two natures after the union'; whereas he could prove from Athanasius, Gregory, and Cyril, that after the union we ought to speak of only one incarnate nature of the Logos. " I am rejected ", he cried, " with the Fathers; but I defend the doctrine of the Fathers, and swerve from it in no respect." He

---

[1] Leo now wished to dispense with a Council, and simply by his legates, in conjunction with Anatolius, receive into communion all suspected bishops who would make profession of the orthodox faith. Even earlier he had apparently wished to adopt this course, and only to hold a Council if it failed.

[2] Yet the West was represented only by the Roman legates and two African bishops.

[3] Theodoret had written a dialogue (satirizing the monks, Cyril's supporters, and accusing the whole party of being mere Apollinarians) between Ἐρανιστής (a scrap-collector—one who picks up scraps of heresies, like Eutyches) and Ὀρθόδοξος.

was willing to accept the expression ' *of* two natures ' (*i.e.* formed out of the two), but not to say ' two natures ' still (*i.e.* existing *in* two natures), since after the union there were no longer two.

By the close of the first session a large majority of the Council agreed that Flavian had been unjustly deposed, and that it was right that the same punishment should be meted out to Dioscorus.

At the second session the Creed of Nicaea was read and received with enthusiasm as the belief of all, and the Creed then first attributed to the Council of Constantinople was approved, and after it the second letter of Cyril to Nestorius and his letter to John of Antioch. Then came the letter of Leo to Flavian, in a Greek translation. This too was received with approval as the faith of the Fathers—" Peter has spoken by Leo ; thus Cyril taught ! Anathema to him who believes otherwise." But the letter did not pass at once. Some passages seemed to some of the bishops ' Nestorian ', and it was only after discussion and explanation that it was accepted.[1]

At the third session, on October 13, the formal deposition of Dioscorus was pronounced, and at the fourth the condemnation of Eutychianism was renewed.[2] At the fifth session, on October 22, a definition of the faith was agreed to, not to add to the faith in any way or substitute a new confession for the old ones (which a canon of the Council of Ephesus forbade), but to refute the innovations of Nestorius and Eutyches.[3] The formula was drawn up by a committee of bishops in consultation, and begins with a declaration of the sufficiency of the Creeds of Nicaea and Constantinople, had not some attempted to do away with the preaching of the truth and to pervert the mystery of the incarnation of the Lord, and denied the term God-bearer as used of the Virgin ; while others introduced a confusion and mixture, and senselessly imagined that there was only one nature of the flesh and of the Godhead, and rashly maintained that the divine nature of the Only-begotten was

[1] Discussion, and ultimate acceptance on its merits, was not quite what Leo would have wished.

[2] Dioscorus, deposed and exiled, died in Paphlagonia in September 454. Eutyches was also exiled, but probably died before the sentence was carried out.

[3] The statement is given in Heurtley *de Fide et Symbolo* p. 23 ff., a translation and part of the Greek in Hefele *Councils* vol. iii p. 346 ff., and the decisive clauses of the definition in Hahn [3] p. 166.

become passible by the confusion or mixture. Therefore, the synod " opposes those who seek to rend the mystery of the incarnation into a duality of Sons, and excludes from participation in the holy rites (*or* from the sacred congregation) those who dare to say that the Godhead of the Only-begotten is capable of suffering. It sets itself against those who imagine a mixture or confusion in regard to the two natures of Christ, and drives away those who foolishly maintain that the form of a servant which was assumed from us is of a heavenly essence or any other than ours ; and it anathematizes those who fancy two natures of the Lord before the union and imagine only one after the union.

" Following, therefore, the holy Fathers ", the declaration runs, " we confess and all teach with one accord one and the same Son, our Lord Jesus Christ, at once perfect (complete) in Godhead and perfect (complete) in manhood, truly God and truly man, and, further, of a reasonable soul and body ; of one essence with the Father as regards his Godhead, and at the same time of one essence with us as regards his manhood, in all respects like us, apart from sin ; as regards his Godhead begotten of the Father before the ages, but yet as regards his manhood—on account of us and our salvation—begotten in the last days of Mary the Virgin, bearer of God ; one and the same Christ, Son, Lord, Only-begotten, proclaimed in two natures, without confusion, without change, without division, without separation ; the difference of the natures being in no way destroyed on account of the union, but rather the peculiar property of each nature being preserved and concurring in one person and one hypostasis—not as though parted or divided into two persons, but one and the same Son and Only-begotten God the Logos, Lord, Jesus Christ, even as the prophets from of old and the Lord Jesus Christ taught us concerning him, and the Creed of the Fathers has handed down to us.

In this definition the Church at length pronounced a final verdict on both extremes of Christological opinion, clearly repudiating Apollinarian, Nestorian, and Eutychian teaching, and stating positively in few words the relation between the two natures in the one person :—the relation which was more fully expressed in the statements of Cyril and Leo, to which, by recognition on this occasion, conciliar authority was given.

The Letter of Leo to Flavian

The letter of Leo well supplements the earlier statement of Cyril, and a summary of it may elucidate some points in the controversy which it helped to close.[1]

It is written all through in the tone of calm judicial decision and direction, and treats Eutyches as imprudent and lacking in sound judgement and understanding of the Scriptures. The very Creed itself refutes him : old as he is, he does not comprehend what every catechumen in the world confesses. To declare belief in " God the Father all-ruling and in Jesus Christ His only Son, our Lord, who was born of the Holy Spirit and [2] the Virgin Mary " is really to overthrow the devices of almost all heretics. These three clauses declare the Son to be God derived from God,[3] co-eternal and co-equal and co-essential with the Father. The temporal nativity in no way detracted from the divine and eternal nativity, and added nothing to it, but was solely concerned with the restoration of man and the need for the assumption of our nature by one whom sin could not stain nor death keep in his hold.[4]

[1] The Letter is often styled the 'Tome' of Leo—the term τόμος, meaning a section or a concise statement, being commonly applied to synodical letters—cf. Athanasius, *Tomus ad Antiochenos*. It is given in Heurtley *de Fidè et Symbolo*, and in Hahn[3] pp. 321–330 (Translation in Hefele *Councils* vol. iii p. 225 ff. and Bright *St Leo on the Incarnation* p. 109 ff.). Dorner (*Doct. of Person of Christ* Div. ii. vol. i p. 85) describes Leo as "more skilled in the composition of formulas of a full-toned liturgical character than capable of contributing to the scientific developement of a doctrine", but at all events he was able to give very clear expression to the doctrine which he received.

[2] The Latin text has *et*. Hefele suggests *ex*, but the simple co-ordination of the Holy Spirit and the Virgin is no doubt original in the Roman Creed—see the forms in Hahn[3] p. 22 ff.

[3] He uses the Nicene phrase 'de Deo Deus', which was not in the Constantinopolitan Creed, but was eventually inserted in the West, *e.g.* at Toledo in 589.

[4] The actual birth as well as the conception took place without loss of virginity. The title ἀεὶ παρθένος is found as early as Clement of Alexandria (*Strom.* vii 16) who reports that some in his day said the fact was known by examination ; anyhow he deems it true. On the other hand, Tertullian about the same time says she was *virgo* till the birth, but that the birth made her *mulier*, and that St Paul implied this, "cum non ex virgine sed ex muliere editum filium dei pronuntiavit, agnovit adapertae vulvae nuptialem passionem "; and so he says, "etsi virgo concepit, in partu suo nupsit" (*de carne Christi* 23). The doctrine here laid down by Leo seems to have been generally held in the Church from early times (Tertullian *l.c.* and Helvidius in the fourth century being exceptions—though doubtless finding followers). Athanasius uses the title *Or. c. Ar.* ii 70, and Augustine declares she was 'virgo concipiens, virgo pariens, virgo moriens' *Cat. rud.* 40. The best account of the different theories will be found in J. B. Mayor's edition of the *Epistle of St James*. See also Bright *St Leo on the Incarnation* p. 137.

If the Creed was not enough he might have turned to the
pages of Scripture and have learnt that as the Word was
made flesh, and born from the Virgin's womb, so as to have the
form of man, so he had also a true body like his mother. "That
generation peerlessly marvellous and marvellously peerless is
not to be understood as though through the new mode of the
creation the peculiar properties of the kind (man, or the
human race) were done away." It is true that the Holy Spirit
gave fruitfulness to the Virgin, but it was from her body that
the Lord's body was produced, animated by a reasonable soul
(§§ i, ii). "Thus the properties of each nature and essence
were preserved entire, and went together to form one person ;
and so humility was taken up by majesty, weakness by strength,
mortality by eternity ; and for the purpose of paying the debt
which we had incurred, the nature that is inviolable was
united to the nature that can suffer, in order that the conditions of our restoration might be satisfied, and one and the
same Mediator between God and men, the man Jesus Christ,
might be able to die in respect of the one and not able to die in
respect of the other.[1]   Accordingly, there was born true God in
the entire and perfect nature of true man, complete in his own
properties, complete in ours. By 'ours' we mean those which
the Creator formed in us at the beginning—and which he took
upon him to restore. For of those properties which the deceiver
brought into our nature, and man by the deception allowed to
enter, there was no trace in the Saviour. And it must not be
supposed that by entering into fellowship with human weaknesses
he became a sharer in our sins. He took upon him the form of
a servant without the defilement of sin, making the human greater
and not detracting from the divine ; for that 'emptying of himself'[2] by which the invisible presented himself as visible, and
the Creator and Lord of all things willed to be one of the
mortal, was a condescension of compassion and not a failure
of power. He who, while continuing in the form (essential
character) of God, made man, was made man in the form
of a servant. For each nature keeps its own characteristics
without diminution, and as the form of God does not annul
the form of a servant, so the form of a servant does not
impair the form of God" (§ iii).

[1] See Note 'Communicatio Idiomatum' p. 293.
[2] See Note 'The κένωσις' p. 294.

19

The Son of God in this way comes down to this lower world from his heavenly throne without retiring from his Father's glory—born by a new order and form of birth, "continuing to be eternally while beginning to be in time." But the new order, the new nativity, in no way implies a nature unlike ours. He is true God, but also true man, with flesh derived from his human mother; and "in the unity which results there is no deception, while the lowliness of man and the majesty of Deity are alternated;[1] for just as the Godhead is not changed by its compassion, so the manhood is not swallowed up by its acquired dignity. For each of the 'forms' (sc. the form of God and the form of a servant) acts in communion with the other its appropriate part —the Word effecting what is proper to the Word and the flesh carrying out what is proper to the flesh. The one shines out brightly in miracles, the other submits to insults.[2] Just as the Word does not retire from equality in the glory of the Father, so the flesh does not desert the nature of our kind (species). For one and the same person . . . is truly Son of God and truly Son of Man." Leo then goes on to point out how the characteristics of the two natures are respectively shewn in the different experiences of the one person—which are conditioned now by the one nature, now by the other. "It does not", he says, "belong to the same nature to say 'I and the Father are one', and to say 'the Father is greater than I'. For although in the Lord Jesus Christ there is one person of God and man, yet there is one source of the contumely which Godhead and manhood share, and another source of the glory which they also share. From our properties comes to him the manhood inferior to the Father; from the Father he has the divinity equal with the Father (§ iv).[2] On account, therefore, of this unity of person, which is to be understood to exist in both natures, we read, on the one hand, that the Son of Man came down from heaven, since the Son of God took upon him flesh from the Virgin from whom he was born; and, on the other hand, the Son of God is said to have been crucified and buried, inasmuch as he suffered thus not in the divinity itself (in which the Only-begotten is co-eternal

---

[1] 'Invicem sunt'—this probably means 'are by turns', as explained in the following attribution of different operations to the different natures: now one and now the other is active. But a possible meaning would perhaps be "are mutually or reciprocally", which would give the sense "have penetrated each other" (as Hefele tr.).

[2] See Note 'Communicatio Idiomatum' p. 293.

and co-essential with the Father) but in the weakness of human nature." Passages are cited from the New Testament to shew that experiences only possible in virtue of the human nature are predicated of the one person, under the title which is his in virtue of his deity; and experiences only possible in virtue of the divine nature are predicated under the title which belongs to him as human.[1] And further evidence is adduced to prove that the distinction of the natures remained in the one person even after the resurrection. It was just to prove that the assumption of manhood was permanent, and that the divine and the human natures still remained in their distinct and individual characters, that the Lord delayed his ascension forty days, and conversed and ate with his disciples, and shewed the marks of his passion saying, "See my hands and my feet, that it is I. Touch and see, for a spirit hath not flesh and bones, as ye see that I have". And so we should be saved from the error of identifying the Word and the flesh, and should confess both Word and flesh together to be one Son of God. The blessed Apostle John declares: "Every spirit which confesses Jesus Christ to have come in flesh is of God; and every spirit which parts (divides or unmakes) Jesus is not of God, and this is anti-Christ";[2] and to 'part' Christ is just to separate the human nature from him, and by

[1] The two passages are 1 Cor. 2[8] "for if they had known they would never have crucified the Lord of majesty"—a passage that Augustine had previously cited (de Trin. i 28) as shewing that the filius hominis propter formam servi and the Filius Dei propter Dei formam are one and the same—and Matt. 16[13] "who do men say that I the Son of Man am?"

[2] 1 John 4[3] 'qui solvit Jesum'=ὃ λύει τὸν Ἰησοῦν. No extant Greek MS. has this reading, but Socrates (H.E. vii 32) says it was so written in the ancient copies, which were altered by those who wished to separate the deity from the manhood in the Incarnation, and that ancient commentators noted that the epistle had been tampered with to further this design. Of Greek fathers Irenaeus and Origen alone attest the reading (in both cases we have only the Latin translation); Irenaeus quoting the passage against those who imagine a plurality of gods and fathers, and divide into many the Son of God; and Origen, while maintaining the characteristics of each 'substance', disclaiming any partition such as this passage has in view (see Iren. adv. Haer. iii 16, 8 and Orig. ad loc.). The reading is also found in Augustine (Hom. in 1 John 6[14], but elsewhere he treats the reading as qui non confitetur or qui negat), Fulgentius, Lucifer, Tertullian (adv. Marc. v 16 and cf. de Carne Christi 24, as Irenaeus supra), and in the Vulgate. Westcott and Hort and the Revisers place it in the margin.

The Textus Receptus ὃ μὴ ὁμολογεῖ (Lat. qui non confitetur) besides having the support of all Greek MSS. and the versions other than the Vulgate, seems to be implied by Polycarp, Cyril, Theodoret, Theophylact, Cyprian, Didymus (lat.). (Unless the text is exactly quoted it might be that the writer was only drawing the negative conclusion to which the first clause points.)

shameless fancies to make void the mystery through which alone we have been saved. "For the Catholic Church lives and grows by this faith—that in Christ Jesus there is neither humanity without true divinity, nor divinity without true humanity" (§ v).

In conclusion Leo comments on the impiety and absurdity of the saying of Eutyches—"I confess that our Lord was of two natures before the union; but after the union I confess one nature"; and insists that it is as wicked and shocking to say that the Only-begotten Son of God was of two natures before the Incarnation (when of course he was God only and not man) as to assert one only nature in him after *the Word was made flesh* (§ vi).

The Later History of Eutychianism—the Monophysites

Thus was the Creed of the Church defined; and "writing, composing, devising, or teaching any other creed" was forbidden under penalties—bishops and clergy to be deposed, monks and laymen anathematized. The Eutychian conception was, however, by no means suppressed. Large bodies of Christians refused to accept the doctrine of two natures as proclaimed at Chalcedon, though ready to condemn the teaching that the human nature was absorbed in the divine. Accordingly, numerous secessions from the Church took place, the seceders asserting one nature only (though not explaining the manner of the union) and being therefore styled Monophysites. In Palestine and in Egypt serious rioting and bloodshed followed—large numbers of the monks and others endeavouring to drive out the bishops who accepted the Council; and when, after many years, some measure of peace and unity was restored to the Church, she had lost her hold upon wide districts which had been hers before.[1]

[1] For the details of the history see Hefele *Councils* vol. iii p. 449 ff. Nearly a hundred years after the Council of Chalcedon (in 541) Monophysitism was strenuously revived and organized by a Syrian monk, named Jacob Baradai, and Monophysite bishops were appointed wherever it was possible. In particular he revived the Monophysite patriarchate of Antioch, which is still the centre of all the Monophysite churches of Syria and other Eastern provinces. From him the name 'Jacobite' Christians, adopted by all Monophysites, was derived. Monophysites have maintained their position down to the present time—(1) in parts of Syria, Mesopotamia, Asia Minor, Cyprus, and Palestine—subject to the Patriarch of Antioch (who now resides near Bagdad) ; but some of these were united with Rome in 1646 and a patriarchate of 'Catholic' Syrians ('Uniates') was established at

COMMUNICATIO IDIOMATUM

To three passages in Leo's letter (pp. 289 n. 1, 290 n. 2) objection was taken at the Council by the Bishops of Illyricum and Palestine, on the ground that they seemed to express a certain separation of the divine and the human in Christ. But the objection was dropped when almost identical statements were cited from Cyril's letters, and the papal legates declared that they did not admit any such separation, and anathematized all who did, and protested their belief in one and the same Lord and Son of God. The passages together in their context express what is commonly called the *communicatio idiomatum* (ἀντίδοσις τῶν ἰδιωμάτων, or τῶν ὀνομάτων). But this technical term is used in somewhat different senses. The teaching of Cyril and Leo (which alone has the authority of a General Council, and is in harmony with the teaching of Origen and Athanasius referred to in connexion with Cyril's letters p. 269 *supra*), is clear. There is one person, and there are two natures. These two natures, though truly (mysteriously) united in the one person, remain distinct, each retaining its own properties. The properties of each nature belong to and are rightly predicated of the one person—he exists at the same time in the divine nature and in the human nature, he lives always in both spheres. The experiences which are strictly divine, and the experiences which are strictly human, are alike his experiences. But they are his in virtue of the different natures—the one set of experiences because he is divine, the other set of experiences because he is human. Furthermore, the one person has different appellations, corresponding to the different natures. In virtue of the divine nature he is the Son of God; in virtue of the human nature he is styled Son of man. It does not matter by which name he is called—it is one and the same person only to whom reference is made: and therefore the experiences which the one person undergoes in virtue of his divine nature may be predicated of the Son of Man; and equally the experiences which he undergoes in virtue of his human nature may be predicated of the Son of God. This is all that Cyril and Leo say; and if the term *communicatio idiomatum* be applied to their (the Chalcedonian) teaching, it must be only in this sense. The one person shares equally in both names and the properties and experiences of both natures.

At a later time, the union of the two natures being thought of as so

Aleppo; (2) in Armenia, under the Patriarchate of Etshmiadsin (in 1439 some of these were united with Rome and these Uniates have their patriarch at Constantinople); (3) in Egypt, where out of hatred to the Byzantines they gave up Greek and adopted the vernacular (so called Copts or Coptic Christians), and in 640 helped the Saracens and were reinstated by them: they number now more than 100,000; (4) in Abyssinia, which was under the Patriarchate of Alexandria and so was involved in the Monophysite heresy.

close, they were held to interpenetrate each other in so intimate a union (the fellowship of each with the other to be so complete) that the properties of one might be predicated of the other. It is difficult to discriminate this conception from the mixture of natures which has been repudiated, but in any case it cannot claim support from Cyril, Leo, or Chalcedon. Dorner notes that the doctrine of a real *communicatio idiomatum*, as taught by the Lutheran Church, is not in harmony with Leo's letter; but the fact is sometimes ignored.

CHRIST'S HUMAN NATURE IMPERSONAL

The solution of the Nestorian difficulties, so far as it was a solution, was reached, as we have seen, in the teaching that it was not the person of *a* man that was assumed by the Logos, but *man*; *i.e.* human nature, human characteristics and attributes, which could be taken up by the divine Person, the Logos, and entered upon and made his own.

This teaching is fully expressed in the passages quoted *supra*, especially perhaps in Cyril's letter p. 268. Later expressions of it and the introduction of more abstract terms have not tended to elucidate the doctrine further (*e.g.* the term ἀνυποστασία to express this 'impersonal existence' of the human nature of Christ, and ἐνυποστασία to express its existence in the Person of the God-Word).

The centre of personality of Him who was God first and became man is necessarily to be found in the Godhead. That must be personal, and the manhood must therefore be impersonal. (See further Note 'Communicatio Idiomatum' p. 293.) In no other way apparently could the Nestorian theories be excluded, and in no other way, it seemed, could the redemptive work of Christ be effective for the whole human race. Otherwise it would have been one individual only who was redeemed.

The Person who enters upon the conditions of human life, and accepts the limitation of his divine life which is involved by those conditions, is divine; but all the human experiences are his, and in that sense he is human too.

The enquiry as to what constituted personality was not pushed. The existence of a human will in Christ was recognized, but its recognition was not regarded as incompatible with the doctrine.

THE κένωσις

The doctrine of the κένωσις can only be touched upon here so far as concerns the history of the Christological controversies of the fourth and fifth centuries.[1] It was not, apparently, till that time that enquiry was much directed to the consideration of the extent and character of the limitation of the divine powers which the Incarnation necessitated, and even then the enquiry is made in another form. For it is this question in effect that lies at the back of the discussion as to the human soul and will in Christ and the relation between the two natures.[2]

The general idea of a κένωσις no doubt is implied in all the 'orthodox' attempts at interpretation of the Person of Christ, all through the period which has been reviewed, as it is also in the New Testament. He who was God became man. The Infinite condescended to be in some way limited, and to enter upon the sphere of human life and experiences, and in so doing to forgo in some sense the full exercise of the Godhead which was his. This idea underlies the teaching of most of the books of the New Testament, though it is to St Paul that the particular expression of it is due (see especially Phil. 2⁶⁻⁸ ὃς ἐν μορφῇ θεοῦ ὑπάρχων . . . ἑαυτὸν ἐνένωσεν . . . καὶ . . . ἐταπείνωσεν ἑαυτὸν γενόμενος ὑπηκοος, and 2 Cor. 8⁹ ἐπτώχευσεν πλούσιος ὤν—cf. Rom. 8³).

St Paul's expression of the doctrine is merely incidental, and the purpose with which he introduces it is to press upon the Philippians the ideal of humility and renunciation of selfish aims. It is to a moral rather than a metaphysical motive that the statement is due.

St Paul declares of Christ Jesus that he was originally and essentially God, living under divine conditions (the μορφὴ θεοῦ) on an equality with God; but that he was willing to forgo (οὐχ ἁρπαγμὸν ἡγήσατο) this life on an equality with God. So he 'emptied' himself and took the life of service with its conditions (the μορφὴ δούλου), and came to exist in the likeness of men. That is the first great act of the κένωσις. It is followed, so to speak, by a second stage. Having entered upon the external conditions of human life (σχήματι εὑρεθεὶς ὡς ἄνθρωπος), he 'lowered' himself and became subject even unto death, and that death on the cross.

Whatever the precise meaning of μορφή may be, there is clearly implied here that the μορφὴ θεοῦ is for the time renounced, in order that the μορφὴ δούλου may be assumed and the life may be lived as man. A limitation is voluntarily chosen and accepted. And a further lowering or humbling takes place, till the lowest level is reached in a

---

[1] It may be noted that the chief subject of enquiry is not the particular aspect of the matter which has most engaged attention in recent times, namely, the limitation of our Lord's knowledge as man. But see Irenaeus *adv. Haer.* ii 28. 6–8, Athanasius *Or. c. Ar.* iii 51–54, Basil *Ep.* 236, Greg. Naz. *Or. Theol.* iv 15.

[2] Arian or Arianizing thinkers had seized upon N.T. passages bearing on the question as proof that Christ was not really God, without attempting to understand them as expressive of the limitation of the Godhead under conditions of human existence.

death which is shameful in the eyes of men. It is all to be followed, as St Paul goes on to say, by a corresponding exaltation. But this only serves to mark more plainly the reality of the previous renunciation and emptying and humbling.

As to what was the exact nature and extent of the self-limitation of the divine majesty, St Paul says nothing. Only it is clear that the κένωσις is regarded by him as a moral act of God and Christ, a free act of will, a voluntary humiliation and self-surrender culminating in the death on the cross. It is to this passage that all later expressions go back.

Only a few can be cited here.

One of the earliest references to the question is made by Irenaeus (adv. Haer. iii 19. 3). "For just as he was man in order that he might be tempted, so too he was Logos in order that he might be glorified. When he was being tempted and crucified and dying, the Logos remained quiescent (ἡσυχάζοντος τοῦ λόγου); when he was overcoming and enduring and performing deeds of kindness and rising again and being taken up, the Logos aided the human nature (συγγινομένου τῷ ἀνθρώπῳ)."

Here we have a definite expression of the conception that the Godhead was in abeyance during the processes and experiences proper to the manhood. Free play, so to speak, was allowed the human nature. The Logos forbore to exercise his functions. But at the same time he was there. In these few words Irenaeus expresses, perhaps, as much of explanation of the problem as is attainable.[1] Hilary's later and more elaborate statement of the theory is on the same lines.

But another point of view is represented by Origen.

As Origen describes it (see contra Celsum iv 15), though the κένωσις is conditioned by God's great love for men, its special purpose is to render the divine glory comprehensible to men. So far, at all events, the Incarnation was a weakening and obscuring of the divine glory (cf. C. Bigg Christian Platonists p. 262). "That which came down to men", he writes, "was originally in the form of God (i.e. existed at the beginning as God—ἐν μορφῇ θεοῦ ὑπῆρχε); and because of his love toward men he emptied himself (ἑαυτὸν ἐκένωσε), in order that he might be able to be comprehended by men (ἵνα χωρηθῆναι ὑπ᾽ ἀνθρώπων δυνηθῇ); . . . and he humbled himself (ἑαυτὸν ἐταπείνωσεν). . . . Out of condescension to such as cannot look upon the dazzling radiance of the

---

[1] Reference should be made to Tertullian's reply (adv. Marc. ii 27) to the criticisms of Marcion in regard to the 'unworthy' characteristics of the God of the O.T. In attributing all these to the Son who represented God to men always, Tertullian seems to conceive of a 'kenotic' process, a limitation for the purpose of revelation, dating from the first example of it in the creation of the universe and of man.

Godhead, he becomes as it were flesh, being spoken of in corporeal fashion, until he that received him in this guise, being lifted up little by little by the Word, becomes able to contemplate also what I may call his inherent Godhead (τὴν προηγουμένην μορφήν, referring to ἐν μορφῇ θεοῦ ὑπῆρχε which precedes)."

In these two sentences the κένωσις is described. But the chapter in which they occur is concerned with the objection of Celsus that the Incarnation involved a change in the being of God and exposed him to πάθος, and in meeting that objection Origen lays stress on the permanence of the divine state along with the κένωσις. When the immortal God-Word took upon him a mortal body and a human soul, he did not undergo any change or transformation (ἀλλάττεσθαι καὶ μεταπλάττεσθαι), or any passage from good to evil, or from blessedness to the reverse; but "remaining essentially (τῇ οὐσίᾳ) the Word, he is not affected by any of the things by which the body or the soul are affected". Even a physician may come into contact with things dreadful and unpleasant, and be unaffected by them; but whereas the physician may fall a victim, *he*, while healing the wounds of our souls, is himself proof against all disease.

The theory of the κένωσις is thus very little worked out by Origen. It is little more than a veiling of the divine majesty which he expresses by it, and he goes far towards representing it as something quite external, and he describes it elsewhere (*ibid.* iv 19) as a device which would not have been chosen by God of set purpose but was made necessary by the circumstances of the case.

It is a much more reasoned theory that is expressed by Hilary (see *de Trinitate* ix 14, xi 48, 49, xii 6, and Dorner *Doctrine of the Person of Christ* Eng. tr. div. I ii p. 405 ff.). He definitely considers (*de Trin.* ix 14) the question how it is possible for him who is God to begin with, and who does not cease to be God, to take the 'form of a servant', through which he was obedient even unto death. He who is 'in the form of a servant' is one and the same person as he who is 'in the form of God'. Taking the form of a servant and remaining in the form of God are different things—the one form is incompatible with the other form; and he who remained in the form of God could take the form of a servant only by a process of self-renunciation (*per evacuationem suam*). (The form of God excludes obedience unto death, the form of a servant excludes the form of God.)

But it is obvious that it is one and the same Person all through, who emptied (*exinanivit*) himself and who took the form of a servant (for only one who already subsists can take).

Therefore the renunciation (*evacuatio*) of the form does not involve the abolition of the nature, for he who renounces himself does not lose his own existence (*non caret sese*), and he who takes is still there (*manet*).   In renouncing and in taking he is himself.   In this there is a mystery (*sacramentum*), but there is nothing to prevent him remaining in existence while renouncing, and existing while taking.   Accordingly, the renunciation of 'the form of God' goes just far enough to make 'the form of a servant' possible; it does not go so far that Christ, who was in the form of God, does not continue to be Christ; for it was none other than Christ who took the form of a servant.   The change of 'fashion' (*habitus, i.e.* outward visible guise) which the body denotes, and the assumption of human nature, did not destroy the nature of the divinity which still continued.   The renunciation of self was such that remaining *Spiritus Christus* he became *Christus homo*.

By *forma* Hilary seems to mean *mode* of existence; by *natura* the sum total of attributes.   He does not use the word *substantia* in this context; but the thought seems to be that *substantially* he cannot be other than God—such he remains all through, and as such he must always have the attributes of God (the divine *natura*).   But God can exist in different modes, and he gives up the divine mode of existence so far as is necessary in order to enter on the human mode of existence (*forma servi*).   He personally accepts a limitation.   The 'emptying' of himself (*exinanitio*) takes place just so far as to make the true assumption of the humanity possible; and the renunciation of the use and enjoyment of the *forma Dei* is a continuous process all through his life on earth.   He 'tempers' himself to the form of human fashion.   He is always forgoing the *forma Dei*, while all the time the divine *natura*, which is absolutely his, is—under that limitation—in operation for the benefit of mankind.   (See *ibid.* xi 48.)

It cannot be said that the extent of the limitation is clearly defined by Hilary.   And when, elsewhere (*ibid.* x 47, 48), he considers in what sense the only-begotten God could undergo the sufferings of men, he has been understood to speak of our Lord's body as endued with impassibility (*indolentia*), and of his soul as not obnoxious to human affections of fear, grief, and the like.   His language is not quite satisfactory; he seems to denote the sufferings as *ours* rather than his, while the triumph through and over them is *his*.   He draws a distinction between suffering and feeling pain (*pati* and *dolere*), feeling pain on behalf of us and feeling pain as we feel it (*pro nobis dolet, non doloris nostri dolet sensu*).   But his saying *quidquid patitur, non sibi patitur* gives the clue to his meaning, and he would probably have accepted Cyril's explanation of the matter (see *supra* p. 268).

He is only trying to guard the impassibility of the Godhead in itself, while recognizing the sufferings of the Incarnate God in his human nature; and he styles it all a *sacramentum* or a *sacramentum dispensa-*

tionis,[1] and a voluntary act. Hilary's whole presentation of the matter recognizes the 'mystery' or the 'economy' as ethical, the outcome of free volition and self-sacrificing love;[2] the manifestation not of weakness but of immeasureable and unfailing strength.

What further advance was made in the enquiry during the Apollinarian controversy may be in some measure gathered from the discussion as to the human soul and will in Christ (see Notes *supra* pp. 247, 249).

The opponents of Nestorianism were chiefly concerned to assert the single personality, and the κένωσις is only touched on from this point of view.

Thus Cyril expresses his conception in the following words (*Ep.* iii ad Nestorium) : "The only-begotten Word of God himself, he that was begotten of the very substance of the Father . . ., he by means of whom all things came into being . . ., for the sake of our salvation came down, and lowered himself to a condition of self-renunciation (καθεὶς ἑαυτὸν εἰς κένωσιν)." But he goes on at once to add, "and he came forth man from woman, not having put away from him (*or* 'lost') what he was (οὐχ ὅπερ ἦν ἀποβεβληκώς), but although he came into being sharing flesh and blood, even in that state remaining what he was (καὶ οὕτω μεμενηκὼς ὅπερ ἦν), namely, God both in nature and in reality . . . for he is unchangeable and unalterable, perpetually remaining always the same, according to the Scriptures. But while visible, and an infant, and in swaddling-clothes, and still in the bosom of the virgin who bare him, he was filling all creation, as God, and was seated by the side of Him who begat him." (Cf. also Cyril's letter to John of Antioch —Heurtley p. 202.)

Nor did the subsequent Eutychian controversy contribute much to the elucidation of this particular problem.

Leo's letter to Flavian does not do more, in this respect, than assert concisely the maintenance of the personal identity and of the divine power through the process of the Incarnation, while declaring it to be an act of condescension. (See the passage *supra* p. 289 Lat. *humana augens, divina non minuens . . . exinanitio illa . . . inclinatio fuit miserationis, non defectio potestatis: . . . qui manens in forma Dei fecit hominem, idem in forma servi factus est homo: . . . tenet sine defectu proprietatem suam utraque natura.*) By this act of compassionate condescension he made himself visible and voluntarily subjected himself to the conditions of human life. But Leo does not define the extent

---

[1] These considerations should correct Harnack's depreciating criticism (*DG.* Eng. tr. vol. iv p. 140) "When dealing with the idea of self-humiliation, Hilary always takes back in the second statement what he has asserted in the first, so that the unchangeableness of God may not suffer."

[2] Cf. John 10[18].

or character of the limitation which the 'emptying' involves. He is content with an edifying statement, and there is no such attempt at accurate scholarly discrimination of terms as Hilary made. (Leo apparently regards the *forma Dei* and the *forma servi* as existing together side by side, whereas Hilary declared that the two 'forms' could not coexist.)

Hilary's statement remains the one direct attempt which was made during this period to understand and explain the nature of the κένωσις.

(Augustine deals with the matter in part *de Trin.* v 17 and vii 5. See further on the whole subject Ottley *Doctrine of the Incarnation* vol. ii p. 285 ff., and Gore *Dissertations* 'The Consciousness of our Lord'.)

CHAPTER XVII

PELAGIANISM

NOWHERE probably in the course of the history of doctrines are fundamental antitheses more sharply marked than in the controversies of the fifth century, as to the nature of man and sin and grace. The different conceptions which then emerged seem to be due to different points of view, corresponding to deep-rooted differences of individual constitution and experience. One man is inclined to natural explanations, another to supernatural; one to lay stress on the human power of good, another on the human power of evil and inability to secure the good. The two tendencies may be detected in ancient philosophies and religions, and they are seen as clearly when men began to face the facts of their experience in the light of the Christian revelation. Conscious of sin and of the need of a force that was not his own to save him from himself, and at the same time conscious of power of his own which he must exercise himself; conscious of personal responsibility, and, at the same time, of almost irresistible forces marshalled against him—how was the Christian to express his experiences in terms consistent with the doctrine of God which he had learnt?

The problem was scarcely faced till the time of Augustine. The antithesis which St. Paul had recognized when he urged the Philippians, " Work out your own salvation, for it is God that worketh in you ", was not made the subject of theoretic treatment. Free will and guiding grace went side by side in the thought, as in the life, of Christian men. Both are apparently recognized by the writers of the New Testament: on the one hand, the gracious purpose of God, and, on the other, man's power to fulfil or to defeat God's purpose. Sometimes Church teachers laid more stress on the corruption of man's nature, on the opposition between grace and nature, and on the all-essential need of the divine grace. Sometimes, against what seemed an extravagantly supernatural tendency, they gave special prominence to human freedom and power of self-recovery. But the relation between free will and grace, and the exact nature and origin of sin in individuals, were not reasoned out. The question did not attract the attention of the Church as a whole, and did not become prominent enough to call for authoritative settlement. But various individual opinions were formed and expressed on questions which really lie at the root of the whole matter; such questions as the origin of the soul and the effects of the Fall. A short review of early thought and teaching in the Church, in regard to these subjects, will be the best introduction to the consideration of the controversy which was roused by the teaching of Augustine and Pelagius.

Origin of the Soul—Different Theories

Three different theories of the origin of the soul were held in the early Church—Pre-existence, Creationism, Traducianism.

(*a*) ' Pre-existence ' was taught by Origen. All human souls were created at the beginning of creation, before the worlds, as angelic spirits. They sinned (except the one which remained pure and was in Jesus), and in consequence of their apostasy were transferred into material bodies. This existence is thus only a disciplinary process, on the completion of which the soul, having passed if necessary through many bodily lives, will be restored to its original condition. The bodies of men come into being in the ordinary course of physical propagation.

This theory seems to carry with it the theories of Metempsychosis (as regards human beings) and Anamnesis (Transmigration of souls and Recollection); but Origen makes little use of either. It was no doubt suggested to him by Platonism, though he defended it on scriptural authority.[1]

The theory secures individual responsibility and accounts for ' original ' sin [2]; but it makes the soul the real man, and

---

[1] *E.g.*, particularly, John 9[2], "Master, who did sin, this man or his parents, that he was born blind", and the allegorical account in Genesis of the fall of the finite pre-existent spirit from the higher to the lower sphere, and the hope of restoration (Rom. 8[19]); and he explained the choice of Jacob in preference to Esau as the result of merit acquired in a preceding stage of existence (cf. Rom. 9[11 ff.]).

[2] In his later works, during his life at Caesarea, Origen seems to have accepted the Church theory of original sin, in consequence, however, of the prevalent practice of infant baptism, rather than of his own theory of ' pre-existence '. See Bigg *Christian Platonists* pp. 202, 203.

the body merely a temporary prison—no constituent element of humanity. Further, it is an extreme form of individualism; each soul being a pure unit created by a distinct *fiat*, and having no connexion with other souls, there is no created species, no common human nature, no solidarity of mankind.[1]

(b) 'Creationism' was the prevalent theory among the Eastern fathers, and was held by Jerome and Hilary. Each individual soul was a new creation by God *de nihilo* (at the time of birth, or whenever individual existence begins) and was joined to a body derived by natural process of generation from the parents.[2]

Thus the physical part of every man is derived by procreation and propagation from the originally created physical nature of the first man—and so the solidarity of the physical nature is upheld, going back to the first creative act. But the spiritual part is a new divine act and must therefore be pure, and so evil must have its seat in the body only, that is, in matter.[3]

(c) 'Traducianism' was generally accepted in the West (Leo (*Ep.* 15) asserted that it was part of the Catholic faith), and in the East by Gregory of Nyssa. Tertullian, in particular, gave forcible expression to the theory. The first man bore within him the germ of all mankind; his soul was the fountain-head of all human souls; all varieties of individual human nature were only different modifications of that one original spiritual substance. Creation was finally and completely accomplished on the sixth day. As the body is derived from the bodies of the parents, so the soul is derived from the souls of the parents—body and soul together being formed by natural generation.[4]

This theory entirely accounts for the unity of mankind and the transmission of sin through the parents (*tradux animae tradux peccati*). All human nature became corrupt in the original father of the race and inherits a bias to evil. This is the *vitium originis*, the blemish or taint in the stock which necessarily affects the offspring, so that all are born with its stain upon them. But against this theory objections are urged, that it

---

[1] This theory was condemned by the Council of Constantinople in 540.

[2] So Jerome *ad Pammachium* "God is daily fashioning souls"—supported by John 5[17], Psalm 33[15], Zech. 12[1], and Hilary *Tract on Ps.* 91 § 3.

[3] And infants before committing any actual offence would be sinless; see Augustine on the theory, *infra* p. 304.

[4] The biblical basis of this theory was St Paul's teaching on the connexion of the race with Adam and the origin of sin, Rom. 5[12-19]; cf. 1 Cor. 15[22], Eph. 2[3], Heb. 7[10], Ps. 51[5], Gen. 5[3].

makes man the product of previous circumstances, allows no room for individual free will, and seems to materialize the soul.

Augustine, who probably contributed most to its currency, nowhere definitely teaches it. But the view which he held of sin and its origin and transmission seems to imply the transmission of the soul that sins. He argues (*de Anima* bk. i, against a work of Vincentius Victor on Creationism) that no texts demonstrate Creationism, and insists that anyone holding that theory must avoid the four following errors—(i) that souls so created are made sinful by an infusion of a sinful disposition, not truly their own, at the moment of birth; (ii) that infants are destitute of original sin and do not need baptism; (iii) that souls sinned previously, and therefore are imprisoned in sinful flesh; (iv) that souls of those who die in infancy are only punishable for sins which it is foreknown they would have committed later. All passages from the Holy Scriptures prove, he says, that God is the creator, giver, framer of the human soul; but *How*— whether by in-breathing it newly created or by the traduction of it from the parent—they nowhere say.

In the Middle Ages Traducianism fell into disrepute, as conflicting with the soul's immortality, and materializing it, and not being needed by the form of anthropology which then prevailed—a form which was more closely allied to Greek than to Latin thought.[1]

These different theories would involve different conceptions of the atonement. According to the first, evil is a fall from a higher to a lower state of being, and the atonement would be spiritual but individual—a rescue of individual souls one by one from the material bodies in which they were imprisoned. According to the second, evil is material, and the atonement would concern the physical nature only, unless the soul be regarded as becoming tainted by its association with the body. According to the third, evil is inherent in body and soul alike, and the atonement would be an almost magical 'new creation'.

Note.—Though it is no part of the purpose of this sketch of the history of doctrine to justify or criticize the doctrines which are dealt with, it may be pointed out that the Traducian theory is the only one which modern biological knowledge supports. Though it is impossible to dissect a man in any stage of his existence into body and soul, it is impossible to point to any moment when the soul begins to be. From the first, in human experience, both are one, and both alike are—as one

---

[1] See *infra* pp. 307, 325.

—derived from the parents. The *whole man* is derived from the parents. But if it be right to speak of body and soul as his constituents, it is not right to declare that this process 'materializes' the soul. It is at least as probable that it is all through the soul—in its growth—that determines the body, as that the body determines the soul. The matter cannot be proved either way, and in the present stage of knowledge, when such terms as 'spirit' and 'matter' and the relations between them are so ambiguous, it is impossible to feel confidence in the current criticisms of the Traducian theory.

Different Conceptions of the Fall and its Effects

Similarly, different conceptions of the effects of the Fall were current. On the whole, in the early Church, in spite of a keen sense of the opposition between the ideal and the real, the more hopeful view of human nature and its capacities prevailed. Of sin and its origin there was no exact idea (so that the Gnostics could refer it either to the Demiurge or to matter).[1] The accounts in the 'Mosaic' books were the historical foundation— some (as Tertullian) regarding them as strictly literal, others (Origen, Irenaeus, the Gnostics) as allegorical, while Augustine held the story of the Fall to be both historical and symbolic. In any case the temptation was regarded as a real temptation to sin, and the transgression of the command as a fall from a state of innocence which was followed by disasters to the human race, death and physical evils being the result;[2] though the more spiritual view was put forward by such men as Origen, who wrote on one of the key-passages, "The separation of the soul from God, which is caused by sin, is called death".[3]

Individual sin, however, was still regarded as the free act of man's will: rather a repetition than a necessary consequence of the first sin—not simply the result of a hereditary tendency. The Fall was not regarded as destroying human freedom of will. The power of self-determination, held to be inherent in the

[1] Sin, though in some sense a fact of universal experience, cannot be said to have been fully realized till it was felt (as by Jews and Christians) as an offence against an Eternal Holiness. The true idea of sin was first grasped side by side with the idea of redemption. The idea of redemption implies a sense of being rescued from some alien power, and, at the same time, a sense of possessing capacity for the higher life to which such a rescue leads. It implies, that is, the corruption of human nature from a state in which it is capable of reaching holiness, so that in its present state it needs some stimulus to its innate capacity, to enable it to regain and realize the condition which it has lost.

[2] Cf. Iren. *adv. Haer.* iii 23 ; v 15, 17, 23.   [3] Origen *on Rom.* lib. vi § 6.

human soul, was the manifestation of the image of God in man. To this freedom of man to choose good or evil the early apologists and Fathers, and even Tertullian, unanimously testify. Thus Justin says,[1] " If it has been fixed by fate that one man shall be good and another bad, the one is not acceptable, the other not blameable. And, again, if the human race has not power by a free moral choice to flee from the evil and to choose the good, it is not responsible for any results, whatever they may be ". And Origen declared that if the voluntary character of virtue were destroyed, the very thing itself was destroyed.[2] As in sin, so too in the work of redemption, man had his part to play—his own free will to exercise: " As the physician offers health to those that work with him with a view to health, so too God offers eternal salvation to those that work with him with a view to knowledge and right conduct." [3] This moral power of choice in all men was, for example, strenuously maintained against the Gnostic teaching, that capacity for redemption and power of moral freedom belonged only to one class of men (the πνευματικοί), and that the schism in man was something necessary in the evolution of existence.[4] Tertullian, approaching the problem from the Traducian theory, was the first to use the expression *vitium originis* to describe the stain or blemish or defect from which man's nature suffered since the Fall ; so that while his true nature is good, evil has become a second nature to him. But this ' original sin ' he did not regard as involving guilt—in urging delay of baptism he asks what need there is

---

[1] *Apol.* i 43 ; cf. Tatian. *Or.* 7 ; Athenag. *Leg.* 31 (God did not create us as sheep or brute beasts, so it is not natural that we should will to do evil (ἐθελοκακεῖν)) ; Theophilus *ad Autol.* ii 27.

[2] *C. Cels.* iv 3.   [3] Clem. Al. *Strom.* vii 7.

[4] The Gnostics were the first to frame the dilemna—"If the first man was created perfect, how could he sin ? If he was created imperfect, God is Himself the author of sin." It cannot be said that any sufficient answer was given on the side of the Church. Clement, indeed, denied that man was created perfect, declaring that he was made with the capacity for virtue, but that its cultivation depended on himself (*Stromateis* vi 12). And others drew a distinction between the εἰκών (the image, the original capacities which were indestructible), and the ὁμοίωσις τοῦ θεοῦ (the likeness of God, which was to be realized by the right use of these capacities in due developement). The perfection was ' ideal', and there was also freedom of the will ; and it was in the will that the source of sin was found, the actual development of the innate capacity falling short of the ideal. Most of the fathers also held that for the realization of the ideal there was needed a third principle, which was supernatural in character, namely, fellowship with God, so that without this co-operation man could not attain to his destiny.

for 'innocent' children to hurry to the remission of sins.[1] And though laying stress on the moral depravity of man resulting from inherited sin, and on the need of the grace of God to effect his redemption, he expressly taught the inherent capacity of the soul for communion with God in virtue of its proper nature.[2] Origen, by his theory of the origin of human souls, according to which they were all stained by sin in a previous stage of existence, might seen to favour the idea of original sin;[3] but his assertion of the freedom of the will is in strong contrast with Augustine's teaching, and he maintained that guilt arises only when men yield to sinful inclinations.[4] The moral powers might be enfeebled by the Fall, but with one voice, up to the time of Augustine, the teachers of the Church declared they were not lost. So the Cappadocian fathers taught, and Chrysostom. Gregory of Nyssa definitely finds in the freedom of the will the explanation of the fact that the grace of faith does not come upon all men alike. The call, he declares,[5] comes with equal meaning to all, and makes no distinction (this was the lesson of the gift of tongues), but " He who exercises control over the universe, because of His exceeding regard for man, permitted something to be under our own control, of which each of us alone is master. This is the will ($\pi\rho o a i\rho\epsilon\sigma\iota s$), a thing that cannot be enslaved, but is of self-determining power, since it is seated in the liberty of thought and mind ($\delta\iota\acute{a}\nu o\iota a$)". If force were used, all merit would be gone. " If the will remains without the capacity of action, virtue necessarily disappears, since it is shackled by the paralysis ($\acute{a}\kappa\iota\nu\eta\sigma\iota a$, lack of initiative) of the will." Whatever stress was laid on the need for the introduction into human nature of a new principle,[6] it was reserved for Augustine to represent man as unable to even will what was good and right.[7]

[1] *De baptismo* 18.

[2] See *e.g. de anima* 40, 41, and the treatise on the *testimonium animae nat. Christianae.*

[3] See *de Princ.* iii 5. 4 ; but see also *supra* p. 302 n. 2.

[4] See *de Princ.* iii 2. 2, iii 4 ; cf. Basil *Hexhaem.* II 5, VI 7.

[5] Greg. Nyss. *Or. Cat.* xxx, xxxi ; cf. *Antirrhet.* xxix (Migne xlv p. 1188).

[6] As, *e.g.*, by Athanasius. Man had admitted corruption into his nature and being, and had passed into a state of moral death—it was therefore necessary that incorruption and life should be united with that nature before it could recover. See the *de Incarnatione.*

[7] According to Augustine himself, the Church of Christ had always held the doctrines he taught, and any sayings of the fathers that seemed to favour Pelagian conceptions were but *obiter dicta*, the Pelagian inferences from which would have been repudiated at once (Pelagianis nondum litigantibus securius loquebantur).

The Teaching of Augustine

Augustine was, it is true, the first great teacher who dealt with anthropology—the developement of which was peculiarly Western, as the result of practical experience and needs. The conception of redemption implies at once a sense of moral insufficiency and a sense of moral freedom on the part of those who seek redemption—a freedom which recognizes its own guilt and appropriates the means of redemption. According as the one or the other sense is the more active, Christianity appears either as a new creation, a new element in life, changing and ennobling the entire nature, or, as a higher power, calling out all that is best in human nature and freeing it from impediments to its due and destined developement. Those who experience a sudden crisis, or from a turbulent consciousness of guilt, are brought to the sense of pardon and peace, naturally tend to the former conception, while those who reach the goal by a more quiet and gradual process will recognize the latter conception as true to the facts they know.

The two courses and tendencies are represented in Augustine and Pelagius respectively. Of Augustine it has been well said, that " he could do neither good nor evil by halves. From a dissolute youth he recoiled into extreme asceticism, and from metaphysical freedom into the most stringent system of authority. He was the staunchest champion of orthodoxy . . . he did not sufficiently respect the claims of conscience. . . . He sacrificed the moral element to God's sovereignty, which he maintained unflinchingly." [1] He was specially conscious of the difficulty of the struggle for holiness, of the opposition between that which issued from nature left to itself, estranged from God, and the fruits of the new divine principle of life imparted by union with Christ. Different stages in the developement of his views may be detected, but the final form they assumed is the most characteristic, and has been the most influential. Justice can hardly be done to the views of so profound a thinker in a summary; but the ideas of human nature, of sin, and of grace which dominated his thought, may be concisely stated in their main aspects.

[1] De Pressensé, Art. 'Augustine' *D.C.B.*—an excellent approciation of Augustine, in which full weight is also given to othor clements in his nature, espccially his "love for Christ and for the souls of his brother men ".

As to human nature, he held the 'fall' of man to have been complete, so that the power of spiritual good is entirely lost, and ever afterwards he wills nothing but evil and can do nothing but evil.[1] The fall was not limited to Adam—in him all have sinned [2] and all have been condemned. By birth all receive the taint of the ancient death which he deserved.[3] Adam, as the stem of the human family, infected and corrupted his entire posterity. The whole race shares his guilt, and cannot by any efforts of its own escape the penalty which is due. It shares his guilt, because it was already in existence potentially in him, so that it really sinned when he sinned. It is only by a very resurrection—a second creation in effect—that it can recover the divine life which it had in Adam before the Fall.

As to sin, he held that human nature as originally created, was free from sin, designed for communion with God and able to realize the end of its being, though having also the capacity for sin. Sin was contrary to the law of human nature, but ever since the first sin it has been present in every one as a disease eating out all true life, and only a radical cure can overcome it. A new life must be given to men, planted in them afresh.

As to grace, he maintained that this power to recover life, which is really a new gift of life, is entirely the free gift of God drawing men to Christ.[4] No human power can deliver man from

---

[1] Action follows the strongest motive. This is given either by God or by Nature. Nature being tainted, the strongest motive must always be evil, prior to God's gift of grace.

[2] So he interpreted Rom. 5[12] 'in quo omnes peccaverunt'—a possible meaning of the Latin but not of the Greek ἐφ' ᾧ. See contra duas epp. Pel. iv 7 c. 4. But the conception of a 'race' life and a 'race' guilt (in which every individual is involved) does not depend only on a mistaken interpretation of this passage. Augustine conceived of Adam as originally perfect (the 'original righteousness' of the race), possessing free will (liberum arbitrium), but capable of using his freedom to the injury of his highest interests. He might have persevered had he wished; his will was free, so as to be able to wish well or ill (de Corrept. et Gratia 11); but since, through free will, he deserted God, he experienced the just judgement of God—was condemned with his whole stock, which was then contained in him and sinned with him (shared in his sin) (ib. 10), and so lost the gift of original righteousness which could only be restored by a second gift of supernatural grace.

[3] Augustine found the support of tradition for the doctrine of original sin in the rite of exorcism, which he believed to be of apostolic origin (c. Julian. vi 5 11).

[4] At an earlier time Augustine had held that the first step by which man was qualified to receive the gift of grace was his own act, the act of faith on his own part (de Praedest. iii 7). Cf. what he says, when reviewing the history of his thought, Retract. II i 1 "to solve this question we laboured in the cause of freedom of the human will, but the grace of God won the day".

his hereditary depravity. In the process man is completely passive—as passive as the infant child in baptism. In a sense it is true to say, that the human will plays no part in it at all; it has no power of initiative, and when the new gift is given it has no power of resistance. But, on the other hand, it is evident that this was not Augustine's real meaning. The grace given is a new gift; and it renews the will in such a way that the will is set free to choose the good and to follow it unswervingly. And the grace thus given is irresistible, in the sense that the will, which has thus had true freedom restored to it, has no desire to resist the good.

Of all Augustine's most characteristic conceptions, none perhaps is more significant than this conception of true freedom as connoting inability to sin. Man is only really free when nothing that could injure him has any power over him. The highest virtue is the fixed habit of good, when man feels no wish to sin and cannot sin. Then and then only does man enjoy true freedom of will. The finest expression to this thought is given incidentally, in writing of the eternal felicity and perpetual sabbath of 'the city of God',[1] when evil will have lost all power of attraction. "It is not the case that they will not have free will, because sins will not have power to delight them. Nay, the will will be more truly free, when it is set free from the delight of sinning to enjoy the unchangeable delight of not sinning. For the first free will which was given to man, when he was first created upright, had power not to sin, but had power also to sin. This latest free will, however, will be all the more powerful because it will not have power to sin—this too by the gift of God, not by its own unaided nature. For it is one thing to be God, and another thing to partake of God. God by his very nature is not able to sin; but one who partakes of God has received from Him the inability to sin. . . . Because man's nature sinned when it was able to sin, it is set free by a

---

[1] *De Civitate Dei* xxii 30. To some extent it is true that there is here a paradox, or a confusion of sense. There is never really freedom of will. Prior to grace, man can only do evil; after grace given, he cannot do evil. This confusion of sense is plainly seen in another passage *De gratia et libero arbitrio* 15. "The will (*voluntas*) in us is always free, but it is not always good. It is either free from righteousness (*justitia*) when it serves sin, and then it is evil: or it is free from sin when it serves righteousness, and then it is good. But the grace of God is always good, and through this it comes about that a man is of good will who before was of evil will." 'Free' here simply means unimpeded by any power that thwarts the inclination.

more bounteous gift of grace, to lead it to that liberty in which it is not able to sin. Just as the first immortality, which Adam lost by sinning, was the ability to escape death, and the latest immortality will be the inability to die; so the first free will was the ability to escape sin, the latest the inability to sin. The desire for piety and equity will be as incapable of being lost as is the desire for happiness. For, assuredly, by sinning we retained neither piety nor happiness, and yet even when happiness was lost we did not lose the desire for happiness. I suppose it will not be said that God Himself has not free will, because he cannot sin."

This conception of freedom, *the beata necessitas non peccandi*— well summed up in the motto of Jansenism, *Dei servitus vera libertas*, and the familiar phrase of the 'Collect for Peace', *whose service is perfect freedom*—was supported, or accompanied, by other novel teaching: novel at all events in the form it assumed. Clearly the question had to be faced, if man has entirely lost the power of self-recovery and self-determination, and salvation depends absolutely on the free gift of God; what is it that determines the disposal of this gift? To this question Augustine could only answer that the difference between men, in their reception of the divine grace, depends on the decree of pre-destination which determines the number of the elect who are to replace the fallen angels. God's will, God's call, alone decides the matter. All men are debtors. He has a right to remit some debts and to demand payment of others. We cannot know the reason of His choice: why the gift of grace, the new principle of life which restores to men their true free will, is given to some and withheld from others. By the divine decree, without reference to future conduct, some are elected as *vasa misericordiae* to redemption (*praedestinatio*), and others are left as *vasa irae* to condemnation (*reprobatio*). The latter are simply left.[1] The former are kept faithful by the further gift of 'perseverance' by which fresh supplies of grace are bestowed— this again being beyond man's comprehension. "Why to one

---

[1] So Augustine put the matter. In this respect, at all events, he would not go beyond the words of St. Paul, who speaks of the "vessels of mercy" as "afore pre-pared unto glory" by *God*, but of the "vessels of wrath" as "fitted to destruction" without attributing the fitness directly to God (Rom. 9$^{22\cdot23}$). But naturally some of his followers (notably the monks of Adrumetum in North Africa) applied to the *vasa irae* the positive principle, and taught the twofold predestination (*praedestinatio duplex*) to sin and evil, as well as to life.

of two pious men perseverance to the end is given, and is not given to the other, is only known to God's mysterious counsels. Yet this much ought to be regarded as certain by believers— the one is of the number of those predestinated (to life), the other is not."[1]

The two ideas of predestination and of grace are clearly expounded in his letter to Sixtus,[2] a priest of the Roman Church. He sets forth the conception of a Will absolute, which out of a 'mass' of souls, all alike deserving of perdition (*massa perditionis*) on account of original sin (apart from sins of their own commission), selected a minority to be vessels of divine mercy, and abandoned the majority as vessels of wrath, without any regard to foreseen moral character.[3] The purpose of God thus formed cannot be frustrated. The grace which is given is irresistible and indefectible. It must achieve its object : it cannot fail. The souls of those predestinated or elected to salvation it so bends to its own pleasure, as literally to make them respond and obey.[4]

The plain assertion of St Paul that "God wills all men to be saved" he interpreted as meaning that he is no respecter of persons, and that all classes, ages, and conditions of mankind, are to be found among the elect.

Opposition of Pelagius—his Antecedents

' Pelagianism ' was really a reaction against Augustine's system and the tendency which it represents. The experiences of Pelagius, in all the circumstances of his life, had been very

---

[1] The divine counsels are inscrutable. Again and again Augustine is brought to this confession of human ignorance ; but he is very far from admitting anything arbitrary or unjust in the methods and acts of God. All are the outcome of justice, wisdom, and love, and are governed by an eternal purpose of good. Yet how ' predestination ' is consistent with the love of God, he does not expressly attempt to shew.

[2] Written in 417 or 418.

[3] In earlier years he had regarded the choice as conditional on man's free will and faith, foreknown by God—see the reference in *de prædest.* 7 ; but the doctrine of grace, as described above, requires a doctrine of predestination independent of man's initiative.

[4] The relation between free will and grace is also set forth in the letter to Vitalis, *Ep.* 217 (Migne xxxiii p. 978 ff.), especially ch. vi, where he insists that the doctrine of grace in no way destroys the freedom of the will, inasmuch as it is grace only which makes the will free to choose and to do what is good—the conception which has been referred to *supra* p. 310.

different from Augustine's; and it seemed to him that such conceptions as Augustine's were alike unscriptural and immoral. It is said that he was greatly shocked when a bishop quoted to him from the *Confessions* of Augustine,[1] which had just been published, the famous prayer, *Da quod jubes et jube quod vis* (give what Thou biddest and bid what Thou wilt), since it seemed to exclude man's part in his own salvation.   But his point of view was altogether different.   A monk of Britain and a layman, he had lived all his life in the peace and solitude of a monastery, a regular life under the shelter of the cloister walls.   He had probably passed through a quiet course of developement, without experience of the darker sides of human existence and the depth of evil to which human nature can sink.   He had not been called on to engage in any such struggles as those which Augustine went through; and the character built up by his experience was predominantly sober and discreet, well-balanced on the whole, although perforce somewhat lacking in sympathy with emotions in which he had had no share.   Of learning and moral earnestness he had full measure.

The weakness of the monastic ideal has often been pointed out.   Like all other rules of life, though designed to govern the inner man, it is in danger of concentrating attention on the surface of life.   Individual sins are battled against and conquered, and outbreaks of sinful impulses checked by constant watchfulness.   The conquest of sins may be mistaken for the conquest of sin.   Again, high moral ideals have different effects on different temperaments.   Some are led by them to deeper self-examination and inner spiritual life, to fuller realization of the opposition between the ideal outside and the actual within. They are stimulated to seek to remove the opposition, and yet, distrusting self, to realize the need of the aid of a power not their own.   Others, conscious of victory over the temptations of sense, of successes already effected in the struggle, may be led to confide in their own moral efforts and to think they have produced great results, while really the evil may be in no true sense eradicated.

---

[1] Confess. x 40.   Cf. what Augustine says about it *de dono persev.* 20, 53 (Migne *P. L.* xlv p. 1026).   He defends the prayer on the ground that God's chief command to man is to believe in Him, and that faith in Him is His own gift, and that by grace He turns the wills of men, even when actively hostile, to the faith which He requires.

The Chief Principles maintained by Pelagius

If Pelagius rose above the worse consequences of the monastic ideals, yet the life he had led no doubt exerted an influence on his views. One far-going principle, which resulted from the life of obedience to detailed rules,[1] was the distinction he drew between what was enjoined (*praecepta*—obligatory) and what was only recommended as an object of higher perfection (*consilia*—optional). By abstaining from what was permitted you could become entitled to a higher reward, there being different grades of merit and of Christian perfection.

On the study of Scripture Pelagius laid great stress, insisting wherever possible on the literal interpretation of its teaching. "If you choose to understand precepts as allegories, emptying them of all their power, you open the way to sin to all." The injunction "Be ye perfect even as your Father which is in heaven is perfect", was enough to prove that perfection is possible for men. What the Lord said, he meant. The giving of the command presupposes the power to obey it. And when the apostle declared to the Christians of Colossae that the purpose of the reconciliation which God designed was to present them "holy and unblameable and unreproveable in his sight" (Col. 1²²), Pelagius rejects with scorn the notion that he knew he had enjoined on them what was impossible.

But his principles were really evolved in opposition also to the practical evils of the time. Much of the Christianity of those days was very worldly. The distinction between the spiritual and the secular was employed as an excuse for a lower standard of life. The corruption and weakness of human nature was used as a plea for indulgence. "We say", Pelagius replies, "it is hard, it is difficult; we cannot, we are but men. . . . Oh what blind madness! It is God we impeach!"[2] And so his

---

[1] But see *infra* p. 353, Note 'The Doctrine of Merit'.

[2] In the letter to Demetrias (§§ 7, 8 Migne *P.L.* xxx p. 22) he insists that the Scriptures never excuse those who sin, on the ground that they cannot help themselves, but put the burden on their lack of will (*peccantes ubique crimine voluntatis gravant, non excusant necessitate naturae*): all through they write alike of good and of evil as voluntary. And he explains that his anxiety to defend 'the good' of nature is due to his desire to repudiate the idea that we are driven to evil through the defect of nature, whereas we really do neither good nor evil except by the exercise of our own will—we are always free to do one of two things. (This is his conception of the freedom of the will—the power of choosing at any moment one course or another, good or evil.) He says that the argument involved in the plea

first concern was to make men see that they were not in want of any of the faculties which are necessary for the fulfilment of the divine law. Even among pagans there were great examples of virtue which proved how much human nature unaided could do. It was not their nature, but their will, that was to blame. Men had it in their power to reach perfection, if they would use the forces which they had at hand. The power and freedom of choice possessed by men he specially emphasized against the doctrine of irresistible grace and predestination. It is the use which is made of it which determines the issue, whether a man succumbs to or conquers temptations.

And thus, in the interest of the power of self-determination, and against the fatalistic acquiescence in a low morality, he was led to deny the 'corruption' of human nature—a doctrine which seemed to him to encourage moral indolence. "Neither sin nor virtue is inborn, but the one as well as the other developes itself in the use of freedom and is to be put to the account only of him who exercises this freedom." Each individual is a moral personality in himself, apart from others, endowed by the Creator with reason and free will; and the only connexion between the sin of Adam and the sin of men is the connexion between example and imitation. He could not acknowledge sin propagated by generation (*peccatum ex traduce*), and believed the soul to be a new creation from God, contemporaneous with the body and therefore untainted and pure (Creationism). God has given all the power to reach perfection—they have only to will and to work it out. The widespread existence of sin in the world is due to education and example. Augustine, on the other hand, with a much stronger sense of the solidarity of the human race, regarded the sin of Adam as involving so vast a change as to affect his whole posterity.[1]

that we have no power to fulfil the divine commands (it is hard, it is difficult . . . § 16) really implies that God orders us what is impossible for us to do, and then condemns us for not doing it; as though he sought our punishment rather than our salvation. He is *justus* and *pius*—it is impossible that a theory which has such consequences can be true.

[1] Pelagius apparently recognized no criterion of sin but acts which are the products of the individual's own volition. For these only is he responsible. 'Hereditary' sin would therefore be impossible. Augustine, on the contrary, with a strong sense of the solidarity of the human race, regarded sin as present since the fall, in the disposition or nature of man, prior to any individual conscious act. The individual's volition was exercised once for all by Adam, and every man had inherited ever since an evil disposition, the acts of which must necessarily be evil.

These two negations of Pelagius—(1) the denial of the necessity of supernatural and directly assisting grace for any true service of God on the part of man; and (2) the denial of the transmission of a fault and corruption of nature, and also of physical death, to the descendants of the first man in consequence of his transgression—found expression in the commentaries he composed on the Epistles of St Paul,[1] and attracted attention during a visit which he paid to Rome in the early years of the fifth century.

The Pelagian Controversy—Coelestius

Pelagius was little inclined for controversy, but while at Rome he converted to the monastic life an advocate, Coelestius, who eagerly adopted his ideas and wished to defend and propagate them against all others. It was Coelestius, rather than Pelagius himself, who was the immediate cause of the outbreak of the controversy.. Three stages in it may be noted.[2]

The First Stage at Carthage.—The scene of the first stage was Africa. Pelagius was on his travels to the East, and left Rome with Coelestius in the year 409, and after a stay in Sicily went to Carthage in the year 411. When he left, Coelestius stayed behind and wished for ordination to the priesthood there, but rumours of his peculiar views were current, and a discussion ensued at a synod held at Carthage in 412 (or possibly the previous year). He was charged with six heretical propositions,[3] the chief and centre of which were—(a) that the sin of Adam had injured himself only and not the whole human race, and (b) that children come into

---

The origin of sin is thus not separated from volition, and though the volition of the individual is determined by the sin of the first man, yet he is himself responsible. It is from a disposition or nature already sinful that sinful acts proceed.

[1] Migne *P.L.* pp. xxx 645-902. On the curious literary history of this book see Art. 'Pelagius' *D.C.B.*

[2] See Art. 'Pelagius' *D.C.B.*, and Hefele *Councils* vol. ii pp. 446 ff. See also, for the whole question, Art. 'Augustine' by Dr. Robertson in the new volume of *D.C.B.*

[3] These were—1. Adam was created mortal, and would have died whether he had sinned or not. 2. The sin of Adam injured himself alone, not the human race. 3. Little children, born into the world, are in the condition in which Adam was before the Fall. 4. It is not through the death or the fall of Adam that the whole race of men dies, nor through the resurrection of Christ that the whole race of men rises again. 5. The law, as well as the gospel, conducts to the kingdom of heaven. 6. Even before the coming of the Lord there were men who were free from sin. (In another account, 5 is combined with 6, and in its place is given—Infants, although they be not baptized, have eternal life.)

life in the same condition in which Adam was before the Fall. Against the accusation, he insisted that the orthodox were not agreed upon the manner in which the soul was propagated, and whether sin was inherited or not. The issue was merely speculative and not a matter of faith. It was an open question in the Church. It was enough that he maintained the necessity of baptism. For the bishops, however, this was not enough ; and, as he refused to condemn the views attributed to him, he was excluded from communion. Against the sentence he appealed to the judgement of his native Church, and going on to Ephesus obtained the ordination which he wished.[1]

The Second Stage in Palestine.—The scene of the next stage of the controversy was Palestine, whither Pelagius had gone. There he found an opponent in Jerome,[2] and in a Spanish priest, Orosius, sent to Bethlehem by Augustine to stay the progress of Pelagian teaching. Accordingly, at a synod at Jerusalem in 415 under the bishop, John, he was called on to explain. Orosius reported what had happened at Carthage, and said that Pelagius taught "that man can live without sin, in obedience to the divine commands, if he pleases". Pelagius admitted that he taught so; and God's command to Abraham to walk before him and be perfect (Gen. 17[1]) was cited by the bishop himself, as presupposing the possibility of perfection in a man. But, in reply to questions, Pelagius declared that he did not exclude the help of God, but held that everyone who strove for it received from God the power to be entirely sinless. In the East, at all events at this time, men were not accustomed to fine distinctions between grace and free will, and were not anxious to define precisely the limits of each agency, and were not prepared to accept without discussion the decisions of the synod to which Orosius appealed.[3] They were satisfied by general statements of belief

---

[1] Soon after this a book of Pelagius *de Natura* was given to Augustine, and he replied to it in his tract *de Natura et Gratia* (which contains all that is extant of the work which it answers). He had previously written the tract *de Spiritu et Litera.*

[2] Jerome was in agreement with Augustine, and referred Pelagianism to the influence of Origen and Rufinus, and wrote against it. See *ad Ctesiphontem* (*Ep.* 133, Migne *P.L.* xxii p. 1147) and *Dialogus contra Pelagianos* (Migne *P.L.* xxiii 495–590).

[3] They resented as a rudeness the curt reply Pelagius made (What have I to do with Augustine ?), when asked if he had really propounded the doctrine which Augustine opposed ; but they were not ready to consider even the support of his great name decisive. The Bishop of Jerusalem had been 'suspect' for 'Origenistic' leanings, and therefore was not likely to be a *persona grata* to Jerome or Augustine. See his defence—Hahn [3] p. 294.

in the need of divine assistance, and were ready to admit Pelagius as orthodox when he assented to the need.[1] Orosius, however, demanded that, as the question had originated in the West,[2] it should be left to the Latins to determine ; and deputies and letters were sent to Innocent, Bishop of Rome, requesting him to hear and decide the case.

Nevertheless, a few months later in the same year, Pelagius appeared before a second synod in Palestine, at Diospolis or Lydda, to answer to a paper of complaints put in against him by two Gallican bishops, who had been driven from their sees and made their way to Palestine.[3] Many of the theses alleged against him he was able to explain to the satisfaction of the Palestinian bishops ; others he declared he did not teach, although Coelestius might maintain them. For these he had not to answer ; but he was ready to declare that he rejected them, and to anathematize all who opposed the doctrines of the holy Catholic Church.[4] He acknowledged and maintained both grace and free will, and professed that his assertion that " man, if he pleases, can be perfectly free from sin " was meant to apply to one who was converted—such an one being able to live without sin by his own efforts and God's grace, although not free from temptation to sin. This was enough for the synod. It declared Pelagius worthy of communion, and earned from Jerome the epithet 'miserable'.[5]

The Third Stage—Appeal to Rome.—So far, Pelagius had won the victory ; but his opponents were not to be silenced. In North Africa they would not rest content with these decisions of the East. Two synods met in the following year

---

[1] The difference between Pelagius and Augustine is tolerably clear. Pelagius regarded the grace of God as an essential aid, a reinforcement from without, to second the efforts which were put forth by the free will of man. To Augustine grace was a new creative principle of life, which generates as an abiding good that freedom of the will which is entirely lost in the natural man.   What it meant exactly to Pelagius is not clear. He does not seem to have conceived it as an inner spiritual illumination, but rather as some external stimulus applied to the natural faculties—so that Augustine could represent him as recognizing little more than the influence of teaching and example in it ('law and doctrine'—*de gratia Christi* 11).

[2] Orosius could only speak Latin, and the bishop only Greek ; so misunderstandings might easily arise.

[3] Heros of Arles and Lazarus of Aix.   They were perhaps 'put up' by Jerome.

[4] Hereby he was said to have anathematized himself.   His desire was for peace and freedom from doctrinal disputes.   The practical moral aspect of the question was what he really cared for.

[5] The treatise of Augustine *de gestis Pelagii* deals with the proceedings at this synod.

(416),[1] and renewed the previous condemnation of Coelestius, and announced their decisions to the Bishop of Rome, Innocent I, begging him to help to stay the spread of the Pelagian errors.

In its third stage, accordingly, the controversy was enacted mainly at Rome. The bishop accepted fully the African view, praised the synods for their action, and confirmed the sentence of excommunication pronounced against Pelagius and Coelestius. But immediately afterwards Innocent died; and Zosimus, his successor, received from Coelestius in person,[2] and from Pelagius by letter,[3] confessions of faith, by which he declared that they had completely justified themselves ; and he wrote to the African bishops, blaming them for their hasty condemnation (Sept. 417), and declaring that the opponents of Pelagius and Coelestius were wicked slanderers.

The Fourth Stage—Final Condemnation by Councils in Africa and at Rome.—The African bishops assembled in all haste in synod (late in 417 or early in 418), and protested that Zosimus had been misled, that " he should hold to the sentence pronounced by Innocent against Pelagius and Coelestius, until both of them distinctly acknowledged that for every single good action we need the help of the grace of God through Jesus Christ; and this not only to perceive what is right, but also to practise it, so that without it we cannot either possess, think, speak, or do anything really good or holy." To this Zosimus replied that he had already fully considered the matter; but he sent the documents regarding it to the Africans, that there might be consultation and

---

[1] One at Carthage for the province of Africa (a local synod—at which, therefore, Augustine was not present, his see belonging to the ecclesiastical province of Numidia), and one at Mileve (Mileum), for the Numidians, at which Augustine was present. See the synodal letters in Aug. *Epp.* 175, 176 (Migne xxxiii pp. 758 ff.).

[2] For fragments of his creed see Hahn[3] p. 292. He argues that "infants ought to be baptized unto remission of sins ", but repudiates Traducianism as alien from the Catholic conception, on the ground that "the sin which is afterwards practised by man is not born with him, for it is proved to be a fault, not of nature, but of will". And he denies that he claims the authority of a dogma for his inferences from the teaching of prophets and apostles. On the contrary, he submits them to the correction of the apostolic see.

[3] See Hahn[3] p. 288. It had been addressed by Pelagius to Innocent, and went at length into most articles of the faith, concluding with an appeal to him to amend anything in it that might have been less skilfully or somewhat incautiously expressed. On the special questions at issue he wrote as follows : " We confess that we have free will, in the sense that we always are in need of the help of God, and that they err who say . . . that man cannot avoid sin, no less than they who . . . assert that man cannot sin ; for both alike destroy the freedom of the will. We, however, say that man can sin and can not sin (is able to sin and able not to sin), in such wise as always to confess that we possess free will."

agreement. A council of two hundred bishops was speedily
held at Carthage (in April 418), at which nine canons were
drawn up, with anti-Pelagian definitions of the points in question.[1]   What were regarded as Pelagian compromises are
definitely faced and detailed, and declared anathema.   The
absolute necessity of baptism to effect regeneration, and to counter-
balance the corruption of nature and stain of sin that is innate—
the powerlessness of the human will unaided, and the vital need
of grace to enable us to fulfil the commands of God—are insisted
on.   No ingenuity of any adherent of Pelagius or Coelestius
could evade the significance of this pronouncement.   Imperial
edicts against the Pelagians were also procured from Honorius
and Theodosius (banishing Pelagius and Coelestius and their
followers) ; and the Bishop of Rome was obliged to reopen the
case.   He summoned Pelagius and Coelestius, and, when they
did not appear, condemned them in their absence and issued a
circular letter (*epistola tractoria*) accepting the African view of
the matter.   This he ordered should be subscribed by all bishops
under his jurisdiction.   Eighteen refused, and were deposed and
banished from their sees, while many probably signed unwillingly.

The Ultimate Issue of the Controversy. — In this way
Pelagianism was stifled, by force rather than by argument ; and
at the next General Council of the Church (at Ephesus in 431)
Pelagius was anathematized in company with Nestorius.[2]   But
in modified forms the Pelagian conceptions continued, and have
always found some place in the Church.

It must, indeed, be noted that, while the negations of Pelagianism were rejected, and Pelagianism was condemned (*i.e.* the
denial of inherited sin and of the need of baptism of children for
remission of sins), yet the positive side of Pelagian teaching (the
point of departure of Pelagius himself) found sympathy in deep-
rooted Christian sentiment and convictions ; and Augustine's anti-
Pelagian theories did not win wide acceptance.[3]

---

[1] Hahn [3] p. 213.

[2] All that is known as to the consideration of Pelagianism at Ephesus is contained
in the synodal letter to Coelestine of Rome, which states that the Western Acts on
the condemnation of Pelagius, Coelestius, and their adherents were read and
universally approved.   Little is known of the history of Pelagius after his condemnation by Zosimus.   He is said to have died in Palestine when seventy years of age
(? c. 440).   Of Coelestius, too, nothing more is known.

[3] Cf. Loofs *Leitfaden* p. 260.   In the Greek Church Augustinianism never took
root.   Many were ready to sympathize with the eighteen bishops, of whom Julian

" *Semi-Pelagianism* " [1]

The attempt to mediate between the two extremes—to express, that is, a theory of human nature and of sin and grace which should be more in harmony with the general conceptions that had been prevalent among Churchmen in earlier ages—was made by John Cassian and Faustus of Rhegium, as representatives of a considerable number of Gallican churchmen.

(*a*) *John Cassian*

Like Pelagius, Cassian passed a large part of his life from boyhood onwards in a monastery. A friend and admirer of Chrysostom, after some years spent at Constantinople he was sent about 405 on an embassy to Rome, to enlist the support of Innocent; and perhaps he stayed on at Rome and met Pelagius. On the invasion of the Goths he retired, and ultimately made his home near Massilia (Marseilles), where he founded two monasteries (for men and for women), and—probably as abbot of one of them—devoted himself for many years to study and writing. As a framer of monastic rules and ideals his influence on Western monasticism was long-lived; [2] and the Semi-

of Eclanum in Campania became the chief mouthpiece—a man of high character and generous benevolence and ample learning and ability, who was firmly convinced that the cause of the Christian faith and of morality itself was endangered by the Augustinian doctrine. He did not shrink from charging that doctrine with Manicheism, considering that its teaching as to the taint which had permeated human nature was equivalent to the Manichean theory that its material part was essentially evil; and he wrote at length against Augustine and his conceptions, and tried to enlist bishops and the emperor (Theodosius II) on his side—not altogether unsuccessfully at first. Both Theodore of Mopsuestia (see *supra* p. 256) and Nestorius endeavoured to shield him; but in 429 he was driven from Constantinople (which had been his refuge for a short time after his deposition by Zosimus and his banishment) by an imperial edict. This was largely through the instrumentality of Marius Mercator, who opposed Pelagianism as well as Nestorianism. And later on he was again condemned by a Council at Rome under Celestine and by successive bishops. He died in 454 in Sicily. His writings are known to us only from Augustine's replies. See especially the four books *Contra duas epistulas Pelagianorum* (420), and the six books *Contra Julianum Pelagianum*. [See the Art. 'Julianus of Eclanum' *D.C.B.*]

Julian was a thoroughgoing supporter of Pelagianism. A more conciliatory position was taken by John Cassian.

[1] The familiar term may be retained, but Semi-Augustinianism would be at least as accurate a designation, and would beg no question.

[2] His works on these subjects were "highly prized all through the Middle Ages as handbooks of the cloister-life".

2 I

Pelagianism [1] which he taught has always numbered many adherents.

Above all else he was inspired by a moral interest and a profound sense of the love of God. As, in his counsels to his monks, he insisted that no outward obedience to rule availed without purity of intention and consecration of the inner life; so he believed that the doctrine of grace was to be known and understood only by the experience of a pure life.

He was repelled equally by the assertions of Pelagius (which he styled profane and irreligious) as by those of Augustine. Against Pelagius he held the universal corruption of human nature as a consequence of the first transgression of the father of the race, and so far accepted the Augustine conception of grace. On the other hand, he was entirely opposed to the denial of free will and of man's power to determine in any way the issues of his life. In the renovation of the human will there are, he held, two efficient agencies—the will itself and the Holy Spirit. The exact relation between the two—free will and grace —is not capable of definition; no universally applicable rule can be laid down; sometimes the initiative is with man, sometimes with God. Nature unaided may take the first step towards its recovery:—If it were not so, exhortations and censure would be alike idle and unjust. 'Predestination' he rejects—it is a shocking 'impiety' to think that God wishes not all men universally, but only some, instead of all, to be saved.[2]

[1] It must be remembered that Semi-Pelagians (so-called) were in full agreement with the Church at large in repudiating the chief Pelagian propositions. It is only when Augustine's teaching is taken as normal that the name is valid.

[2] *Collationes* xiii 7 : Quomodo sine ingenti sacrilegio putandus est [Deus] non universaliter omnes sed quosdam salvos fieri velle pro omnibus? Other significant passages on the subject are—§ 8 " When He (*sc.* God) sees in us any beginning of good will, straightway He enlightens it and strengthens it and stimulates it to salvation, giving increase to that good will which He planted Himself, or sees has sprung up by our own effort"; § 9 "in order, however, to shew more clearly that the first beginnings of good desires (good will) are sometimes produced by means of that natural goodness (*naturae bonum*) which is innate in us by the gift of the Creator, and yet that these beginnings cannot end in the attainment of virtuous acts unless they are directed by the Lord, the Apostle bears witness and says, 'for to will is present to me, yet how to accomplish the good I find not' (Rom. 7[18])"; and § 11 "if, however, we say that the first beginnings of good will are always inspired by the grace of God, what are we to say of the faith of Zacchaeus and of the piety of the crucified thief, who, applying force, as it were, to the kingdom of heaven by their own longing desire, anticipated the special monitions of the call." The *Collationes* (conferences of Egyptian monks on true asceticism) were written about

The most that can be rightly said is that God knows beforehand who will be saved (*praescientia*—foreknowledge). He thus really departs a long way from the Augustinian conceptions, connecting the idea of grace with a dominant purpose of divine love which extends to all men and wills the salvation of all; whereas to Augustine election and rejection alike were divine acts[1] entirely unconditioned by anything in the power of the individuals elected or rejected.

(b) *Faustus of Rhegium*

Similar teaching to that of Cassian was given also by another of the greatest monks and bishops of Southern Gaul—Faustus, a member, and from about 433 abbot, of the famous monastery of Lerinum (Lerins), and afterwards Bishop of Rhegium (Riez in Provençe), most highly honoured for his learning and his ascetic and holy life of self-sacrificing labours and active benevolence.[2] A staunch champion of the Nicene faith against Arianism—the religion of the Visigoths into whose power his diocese passed—and therefore driven from his see, he yet did not escape criticism for his anthropological doctrines from some of his contemporaries, and still more from theologians of the next generation. Neither Augustine nor Pelagius seemed to him to express the whole truth. Pelagius indeed he severely condemns as heretical; but at the same time he expresses fear of teaching which, in denying man's power as a free agent, becomes fatalistic. He anathematizes anyone who says that the 'vessel of wrath' cannot ever become a 'vessel of honour', or that Christ did not die for all men, or does not will that all should be saved, or says that anyone who has perished (being baptized, or being a pagan who might have believed and would not) never had the opportunity of being saved; and he strongly urges the need of human endeavour and co-operation with the divine grace. 'He that

425-428. The third and thirteenth are on Grace and Free Will and were impugned by Augustine, and by Prosper *De gratia Dei et libero arbitrio contra Collatorem* (Migne *P.L.* li p. 213).

[1] Cf. his *de Praedestinatione Sanctorum* and *de Dono Perseverantiae*.

[2] He was born in Brittany (or perhaps Britain) early in the fifth century, and lived nearly to the end of it. His local reputation was so great that the title of Saint was given him, and his festival was observed, in spite of the weight of Augustine's authority. In more modern times Jansenist historians and editors naturally impugn his right to canonization, while learned Jesuits defend him.

hath, to him shall be given'—he has the power and must use it. The doctrine of predestination, in particular, called forth his energetic protests, and he strongly denied the assumption of any such 'special and personal' grace (*grátia specialis* and *personalis*) as Augustine's theory of predestination involved; though at the same time he speaks of a precedent grace (*gratia praecedens*) of a general character.[1]

A presbyter of Gaul named Lucidus had roused uneasiness by his advocacy of these and other Augustinian conceptions, and Faustus was requested by Leontius, the Archbishop of Arles, to write upon the subject;[2] and at a Council held at Arles in 472 (or 473) his writing was formally approved and signed by the bishops present, who also agreed to six anathemas against the extremer teaching on either side.   What is commonly known as the 'Semi-Pelagian' position is set forth in these anathemas.[3] They condemn the Pelagian ideas that man is born without sin and can be saved by his own efforts alone without the grace of God, and, along with the anti-Pelagian conceptions already noted, the view that it is the fault of original sin when a man who has been duly baptized in the true faith falls through the attractions of this world.   And they further reject the compromise by which many were satisfied to speak of God's foreknowledge rather than of predestination,—it is not even to be said that the foreknowledge of God has any effect on the downward course of a man towards death.

The later History of the Doctrine

Teaching to this effect prevailed in Gaul for some time.   But synods at Orange (Arausio)[4] and Valence[5] in 529 decided for the

---

[1] See the *Letter to Lucidus* (Migne *P.L.* liii p. 683).   It appears that he did not mean to express the need for a definite 'prevenient' grace (as positively requisite before any step towards salvation was possible) in the Augustinian sense, as something altogether external to the human will, but rather an awakening of the will so that it was able to co-operate at once in the work, which, however, could never be successfully completed but for the divine grace.

[2] He wrote first a letter to Lucidus and afterwards to the same effect a more formal treatise entitled *De gratia Dei et humanae mentis libero arbitrio* (Migne *P.L.* lviii p. 783 ff).

[3] Hahn³ p. 217.

[4] Under the presidency of Caesarius of Arles, sometime abbot of Lerinum.

[5] The priority of these Councils is disputed (see Hefele).   Arnold *Caesarius von Arelate* p. 348 n. 1129 puts that of Valence first.

Augustinian doctrine, with the limitation that predestination to evil was not to be taught (Augustine himself did not really teach it in words at least), and accepted canons which had been drawn up at Rome in accordance with the teaching of ancient Fathers and the holy Scriptures.[1]   The decisions of this Council were confirmed by the Bishop of Rome, Boniface II, in the following year.   But, on the whole, Semi-Pelagianism prevailed in the West—that is to say, the theory of inherited evil and sin, the somewhat uncertain acceptance of the necessity of grace as ' prevenient ' to the first motions of goodness in man, and the belief in the power of man to aid in the work of divine grace within himself (' synergistic ' regeneration, man co-operating with God).

During the Middle Ages individuals—as Gottschalk (with strong assertion of twofold predestination), Bede, Anselm, Bernard —represented the Augustinian teaching.   And it was revived in its harshest forms by Calvin—to arouse the opposition of Arminians and Socinians.   Luther was only to some extent Augustinian in this respect.   He believed that the fall of man changed his original holiness into absolute depravity, exposing the whole race to condemnation ; but the divine grace, which is indispensable to conversion, he taught was proffered to all men without distinction, but might be rejected by them.   Free play was thus allowed for human responsibility, and the only predestination possible was such as was based on foresight as to the faith and obedience of men, on which the decrees of God were held to be conditional.   It is certainly not the doctrine of Augustine that was stated at the Council of Trent.   That man's free will alone is insufficient, and that without prevenient grace he cannot be justified, and without its inspiration and assistance cannot have faith or hope or love or repentance, is asserted in plain terms.[2] But no less clearly it is maintained that man himself has something to contribute to the process of salvation : he can receive and he can reject the inspiration and illumination of the Holy Spirit, and he does so according to his own proper disposition and co-operation.[3]   The fall of man caused the loss of the gift of divine grace originally bestowed upon him, and its consequence

---

[1] See the canons of the Council of Orange—Hahn[3] pp. 220–227, esp. canon 25 p. 227.   They insist with emphasis that human nature is unable to make any kind of beginning of faith and goodness, or to invoke the divine aid, without the grace of God.   The giving and reception of grace depends solely on God's initiative.

[2] Sess. vi cap. 3.   [3] Sess. vi cap. 4, 5, 7.

was weakness and imperfection. His freedom of will was weakened and turned aside, but not lost and extinguished. Roman orthodoxy thus recognizes *gratia praeveniens*, and *gratia co-operans*, and the human power of self-determination. Similarly, as opposed to the theory of predestination, the Council of Trent declared the universality of grace ; and, when the Jansenists attempted to revive the doctrines of Augustine, predestination was still more decisively rejected.

AUGUSTINE'S CHIEF ANTI-PELAGIAN WRITINGS (see Robertson
Art. 'Augustinus' *D.C.B.* new volume)

A.D.

412 *De pecc. meritis et remiss.* lib. iii, and *De spiritu et litera* (to
 Marcellinus).

415 *De natura et gratia*, and *De perfectione iustitiae hominis* (against
 the teaching of Coelestius).

417 *De gestis Pelagii* (on the proceedings in Palestine), and *Epp.* 176,
 177, and *Serm.* 131.

418 *De gratia Christi et de peccato originali* lib. ii.

419 *De nuptiis et concupiscentia* lib. ii, and *De anima eiusque origine*
 lib. iv (on the transmission of original sin and on the origin of
 the soul).

420 *Contra duas epp. Pelagianorum* lib. iv. (a reply to Julian's attack
 on the treatise *De nuptiis*).

421 *Contra Julianum* lib. vi.

426-7 *De gratia et libero arbitrio* and *De correptione et gratia*

428-9 *De praedest. sanctorum* and *De dono perseverantiae*

(against the arguments of the Semi-Pelagians).

CHAPTER XVIII

Introductory

WHAT we have seen to be true in the case of other doctrines is even more noteworthy in regard to the Atonement. The certainty that the life and death of Christ had effected an Atonement between God and man was the very heart and strength of the faith of Christians from the earliest days. They did not need to theorize about it; they were content to know and feel it. So it was long before any doctrine of the Atonement was framed. Various points of view, no doubt, are represented in the various books of the New Testament; but the allusions are incidental and occasional. And it is now from one point of view and now from another that we find the mysterious fact of the Atonement regarded in such writings of Christians of the first four centuries as happen to have been preserved. If more had come down to us there might have been more points of view to claim consideration. But nothing like a definite theory is propounded in the earlier ages—nothing that can be said to go beyond the expressions of the apostolic writers—except perhaps by Irenaeus and Origen. They indeed were conscious of questions which the New Testament does not answer;[1] they wanted to define more closely the why and the wherefore, and they let the spirit of speculation carry them further than others had tried to penetrate. The solution of some of the unsolved problems which they reached satisfied many of the ablest theologians of their own and later generations, though in the process of time they came to be regarded as erroneous, and have for us now a merely historical interest. But apart from these particular theories, which we must notice in their place, we have no attempt at formal statement of a doctrine, and can only record incidental references and more or less chance phrases which indicate, rather

[1] See *supra* Chapter II pp. 20, 21.

than express, the conceptions of the earlier exponents of Christian teaching.[1] They are in all cases only personal attempts to set forth and illustrate experiences and emotions that were still personal, however widely they were shared among those who were fellows in faith. How far they were generally received, or what—if any—measure of official sanction was given them, it is impossible to say. Only, it is clear that every theologian was free to give expression of his own to the feelings which stirred him at the moment, and it would be a mistake to suppose that he emptied his whole thought on the mystery of the Atonement into such utterances as have been preserved. Nor must it be supposed that any such utterances in any way committed more than the writer himself. Later thinkers were still free to take them or to leave them ; just as, for example, Athanasius is apparently quite untouched by the modes of thought which are commonly regarded as characteristic of Irenaeus and Origen, and Gregory of Nazianzus expressly rejects the theory which his friend Gregory of Nyssa handed down to later ages.

It is then as individual answers to speculative questions, or as personal utterances of faith and hope, suggestive and illustrative of larger conceptions than are expressed, that we must take such expressions of the doctrine as we find.

Of the various aspects of the Atonement which are represented in the pages of the New Testament,[2] the early Fathers chiefly dwell on those of sacrifice (and obedience), reconciliation, illumination by knowledge, and ransom. Not till a later time was the idea of satisfaction followed up.[3]

The Apostolic Fathers

Outside the New Testament the earliest references to the doctrine are to be found in the *Epistle of Clement.* They are only incidental illustrations in his exposition of ' love '

[1] Of books on the history of the doctrine of the Atonement see H. N. Oxenham *The Catholic Doctrine of the Atonement.* For special points of view see also R. C. Moberly *Atonement and Personality* ; R. W. Dale *The Atonement* ; B. F. Westcott *The Victory of the Cross,* and the notes to his edition of the *Epistles of St John* ; M'Leod Campbell *The Nature of the Atonement,* and J. M. Wilson *The Gospel of the Atonement.*

[2] See *supra* Chapter II p. 19.

[3] The only ' satisfaction ' which was thought of was the satisfaction which the penitent himself makes. There is no suggestion of any satisfaction of the divine justice through the sufferings of Christ.

(ἀγάπη).[1]   Through the love which he had towards us, Jesus
Christ our Lord, in the will of God, gave his blood on behalf of
us, and his flesh on behalf of our flesh, and his life on behalf
of our lives.   So it is that we are turned from our wander-
ing and directed into the way of truth, and through the
benevolence of the Word towards men we are become the
sons of God.   His blood, which was shed for the sake of our
salvation, brought to all the world the offer of the grace of
repentance.   So it is not by works which we have done in
holiness of heart that we are justified, but only by faith; though
he adds at once "let us then work from our whole heart the
work of righteousness".

Incidental though the references are, they shew that Clement
taught that the motive of the whole plan of redemption was the
love of God and the spontaneous love of Christ fulfilling the
Father's will, and that by the sacrifice of himself—by his blood
—is offered both the grace of repentance and the knowledge of
the truth to all men.

In the *Epistle of Barnabas*[2] there are many allusions to the
passion and sufferings of Christ as effecting our salvation—the
remission of sins by the sprinkling of his blood.   The Son of
God could not suffer except only on account of us.   Incidents
in the history of Israel and prophecies are cited, which find
their fulfilment and real meaning in the passion of the Lord.
For instance, the account of Moses stretching out his hands,
while the Israelites prevailed against the Amalekites, is a type
of the Cross, and is designed to teach that unless men put their
hope and faith in it they will not conquer and cannot be saved.
But perhaps most prominence is given in the Epistle to the idea
of a new covenant founded by Christ's life and death, by which
the way of truth is exhibited for our knowledge; and the special
need for the coming of the Saviour in the flesh is found in
human weakness, requiring an unmistakeable revelation visible
to the naked eye.   "For had he not come in flesh, how could
we men *see* him and be saved?"

In *The Shepherd of Hermas*[3] there is only one clear reference
to the doctrine, but it has special interest as connecting the
value of the work of the Saviour with his obedience to the
Father's will and laws.   The thought is expressed in the form
of a parable of a vineyard, which represents God's people, in

[1] 1 *Ep.* 49.   [2] See esp. chs. 5, 7, 12.   [3] *Similitude* v 6.

which the Son is bidden to work as a servant, and in which he labours much and suffers much to do away their sins, and then points out to them the way of life by giving them the law which he received from his Father. The perfect fulfilment of the Father's will, at the cost of toil and suffering, on the one hand, and on the other hand, the revelation of that will to men; that is, obedience, active as well as passive, on his own part, and the instruction of men that they may render a similar obedience on their part, are represented here as being the two main elements in the work of Christ.

In the *Epistles of Ignatius* the reality of the sufferings of Christ is emphasized again and again against docetic teaching, and it is clear that the writer attached unique importance to the passion, although it is the reality of the manhood as a whole that he is all through concerned to uphold. All in heaven and in earth, men and angels, must believe in the blood of Christ if they are to escape condemnation.[1] But how the redemption is effected, and precisely what value is to be attributed to the sufferings of the Redeemer, is naturally not expressed. It was no part of the task of Ignatius to expound the doctrine of the Atonement, but only to appeal to the deepest convictions of those that he addressed, based on the teaching they had already received. But he insists on the supreme need of faith and love toward Christ on the part of men; and he seems to regard the death of Christ as operative in bringing the human soul into communion with him, as the means of imparting the principle of spiritual life, and as a manifestation of love by which a corresponding affection is generated in the believer's heart. In this way he has in mind perhaps the 'sanctification' more than the 'justification' of mankind.[2]

Justin

No systematic treatment of the subject is to be found either in Justin's *Apologies* or in the *Dialogue with Trypho*; but enough is said to shew that various aspects of the work of Christ were clearly present to his thought. The reason why the Logos became

---

[1] *Ad Smyrn.* 6.

[2] The idea of 'justification' is hardly present, though the verb occurs twice *Philad.* 8 and *Rom.* 5 (with reference to 1 Cor. 4⁴). He speaks also of 'peace' through the passion (*Eph. inscr.*) and of deliverance from demons through Christ (*Eph.* 19).

331 THE DOCTRINE OF THE ATONEMENT

man, it is declared on the one hand, was that he might share our
sufferings and effect a cure,[1] cleansing by blood those that believe
in him.[2]   But on the other hand, Justin emphasizes more than
other writers of the time the didactic purpose of the Incarnation.
The Saviour saves by teaching men the truth about God and
withdrawing them from bondage to false gods.   " Having become
man he taught us . . ."[3]   "His mighty Word persuaded many
to leave demons, to whom they were enslaved, and through him
to believe on the all-sovereign God."[4]   "We beseech God to
keep us safe, always through Jesus Christ, from the demons
who are contrary to the true religion of God, whom of old we
used to worship; in order that after turning to God through
him we may be blameless."[5]   The intellectual purpose issues
in the moral reformation, the knowledge of God in the blameless life.

J ustin also alludes to the conquest of Satan as one of the
consequences of the Passion, and seems to attribute the ultimate
responsibility for the sufferings of Christ to the devils who
prompted the Jews,[6] so that his triumph over death was a
victory over Satan himself.   But he does not express the idea
of any kind of ransom to Satan.

And though he speaks of 'sacrifice', he does not refer it to
the idea of justice, and he is far from any theory of satisfaction
of an alienated God.   His thought is shewn in his treatment of
the passage 'Cursed is everyone that hangeth on a tree' (Gal. 3[13]).
All mankind, he says, is under a curse, and God willed that
Christ, his own Son, should receive the curses of all.   Christ
also willed this, and all who repent of their sins and believe in
him will be saved.   But the curse which he takes upon him is
not God's curse.[7]   "In the law a curse is laid on men who are
crucified.   But God's curse does not therefore lie upon Christ,
through whom he saves all those who have done things deserving
a curse."[8]   Rather, the words of Scripture indicate God's foreknowledge of what was destined to be done by the Jews and
others like them.   It was by the Jews, and not by God, that he

[1] Apol. ii 13, and esp. (the chief passage) Dial. c. Tryph. 40-43 and 95.
[2] Apol. i 63.   [3] Ibid. i 23.
[4] Dial. c. Tryph. 83.   [5] Ibid. 30.
[6] See Apol. i 63 "he endured to suffer all that the devils disposed the Jews to do
to him ".
[7] Indeed, he styles it only an 'apparent' curse (Dial. c. Tryph. 90).
[8] Ibid. 94.

was accursed. For all who have faith in him there hangs from the crucified Christ the hope of salvation.[1]

The Writer to Diognetus

Some fine passages in the *Epistle to Diognetus* shew the writer's conception of the Atonement as essentially an act of compassion which is prompted by the unalterable love of God, and insist on the perfect union of will between the Father and the Son. "God, the Master and Maker of all things, who created all things and set them in order, was not only a lover of man but also long-suffering. He indeed was always and will be such, gracious and good, and uninfluenced by anger and true. He alone is good, and he conceived the great inexpressible design which he communicated only to his Son."[2] The Son carries out the Father's will, but it is his own will too. It is the Father's love that finds expression in the self-sacrifice of the Son. "When our unrighteousness (iniquity) was fully wrought out, and it was fully made manifest that its wages, punishment and death, were to be expected, and the time was come which God fore-appointed to make manifest His goodness and power—Oh the surpassing kindness towards men and love of God! He did not hate us or thrust us from Him or remember our evil deeds against us, but He was long-suffering, He was forebearing, and in His mercy He took our sins upon Himself. He Himself gave up His own Son as a ransom on behalf of us :—the holy on behalf of lawless men, him who was without wickedness on behalf of the wicked, the righteous on behalf of the unrighteous, the incorruptible on behalf of the corruptible, the immortal on behalf of the mortal. For what else but his righteousness was able to cover our sins? In whom, except only in the Son of God, was it possible for us, the lawless and impious, to be declared righteous (justified)?"[3] But it is no external act or transaction that effects the object in view. It is a real inner change that is wrought in man. God sent His Son with a view to saving, with a view to persuading, not with a view to forcing: for force is not the means God uses.[4]

---

[1] *Dial. c. Tryph.* 96, 111. A similar view of the curse was held by Tertullian (*adv. Judaeos* 10).

[2] Ch. 8. [3] Ch. 9. [4] Ch. 8.

Tertullian

From Tertullian, if from any one, we should have expected a theory of atonement based on legal conceptions and forensic metaphors.[1] But he has no more definite theory than the writers before him. He is the first to use the term 'satisfaction', it is true, but he never uses it in the sense of vicarious satisfaction which afterwards attached to it. He means by it the amends which those who have sinned make for themselves by confession and repentance and good works.[2] He does not bring the idea into connexion with the work of Christ, but with the acts of the penitent.[3]

Similarly he insists[4] that the curse which was supposed to attach to the crucified Christ, in accordance with the application of the words of Deuteronomy (21^{32})—'Cursed is he that hangeth on a tree', was not the curse of God but the curse of the Jews. They denied that the death upon the cross was predicted of the Messiah, basing their denial on that passage; but he argues that the context shews that only criminals justly condemned were meant—the curse is the crime and not the hanging on the tree, whereas in Christ no guile was found: he shewed perfect justice and humility. It was not on account of his own deserts that he was given over to such a death, but in order that the things which were foretold by the prophets as destined to come on him by the hands of the Jews might be fulfilled. All those things which he suffered,[5] he suffered not on account of any evil deed of his own, but that the Scriptures might be fulfilled which were spoken by the mouth of the prophets.[6]

Irenaeus

When we pass to consider the conceptions of Irenaeus we must note at the outset that no one has ever more clearly

---

[1] So Oxenham points out *op. cit.* p. 124.

[2] See Note on the 'Doctrine of Merit' p. 353.

[3] This is evident from the references in *de Poen.* 5, 7, 8, 9, 10 ; *de Pat.* 13 ; *de Pud.* 9 ; *de Cult. Fem.* i 1 ; *adv. Jud.* 10.

[4] See *adv. Judaeos* 10.

[5] That the highest value attached to the sufferings of Christ in Tertullian's judgement is shewn by his argument against docetic teaching (*adv. Marc.* iii 8). If his death be denied, he says (and a phantasm could not really suffer), the whole work of God would be overthrown and the whole meaning and benefit of Christianity rejected.

[6] It was only dimly that the mystery (*sacramentum*) of his passion could be

grasped the fundamental truth of the 'solidarity' of humanity. No principle is more characteristic of Christian theology than this, that the race of men is a corporate whole—all members of it being so closely bound together in a union so intimate that they form together one living organism. To this conception Irenaeus gives the clearest expression, and following up the meaning of the title 'Son of Man' which St Paul had been the first to expand,[1] he points to Christ as the great representative of the race, in whom are summed up all its ripe experiences as they were contained in germ in Adam. What Christ achieves the whole race achieves. Just as mankind in Adam lost its birthright, so in Christ mankind recovers its original condition. The effect of Adam's acts extended to the whole company of his descendants, and the effect of Christ's acts is equally coextensive with the race. In each case it is really the whole race that acts in its representative.

It is this that the Incarnation means. "When he was incarnate and made man, he summed up (or recapitulated) in himself the long roll of the human race, securing for us all a summary salvation, so that we should regain in Christ Jesus what we had lost in Adam, namely, the being in the image and likeness of God."[2] And again, "This is why the Lord declares himself to be the Son of Man, summing up into himself the original man who was the source of the race which has been fashioned 'after woman'; in order that, as through the conquest of man our race went down into death, so through the victory of man we might mount up to life."[3] And again, "For in the first Adam we stumbled, not doing his command; but in the second Adam we were reconciled, shewing ourselves obedient unto death."[4] These passages shew clearly that the writer's

shadowed forth in the O.T. (in order that the difficulty of interpretation might lead men to seek the grace of God), in types such as Isaac and Joseph, and in figures like the bull's horns and the serpent lifted up. See also *adv. Marc.* v 5.

[1] See such passages as Rom. $5^{12\text{-}21}$, 1 Cor. $15^{20\text{-}22}$, Eph. 1^{10}.

[2] *Adv. Haer.* iii 19. 1. The thought expressed by the words *recapitulare, recapitulatio*, applied in this way to Christ, is the chief clue to the full conception of the writer, both as to the Incarnation and as to the Atonement. The doctrines are one and the same: the Incarnation effects the Atonement. It brings to completion the original creation, and is its perfecting as much as its restitution. From this point of view the Incarnation is the natural and necessary completion of the self-revelation of God even apart from sin.

[3] *Ibid.* v 21. 1.

[4] *Ibid.* v 16. 2. Compare the striking passage (*ibid.* ii 33. 2) in which Irenaeus

thought was as distinct as possible. The whole race is *solidaire*: it exists as a whole in each of its great representatives, Adam and Christ. As a whole it forfeits its true privileges and character in Adam; as a whole it recovers them in Christ. The thought is not that Adam loses *for us*, and Christ regains *for us*; but that we ourselves lose in the one case, and we ourselves regain in the other case.

Whatever else Irenaeus says in regard to details of the work of atonement must be interpreted in the light of this principal conception, in his treatment of which he has in mind particularly such passages as Rom. 5^{19} ' As by one man's disobedience the many were made sinners, so by the obedience of one shall the many be made righteous'. It is in connexion with another passage (Heb. 2^{14} ' destroying him that hath the power over death, that is the devil') that he gives expression to the idea which was emphasized by later thinkers and became for centuries the 'orthodox' opinion among theologians. Man, in the free exercise of his will, had yielded to the inducements set before him by Satan, and had put himself under his dominion; and the justice of God required that this dominion should not be violently overthrown, but that Satan himself should be met, as it were, on equal terms, and induced to relinquish his possession. "The powerful Word and true man", he writes,[1] " by his own blood ransoming (*or* redeeming) us by a method in conformity with reason, gave himself as ransom for those who have been led into captivity. And since the 'apostasy' (*i.e.* the spirit of rebellion, *or* Satan himself) unjustly held sway over us, and, though we were Almighty God's by nature, estranged us in a manner against nature, making us his own disciples; the Word of God which is powerful in all things and not wanting in justice of his own, acted justly even in dealing with the apostasy itself, ransoming (buying back) from it what is his own, not by force in the way in which it gained sway over us at the beginning, snatching greedily what was not its own; but by a method of persuasion, in the way in which it was fitting for God to receive what he wished, by persuasion and not by the use of force, so that there might be no infringement of the principle of justice, and yet God's ancient creation might be

describes the passing of Christ through the different stages of human growth and developement in order that he might redeem and sanctify each age.

[1] *Adv. Haer.* v 1. 1.

preserved from perishing." To achieve the end in view man must render perfect obedience as a first condition, and that is one chief reason for the Incarnation, in order that the obedience may be at once man's and perfect.[1] "For if it had not been man who conquered the adversary of man, he would not have been justly conquered."[2]

He speaks of the obedience as being specially shewn in the three temptations:[3] "And so by conquering him the third time he drove him away for the future as having been legitimately conquered; and the violation of the command which had taken place in Adam was cancelled (or compensated for) by means of the command of the law which the Son of Man observed, not transgressing the command of God."[4]

The redemption, however, of man from the devil's dominion is finally won by the Redeemer's death. "By his own blood, therefore, the Lord redeemed us, and gave his soul on behalf of our souls, and his own flesh instead of our flesh; and poured out the Spirit of the Father to effect the union and communion of God and man, bringing down God to men through the Spirit, and at the same time bringing up man to God through his incarnation, and in his advent surely and truly giving us incorruption through the communion which he has (or we have) with God."[5]

While, therefore, the thought of man's bondage to the devil (of Satan's dominion as a real objective power) is thus clearly present to the mind of Irenaeus, and the additional thought that the 'justice' of God required that man should be 'bought back' from the devil by consent, he does not attempt to describe in

---

[1] *Adv. Haer.* iii. 19. 6. Cf. v 1, v 16. 2.

[2] It is to God, of course, that the obedience is due. Cf. *ibid.* v 16. 2, 17. 1–3.

[3] The temptations of Jesus are the counterpart of the temptation of Adam, as the obedience of the mother of Jesus is the counterpart of Eve's disobedience, and the birth from the Virgin Mary the counterpart of Adam's birth from the virgin earth.

[4] *Ibid.* v 21. The Latin "soluta est ea quae fuerat in Adam praecepti praevaricatio per praeceptum legis quod servavit filius hominis" is not quite clear, but the translation given above seems to convey the full meaning of the words. The technical legal sense of *praevaricari* (of an advocate who so conducts his case as to play into the hands of his opponent) can scarcely be maintained, and certainly there is no idea in *soluta est* of the payment of a price (cf. parallel expressions 'dissolvens (or sanans) . . . hominis inobedientiam' v 16. 2, 'nostram inobedientiam per suam obedientiam consolatus' v 17. 1).

[5] *Ibid.* v 1. 2 (the conclusion of the passage quoted *supra*), but the idea of the blood of Christ as ransom does not seem to occupy a very prominent place in the whole work of atonement and redemption.

THE DOCTRINE OF THE ATONEMENT 337

any detail the nature of the transaction which is implied. These are certainly not the aspects of the matter which appeal to him most, or which he cares to emphasize. Any unscriptural conclusions that might be drawn from them were for Irenaeus himself, it seems, effectively precluded by the other conceptions which he grasped so firmly.[1]

Nevertheless difficult questions were bound to be put, coarsely and crudely perhaps, but anyhow questions which had to be met. In what sense could it be said that the justice of God required such a method of working?[2] and how was it that the devil came to make so bad a bargain?

Origen

Origen met the latter question with an answer more frank than satisfactory. The devil accepted the death of Christ (or his soul) as a ransom, but he could not retain it in his power, and so he found himself deceived in the transaction. The arrangement was conceived of as between God on the one side and the devil on the other, and so the author of the deception was God Himself, who in this way made use of Satan as the means of the destruction of his own power. He thought that by compassing the death of Christ he would prevent the spreading of his teaching, and by getting possession of his soul as an equivalent ($\dot{a}\nu\tau\dot{a}\lambda\lambda\alpha\gamma\mu\alpha$) would secure his control over men for ever. He did not perceive "that the human race was to be still more delivered by his death than it had been by his teaching and miracles". He did not realize that the sinless soul of Christ would cause him such torture that he could not retain it near him. So he over-reached himself. The issue was, of course, all along known to God; and Origen does not face the question how this deception was consistent with the recognition of Satan's rights.[3]

[1] So Harnack writes: "Irenaeus is quite as free from the thought that the devil has real rights over man as he is free from the immoral idea that God accomplished his work of redemption by an act of deceit" (*DG.* Eng. tr. vol. ii p. 290).
[2] The kingdom had been established in the first instance by injustice and usurpation,—how could this inveterate wrong become a right?
[3] This theory is expressed or alluded to in various writings of Origen. *E.g. Comm. in Joann.* tom. ii 21, *in Matt.* xvi 8, *in Rom.* ii 13. But the notion of intentional deception on the part of God (expressed *in Matt.* tom. xiii 9) is not prominent in Origen. His idea was rather that the devil deceived himself, imagin-

22

However, this particular point is only quite a subordinate element in the doctrine which Origen held on the whole matter. He dwells at greater length on other more important aspects of the Atonement.

Thus he sees in the Incarnation the beginning of an intimate connexion between the divine and the human, which is to be developed progressively in men. " Since the time of the Incarnation the divine and the human nature began to be woven together, in order that the human nature might become divine through its communion with the more divine not only in Jesus but also in all those who along with belief receive life which Jesus taught.[1] Redemption is thus effected by joining in one the divine and the human nature.

The death, too, was his own act. St Paul had written (Rom. 8[32]) of the Father that he spared not his own Son, but delivered him up for us all; and Origen's comment on the passage is this. " The Son too gave himself unto death on behalf of us, so that he was delivered up not only by the Father but also by himself." [2]

This death is described as the chastisement which we deserved, the discipline which was to lead to peace. He took our sins and was bruised for our iniquities, that we might be instructed and receive peace.[3] So the death is regarded as the expression of voluntary penance which cleanses [4] from sin, and in its inmost sense it must be experienced by every Christian. " So now if there be any one of us who recalls in himself the consciousness of sin, . . . let him fly to penitence, and accept a voluntary doing to death of the flesh, that cleansed from sin

ing that he could retain possession of the Son of God. (Contrast with Origen's words on the subject, Gregory of Nyssa's ἀπάτη τίς ἐστι τρόπον τινά on the part of God, that Jesus veiled his divine nature, which the devil would have feared, by means of his humanity, so that the devil was outwitted in spite of all his cunning.

[1] c. Cels. iii 28.

[2] In Matt. tom. xiii 8.

[3] In Joann. tom. xxviii 14 (Opp. iv p. 392, Migne). Thus he explains Isaiah's prophecy of the discipline of our peace being laid upon Christ as the chastisement due to us for our discipline, our peace-producing discipline, not a retributive punishment but a remedial chastisement. (This is Origen's conception of all punishment of sin, which therefore he could not think of as endless.)

[4] Jesus, who alone was able to bear the sins of the whole world, also removed judgement from the whole world by his own perfect obedience. In this conception may be seen perhaps, in germ, the later Anselmic theory of the need of redemption by obedience—paying back a debt to God, man having deprived him of honour by disobedience. For the stress laid on obedience by Irenaeus see supra p. 336.

during this present life our spirit may find its way clean and pure to Christ." [1] This 'moral interpretation' of the death of Christ is very significant. Its purpose, thus understood, was not to save us from suffering, but to shew us the true purpose of suffering, to lead us to accept it in a spirit of docility—the spirit which transforms pain into gain. "For he did not die for us in order that we may not die, but that we may not die for ourselves. And he was stricken and spat upon for us, in order that we who had really deserved these things may not have to suffer them as a return for our sins, but suffering them instead for righteousness sake may receive them with gladness of heart." [2]

At the same time, the death is described as an atoning sacrifice for sin, resembling in kind, though infinitely transcending in degree, the sacrifices of those men who have laid down their lives for their fellow-men, and is designed to act as a moral lever to elevate the courage of his followers. [3] It is from this point of view a sacrifice to God, and on Rom. 3[24] he comments thus: "God set him forth as a propitiation, in order, that is, that by the sacrifice of his body he might make God propitious to men." And elsewhere he speaks of Christ as by his blood making God propitious to men and reconciling them to the Father. [4] This conception of a sacrifice to God he does not seem to bring into correspondence with the idea of a ransom to the devil; and the allusion to a change effected by it in God's attitude to men, merely incidental and passing as it is, must be interpreted in harmony with his main conception, according to which he regularly ascribes the whole work of redemption to the love of God for men. [5]

From the time of Origen to the end of our period the two ideas of a ransom to Satan and a sacrifice to God remain unreconciled. [6] The idea that man needs to be rescued from the

[1] *In Levit. Hom.* xiv 4.
[2] *In Matt. Comment.* series 113, vol. iii p. 912 (Moberly *op. cit.*). *Serm. in Matt.* 912.
[3] See *in Num. Hom.* xxiv 1 ; cf. tom. *in Joann.* xxviii 393 ; *c. Cels.* i 1, ii 17 (Socrates).
[4] *In Lev. Hom.* ix 10.
[5] Similar expressions elsewhere (*e.g.* Iren. *adv. Haer.* v 17. 1 *propitians quidem pro nobis Patrem*, and Ath. *Or. c. Ar.* ii 7) seem to shew that such language was not regarded as unnatural; while at the same time it was kept subordinate to the idea of the love of God in sending His Son, and no theory of propitiation was framed.
[6] But a second attempt to mediate between the two notions was made by Athan-

power of evil and the penalty of sin is dominant. It is in that need that the later Fathers find the reason for Christ's death as the only sufficient ransom that could be paid. And the power of evil is no abstract idea, but a personal power—Satan, who is regarded as having acquired an actual right over men. This conception controlled the thought of the ages till the time of Anselm, along with the idea that the devil was deceived, and deceived by God,[1] as the explanation of the problem, although voices were raised against it.

The conception was expressed more precisely a century after Origen by Gregory of Nyssa and Rufinus, and repudiated at the same time by Gregory of Nazianzus.[2]

Gregory of Nyssa

The theory that Gregory of Nyssa framed is in some respects so characteristic and won such long acceptance that it must be stated at some length.[3]   He begins by shewing the reasonableness of the Incarnation.   Man had been created in the image of God, because the overflowing love of God desired that there should exist a being to share in His perfections.   He was bound, therefore, to be endowed with the power of self-determination, and in virtue of this freedom was able to be misled and to choose evil rather than good (or, more accurately, to turn aside from good), inasmuch as having come into being, and so passed through a change, he was susceptible of further change.   Such a change or deviation or fall from good took place, and to counteract its effects the Giver of life himself became man— the divine nature was united to the human.   *How*, we cannot

asius when he emphasized the necessity of God's fulfilment of the sentence pronounced on Adam's sin.   (It is deliverance from Death rather than from Satan that Athanasius conceives as effected, see *infra* p. 345 n. 3.)

[1] The first trace of the idea that the Deceiver of man was himself in turn deceived by God's plan of Redemption is to be found in the famous passage in the Ignatian Epistles (*Eph.* 19) on the three secrets, wrought in the silence of God, which were to be proclaimed abroad, namely, the virginity of Mary, her child-bearing, and the death of the Lord.   These, it is said, "deceived the prince of this world".   [Some would regard the idea as implied in St Paul's allusion to the rulers of this world (1 Cor. 2⁸) to be interpreted as meaning not earthly rulers but spiritual powers (as it was by many ancient commentators).   Ignatius has referred to the passage just before.   (See Lightfoot's note *l.c.*).]

[2] For an excellent criticism of this theory see Oxenham *op. cit.* p. 150 ff.

[3] See the *Oratio Catechetica*, esp. chs. xxi–xxvi—ed. J. H. Srawley (Eng. tr. in 'Gregory of Nyssa' *N. and P.-N.F.*).

understand; but the fact of the union in the person of Jesus is
shewn by the miracles which he wrought.   Human life was
purged by this union and set free again to follow a course of
freedom.   This divine scheme of redemption must be characterised by all the attributes of the Deity, and display alike goodness and wisdom and power and justice.   The first three were
clearly shewn,—it is in regard to the fourth that Gregory's
exposition is most noticeable.   Man was intended always to
move in the direction of the highest moral beauty.   But in the
exercise of his own free will he had allowed himself to be
diverted from the true line of developement and to be deceived
by a false appearance of beauty.   He had thus delivered himself
over to the enemy (the devil) and bartered away his freedom.
Justice therefore required that the recovery of his freedom
should be effected by a transaction as voluntary on the side
of the enemy as the fall had been on the side of man.   Such
a ransom must be paid as the master of the slave would agree
to accept in exchange for his slave.   In the Deity invested with
flesh he recognized a unique object of desire, the flesh veiling
the Deity sufficiently to preclude the fear which the devil
would otherwise have felt.   He eagerly accepted the proffered
exchange, and, like a ravenous fish, having gulped down the bait
of the flesh, was caught by the hook of the Deity which it
covered.[1]   That the wish to recover man proclaims the goodness
of God, and the method adopted his power and wisdom, Gregory
regards as obvious; but he notes that some one might think that
it was by means of a certain amount of deceit that God carried
out this scheme on our behalf; and that the veiling of the Deity
in human nature was 'in some measure a fraud and a surprise'.
The deception he admits, and justifies.   He argues that the
essential qualities of justice and wisdom are to give to everyone
his due, and at the same time not to dissociate the benevolent
aim of the love of mankind from the verdict of justice; and in
this transaction both requirements were satisfied.   The devil
got his due, and mankind was delivered from his power.   "He
who first deceived man by the bait of sensual pleasure is himself
deceived by the presentment of the human form."   The deceiver
was in his turn deceived—this was entirely just, and the inven-

---

[1] This strange simile is found again in regard to Death, John Damasc. *de
Fid.* iii 27.   Leo (*Serm.* xxii 4) expresses himself to much the same effect as
Gregory.

tion by which it was effected was a manifestation of supreme wisdom.[1]

Rufinus

A very similar account is given by Rufinus. He expresses his conception in his exposition of the Creed,[2] on the article ' He was crucified . . .' He speaks of the Cross as a signal trophy, and token of victory over the enemy. By his death he brought three kingdoms at once into subjection under his sway —'things in heaven, and things on earth, and things under the earth'. And the reason why the special form of death—the Cross—was chosen was that it might correspond to the mystery : in the first place, being lifted up in the air and subduing the powers of the air, he made a display of his victory over those supernatural and celestial powers ; in the second place, 'all the day long he stretched out his hands' to the people on the earth, making protestations to unbelievers and inviting believers ; and finally, by the part of the Cross which is sunk under the earth, he signified his bringing into subjection to himself the kingdoms of the nether world. Rufinus then touches on what he styles some of the more recondite topics, particularly how at the beginning, having created the world, God set over it certain powers of celestial virtues, to govern and direct the race of mortal men. But some of these, particularly he who is called the Prince of this world, did not exercise the power committed to them as God intended, but on the contrary, instead of teaching men to obey God's commandment, taught them to follow their own perverse guidance. Thus we were brought under the bonds of sin. Christ triumphing over these powers delivered men from them, and brings them (who had wrongfully abused their authority) into subjection to men. And thus the Cross teaches us to resist sin even unto death, and willingly to die for the sake of religion ; and sets before us a great example of obedience, to be rendered even at the cost of death.

Having laid down these main principles and lessons, Rufinus goes on to the special topic of the snare by which the Prince

---

[1] The crudity of Gregory's conception is somewhat modified by his comparison of God's act of deception with the procedure of the physician who deceives his patient for a beneficent purpose. Satan himself shall profit by the deception and be healed. See *Or. Cat.* xxvi.

[2] Rufinus *Comm. in Symb. Apost.* § 14 ff.

of this world was overcome. "The object," he says, "of that mystery of the Incarnation which we expounded just now was that the divine virtue of the Son of God, as though it were a hook concealed beneath the fashion of human flesh (he being, as the Apostle Paul says, found in fashion as a man, Phil. 2⁸), might lure on the Prince of this world to a conflict; so that, offering his flesh as a bait to him, his divinity underneath might catch him and hold him fast with its hook, through the shedding of his immaculate blood. For he alone who knows no stain of sin hath destroyed the sins of all—of those at least who have marked the doorposts of their faith with his blood. As, therefore, if a fish seizes a baited hook, it not only does not take the bait off the hook, but is itself drawn out of the water to be food for others; so he who had the power of death seized the body of Jesus in death, not being aware of the hook of divinity enclosed within it; but, having swallowed it, he was caught forthwith; and the bars of hell being burst asunder, he was drawn forth as it were from the abyss to become food for others." And so it was not with any loss or injury to the divinity that Christ suffers in the flesh; but by means of the flesh the divine nature descends to death in order to effect salvation by means of the weakness of the flesh—not to be kept by death in its power as mortals are, but to rise again through his own power and open the gates of death; just as a king might go to a prison and open the gates, and unlock the fetters, and bring out the prisoners and set them free, and so he would be said to have been in the prison, but not in the sense in which the others were.

Gregory of Nazianzus

The idea of a ransom paid to Satan was indignantly repudiated by Gregory of Nazianzus, the intimate friend of Gregory of Nyssa. Head and heart alike reject it, though logic seems to require it. "We were," he says,[1] "under the dominion of the

---

[1] *Orat.* xlv 22. For an excellent criticism of the theory see Oxenham *op. cit.* p. 150 ff. It involves great difficulties, intellectual and moral. The notion of deception cannot be harmonized with the notion of a bargain struck and a price paid to satisfy a just claim. If the devil was tricked into forfeiting his just rights by grasping at rights where he had none, how was compensation made to him? And how could the blood, or the soul, or the death, of the Redeemer be an equivalent to him at all for the empire which he lost, when it gave him no real power over him who only died to rise again at once from the dead. And again, the theory makes the God of truth choose

wicked one, and ransom is always paid to him who is in possession of the thing for which it is due. Was the ransom then paid
to the evil one? It is a monstrous thought. If to the evil
one—what an outrage! Then the robber receives a ransom, not
only from God, but one which consists of God Himself, and for
his usurpation he gets so illustrious a payment—a payment for
which it would have been right to have left us alone altogether."
That, at all events, cannot be. Was it then paid to the Father?
But we were not in bondage to Him: and again, How could it
be? Could the Father delight in the blood of His Son?

Yet though his moral and intellectual insight led him
surely to reject the notion of a ransom, either to the devil or
to the Father, Gregory has no certain positive answer to give.
He can only fall back on the mystery of the 'economy' of God.
The Father received the sacrifice "on account of the providential
plan, and because man had to be sanctified by the Incarnation,
so that, having subdued the tyrant, he might deliver and reconcile us to himself by the intercession of his Son". The death of
Christ is thus regarded as a sacrifice offered to and accepted by
the Father; but no theory of satisfaction is put forward, and it
would seem that the great theologian deprecated any closer
scrutiny of the divine 'economy'.[1]

No solution of these problems, it is true, was found by the
thinkers of the Church of those days; but it was not to such
details, however important, that the greatest of them directed
their deepest thought.

As representatives of the best of that thought we may

as his instrument deception, and represents the end as justifying the means (and a
parallel is drawn between the deceit which ruined man and that which redeemed
him). An unjust victory could confer no claims, nor could wrong, because successful,
become the ground of an immoral right. And further, the theory implies the acceptance of dualism—two independent powers set over against one another, a kingdom
of light and a kingdom of darkness, with jurisdictions naturally limited by conflicting
claims : instead of treating evil as a temporary interruption of the divine order.

[1] One striking passage, however, as Mr. C. F. Andrews has reminded me, must
not be overlooked, viz. *Or.* xxx 5, 6 (*The Theological Orations of Gregory* ed. A. J.
Mason p. 114 ff.). Gregory here emphasizes the representative character of the
human experiences and sufferings of Christ—the 'learning obedience', the 'strong
crying', and the 'tears'. Ἁ δραματουργεῖται καὶ πλέκεται θαυμασίως ὑπὲρ ἡμῶν is the
remarkable phrase he uses of them. The Saviour endures them as representing
mankind : he makes what is ours his own, and his is ours—in him. He imperson-
ates and plays the part of the human race, entering into a full realization of our
circumstances. It is our state that is described and represented in his experiences ;
and Gregory implies that, till we have fully made his experiences our own, our
salvation is not fully accomplished—we are not σεσωσμένοι.

fairly take, among Greek Fathers, Athanasius, and among Latin, Augustine; and this sketch of the conceptions of Atonement which were prevalent among Christians during the first four centuries of the life of the Church may be concluded with a brief account of the ideas and teaching of Athanasius and Augustine.

Athanasius [1]

No more fresh and bracing treatment of the doctrine of the Atonement is to be found in the literature of the early Church than that which Athanasius gives in his writing *On the Incarnation of the Word*.[2] The necessity for the redemption of men he finds in the goodness of God, and in this main thought he is entirely at one with Augustine. But his conception of 'goodness' includes the consistency and honour of God, which make it requisite that his decrees should be maintained and put in force, and thus the principle of justice is recognized under the wider concept. He had appointed rational beings, his creatures, to share in his life, and he had ordained the sentence of death as the penalty of transgressions.[3] By transgression man lost the life which was ordained by the plan of God to be his, and redemption became necessary. But no plan of redemption would be admissible which did not do away with the transgression and also restore the life which had been lost (*e.g.* repentance would do the one, but could not avail to effect the other).[4] The only way in which the corruption, or mortality, of man could be overcome was by the introduction of a new principle of life which should overpower and transform the corruption. As, therefore,

---

[1] See Harnack *DG*. Eng. tr. vol. iii p. 290 ff., and Moberly *Atonement and Personality* p. 349 ff. (a full and sympathetic and discriminating appreciation of the teaching of Athanasius). I cannot think that the tradition which ascribes this work to Athanasius has been in any way shaken by the elaborate arguments of Dr. Dräseke (*Theol. Stud. u. Krit.* 1893, and *Zeitschrift f. wiss. Theol.* 1895).

[2] And in frequent references to the doctrine elsewhere, particularly in the Orations against the Arians, esp. ii 67–70.

[3] It is said that a personification of Death takes the place of the devil in the thought of Athanasius, and that his conception has thus much kinship with the idea of a ransom to the devil : but it will be seen that he has really very little in common with such an idea. It is nearer perhaps to the thought of Athanasius to describe the penalty as paid to the justice of God in close connexion with the demands of His veracity. But it is difficult to grasp exactly what Athanasius means by Death in this connexion, if he had an exact idea himself.

[4] Athanasius speaks of it as unthinkable (ἄτοπον ἦν) that mere penitence should compensate for sin and restore the tainted nature.

the Logos had originally made all things out of nothing; so it was fitting and necessary that he should take human nature to himself, and recreate it by assuming a human body, and once and for all overpowering in it the principle of death and corruption. This, therefore, is the first and chief effect of the Incarnation: [1] the principle of corruption is annihilated. And it is in virtue of the inherent relation of the Logos to the human race that he effects its restoration.[2] He is able to represent the whole race and to act on its behalf.

To secure the purpose in view the death of the humanity thus assumed was necessary, to pay the debt that was due from all.[3] Exactly why, or how, Athanasius does not clearly define or discuss. But it is the death of all mankind that is owed, and it is the death of all mankind that is effected in his death. And, in like manner, in his conquest over death and the resurrection which ensued, it is the conquest and resurrection of all mankind that is achieved. And the death is called a sacrifice. The Logos is said to have " offered the sacrifice on behalf of all, giving up to death in the stead of all the shrine of himself (*i.e.* his human body or humanity), in order that he might release all from their liability and set them free from the old transgression, and shew himself stronger even than death, displaying his own body incorruptible as the first-fruits of the resurrection of all ". [3] So he suffers on behalf of all, and can be ambassador to the Father concerning all.[4] Athanasius does not expand the conceptions of ' debt' and ' sacrifice '. But his whole presentation of the matter shews that he regards the incarnate Logos as achieving all his work of redemption as the representative, not as the substitute, of man.[5] The argument is carefully elaborated, with the main

[1] See the famous simile in ch. ix. "Just as when a great king has entered some great city and takes up his dwelling in the houses in it, such a city is certainly deemed worthy of much honour, and no enemy or bandit any more attacks it and overpowers it, but it is counted worthy of all respect because of the king who has taken up his dwelling in one of its houses ; so it has happened in the case of the King of All. For since he came into our domain and took up his dwelling in a body like ours, attacks of enemies upon men have entirely ceased, and the corruption of death which of old prevailed against them has vanished away."

[2] See chs. iii and viii.   [3] Ch. xx ; cf. *Or. c. Ar.* ii 69.

[4] Ch. vii ; cf. ch. ix.

[5] Phrases are used which by themselves might suggest substitution, but the whole drift of the argument shews that representation is meant. *E.g.* ch. ix ἡ προσφορὰ τοῦ καταλλήλου, τὸ ὀφειλόμενον, ἀντίψυχον—but they are ὑπὲρ πάντων. The phrase ἀντὶ πάντων is, I think, used once only (ch. xxi), and then in the mouth of an objector to the argument.

purpose of shewing that no mere external act done by another would suffice. And elsewhere, in referring incidentally to the manner of redemption, Athanasius emphasizes the thought. " If the curse had been removed by a word of power, there would have been indeed a manifestation of the power of God's word ; but man would only have been (as Adam was before the fall) a recipient from without of grace which had no real place within his person ; for this was how he stood in Paradise. Or rather, he would have been worse off than this, inasmuch as he had already learned to disobey. If under these conditions he had again been persuaded by the serpent, God would have had again to undo the curse by a word of command ; and so the need would have gone on for ever, and men would never have got away one whit from the liability of the service of sin ; but for ever sinning they would for ever have needed to be pardoned, and would never have become really free, being flesh for ever themselves, and for ever falling short of the law because of the weakness of their flesh." [1]   No eternal change, no remission of penalty or equivalent compensation, no *fiat* of God, no change in Him, if that were conceivable, would have sufficed : there was needed a change in man himself. And again : " That henceforth, since through him all died, the word of the sentence on man might be fulfilled (for ' in Christ all died ') ; and yet all might through him be made free from sin and the curse upon sin, and remain for ever truly alive from the dead and clothed in immortality and incorruption." [2]   It is not only the penalty for sin, but sin itself, from which man must be freed : the condition of deadness within him must be quickened into life.[3]   This double end could only be achieved by one who could go through the process of dying, by which alone sin could be eliminated, and yet—paradox as it sounds—escape annihilation, and overpower death by a superior energy of life.   So it was that the Logos, being the Son of the Father and incapable of death, " when He saw that there could be no escape for men from destruction without actually dying, . . . took to Himself a body which could die ; in order that this, being the body of the Logos who is over all, might satisfy death for all, and yet by virtue of the indwelling Logos might remain itself imperishable, and so destruction might be

---

[1] *Or. c. Ar.* ii 68 (Dr. Moberly's translation).   [2] *Ibid.* ii 69.

[3] Cf. Gregory of Nyssa's idea that the ailing part must be ' touched ' in order to be healed—*Or. Cat.* xxvii.

averted from all by the grace of the resurrection. . . . Thus he
abolished death at a stroke from his fellow-men by the offering of
that which stood for all. . . . For the destruction which belongs
to death has now no more place against men, because of the
Logos who through the one body indwells in them." [1]   This
special immanence of the Logos in humanity since the Incarnation is known and recognized by the presence of his Spirit in his
followers.   It is we ourselves who receive the grace.   " By
reason of our kinship of nature with his body we ourselves also are
become a temple of God, and have been made from henceforth sons
of God; so that in us too now the Lord is worshipped, and those
who see us proclaim, as the apostle said, that ' God is in truth
in them '." [2]   " The descent of the Spirit, which came upon him
in Jordan, came really upon us, because it was our body that he
bore. . . . When the Lord, as man, was washed in Jordan, it was
we who were being washed in him and by him.   And when he
received the Spirit, it was we who were being made by him
capable of receiving it." [3]

Such are the thoughts which specially characterize the teaching of Athanasius and give it its peculiar value.   But he does
not, of course, ignore other aspects of the work of Christ, and he
lays particular stress on his mission of revelation of God.
Through the Incarnation of the Logos the true knowledge of God,
which they had lost, was restored to men.   They had not been
able to recover it from the works of God in creation; they had
their eyes cast downwards, fallen low down in the depths as
they were, and looking for him only in the objects of sense. [4]
' Therefore the compassionate Saviour of all, the Logos of God,
took to himself a body and lived as a man among men, and
assumed the experiences which are common to all men, in order
that they who conceived that God was to be found in the domain
of the body might perceive the truth from the actions of the
Lord through the body, and thus by those means might form a
conception of the Father." [5]   So, as Athanasius holds, in one
who lived among them under the same conditions as their own,
one who was at the same time God, it was possible for men to

[1] Ch. ix.   That all his experiences are really in a true sense *ours*, and that his
immanence in humanity is of widest consequence, is further argued *Or. c. Ar.* i 41,
iii 33, iv 67.
[2] *Or. c. Ar.* i 43.   [3] *Ibid.* i 47 ; and again *ibia.* ii 48, 49.
[4] *De Incarn.* ch. xiv.   [5] *Ibid.* ch. xv.

gain a true knowledge of God, which they could not have gained in any other way. The invisible thus became visible, and made himself known as he really was.

So, at the end of his book, Athanasius sums up his exposition. "He became man, in order that we might become divine; and he manifested himself through the body, in order that we might get a conception of the unseen Father; and he endured the outrage which befell him at the hands of men, in order that we might inherit immortality." [1]

Augustine's Conception

Augustine was perhaps the first of the Fathers to definitely face the question *Cur Deus Homo?* which was to occupy the acutest minds of the Middle Ages, and to attempt to shew the inherent necessity of the particular form of Atonement which was adopted. His discussion of the question is incidental, in connexion with his exposition of the doctrine of the Trinity and the analogies to illustrate it which are furnished by the phenomena of human thought and other experiences. [2]

He states the objection which was already urged—Had God no other way of freeing men from the misery of this mortality than by willing that the only-begotten Son—God co-eternal with Himself—should become man and, being made mortal, endure death? In reply, it is not enough, he says, to shew that this mode is good and suitable to the dignity of God : we must shew that there was not, and need not have been, any other more appropriate mode of curing our misery. [3] This he aims at shewing by pointing to the primary condition of our rescue. The first thing to do was to build up our hope and free us from despair. The most effective means of doing this was to shew us at how great a price God rated us, and how greatly He loved us; and in no way could this be shewn more clearly than by the Son of God entering into fellowship with our nature and bearing our ills. Good deserts of our own we have none—they are all His gifts. We were sinners and enemies of God. But through the means

---

[1] *De Incarn.* ch. liv.   [2] *De Trinitate* xiii § 13 ff.
[3] It is in this sense that the Fathers of this time speak of the *necessity* of the particular mode of atonement which was adopted, not as absolute but as conditioned by God's purposes. That God might have chosen other methods is recognized by all. (See Oxenham *op. cit.* p. 149.)

devised we are saved: we are justified by the blood, and reconciled by the death, of the Son of God; we are saved from wrath through him, saved by his life.

Augustine then faces the difficulty—How are we justified in his blood—what power is there in the blood? and how are we reconciled by the death of the Son? It could not be as though God the Father was wroth, and was appeased by the death of His Son; for on that supposition the Son must have been already appeased, and there would be implied a conflict between the Father and the Son. And St Paul (Rom. 8[31, 32]) represents the Father as delivering up His Son, not sparing him—so shewing that the Father was already appeased. And indeed there could be no doubt that God had always loved us. And the Father and the Son work all things together harmoniously and equally (there could be no kind of conflict or difference between them). We must look elsewhere for the solution of the problem.

The fact is, that the human race was delivered over into the power of the devil by the justice of God, inasmuch as the sin of the first man passed over by nature[1] into all who are born by natural process from him, and the debt incurred by the first parents binds all their posterity. But though the race was delivered over to the power of the devil, yet it did not pass out of God's goodness and power. And as surely as the commission of sins subjected man to the devil, through the just anger of God; so surely the remission of sins rescues man from the devil, through the gracious reconciliation of God.

But further reasons for the Incarnation may be seen. Justice (righteousness) is greater than might, and it pleased God that the devil should be conquered by justice rather than by might, so that men also, imitating Christ, might seek to conquer the devil by righteousness rather than by might. And the way in which the devil was conquered was this. Though finding in Christ nothing worthy of death, he slew him: he shed innocent blood, taking that which was not owed him; and so it was mere justice that he should be required to surrender and set free those who were owed to him—the human race over whom he had acquired rights.

Christ—the Saviour—had to be man in order to die, and he

---

[1] The word used is *originaliter*. It is explained immediately as meaning 'by nature', *i.e.* as it has been depraved by sin, not as created upright (*recta*) at the beginning.

had to be God in order to prove that the choice of righteousness was spontaneous (*i.e.* to shew that the Saviour *could* have chosen the way of might rather than the way of justice); and this voluntary humility made the righteousness the more acceptable.

Although it was only death for a time that the devil secured, the blood of Christ was of such price that release from sins was fairly bought by it. The death of the flesh and other ills still remain for man, even when sin is forgiven; but they give opportunity for pious endurance, and set off the blessedness of eternity.

The manner in which it was all accomplished was also a great example of obedience to us: and it was fair that the devil should be conquered by one of the same rational race as that which he held in his power.

Augustine's main conceptions of the Atonement are clearly revealed in this discussion. The claims of the devil are recognized; and the death of Christ has for its final end the release of mankind from the devil's power. The satisfaction of justice is in view throughout. There is a great principle involved. Might could have set aside the claims of justice, but God's action is determined by right. Above all else, it is the love of God for men that is the motive power that originates and guides the whole plan of redemption. Certainly, Augustine had no conception of an angry God needing to be appeased. It is only on the part of man that love is wanting; and the plan of Atonement was chosen just because it was peculiarly fitted to reveal to men the depth of the love of God, and so to arouse in them a corresponding emotion.[1]

From this review of the teaching of the Church it will be seen that there is only the most slender support to be found in

---

[1] Harnack (*DG.* Eng. tr. vol. iii p. 313) describes the propitiation of an angry God by a sacrificial death as the characteristic Latin conception of the work of Christ. It is clearly not the conception of Augustine. As to the conceptions of Tertullian and Cyprian see *supra* p. 333. With the passage cited above may be compared the treatment of the passage John 17²¹⁻²⁹ (*Tract. in Joh.* cx 6): "For it was not from the time that we were reconciled unto Him by the blood of His Son that He began to love us; but He loved us before the foundation of the world. . . . Let not the fact, then, of our having been reconciled to God through the death of His Son be so listened to, or understood, as if the Son reconciled us unto Him in such wise that He now began to love those whom He formerly hated, as enemy is reconciled to enemy, so that on that account they become friends and mutual love takes the place of mutual hatred; but we were reconciled unto Him who already loved us, but with whom we were at enmity because of our sins."

the earliest centuries for some of the views that became current at a later time. It is at least clear that the sufferings of Christ were not regarded as an exchange or substitution of penalty, or as punishment inflicted on him by the Father for our sins. There is, that is to say, no idea of vicarious satisfaction, either in the sense that our sins are imputed to Christ and his obedience to us, or in the sense that God was angry with him for our sakes and inflicted on him punishment due to us. Wherever language that seems to convey such notions is used, it is safeguarded by the idea of our union with Christ, so peculiarly close and intimate that we are sharers in his obedience and his passion, and only so far as we make them our own do we actually appropriate the redemption which he won for us. Also, in spite of a phrase or two suggesting another conception, it is clear that the main thought is that man is reconciled to God by the Atonement, not God to man. The change, that is, which it effects is a change in man rather than a change in God. It is God's unchangeable love for mankind that prompts the Atonement itself, is the cause of it, and ultimately determines the method by which it is effected.

Furthermore in the light of the teaching which has been reviewed, it is difficult to avoid the conclusion that the death was regarded as in itself of high value and importance—as an integral part of the work of Atonement and not only as the entrance to a new and greater life.

As to the scope of the Atonement, no limit seems to have been thought of (except by the Gnostics) till the theory of predestination was worked out. Redemption was effected for all men (according to Origen, for all rational orders of being), though individuals must come within the range of its influence by an act of volition (and Origen and Gregory of Nyssa, at least, believed that ultimately all men would be redeemed). The theory of predestination carries with it a limitation of the scope of the Redeemer's work, however the limitation may be disguised.

'HERETICAL' CONCEPTIONS OF THE ATONEMENT

In the foregoing review of early conceptions of the Atonement no notice has been taken of 'heretical' thought upon the subject. It is, however, worth noting briefly in what points the doctrine would be affected by the different christological conceptions of some of the leading heretics.

E.g. to Gnostics, who denied the reality of the human nature, the sufferings which were only apparent could have no value or effect of any kind: redemption was accomplished by teaching, by knowledge. To Ebionites, who acknowledged the human nature only, the death of Christ could not be regarded as availing for others: the infinite value attributed to his acts and sufferings as man, in virtue of the hypostatic union of the divine and the human, could not enter into their conception of the matter. The Arians conceived of Christ as a supernatural being sent to announce redemption, and put the reconciliation in the bare proclamation of forgiveness. Apollinarian teaching, as it was understood, excluding the human soul from the constituents of the Redeemer's person, deprived him of one of the chief qualifications for his mediatorial work and made him unable to act as the representative of men. The Nestorian conception of the junction of two persons was inconsistent with the idea of the true reconciliation of God and man as actually effected in the Incarnation, while a similar consequence followed from the confusion of the substances involved in the teaching of Eutyches (see also *supra* pp. 247, 274).

THE DOCTRINE OF MERIT

Tertullian and Cyprian

Tertullian's conception of merit is based on the idea that in some spheres of life and conduct God imposes no law on men. He 'wills', it is true, some things; but He 'permits' others. Man is therefore free, either to avail himself of this permission (*indulgentia*) and follow his own natural inclinations, or to forgo what God permits and follow instead the guidance of His will (*voluntas*). That is to say, he can choose between the *indulgentia* and the *voluntas* of God. And to forgo what He permits, and to follow instead what He wills, is to acquire merit.

It is, of course, self-evident that no one may do what God has directly forbidden. Tertullian treats it as equally self-evident that it is possible for a man to do meritorious acts, and on the strength of them have a claim for reward from God; because to take advantage of God's *indulgentia* (or *permissio* or *licentia*) is in no way sin. It may at times be even *good*, relatively to actual sin; though there is a *better*, *i.e.* a good in the full sense of the word, viz. *abstinentia*. God gives the opportunity both to use and not to use, and our choice not to use earns us merit.

This earning of merit through renouncing that which is allowed by the *indulgentia Dei* and doing instead the *voluntas Dei* is, however, passive in character. In contrast with it is the active presentation of the matter, viz. the doctrine of merit resting on the idea of *satisfactio*,

This idea depends on other considerations. God is the lawgiver before whose authority man must bow in unconditional obedience. His will is set before men in the Old and in the New Testament (both of which Tertullian styles *lex*), and in the order of Nature, as also in the ecclesiastical discipline and in the tradition. Herein, from these sources of knowledge, can be found what is pleasing to God and what is not pleasing but forbidden. To 'satisfy' or content God is to do what is pleasing to Him, and not to do what is forbidden. Otherwise a sin is incurred. No recourse to the indulgence of God is admitted here. But men are always falling into sin, and each sin incurs guilt, and God in accordance with His righteousness must take vengeance, must exact punishment. (Baptism washes away inherited sin and all sins actually committed by the individual before baptism, but after baptism a man must do God's will—must 'satisfy' God—or he ceases to be a Christian.) The punishment, the suffering which is due for sin committed, man can take voluntarily upon himself. It is accepted by God as equivalent to the fulfilment of the law, and in this way man can *in effect* fulfil the law and escape God's punishment. This *satisfactio* may be accomplished in various ways—*e.g.* by bodily castigation, by fasting, by voluntarily stripping oneself of wealth, in order to give alms and endure poverty, and especially by death in martyrdom. All such satisfying suffering is a debt due to God, by which the deficit on man's part is balanced (it is styled *pro Deo, pro Christo*). It is an expiatory sacrifice, and the amount of the sacrifice required is in exact correspondence with the offence. If more than is needed is offered, the surplus is deemed a meritorious offering or 'good work' (*bonum opus*), and counts as merit. These *bona opera* put God in our debt (*habent Deum debitorem*).

The religious motive which prompts us to acquire merit with God is furnished by the hope of temporal and eternal reward on the one hand, and the fear of temporal and eternal punishment on the other hand; of both of which—reward and punishment—there will be various grades, proportioned to the merit or guilt acquired here.

Such, in outline, is the doctrine of merit which is expressed and implied in Tertullian's writings; which Cyprian reproduced, and which through Cyprian so profoundly affected the ethical system of the Church of the West in later times.

Tertullian was the first to 'formulate' the conception, while Cyprian was the first to 'naturalize' it fully in the system of church doctrine.

Two presuppositions of the doctrine must, of course, be borne in mind: (1) it is only man regenerate by baptism who is thought of as able to do good works (all that Tertullian and Cyprian say on the subject has reference only to those who have undergone the supernatural change of moral personality which they believed the sacrament of baptism effected); (2) there is no suggestion that the baptized Christian who does good works has any claim for reward apart from God's own promise.

An important developement of the conception is to be noted in the teaching of Cyprian, for whom, it will be remembered, the question how to deal with Christians under penance, or even excommunicate, to whom martyrs or confessors had given *libelli pacis*, was a very pressing practical difficulty. It is possible, he held, by special sanctity (or by martyrdom) to acquire an accumulation of merit over and above what is needed for the highest grade of the heavenly reward. This surplus of merit may pass over to the benefit of others, through the intercession of those to whose credit it stands; though the benefit can only be obtained by an act of God's grace, conditioned by the relative worthiness of those for whom intercession is made by the saints. He can grant indulgence and He can refuse it: and the bishops and priests of the Catholic Church may be used as the means through which He gives it. The efficacy of the intercession of the Saints shews itself in two ways: here, on earth, in the restoration of the fallen to the privileges of church membership; and afterwards, on the Judgement day, when the merits of the martyrs and the works of the just may have great weight with the Judge.

It is evident that all the germs of the mediaeval theory are here. Such scriptural basis as they have is to be found in passages in the Gospels in which a reward is promised, so that if by the grace of God the conditions are fulfilled the reward may be claimed; in St Paul's teaching to the Corinthians (1 Cor. 7), where he draws a distinction between the commandment of the Lord (*praeceptum*) and his own judgement or advice (*consilium*)—all must obey *praecepta*, but in matters with regard to which there were no *praecepta* special merit might be acquired by doing more than was obligatory; and in passages such as Rom. 12[5], 1 Cor. 12[26], Col. 1[24] which seem to imply that the faith and piety and good works and sufferings, done and borne in Christ, of some of the members of his Body—the Church—may in some sense pass over to and affect the condition of others, who are united to them in so close and intimate a union.

An admirable collection of the passages in the writings of Tertullian and Cyprian which shew their conceptions will be found in *Der 'Verdienst'-Begriff* by Dr. Wirth (Leipzig 1892 and 1901), on whose exposition this note is based. For some considerations which would modify his presentation of the matter as a whole, see a notice of his work contributed to the *Church Quarterly Review* October 1902 p. 207, a considerable part of which is here reproduced.

CHAPTER XIX

THE CHURCH

OF the doctrine of the Church, as of other doctrines which have been reviewed, there was for some time no clear definition framed. The limit-line was not drawn. There was a general sentiment about it, in keeping with the conceptions expressed in the New Testament, but it was not easily fixed in words.

Till the time of Cyprian no special treatise on the Church was written, and the general sentiment about it must be gathered from the evidence of incidents and occasional phrases and allusions.[1] It must also be remembered that whatever importance was attributed to the Sacraments attached also to the Church, without which the Sacraments could not be had;[2] and that, when evidence of definite theories as to the powers of the Church is wanting, practical proof of her authority over her members was being given all along in the system of discipline and penance which—however great its developements in later ages—was in existence from the earliest times.[3]

The idea of a new spiritual society which was potentially world-wide, united by a common faith and worship and pledged to definite moral standards of life, enjoying a real spiritual union with Christ himself, permeated and sustained by the Holy Spirit and his various gifts of grace, is implied from the first.[4]

This new spiritual society was the visible organization to which baptism gave admission. The attempt to distinguish

---

[1] Any attempt at summary statement must therefore be received with caution—as *e.g.* in regard to Clement Al. *infra* p. 362.

[2] This was clearly seen in the matter of heretical baptism. No Church, therefore no Sacrament. See *infra* p. 386.

[3] See *infra* p. 372.

[4] See the picture of a Church as it should be in the *Epistle of Clement* 1, 2, 59. Cf. *Didache* 9, 10 ; Barn. *Ep.* 3, 6. All were brethren 'according to the spirit and in God' (Aristides *Apol.* 15). Mutual love was, to outsiders, the most striking feature of the society. They were a new people.

between the two, to recognize an invisible Church within the visible, does not belong to the earliest thought. Precise definition is indeed wanting, but the Church is regarded always as at once a spiritual society and an external organisation. Though St Paul addressed the first generation of Christians as 'saints' or 'holy', it is clear from his letters to them that they were so potentially only, and that he applied the term to them as set apart (called out from the rest of men) for a holy purpose, rather than possessed of personal holiness.[1]

The authority of the Church was guaranteed ultimately by its connexion with the Holy Spirit himself; but the continuity of this authority was preserved through the bishops, the successors of the Apostles, or the living representatives of Christ upon earth. It was this unbroken succession that gave the assurance that the Church was still the society founded by Christ.[2]

It was in and through this Society and its ordinances that all the benefits of the life and death of Christ were to be obtained.[3] In the Society were vested all the means of grace.

The four epithets which were at a later time applied to the Church—one, holy, catholic, apostolic—truly represent the earliest conceptions, although the experience of growth and new conditions of life and controversy gave fresh force and meaning to some of them as time went on.

We may, accordingly, simply note a few characteristic expressions of the earlier writers, and consider a little more fully the more exact and elaborate treatment of the matter by the later writers, who set themselves the task of expounding a definite theory in view of opinions or actions that threatened disunion and disruption.

Ignatius

Thus Ignatius insists above all else on the unity of the Church, the security for which he finds in the bishop, who is the representative of Christ, or God, and the head of the

[1] 'Set apart', 'devoted to sacred purposes' is the primary meaning of ἅγιος. The problem how to reconcile the holiness of the society as a whole with the unholiness of its individual members was bound to arise; but the relation between 'the true body' and 'the mixed body' (corpus verum and corpus permixtum) was thoroughly considered for the first time by Augustine in the controversy with the Donatists. See infra p. 369 n. 1.

[2] See infra and Note on the Bishops as centre of the Church p. 373.

[3] Cf. e.g. the African Creeds, 'remissionem peccatorum . . . et vitam aeternam per sanctam ecclesiam' (Hahn[3] pp. 59 ff.).

organization, administration, discipline, and worship of each
local Church.[1] The bishop and, with him, the body of presbyters
and deacons are essential to the existence of a Church. Apart
from them the Sacraments cannot be validly performed. The
bishop is, he argues, the centre of each individual church, as
Jesus Christ is the centre of the Catholic Church.[2]

The people must be united to the bishop as the Church is to
Jesus Christ, and Jesus Christ to the Father. And as he insists
thus strongly that the bishop is the head of the local church,
so he shews, by an incidental allusion, that he is familiar with
the conception of the relation between Christ and the Church
as that of the Head to the Body.[3] The Body is to be characterized by the incorruptibility of the Head; but it is itself
composed of various members whose union is guaranteed by

---

[1] It is clear the conception is the same whether the bishop's charge (the
'Church' of which he is chief) be merely a town and its vicinity, as in the time
of Ignatius, or a larger area like the diocese of a later age; and whether the
presbyters and deacons are expressly included or not. See further Note on the
Bishops as the Centre of Union of the Church *infra* p. 373.

[2] Nearly every letter has repeated statements and exhortations to this effect.
See *e.g. Eph.* 5, 6; *Smyrn.* 8; *Trall.* 2, 3; *Magn.* 3, 6; *Philad.* 7. This
(*ad Smyrn.* 8) is the first instance of the use of the epithet '*Catholic*' (universal)
applied to the Church. The word was in common use in the sense of 'universal'
or 'general' as opposed to partial or particular; and Ignatius follows here the
current usage. "Wherever Jesus Christ is, there is the universal Church"—so
Ignatius writes, and therefore (though he expresses himself in the form of exhortation), wherever the bishop is seen, there is the body of Christian people which
constitutes a particular local church. That is to say, just as the Church universal
spread throughout the world is to be recognized by the presence of Jesus Christ,
so the church particular is to be known by the presence of the bishop (that is, the
bishop and the congregation that gathers round him is the local church—not
the congregation without the bishop). This is the primary sense of the words
'Catholic Church', denoting extension over space. So it is used again in the
Letter of the Symrnaeans inscr. §§ 8, 19. But in view of heresies, or errors of
particular bodies of men or churches, it soon acquired a special doctrinal sense.
The appeal is made to the *consensus fidelium*, the Church universal, against the
opinions of individuals. And so, a little later, this technical sense, denoting
doctrinal exactitude and fullness of truth, as contrasted with inaccuracy and error
or partial understanding, is found in the *Muratorian Fragment of the Canon*,
which declares of heretical writings that they cannot be received into the 'Catholic'
Church. Cf. also Clem. Al. *Strom.* vii 17. The two ideas of local extension and
comprehensiveness of doctrine (or 'orthodoxy') remained combined, and later writers
delighted to draw out still deeper meanings of the word. Cf. Cyril of Jerusalem
Cat. xviii 33, cited *infra* p. 366.

[3] *Eph.* 17, "the Lord received the ointment upon his head, in order that he
might breathe the odour of incorruptibility upon his (the) Church." See Von der
Goltz *Texte u. Unters.* xii 3, and J. H. Srawley *Epistles of St Ignatius* S.P.C.K.
ad loc.

their relation to the Head.[1]   They must be seen as true branches of his Cross, bearing incorruptible fruit.

Again and again Ignatius insists on the need for visible unity.   He knows nothing of any distinction between a visible and an invisible Church.   Just as all through his teaching he insists on the Incarnation as the very union of the seen and the unseen, of the flesh and the spirit, of man and God; so that Jesus Christ is really God existing as man, the spiritual revealed in the material, the unseen become seen; so the Church is at once both flesh and spirit, and its union is the union of both.[2]   The Church thus clearly represents to Ignatius the very principle of which the Incarnation is the great expression, and in and through its unity that principle is set forth.   The life of faith and love to which Christians are pledged is a practical evidence of the union of spirit and flesh,[3] but it is in the Church itself that the union is most manifestly realized.

The independence of local churches under their bishops, and at the same time the intimate interdependence of one Church on another, and the closeness of the tie of brotherhood which bound them together—the consciousness of essential union in one society —is plainly revealed in these letters of Ignatius.   The Church as a whole is, as it were, focused in each particular Church.

Irenaeus—the Church as Teacher and Guardian of the Faith

Another point of view comes before us in the writings of Irenaeus.

The needs of his argument against heresies of various kinds led Irenaeus to speak of the Church, particularly in its aspect as a teacher, as the home of faith—the treasure-house amply filled by the Apostles, so that every one who will may take from it the draught of life.   It is the entrance to life: and had there been no writings left to future generations by the Apostles the traditional teaching preserved in the Church would have sufficed.[4]

---

[1] See esp. *Trall.* 11.   [2] *Eph.* 10, *Magn.* 13, *Smyrn.* 12.
[3] Heretics, who fail to realize this, prove themselves thereby opposed to the mind or purpose of God—*Smyrn.* 6.   Cf. *Eph.* 14.
[4] *Adv. Haer.* iii 4. 1 ; cf. iv. 48. 2, where he sees in Lot's wife, become a pillar of salt, a type of the Church which is the salt of the earth, and is left behind on the confines of the world, enduring all that falls to human lot.   And, often as members are taken from her, she yet remains whole—a pillar of salt, the strength of the faith, strengthening and sending on her sons to their Father.

This teaching of the faith (always and everywhere constant and persistent, always young and strong, endowed with perennial youth, and making the vessel in which it is young) is a trust committed to the Church by God, to give life to all that share it.[1] It is only in the Church that communion with Christ, *i.e.* the Holy Spirit, can be obtained—the Holy Spirit which is the guarantee of immortality, the security of our faith, and the ladder by which we mount to God.   Where the Church is, there too is the Spirit of God: and where the Spirit of God is, there is the Church and every operation of grace; and the Spirit is Truth.[2] Those who do not share in that are without the vital nourishment of their mother's milk and the pure waters that flow from the body of Christ.   They are aliens from truth, and doomed to wander in all directions.   They have no rock as their foundation, but only sand and stones.   The light of God never shines upon them.[3]

The true Church is distinguished by its unity.   Though diffused through the whole inhabited world to the ends of the earth, it has one and the same faith everywhere, derived from the Apostles.[4]

It is endowed with miraculous powers to cleanse from evil spirits, to foresee the future, to heal the sick, and even to raise the dead: and all these spiritual gifts it ministers freely, as freely it received them.[5] So it follows that, inasmuch as the Church alone has the true faith, it alone can bear witness to it; and so it is only the Church that can furnish examples of true martyrdom—for the love it has toward God.[6]

Tertullian's Conception of the Church

Tertullian has much in common with Irenaeus, though he deals with fresh aspects of the matter.   His conceptions underwent a change after his conversion to Montanism.   In his earlier days, against heretics, he defended the claim of the Church to be the sole repository of the truth, the 'witness and keeper of holy writ', in such a sense that no one outside the Church had any right to attempt to put his own inter-

---

[1] See *adv. Haer.* i 3, 4 ; iii 12. 9 ; v 20.   So the *magisterium* and the *charisma veritatis*, a ' succession' of truth, belong to the bishops.

[2] *Adv. Haer.* iii 38. 1.   [3] *Ibid.* iii 38. 2.   [4] *Ibid.* i 2, etc.

[5] *Ibid.* ii 48. 3, 4 ; 49. 3.   [6] *Ibid.* iv 54.

pretation on it. As the Church is made up of many individual Churches, the test of truth is ultimately to be found in the consent of those which were of apostolic foundation, which received, that is, their doctrine from the Apostles, who received it from Christ, as Christ received it from God. Yet many Churches of much later origin, which can point to no apostolic founder but agree in the same faith, deserve the name in virtue of this consanguinity of doctrine.[1] From this point of view the chief function of the Church is the preservation of the first tradition, which is derived from God through Christ and the Apostles. The Church has thus a divine origin and a divine authority. No mention is made of the bishops; but it is essentially a visible external Church that Tertullian has in view, and its rulers were bishops.

In other connexions he shews, by a merely incidental reference, that the conception of the Church as the body of Christ was familiar to him. In baptism, he says,[2] not only Father, Son, and Holy Spirit are named, but also the Church; because wherever there are the three, Father, Son, and Holy Spirit, there is the Church, which is the Body of the Three.

And quite in keeping with the general thought that underlies this saying is another incidental description of the Church in connexion with the first clause of the Lord's Prayer. As we therein recognize God as our Father in heaven (and in invoking Him address at the same time the Son who is one with Him), so we have in mind the Church our Mother.[3] That is to say, Tertullian conceives of the motherhood of the Church as corresponding upon earth to the Fatherhood of God in heaven, as though without the agency of the Church we could not have the Fatherhood of God. It is through her that we become his sons.

Later, when a Montanist,[4] Tertullian still conceived only of an outward visible Church; but, as a spiritual society essentially pure and holy and undefiled, it must be composed exclusively of spiritual men. The Church, he declares, is in its essential nature and fundamentally Spirit:—Spirit in which exists a Trinity of one and the same divinity—Father, Son, and Holy Spirit. . . . Accordingly the whole number of those who agree together in this faith in the Trinity are counted as the Church

---

[1] *De praescr. haeret.* 21, 32, 37.   [2] *De Bapt.* 6.   [3] *De Orat.* 2.
[4] See especially *de Pudicitia* 21, and the whole argument.

by its founder and sanctifier. To this Church belongs the power of forgiveness of sins—but it is a Church which is Spirit and acts through a spiritual man, not a Church which consists in a body of bishops. For the right of decision is the Lord's, and not his servant's: it belongs to God Himself, and not to His priest.

Here, then, we have Tertullian utterly repudiating the theory that any but the spiritually minded could ever constitute the Church, and insisting that episcopal office in itself conferred no authority to absolve from sin.

It is thus entirely a spiritual and inward criterion that he adopts, though it is not obvious how the test would be applied. Only, it is clear that he finds no guarantee in the outward organization and the continuity of bishops.[1]

It was in the West always, rather than in the East, that the social conceptions which underlie any idea of the Church were felt with most force; and if we turn from Tertullian in Africa to his contemporaries in the East—to Clement, for example, at Alexandria, we do not find much help towards a clearer definition.

Clement and Origen

To Clement[2] every person who has been baptized, and has not forfeited the privileges which were then obtained by any judicial sentence, is a member of the Church on earth—the one, true, ancient catholic apostolic Church,[3] a 'lovely body and assemblage of men governed by the Word', 'the Company of the Elect', the Bride of Christ, the Virgin Mother, stainless as a Virgin, loving as a Mother. But that Clement's chief thought of the Church was as the mystical Body of Christ[4] is shewn by the distinction

---

[1] It is noteworthy that in this connexion he insists that the Lord's sayings to Peter were to him personally, and that the bishops or Church of Rome (of whom he is writing) have no right to take them to themselves. To regard the authority and powers entrusted to Peter as extending to others is to change the plain intention of the Lord who said, 'On *thee* I will build my Church' and 'I will give the keys to *thee*', not to the Church (*de Pudicitia* 21). With this interpretation cf. the view of Cyprian (*infra* p. 364) that the commission and the authority was given equally and fully to all the Apostles and their successors the bishops. Tertullian and Cyprian are at one in rejecting the idea that any special authority or power was inherited by Peter's successors in the Roman see.

[2] See C. Bigg *The Christian Platonists of Alexandria* p. 100 f.

[3] *Strom.* vii 17 (Migne ix p. 548). Other references given by Bigg (p. 99) are *Strom.* vii 26, vii 5, iii 6, 11; *Paed.* i 6.

[4] *Strom.* vii 14 (Migne ix p. 521).

which he recognized between the persons, the members, composing it—a distinction corresponding to that between the flesh and the spirit. Those who, though members of the Body, still live as do the Gentiles are the flesh; those who truly cleave to the Lord and become one spirit with Him—the Sons of God, the Gnostics —are the Holy Church, the Spirit. This Church, which is thus composed of those who are called and saved, is the realized purpose of God.[1] On the oneness of the Church he naturally lays stress in this connexion. The Virgin Mother is one, alone; just as the Father is one, and the Word one, and the Holy Spirit one and the same everywhere.

Yet the distinctions he marks almost amount to a division of the one Church into two parts. He does not seem to attempt any real reconciliation of the antithesis.

Origen certainly insists that outside the Church no one is saved;[2] but the terms in which he describes the true Church preclude the identification of it with the outward visible Church. "Christ is the true light, and it is with his light that the Church is lighted up and made the light of the world, lightening those who are in darkness. Even so Christ himself testified to his disciples when he said, Ye are the light of the world: for that saying shews that Christ is the light of the Apostles, and that the Apostles are the light of the world. For those who have not spot nor wrinkle, nor anything of the kind, are the true Church."[3] Some of Origen's other references to the Church have been already noticed.[4]

Cyprian's Conception of the Church

Turning from Egypt towards the West again, we find a further developement of the doctrine of the Church worked out by Cyprian.

The first treatise which expressly deals with the subject in view of practical difficulties which had arisen is Cyprian's *On the Unity of the Church*.

His conception of the Church is expressed, for the most part, in his attempt to find the true solution of the new problem by which his generation was perplexed—the problem of secession

---

[1] *Paed.* i 4. 6; cf. *Strom.* i 18, vii 6.
[2] *Hom.* iii *in Jos.*   [3] *Hom.* i *in Gen.*
[4] See, *e.g.*, his reference to its authority as the vehicle of tradition and so the standard of truth *supra* ch. iv p. 58.

upon questions not originally doctrinal, when "with teaching identical, amid undoubted holiness of life, there was seen Altar against Altar, Chair against Chair ".[1]   Where was the seat of authority, the guarantee of unity, to be found ?   This is the question which Cyprian deals with in his tract *On the Unity of the Church*; and his answer to it shews clearly, not only what he held to be the basis of authority in the Church and the nature and safeguard of its external constitution, but also incidentally his conception of the inner character and functions of the Church itself.

On the first point he says the answer is quickly given (§ 4).   It is found at once in the Lord's commission given in the first place to Peter, both before and after the crucifixion and resurrection, and in the second place after the resurrection in similar terms to all the Apostles alike as peers, conferring the same power on them all.   This commission is conclusive.   An equal partnership in honour and power was bestowed on all alike, but without any sacrifice of unity.   It was in order to shew and to preserve the unity of the Church that a unit (one) was made the starting-point.   This was the reason for Peter's selection and the commission to him individually to begin with.[2] How then can anyone who does not hold this unity of the Church think that he holds the faith ?   Bishops, above all others, ought to hold fast and assert this unity, to shew that the episcopate is one and undivided.   For the episcopate is one, and each bishop enjoys full tenure of episcopal authority and rights [3] —that is to say, the authority of each is perfect in itself and independent, yet it is in the body of bishops as a whole that the unity is found : the existence of many bishops in no way impairs the essential oneness of the office and of the Church. A number of similes are given to illustrate this unity :—the sun and its rays, all one light; the branches of a tree and the tree; the fountain and the many streams that flow from it. The common source is in each case the safeguard of unity.

[1] Abp. Benson *Cyprian* p. 181. See the whole chapter.

[2] On the interpolations here see Abp. Benson *op. cit.*

[3] *Episcopatus unus est, cuius a singulis in solidum pars tenetur* ('like that of a shareholder in some joint property'—Benson). This conception of the full and independent authority of each bishop, so that no one could force his will upon another, while nevertheless isolated action endangered the unity of the body, was the controlling principle of the whole of Cyprian's treatment of the question. On the episcopate as constituting the unity of the Church see also *Ep.* 66. 8.

Separate any one of the derivatives from its source and it perishes; the branch cannot bud, the stream is dried up. So the Church spreads her rays throughout the world; yet the light which is shed in all places is one and the same, and the unity of the body is not impaired. She stretches forth her branches over the whole earth, she broadens out more and more widely the flow of her ample streams; yet there is one head and one source and one mother, ever prolific as birth follows birth. It is of her that we are born, her milk by which we are fed, her breath by which we live. She is the bride of Christ, who knows but one home, and preserves with chastity and modesty one bed inviolate. She it is who keeps us safe for God, and puts upon the sons she bore the seal that marks them for the kingdom. Whoever separates himself, and leaves the Church, is separated from the promises which are hers and will not attain to the rewards that Christ bestows. He cannot have God as Father who has not the Church as Mother. If anyone outside the ark of Noah could escape, then too he who has been outside the Church escapes.

Cyprian unhesitatingly applies to the Church the Lord's saying, 'He that is not with me is against me, and he that gathereth not with me scattereth abroad', and declares that the separatist is scattering the Church of Christ, and that the unity of the Church has its analogue in the unity of the three divine persons of the Godhead.[1]

Further than this it is impossible to go. The doctrine of the unity of the Church is raised to the very highest plane of thought and existence. It is founded in the very nature and being of God. So he who does not keep this unity does not keep the law of God, nor the faith in Father and Son, nor life and salvation. Scripture is full of symbols and illustrations of this unity,[2] and apostolic precepts and injunctions insist on it.

It only remains to note some practical consequences which Cyprian deduces. Good men cannot withdraw themselves from

---

[1] At the end of the treatise (§ 23) he tersely sums up his teaching in the words: "There is one God, and one Christ, and one Church of Christ, and one faith and people linked together by the glue of concord so as to be a unity compact and corporate." Cf. *Ep.* 66. 8.

[2] He cites the seamless vest (§ 7), the one flock (§ 8), the one house of Rahab undestroyed, the one house in which the paschal Lamb must be eaten, the men of one mind in a house, the Spirit in the form of a dove (shewing the character which the Church must have).

the Church. It is the chaff only that is blown away and separates from the wheat.[1] No support for separation can be derived from the Lord's promise to be with two or three who were gathered together in his name : the whole point of the saying was to teach the power of unanimity and common (not separate) action. Such men may be put to death for the name of Christ, but they are not martyrs (§ 14); they have violated the primary principle of love ; and though they give their bodies to be burnt, it will not profit them. Only a Churchman can be a martyr.[2] The separatist is in many ways worse than the apostate in time of trial. The latter has sinned once, and may certainly purge his sin by repentance and martyrdom ; but the separatist sins daily and glories in his sin.

Co-heirs of Christ must remain in the peace of Christ : sons of God must be peacemakers.

Of old this unanimity and unity was realized. That it was so no longer Cyprian avers to be due to loss of faith, and the selfishness which results from the weakening of moral force that follows loss of faith and of fear.

The theory of the Church which Cyprian laid down became, if it was not already at the time at which he wrote, normal for the West; and no Latin writing on the subject calls for notice till fresh circumstances called forth a fresh expression of the theory from Augustine.

The kind of teaching which was given in the East may be fairly inferred from the Catechetical Lectures of Cyril of Jerusalem in the middle of the fourth century.[3]

Cyril of Jerusalem

According to the teaching which Cyril of Jerusalem gave his catechumens, the Church into which they were about to be admitted was a society and an institution of unrivalled excellences and powers.

The Church is spread throughout the whole of the inhabited world, from end to end of the earth ; it teaches, without deficiency of any kind, all the doctrines which men ought to know, about

---

[1] The only part heresies play is the part of testing and distinguishing the faithful from the unfaithful (§ 10). Those who thus withdraw stand, as it were, self-convicted as aliens.

Cf. *Ep.* 55. 24.   [3] Cyril of Jerusalem *Cat.* xviii 23–28.

things visible and invisible, celestial and terrestrial. It brings
the whole of the human race into obedience to godliness (true
religion), rulers and those they rule, learned and ignorant alike.
It heals and cures every kind of sin of soul and body, and possesses every description of virtue in word and deed, and all
varieties of spiritual gifts.[1]

It calls and collects together all,[2] that they may hear the
words of God and learn to fear Him and make confession to Him
and praise His name. It is, as Paul described it, the Church of
the living God, the pillar and foundation of the truth.

Other gatherings of men have had the same name Church.[3]
The catechumen must remember that this is the Church to which
alone the name ' One Holy Catholic ' belongs. It is to the Catholic
Church he must always betake himself—the Holy Church,
Mother of us all; the bride of our Lord Jesus Christ, corresponding to the heavenly Jerusalem; the parent of many children.
In this Church God has set not only the various ministries
which St Paul described (1 Cor. 12[28]),[4] but also every sort of
virtue of all kinds:—wisdom and understanding, temperance and
righteousness, compassion and philanthropy, and invincible endurance in times of persecution. Armed with the weapons of
righteousness on the right hand and on the left, it has passed
through honour and dishonour; in the days of persecution it
crowned the martyrs with the flowers of patience, and now in the
season of peace it has won from kings and rulers and all mankind the honour that is its due, inasmuch as while their authority
is limited, it alone has power illimitable extending over the whole
inhabited world. For all who are taught in this Holy Catholic
Church and lead good lives, there is in store the kingdom of
heaven and the inheritance of eternal life.

There is no doubt a touch of rhetoric in this panegyric; but
Cyril meant it all; and the description which he gives would
not have seemed artificial to those who heard it. It is an
eminently spiritual and ethical conception of the Church that

---

[1] It is for these reasons that it is called ' Catholic ' or universal.

[2] Therefore it is aptly named *Ecclesia* or ' Convocation '. Cyril all through refers
to the Jewish *ecclesia* as the first, and the Christian as the second, made necessary
because the first proved to be an " *ecclesia* of wicked men ".

[3] Cyril mentions Marcionites and Manichaeans, and calls them 'abominable'
assemblies of wicked men.

[4] It is notable that Cyril does not name bishops or priests, but only apostles,
prophets, teachers and the rest, as stated by St Paul.

is set forth. External 'notes', such as constitution and ministry, are scarcely hinted at; but really it is clear that Cyril identified the spiritual society which he describes with the external society of which he was a presbyter, and which alone he thought of as endowed with such gifts of grace in this world and with the promise of life eternal hereafter.

Augustine

The most careful and complete consideration of the whole question of the Church was forced upon Augustine by the exigencies of the times and by his own experience; but his conception of the Church was so many-sided, and affected by his peculiar conceptions as to predestination, the kingdom of God, and the process of justification,[1] that it is difficult to feel confidence in the accuracy of any summary statement. Though he was "the first Christian writer who made the *Church*, as such, the subject of systematic thought",[2] yet the distinctions which he drew were not always clearly defined.

In the strongest terms he maintained the belief that outside of the Church there was no salvation, that love could only be obtained in the Church, and could only be preserved in the unity of the Church. So, too, it was only in this same unity that any of the benefits of the sacraments could be obtained,[3] and the Holy Spirit possessed.

In these and similar assertions he has in mind the Catholic Church, in contrast with heretical or schismatic societies of Christians; and so far it is clear that the Church of which he speaks is the outward and visible society, with its ordered system and organic life, and its practical endeavour to realize the Christian ideal—the society which had made its irresistible appeal to him and convinced him of the truth of the Gospel.[4]

---

[1] Cf. Harnack *DG.* Eng. tr. vol. vi p. 133: "Augustine combined the old Catholic notion of salvation as the *visio et fruitio Dei* with the doctrine of pre-destination on the one hand and the doctrine of the *regnum Christi* and the process of justification on the other."

[2] A. Robertson Art. 'Augustinus' *D.C.B.*

[3] See the interesting distinction he drew between *habere* and *utiliter habere* in this connexion—Note on "Heretical Baptism" *infra* p. 388.

[4] "I should not believe the Gospel, did not the authority of the Catholic Church induce me" *c. ep. Man.* v 6. Faith rests, for Augustine, on authority; and authority is embodied in the visible Church, with its accumulated experience of the power of the Gospel over the lives of men.

But, on the other hand, he maintained that no one could belong to the unity of the Church who had not love; and he distinguished between the external society, the visible Church—the general body of Christians, good and bad [1]—(*externa communio*), and the spiritual society (*communio sanctorum*), which was composed of those who were predestined to salvation, the elect, the members of the Church who were worthy of their calling. The latter were known to God alone and might not be distinguishable from the former, and indeed they might be found outside the visible society; but, whether within or without the *externa communio*, they were 'the Church' in the true and real sense.[2]

[1] Controversy with the Donatists gave occasion for the expression of Augustine's theory of the Catholic Church as including good and bad alike, and as alone possessing efficacious means of grace.

As regards the unity of the Church, Optatus, Bishop of Milevis, in controversy with Parmenian, the successor of Donatus, had clearly maintained the principle that the Church and sacraments and priesthood were independent of individual personal worthiness. And Augustine does little more than reiterate what Optatus had urged, when he himself was called upon to meet the arguments of Petilian the Donatist Bishop of Cirta. The difference between the two conceptions of the Church is seen, in the first place, in Augustine's contention, that the validity of the sacraments is independent of the personal character of the human agent who administers them (the sacrament is God's sacrament, not man's, and the medium through which it is conveyed cannot destroy the gift); and, in the second place, in the different interpretations of the parables of the field and the draw-net. The Donatists insisted that the mixing of good and evil was in the world, and not within the Church; or at all events that, if the Church was meant, the reference was simply to the mixing of secret sinners with the saints (and they only wanted the manifestly vicious to be excluded); and they cited St Paul's injunction to the Corinthians (1 Cor. 5[13]), and other passages which refer to avoiding the company of the wicked, as meaning that those who were known by open sins to be unworthy members were to be cast out from the Church and cut off from all external intercourse. So, according to their conception, a Church which tolerated unworthy members within its ranks was itself polluted and ceased to be a true Christian Church at all. On the other hand, Augustine understood the field with its wheat and tares, and the draw-net with its good fish and bad fish, of the Church itself. Complete separation was not practicable in this world, and must be deferred till the final judgement. The few individuals whose sins and vices were rare and universally known might be excluded; but the Church was intended to be a training school for men, and there was greater chance of amendment of life for those who fell into sin if their relations with the Church were maintained.

[2] To Augustine, as an idealist, it is only the timeless, the immaterial, the good, that has reality; and his metaphysical theory of being must be borne in mind in attempting the "very delicate analytical problem of disengaging two really disparate strains of thought in Augustine's mind, with a view to assign to them their relative predominance" (A. Robertson *Regnum Dei* p. 196, whose discussion of the whole question should be carefully studied). From the point of view of this idealistic definition of the Church it is of course a mere truism to say that "outside the Church there is no salvation".

24

Though it is difficult to harmonize this conception of the real Church with the stress which is laid by Augustine on the need of participation in the daily life and discipline of the visible Church, and in the means of grace which it dispenses,[1] yet it is clear that he really held it as part of his whole thought on the subject. It is true that he seems to assume that the elect who were outside the Church were destined to come inside before their death. But, on the other hand, he did not conceive that salvation through Christ was limited to believers in the historical Christian religion. It has been made accessible to those who were worthy in all ages, though less clearly in the past than in the present.[2] From this point of view the true Church has always existed, though it had no outward and visible form. And it is apparently because he more or less unconsciously transfers to the visible Catholic Church, with its organization and teaching and worship, which all the world could recognize, the high prerogatives that properly belong only to the ideal spiritual society—the communion of saints—that he is able to appreciate it so highly.[3]

But Augustine's conception of the Church cannot be separated from his conception of the *civitas Dei* in contrast with the *civitas terrena*.[4] To a large extent the *civitas Dei* is identified with the visible Church on earth, while the *civitas terrena* is the secular empire—the civil society. In idea, in principle and aim, the two are represented as fundamentally opposed.[5] The one is the home of all spiritual aspiration and power, the other is the embodiment of merely carnal and selfish ideals and physical force:—it is the kingdom of the devil. But, on the other hand,

---

[1] So Loofs *op. cit.* p. 210 discriminates the two conceptions of the Church as— (1) the common Catholic conception of it as an institution whose object is the salvation of men, and which, in accordance with the Lord's saying "compel them to come in", may use force to lead straying sheep to salvation; and (2) an ethical religious conception, as not identical with the visible Church, but the congregation of saints contained within the visible Church and not separable from it by men. And he notes that the two conceptions are not necessarily mutually exclusive.

[2] *Ep.* 102; *de Civ. Dei* xviii 47.

[3] He also uses the image of the Body—"the members of Christ are linked together by means of love that belongs to unity, and by means of it are made one with their Head " (*de Unit. Eccl.* ii 2).

[4] The two *civitates* are treated of in the second half of the work *de civitate Dei* xi–xxii. See esp. Loofs *Leitfaden* § 52, and A. Robertson *Regnum Dei* and Art. 'Augustinus' in *D.C.B.* new volume.

[5] In his own words, *amor sui usque ad contemptum Dei* constitutes the earthly state, *amor Dei usque ad contemptum sui* the heavenly (*ibid.* xiv 28); and their founders were Cain and Abel respectively.

whatever they are in idea, in practical experience the two states are not so separate, but each depends on the other. For all temporal and earthly purposes the *civitas Dei* requires the support of the civil power ; and, without the aid of all the moral influences which the *civitas Dei* alone possesses, the *civitas terrena* could not thrive. And so, in spite of the sharply defined distinction between the two states, the earthly state—so far at least as it is subject to the moral influences which it derives from the *civitas Dei*—tends to become merged in the Church, which is the only true *civitas* which exists on earth. And if the earthly state be Christian, then it is bound to attempt to give practical effect to the ideals of the Church,[1] and to support by its own means the aims which the Church pursues.

In this way the Church is invested with high authority, as the arbiter and director of the aims and forces of the civil society. She is the repository of all goodness and truth of life—for practical purposes. Infallible authority, ultimate truth, belongs to her only ideally. Neither can be actually realized on earth. But such authority (relative authority) as is possible is to be found in the Church and nowhere else.[2]

Augustine's teaching on the sacraments, which will be considered later, throws some further light on his conception of the Church.[3] It is in special connexion with the effective ministration of the sacraments that the holiness of the Church is emphasized by him, but particularly on the ground that it alone possesses the Spirit of peace and of love, which alone, as he held, makes the sacrament a means of grace.[4] Against the Donatists it was impossible to insist on the unity of the Church, because they claimed that note for their own communion ; or on the episcopate, because their orders were indisputable. Sacraments they undoubtedly possessed, but *caritas* they lacked ; and so Augustine was led to argue that, by breaking the bond of love, they deprived their sacraments of all their virtue. An essential

[1] This is the first expression of the idea which was the centre of the ecclesiastical system of the Middle Ages.

[2] Of this authority, however, no clear definition is to be extracted from Augustine's works. It rests on agreement, on tradition, on Scripture ; but sometimes he lays all stress on one, sometimes on another, of these three supports. It is to be found in the episcopate, especially when acting together in councils, but smaller and earlier councils are liable to correction by more general and later ones.

[3] See *infra* Note on "Heretical Baptism" p. 388.

[4] It is this which seems to differentiate his conception of holiness in this respect from that of the Donatists.

mark of the Catholic Church, in which alone efficacious sacraments could be ministered, was love; and it is his insistent advocacy of this view that gives to Augustine's conception of the Church its special spiritual character.

So he was able to maintain in its fulness the belief he had received in the Church as one, holy, catholic, and apostolic.

THE PENITENTIAL SYSTEM

The authority of the Church is most readily seen in the system of discipline which it exercised. As an organized society, it had from the first its outward and visible government, with its recognized rule of life for all its members; and as such it had, and exercised, the right to suspend, in part or in whole, from the advantages of the society, such members as offended against the rule of life. Such a jurisdiction was recognized in the earliest days, under the personal authority of our Lord (Matt. 8^{18}, John 16^2, Luke 6^{22}), and exercised in the earliest churches which were established (1 Cor. 5$^{3\text{-}5}$, 2 Cor. 13^{10}, 1 Tim. 1^{20}, Tit. 3^{10}), and ever afterwards in the Church over all its members of whatever class or rank in life. (Such conspicuous instances as the condemnation of the governor of Libya by Athanasius, the refusal of communion to Theodosius by Ambrose, and the excommunication of Andronicus by Synesius of Cyrene,[1] were no doubt rare, but they serve to shew the principle which was followed.)

The discipline was essentially moral and spiritual, intended in all but extreme cases to excite a perfect repentance, and to lead the offender to the full Christian life. It was graduated according to the character and degree of the offence, though the principles which were followed varied at different times and in different places. Three forms of censure were common at first—(1) the lightest form, exclusion for a period from the right of receiving the holy communion, but not from participating in the rest of the service; (2) exclusion from all the eucharistic service; (3) the heaviest form of censure, exclusion from the Church altogether. (See *Apost. Const.* ii 16, Tert. *Apol.* 39, *de poenit.* 9.) During the period of exclusion penitential acts were to be performed (such as public prostration and other expressions of sorrow, and fasting and abstinence from pleasures, and works of service and almsgiving), and restoration was only to be effected when penitence was complete. The period was short at first, a few weeks sufficing; but by the middle of the third century a sentence could run to one or two years, and after the fourth century even to ten or twenty years for grave offences.

That men would undergo such discipline shews, perhaps more clearly than any other evidence that is available, the general feeling as to the

---

[1] See J. O. Nicol *Synesius of Cyrene* (Hulsean Essay 1886) pp. 64–69.

necessity of membership of the Church and of participation in the aids to Christian life which could be had only in communion with the Church.

On the different stages through which they had to pass (mourners, hearers, kneelers, bystanders), and the different dress to be worn, and the positions in the Church, see *D.C.A.* Art. 'Penitence'.

In the earlier times it was only what were called 'mortal sins' that had to be purged by this public penance, that is, all kinds of idolatry, murder, and adultery; and the former sin is the one which had to be dealt with most commonly (Cyprian's references are almost entirely to the *lapsi*). For lighter sins of daily life, private prayer and repentance, and the use of the ordinary means of grace, were held to suffice. The three sins named were held to cover all that could be regarded as in the same class; and covetousness, robbery with violence, and spoiling of graves, are mentioned as included in the list.

But different estimates of the power of the Church in this respect were held, and led to controversy. The infliction of penance implied, or was generally understood to imply, that the Church had power to grant forgiveness for the sins for which penance was inflicted. But the idea that the Church had power to forgive mortal sins was strongly opposed by the Montanists and Tertullian, who regarded such an idea as destructive of morality, and maintained that for such sins no hope of forgiveness in this world should be held out: they should be punished by perpetual exclusion from the Church (see *e.g.* Tert. *de Pudicitia* 12). What the earliest practice was in such matters is uncertain; but as early as 169 Dionysius of Corinth had written to this effect—that no sin should involve perpetual excommunication (Euseb. *H.E.* iv 23). Zephyrinus had admitted to communion, after penance, some who had been guilty of adultery and unchastity; and against him Tertullian wrote his treatise. Callistus apparently went further, and extended the hope of readmission to those who were guilty even of idolatry, apostasy, and murder, and by so doing roused the indignation of Hippolytus. It was the Puritan conception of the Church that really prompted the opposition of both Tertullian and Hippolytus to what seemed a relaxation of discipline. [See also Dr Swete's article *J.T.S.* vol. iv no. 15.]

THE BISHOPS AS THE CENTRE OF UNION OF THE CHURCH

Ignatius was the first to give expression to the theory of the Church, which was the basis of Cyprian's conception, namely, that the bishop is the centre of unity; and though Ignatius deals with individual churches and their rulers,[1] while Cyprian rather thinks of the Church as a whole, and

---

[1] So far as Ignatius recognizes a corporate whole in this connexion, it is probably still in regard to the individual church which had its body of presbyters, one of whom

bishops as a body, yet his theory is essentially the same as Cyprian's: "Do nothing without the bishop" (*ad Trall.* 2) ; "Be subject to the bishop" (*ad Magn.* 13) ; "Look to the bishop as to the Lord himself" (*ad Eph.* 6)—this is the burden of exhortation after exhortation ; though he frequently joins with the bishop the body of presbyters and the deacons too, speaking of the former, in one case at least, as harmoniously related to the bishop as the strings are to the lyre (*ad Eph.* 4). He bids all "follow the bishop as Jesus Christ followed his Father" (*ad Smyrn.* 8), but he adds also "and the body of presbyters as the apostles ; and reverence the deacons as the commandment of God". And elsewhere he bids them reverence the deacons *as Jesus Christ*, even as the bishop who is a type of the Father, and the presbyters as the council of God and the uniting bond of the apostles. Apart from these, he says, you cannot speak of a Church (*ad Trall.* 3).

It is thus the same conception that is in Cyprian's mind, when he declares that Christ's Church is constituted by the people united to the bishop and the flock clinging to its shepherd. The bishop is in the Church and the Church in the bishop. Any one who is not with the bishop is not in the Church. The Church is not rent and divided, but bound and linked together by the bishops who form together, one with another, a solid body.[1] They are a *collegium*, and on their unity the unity of the Church rests. They are the successors of the apostles, and according to Cyprian's teaching personal holiness is requisite for the due administration of their office (*Ep.* 65. 4 ; 66. 1). All true members of the Church will obey them—opposition to the bishop is opposition to God.

In this conception there is no real identification of the Church with the organization, the hierarchy. The Church is still regarded as the society of the faithful. But it is the society regarded as grouped round the bishops, in such a sense that the bishops are essential to its existence.

So, too, the fact that the bishop was always the agent in discipline, the judge and arbiter of penance, through whom the restoration of the penitent was effected, even though his presbyters were often associated with him, must have aided the conception of him as the centre of the practical life of the Church.

Augustine's conception of the bishops as the successors of the apostles, and the guarantee, accordingly, that the Church over which they preside is the Church of the apostles, is similar to Cyprian's ; but

---

in particular exercised the 'episcopal' function of oversight. Cf. *ad Trall.* 2, where to "Do nothing without the bishop" he adds, "Be in subjection to the body of presbyters too, as to the representatives (ἀπόστολοι) of Christ".

[1] Connexa et cohaerentium sibi invicem sacerdotum glutino copulata, *lit.* "joined and linked together by the glue of the bishops who stick together each to each" (Cyprian *Ep.* 66. 8).

he lays less stress on the bishops as the centre of unity, in proportion as he emphasizes more the thought, that the presence of the Holy Spirit and of love are the essential notes of the Church. He seems to be much less affected by any hierarchical interest.

By the Donatists the bishops were regarded as the safeguards of the purity rather than of the unity of the Church; hence the need of their personal holiness.

In like manner Vincent of Lerinum finds little place for the episcopate in this connexion.

The later theory, which would see the centre of unity in the Papacy, can claim little general support in the earlier ages with which we have to do; but traces of it are to be found in regard to doctrine as in regard to practice, at least from the time of Stephen, though the idea of an *episcopus episcoporum* was then indignantly repudiated. Yet it was as successors of Peter that the bishops of Rome asserted their authority, and, as such, obtained what was conceded them; and as the chiefs of the only apostolic See in the West they naturally acquired their primacy over the other bishops of the Western Church. But it was as being in this way the embodiment of tradition, representing apostolic teaching, that the claim to be the successors of Peter had weight. [The *nihil innovetur* of Stephen, with regard to the question of baptism, truly represents the appeal to tradition. So Leo the Great, who wished his letter to Flavian to be taken as an authoritative statement of doctrine, and to form a test of membership of the Catholic Church, expressly referred to the Apostles' Creed as its basis, and only summed up the traditional teaching of western theologians.[1] And it was as such that it was considered and received, on its merits, not on any personal authority of its writer—see *supra* p. 286.] But at Ephesus, in 431, the papal legates had asserted this claim, with the more personal touch, "Peter always, down to the present time, lives and adjudicates in his successors". And Jerome pointed clearly to the Pope as the centre of unity in the later sense, when he declared, with reference to the special commission to Peter, "one is chosen from among the Twelve, just in order that by the appointment of a head there might be left no opportunity of schism" (*adv. Jovin.* i. 26)—a saying in accordance with the claim of Zosimus and his successors to receive appeals on the strength of a supposed canon of Nicaea. On this see A. Robertson *D.C.B.* 'Augustinus', and C. H. Turner *The Genuineness of the Sardican Canons, J.T.S.* vol. iii no. 11.

---

[1] Mr. Burn suggests that probably the 'Constantinopolitan' Creed was taken up so warmly because it had the words σαρκωθέντα ἐκ πνεύματος ἁγίου καὶ Μαρίας τῆς παρθένου which formed a parallel to the *natus est de Spiritu sancto et Maria Virgine* of the Old Roman Creed quoted by Leo (see *supra p.* 288 n. 2): and he thinks that Leo's references to the 'one faith' may imply acceptance of this "Apostles' Creed" of Constantinople, parallel as a baptismal creed to his own.

CHAPTER XX

BAPTISM

The General Conception of a Sacrament—The Use of the Term

AT the outset of any account of the Sacraments of the Church, it must be noted that in early times there were no formulated doctrines about them. There was neither close definition of the term itself nor desire to explain with any precision the exact nature of the rites and the manner in which their action was effected; and in the following pages no attempt at systematic treatment will be made.

The practices were there: the facts were realized: but controversy had not arisen.[1]

From the earliest days Baptism had been conferred and the Lord's Supper had been administered, and certain privileges and gifts were known to be obtained by baptism and by the Eucharist; but the realities, the things themselves, were in use long before a special term was needed to describe them.

At first there were sacraments many: the term was used in a wider sense. It represented the Greek word 'mystery' (μυστήριον) as used in the New Testament of a 'secret', long-hidden and still hidden from the mass of men, but revealed to Christians. Everything which could be called a 'mystery' was to Latin Christians a 'sacrament', while the Latin associations of the word 'sacrament' gave it a still wider range of meaning, so that it covered much to which the Greek term could not have been applied.[2]

---

[1] Such qualifications of this statement as may suggest themselves, in particular with regard to some points connected with baptism, are noted later.

[2] *Sacramentum* meant originally a "pledge or deposit in money" which in certain suits was required by Roman law—in the form of a wager as to the right; then it was used of the pledge of military fidelity, voluntary at first but afterwards exacted —an oath of allegiance; and so of any solemn oath or obligation taken on oneself. The ecclesiastical use was probably determined by its adoption in the Latin Versions as the rendering of μυστήριον—*e.g.* Eph. 5³², 1 Tim. 3¹⁶.

The earliest instance of its use in relation to the Lord's Supper is probably to be seen in Pliny's Letter to Trajan in which he speaks of the Christians binding themselves by a ' sacrament', using no doubt the term which they had used to him, though understanding it in the narrower Latin sense. Tertullian is the first to use the phrase " the Sacrament of baptism and of the Eucharist ",[1] and he also uses the word in the use of oil and of milk and honey;[2] but he readily employs it in a more general sense, in considering passages of Scripture where it represents the Greek word ' mystery'.[3] With Cyprian it has the sense of a sacred bond, or a symbol or its meaning;[4] with Augustine of a sign pertaining to divine things, with or without a gift of grace attached;[5] and Leo uses it frequently of any sacred act or rite or meaning or observance. It means then, always, something to be kept sacred, whether a secret or a revelation or a mystery or an act or operation symbolical of a spiritual force.

At a later time, as is well known, the use of the term was narrowed down, and more precise definitions were framed. But the subject did not come before Councils of the Church during the first few centuries (except in regard to some details of the administration of baptism), and it is only the thought of individual teachers and thinkers that can be presented here, in regard to what were always held to be the chief sacraments— Baptism and the Lord's Supper.[6]

[1] Tert. *adv. Marc.* iv 34, cf. *de Cor.* 3.

[2] See the striking passage *adv. Marc.* i 14, in which against Marcion he argues that the Lord himself never despised the use of any of the works of God's creation.

[3] *E.g. ibid.* v. 18.   [4] Cyprian *de Lapsis* 7, *de Unitate* 7, *de Orat.* 9, 28.

[5] See *e.g. Ep.* 137, 15, *Serm.* 272, *de Cat. Rud.* 26. He uses the term of Jewish ordinances, salt given to catechumens, the Lord's Prayer and the Creed, chrism and imposition of hands, orders, marriage, baptism, and the Lord's body and blood. He gives various partial definitions of the terms, as that " one thing is seen, another understood " (*aliud videtur, aliud intelligitur,* cf. " the outward and visible sign of an inward and spiritual grace "), "something is signified which must be reverently received", "what is seen has a bodily appearance, what is understood has spiritual fruit". He lays stress on the part played by the Word, which effects the sacrament (*accedit verbum ad elementum et fit sacramentum, etiam ipsum tanquam visibile verbum*), and asks "what is a corporeal sacrament but a kind of visible word?" The signs of divine things are visible, but the things themselves which are invisible are honoured in them. [See also the note on the history of the word in Bright *St Leo on the Incarnation* p. 136.]

[6] The idea that divine grace is conferred by these sacraments was often so stated in early times, that the inference might easily be drawn that it was supposed that grace was limited to the sacrament, so that without the sacrament there would be

The Sacrament of Baptism

With regard to baptism scarcely any developement can be seen during the period with which we are concerned. It is the doctrine of the New Testament writings that is repeated almost *verbatim* by the earliest fathers to whom we can refer, and by the writers of the fourth and fifth centuries. Developement was only in the application of principles to new circumstances, and in the accompaniments of the rite. The latter do not concern us here, except so far as they serve to throw light on the doctrinal conceptions which they represent.

And it must suffice to take only representative examples of teaching, and earlier rather than later examples.

Early Conceptions of Baptism

The real import of baptism in early days is no doubt to be seen in the fact that it was the visible mark of acceptance of Christ as Saviour,[1] and of entrance into the Church which he founded to be the guardian of the salvation he gave (Acts 2⁴¹). But it is very much more than a mere ceremony of initiation. It was regarded as in itself conveying the blessings and the grace which were bestowed. It was the medium by which the power of the life and death of Christ was made effective to individual experience. And as the habit of post-

---

no gift of grace. The inference would be at all events an uncertain one ; but that a wider conception prevailed in the Church was in large measure due to the dominant influence of Augustine's teaching. "Augustine left a permanent, an indelible stamp, upon ecclesiastical life and thought. The conception of grace was thenceforth never in the West so nearly limited to sacraments as it practically remained in the Greek Church. The sacraments were held in a deepened sense, with a context of grace, preventing, predisposing, concomitant, which conditioned the grace of the sacrament itself" (A. Robertson *Regnum Dei* p. 193).

[1] So baptism was perhaps originally into the name of Jesus only (Acts 2³⁸, 8¹⁶, 10⁴⁸)—though, in view of the full form given in Matt. 28¹⁹, the expressions used in Acts may possibly signify Christian baptism without denoting any particular form of words (see *supra* p. 25 n. 1). And in the third or fourth centuries there were still some who held the one name by itself to be sufficient (see Cyprian *Ep.* 73, 4 and 75, 5, 16–18, Ambrose *de Spiritu S.* i 3). But the full name of the Trinity is found in Justin Martyr's account of the rite (*Apol.* i 61 f.), in Tertullian (*de Bapt.* 13, *adv. Prax.* 26), and is insisted upon by Cyprian (*loc. cit.*) and some other writers on the subject (*e.g.* Augustine *de Bapt.* vi 25). (The early practice of baptism into the name of Jesus only was defended on the ground that the whole Trinity was implied in each of the persons—the περιχώρησις. See Cyprian *Ep.* 73, 17, and Ambrose *loc. cit.*)

poning baptism grew up, and the unbaptized were regarded as belonging to the Church, the rite was less and less considered as an act of initiation, and its other aspects and effects were emphasized. It might even come to seem the completion rather than the beginning of the Christian life.[1]

The general sentiment in regard to it is reflected in the names by which it was known.[2] It was the bath in which all the pollution of sin was washed away; the illumination, by which all the darkness of ignorance was dispelled and the light of the truth shed over the soul; it was the seal, God's mark to attest forgiveness and all the benefits which were to follow and to prove the recipient his own; it was the new birth or regeneration, by which the new life was begun. It conferred forgiveness of sins and established actual sinlessness.

Repentance and faith on the part of the person to be baptized must obviously precede the baptism; but it was through the rite itself that forgiveness was bestowed. So closely was forgiveness of past sins connected with the rite of baptism that, as baptism could not be repeated, it was widely deemed expedient to delay it as long as possible, lest sins committed after baptism should fail to find forgiveness. The opposition to infant baptism was based upon this feeling,[3] strengthened by the conviction that the guilt of sin after baptism was peculiarly great;[4]

[1] Cf. Augustine *Confess.* vi 4.

[2] Names commonly found are λοῦτρον, φωτισμός, σφραγίς, ἀναγέννησις, descriptive of various aspects of the βάπτισμα. It was also viewed as taking the place of circumcision—*e.g.* Justin *Dial. c. Tryph.* 43. (σφραγίς, the 'seal', specially applied to the chrism or confirmation, is also used of baptism proper.)

[3] The evidence of the New Testament is not decisive as to the custom of the first generation, and probably all allusions are to the baptism of adults, though 1 Cor. 7[14], and Eph. 6[1], may imply the baptism of children. (See Mark 10[14], Matt. 18[4, 6], Acts 2[38] 10[48], 1 Cor. 1[16].) The baptism of infants was not universal in the time of Tertullian, who opposed it and argued against it (see *de Bapt.* 18) on the ground that delay was safer and more expedient; but Irenaeus *adv. Haer.* ii 33. 2 seems to attest it; Cyprian advised it as soon as possible on account of its beneficial effects (*Ep.* 64, 5); and Origen called it a tradition from the apostles (*Comm. in Rom.* 5[9]). That many, however, preferred to postpone it, is shewn by the case of Constantine, and still later by Chrysostom's exhortations. Probably the practice of immediately baptizing children of Christian parents was generally followed from an early time, though postponement in the case of adult converts was common even in the fifth century.

[4] Such was the interpretation of the severe passages in the Epistle to the Hebrews, *e.g.* Heb. 6[4-6], and Rom. 2[17, 21]. See, for example, Irenæus iv 42. 4. "We ought therefore . . . to be afraid lest haply, if after the recognition of Christ we do aught unpleasing to God, we have no longer forgiveness of our sins but are shut out from his kingdom" (but cf. also iv 46. 1). Cf. Tert. *de Bapt.* 8.

so that it seemed desirable to save the child from the risk of incurring such guilt.[1]

Justin Martyr on Baptism

Outside the New Testament the earliest description of the meaning of the rite is that which Justin gives.[2] " All who are convinced and believe that what is taught and said by us is true, and promise that they can live accordingly, are taught to pray and to ask from God, with fasting, forgiveness of their past sins, while we pray and fast with them. Then they are taken by us to a place where is water, and are regenerated with the kind of regeneration with which we ourselves were regenerated; for the bath, which they then have in the water, they make in the name of the Father and Lord God of the Universe, and of our Saviour Jesus Christ, and of the Holy Spirit.[3] For Christ said, ' Unless ye be regenerated, ye shall not enter into the kingdom of heaven.' " Justin then notes that, while it is impossible to be literally born again, the prophet Isaiah had pointed to the way of escape from sins by the cleansing of water; and he goes on to contrast the first birth, in regard to which we have neither consciousness nor volition, after which we live in bad and wicked ways and habits, with the new birth by which we cease to be children of compulsion and ignorance, and become children of moral purpose or choice and knowledge, and obtain remission of sins which we have sinned before :—when over him who has chosen to be regenerated, and has repented of the sins he has committed, the name of the Father of the universe—the Lord God—is called in the water (for this is all that is said by him who brings to the bath him who is to be washed). " And this bath ", he adds, " is called illumination, inasmuch as those who learn these things are being illumined in understanding. And he who is illumined is washed in the name of Jesus Christ, who was crucified under Pontius Pilate, and in the name of the Holy Spirit, who proclaimed beforehand, by means of the

[1] It was thus in the interests of the adult that delay was counselled, rather than from any notion of the child's incapacity to receive the benefit of the sacrament.

[2] Justin *Apol.* i 61f. There are mere references, however significant, earlier, *e.g. Did.* 7; Barn. 11, 16; Hermas *Vis.* iii 3, *Mand.* iv 3, *Sim.* ix 16; Ignatius *Eph.* 18, *Polyc.* 6.

[3] The amplification of the actual formula is probably intended as an aid to heathen readers.

prophets all things concerning Jesus." From this account it is clear that Justin sees in the rite—on the part of the baptized —the conscious recognition of a new ideal of life and repentance for the past, and—on the part of God—the gift of remission of sins and spiritual enlightenment. He is cautious and guarded in his expressions, as writing for other than Christians ; but there is no concealment of the main conceptions. He goes on further, after a short digression, to state that the newly baptized is then taken to the assembly of the brethren, who join in prayers for him and themselves, and all others, that, having learned the truth, they may be found keepers of the commandments and be saved with the eternal salvation. Then follows the communion. It is probable that these prayers, which seem to be regarded as completing the baptism, included the laying on of hands, or confirmation.

Tertullian on Baptism

Tertullian, whose tract *On Baptism* is valuable to us for the light it throws on details of practice as well as for the exposition of doctrine, boldly declares that no one can obtain salvation without baptism [1]; and with eloquent eulogy of the virtues of water, while contrasting its simplicity with the great thing it effects, he speaks of it as conferring eternal life.[2] It is in water that we are born, and only by staying in water that we can be saved.[3] The water itself, hallowed by the Holy Spirit, drinks in the power of hallowing.[4] It prepares man for the reception

---

[1] Tertullian *de Baptismo* 12, 13, with reference to John 3[5] and the baptismal commission Matt. 28[19]. 'Faith' alone therefore is not enough. So Augustine, Serm. 294, 8, 16, 19. Infants dying unbaptized would be excluded from heaven, though they would have the lightest punishment (*Ep.* 215 § 1, cf. *Ep.* 166 § 5).

[2] *Ibid.* 1, 2.

[3] He fears that if he describes fully all the beneficial qualities and powers of water, he will seem to have detailed the praises of water rather than the principles of baptism.

[4] § 4. It is an unsympathetic criticism that styles Tertullian's conception 'magical'. His strong expressions about the water must be taken in close association with the rite as a whole. This consecration of the water (to which allusions are frequent afterwards—by invocation of the Spirit or by prayer) is first mentioned by Tertullian. Cyprian goes further (*Ep.* 70. 1), in saying the water must be sanctified by a priest, by one who is himself clean and has the Holy Spirit. Cyril of Jerusalem (*Cat.* iii 3) expresses the same belief in a sacred efficacy attaching to the water which has received the invocation of the Holy Spirit and of Christ and of the Father, and so has ceased to be mere water, and become able to hallow both body and soul. And Cyril of Alexandria carries on the traditional teaching in somewhat

of the Holy Spirit and restoration to the image of God which he had lost. The anointing with holy oil and the imposition of hands that follow complete the rite and its spiritual benefit.[1]

Cyprian on Baptism

Cyprian's references to baptism shew the same conceptions,[2] particular points being emphasized in connexion with the controversy as to heretical baptism, which became so acute in his time.[3] To him baptism was a real illumination, following upon the cleansing from sins, and he gives enthusiastic expression to his own experience. He had been enslaved to faults and errors, from which he could not free himself, and despaired of better things; but baptism gave him freedom and new life and power. "As soon as by help of the water of birth the stains of my former life were wiped away, and calm pure light from on high was shed upon my heart, now cleansed; as soon as I had drunk in the Spirit from heaven, and a second birth had restored me and made me a new man: forthwith, in marvellous wise, what had been doubtful received assurance, what had been shut from me was laid open, what had been dark was illumined; a way was opened out for what before seemed difficult, what was thought impossible could be done; what had been born of the flesh and lived before in bondage to its pleasures confessed that it was of the earth, and what the Holy Spirit now quickened in me began to be God's own." [4]

more technical terms, when he says "by means of the operation of the Spirit the natural water (αἰσθητὸν ὕδωρ) is transelemented to a *quasi*-divine and mysterious power" (Harnack *DG.* Eng. tr. vol. iv p. 284 n.—but the expressions used scarcely warrant the statement that a change of the water into a divine "material" is taught). Yet, though the description is fuller, the thought is no deeper than that which was familiar to Ignatius when he wrote incidentally that Jesus was himself baptized "in order to purify water by his passion" (*Eph.* 18).

[1] See Note on 'Confirmation' *infra* p. 390. Tertullian is the first to speak of the seasons of Easter and Pentecost as specially appropriate for baptism (§ 19), but he is careful to add that no time is unsuitable, and that the grace given is the same. And elsewhere he alludes to the threefold immersion then customary (*de Corona* § 3), and explains the custom as having direct reference to the Trinity (*adv. Prax.* § 26). He also marks the parallel (as Justin before him) between baptism and the pagan mysteries—see *de Bapt.* 5 and *de Praescr.* 40. Other interesting references to Baptism occur in *de Praescr.* 36, *de Res. Carn.* 8.

[2] See esp. *Ep.* 70–74.

[3] On these points see Note on 'Heretical Baptism' *infra* p. 387, and on 'Confirmation' p. 391.

[4] *de Gratia Dei* § 4.

And more than once, besides, he declares that the gift of the
Holy Spirit is not bestowed by measure, but that he is given
in, his plenitude to all alike in connexion with the rite
of baptism.[1] Baptism is the beginning of all faith, and of the
saving entrance on the hope of eternal life and of the divine
condescension to purify and quicken the servants of God.[2]

Cyril of Jerusalem on Baptism

The ideas and the ritual connected with baptism find full
expression in the Catechetical Lectures (*Cat. Myst.* i–iii) of Cyril
of Jerusalem (*c.* 348 A.D.), though nearly all can be seen in the
time of Tertullian.

His exposition deals first with the renunciation of Satan
and all his works, which the candidate for baptism pronounced
with stretched out hand, facing the west. The meaning of the
renunciation is drawn out in some detail and applied to daily
life. Then, turning to the east, the candidate recited his belief
in Father, Son, and Holy Spirit, and in one baptism of repentance ; turning to the east, because it is the place of light. This
is done in the outer building.[3]

Then inside the baptistery the candidate puts off his clothes
—a symbol of the putting off of the old man with his doings.
Naked, like Christ upon the cross, leading principalities and
powers in triumph ; like the first man Adam, in the garden, and
not ashamed ; he is anointed from head to foot with the
exorcised oil, which has power, not only to burn and purge
away the marks of sins, but also to put to flight all the
invisible powers of the evil spirit. He is then questioned as to
his faith, and thrice immersed in the water—even as Christ
was three days in the grave. So he goes down into darkness
and emerges (as by a resurrection) into the light of day. The
water is at once both " a grave and a mother ". It is only by

---

[1] *E.g. Ep.* 69. 14, 64. 3.   [2] *Ep.* 73. 12.

[3] In contrast with the previous reign of the devil and of death, Cyril declares
that in the holy laver of regeneration God has taken away every tear from every
face. " For no longer wilt thou mourn, now that thou hast been stripped of the
old man, but thou wilt keep festival, clad in the vesture of salvation, even Jesus
Christ." Earlier in his lectures (*Cat.* iii 3, 4) he has insisted on the sanctifying
power of the water, and declared that whatever good works a man may do, he will
not enter into the kingdom of heaven unless he receive the seal which is given by
water.

imitation that he shares in the cross and the grave, but salvation is thus really and in very truth bestowed upon him. He becomes conformed to the Son of God, a partaker in Christ, himself an anointed one (a 'Christ'), having received the mark of the Holy Spirit. Everything is done in his case in image, because he is an image of Christ. So when he comes from the water, just as the Holy Spirit descended upon Christ after his baptism, he is anointed with the ointment (the chrism), which corresponds to the Spirit wherewith Christ was anointed, the oil of gladness. Cyril warns his pupils against supposing that this chrism is mere plain oil, and tells them that just as the bread of the Eucharist, after the invocation of the Holy Spirit, is not simple bread, but is the body of Christ, so this holy ointment is no longer anything plain and ordinary, after the invocation of the Spirit, but the spiritual gift of Christ and of the Holy Spirit, made efficient by his divine presence ; so that when the body is anointed with the visible ointment, the soul is hallowed with the holy and life-giving Spirit.[1] This spiritual unction is a reality, and gives its recipients full right to the name of Christians.[2] The holiness of Christ will pass over to them.

Real union with Christ would thus seem to be the chief effect of the rite of baptism as a whole, according to Cyril's conception.[3]

Ambrose on Baptism

Ambrose, in his treatise *on the Mysteries*,[4] contributes little fresh that is of doctrinal importance, though he gives some interesting interpretations of the ritual, as, for example, that the unction which follows baptism (the chrism) is parallel to the unction of Aaron, to make a chosen race, priestly and

[1] He is anointed on the forehead, the ears, the nostrils, the breast, in order that every power and sense may be consecrated and armed. See, further, Additional Note on " Confirmation " *infra* p. 390.

[2] So Tertullian (*de Bapt.* 7) had noted that the name of Christ himself was derived from the anointing, the chrism. And still earlier (*c.* 180 A.D.) Theophilus (*ad Autol.* i. 12) wrote " We, therefore, are called Christians on this account, because we are anointed with the oil of God ".

[3] Cf. Rom. 6³⁻¹¹ and see *supra* p. 25. This conception of St Paul is the starting-point of the teaching of Cyril, as of that of Gregory of Nyssa *Or. Cat.* 33–36, on which see *infra* p. 411.

[4] There seems no sufficient reason to question the genuineness of this treatise, though its date is uncertain. The six sermons *de Sacramentis*, on the other hand, seem to be a later composition based on the *de Mysteriis*, but whether by Ambrose himself or by some later writer is uncertain.

precious; for we all are anointed with spiritual grace into the kingdom of God and the priesthood.[1] He also insists that the merits of the ministrant are not to be taken into account in the sacrament, inasmuch as the Lord Jesus, invoked by the prayers of the priest, is present himself. One fresh doctrinal idea in his treatise must be noted, though its meaning is obscure. In connexion with the text "He who is washed (*lotus*) has no need save to wash his feet (*ut pedes lavet*), but is wholly clean" (Jn 13[10]), he refers to the practice of washing the feet of the newly baptized.[2] In regard to Peter he gives the explanation that, though Peter was clean, he still had the sin of the first man derived by descent, and "the sole of his foot was therefore washed, that inherited sins might be done away, for it is our own sins that are removed by baptism". He says no more about it, and he certainly speaks elsewhere as though baptism removed all trace of sin, yet, so far as this *obiter dictum* goes, it implies the theory that 'original sin' is removed by the subsequent washing of the feet. For this theory there is no other evidence.[3]

From the end of the fourth century no questions arose in regard to baptism except such as have been considered already in connexion with the Pelagian controversy, and some points of detail which are referred to in the following notes.

[1] He also adds mention of the white garment put on immediately after baptism, to symbolize the new purity of soul; and he gives all through references to 'types' of baptism and explanations of the ritual from incidents in the Old and New Testaments.

[2] This ceremony was a recognized part of the ritual of baptism in the Gallican churches (see Art. 'Baptism' *D.C.A.* vol. i p. 164[b]), and was evidently in use at Milan (cf. *de Sacr.* iii ch. i), but there is no evidence for it elsewhere. Ambrose speaks of it here as specially designed to teach humility.

[3] What Ambrose really meant, and what conception of baptism underlies this passage, seems very obscure. Peter had not received Christian baptism; yet he was *lotus* and *mundus*. Perhaps, as Westcott suggests (*ad loc.*), his baptism had been his "direct intercourse and union with Christ". Ambrose implies that he was free from sin of his own conscious initiative; but there was still the stain of birth, and that was removed by the washing of the feet. (This is a reversal of the interpretation which would distinguish λελουμένος and νίψασθαι, and see in the former the full cleansing, and in the latter the partial washing, which removes "the stains contracted in the walk of life" (Westcott). The Latin does not discriminate between the two verbs.) If Ambrose intended any analogy, he teaches that we, in like manner, receive cleansing from our own sins by baptism, but from our original sin by the washing of the feet which follows. The editors, however, naturally shrink from attributing this theory to him, in view of his other utterances on the subject in general, and of the local character of the rite; but no satisfactory explanation of the passage has been given. That he regarded the rite as conferring at least some special grace seems clear.

25

MARTYRDOM AS BAPTISM

That martyrdom might take the place of baptism was an accepted principle, even with those who laid most stress on the necessity of baptism for salvation.

Thus Tertullian, having insisted that faith is not enough without baptism, that baptism can be received only in the orthodox Church, once for all, and is not to be repeated (contrasting it with the frequent 'washings' of the Jews), goes on to declare that Christians have, however, a second laver, which is the baptism of blood. He sees a reference to it in our Lord's saying, that he had a baptism to be baptized with, when he was already baptized (Lk. 12^{50}), and in St. John's description of him as having come by water and by blood (1 Jn. 5^{6}); and he declares that from the spear-wound in his side there issued these two baptisms. So martyrdom is a baptism which bestows in full the laver, if not yet received, and restores it if lost (*de Bapt.* 15, 16).

And Cyprian follows him closely (*Ep.* 73. 22), speaking of martyrdom as the chief and most glorious baptism, and citing the case of the penitent robber as shewing that those who are baptized by their own blood, and hallowed by suffering, obtain the promised benefits.

That martyrdom could be in this way a substitute for baptism was acknowledged with equal heartiness by Augustine, with reference to Cyprian's proof; though he is conscious that Cyprian's instance is not very apposite, and points out that the robber was crucified, not for Christ's sake, but for his own crimes, and that he did not suffer because he believed, but believed in the course of suffering. And so Augustine is led to say that faith and conversion of heart also (as well as martyrdom) may compensate for the want of baptism when there has not been opportunity of receiving baptism (*de Bapt. c. Don.* iv 29).

HERETICAL BAPTISM

Whether baptism be regarded as admission to the Christian society, entrance into the Church as an organized body, or as a sacrament, the administration of which (and of all the benefits it conveys) was committed by Christ to his apostles, it might naturally be inferred that only those who were members of the Christian society or the Church could give admission to their body, and only those who fulfilled the conditions of a true faith in Christ could receive the benefits of the sacrament.

Accordingly, at an early date it was maintained that heretics could not confer valid baptism. Tertullian (*de Bapt.* 15) argues, on the basis of the text "One Lord, one faith, one baptism", that heretics have no part in the faith of the Church, as their exclusion from communion shews. Their God is not the God of the Church; nor have they the one Christ; and therefore they have not got the one baptism.

To the same effect Cyprian (e.g. Ep. 73; cf. Ep. 69, 70, 71) insisted that there was nothing in common, as regards baptism, between heretics and orthodox; just as they had not got in common either God the Father, or Christ the Son, or the Holy Spirit, or the faith, or the Church itself. Those, therefore, who had received baptism from heretics had not really been baptized at all; he even says (de Unit. Eccles. 11) that such a baptismal birth bears sons, not to God, but to the devil, as father; and, when they wished to join the Church, they must receive the rite in full. It was not a question of rebaptizing them, which, of course, could not be thought of. Anyone who had been baptized in the Church and had then fallen into heresy, and afterwards desired to return to the truth and his mother Church, would be received with imposition of hands alone (see e.g. Ep. 71. 1, 2). There is no such thing as baptism outside the Church. There is one Lord, one faith, one Church, one baptism. The grace depends upon the faith (ibid. 73. 4). If there is not the true faith, there cannot be obtained the remission of sins and the grace of divine forgiveness. The authority to confer it was given primarily to Peter, and afterwards to the other apostles, and is only to be found among the ministers of the Church. The heretic who has lost the Holy Spirit cannot perform spiritual acts or give what he does not himself possess (Ep. 70).

In this conception Cyprian was supported by all the African bishops and by strong feeling in the eastern Church, as well as at Alexandria (cf. Firmilian of Caesarea in Cypr. Ep. 75, Clem. Al. Strom. i 19, and Dionysius Euseb. H.E. vii 7). Against Cyprian's conception the treatise de Rebaptismate (printed among Cyprian's works) was written in favour of the validity of heretical baptism.

The Roman opposition, headed by Stephen (who claimed the anthority of tradition for his view), recognized the security for the essence of Church membership in the institution rather than in the person, in the opus operatum—the objective form of the sacrament. The sacrament was God's, and the human organ through which it was administered could not affect it. The Councils of Arles and of Nicaea gave sanction to this opinion rather than the other, provided that the baptism had been given in the name of the Trinity—a limitation, however, which does not seem necessarily to require a true faith on the part of the ministrant, even in this important particular.

This view, which is summed up in Augustine's non est cogitandum quis det sed quid det (de Bapt. iv 10. 6) prevailed in the West, but only partially in the East. Thus Cyril of Jerusalem (Procat. 7) says simply "heretics are rebaptized, because their former baptism was not baptism"; and Athanasius (Or. c. Ar. ii 42, 43) insists that it is not enough to say the names only, if they have not the right intention, and that baptism by Arians and others who have not the true faith in the Father and the Son is vain and unprofitable, so that "he who is sprinkled by them is rather defiled in ungodliness than redeemed". And though distinctions were drawn, the practice of rebaptizing heretics seems to have remained in the East, where it is still the custom.

Augustine's attitude towards the question seems to shew a strange acceptance of the established practice and denial of the principles which it implied. He maintained, on the one hand, that heretical or schismatical baptism was valid, but, on the other hand, that it did not confer remission of sins, or any saving grace, until the heretics so baptized abjured their errors and joined the Church.[1] Hereby he held that he avoided violation of the sacrament of God, while securing the right state of mind on the part of the person baptized—"intellectum hominis corrigo, non Dei violo sacramentum" (contra Petil. de unico baptismo § 3). Wherever the sacrament was administered, it was God's sacrament—holy in itself—and it conferred on the recipient of it a 'character' or mark which nothing could destroy; but it was only in union with the Catholic Church that he could actually enjoy its benefits. (This distinction between habere and utiliter or salubriter habere was apparently forged as a weapon against the Donatists.) And, similarly, against the theory that the ministrant of the sacrament must be holy, he insisted that the conscience of man was often unknown to him, but he was certain of the mercy of Christ (c. litt. Petil. i 8), and that the important matter was "not who gives, but what he gives" (de Bapt. iv 16 "non cogitandum quis det sed quid det").

BAPTISM BY LAYMEN

No rule seems to have been laid down as to the qualifications requisite in one who was to administer the rite. Neither the twelve nor the seventy were commissioned to baptize (Lk. 9 and 10), and only one gospel includes baptism in the final commission to the eleven (Mt 28[19]). It seems probable that the apostles took part in baptizing converts (cf. Acts 2[41] and 1 Cor. 1[14]); but there is no direct evidence that they did so in the Acts of the Apostles, and St Paul's incidental allusion to the fact that he himself only occasionally baptized a convert proves that the practice was not common, and that he regarded himself as sent by Christ "not to baptize, but to preach". The baptism of the eunuch by Philip (doubtless the Philip who was one of 'the seven') and of St Paul—as it seems—by Ananias (who probably held no 'official' position) is enough to shew that there was no monopoly of the right to

---

[1] See de Bapt. c. Don. i 15–18 and iv 23 ff., and elsewhere.

confer baptism, and probably any believer in Christ was deemed to be competent to admit another to the Church and so secure to him remission of sins. This right of laymen has never been denied by the Church. But the special commission to the apostles (Mt 28[19]) distinctly favours the theory that it is only as the representative of them and their successors that a layman acts. The theory is plainly expressed by Ignatius (*ad Smyrn.* 8)—" Without the bishop it is not lawful to baptize ". And it must be noted that the chrism and imposition of hands (see note following), whereby the rite of baptism was completed, could never be given by any other than a bishop; or, at all events, even when a presbyter might in this way complete the rite (as in the Eastern Church in later times), the chrism which he used had been consecrated by a bishop. And Tertullian shews his acceptance of the theory when, while vindicating the rights of laymen in emergencies, he says (*de Bapt.* 17): "The chief priest, who is the bishop, has the right of conferring baptism (*jus dandi*); and next the presbyters and deacons—not, however, without the licence (*sine auctoritate*) of the bishop, for the sake of the honour of the Church, which must be safeguarded as the safeguard of peace. With this limitation, the right belongs to the laity too (for what is received by all alike can be given by all alike), unless bishops or presbyters or deacons *discentes* (? late Lat. = licensed to teach, *i.e.* deacons with more than the usual ecclesiastical powers of deacons—as to which see Cheetham Art. ' Deacon ' *D.C.A.* esp. pp. 530, 531) are invited. The word of the Lord ought not to be hidden from any one. Likewise baptism, which is equally God's own, can be administered by all. But the practice of modesty and moderation is all the more incumbent on the laity because it is required of their superiors, so that they may not take upon themselves a duty of the episcopate assigned to bishops. Ambition is the mother of schisms. The most holy apostle said that all things were permitted but not all things were expedient. Be satisfied, therefore, to use the right in emergencies in any case in which the circumstances of place, or time, or person require." (Cf. Cyprian *Ep.* 73. 7, and the *de Rebapt.* 10.) Cyril's evidence (*Cat.* 17. 35) is to like effect, when he speaks of the baptizand coming before the bishops or presbyters or deacons, but immediately adds words implying that anyone could confer the gift of grace, since it is not derived from men but from God, and is only administered through the agency of men. The right of women to baptize was, however, strenuously repudiated by Tertullian in his pre-Montantistic days (*de Bapt.* 17; cf. *de Virg. Vel.* 9, and *de Praescript.* 41), and this was the accepted view in the Church.

Bishop, priest, and deacon were all mentioned as present by Ambrose (*de Myst.* ii). Cyprian (*Ep.* 73. 7) regards the authority to declare remission of sins as strictly limited to the Church, and apparently to its ordained ministry.   Cf. also Jerome *adv. Lucif.* 9, and Augustine *contra ep. Parm.* ii 29 and *de Bapt. c. Don.* v 14.

CONFIRMATION

Of 'Confirmation' as a distinct rite, separated and disconnected from baptism, there is no other evidence during the first five centuries than that which the New Testament itself supplies (as to which see *supra* p. 24 n. 8). But in close connexion with baptism, as an essential part of the rite, with which the benefits of baptism itself were directly associated, there was the chrism and imposition of hands, which at a later time (when dissociated from the baptism proper) became the separate rite of confirmation. (The name βεβαίωσις τῆς ὁμολογίας is applied to the chrism in *Const. Apost.* iii 17, and the consecration of the chrism was always deemed to be an episcopal act.) It is from the first with this ceremony of the chrism rather than with the actual baptism—*i.e.* with this particular part of the whole rite of baptism—that the reception of the Holy Spirit is associated. Baptism effected the cleansing needed for the moment, giving full remission of sins ; but the special gift of grace which was required to sustain a man through his future life was only to be obtained through the subsequent rite.

It is not clear whether the rite of chrism was used by the apostles. The references in 2 Cor. 1[21] and 1 Jn. 2[20] are to the inward unction of the Holy Spirit. Whether there was also an outward and visible act which symbolized this inward unction or not, cannot be determined. The argument that the early use of the rite indicates apostolic origin is weighty, but not decisive.

Although Tertullian is the first who clearly states the use of unction in baptism in the Church, yet Irenæus mentions it as one of the rites of initiation employed by some of the Gnostic schools, who used a special kind of unguent immediately after baptism (or unguent mixed with water as one rite instead of baptism and unction), and it is most probable that their use was based upon a practice of the Church (see *adv. Haer.* I xxi 3, 4). So elsewhere (*ibid.* IV lxii, lxiii) he clearly associates the gift of the Spirit with the imposition of hands, and not with baptism. And again (*ibid.* III xviii 1) he seems to consider the baptism with water as affecting the body, while it is the gift of the Spirit afterwards that renews the soul (so Didymus and Cyril of Alexandria afterwards).

Tertullian is the first to definitely mention the unction (after baptism) and the imposition of hands which followed, clearly discriminating the intention and effects of the two parts of the whole rite. He says plainly (*de Bapt.* 6) that we do not obtain the Holy Spirit in the water. As John was the forerunner of the Lord, preparing his ways ;

so baptism prepares the way for the Holy Spirit, by the washing away of sins which faith, sealed in the Father, Son, and Holy Spirit, secures. Baptism gives remission of sins, but the gift of the Holy Spirit comes with the unction and the imposition of hands that follow.

Cyprian insists that this unction is necessary to a valid baptism. One reason why heretical baptism was not valid was, that having neither church nor altar, they could not consecrate the oil (*Ep.* 70. 2). And he says that it was by the bishop's prayer and imposition of hands that those who were baptized in the Church obtained the Holy Spirit and were consummated with the seal of the Lord (*Ep.* 73. 9). Whether the bishop's prayer and imposition of hands may be sufficient for this purpose without the unction, or not, it seems clear that to Cyprian they were parts of one and the same rite, but that the imposition of hands was by far the more important part. He mentions it frequently, the unction seldom. (Augustine speaks of both as conveying the Holy Spirit. They are equivalent rites, used together and for the same purpose—the unction more closely connected with the baptism and therefore not necessarily repeated in the case of heretics, in which case fresh imposition of hands would be enough.)

Just the same teaching was given by Cyril to his catechumens (see the passage quoted *supra* p. 384 n. 1). The exorcised oil before baptism has power to purge away the marks of sin, but it is the chrism afterwards that is associated with the bestowal of the Holy Spirit.

And in keeping with this conception was the practice by which heretics coming over to the Church, if their baptism was recognized, were received by the chrism and imposition of hands (which could be respectively prepared and given only by a bishop of the Church)—a separate rite being thus in effect instituted, though it was regarded merely as the completion of an imperfect sacrament. So Cyprian (*Ep.* 72. 1, 2) declared "It is not enough to lay hands on them that they may receive the Holy Spirit, unless they receive also the baptism of the Church; for only when they are born by each sacrament can they become fully sanctified and be sons of God, since it is written, Unless a man be born again of water and Spirit, he cannot enter into the kingdom of God". (The interpretation of the saying is probably erroneous—it probably refers to the outward visible sign and the inward gift of grace: but Cyprian's conception is clear.) Cf. *Sentent. Episc.* 5. And Cornelius of Rome (Euseb. *H.E.* vi 43. 15) denied that Novatus could have received the Holy Spirit, because, though baptized on his bed in a dangerous illness, he did not afterwards receive the other things which were necessary, according to the canon of the Church, among which was the being sealed by the bishop (unction *and* imposition of hands are doubtless meant).

[The earliest canons on the subjects are the 38th and the 77th of Elvira (306 A.D.). Cf. the 8th of Arles (314). The practice of the Church is also shewn by the 7th, 8th, and 48th canons of Laodicea (between 333 and 381), and the so-called 7th of Constantinople (381 A.D.)—see Hefele *Councils*, vol. i pp. 152, 169 ; vol. ii pp. 302, 368.]

On the later practice in the time of Augustine, in relation to the Donatists, and on Hilary's and Augustine's views see Mason *The Relation of Confirmation to Baptism*, p. 133 ff.

See also the treatise *de Rebaptismate* (on the Roman side) in Migne's *Cyprian* and Mason *op. cit.* p. 122 ff.

The first unqualified use of the term is found in Faustus, viz. 'confirmati' (*de Sp. S.* ii 4) and 'confirmatio' (*Homily*)—see Mason *ibid.* p. 191.

CHAPTER XXI

THE EUCHARIST

NOTE

THE following account of early teaching on the Eucharist will be better understood, and the teaching more readily appreciated in its true proportions, if regard is had to the various forms in which the doctrine was expressed in later times. The different theories which have been widely held may be summed up as follows:—

1. *Transubstantiation.*—This, though not officially recognized till the Council of the Lateran in 1215, was no doubt the doctrine most widely current for some time before and after in the Church. It was the doctrine enforced in England by Henry VIII and Mary. The term itself was in use at the beginning of the twelfth century, occurring in a sermon of Hildebert of Tours, no. 93, Migne clxxi p. 176.

The statement of the Council of the Lateran was as follows: "There is moreover one universal Church of the faithful, outside which no one at all is saved, in which Jesus Christ is himself at once the priest and the sacrifice, whose body and blood are truly contained in the sacrament of the altar, under the forms of bread and of wine (*sub speciebus* panis et vini), the bread being *transubstantiated* into the body and the wine into the blood, by divine power, so that for the accomplishment of the mystery of unity we ourselves receive from his what he himself received from ours."

And the decree of the Council of Trent ran in equivalent terms, declaring that the God-man is present truly, really, and substantially in this sacrament, under the form of things sensible (vere, realiter, et substantialiter sub specie rerum sensibilium). "By the consecration of bread and wine a conversion takes place of the entire substance of the bread into the substance of the body of Christ our Lord, and of the entire substance of the wine into the substance of his blood. And this conversion is fittingly and appropriately styled by the Holy Catholic Church transubstantiation." At the same time, the significance of this definition was fortified by an anathema on any one who believes that the substance of the elements remains after the consecration. The supernatural presence is thus regarded as annihilating its natural vehicle, except in appearance to the senses.

This definition, at least in the mouth of expert theologians, depends upon a particular philosophical theory of existence, according to which everything consists of two parts—(1) *substance*, which is invisible and imperceptible, and constitutes the essential reality of the thing; and (2) *accidents*, which are visible and tangible, and give the thing its outward form, shape, taste. (To take a rough illustration. In the case of a man, the real man would not be the outward flesh and blood and bones and body—these would be the 'accidents': he himself would be really the invisible something behind them all.) So, in regard to the Eucharist, the theory was that the substance of the bread and wine (the invisible) became by consecration the actual substance of the Body and Blood of Jesus Christ, while the accidents (the visible) remained unaltered, what they were. (The substance of the bread and wine thus wholly ceased to be, and a new substance took their place. The accidents, however, continue to exist without their substance. And it was the metaphysical difficulty involved in this conception of *accidentia per se (sine subjecto) subsistentia*, more than anything else, that roused opposition to the doctrine. This was the point to which both Wyclif and Luther took exception, as did Berengar before them.) The doctrine of transubstantiation, accordingly, as the official doctrine of the mediæval Church, is only to be understood by experts in philosophical terms, in connection with a highly technical theory of existence. It was probably never understood by the masses of the people. At all events, in the sixteenth century, it seems certain that 'substance' did not convey to any but experts any special metaphysical sense, and was generally regarded as equivalent to the 'substance' and the 'accidents' together, so that the theory of transubstantiation seemed to destroy the reality of the outward and visible sign (cf. Article xxviii 'overthroweth the nature of a sacrament'—directed probably against the popular conception of the doctrine, though it may be questioned whether, even according to the technical definition, the reality of the outward and visible sign was preserved when the substance disappeared and only the accidents remained).

2. *Consubstantiation.*—Luther, as Wyclif before him and others who rejected the theory of *accidentia sine subjecto*, held that, in the Eucharist, while the natural substance of the bread and wine remain, there is present also at the same time the Body and Blood of Christ. In and under the consecrated elements Christ is therefore actually present, his very body and blood: and every one who receives the elements receives Christ, to his benefit or to his hurt. "Though it be a rogue who takes or gives the sacrament, it is the right sacrament, that is Christ's body and blood" (Luther—"The Greater Catechism").

Luther was chiefly concerned to maintain that there is a real presence in the sacrament, while denying that the theory of transubstantiation was necessarily the true explanation of that presence. He argues (*Babylonish Captivity of the Church*) that it is not necessary to comprehend altogether the manner of the divine working; that the laity could not understand the philosophical distinction between substance and accidents; and that Christ is able to include his body within the substance of bread as well as within the accidents. Luther seems to have avoided speaking of the 'substance' of the body and blood, though his argument implies it; but in the *Formula Concordiae*, drawn up in 1577, it is declared that in the holy supper two different substances, the natural bread and the true natural body of Christ, are present (just as in Christ two distinct natures are inseparably united, unchanged)—and the word *consubstantiation* was coined, on the analogy of *transubstantiation*, to denote this coexistence of the two substances together. (The word has, of course, no relation to the Latin representative of ὁμοούσιος.)

3. *The Sacramentarian theory*, on the contrary, denies any actual presence of the body of Christ, and regards the Eucharist as, above all else, a commemoration of the passion—a pledge (*sacramentum*, in the early Latin sense), a seal of grace, but not the means by which it is received. The words "This is my body" were merely symbolic and metaphorical ('is' means 'signifies'); by "eating his flesh and blood" Christ meant simply "trusting in him". There was thus no mystery about the rite; the bread and wine were in no way changed by consecration, though becoming 'holy' by association with the rite. The presence of Christ was only granted to faith and contemplation; it was not connected with the elements; and communion was an act of obedience to the Lord's ordinance, rather than the means of union with him. These views were expressed by Zwingli, and held by the early Swiss and Dutch reformers, spreading to England from Holland in the time of Henry VIII. They were the opinions for which Frith, Lambert, Anne Askew, and others were put to death.

4. *The Receptionist theory*, to which Calvin gave currency, is closely allied to the 'Sacramentarian' in that it holds to a merely figurative sense of the words of institution, and recognizes no effect produced on the bread and wine by consecration, and no objective presence of Christ in the sacrament. But Calvin believed the Eucharist to be more than a commemorative rite, and taught that special grace was imparted in it to the soul of the communicant who receives faithfully and worthily. Such a communicant enjoys spiritual participation in Christ, receiving in his soul a subjective presence which depends on his fitness when he takes into his mouth the bread and wine. By this theory the presence of Christ, though subjective and

individual and conditional, and not in any sense contained in the bread and wine, is associated with reception of the elements; but the rite is regarded in the main as a pious exercise of personal devotion. Its efficacy, though ultimately due to Christ's promise, depends as much on the recipient as on Christ or God. This theory was maintained by Peter Martyr, Martin Bucer, and Ridley, and through their influence was accepted by Cranmer. The exiles returning from Geneva in the time of Elizabeth commonly held the same opinion. Hooker plainly asserts it [1]—"The real presence of Christ's most blessed body and blood is not to be sought for in the sacrament, but in the worthy receiver of the sacrament" and "by the sacrament Christ doth really and truly in us perform his promise"; and it became widely current in England both in the Church and among Protestant Nonconformists; though Andrewes, and others like-minded with him, did their best to maintain the doctrine of the real presence in the sacrament.

5. The formularies of the Church of England must therefore be held to be patient of the 'Receptionist' interpretation, in its positive aspect at least, though no expressions are used which suggest the inference that the presence is separate from the consecrated elements and only existent *in usu*. On the contrary, all the expressions used are compatible with the doctrine that the presence is to be found actually in the sacrament. The Catechism clearly asserts that the bread and the wine are the vehicles of the grace that is given, the means whereby the body and blood of Christ are verily and indeed *taken and received* (the thing signified is not conceived of as separate from the outward part or sign). And elsewhere, alike in the devotional language of the Communion Service and in the more formal descriptions of the Articles, the consecrated bread and wine are consistently described as the body and blood of Christ which every communicant receives, though he can only by faith become really a partaker of Christ. The presence of Christ is declared to be a spiritual and not a material presence; but the teaching that there is an objective presence of Christ in the elements themselves, which becomes, in the case of every worthy recipient, a subjective presence in the soul, is certainly a legitimate inference from the plain and simple sense of the terms that are used. In any case it is clear that the popular materialistic conceptions of the doctrine of transubstantiation are expressly repudiated, and technical definitions and scholastic terminology are carefully eschewed; but the doctrine that in the Eucharist Christ is verily present is firmly upheld, without attempt to define precisely the mode in which he is present, or to explain how that which still remains bread and wine can at the same time be the body and blood of Christ. (Cf. Bishop Ken's *Exposition of the Church Catechism.*)

[1] *Eccles. Pol.* V lxvii 6.

The Agape

The Eucharist [1] in the apostolic age was part of the common supper of the brotherhood—the love-feast (*agape*) which they held in imitation of the last supper of the Lord with his disciples. The supper apparently came first, and then the special acts and rites which made the celebration of the Eucharist.[2] The same practice is implied in the Didache,[3] and and was still followed when Ignatius wrote his letters urging the need for the presence of the bishop if there was to be a valid Eucharist.[4]

In the following sketch of early conceptions of the Eucharist no attempt is made to label the teaching of different fathers and writers 'symbolic', 'spiritual', 'materialistic', and the like; nor to give a complete *catena* of extracts from their writings on the subject;[5] nor yet, as a rule, to trace developement of teaching from one to another. There is simply stated, as much as possible in their own words and as briefly as possible, what seems to be characteristic or noteworthy.[6]

Early Conceptions of the Effect of Consecration— Ignatius, Justin, Irenaeus

The effect which consecration of the bread and the wine— the giving of thanks—was believed to have upon them is conceived in the prayer in the *Didache* as making them spiritual food and drink, which gives eternal life.[7]

Pliny's informants only spoke to him of the bread and wine

---

[1] The names familiar to the first Christians were clearly rather "the breaking of the bread" (Luke 24[35], Acts 2[42 46] 20[7]) and "the Lord's Supper" (1 Cor. 11[7]); and St Paul calls it "the cup of blessing" rather than "of thanksgiving"; but the term "Eucharist" is used *Didache* 9; Ignatius *Philad.* 4, *Smyrn.* 6, 8, *Eph.* 13; and by Justin's time had become usual (*Apol.* i. 66).

[2] See 1 Cor. 11[17] ff. and Acts 20[7], and Lightfoot note *infra.*   [3] See ch. x.

[4] *E.g. Smyrn.* 8: "It is not lawful without the bishop either to baptize or to hold a love-feast"—where the two great sacraments of the Church seem to be intended, although the Eucharist has been specially mentioned in the preceding context. See Lightfoot's note, *Apostolic Fathers* part II vol. ii p. 313. (The interpolator afterwards, when the Agape and the Eucharist had been long separated, added "or to make oblations or to present the sacrifice".)

[5] For this see *e.g.* Pusey *The Doctrine of the Real Presence.*

[6] The chapter is therefore little more than a series of notes. I do not think that fuller or more connected treatment of the subject can be attempted with advantage here.

[7] *Didache* 10 (I assume this is the post-communion prayer, but possibly it is

as ordinary simple food.[1] To *Ignatius* the Eucharist is the one great bond of union of Christians with one another,[2] but only so because it brings them into closest relation to the Lord. To partake of his one flesh and of the one cup of his blood is to live one life.[3] It is this participation which really makes the whole Church one body. It is breaking one bread which is a medicine of immortality, a cure against death giving life in Jesus Christ for ever.[4] So with the food of corruption and the pleasures of this life are contrasted the bread of God, which is the flesh of Christ, and his blood, which is love incorruptible.[5] With less direct reference to the Eucharist, faith is said to be the flesh of the Lord, and love the blood of Jesus Christ.[6] To be without participation in the true and valid Eucharist is to be outside the body of Christ.

From *Justin*, although his account was meant for pagan ears, we get the first plain statement that a mysterious change was effected by the words of consecration.[7] After saying that the food of which he has spoken is called among Christians 'Eucharist', and that none are permitted to partake of it but believers who have been baptized, and who live as Christ prescribed, he gives the reason. "For we do not receive these as common (ordinary) bread and common drink. But, just as Jesus Christ our Saviour, when made flesh by the word of God, had both flesh and blood on behalf of our salvation, so too we were taught that the food which has been made a Eucharist [8]

only the grace after the Agape, if the words "If any be holy let him come", indicate that communion follows—as Swete *Services and Service Books before the Reformation* p. 78). It is difficult to decide the question whether the directions of the *Didache* refer to the Eucharist proper, or to the social meal from which the Eucharist is not yet separated.

[1] Pliny to Trajan *Ep.* 96 (ed. E. G. Hardy). They probably told Pliny that they believed it to be the body and blood of the Lord, but the practical Roman was content to know that only ordinary articles of food were used ; their belief about the bread and wine was merely part of their "degraded and extravagant superstition", which was the only thing in them he could find blameworthy. (But the reference may be to the Agape.)

[2] See *Eph.* 13, *Magn.* 4, *Philad.* 4, *Smyrn.* 6, 8.

[3] See esp. *Philad.* 4, cf. *Smyrn.* 6.

[4] *Eph.* 20 φάρμακον ἀθανασίας, ἀντίδοτος τοῦ μὴ ἀποθανεῖν ἀλλὰ ζῆν ἐν Ἰησοῦ χριστῷ διὰ παντός. No distinction is made by Ignatius between the body and the spirit. It is the whole self that receives the gift of immortality.

[5] *Rom.* 7.

[6] *Trall.* 8. So a certain mystical tendency must be recognized in Ignatius.

[7] Justin M. *Apol.* i 66.

[8] εὐχαριστηθεῖσαν "over which thanks have been given".

by prayer of the Word which comes from him (from which our blood and flesh are fed by a process of change) is both the flesh and blood of that Jesus who was made flesh." The prayers said over the elements of bread and wine, perhaps with invocation of the Spirit,[1] change then from ordinary bread and wine into the flesh and blood of the incarnate Jesus. They are still capable of nourishing the human body, but they are much more besides.[2]

There can be no doubt that Ignatius conceives of the gift which is received in the Eucharist as being the gift of Jesus Christ himself—his very life and spirit. And this conception underlies and prompts the language of nearly all ecclesiastical writers after him. Only here and there an individual may be found who tends to refine away the full meaning of the flesh and blood, and to limit the scope of the sacrament either to the spirits (*e.g.* Origen) or to the bodies (*e.g.* more or less precisely, Irenaeus, Tertullian, Cyril of Jerusalem, and Gregory of Nyssa) of those who partake in it, or else to distinguish the Eucharistic body and blood of Christ as 'spiritual' from his real self (*e.g.* Clement of Alexandria, Jerome). But these are different individualistic tendencies, in regard to particular points, which do not influence the main stream of thought in the Church as to the doctrine as a whole.[3]

The conceptions of *Irenaeus*[4] are revealed most plainly—all the more so perhaps because each mention of the Eucharist is incidental. He does not write to explain the nature of the sacrament. He is concerned to refute two grievous errors of Gnostic speculation—one, the Marcionite conception of matter,

---

[1] It is the Holy Spirit who makes the elements the body and blood of Christ, and thus it is that the prayers for his descent, rather than the recital of the words of institution, are regularly regarded in early times as the essential part of the rite of consecration. This seems to me the natural meaning of the words δι᾽ εὐχῆς λόγου τοῦ παρ᾽ αὐτοῦ εὐχαριστηθεῖσα, *i.e.* by invocation of the Logos which comes from him (namely, the Holy Spirit), for Justin—as others—does not clearly discriminate the title Logos. See *Apol.* i 33 τὸ πνεῦμα οὖν καὶ τὴν δύναμιν τὴν παρὰ τοῦ θεοῦ οὐδὲν ἄλλο νοῆσαι θέμις ἢ τὸν λόγον. So in Sarapion's *Sacramentary* it is the Logos whose descent upon the elements is prayed for, and probably the same use is implied in the account which Irenaeus gives, see *infra* p. 401 n. For other interpretations of the words of Justin see Gore *The Body of Christ* pp. 6, 289, and Swete 'Eucharistic Belief in the Second and Third Centuries' *Journal of Theological Studies* vol. iii no. 10 pp. 170, 171.

[2] Cf. also the passages cited *infra* p. 405 in regard to the sacrificial conception.

[3] See Gore *The Body of Christ* pp. 59 and ff.

[4] See in particular the *Introduction* to Harvey's edition, vol. i p. clxxiii.

denying that the creation, and the good gifts of God stored up in it, are the work of the supreme Deity or of the divine Word; the other, the Valentinian belief that the created universe was the product of ignorance and a mere abortion. It is merely in illustration of the general course of his argument that he refers to the well-known teaching of the Church in this particular. But the incidental appeal depends for all its force on the fact that the Church believed that the body and blood of Christ are verily and indeed taken and received in the Lord's Supper; the bread and the wine are the very body and the very blood of the incarnate Word of God. When Christ himself consecrated bread as his body, and blessed the cup as his blood, how can it be maintained that bread and wine are creatures not of the Word, not of God the Father, but of some subordinate Demiurge, half malignant and wholly ignorant? Then were the body and blood of Christ the products of the workmanship of the Demiurge.

And again, against the teaching that the Saviour's body was phantasmal (docetic), the reasoning runs: We know that our own bodies are real flesh and blood, and that the bread and wine which we receive in the Eucharist do nourish and strengthen and increase our own real bodies. Therefore the bread and wine are real. But further we know (such is the teaching of the Church derived from the words in which Christ instituted the sacrament) that by consecration they become the very body and blood of Christ. Therefore Christ was no incorporeal appearance, but had real body and blood.

In each allusion, without reference to the process and the manner of the change, it is assumed that consecration makes what was bread and wine into the very body and blood of Christ, which, just because of its reality, is able to nourish our body and blood, while at the same time, because it is the Lord's body, it imparts to our bodies the gift of eternal life.[1]

---

[1] The actual words of Irenaeus are as follows: "How can they say that the flesh, which is nourished from the body of the Lord and his blood, passes into corruption and does not partake of life? Either let them change their opinion, or let them refuse to offer up [the body and the blood]. But our opinion is in harmony with the Eucharist, and the Eucharist confirms our opinion. We offer up to him that which is his own, concordantly proclaiming communion and union of flesh and spirit. For just as bread which comes from the earth, when it has received the invocation of God upon it, is no longer common bread, but a Eucharist, composed of two factors, an earthly and a heavenly; so too our bodies, when they participate in the Eucharist, are no longer perishable, since they possess the hope of the eternal

At other times, in a different vein, Irenaeus could write of the spiritual character of the sacrifice offered in the Eucharist, which replaced for Christians the ancient offerings of the sanctuary. There is apparently in view the objection that it was itself a 'Judaistic' rite. "These offerings", he says, [1] "are not after the law (its bond the Lord blotted out and took away), but after the Spirit, for in spirit and in truth we must worship God. And for this reason the offering of the Eucharist is not fleshly but spiritual, and therein pure. For we offer to God the bread and the cup of blessing, giving thanks to him,[2] for that he bade

resurrection (cf. *adv. Haer.* iv 31. 4). And again (*ibid.* iv 51. 1) he declares that the Lord could not have taken bread and professed that it was his body, and declared the wine and water mixed in the cup to be his blood, unless he had a human body like ours.

Again, he meets the argument for a merely spiritual salvation and resurrection by a *reductio ad absurdum*, thus: "If, however, this flesh is not to be saved; then the Lord did not redeem us by his blood, and the cup of the Eucharist is not the communication of his blood, and the bread which we break is not the communication of his body. For blood can only come from veins and flesh and all the rest of that which makes man what he is, of which the Word of God who redeemed us by his blood was truly made. . . . Since we are his members, we are nourished by means of his creation (creatures). He bestows upon us his creatures—causing his sun to rise, and raining as he wills: the cup which was derived from his creatures he declared to be his own blood, from which he bedews our blood; and the bread derived from his creatures he affirmed to be his own body, from which he gives increase to our bodies. Whenever, then, the mixed cup and the bread which has been made receive the Word of God [τὸν λόγον τοῦ θεοῦ, where λόγον is probably personal, though it may mean only the word, in the sense of the whole prayer of consecration], and the Eucharist becomes the body of Christ, and out of those our flesh maketh increase and is compacted:—how can they say that the flesh is incapable of receiving the gift of God, which is eternal life, when it is nourished (fed) by the body and blood of the Lord, and is a member of him? Even as the blessed Paul says, in his epistle to the Ephesians, 'We are members of the body, of his flesh and of his bones' (Eph. 5[2]); not saying this of a spiritual and invisible man—'for spirit hath neither bones nor flesh' (Luke 24[39]), but of the dispensation which follows the law of very man, which consists of flesh and nerves and bones; which also is nourished from the cup—which is his blood, and is increased from the bread which is his body" (*ibid.* v ii 2).

The tendency, which has been referred to above p. 399, to regard the effect of the sacrament as primarily exercised on our bodies, bestowing immortality, the hope of eternal resurrection, is obvious in these passages. The effect is represented as direct, rather than mediate, through the influence of the sacrament on the spirit primarily, and then through the spirit on the body. But it must be borne in mind that Irenaeus is not writing a treatise on the Eucharist; he is only drawing from it an argument against Gnostic ideas. And so he may well emphasize one aspect of the matter—enough for his immediate purpose.

[1] Fragment xxxvi (Harvey vol. ii pp. 500–505). This, however, is the second of the Pfaffian fragments, which Harnack believes to be forgeries by Pfaff, in the interests of the Lutheran doctrine (*Texte u. Unters. N.F.* v 3 p. 56 ff.).

[2] εὐχαριστοῦντες αὐτῷ.

the earth bring forth these fruits for our food. And then, when we have finished the offering (oblation), we invoke the Holy Spirit to proclaim this sacrifice, and the bread the body of Christ, and the cup the blood of Christ, in order that by partaking of these symbols we may obtain forgiveness of sins and eternal life. So then they who take part in these offerings in remembrance (or in the memorial) of the Lord do not follow after the ordinances of the Jews, but worshipping in spiritual fashion they shall be called sons of wisdom."

The Conception of the Elements as Symbols

It will be noted that Irenaeus here uses a word [1] which is rendered 'symbols'. Yet how the bread and wine could be the body and blood of Christ does not seem to have been regarded as a problem calling for solution. There is no trace of any widespread conception of the elements as symbols. In some way, undefined if not undefinable, they *were* what they represented.[2]

There might perhaps, for the sake of argument, be some distinction drawn, as when Tertullian, arguing against the docetic conception of Christ's person, says:[3] "He made the bread, he took and distributed to his disciples his body, saying 'This is my body', that is a figure (*figura*) of my body. It would not, however, have been a figure, unless the body were a real body (*i.e.* no phantom body could have a *figura* of itself)." And again, when he interprets the passage of Jeremiah "Come, let us cast wood at his bread"[4] of the crucifixion, explaining that this 'bread' means 'his body', and that the Lord so interpreted the

---

[1] The word used is ἀντίτυπον, an answering pattern, which is found in two senses; either (1) where the τύπος is the archetype (the reality) of which the ἀντίτυπον is the copy or symbol (as in Heb. 9²⁴); or (2) where the τύπος is the symbol pointing forward to the ἀντίτυπον which is the reality (as in 1 Pet. 3²¹).

[2] So Harnack *DG.* i p. 360; Eng. tr. vol. ii p. 144: "The symbol is the mystery, and the mystery was not conceivable without a symbol. What we nowadays understand by 'symbol' is a thing which is not that which it represents; at that time 'symbol' denoted a thing which in some kind of way really is what it signifies." Really, except perhaps in Tertullian (who, however, Harnack says, is erroneously credited with a 'symbolical' doctrine), there is no suggestion of symbol in any way, I believe. The consecrated elements *are* (not 'are a symbol of') the flesh and blood of Christ. So, as Harnack concludes his statement, 'the *distinction* of a symbolic from a realistic conception of the Supper is altogether to be rejected'.

[3] Tert. *adv. Marc.* iv 40.

[4] *Jerem.* 11¹⁹ LXX: Δεῦτε καὶ ἐμβάλωμεν ξύλον εἰς τὸν ἄρτον αὐτοῦ—Tert. *adv. Marc.* iii 19: Venite, mittamus lignum in panem eius.

saying when he called bread his body, bread being a 'figure' of his body. Or again, when shewing how for the very sacraments it was necessary to make use of the works of creation which Gnostics despised, he says that the Lord " exhibits (*repraesentat*) his very own body " by bread.[1] There is no idea, in any of these passages, of making the bread a mere material symbol of the spiritual force of Christ conveyed by it.

So it is that, in expounding the intimate relation between the soul and the flesh in men, Tertullian argues that it is in and through the flesh that the soul is reached. " The flesh is washed, that the soul may be cleansed from stain; the flesh is anointed, that the soul may be hallowed; the flesh is signed with the cross, that the soul too may be guarded; the flesh is overshadowed by the imposition of the hands, that the soul too may be enlightened by the Spirit; the flesh feeds on the body and blood of Christ, that the soul too may be made full of God. They are joined together in action, they cannot therefore be separated in reward."[2] Here the idea is plain—it is really the body and blood of Christ that nourish the flesh, and so at the same time feed the soul. And, in like manner, in placing a spiritual interpretation on the clause of the Lord's prayer " Give us this day our daily bread ", he says " Christ is our bread, for Christ is life and bread is life. He says 'I am the bread of life'; and just before ' The bread is the Word of the living God, he who cometh down from heaven'. And, besides, to shew that his body is regarded as bread, there is the saying ' This is my body'. So, in making petition for daily bread, we are asking for continuance in Christ and inseparability from his body."[3] Clearly the conception is here, also, that participation in the consecrated bread is union with the body of Christ. The two are not distinguished except in thought.

[1] Tert. *adv. Marc.* i 14. The verb *repraesentare* does not suggest any imaginary or illusive portraiture or any kind of unreality (*e.g.* it is " to pay down in cash " and "to win back" completely something lost); see the Lexicons. See, however, also Swete *l.c.* p. 173 n. 5.

[2] Tert. *de Res. Carn.* 8. Yet, with reference to the saying that they must eat his flesh, he insists on other sayings, which contrast the flesh as profiting nothing with the life-giving Spirit, and protests that it was really the Word which was meant, and that the Lord only called it his flesh because the Word was made flesh (*de Res. Carn.* 37, though the argument is not obvious). [On the patristic interpretation of Jn. 6[63] see Gore *Dissertations* p. 303 ff.]

[3] Tert. *de Orat.* 6. quod et corpus eius in pane censetur ('is spoken of or reckoned in the class or category of bread').

The Conception of the Eucharist as a Sacrifice.
Clement, Ignatius, Justin, Cyprian

That the Eucharist was from the very first regarded as a sacrifice is certain—as the 'pure offering' which the prophet of old had declared should be offered to the name of the Lord in every place.[1]

Clement of Rome presupposes this idea, and describes the offering of the gifts as the chief function of the Christian ministers.[2] 'Sacrifice' is the term used in the *Didache* of the breaking of bread and giving of thanks,[3] and special reference is made to the prophecy of Malachi as " spoken by the Lord" about it. Ignatius does not actually apply the word itself to the celebration of the Eucharist, but the terms which he uses in connexion with it shew conclusively that his whole conception of the rite was coloured by this idea. "Take heed that ye keep one Eucharist only", he says, "for there is one flesh of our Lord Jesus Christ, and one cup of his blood to make all one : one place of sacrifice, as there is one bishop." [4] " Unless a man be within the place of sacrifice he is deprived of the bread of God." [5]

With Justin, in the chief account of the service which he gives,[6] the idea of sacrifice is latent rather than expressed. He represents the rite more particularly as one of grateful recognition of the saving work of Jesus and a memorial of his life, and the

[1] Mal. 1¹¹. Harnack, *DG.* Eng. tr. vol. i p. 269 notes various facts which would naturally lead to this view. The fulfilment of prophecy demanded a solemn Christian sacrifice. All prayers were regarded as sacrifice. The words of institution τοῦτο ποιεῖτε would naturally be understood by Gentile Christians in the sacrificial sense (ποιεῖν=θύειν), and anyhow denoted a definite religious act which must be a sacrifice. The offerings of bread and wine could only be regarded as προσφοραί for the purpose of a sacrifice. [For the term 'sacrifice' of praise and self-consecration see Rom. 12¹, Phil. 2¹⁷, Heb. 13¹⁵, 1 Pet. 2⁵.]
[2] Clem. Rom. *Ep.* 44, in connexion with the parallel he draws between them and the priests and Levites of old.
[3] *Didache* 14. The Eucharistic prayers in the *Didache* (9, 10) are probably the earliest extant.
[4] ἐν θυσιαστήριον, ὡς εἷς ἐπίσκοπος (sc. to offer the sacrifice) *Philad.* 4.
[5] *Eph.* 5, cf. *Trall.* 7, *Magn.* 7 (cf. *Rom.* 2, of the place of martyrdom). Lightfoot *ad. loc.* says, it would be an anachronism to suppose that Ignatius by the 'altar' means 'the Lord's table', and that the term is always metaphorical with him. But he shews that it means 'the place of sacrifice'; and it is certainly used by Ignatius in such peculiarly close association with the Eucharist as to prove that he deemed the Eucharist in some true sense a sacrifice. If he did not, why choose such a word at all ?
[6] Justin *Apol.* i 66.

means by which the power of that life is still communicated to his followers. As on behalf of our salvation he was incarnate, and took flesh and blood, so the Eucharistic food, his flesh and blood, still nourishes us.[1] But elsewhere [2] in incidental allusions, he speaks of the " sacrifices which Jesus Christ appointed to be made through his name, namely, in the Eucharist of the bread and cup ", and insists that it was to the Christian sacrifices that Malachi referred,[3] and not, as the Jews maintained, to the sacrifice of prayer offered by their brethren of the ' Dispersion throughout the world '; though he admits that prayers and thanksgivings made by those who are worthy are the only perfect sacrifices acceptable to God.

The allusions of Irenaeus to the sacrament reveal the same point of view. The Eucharist was certainly a sacrifice.[4]

The sacrificial aspect of the Eucharist is prominent also in Cyprian's conception of the rite. It is as a sacrifice and an offering, fulfilling types and prophecies of old, that he refers to it all through the letter he wrote to protest against the practice of using only water in the cup.[5] The mixture of water with the wine is right and significant; it ought not to be omitted.[6] But if the wine be omitted, there ceases to be the blood of Christ. Several arguments are adduced; but the really conclusive proof

---

[1] Cf. *Dial. c. Tryph.* 70.   [2] *Ibid. Dial. c. Tryph.* 117.

[3] *Dial. c. Tryph.* 41. "He foretells concerning the sacrifices which are offered to him in every place by the Gentiles, that is, the bread of the Eucharist and likewise the cup of the Eucharist." So this section opens with the saying that the offering of the meal, after cure from leprosy, was a figure of the bread of the Eucharist which our Lord commanded us to offer as a memorial of his passion . . . (τύπος τοῦ ἄρτου τῆς εὐχαριστίας, ὃν . . . ποιεῖν. Ποιεῖν seems to be used here in the sacrificial sense, but possibly the stress is on the εὐχαριστία and the act as a whole.)

[4] See the passages cited *supra* p. 401, and *adv. Haer.* iv 29. 5.

[5] *Ep.* 63.

[6] The cup which the Lord offered, he says, was a mixed cup, and it was wine that he said was his blood. Therefore it is clear that the blood of Christ is not offered, if wine be absent from the cup (*unde apparet sanguinem Christi non offerri, si desit vinum calici*). There is, of course, no doubt that—in accordance with custom at the time—the cup which was blessed by the Lord was wine diluted with water ; and it is not likely that water was ever omitted till much later times. See, particularly, the account of the service given by Justin, *Apol.* i 65 ; and the argument of Cyprian, *Ep.* 63. 13, here cited, in which he insists that both water and wine are needed to make the "cup of the Lord" (the water he says represents the Church or people, and the blood Christ, and the mixture of water and wine the union of his people with Christ). Harnack *Texte u. Unters.* vii 2, p. 117 ff. has endeavoured to shew that the use of water alone without wine was common in the second century ; but the use seems to have been exceptional and limited to ' heretical' circles.

is derived from the conception of the sacrifice. The sacrament is the sacrifice of Christ—the sacrament of the passion of the Lord and our redemption, and therefore it must be offered as he himself offered it. Human tradition must not infringe, or change into something else, a divine institution. "For if Jesus Christ our Lord and God is himself the High Priest of God the Father, and first offered himself as a sacrifice to the Father, and commanded that this should be done in commemoration of himself, it is clear that the priest who truly plays the part of Christ is he who imitates what Christ did, and that only then does he offer in the Church a true and full sacrifice to God the Father when he begins the offering as he sees that Christ himself made it." [1]

The idea of sacrifice, which was thus present from the first, may be traced through all subsequent ages.

The Nature of the Sacrifice

The nature of the sacrifice is regularly described as 'spiritual' or 'bloodless', in contrast with the material fleshly sacrifices of Jews and Gentiles alike, and as 'pure' and 'rational' service. It is a sacrifice of prayers and thanksgivings.

But none the less it is the body of Christ that is offered; and inasmuch as the Church is also in a true sense his body, it is an oblation of herself too that is made by the Church in the sacrament—by the Church, through her representative the celebrating priest, the Church identifying herself in this way with the sacrifice of Christ who is her Head.[2]

Clement of Alexandria

In the time of Clement the Eucharist was not, it seems, at Alexandria formally separated from the primitive Supper of the Lord—the Agape or Love-Feast—though formal separation had been made at an earlier date elsewhere. It was still held in the evening, whether publicly in church or privately in

---

[1] Cyprian *Ep.* 63. 14. The sacrifice offered is thus the passion of the Lord (*ibid.* 17). The phrase *quod Christus fecit imitatur* is noteworthy. There is no idea of a *repetition* of the act of Christ.

[2] See further, in regard to the nature of the sacrifice, Gore *The Body of Christ* esp. chap. iii. Though the actual expression 'offering the passion of the Lord' first appears in Cyprian, the conception seems to be earlier, if not original.

houses. The former was the public feast (δημώδης ἐστίασις),[1] probably already tending towards the form of the 'charity' supper, which was also held by invitation and alone survived in the later charitable doles and meals. The Agape in private houses was the ordinary family supper, hallowed by its connexion with the reading of Scripture, and intercession, and psalms and hymns—the family prayers—which made it a Eucharist.[2] At the former, no doubt, there would be present always the priest and the deacons; the latter, if it was as universal as it seems, can seldom have been attended by others than the members of the particular household.[3] In both cases alike the bread and the wine were hallowed by blessing and thanksgiving before the Supper which followed. In the case of the public Agape, the consecrated bread and wine were first distributed by the deacons, and in like manner the supper also afterwards.[4] The supper itself is a Eucharist. "He that eateth eateth unto the Lord and keepeth Eucharist with God . . . so that the food which is piously taken (τὴν δικαίαν τροφήν) is a Eucharist."[5]

But the terms in which this conception is expressed show clearly that Clement did distinguish between the Eucharist proper and the supper—the family or social meal—which to the Christian should assume the character of the higher rite. He is comparing the less with the greater. It is from God that all gifts come; the recognition by the Christian of the source from which they come makes the enjoyment of all alike—the less and the greater—a religious act. He uses, however, expressions which are clearly applicable only to the Eucharist in the higher sense.

The elements of bread and wine are 'hallowed food', the flesh and the blood of Christ; and he who eats receives into himself Christ's perfect self, and thereby incorruption and immortality. In a sense the elements are an allegory, and Clement's teaching has been supposed to be almost Zwinglian.[6] But anxious as he

---

[1] See Clement *Paed.* II i 12 (Dindorf's edition).   [2] *Ibid.* II i 10 (*ib.*).

[3] Similarly, in Cyprian *Ep.* 63. 16, the ordinary evening meal, which can be made a Eucharist (like the last supper), is contrasted with the morning Eucharist proper (at which the resurrection of the Lord is celebrated); and Cyprian expressly notes that the whole brotherhood could not be present at it. For the Agape see especially *Paed.* II i 10, 12 (*ib.*), and Bigg *Christian Platonists.*

[4] *Paed.* II i 11.   [5] *Ibid.* II i 10.

[6] See Bigg (*op. cit.* pp. 106, 107), who lays special stress on passages in which Clement speaks of the Gnosis as our reasonable food, and the eating and drinking of

always was to draw out the inner significance of all rites and ceremonies, and to emphasize the antithesis of the flesh (the letter) to the spirit, the phrases cited do not justify the Zwinglian interpretation. The consecrated elements are to Clement much more than the symbols—he clearly states that the bread, when "hallowed by the potency of the name", is not the same as it was, but "has been changed by potency into a spiritual potency".[1]

Origen

Origen speaks of the Eucharist in terms that are only compatible with the highest conceptions of it. The bread becomes "by reason of the prayer a kind of holy body and one that hallows those that with sound purpose use it";[2] it is "the body of the Lord" and not a particle of it must be dropped.[3]

But, on the other hand, he puts a purely spiritual interpretation on the words 'body' and 'blood', dealing with the bread and the wine as allegories or symbols of the spiritual illumination and knowledge which Christ confers on those who enter on the higher life.[4]

the divine Logos. The tendency in Clement "to distinguish the eucharistic body and blood of Christ from that in which He was born and suffered and died, as being 'spiritual' and not 'natural' or 'real', and thus a different body" (Gore *The Body of Christ* p. 61), must be taken into account here too. Later writers, who used similar expressions, intended by them only to mark the spiritual or heavenly manner in which the body and blood of Christ are bestowed upon us—the body which Christ now has (*i.e.* the risen and ascended body) being *the same* as that which suffered and died, *but glorified*, and this glorified body being that which is given in the Eucharist. It is the same body, the same manhood, but the manner of its existence and of its bestowal is heavenly and spiritual. The flesh and blood are the flesh and blood of the one living person who died and rose again.

[1] *Excerpta* 82, and see *Paed.* II ii 19, 20.

[2] *Contra Cels.* viii 33. [3] *In Exodum* Hom. xiii 3.

[4] See in *Matt. Com. Series*, 85, quoted by Bigg *op. cit.* p. 221. So it has been said that "whenever he speaks of the Supper, or indeed in a more general sense of the eating of the flesh or of the drinking of the blood of Christ, he does this without any reference to the body which he had as man, or to the blood which flowed in the veins of this body". In Origen's view 'the eucharistic body' was not really the Word himself, but a substitute for his appearance in the flesh ; and the bread was a symbol of this eucharistic body, rather than of his body offered up on the Cross. As under the old covenant the shewbread was placed before the eyes of God as a propitiatory memorial object, so the Church puts before God a bread which has a great propitiatory power—the commemoration of the passion and death of Christ.—Steitz, quoted by Harnack *DG.* Eng. tr. vol. iv p. 290.

Dr. Gore (*The Body of Christ* p. 60) points out that Origen witnesses against

Yet the body and the blood are none the less real on this account. If the interpretation be mystical or spiritual, yet the reality of the presence of Christ and of his gifts of spirit and life and immortality in the Eucharist is none the less certain. He gives himself to be eaten, and the eating is actual.

Cyril of Jerusalem

After the time of Origen the first important writing dealing with the Eucharist that calls for study [1] is the work of Cyril of Jerusalem. His catechetical lectures form indeed the first

himself that his special conception was not the common faith of the Church ("Let the bread and the cup be conceived by the simple according to the commoner acceptation of the Eucharist; but to those who have learned to hear with a deeper ear, according to the divine promise, even that of the nourishing word of the truth . . ."), and that his depreciation of the 'flesh' is part of his allegorism and general depreciation of the merely historical sense of Scripture.

[1] Harnack notes that with Eusebius (*Demonstr. ev.* i 10 and *de eccles. theologia* iii 12) the offering of the memorial of the body passes over into the offering of the body; the consecrated elements possess the value of symbols of the actual body which was once offered up. As to Athanasius, he says it is impossible to extract a doctrine from his confused statements, but that he probably comes near to Origen in his conceptions. (The references in Athanasius to the sacrament are few.) See *Ep. ad Serap.* iv 19 (written some years after Cyril's lectures) with regard to the saying 'It is the spirit that maketh alive, the flesh profiteth nothing; the words which I have spoken to you are spirit and life'. "He used both expressions, flesh and spirit, of himself, and he distinguished the spirit from the flesh, in order that believing not only that which is visible of him, but also that which is invisible, they might learn that what he said is not fleshly but spiritual. Why, for how many men would his body have sufficed for meat, that it might become food for the whole world? It was just on this account that he spoke of the ascending up into heaven of the Son of Man, to draw them away from the corporeal conception, so that they might learn that the flesh of which he spoke was heavenly meat from above, and spiritual food given by him. For, What I have spoken to you, he says, is spirit and life. And this is equivalent to saying: What is exhibited and given on behalf of the salvation of the world is the flesh which I bear: but this and its blood shall be given you spiritually by me as food, so that spiritually this shall be distributed in each of you and become for all a safeguard for the resurrection to life eternal." This passage might seem to imply that the body and blood of Christ were not really, but only spiritually, received in the Eucharist. But according to the interpretation which Athanasius follows in the immediate context, the flesh represents the outward and visible (the body—the bread), and the spirit the inner invisible (the divinity— the divine person or nature); so that a truer inference would be that the body of Christ with the divinity was present in the Eucharist, and that the invisible part was no less to be believed than the visible which was apparent. (So B. de Mont-faucon *ed.* Philo.)

Besides this passage there is only a phrase or two, shewing the reality of the rite, but not further elucidating the conception of the relation between the outward and the inward.

deliberate attempt with which we are acquainted to provide a formal exposition of the teaching of the Church for catechumens on this and other fundamental doctrines, though doubtless every catechist was accustomed to give similar instruction to his pupils in his measure.

Cyril teaches that those who are permitted to share in the mysteries of the Eucharist become of one body and one blood with Christ.[1] In accordance with his own words, the bread and wine must be held to be his body and blood. As he changed the water into wine at Cana, so he changes the wine into blood. In the figure ($\tau\acute{\nu}\pi\circ\varsigma$) of bread is given the body, and in the figure of wine is given the blood. So we become Christ-bearers, when his body and his blood are distributed into our members,[2] and partakers of the divine nature. The heavenly bread and the cup of salvation hallow soul and body. To sense and taste, no doubt, the bread and the wine remain what they were; but faith in the declaration of the Lord assures us that we have bestowed upon us his very body and blood. It was to this table, this cup, this bread that prophets and psalmists of old looked forward—here is found the mystic or spiritual meaning of their sayings. That which appears to be bread is not bread (even though it is so to the sense of taste), but the body of Christ; and that which appears to be wine is not wine (even though the taste will have it that it is), but the blood of Christ.

The time of communion is said to be an hour most awe-inspiring.[3]

The invocation of the Holy Spirit and his descent upon the elements set out upon the altar hallows them, and changes them into the body and blood of Christ.[4]

Then the rite is completed. It is a spiritual sacrifice, a bloodless service,[5] a propitiatory sacrifice, offered by way of intercession for all who are in need of help. It is a holy and most awful sacrifice that is set forth—it is nothing less than Christ slain on behalf of our sins that is offered.[6]

---

[1] σύσσωμοι καὶ σύναιμοι τοῦ χριστοῦ *Cat. Myst.* iv 1.

[2] Or *v.l.* "having received of his body . . . into our members". See Gifford 'Cyril of Jerusalem' *Nicene and Post-Nicene Fathers, ad loc.*

[3] *Cat. Myst.* v 4. Cyril's addresses throughout, it must be remembered, have a devotional character. His object is as much edification as scientific exposition.

[4] *Ibid.* 7 (μεταβάλλειν is the verb used, as above).

[5] *Ibid.* 8. πνευματικὴ θυσία, ἀναίμακτος λατρεία, θυσία ἱλασμοῦ.

[6] *Ibid.* 10.

So when bidden to " taste and see that the Lord is good ", the testing must be entrusted to undoubting faith ; for that which is to be tasted is the sacrament of the body and blood of Christ,[1] to be received as a king in the hands prepared as a throne, more precious than gold and precious stones.

In this exposition the conception of a real offering of the body and blood of Christ himself as slain for sins is clear. The elements have been changed and have become what they were not before, though to the senses still the same. That is to say, the outward and visible sign is still there—to the senses which deal with the outward and visible only ; but he who receives the outward and visible sign really receives the very body and blood of Christ. *How*, Cyril does not attempt to say.

The new points in this teaching, or rather the developments of the expression and interpretation of the traditional — not always articulate — belief of the Church, are obvious.

By Gregory of Nyssa, a little later, the ideas of Cyril are carried on, and fresh lines of interpretation are opened out.

Gregory of Nyssa

The exposition of the sacraments which Gregory of Nyssa gives in his apologetic statement of the faith,[2] written about 385, is intended to commend the teaching of the Church by analogies from ordinary human experience. Through the sacraments man is brought into special relation to God, as he is in other respects through other means. Baptism unites the soul to God; the Eucharist unites the body to God. That it is necessary for mankind to partake in both he does not certainly say, but he declares that those who have no part in the cleansing from sin which the 'mystic water' gives must be cleansed hereafter by fire (ch. xxxv).

In the first generation of a man it is from moisture that God gives life and produces man (ch. xxxiii), without prayer or invocation of his aid on the part of the parents, from a very small beginning. Similarly in Baptism, by a higher generation, effected through water with prayer to God and invocation of heavenly

---

[1] ἀντίτυπον σώματος κ.τ.λ. (the *sign* . . .).

[2] *Oratio Catechetica* ch. xxxiii–xxxvii (Eng. tr. 'Gregory of Nyssa' *N. and P.-N. F.*). See the edition with notes by J. H. Srawley.

grace [1] and faith, new life is given and a transformation into a spiritual state effected. "The presence of a divine influence refashions what is born with a corruptible nature into a state of incorruption." The whole process of Baptism represents the process through which the Author of our life and Captain of our salvation himself passed ; the trine immersion corresponding to the death, the burial, the resurrection (ch. xxxv). In this way the soul of man is fused into him, and the act of union with the life implies a fellowship with the life.[2] Similarly, in another way, through the Eucharist (ch. xxxvi), the body comes into fellowship with him. We have received poison into our bodies,[3] and we need some antidote to undo the mischief introduced into the body by the poison. This antidote can only be the very Body which has been shewn to be superior to death, which— when it is in ours—changes and translates the whole into itself (πρὸς ἑαυτὸ μεταποιεῖ καὶ μετατίθησιν). The antidote can only be appropriated by being eaten. So that one body is always being distributed to the faithful throughout the world; though given in portions it enters whole into each individual, and it still remains whole in itself. How this is done it is not easy

[1] Gregory contrasts the work of God in the birth of a man, when his aid is not invoked, with his work in Baptism, when he is specially invoked. He might be understood to say (in ch. xxxiv) that the grace of Baptism is independent of the prayers offered. But the general argument must determine the meaning of incidental phrases, and his argument is that God (through Christ) promised his presence in Baptism when invoked—that is, when he ordered his disciples to baptize into the name of the Father, Son, and Holy Spirit. The use of the name of the Trinity is an invocation, and in effect a prayer for the promised presence ; and it was ordered as an essential part of the rite. Those, therefore, who argue that, because God is universally present, it is not necessary to invoke his presence in Baptism, or that there is no special guarantee of his presence when invoked, are mistaken.

[2] The proof that the Holy Spirit is really given in baptism he finds in the essential truthfulness of God, who in the person of Christ (whose miracles prove that he was God come in the flesh) promised that if called in a particular way (as he is in baptism) he would come (ch. xxxiv). The resurrection to the new life, therefore, undoubtedly takes place in baptism, but human nature is so weak that it can only realize its full effect gradually and by strenuous moral effort.

[3] The poison of sin and corruption which entered when the apple was eaten, cf. the phrase of Ignatius ἀντίδοτος τοῦ μὴ ἀποθανεῖν. Only with Gregory the whole force of the sacrament seems to be regarded as directed to the *bodies* of men. Baptism secures the communication of the divine life to the *soul*, but the corruption of the *body* is only to be counteracted by the gift of the Eucharist—the communication, that is, to the bodies of men of the body which has overcome death. The tendency to regard this as the special virtue of the Eucharist, which we have seen in Irenaeus and Cyril, finds its strongest expression in this teaching of Gregory.

to understand, but an analogy may help. The human body remains in existence simply through a force called nourishment, that is introduced into it, which is changed into the 'nature' (or 'form') of the body. This nourishment (bread and wine) may therefore be said to be the body. Now the body of the incarnate Christ was nourished and sustained by bread and wine, and, by the indwelling of God the Word, was transmuted to the dignity of the Godhead. In the same way the bread which is consecrated by the word of God is changed into the body of God the Word — not by the process of eating, but at once.[1] The bread and wine together form his flesh (the bread becomes body, and the wine becomes blood), and by means of it he implants himself in every believer. He gives these gifts by virtue of the benediction through which he 'transelements' the natural quality of these visible things to that immortal thing.[2] That is to say, the consecrated bread and wine are the flesh of Christ,

---

[1] πρὸς τὸ σῶμα μεταποιούμενος. μεταποιεῖν 'transmake' is used by Gregory (see Pusey *The Doctrine of the Real Presence as contained in the Fathers* p. 162 ff.) of various kinds of change:—of our own bodies, which while yet mortal and corruptible, receive the principle of immortality, by union with our Lord's body; of our Lord's own human body to a divine dignity by the indwelling of the Word; of the food eaten by our Lord being assimilated to his human body; of the sacramental change of the elements; of the change effected through regeneration in Baptism. It therefore clearly does not in any special way denote any material change. (μετατιθέναι and μεθιστάναι are used as practically synonyms.)

[2] μεταστοιχειώσας τὴν φύσιν. The word μεταστοιχειοῦν (see Pusey *op. cit.* p. 180 ff.) is used of the Eucharist by Gregory only, in this one passage; though it is frequently used in other connexions by him and by others, always of changes of condition (moral or spiritual), not of substance or of matter. Thus Gregory uses it of the change of condition of our Lord's human nature after the resurrection, of the religious change of nature in us, of the change of the body to incorruption, of the regeneration in Baptism: and similar usages are found in Cyril Al. and other writers of the fourth and fifth centuries, as also of the word ἀναστοιχειοῦν. In neither word, Pusey maintains, is there any reference to the 'elements' of which a thing is composed: neither, by the mere force of the word, has reference to any physical change. Pusey's argument is conclusive as regards the terms, but Mr. Srawley thinks he hardly does justice to Gregory's treatment as a whole: the crucial point in which is the statement that bread and wine become actually and immediately the Body and Blood of the Lord, in contrast with the process of digestion by which when eaten they become human body, the elements (στοιχεῖα) being rearranged under a new form (εἶδος). The idea seems to be not the substitution of one element for another, but the rearrangement of the same elements and the imposition upon them of a new 'form', due to the new relation into which the elements of bread and wine have been brought, resulting in their possession of new qualities or properties. (This is practically the change of condition of which Pusey speaks.)

The στοιχεῖα are of course the constituents of the bread and of the wine, not the 'elements' in the modern sense in connexion with the Eucharist.

and through that flesh he blends himself with the bodies of believers, who thus by union with the immortal (*i.e.* the body of Christ) become sharers in incorruption.

This is in effect the teaching of Cyril of Jerusalem, that by partaking of the body and blood of Christ a believer becomes σύσσωμος καὶ σύναιμος αὐτοῦ (*C. M.* iv 3) and χριστοφόρος; but he developes the view of the change in the elements in a way that has seemed to some to be identical in idea, though not in word, with the mediaeval doctrine of transubstantiation. As, however, the expression of that doctrine depends entirely on a particular metaphysical terminology, and Gregory speaks of a change of form only, and not of a change of substance as well, the term 'transformation' expresses his teaching with less risk of misunderstanding.

But perhaps the most characteristic feature in the teaching of Gregory is the more exact expression which he gives to the conception of the Eucharist as the means by which the special purpose of the Incarnation is still being worked out in the world. This thought, no doubt, underlies the earlier teaching which has been reviewed, but with Gregory of Nyssa it becomes explicit. The Eucharist is in a special sense the extension of the Incarnation. As the Church is the body of Christ, and through the Church he still works, as of old he worked through his visible body on earth, carrying on through it the process which he then began, so in a special sense in the Sacraments is the process of the Incarnation continued. Gregory does not speak of the Church in this connexion, but he marks the conception clearly both in regard to Baptism (ch. xxxv) and in regard to the Eucharist (ch. xxxvii)—the sacraments which are enjoyed only by the ministry of the Church,—in both of which alike, though in different ways, we become partakers of Christ. The special purpose of the Incarnation is the redemption of man, which Gregory conceives as the 'deification' of human nature (chs. xxxii–xxxv), through the union of Christ with humanity. That union was effected in the Incarnation, and is still being effected through Baptism and the Eucharist, in which accordingly the work of redemption is still being carried on.[1]

The body which the Lord bore, so Gregory argues, was sustained as all other human bodies are sustained, that is, by bread. The bread enters the body, and becomes part of it, so

[1] The same conception is expressed by Hilary of Poictiers see Note p. 425.

that it may indeed be truly said that the body is what its chief constituent is. The body of the Lord was therefore bread, and the body was transformed to a divine dignity by the dwelling in it of the word of God. So in the Eucharist the bread, by God's word and command, is hallowed and sanctified and transformed into the body of the Lord. It is true the analogy is not quite exact. The bread which sustained, and thus made, the body which the Lord bore upon earth required to be eaten; only through the process of eating could it become his body. But in the Eucharist the change is immediate without any process of eating.[1]

Chrysostom

Still stronger expressions are used by Chrysostom. The bread and wine become the very body and blood of Christ, 'the body pierced with nails'. We bury our teeth in his flesh; by his most awful blood our tongue is reddened.[2] Chrysostom would have the sacrifice and feast approached with awe and devotion, and he lets his emotions and warm imagination have free expression in language calculated to arouse the proper feelings and make the worshipper vividly conscious of the sacrifice and presence of Christ. Of the consecration he says, "Christ is present, and he who arranged that first table, even he arranges this present one. For it is not man who makes the things which are set before us become the body and blood of Christ; but it is Christ himself, who was crucified for us. The priest stands fulfilling his part by uttering the appointed words, but the power and the grace are of God. 'This is my body' he says. This expression changes [3] the elements; and as that sentence 'increase and multiply', once spoken, extends through all time and gives to our nature the power to reproduce itself; even so that saying 'this is my body', once uttered, does at every

---

[1] This is not said with reference to the recipient of the consecrated elements in communion, but only to mark the instantaneous character of the change effected, in contrast with the natural process by which the bread became the body of the Lord on earth. (It is, however, obvious that Gregory held that the elements became the body of the Lord prior to and independently of any reception by communicants. The presence was objective τῇ δυνάμει τῆς εὐλογίας and unconditioned.)

[2] See passages cited by Harnack *DG*. Eng. tr. vol. iv p. 297. The licence of the rhetorical 'popular' preacher must be borne in mind in considering Chrysostom's language.

[3] μεταρρυθμίζει *i.e.* re-orders : elsewhere μετασκευάζει *i.e.* re-fashions.

table in the Churches from that time to the present day, and even till Christ's coming, make the sacrifice complete."[1] Of the sacrifice too he speaks in no uncertain tone. It is a real sacrifice that is offered daily;[2] but it is not one victim to-day and another to-morrow, but always the same; and therefore the sacrifice is one. "There is one Christ everywhere, complete both in this world and in the other; one body. As then, though offered in many places, he is but one body, so there is but one sacrifice. . . . We offer that now which was offered then; which is indeed inconsumable. . . . We do not then offer a different sacrifice as the high priest formerly did, but always the same; or, rather, we celebrate a memorial of a Sacrifice." Thus, in the same breath, while insisting that it is a sacrifice that is offered daily in the Eucharist, he also calls it, rather, a memorial of a sacrifice. And while styling it a sacrifice, he lays no less stress on it as a holy feast, which feeds and hallows those who partake of it.

Ambrose and Augustine

No further developement of the doctrine took place till later times. Ambrose and Augustine do not really make any fresh contribution to the subject, though Ambrose[3] ransacks the Old

---

[1] *De Prod. Jud.* vol. ii, *Hom.* i c. 6—Stephen's *Life of St Chrysostom* p. 413.

[2] *In Ep. ad Hebr. Hom.* xvii c. 3 (*ibid.*). See note on ʻDaily Celebrationʼ *infra* p. 419.

[3] The teaching of Ambrose is given in his treatise *De Mysteriis* o. viii ff. (§ 43). Lest any one should in any way disparage the gift of the sacrament, judging by what he sees (since the invisible things of it cannot be perceived by human eyes), and remembering the gift of manna to the Jews of old; he first essays to prove that the sacraments of the Church are older and more imposing than those of the synagogue. He finds the origin of the Eucharist in the bread and wine which was given to Abraham by Melchisedek, who was Christ himself (sine matre secundum divinitatem . . . sine patre secundum incarnationem); and, in contrasting the bread of the Eucharist with the manna, he describes it as giving eternal life and incorruptibility. The manna and the water from the rock were wonderful enough, but they were only the shadow and figure of the light and the reality which were to come. The Jews had figures (? types, symbols) of the body and blood of Christ, but Christians have the realities themselves.

In the search for parallels which follows, he asks whether the word of Christ, by which the sacrament is effected, is not able to change the species of the elements, to change things into something different from what they were, when it was able to make all things out of nothing. (By ʻelementsʼ he means the ʻconstituentsʼ of the bread and of the wine—the $\sigma\tauο\iota\chi\epsilonῖα$ of Gregory of Nyssa, and by ʻspeciesʼ the distinctive natures or ʻkindsʼ.) It is not of course the natural order of experience that is seen in the sacrament which gives us the body of Christ, but how could that be expected when the birth itself was outside the natural order of experience?

Testament to find figures of the Sacrament, and Augustine [1] gives graphic expression to ideas which earlier writers and teachers had made familiar, and accident has connected with his name in particular. In doing this he shews the ambiguities and uncertainties which are characteristic of early exposition of the sacraments, perhaps because he gives more definite expression than some of the earlier writers to the various aspects in which the sacraments can be regarded; and therefore the authority of his name is claimed for every theory of the Eucharist which has been suggested.

But the flesh of Christ was real flesh, and the sacrament is really the sacrament of his flesh. The body which we make (in the Eucharist) is the body born of the Virgin. (The principle of the Incarnation is carried on in the Sacrament.) "The Lord Jesus himself exclaims 'This is my body'. One *species* is named before the benediction of the heavenly words; after the consecration it is signified as the body. He himself says his blood. Before consecration one thing is said, after consecration it is called blood. . . . With these sacraments Christ feeds his Church, and by them the soul is strengthened." Christ is in the Sacrament because it is the body of Christ, and therefore it is spiritual food, not material (corporalis); for the body of God is a spiritual body, and the body of Christ is the body of the divine spirit, because Christ is Spirit. There is nothing here of the natural order, it is all the excellency of grace.

From this exposition it is clear that Ambrose believed, as all at the time believed, that Christ was really present in the sacrament; that the bread and wine were 'changed' by consecration, becoming what they were not before; that the whole experience was outside the order of nature and belonged to the spiritual sphere.

The instances taken from the O.T. are the rod of Moses becoming a serpent, the rivers of Egypt changed into blood, the passage of the Jordan, the water from the rock, the bitter water made sweet, the iron axe-head made to swim. The two last cases are brought by Ambrose into the closest relation with his argument. The *nature* of the water, the *species* of the iron, are changed; but the water and the iron are still the same (*i.e.* they have only acquired a new character). The inference would be that the bread and wine are still bread and wine, though they have become the body and blood of Christ as our spiritual food. This is probably all that he meant by the phrase "hoc quod conficimus corpus" (§ 53); at least, it is not sufficient evidence that Ambrose taught that Christ's body was really offered anew by the priest.

[1] Some of Augustine's definitions and phrases that apply to sacraments in general have been already cited.

Many of the expressions he used justify the description of his conception of the Eucharist as decidedly 'symbolical' (Loofs *Leitfaden*[3] p. 224).

He cites the words of institution as an example of figurative speech ("the Lord did not shrink from saying 'This is my body' when he was giving the sign of his body"). He finds the significance of the Lord's Supper in the discourse in John 6— "to have faith in him, *that* is to eat living bread". The 'Communion of the body of Christ' is the association of love which is found in the Church, which is the body of Christ; and in like manner the sacrifice of the body of Christ, which is represented in the Eucharist, is the self-sacrifice of the Church (*in Joh.* xxvi 1).

That is to say, he speaks as though eating the flesh of Christ and having a living faith were one and the same thing (cf. 'believe, and thou hast eaten', *in Joh.* xxv 12); and he declares that he who does not abide in Christ, and in

27

INFANT COMMUNION

The practice probably goes back as far as the universal acceptance of infant baptism; but the first mention of it is by Cyprian in his account of an infant girl taken by its nurse to taste the heathen sacrifices in time of persecution and afterwards by its mother, in ignorance of what had happened, to the Christian Eucharist (*de Lapsis* 25). The child by divine instinct, though unconscious of the enormity and unable to speak, refused to open her mouth. The deacon insisted, and poured in some drops of wine: but the Eucharist refused to remain in the polluted body and mouth of the child. Infant communion was clearly then the recognized practice of the Church of Africa. To eat the flesh of the Son of Man and to drink his blood was necessary in order to have life (cf. *Testim.* iii. 25).

So too in the order of the service prescribed in the *Apostolical Constitutions* (viii 12), directions are given to the mothers to take to

---

whom Christ does not abide, certainly neither eats his flesh nor drinks his blood, though he does eat and drink the sacrament (*ibid.* xxvii 18). He insists that ' what is visibly celebrated must be invisibly understood' (*in Ps.* 98⁹). So it is fairly said that support for the 'receptionist' theory can be obtained from him, while he resists the realistic interpretation.

Yet elsewhere, with reference to St Paul's words to the Corinthians (1 Cor. 9²⁹), he says that to all alike it is the body of the Lord and the blood of the Lord (*de Bapt. c. Don.* v 9); and in other passages he seems to identify the sacramental body of the Lord with the real body. (Harnack thinks no passages clearly support this view, though they can be at a first glance, and soon were, understood in this way.)

Apparently the dominant conception of the effects of this Sacrament in Augustine's mind was that it effected incorporation into Christ's body, that is, into the Church. The full significance of this conception can only be realized when it is remembered that at the same time he held firmly the belief that outside the Church there was no salvation; that no one could belong to the unity of the Church who had not love; and that love could only be obtained in the Church, and could only be preserved in the unity of the Church. It is the union of these conceptions with the unhesitating assertion of the objective validity of the sacrament in itself, independently of the personal character of the ministrant (see note on Heretical Baptism *supra* p. 388), that specially characterizes the teaching of Augustine. (So Loofs *op. cit.* p. 207 says he must be regarded as the founder of the Western doctrine of the Sacraments, though he scarcely altered at all the old conception of what a Sacrament was.)

[Gore *Dissertations* p. 233 summarizes Augustine's doctrine of the Eucharist under three heads as follows:—(1) the consecrated elements are signs of the body and blood, and not in themselves the things they signify; (2) the spiritual gift of the Eucharist is really the flesh and blood of Christ; the same flesh and blood in which he lived on earth, but raised to a new spiritual power, become 'spirit and life'; (3) this gift he sometimes speaks of as given to all, good and bad, alike; but at other times he explicitly identifies 'eating the flesh of Christ' with 'abiding in Christ' and with a living faith.]

them their children (when all non-communicants are bidden to withdraw); a clause on behalf of 'the infants of thy people' is included among the petitions to God for the congregation then present; and a special place is assigned for the communion of the children (after the various 'orders' and before the general body of the people). It was thus the custom of the Churches of the East also, probably as early as Cyprian's time.

The evidence available comes from the East and from Africa, but there is no reason to suppose that these Churches were peculiar in their use. (There was no movement within the Church against the practice till the ninth century—see Art. 'Children' *D.C.A.* It is still retained in the Greek Church.)

DEATH-BED COMMUNION

The conception of the Eucharist as a means of spiritual food and strengthening, the channel of eternal life (cf. Ignatius φάρμακον ἀθανασίας), as well as of the closest union with the Lord, led naturally to the desire for it when death was imminent.

The Council of Nicaea (Canon 13) declared the custom to be the ancient and canonical law of the Church, and ordered that no one at the point of death should be deprived of this last and most necessary *viaticum* (τοῦ τελευταίου καὶ ἀναγκαιοτάτου ἐφοδίου μὴ ἀποστερεῖσθαι).

DAILY CELEBRATION OF THE EUCHARIST

The passage from one of Chrysostom's homilies cited in the text (p. 416) shews incidentally the practice. There are frequent references to it in his sermons, particularly in connexion with the neglect of the people to take advantage of their opportunities. The customs of different Churches varied. From the earliest times the faithful received once a week, on the Lord's day, and probably on other days as well, by no fixed rule. The anniversary festivals of martyrs were probably always kept in this way. Certainly they were in Tertullian's time, and the stationary days —Wednesday and Friday—in every week as well (cf. Tert. *de Orat.* 14), and every day from Easter to Pentecost. In other Churches Saturday too was observed, at least in the fourth century (see Basil *Ep.* 219 and *Ep.* 93 *infra* p. 421). From the time of Cyprian the greater Churches, at all events in Africa, had daily celebrations (see Cypr. *de Orat. Dom.* 18), as they had in Augustine's time (Aug. *Ep.* 118, *in Joan. Tract.* xxvi 15), and, by the testimony of Jerome, at Rome and in Spain (*Epp.* 50, 28). For other references see Bingham *Antiquities* bk. xv ch. ix (*e.g.* Eusebius and Ambrose shew the same custom).

RESERVATION OF THE SACRAMENT

That reservation of the consecrated elements was freely practised is clearly shewn by the comments of the earliest writers to which we can appeal.

Justin Martyr, in the passage already quoted (p. 398), says,[1] "Those who are called deacons among us give to every one who is present some of the eucharistic bread and wine and water to partake of, and to those who are not present they take it away ". The words are clear and simple, but the course of procedure actually followed cannot be regarded as certainly ascertained. We naturally infer that those who were present at once consumed what was given them, and it is possible that the deacons bore the elements at once to those who were not present and that they received them from their hands and at once consumed them in like manner.[2] But it is equally consistent with the words which are used if the worshippers present reserved for later use all or part of that which they received, and if those who were absent in like manner reserved for a convenient opportunity (their time of private prayers) the consecrated elements which were brought to them. (There is no reason to suppose that it was only to the sick that the deacons went; in those days at least there might be many good reasons for absence.) And it is a practice of this kind that we meet with in the next reference to customs connected with the Eucharist which has to be considered.

Tertullian in his tract on Prayer[3] refers to the objection which some felt to taking part in the sacrificial prayers (the service of the Eucharist) on vigil-days,[4] thinking that the vigil would be broken by reception of the Body of the Lord. In reply to this objection Tertullian asks whether the Eucharist destroys the allegiance vowed to God, or rather binds it closer to Him. "Will not", he says, "your vigil-day be all the better kept if you have also stood at the altar of God? By receiving the Body of the Lord and reserving it you will secure both ends—participation in the sacrifice and performance of your obligation. If

---

[1] Justin *Apol.* i 65.

[2] Thus Bishop Westcott could write 'It is clear to me Justin Martyr describes coincident and not subsequent administration to the absent' (*Life and Letters* vol. ii p. 274).

[3] Tert. *de Orat.* 14 (19).

[4] The days to which the term *statio* (*stationes*) was applied. The name is undoubtedly connected with the military use of the word for 'encampment' or 'post', set for watch or guard. So Christians adopted the practice of setting apart special days (Wednesday and Friday in each week, it seems) on which by prayer and fasting they kept their watch. That fasting was part of the observance seems to be shewn by other references in Tertullian (*de Jejun.* 10, 13, 14); but as the *stationes* of Wednesday and Friday seem to be in some way distinguished from the *jejunia* of Saturday, it is better to render 'vigil day' than 'fast-day'. In this passage Tertullian plays on the derivation of *statio* from *stare* 'to stand'.

'vigil' gets its name from a practice of soldiers (and surely we are the soldiers of God), it is certain that no rejoicing and no sorrow which a camp experiences interferes with the soldiers' vigil (watch). The only difference is that the practice is observed more willingly in time of rejoicing, more anxiously in time of sorrow." That is to say, Tertullian argues that it is better to attend the celebration of the Eucharist—to participate in the sacrifice, and to receive the consecrated elements, yet not to consume them on the spot, for that would be to break the 'vigil' —but to take them home (and, doubtless when the vigil was over, to partake of them at the time of private prayers). Their vigil need not be sorrowful and anxious; the rejoicing which may be theirs, by sharing in the early morning Eucharist, will carry them more willingly and gladly through the hours of the vigil-day.

The only question which is left undetermined by the evidence of these two passages is, when and how the elements so reserved were used. From another passage in Tertullian's writings it would appear that some were accustomed to take a morsel of the bread before each meal, or before any other food in the morning.[1]

A little later Cyprian bears witness to the practice of reservation by an incidental illustration of the thesis that the vengeance of God falls on sinners who elude the notice of their fellow-men. He tells the tale[2] of a woman who tried to open with unworthy hands the casket in which she had 'the holy of the Lord' (*Sanctum Domini*), but a flame of fire shot out from it and frightened her from daring to touch it,—a reference which clearly shews a practice so established that a special vessel for the purpose was in use.

That this custom of reservation by private persons in their own houses for their own use continued without check or hindrance from ecclesiastical authority is shewn remarkably by a letter of Basil[3] late in the fourth century (372 A.D.).

"It is good and beneficial", writes Basil, "to communicate every day, and to partake of the holy body and blood of Christ. For he distinctly says 'He that eateth my flesh and drinketh my blood hath eternal life'. And who doubts that to share frequently in life is the same thing as to have manifold life? I indeed communicate four times a week: on the Lord's day, on Wednesday, on Friday, and on the Sabbath, and on the other days if there is a commemoration of any saint. It is needless to point out that for any one in times of persecution to be compelled to take the communion in his own hand without the presence of

---

[1] Tert. *ad Uxorem* ii 5 (the case of a Christian wife and a heathen husband) "Will not your husband know what it is you take a morsel of secretly before all other food (*ante omnem cibum*)?—and if he knows it is bread, he will not believe it is the bread you say it is."

[2] Cyprian *de Lapsis* 26 (21). [3] *Ep.* 93

a priest or minister is not a serious offence, as long custom sanctions this practice from the facts themselves. All the solitaries in the desert, where there is no priest, take the communion themselves, keeping communion at home. And at Alexandria and in Egypt each one of the laity, for the most part, keeps the communion at his own house, and participates in it when he likes. For when once the priest has completed the offering and given it, the recipient participating in it each time entire is bound to believe that he properly takes and receives it from the giver. And even in the Church, when the priest gives the portion, the recipient takes it with complete power over it, and so lifts it to his lips with his own hand. It has the same validity whether one portion or several portions are received from the priest at the same time " (Trans. *N. and P.-N.F.*).

The recipient of this letter had evidently no scruple on the subject of reservation of the Sacrament in general; his only doubt was whether it was right to partake without the presence of a priest who would administer as in the Church.

But the custom, it is obvious, might easily be abused, and it was prohibited by the Council of Saragossa in 380, the third canon of which declares anathema " whoever does not consume the holy Eucharist given him in church", though it is not certain whether the Council intended to forbid the practice as a whole or only some particular mode of it.[1] By degrees the custom dropped into desuetude—so far as regards reservation by lay people.[2]

Reservation even by priests, for the purpose of communicating the laity, is said to have been prohibited by an Armenian canon of the fourth century;[3] but the practice of reserving, by the clergy, at least for the sick and for sudden emergencies, if not for their own use,[4] appears to have been universal. There is no trace of reservation for the purpose of adoration.

OBLATIONS FOR THE DEAD

The conception of the Eucharist as the sacrifice of the Cross (*passio est enim Domini sacrificium quod offerimus*, Cyprian *Ep.* 63. 17), and the propitiatory value which was believed to belong to the Eucharistic commemoration of the death of Christ, are illustrated by the practice of associating the faithful departed with the living in the Eucharistic

---

[1] See Hefele *Councils* vol. ii p. 293 (Eng. tr.).

[2] It was still normal in the time of Jerome (see *Ep.* 48 *ad Pammach.* § 15).

[3] See W. E. Scudamore Art. 'Reservation' *D.C.A.* Exception was made in case of sickness.

[4] Bishops, priests, and monks are known to have carried the reserved elements with them on journeys. See further the Art. in *D.C.A.*

prayers. How far back the practice goes cannot be determined. Its origin is perhaps to be found in the solemn commemoration of martyrs which was held at their tombs on the days of their death (their 'birthdays'), in which thanksgiving for their examples and the constancy of their faith came to be combined with prayer for their present welfare. (See *e.g. The Martyrdom of Polycarp* 18.) From the time of Tertullian, in the Church of Africa, at all events, the Eucharist was expressly offered for the departed and was believed to be of special benefit to them. Tertullian several times refers to the custom, evidently as nothing new, but as the established practice of the Church. ' We make oblations annually ' he says ' for the departed, for their birthdays ' (*de Cor.* 3). A husband who has lost his wife prays for her spirit and offers annual oblations for her (*de exhort. cast.* 11, where the practice is referred to as an impediment to second marriages). So too a woman prays for the soul of her husband, and implores for him a time of refreshment (*refrigerium interim adpostulat ei*) and a share in the first resurrection, and makes an oblation each year on the day of his decease (*de Monogam.* 10). And Cyprian, in like manner, speaks of oblations and sacrifices being offered, with annual commemoration, for martyrs and other deceased members of the Church (*Epp.* 12. 2, 39. 3, 1. 2). So normal was the practice that a man might be punished for violating an ecclesiastical law (*e.g.* by appointing a priest as his executor), by being deprived of the oblation for the repose of his soul (*ibid. Ep.* 1. 2), just as exclusion from participation in the Eucharist was the severest penalty that could be inflicted on him in his lifetime. And Augustine [1] at a later time could claim the universal custom of the Church and the tradition of the fathers in support of the practice of offering the sacrifice for those who had died in the communion of Christ's body and blood, declaring that there was no doubt that the dead were thereby helped so that the Lord would deal with them more mercifully than their sins deserved (*Sermo* 172. 2). So he records the earnest entreaty of his mother, Monica, to be remembered when the solemn rites at the altar were performed ; and other references in his writings shew his belief in the expiatory power of the sacrifices of the altar offered by the living for the dead (cf. *Enchiridion* 110, *Confess.* ix 27, 32, 35, *de Cura pro Mortuis* 3).

It is in the sense of this explicit teaching that the expressions used in all the ancient liturgies, and the references to the departed which they contain, must be interpreted. The faithful departed are always mentioned, as well as the living,[2] and so they were brought within the

---

[1] See W. Cunningham *S. Austin* p. 187 note.
[2] The names of the dead and of the living for whom intercession was to be made were written in books for the purpose (the *diptychs* of the living and of the dead).

range of the same intercession and the benefit of the sacrifice passed over to them.[1]

See further *Apost. Const.* viii 12, 41 ; Epiphanius *adv. Haer.* lxxv 7 ; Chrysostom *Hom.* xxi in Act., *Hom.* xli in 1 Cor., *Hom.* iii in Phil. ; and Bingham *Antiquities of the Christian Church* bk. xv ch. iii § 15, bk. xxiii ch. iii §§ 12, 13.

THE ANCIENT MYSTERIES

That the doctrine of the Eucharist was influenced to any important extent by the ideas connected with the ancient mysteries has not been proved and seems to be improbable. In a sense, of course, the whole Christian dispensation was a 'mystery'; that is, a 'secret', revealed to those that had ears to hear and eyes to see, but still hidden from all others. A process of initiation was required before the secret could be understood. This is the sense in which the word μυστήριον is used in the New Testament, and it seems probable that it was from this usage that Christians adopted the word in connexion with the Eucharist, in which the secret may be said to culminate. The Church and the Mysteries had further a common object in view—so far as both aimed at the purification of life under the influence of religious sanctions; and the terminology of the Mysteries found *its* way to some extent into the language used of the Christian Sacraments. But of the influence of the Mysteries on the doctrine of the Sacraments there is no certain trace during the period with which we are concerned.

See Cheetham *Mysteries Pagan and Christian* and references to the subject in Loofs *Leitfaden* §§ 25, 26 and Harnack *DG.* Eng. tr. (see Index 'Mysteries').

---

[1] In the course of time a distinction was made between saints and martyrs, who were regarded as not being in need of such assistance, and the ordinary faithful departed. Thus Cyril of Jerusalem (*Cat. Myst.* v 8), though he instructs his pupils that the sacrifice is offered in memory of all those that are fallen asleep, distinguishes two classes—first, patriarchs, prophets, apostles, and martyrs ; and secondly, holy fathers and bishops and others. In regard to the latter he declares the belief that it will be of greatest advantage to their souls that supplication be offered for them while the holy and awful sacrifice is set forth ; but the former class are mentioned that the living themselves may be aided by them ('in order that by their prayers and intercessions God may receive our supplication').

Augustine's teaching is to the same effect (*Enchirid.* 110, *Tract. in Joann.* 84).

By a natural extension of this distinction, some who had originally been included in the second class might come to be regarded as belonging to the first. Thus, in the Roman liturgy the form of one of the prayers was originally " Grant, O Lord, that this oblation may be of advantage to the soul of Thy servant Leo " ; but at a later time the form was altered to " Grant, O Lord, we beseech Thee, that this oblation may be of advantage to us by the intercession of St Leo ".

THE SACRAMENTS AS THE EXTENSION
OF THE INCARNATION

Hilary of Poictiers

This conception to which Gregory of Nyssa gave expression in the East (see *supra* p. 414) is also explicitly stated by Hilary of Poictiers, in the West, in his treatise *On the Trinity*, in the course of his exposition of the nature of the unity which exists between the Father and the Son. He discusses the meaning of the passage John 17$^{20-23}$ (*de Trinitate* viii 5-19), and argues against Arian or other heretical interpretations of the unity as merely moral or volitional. And the chief evidence in support of his contention, that the unity between the Father and the Son is a unity of nature, he finds in the character of the unity which believers have with the Son (and through him with the Father), as exhibited in the Incarnation and the Sacrament of his flesh and blood. The heretics argued that our unity with Christ was not 'natural', but one of allegiance and of will, and that the union of Christ with God the Father was of the same character as ours with him. Hilary accepts the latter premiss, but insists that believers are united with Christ in the Eucharist *naturaliter*, *carnaliter*, and *corporaliter* (*ibid.* 13-17); so that on the heretics' own shewing the unity between the Father and the Son is one of nature, not merely one of will. And all through his argument he treats the union of believers with Christ in the Eucharist as a continuation or extension of the union which was first effected in the Incarnation. The Word was truly made flesh, and we truly take the Word incarnate (*verbum carnem*) in the Lord's Supper. We must therefore hold that it is *naturaliter* that he abides in us, since he was born as man and took upon him the 'nature' of our flesh to be his inseparably thereafter, and blended the 'nature' of his flesh (*i.e.* our flesh thus assumed) with the 'nature' of eternity in the sacrament by which he communicates his flesh to us (*sub sacramento nobis communicandae carnis*). We are thus all one, because the Father is in Christ, and Christ is in us. Any one who would deny that the Father is 'naturally' in Christ must first deny that he himself is 'naturally' in Christ or Christ in him.

And again he emphasizes the relation of the Sacrament to the Incarnation in the words: "If therefore Christ truly assumed flesh of our body, and the man who was born of Mary is truly Christ, and we truly in a sacred rite (*sub mysterio*) receive flesh of his body (and by this means we shall be one, because the Father is in him and he in us): how can it be maintained that the unity is a unity of will, when the appropriation of nature effected through the sacrament is the sacrament of a complete unity?" And to the same effect are other expressions which follow in the course of the discussion. "He therefore himself is in us through his flesh, and we are in him; while, along with him, that which we are is in God." "Since he is in the Father in virtue of his divine nature, we must be believed to be in him in virtue of his bodily nativity (*per corporalem eius nativitatem*), and he again in us in virtue of the sacred rite of the Sacraments (*per sacramentorum mysterium*) . . . and so we attain to unity with the Father, since we are 'naturally' in him who in respect of his nativity is naturally in the Father—since he himself abides naturally in us." Through the Eucharist, in which he gives us his flesh to eat, the natural and corporal union of Christ and mankind, which was effected when he was born of the Virgin Mary, is continued and perpetuated.

THE DOCTRINE OF THE EUCHARIST IN LITURGIES

In the ritual and prayers of the Communion Service the sentiment of Christians in regard to the Eucharist found free expression. But the unrestrained language of worship—the outcome of the spirit of devotion rather than of exact definition—detracts to some extent from the value of Liturgies as evidence of doctrine. Moreover, of the Liturgies which have been most widely used in later times no manuscripts of the period before the Council of Chalcedon are extant, and the form of liturgy which was in use in the earlier centuries cannot be certainly inferred from them. The tradition which associates some of them with the names of Apostles witnesses to little more than the belief that the Apostles initiated the liturgical forms of the several churches.

There is, however, definite evidence as to the Liturgies in use in several churches in the fourth century. The Liturgy of Palestine in the middle of the fourth century is described in all its main features and parts by Cyril of Jerusalem in his *Catechetical Lectures*. Evidence as to the Liturgy in use in Egypt about the same time is furnished by *Bishop Sarapion's Prayer-Book* (*ed.* Bp. Wordsworth "Christian Classics" S.P.C.K.). From the writings of Chrysostom the Liturgy of Antioch at the end of the fourth century, and the Liturgy of Constantinople in the early part of the fifth century, can be largely reconstructed. The so-called 'Clementine Liturgy', contained in the *Apostolic Constitutions* bk. viii, probably represents the form of Liturgy which was in use in the Syrian Church in the fourth century, though the compiler at the end of that century has worked over and expanded the whole and filled it out with prayers of his own composition.

These Liturgies, so far as their evidence goes, all agree in support of the main conceptions of the Eucharist which have been described in the foregoing account as to the nature of the Sacrament as a whole and the benefits to be obtained by it,[1] and it is probable that they represent in these respects the general, if not universal, use of much earlier times.

See further Brightman *Eastern Liturgies*, Hammond *Liturgies Eastern and Western* (for the Western forms), or for an English translation of some, Warren *Liturgy of the Ante-Nicene Church*.

---

[1] See Note preceding on 'Oblations for the Dead'.

INDEX

(The references are to the pages of the book.)

Printed by MORRISON & GIBB LIMITED, *Edinburgh*

A CATALOGUE OF BOOKS AND ANNOUNCEMENTS OF METHUEN AND COMPANY PUBLISHERS : LONDON 36 ESSEX STREET W.C.

CONTENTS

MAY 1903

MESSRS. METHUEN'S
ANNOUNCEMENTS

BY COMMAND OF THE KING

THE CORONATION OF EDWARD VII. By J. E. C
BODLEY, Author of ' France.' *Demy 8vo.*

This important book is the official history of the Coronation, and has been written by the distinguished author of 'France,' by command of the King himself. The Coronation is the central subject, and of it a detailed account is given. But the book is in no sense an occasional volume, and the Ceremony is treated, not as an isolated incident, but as an event belonging to European and Imperial history. At the end of the work there will be an appendix containing official list of all the persons invited to the Abbey, and also lists drawn up with some historical detail of the Colonial and Indian troops who assisted at the Ceremony. It will therefore be an historical document of permanent value and interest.

THE COMPLETE WORKS OF CHARLES LAMB. Edited
by E. V. LUCAS. With numerous Illustrations. *In Seven Volumes.*
Demy 8vo. 7s. 6d. each.

This new edition of the works of Charles and Mary Lamb, in five volumes (to be followed by two volumes containing the Letters), will be found to contain a large quantity of new matter both in prose and verse—several thousand words in all. Mr. E. V. Lucas, the editor, has attempted in the notes, not only to relate Lamb's writings to his life, but to account for all his quotations and allusions— an ideal of thoroughness far superior to any that previous editors have set before themselves. A Life of Lamb by Mr. Lucas will follow in the autumn.

FLORENCE, HER HISTORY AND ART. By F. A. HYETT.
Demy 8vo. 7s. 6d.

This work is intended to occupy a middle position between the Guides and Histories of Florence. It tells the story of the rise and fall of the Republic consecutively, but more succinctly than the works of Napier, Trollope, or Villari, while it treats of Florentine Art and Letters parenthetically but more systematically than has been done by either of these writers.

THIRTY YEARS IN AUSTRALIA. By Mrs. CROSS (ADA
CAMBRIDGE). *Demy 8vo. 7s. 6d.*

A highly interesting account of a generation in Australia by a distinguished writer. Mrs. Cross's style is picturesque, and the book is more attractive than many novels. The early difficulties of Australian settlers, life in the towns and life on the farms are vividly described.

THE LAND OF THE BLACK MOUNTAIN. The Adven-
tures of Two Englishmen in Montenegro. By R. WYON and G.
PRANCE. With 51 Illustrations. *Crown 8vo. 6s.*

LETTERS FROM A SELF-MADE MERCHANT TO HIS SON. By GEORGE HORACE LORIMER. With Eighteen Illustrations. *Crown 8vo.* 6s.

This book is a masterpiece of humour and sound sense. It purports to be a collection of letters written by J. Graham, head of a great packing company in Chicago, to his son Pierrepont, and it describes in a racy and interesting form the secrets of success in business and in life.

WHEN I WAS A CHILD. By AN OLD POTTER. With an Introduction by ROBERT SPENCE WATSON. *Crown 8vo.* 6s.

THE STORY OF GENERAL BACON: A Short Biography of a Peninsular and Waterloo Veteran. By ALNOD J. BOGER. With Portraits. *Crown 8vo.* 6s.

A BOOK OF THE COUNTRY AND THE GARDEN. By H. M. BATSON. Illustrated by F. CARRUTHERS GOULD and A. C. GOULD. *Demy 8vo.* 10s. 6d.

SHAKESPEARE'S GARDEN. By J. HARVEY BLOOM. With Illustrations. *Fcap. 8vo.* 3s. 6d. ; *leather*, 4s. 6d. *net.*

A CONCISE HANDBOOK OF HERBACEOUS PLANTS. By H. M. BATSON. *Fcap. 8vo.* 3s. 6d.

A very complete and concise guide in alphabetical order.

THE RING OF THE NIBELUNG: An Interpretation embodying Wagner's own explanation, by ALICE LEIGHTON CLEATHER and BASIL CRUMP. *Fcap. 8vo.* 2s. 6d.

A BOOK OF EXMOOR. By F. J. SNELL. Illustrated. *Crown 8vo.* 6s.

This book deals with a variety of topics, embracing legend, folklore, dialect, sport, biography, history, and natural history, and renders accessible to the public a mass of particulars hitherto attainable only in expensive monographs or in scattered periodicals. The author has been at immense pains to consult every known source of information, both printed and oral ; and his aim has been to produce, not so much a guide-book, but something more satisfying and substantial, viz. an exhaustive account of the matters in question. There are numerous illustrations.

CHRISTIAN DOCTRINE. By J. F. BETHUNE BAKER. *Demy 8vo.* 10s. 6d.   [*Handbooks of Theology.*

THE PRECES PRIVATAE OF LANCELOT ANDREWES. Translated with an Introduction and Notes, by F. E. BRIGHTMAN, M.A., of Pusey House, Oxford. *Crown 8vo.* 6s.

This elaborate work has been in preparation for many years, and is the most complete edition that has ever been published of the famous devotions. It contains a long Introduction, with numerous Notes and References.

THE SPIRIT AND ORIGIN OF CHRISTIAN MONASTICISM. By JAMES O. HANNAY, M.A. *Crown 8vo.* 6s.

THIRTEEN SATIRES OF JUVENAL. Translated by S. G. OWEN. *Crown 8vo.* 2s. 6d.   [*Classical Translations.*

THE ENGLISH SUNDAY. By E. R. BERNARD, M.A., Canon of Salisbury. *Fcap. 8vo.* 1s. 6d.

THE EDUCATIONAL SYSTEM OF ENGLAND AND WALES. By JOHN HUGHES. With a Prefatory Note by ELLIS J. GRIFFITH. *Crown 8vo.* 3s. 6d.

THE EDUCATION ACT—AND AFTER. An Appeal addressed to the Nonconformists. By H. HENSLEY HENSON, B.D., Canon of Westminster. *Crown 8vo.* 1*s.*

The Little Library

Pott 8vo, cloth, 1*s.* 6*d. net ; leather,* 2*s.* 6*d. net each volume.*

THE ROMANY RYE. By GEORGE BORROW. With Notes and an Introduction by JOHN SAMPSON.

ESMOND. By W. M. THACKERAY. Edited by STEPHEN GWYNN.

A LITTLE BOOK OF ENGLISH SONNETS. Edited by J. B. B. NICHOLS.

THE SCARLET LETTER. By NATHANIEL HAWTHORNE.

The Arden Shakespeare

General Editor—W. J. CRAIG.

OTHELLO. Edited by H. C. HART. *Demy 8vo.* 3*s.* 6*d.*

CYMBELINE. Edited by EDWARD DOWDEN. *Demy 8vo.* 3*s.* 6*d.*

Little Biographies

Cloth, 3*s.* 6*d. ; leather,* 4*s. net.*

THE YOUNG PRETENDER. By C. S. TERRY. With 12 Illustrations.

ROBERT BURNS. By T. F. HENDERSON. With 12 Illustrations.

CHATHAM. By A. S. M'DOWALL. With 12 Illustrations.

TENNYSON. By A. C. BENSON, M.A. With 12 Illustrations *Fcap. 8vo.*

The Little Guides

Pott 8vo, cloth, 3*s. ; leather,* 3*s.* 6*d. net.*

CORNWALL. By A. L. SALMON. Illustrated by B. C. BOULTER.

KENT. By G. CLINCH. Illustrated by F. D. BEDFORD.

HERTFORDSHIRE. By H. W. TOMPKINS, F.R.H.S. Illustrated by E. H. NEW.

ROME. By C. G. ELLABY. Illustrated by B. C. BOULTER.

The Library of Devotion

Pott 8vo, cloth, 2*s. ; leather,* 2*s.* 6*d. net.*

GRACE ABOUNDING. By JOHN BUNYAN. Edited by S. C. FREER, M.A.

BISHOP WILSON'S SACRA PRIVATA. Edited by A. E BURN, B.D.

THE DEVOTIONS OF ST. ANSELM. Edited by C. C. J. WEBB, M.A.

LYRA SACRA : A Book of Sacred Verse. Selected and edited by H. C. BEECHING, M.A., Canon of Westminster.

Educational Books

AN INTRODUCTION TO THE STUDY OF TEXTILE DESIGN. By ALDRED F. BARKER, Author of 'Pattern Analysis,' etc. With numerous Diagrams and Illustrations. *Demy 8vo.* 7s. 6d.

AGRICULTURAL GEOLOGY. By J. E. MARR, F.R.S. With numerous Illustrations. *Crown 8vo.* 6s.

TECHNICAL ARITHMETIC AND GEOMETRY, for use in Technical Institutes, Modern Schools and Workshops. By C. T. MILLIS, M.I.M.E., Principal of the Borough Polytechnic College. With Diagrams. *Crown 8vo.* 6s.

THE ACTS OF THE APOSTLES. Edited by A. E. RUBIE, M.A., Headmaster Royal Naval School, Eltham. *Crown 8vo.* 2s. [*Methuen's Junior School Books.*]

A JUNIOR FRENCH GRAMMAR. By L. A. SORNET and M. J. ACATOS, Modern Language Masters at King Edward's School, Birmingham. *Crown 8vo.* 2s. [*Methuen's Junior School Books.*]

THE STUDENTS' PRAYER BOOK. PART I. MORNING AND EVENING PRAYER AND LITANY. Edited by W. H. FLECKER, M.A., D.C.L., Headmaster of the Dean Close School, Cheltenham. *Crown 8vo.* 2s. 6d.

Fiction

LORD LEONARD THE LUCKLESS. By W. E. NORRIS. *Crown 8vo.* 6s.

THE BETTER SORT. By HENRY JAMES. *Crown 8vo.* 6s.

ANTHEA'S WAY. By ADELINE SERGEANT. *Crown 8vo.* 6s.

OUTSIDE AND OVERSEAS. By G. MAKGILL. *Crown 8vo.* 6s.

THE SQUIREEN. By SHAN. F. BULLOCK. *Crown 8vo.* 6s.

AUNT BETHIA'S BUTTON. By J. RANDAL. *Crown 8vo.* 6s.

LOVE IN A LIFE. By ALLAN MONKHOUSE. *Crown 8vo. 6s.*

A MIXED MARRIAGE. By Mrs. FRANK PENNY. *Cr. 8vo. 6s.*

THE SWORD OF AZRAEL, a Chronicle of the Great Mutiny. By R. E. FORREST. *Crown 8vo. 6s.*

A FREE LANCE OF TO-DAY. By HUGH CLIFFORD. *Crown 8vo. 6s.*

A STRETCH OFF THE LAND. By G. STEWART BOWLES. *Crown 8vo. 6s.*

THE KNIGHT PUNCTILIOUS. By ARTHUR MOORE. *Crown 8vo. 6s.*

THE POET'S CHILD. By EMMA BROOKE. *Crown 8vo. 6s.*

THE DIVERTED VILLAGE. By GRACE RHYS. With Illustrations by DOROTHY GWYN JEFFRIES. *Crown 8vo. 6s.*

THE RED HOUSE. By E. NESBIT. Illustrated. *Crown 8vo. 6s.*

WORLD'S PEOPLE. By JULIEN GORDON. *Crown 8vo. 6s.*

THE CYNIC AND THE SYREN. By J. W. MAYALL. *Crown 8vo. 6s.*

A BRANDED NAME. By J. BLOUNDELLE BURTON. *Crown 8vo. 6s.*

SILENT DOMINION. By WINEFRIDE TRAFFORD-TAUNTON. *Crown 8vo. 6s.*

THE MACHINATIONS OF THE MYO-OK. By CECIL LOWIS. *Crown 8vo. 6s.*

ABRAHAM'S SACRIFICE. By GUSTAF JANSON. *Crown 8vo. 6s.*

PLAIN AND VELDT. By J. H. M. ABBOT, Author of 'Tommy Cornstalk.' *Crown 8vo. 6s.*

BY A FINNISH LAKE. By PAUL WAINEMAN. *Crown 8vo. 6s.*

A LOST ESTATE. By MARY E. MANN. A New Edition. *Crown 8vo. 6s.*

THE PARISH OF HILBY. By MARY E. MANN. A New Edition. *Crown 8vo. 6s.*

LITTLE TU'PENNY. By S. BARING-GOULD. A New Edition *Crown 8vo. 6d.*

FOUR NOVELS TRANSFERRED

New Editions.   Crown 8vo.   3s. 6d. each.

TALES OF SPACE AND TIME.   By H. G. WELLS.
WHEN THE SLEEPER WAKES.   By H. G. WELLS.
LOVE AND MR. LEWISHAM.   By H. G. WELLS.
THE INVISIBLE MAN.   By H. G. WELLS.

The Novelist

Messrs. METHUEN are issuing under the above general title a Monthly Series of Novels by popular authors at the price of Sixpence.   Each Number is as long as the average Six Shilling Novel.

Jan.   DRIFT.   By L. T. MEADE.
Feb.   THE MASTER OF BEECHWOOD.   By ADELINE SERGEANT.
March. CLEMENTINA.   By A. E. W. MASON.
April. THE ALIEN.   By F. F. MONTRESOR.
May.   THE BROOM SQUIRE.   By S. BARING-GOULD.
June. HONEY.   By HELEN MATHERS.
July. THE FOOTSTEPS OF A THRONE.   By MAX PEMBERTON.

IX. A FLASH OF SUMMER.   By Mrs. W. K. CLIFFORD, *in place of* 'The Adventure of Princess Sylvia.'

Methuen's Sixpenny Library

Jan.   A STATE SECRET.   By B. M. CROKER.
Feb.   SAM'S SWEETHEART.   By HELEN MATHERS.
March. HANDLEY CROSS.   By R. S. SURTEES.
April. ANNE MAULEVERER.   By Mrs. CAFFYN.
May.   THE ADVENTURERS.   By H. B. MARRIOT WATSON.
         THE CEDAR STAR.   By MARY E. MANN.
June. MASTER OF MEN.   By E. P. OPPENHEIM.
         WHEN THE SLEEPER WAKES.   By H. G. WELLS.
July. THE TRAIL OF THE SWORD.   By GILBERT PARKER.

A CATALOGUE OF

MESSRS. METHUEN'S
PUBLICATIONS

---◆---

PART I.—GENERAL LITERATURE

Jacob Abbot. THE BEECHNUT BOOK. Edited by E. V. LUCAS. Illustrated. *Demy 16mo. 8vo. 2s. 6d.* [Little Blue Books.

R. Ashton. THE PEELES AT THE CAPITAL. Illustrated. *Demy 16mo. 2s. 6d.* [Little Blue Books.

W. F. Adeney, M.A. See Bennett and Adeney.

Æschylus. AGAMEMNON, CHOEPHO-ROE, EUMENIDES. Translated by LEWIS CAMPBELL, LL.D., late Professor of Greek at St. Andrews. *5s.* [Classical Translations.

G. A. Aitken. See Swift.

William Alexander, D.D., Archbishop of Armagh. THOUGHTS AND COUNSELS OF MANY YEARS. Selected from the writings of Archbishop ALEXANDER. *Square Pott 8vo. 2s. 6d.*

Aristophanes. THE FROGS. Translated into English by E. W. HUNTINGFORD, M.A., Professor of Classics in Trinity College, Toronto. *Crown 8vo. 2s. 6d.*

Aristotle. THE NICOMACHEAN ETHICS. Edited, with an Introduction and Notes, by JOHN BURNET, M.A., Professor of Greek at St. Andrews. *Demy 8vo. 15s. net.*
'We have seldom, if ever, seen an edition of any classical author in which what is held in common with other commentators is so clearly put, and what is original is of such value and interest.'—*Pilot.*

J. B. Atkins. THE RELIEF OF LADY-SMITH. With 16 Plans and Illustrations. *Third Edition. Crown 8vo. 6s.*

J. B. Atlay. See R. H. Barham.

St. Augustine, THE CONFESSIONS OF. Newly Translated, with an Introduction and Notes, by C. BIGG, D.D., late Student of Christ Church. *Third Edition. Pott 8vo. Cloth, 2s; leather, 2s. 6d. net.* [Library of Devotion.
'The translation is an excellent piece of English, and the introduction is a masterly exposition. We augur well of a series which begins so satisfactorily.'—*Times.*

Jane Austen. PRIDE AND PREJU-DICE. Edited by E. V. LUCAS. *Two Volumes. Pott 8vo. Each volume, cloth, 1s. 6d.; leather, 2s. 6d. net.* [Little Library.

NORTHANGER ABBEY. Edited by E. V. LUCAS. *Pott 8vo. Cloth, 1s. 6d.; leather, 2s. 6d. net.* [Little Library.

Constance Bache. BROTHER MUSI-CIANS. Reminiscences of Edward and Walter Bache. With 16 Illustrations. *Crown 8vo. 6s. net.*

R. S. S. Baden-Powell, Major-General. THE DOWNFALL OF PREMPEH. A Diary of Life in Ashanti, 1895. With 21 Illustrations and a Map. *Third Edition. Large Crown 8vo. 6s.*

THE MATABELE CAMPAIGN, 1896. With nearly 100 Illustrations. *Fourth and Cheaper Edition. Large Crown 8vo. 6s.*

Graham Balfour. THE LIFE OF ROBERT LOUIS STEVENSON. *Second Edition. Two Volumes. Demy 8vo. 25s. net.*
'Mr. Balfour has done his work extremely well—done it, in fact, as Stevenson himself would have wished it done, with care and skill and affectionate appreciation.'—*Westminster Gazette.*

S. E. Bally. A FRENCH COMMERCIAL READER. With Vocabulary. *Second Edition. Crown 8vo. 2s.* [Commercial Series.

FRENCH COMMERCIAL CORRE-SPONDENCE. With Vocabulary. *Third Edition. Crown 8vo. 2s.* [Commercial Series.

A GERMAN COMMERCIAL READER. With Vocabulary. *Crown 8vo. 2s.* [Commercial Series.

GERMAN COMMERCIAL CORRE-SPONDENCE. With Vocabulary. *Crown 8vo. 2s. 6d.* [Commercial Series.

Elizabeth L. Banks. THE AUTO-BIOGRAPHY OF A 'NEWSPAPER

GIRL.' With Portrait of the Author and her Dog. *Crown 8vo. 6s.*
'A picture of a strenuous and busy life, perhaps the truest and most faithful representation of the ups and downs of a lady journalist's career ever given to the public. A very lively and interesting book.'—*Daily Telegraph.*
'A very amusing, cheery, good-natured account of a young lady's journalistic struggle in America and London.'—*Times.*

R. H. Barham. THE INGOLDSBY LEGENDS. Edited by J. B. Atlay. *Two Volumes. Pott 8vo. Each volume, cloth, 1s. 6d. net; leather, 2s. 6d. net.*
[The Little Library.

S. Baring-Gould, Author of 'Mehalah,' etc. THE LIFE OF NAPOLEON BONAPARTE. With over 450 Illustrations in the Text, and 12 Photogravure Plates. *Gilt top. Large quarto. 36s.*
'The main feature of this gorgeous volume is its great wealth of beautiful photogravures and finely-executed wood engravings, constituting a complete pictorial chronicle of Napoleon I.'s personal history.'—*Daily Telegraph.*

THE TRAGEDY OF THE CÆSARS. With numerous Illustrations from Busts, Gems, Cameos, etc. *Fifth Edition. Royal 8vo. 15s.*
'A most splendid and fascinating book on a subject of undying interest. It is brilliantly written, and the illustrations are supplied on a scale of profuse magnificence.' —*Daily Chronicle.*

A BOOK OF FAIRY TALES. With numerous Illustrations and Initial Letters by ARTHUR J. GASKIN. *Second Edition. Crown 8vo. Buckram. 6s.*

OLD ENGLISH FAIRY TALES. With numerous Illustrations by F. D. BEDFORD. *Second Edition. Cr. 8vo. Buckram. 6s.*
'A charming volume.'—*Guardian.*

THE CROCK OF GOLD. Fairy Stories. *Crown 8vo. 6s.*
'Twelve delightful fairy tales.'—*Punch.*

THE VICAR OF MORWENSTOW: A Biography. A new and Revised Edition. With Portrait. *Crown 8vo. 3s. 6d.*
A completely new edition of the well-known biography of R. S. Hawker.

DARTMOOR: A Descriptive and Historical Sketch. With Plans and numerous Illustrations. *Crown 8vo. 6s.*
'A most delightful guide, companion and instructor.'—*Scotsman.*

THE BOOK OF THE WEST. With numerous Illustrations. *Two volumes. Vol. I. Devon. Second Edition. Vol. II. Cornwall. Second Edition. Crown 8vo. 6s. each.*

'Bracing as the air of Dartmoor, the legend weird as twilight over Dozmare Pool, they give us a very good idea of this enchanting and beautiful district.'—*Guardian.*

A BOOK OF BRITTANY. With numerous Illustrations. *Crown 8vo. 6s.*
Uniform in scope and size with Mr. Baring-Gould's well-known books on Devon, Cornwall, and Dartmoor.

BRITTANY. Illustrated by Miss J. WYLIE. *Pott 8vo. Cloth, 3s.; leather, 3s. 6d. net.*
[The Little Guides.
'A dainty representative of "The Little Guides."'—*Times.*
'An excellent little guide-book.'—*Daily News.*

OLD COUNTRY LIFE. With 67 Illustrations. *Fifth Edition. Large Cr. 8vo. 6s.*

AN OLD ENGLISH HOME. With numerous Plans and Illustrations. *Cr. 8vo. 6s.*

HISTORIC ODDITIES AND STRANGE EVENTS. *Fifth Edition. Cr. 8vo. 6s.*

YORKSHIRE ODDITIES AND STRANGE EVENTS. *Fifth Edition. Crown 8vo. 6s.*

STRANGE SURVIVALS AND SUPERSTITIONS. *Second Edition. Cr. 8vo. 6s.*

A GARLAND OF COUNTRY SONG: English Folk Songs with their Traditional Melodies. Collected and arranged by S. BARING-GOULD and H. F. SHEPPARD. *Demy 4to. 6s.*

SONGS OF THE WEST: Traditional Ballads and Songs of the West of England, with their Melodies. Collected by S. BARING-GOULD, M.A., and H. F. SHEPPARD, M.A. In 4 Parts. *Parts I., II., III., 3s. each. Part IV., 5s. In One Volume, French Morocco, 15s.*
'A rich collection of humour, pathos, grace, and poetic fancy.'—*Saturday Review.*

W. E. Barnes, D.D. ISAIAH. *Two Volumes. Fcap. 8vo. 2s. net each.* Vol. I. With Map. [Churchman's Bible.

Mrs. P. A. Barnett. A LITTLE BOOK OF ENGLISH PROSE. *Pott 8vo. Cloth, 1s. 6d. net; leather, 2s. 6d. net.*
[Little Library.

R. R. N Baron, M.A. FRENCH PROSE COMPOSITION. *Crown 8vo. 2s. 6d. Key, 3s. net.*

H. M. Barron, M.A., Wadham College, Oxford. TEXTS FOR SERMONS. With a Preface by Canon SCOTT HOLLAND. *Crown 8vo. 3s. 6d*

C. F. Bastable, M.A., Professor of Economics at Trinity College, Dublin. THE COMMERCE OF NATIONS. *Second Edition. Crown 8vo 2s. 6d.*
[Social Questions Series.

H. M. Batson. See Edward FitzGerald.

A Hulme Beaman. PONS ASINORUM ; OR, A GUIDE TO BRIDGE. *Second Edition. Fcap. 8vo. 2s.*

W. S. Beard. JUNIOR ARITHMETIC EXAMINATION PAPERS. *Fcap. 8vo. 1s.* With or without Answers.
[Junior Examination Series.

Peter Beckford. THOUGHTS ON HUNTING. Edited by J. OTHO PAGET, and Illustrated by G. H. JALLAND. *Demy 8vo. 10s. 6d.*

William Beckford. THE HISTORY OF THE CALIPH VATHEK. Edited by E. DENISON ROSS. *Pott 8vo. Cloth, 1s. 6d. net; leather, 2s 6d. net.* [Little Library.

F. D. Bedford. See E. V. Lucas.

H. C. Beeching, M.A. See Tennyson.

Jacob Behmen. THE SUPERSENSUAL LIFE. Edited by BERNARD HOLLAND. *Fcap. 8vo. 3s. 6d.*

Hilaire Belloc. PARIS. With Maps and Illustrations. *Crown 8vo. 6s.*

H. H. L. Bellot, M.A. THE INNER AND MIDDLE TEMPLE. With numerous Illustrations. *Crown 8vo. 6s. net.*
'A vast store of entertaining material.'—*Liverpool Mercury.*
'A delightful and excellently illustrated book; a real encyclopædia of Temple history.'—*Pilot.*

W. H. Bennett, M.A. A PRIMER OF THE BIBLE. *Second Edition. Crown 8vo. 2s. 6d.*
'The work of an honest, fearless, and sound critic, and an excellent guide in a small compass to the books of the Bible.'—*Manchester Guardian.*

W. H. Bennett and W. F. Adeney. A BIBLICAL INTRODUCTION. *Crown 8vo. 7s. 6d.*
'It makes available to the ordinary reader the best scholarship of the day in the field of Biblical introduction. We know of no book which comes into competition with it.'—*Manchester Guardian.*

A. C. Benson, M.A. THE LIFE OF LORD TENNYSON. With 12 Illustrations. *Fcap. 8vo. Cloth, 3s. 6d.; Leather, 4s. net.* [Little Biographies.

R. M. Benson. THE WAY OF HOLINESS: a Devotional Commentary on the 119th Psalm. *Crown 8vo. 5s.*

M. Bidez. See Parmentier.

C. Bigg, D.D. See St. Augustine, À Kempis, and William Law.

C. R. D. Biggs, B.D. THE EPISTLE TO THE PHILIPPIANS. Edited by. *Fcap. 8vo. 1s. 6d. net.* [Churchman's Bible.
'Mr. Biggs' work is very thorough, and he has managed to compress a good deal of information into a limited space.'—*Guardian.*

T. Herbert Bindley, B.D. THE OECUMENICAL DOCUMENTS OF THE FAITH. With Introductions and Notes. *Crown 8vo. 6s.*
A historical account of the Creeds.

William Blake. See Little Library.

B. Blaxland, M.A. THE SONG OF SONGS. Being Selections from ST. BERNARD. *Pott 8vo. Cloth, 2s.; leather, 2s. 6d. net.* [Library of Devotion.

George Body, D.D. THE SOUL'S PILGRIMAGE: Devotional Readings from his published and unpublished writings. Selected and arranged by J. H. BURN, B.D. *Pott 8vo. 2s. 6d.*

Cardinal Bona. A GUIDE TO ETERNITY. Edited with an Introduction and Notes, by J. W. STANBRIDGE, B.D., late Fellow of St. John's College, Oxford. *Pott 8vo. Cloth, 2s.; leather, 2s. 6d. net.* [Library of Devotion.

F. C. Boon, B.A. A COMMERCIAL GEOGRAPHY OF FOREIGN NATIONS. *Crown 8vo. 2s.*
Commercial Series.

George Borrow. LAVENGRO. Edited by F. HINDES GROOME. *Two Volumes. Pott 8vo. Each volume, cloth, 1s. 6d. net; leather, 2s. 6d. net.* [Little Library.

J. Ritzema Bos. AGRICULTURAL ZOOLOGY. Translated by J. R. AINSWORTH DAVIS, M.A. With an Introduction by ELEANOR A. ORMEROD, F.E.S. With 155 Illustrations. *Cr. 8vo. 3s. 6d.*

C. G. Botting, B.A. JUNIOR LATIN EXAMINATION PAPERS. *Fcap. 8vo. 1s.* [Junior Examination Series.

EASY GREEK EXERCISES. *Cr. 8vo. 2s.*

E. M. Bowden. THE EXAMPLE OF BUDDHA: Being Quotations from Buddhist Literature for each Day in the Year. *Third Edition. 16mo. 2s. 6d.*

E. Bowmaker. THE HOUSING OF THE WORKING CLASSES. *Crown 8vo. 2s. 6d.* [Social Questions Series.

F. G. Brabant, M.A. SUSSEX. Illustrated by E. H. NEW. *Pott 8vo. Cloth, 3s.; leather, 3s. 6d. net.* [Little Guides.
'A charming little book; as full of sound information as it is practical in conception.'—*Athenæum.*

THE ENGLISH LAKES. Illustrated by E. H. NEW. *Pott 8vo. Cloth, 4s.; leather, 4s. 6d. net.* [The Little Guides.

Miss M. Brodrick and Miss Anderson Morton. A CONCISE HANDBOOK OF EGYPTIAN ARCHÆOLOGY. With many Illustrations. *Crown 8vo. 3s. 6d.*

E. W. Brooks. See F. J. Hamilton.

C. L. Brownell. THE HEART OF JAPAN. Illustrated. *Crown 8vo. 6s.*
'These lively pages are full of portraits from the life.'—*Morning Post.*

'It is the work of one who has lived in Japan among the people.'—*Athenæum.*

'A more readable and interesting book about Japan has not been written.'
—*Scotsman.*

Robert Browning. SELECTIONS FROM THE EARLY POEMS OF. With Introduction and Notes by W. HALL GRIFFIN. *Pott 8vo. 1s. 6d. net.; leather, 2s. 6d. net.* [Little Library.

O. Browning, M.A. A SHORT HISTORY OF MEDIÆVAL ITALY, A.D. 1250-1530. In Two Volumes. *Crown 8vo. 5s. each.* VOL. I. 1250-1409.—Guelphs and Ghibellines. VOL. II. 1409-1530.—The Age of the Condottieri.

J. Buchan. See Isaak Walton.

Miss Bulley. See Lady Dilke.

John Bunyan. THE PILGRIM'S PROGRESS. Edited, with an Introduction, by C. H. FIRTH, M.A. With 39 Illustrations by R. ANNING BELL. *Cr. 8vo. 6s.* 'The best "Pilgrim's Progress."'—*Educational Times.*

G. J. Burch, M.A., F.R.S. A MANUAL OF ELECTRICAL SCIENCE. With numerous Illustrations. *Crown 8vo. 3s.* [University Extension Series.

Gelett Burgess. GOOPS AND HOW TO BE THEM. With numerous Illustrations. *Small 4to. 6s.*

A. E. Burn, B.D., Examining Chaplain to the Bishop of Lichfield. AN INTRODUCTION TO THE HISTORY OF THE CREEDS. *Demy 8vo. 10s. 6d.* [Handbooks of Theology. 'This book may be expected to hold its place as an authority on its subject.'—*Spectator.*

J. H. Burn, B.D., F.R.S.E. A MANUAL OF CONSOLATION FROM THE SAINTS AND FATHERS. *Pott 8vo. Cloth, 2s.; leather, 2s. 6d. net.* [Library of Devotion.

Robert Burns. THE POEMS OF ROBERT BURNS. Edited by ANDREW LANG and W. A. CRAIGIE. With Portrait. Second Edition. *Demy 8vo, gilt top. 6s.*

J. B. Bury, LL.D. See Gibbon.

Alfred Caldecott, D.D. THE PHILOSOPHY OF RELIGION IN ENGLAND AND AMERICA. *Demy 8vo. 10s. 6d.* [Handbooks of Theology. 'A lucid and informative account, which certainly deserves a place in every philosophical library.'—*Scotsman.*

D. S. Calderwood, Headmaster of the Normal School, Edinburgh. TEST CARDS IN EUCLID AND ALGEBRA. In three packets of 40, with Answers. 1s. each. Or in three Books, price 2d., 2d., and 3d.

E. F. H. Capey. THE LIFE OF ERASMUS. With 12 Illustrations. *Cloth, 3s. 6d. net; leather, 4s. net.* [Little Biographies.

Thomas Carlyle. THE FRENCH REVOLUTION. Edited by C. R. L. FLETCHER, Fellow of Magdalen College, Oxford. Three Volumes. *Crown 8vo. 6s. each.* [Methuen's Standard Library.

R. M. and A. J. Carlyle, M.A. BISHOP LATIMER. With Portrait. *Crown 8vo. 3s. 6d.* [Leaders of Religion.

C. C. Channer and M. E. Roberts. LACE-MAKING IN THE MIDLANDS, PAST AND PRESENT. With 16 full-page Illustrations. *Crown 8vo. 2s. 6d.* 'An interesting book, illustrated by fascinating photographs.'—*Speaker.*

Lord Chesterfield, THE LETTERS OF, TO HIS SON. Edited, with an Introduction, by C. STRACHEY, and Notes by A. CALTHROP. Two Volumes. *Crown 8vo. 6s. each.* [Methuen's Standard Library.

F. W. Christian. THE CAROLINE ISLANDS. With many Illustrations and Maps. *Demy 8vo. 12s. 6d. net.*

Cicero. DE ORATORE I. Translated by E. N. P. MOOR, M.A. *Crown 8vo. 3s. 6d.* [Classical Translations. SELECT ORATIONS (Pro Milone, Pro Murena, Philippic II., In Catilinam). Translated by H. E. D. BLAKISTON, M.A., Fellow and Tutor of Trinity College, Oxford. *Crown 8vo. 5s.* [Classical Translations. DE NATURA DEORUM. Translated by F. BROOKS, M.A., late Scholar of Balliol College, Oxford. *Crown 8vo. 3s. 6d.* [Classical Translations. DE OFFICIIS. Translated by G. B. GARDINER, M.A. *Crown 8vo. 2s. 6d.* [Classical Translations.

F. A. Clarke, M.A. BISHOP KEN. With Portrait. *Crown 8vo. 3s. 6d.* [Leaders of Religion.

T. Cobb. THE CASTAWAYS OF MEADOWBANK. Illustrated. *Demy 16mo. 2s. 6d.* [Little Blue Books. THE TREASURY OF PRINCEGATE PRIORY. Illustrated. *Demy 16mo. 2s. 6d.* [Little Blue Books.

E. H. Colbeck, M.D. DISEASES OF THE HEART. With numerous Illustrations. *Demy 8vo. 12s.*

W. G. Collingwood, M.A. THE LIFE OF JOHN RUSKIN. With Portraits. Cheap Edition. *Crown 8vo. 6s.*

J. C. Collins, M.A. See Tennyson.

W. E. Collins, M.A. THE BEGINNINGS OF ENGLISH CHRISTIANITY. With Map. *Crown 8vo. 3s. 6d.* [Churchman's Library.

A. M. Cook, M.A. See E. C. Marchant.

R. W. Cooke-Taylor. THE FACTORY SYSTEM. *Crown 8vo.* 2s. 6d.
[Social Questions Series.

Marie Corelli. THE PASSING OF THE GREAT QUEEN : A Tribute to the Noble Life of Victoria Regina. *Small 4to.* 1s.

A CHRISTMAS GREETING. *Sm. 4to.* 1s.

Rosemary Cotes. DANTE'S GARDEN. With a Frontispiece. *Second Edition. Fcap. 8vo. cloth* 2s. 6d. ; *leather,* 3s. 6d. *net.*

Harold Cox, B.A. LAND NATIONAL-IZATION. *Crown 8vo.* 2s. 6d.
[Social Questions Series.

W. J. Craig. See Shakespeare.

W. A. Craigie. A PRIMER OF BURNS. *Crown 8vo.* 2s. 6d.

Mrs. Craik. JOHN HALIFAX, GEN-TLEMAN. Edited by ANNIE MATHE-SON. *Two Volumes. Pott 8vo. Each Volume, Cloth,* 1s. 6d. *net ; leather,* 2s. 6d. *net.* [Little Library.

Richard Crashaw, THE ENGLISH POEMS OF. Edited by EDWARD HUT-TON. *Pott 8vo. Cloth,* 1s. 6d. *net ; leather,* 2s. 6d. *net.* [Little Library.

F. G. Crawford. See Mary C. Danson.

C. G. Crump, M.A. See Thomas Ellwood.

F. H. E. Cunliffe, Fellow of All Souls' College, Oxford. THE HISTORY OF THE BOER WAR. With many Illustrations, Plans, and Portraits. *In 2 vols. Vol. I.,* 15s.

E. L. Cutts, D.D. AUGUSTINE OF CANTERBURY. With Portrait. *Crown 8vo.* 3s. 6d. [Leaders of Religion.

The Brothers Dalziel. A RECORD OF FIFTY YEARS' WORK. With 150 Illus-trations. *Large 4to.* 21s. *net.*
The record of the work of the celebrated Engravers, containing a Gallery of beauti-ful Pictures by F. Walker, Sir J. Millais, Lord Leighton, and other great Artists. The book is a history of the finest black-and-white work of the nineteenth century.

G. W. Daniell, M.A. BISHOP WILBER-FORCE. With Portrait. *Crown 8vo.* 3s. 6d. [Leaders of Religion.

Mary C. Danson and F. G. Crawford. FATHERS IN THE FAITH. *Small 8vo.* 1s. 6d.

Dante Alighieri. LA COMMEDIA DI DANTE. The Italian Text edited by PAGET TOYNBEE, Litt.D., M.A. *Demy 8vo. Gilt top.* 8s. 6d. *Also, Crown 8vo.* 6s.
[Methuen's Standard Library.

THE INFERNO OF DANTE. Trans-lated by H. F. CARY. Edited by PAGET TOYNBEE, Litt.D., M.A. *Pott 8vo. Cloth,* 1s. 6d. *net ; leather* 2s. 6d. *net.*
[Little Library.

THE PURGATORIO OF DANTE. Translated by H. F. CARY. Edited by PAGET TOYNBEE, Litt.D., M.A. *Pott 8vo. Cloth,* 1s. 6d. *net ; leather,* 2s. 6d. *net.*
[Little Library.

THE PARADISO OF DANTE. Trans-lated by H. F. CARY. Edited by PAGET TOYNBEE, Litt.D., M.A. *Post 8vo. Cloth,* 1s. 6d. *net ; leather,* 2s. 6d. *net.*
[Little Library.

See also Paget Toynbee.

A. C. Deane. Edited by. A LITTLE BOOK OF LIGHT VERSE. *Pott 8vo. Cloth,* 1s. 6d. *net ; leather,* 2s. 6d. *net.*
[Little Library.

Percy Dearmer. See N. Hawthorne.

Leon Delbos. THE METRIC SYSTEM. *Crown 8vo.* 2s.
A theoretical and practical guide, for use in schools and by the general reader.

Demosthenes : THE OLYNTHIACS AND PHILIPPICS. Translated upon a new principle by OTHO HOLLAND. *Crown 8vo.* 2s. 6d.

Demosthenes. AGAINST CONON AND CALLICLES. Edited with Notes and Vocabulary, by F. DARWIN SWIFT, M.A. *Fcap. 8vo.* 2s.

Charles Dickens.

THE ROCHESTER EDITION.
Crown 8vo. Each Volume, cloth, 3s. 6d.
With Introductions by GEORGE GISSING, Notes by F. G. KITTON, and Topographical Illustrations.

THE PICKWICK PAPERS. With Illustra-tions by E. H. NEW. *Two Volumes.*

NICHOLAS NICKLEBY. With Illustra-tions by R. J. WILLIAMS. *Two Volumes.*

BLEAK HOUSE. With Illustrations by BEATRICE ALCOCK. *Two Volumes.*

OLIVER TWIST. With Illustrations by E. H. NEW.

THE OLD CURIOSITY SHOP. With Illustrations by G. M. BRIMELOW. *Two Volumes.*

BARNABY RUDGE. With Illustrations by BEATRICE ALCOCK. *Two Volumes.*

G. L. Dickinson, M.A., Fellow of King's College, Cambridge. THE GREEK VIEW OF LIFE. *Second Edition. Crown 8vo.* 2s. 6d. [University Extension Series.

H. N. Dickson, F.R.S.E., F.R.Met. Soc. METEOROLOGY. The Elements of Weather and Climate. Illustrated. *Crown 8vo.* 2s. 6d. [University Extension Series.

Lady Dilke, Miss Bulley, and **Miss Whit-ley.** WOMEN'S WORK. *Crown 8vo.* 2s. 6d. [Social Questions Series.

P. H. Ditchfield, M.A., F.S.A. ENGLISH VILLAGES. Illustrated. *Crown 8vo.* 6s.
'A book which for its instructive and pictorial value should find a place in every village library.'—*Scotsman.*

THE STORY OF OUR ENGLISH TOWNS. With Introduction by AUGUSTUS JESSOP, D.D. *Second Edition. Crown 8vo. 6s.*

OLD ENGLISH CUSTOMS: Extant at the Present Time. An Account of Local Observances, Festival Customs, and Ancient Ceremonies yet Surviving in Great Britain. *Crown 8vo. 6s.*

W. M. Dixon, M.A. A PRIMER OF TENNYSON. *Second Edition. Crown 8vo. 2s. 6d.*
'Much sound and well-expressed criticism. The bibliography is a boon.'—*Speaker.*

ENGLISH POETRY FROM BLAKE TO BROWNING. *Second Edition. Crown 8vo. 2s. 6d.* [University Extension Series.

E. Dowden, Litt.D. See Shakespeare.

J. Dowden, D.D., Lord Bishop of Edinburgh. THE WORKMANSHIP OF THE PRAYER BOOK: Its Literary and Liturgical Aspects. *Second Edition. Crown 8vo. 3s. 6d.* [Churchman's Library.

S. R. Driver., D.D., Canon of Christ Church, Regius Professor of Hebrew in the University of Oxford. SERMONS ON SUBJECTS CONNECTED WITH THE OLD TESTAMENT. *Crown 8vo. 6s.*
'A welcome companion to the author's famous "Introduction."'—*Guardian.*

S. J. Duncan (Mrs. COTES), Author of 'A Voyage of Consolation.' ON THE OTHER SIDE OF THE LATCH. *Second Edition. Crown 8vo. 6s.*

J. T. Dunn, D.Sc., and **V. A. Mundella.** GENERAL ELEMENTARY SCIENCE. With 114 Illustrations. *Crown 8vo. 3s. 6d.* [Methuen's Science Primers.

The Earl of Durham. A REPORT ON CANADA. With an Introductory Note. *Demy 8vo. 7s. 6d. net.*
A reprint of the celebrated Report which Lord Durham made to the British Government on the state of British North America in 1839. It is probably the most important utterance on British colonial policy ever published.

W. A. Dutt. NORFOLK. Illustrated by B. C. BOULTER. *Pott 8vo. Cloth, 3s.; leather, 3s. 6d. net.* [Little Guides.

Clement Edwards. RAILWAY NATIONALIZATION. *Crown 8vo. 2s. 6d.* [Social Questions Series

W. Douglas Edwards. COMMERCIAL LAW. *Crown 8vo. 2s.* [Commercial Series.

H. E. Egerton, M.A. A HISTORY OF BRITISH COLONIAL POLICY. *Demy 8vo. 12s. 6d.*
'It is a good book, distinguished by accuracy in detail, clear arrangement of facts, and a broad grasp of principles.'—*Manchester Guardian.*

Thomas Ellwood, THE HISTORY OF THE LIFE OF. Edited by C. G. CRUMP, M.A. *Crown 8vo. 6s.* [Methuen's Standard Library.
This edition is the only one which contains the complete book as originally published. It has a long Introduction and many Footnotes.

E. Engel. A HISTORY OF ENGLISH LITERATURE: From its Beginning to Tennyson. Translated from the German. *Demy 8vo. 7s. 6d. net.*

W. H. Fairbrother, M.A. THE PHILOSOPHY OF T. H. GREEN. *Second Edition. Crown 8vo. 3s. 6d.*

Dean Farrar. See À Kempis.

Susan Ferrier. MARRIAGE. Edited by Miss GOODRICH FREER and Lord IDDESLEIGH. *Two Volumes. Pott 8vo. Each volume, cloth, 1s. 6d. net; leather, 2s. 6d. net.* [Little Library.

THE INHERITANCE. *Two Volumes. Pott 8vo. Each Volume, cloth, 1s. 6d. net.; leather, 2s. 6d. net.* [The Little Library.

C. H. Firth, M.A. CROMWELL'S ARMY: A History of the English Soldier during the Civil Wars, the Commonwealth, and the Protectorate. *Crown 8vo. 7s. 6d.*
An elaborate study and description of Cromwell's army by which the victory of the Parliament was secured. The 'New Model' is described in minute detail.

G. W. Fisher, M.A. ANNALS OF SHREWSBURY SCHOOL. With numerous Illustrations. *Demy 8vo. 10s. 6d.*

Edward FitzGerald. THE RUBAIYAT OF OMAR KHAYYAM. With a Commentary by H. M. BATSON, and a Biography of Omar by E. D. ROSS. *Crown 8vo. 6s.*

E. A. FitzGerald. THE HIGHEST ANDES. With 2 Maps, 51 Illustrations, 13 of which are in Photogravure, and a Panorama. *Royal 8vo. 30s. net.*

C. R. L. Fletcher. See Thomas Carlyle.

W. Warde Fowler, M.A. See Gilbert White.

J. F. Fraser. ROUND THE WORLD ON A WHEEL. With 100 Illustrations. *Fourth Edition Crown 8vo. 6s.*
'A classic of cycling, graphic and witty.' —*Yorkshire Post.*

J. H. Freese. See Plautus.

W. French, M.A., Principal of the Storey Institute, Lancaster, PRACTICAL CHEMISTRY. Part 1. With numerous Diagrams. *Crown 8vo. 1s. 6d.* [Textbooks of Technology.
'An excellent and eminently practical little book.'—*Schoolmaster.*

Ed. von Freudenreich. DAIRY BACTERIOLOGY. A Short Manual for the Use of Students. Translated by J. R. AINSWORTH DAVIS, M.A. *Second Edition. Revised. Crown 8vo. 2s. 6d.*

H. W. Fulford, M.A. THE EPISTLE OF ST. JAMES. Edited by. *Fcap. 8vo. 1s. 6d. net.* [Churchman's Bible.

Mrs. Gaskell. CRANFORD. Edited by E. V. LUCAS. *Pott 8vo. Cloth, 1s. 6d. net; leather, 2s. 6d. net.* [Little Library.

H. B. George, M.A., Fellow of New College, Oxford. BATTLES OF ENGLISH HISTORY. With numerous Plans. *Third Edition. Crown 8vo. 6s.*

'Mr. George has undertaken a very useful task—that of making military affairs intelligible and instructive to non-military readers—and has executed it with a large measure of success.'—*Times.*

H. de B. Gibbins, Litt.D., M.A. INDUSTRY IN ENGLAND: HISTORICAL OUTLINES. With 5 Maps. *Third Edition. Demy 8vo. 10s. 6d.*

A COMPANION GERMAN GRAMMAR. *Crown 8vo. 1s. 6d.*

THE INDUSTRIAL HISTORY OF ENGLAND. *Eighth Edition.* Revised. With Maps and Plans. *Crown 8vo. 3s.* [University Extension Series.

THE ECONOMICS OF COMMERCE. *Crown 8vo. 1s. 6d.* [Commercial Series.

COMMERCIAL EXAMINATION PAPERS. *Crown 8vo. 1s. 6d.* [Commercial Series.

BRITISH COMMERCE AND COLONIES FROM ELIZABETH TO VICTORIA. *Third Edition. Crown 8vo. 2s.* [Commercial Series.

ENGLISH SOCIAL REFORMERS. *Second Edition. Crown 8vo. 2s. 6d.* [University Extension Series.

H. de B. Gibbins, Litt.D., M.A., and R. A. **Hadfield**, of the Hecla Works, Sheffield. A SHORTER WORKING DAY. *Crown 8vo. 2s. 6d.* [Social Questions Series.

Edward Gibbon. THE DECLINE AND FALL OF THE ROMAN EMPIRE. A New Edition, edited with Notes, Appendices, and Maps, by J. B. BURY, LL.D., Fellow of Trinity College, London. *In Seven Volumes. Demy 8vo. Gilt top, 8s. 6d. each. Also, Crown 8vo. 6s. each.*

'At last there is an adequate modern edition of Gibbon. . . . The best edition the nineteenth century could produce.'—*Manchester Guardian.*

'A great piece of editing.'—*Academy.*

MEMOIRS OF MY LIFE AND WRITINGS. Edited, with an Introduction and Notes, by G. BIRKBECK HILL, LL.D. *Crown 8vo. 6s.*

'An admirable edition of one of the most interesting personal records of a literary life. Its notes and its numerous appendices are a repertory of almost all that can be known about Gibbon.'—*Manchester Guardian.*

E. C. S. Gibson, D.D., Vicar of Leeds. THE BOOK OF JOB. With Introduction and Notes. *Demy 8vo. 6s.* [Westminster Commentaries.

'Dr. Gibson's work is worthy of a high degree of appreciation. To the busy worker and the intelligent student the commentary will be a real boon; and it will, if we are not mistaken, be much in demand. The Introduction is almost a model of concise, straightforward, prefatory remarks on the subject treated.'—*Athenæum.*

THE XXXIX. ARTICLES OF THE CHURCH OF ENGLAND. With an Introduction. *Third and Cheaper Edition in One Volume. Demy 8vo. 12s. 6d.* [Handbooks of Theology.

'We welcome with the utmost satisfaction a new, cheaper, and more convenient edition of Dr. Gibson's book. It was greatly wanted. Dr. Gibson has given theological students just what they want, and we should like to think that it was in the hands of every candidate for orders.'—*Guardian.*

THE LIFE OF JOHN HOWARD. With 12 Illustrations. *Pott 8vo. Cloth, 3s.; leather, 3s. 6d. net.* [Little Biographies.

See also George Herbert.

George Gissing. See Dickens.

A. D. Godley, M.A., Fellow of Magdalen College, Oxford. LYRA FRIVOLA. *Third Edition. Fcap. 8vo. 2s. 6d.*

VERSES TO ORDER. *Cr. 8vo. 2s. 6d. net.*

SECOND STRINGS. *Fcap. 8vo. 2s. 6d.*

A new volume of humorous verse uniform with *Lyra Frivola.*

'Neat, brisk, ingenious.'—*Manchester Guardian.*

'The verse is facile, the wit is ready.' *Daily Mail.*

'Excellent and amusing.'—*St. James's Gazette.*

Miss Goodrich-Freer. See Susan Ferrier.

P. Anderson Graham. THE RURAL EXODUS. *Crown 8vo. 2s. 6d.* [Social Questions Series.

F. S. Granger, M.A., Litt.D. PSYCHOLOGY. *Second Edition. Crown 8vo. 2s. 6d.* [University Extension Series.

THE SOUL OF A CHRISTIAN. *Crown 8vo. 6s.*

A book dealing with the evolution of the religious life and experiences.

E. M'Queen Gray. GERMAN PASSAGES FOR UNSEEN TRANSLATION. *Crown 8vo. 2s. 6d.*

P. L. Gray, B.Sc., formerly Lecturer in Physics in Mason University College, Birmingham. THE PRINCIPLES OF MAGNETISM AND ELECTRICITY: an Elementary Text-Book. With 181 Diagrams. *Crown 8vo. 3s. 6d.*

G. Buckland Green, M.A., Assistant Master at Edinburgh Academy, late Fellow of St. John's College, Oxon. NOTES ON GREEK AND LATIN SYNTAX. *Crown 8vo. 3s. 6d.*
Notes and explanations on the chief difficulties of Greek and Latin Syntax, with numerous passages for exercise.

E. T. Green, M.A. THE CHURCH OF CHRIST. *Crown 8vo. 6s.*
[*Churchman's Library.*

R. A. Gregory. THE VAULT OF HEAVEN. A Popular Introduction to Astronomy. With numerous Illustrations. *Crown 8vo. 2s. 6d.*
[*University Extension Series.*

W. Hall Griffin, M.A. See Robert Browning.

C. H. Grinling. A HISTORY OF THE GREAT NORTHERN RAILWAY, 1845-95. With Illustrations. *Demy 8vo. 10s. 6d.*

F. Hindes Groome. See George Borrow.

M. L. Gwynn. A BIRTHDAY BOOK. *Royal 8vo. 12s.*
This is a birthday-book of exceptional dignity, and the extracts have been chosen with particular care.

Stephen Gwynn. See Thackeray.

John Hackett, B.D. A HISTORY OF THE ORTHODOX CHURCH OF CYPRUS. With Maps and Illustrations. *Demy 8vo. 15s. net.*

A. C. Haddon, Sc.D., F.R.S. HEAD-HUNTERS, BLACK, WHITE, AND BROWN. With many Illustrations and a Map. *Demy 8vo. 15s.*
A narrative of adventure and exploration in Northern Borneo. It contains much matter of the highest scientific interest.

R. A. Hadfield. See H. de B. Gibbins.

R. N. Hall and W. G. Neal. THE ANCIENT RUINS OF RHODESIA. With numerous Illustrations. *Demy 8vo. 21s. net.*

F. J. Hamilton, D.D., and **E. W. Brooks.** ZACHARIAH OF MITYLENE. Translated into English. *Demy 8vo. 12s. 6d. net.*
[*Byzantine Texts.*

D. Hannay. A SHORT HISTORY OF THE ROYAL NAVY, FROM EARLY TIMES TO THE PRESENT DAY. Illustrated. *Two Volumes. Demy 8vo. 7s. 6d. each.* Vol. I. 1200-1688.

A. T. Hare, M.A. THE CONSTRUCTION OF LARGE INDUCTION COILS. With numerous Diagrams. *Demy 8vo. 6s.*

Clifford Harrison. READING AND READERS. *Fcap. 8vo. 2s. 6d.*
'An extremely sensible little book.'—
Manchester Guardian.

Nathaniel Hawthorne. THE SCARLET LETTER. Edited by PERCY DEARMER, *Pott 8vo. Cloth, 1s. 6d. net; leather, 2s. 6d. net.*
[*Little Library.*

Sven Hedin, Gold Medallist of the Royal Geographical Society. THROUGH ASIA. With 300 Illustrations from Sketches and Photographs by the Author, and Maps. *Two Volumes. Royal 8vo. 36s. net.*

T. F. Henderson. A LITTLE BOOK OF SCOTTISH VERSE. *Pott 8vo. Cloth, 1s. 6d. net; leather, 2s. 6d. net.*
[*Little Library.*
See also D. M. Moir.

W. E. Henley. ENGLISH LYRICS. *Crown 8vo. Gilt top. 3s. 6d.*

W. E. Henley and C. Whibley. A BOOK OF ENGLISH PROSE. *Crown 8vo. Buckram, gilt top. 6s.*

H. H. Henson, M.A., Fellow of All Souls', Oxford, Canon of Westminster. APOSTOLIC CHRISTIANITY : As Illustrated by the Epistles of St. Paul to the Corinthians. *Crown 8vo. 6s.*

LIGHT AND LEAVEN : HISTORICAL AND SOCIAL SERMONS. *Crown 8vo. 6s.*

DISCIPLINE AND LAW. *Fcap. 8vo. 2s. 6d.*

George Herbert. THE TEMPLE. Edited, with an Introduction and Notes, by E. C. S. GIBSON, D.D., Vicar of Leeds. *Pott 8vo. Cloth, 2s.; leather, 2s. 6d. net.*
[*Library of Devotion.*

Herodotus: EASY SELECTIONS. With Vocabulary. By A. C. LIDDELL, M.A. *Fcap. 8vo. 1s. 6d.*

W. A. S. Hewins, B.A. ENGLISH TRADE AND FINANCE IN THE SEVENTEENTH CENTURY. *Crown 8vo.*
[*University Extension Series.*

T. Hilbert. THE AIR GUN : or, How the Mastermans and Dobson Major nearly lost their Holidays. Illustrated. *Demy 16mo. 2s. 6d.*
[*Little Blue Books.*

Clare Hill, Registered Teacher to the City and Guilds of London Institute. MILLINERY, THEORETICAL, AND PRACTICAL. With numerous Diagrams. *Crown 8vo. 2s.*
[*Textbooks of Technology.*

Henry Hill, B.A., Headmaster of the Boy's High School, Worcester, Cape Colony. A SOUTH AFRICAN ARITHMETIC. *Crown 8vo. 3s. 6d.*
This book has been specially written for use in South African schools.

G. Birkbeck Hill, LL.D. See Gibbon.

Howard C. Hillegas. WITH THE BOER FORCES. With 24 Illustrations. *Second Edition. Crown 8vo. 6s.*

Emily Hobhouse. THE BRUNT OF THE WAR. With Map and Illustrations. *Crown 8vo. 6s.*

L. T. Hobhouse, Fellow of C.C.C., Oxford. THE THEORY OF KNOWLEDGE. *Demy 8vo. 21s.*

J. A. Hobson, M.A. PROBLEMS OF POVERTY: An Inquiry into the Industrial Condition of the Poor. *Fourth Edition. Crown 8vo. 2s. 6d.*
[Social Questions Series and University Extension Series.
THE PROBLEM OF THE UNEMPLOYED. *Crown 8vo. 2s. 6d.*
[Social Questions Series.

T. Hodgkin, D.C.L. GEORGE FOX, THE QUAKER. With Portrait. *Crown 8vo. 3s. 6d.* [Leaders of Religion.

Chester Holcombe. THE REAL CHINESE QUESTION. *Crown 8vo. 6s.*
'It is an important addition to the materials before the public for forming an opinion on a most difficult and pressing problem.'—*Times.*

Sir T. H. Holdich, K.C.I.E. THE INDIAN BORDERLAND : being a Personal Record of Twenty Years. Illustrated. *Demy 8vo. 15s. net.*
'Interesting and inspiriting from cover to cover, it will assuredly take its place as the classical work on the history of the Indian frontier.'—*Pilot.*

Canon Scott Holland. LYRA APOSTOLICA. With an Introduction. Notes by H. C. BEECHING, M.A. *Pott 8vo. Cloth, 2s.; leather, 2s. 6d. net.*
[Library of Devotion.

G. J. Holyoake. THE CO-OPERATIVE MOVEMENT TO-DAY. *Third Edition. Crown 8vo. 2s. 6d.*
[Social Questions Series.

Horace : THE ODES AND EPODES. Translated by A. GODLEY, M.A., Fellow of Magdalen College, Oxford. *Crown 8vo. 2s.*
[Classical Translations.

E. L. S. Horsburgh, M.A. WATERLOO : A Narrative and Criticism. With Plans. *Second Edition. Crown 8vo. 5s.*
'A brilliant essay—simple, sound, and thorough.'—*Daily Chronicle.*
THE LIFE OF SAVONAROLA. With Portraits and Illustrations. *Second Edition. Fcap. 8vo. Cloth, 3s. 6d.; leather, 4s. net.* [Little Biographies.

R. F. Horton, D.D. JOHN HOWE. With Portrait. *Crown 8vo. 3s. 6d.*
[Leaders of Religion.

Alexander Hosie. MANCHURIA. With Illustrations and a Map. *Demy 8vo. 10s. 6d. net.*

G. Howell. TRADE UNIONISM—NEW AND OLD. *Third Edition. Crown 8vo. 2s. 6d.* [Social Questions Series.

A. W. Hutton, M.A. CARDINAL MANNING. With Portrait. *Crown 8vo. 3s. 6d.* [Leaders of Religion.
See also TAULER.

Edward Hutton. See Richard Crashaw.

R. H. Hutton. CARDINAL NEWMAN. With Portrait. *Crown 8vo. 3s. 6d.*
[Leaders of Religion.

W. H. Hutton, M.A. THE LIFE OF SIR THOMAS MORE. With Portraits. *Second Edition. Crown 8vo. 5s.*
WILLIAM LAUD. With Portrait. *Second Edition. Crown 8vo. 3s. 6d.*
[Leaders of Religion.

Henrik Ibsen. BRAND. A Drama. Translated by WILLIAM WILSON. *Third Edition. Crown 8vo. 3s. 6d.*

Lord Iddesleigh. See Susan Ferrier.

W. R. Inge, M.A., Fellow and Tutor of Hertford College, Oxford. CHRISTIAN MYSTICISM. The Bampton Lectures for 1899. *Demy 8vo. 12s. 6d. net.*
'It is fully worthy of the best traditions connected with the Bampton Lectureship.'—*Record.*

A. D. Innes, M.A. A HISTORY OF THE BRITISH IN INDIA. With Maps and Plans. *Crown 8vo. 7s. 6d.*
'Written in a vigorous and effective style . . . a thoughtful and impartial account.'—*Spectator.*

S. Jackson, M.A. A PRIMER OF BUSINESS. *Third Edition. Crown 8vo. 1s. 6d.* [Commercial Series.

F. Jacob, M.A. JUNIOR FRENCH EXAMINATION PAPERS. *Fcap. 8vo. 1s.* [Junior Examination Series.

J. Stephen Jeans. TRUSTS, POOLS, AND CORNERS. *Crown 8vo. 2s. 6d.* [Social Questions Series.

E. Jenks, M.A., Professor of Law at University College, Liverpool. ENGLISH LOCAL GOVERNMENT. *Crown 8vo. 2s. 6d.* [University Extension Series.

C. S. Jerram, M.A. See Pascal.

Augustus Jessopp, D.D. JOHN DONNE. With Portrait. *Crown 8vo. 3s. 6d.*
[Leaders of Religion.

F. B. Jevons, M.A., Litt.D., Principal of Hatfield Hall, Durham. EVOLUTION. *Crown 8vo. 3s. 6d.* [Churchman's Library.
AN INTRODUCTION TO THE HISTORY OF RELIGION. *Second Edition. Demy 8vo. 10s. 6d.*
[Handbooks of Theology.
'The merit of this book lies in the penetration, the singular acuteness and force of the author's judgment. He is at once critical and luminous, at once just and suggestive. A comprehensive and thorough book.'—*Birmingham Post.*

Sir H. H. Johnston, K.C.B. BRITISH CENTRAL AFRICA. With nearly 200 Illustrations and Six Maps. *Second Edition. Crown 4to.* 18s. net.

H. Jones. A GUIDE TO PROFESSIONS AND BUSINESS. *Crown 8vo.* 1s. 6d.
[Commercial Series.

Lady Julian of Norwich. REVELATIONS OF DIVINE LOVE. Edited by GRACE WARRACK. *Crown 8vo.* 3s. 6d.
A partially modernised version, from the MS. in the British Museum of a book which Mr. Inge in his Bampton Lectures calls 'The beautiful but little known *Revelations.*'

M. Kaufmann. SOCIALISM AND MODERN THOUGHT. *Crown 8vo.* 2s. 6d. [Social Questions Series.

J. F. Keating, D.D. THE AGAPE AND THE EUCHARIST. *Crown 8vo.* 3s. 6d.

John Keble. THE CHRISTIAN YEAR. With an Introduction and Notes by W. LOCK, D.D., Warden of Keble College. Illustrated by R. ANNING BELL. *Second Edition. Fcap. 8vo.* 3s. 6d; *padded morocco*, 5s.

THE CHRISTIAN YEAR. With Introduction and Notes by WALTER LOCK, D.D., Warden of Keble College. *Second Edition. Pott 8vo.* Cloth, 2s.; *leather*, 2s. 6d. net. [Library of Devotion.

LYRA INNOCENTIUM. Edited, with Introduction and Notes, by WALTER LOCK, D.D., Warden of Keble College, Oxford. *Pott 8vo.* Cloth, 2s.; *leather*, 2s. 6d. net.
[Library of Devotion.
'This sweet and fragrant book has never been published more attractively.'—
Academy.

Thomas À Kempis. THE IMITATION OF CHRIST. With an Introduction by DEAN FARRAR. Illustrated by C. M. GERE. *Second Edition. Fcap. 8vo.* 3s. 6d. net; *padded morocco*, 5s.

THE IMITATION OF CHRIST. A Revised Translation, with an Introduction by C. BIGG, D.D., late Student of Christ Church. *Third Edition. Pott 8vo.* Cloth, 2s.; *leather*, 2s. 6d. net.
[Library of Devotion.
A practically new translation of this book which the reader has, almost for the first time, exactly in the shape in which it left the hands of the author.
THE SAME EDITION IN LARGE TYPE. *Crown 8vo.* 3s. 6d.

James Houghton Kennedy, D.D., Assistant Lecturer in Divinity in the University of Dublin. ST. PAUL'S SECOND AND THIRD EPISTLES TO THE CORINTHIANS. With Introduction, Dissertations and Notes. *Crown 8vo.* 6s.

J. D. Kestell. THROUGH SHOT AND FLAME : Being the Adventures and Experiences of J. D. KESTELL, Chaplain to General Christian de Wet. *Crown 8vo.* 6s.

C. W. Kimmins, M.A. THE CHEMISTRY OF LIFE AND HEALTH. Illustrated. *Crown 8vo.* 2s. 6d.
[University Extension Series.

A. W. Kinglake. EOTHEN. With an Introduction and Notes. *Pott 8vo.* Cloth, 1s. 6d. net; *leather*, 2s. 6d. net.
[Little Library.

Rudyard Kipling. BARRACK-ROOM BALLADS. *73rd Thousand. Crown 8vo.* 6s. ; *leather*, 6s. net.
'Mr. Kipling's verse is strong, vivid, full of character. . . . Unmistakable genius rings in every line.'—*Times.*
'The ballads teem with imagination, they palpitate with emotion. We read them with laughter and tears : the metres throb in our pulses, the cunningly ordered words tingle with life ; and if this be not poetry, what is?'—*Pall Mall Gazette.*

THE SEVEN SEAS. *62nd Thousand. Crown 8vo.* Buckram, gilt top, 6s. ; *leather*, 6s. net.
'The Empire has found a singer ; it is no depreciation of the songs to say that statesmen may have, one way or other, to take account of them.'—
Manchester Guardian.

F. G. Kitton. See Dickens.

W. J. Knox Little. See St. Francis de Sales.

Charles Lamb. THE ESSAYS OF ELIA. With over 100 Illustrations by A. GARTH JONES, and an Introduction by E. V. LUCAS. *Demy 8vo.* 10s. 6d.
'This edition is in many respects of peculiar beauty.'—*Daily Chronicle.*
ELIA, AND THE LAST ESSAYS OF ELIA. Edited by E. V. LUCAS. *Pott 8vo.* Cloth, 1s. 6d. net; *leather*, 2s. 6d. net.
[Little Library.
THE KING AND QUEEN OF HEARTS : An 1805 Book for Children. Illustrated by WILLIAM MULREADY. A new edition, in facsimile, edited by E. V. LUCAS. 1s. 6d.
This little book is a literary curiosity, and has been discovered and identified as the work of Charles Lamb by E. V. Lucas. It is an exact facsimile of the original edition, which was illustrated by Mulready.

Professor Lambros. ECTHESIS CHRONICA. Edited by. *Demy 8vo.* 7s. 6d. net. [Byzantine Texts.

Stanley Lane-Poole. THE LIFE OF SIR HARRY PARKES. *A New and Cheaper Edition. Crown 8vo.* 6s.
A HISTORY OF EGYPT IN THE MIDDLE AGES. Fully Illustrated. *Crown 8vo.* 6s.

A 3

F. Langbridge, M.A. BALLADS OF THE BRAVE : Poems of Chivalry, Enterprise, Courage, and Constancy. *Second Edition. Crown 8vo.* 2s. 6d.
'The book is full of splendid things.'— *World.*

William Law. A SERIOUS CALL TO A DEVOUT AND HOLY LIFE. Edited, with an Introduction, by C. BIGG, D.D., late Student of Christ Church. *Pott 8vo. Cloth,* 2s.; *leather,* 2s. 6d. *net.*
[Library of Devotion.
This is a reprint, word for word and line for line, of the *Editio Princeps.*

G. S. Layard. THE LIFE OF MRS. LYNN LINTON. Illustrated. *Demy 8vo.* 12s. 6d.

Captain Melville Lee. A HISTORY OF POLICE IN ENGLAND. *Crown 8vo.* 7s. 6d.
'A learned book, comprising many curious details to interest the general reader as well as the student who will consult it for exact information.'—*Daily News.*

V. B. Lewes, M.A. AIR AND WATER. Illustrated. *Crown 8vo.* 2s. 6d.
[University Extension Series.

W. M. Lindsay. See Plautus.

Walter Lock, D.D., Warden of Keble College. ST. PAUL, THE MASTER-BUILDER. *Crown 8vo.* 3s. 6d.
See also Keble and Westminster Commentaries.

JOHN KEBLE. With Portrait. *Crown 8vo.* 3s. 6d. [Leaders of Religion.

E. V. Lucas. THE VISIT TO LONDON. Described in Verse, with Coloured Pictures by F. D. BEDFORD. *Small 4to.* 6s.
This charming book describes the introduction of a country child to the delights and sights of London. It is the result of a well-known partnership between author and artist.
'A beautiful children's book.'
Black and White.
'The most inimitable verses and interesting pictures.'—*Daily Chronicle.*
'Of quite unusual charm.'
Daily Telegraph.
See also Jane Austen and Mrs. Gaskell and Charles Lamb.

Lucian. SIX DIALOGUES (Nigrinus, Icaro-Menippus, The Cock, The Ship, The Parasite, The Lover of Falsehood). Translated by S. T. Irwin, M.A., Assistant Master at Clifton; late Scholar of Exeter College, Oxford. *Crown 8vo.* 3s. 6d.
[Classical Translations.

L. W. Lyde, M.A. A COMMERCIAL GEOGRAPHY OF THE BRITISH EMPIRE. *Third Edition. Crown 8vo.* 2s.
[Commercial Series.

Hon. Mrs. Lyttelton. WOMEN AND THEIR WORK. *Crown 8vo.* 2s. 6d.
'Thoughtful, interesting, practical.'— *Guardian.*
'The book is full of sound precept given with sympathy and wit.'—*Pilot.*

Lord Macaulay. CRITICAL AND HISTORICAL ESSAYS. Edited by F. C. MONTAGUE, M.A. *Three Volumes. Cr. 8vo.* 6s. *each.* [Methuen's Standard Library.
The only edition of this book completely annotated.

J. E. B. M'Allen, M.A. THE PRINCIPLES OF BOOKKEEPING BY DOUBLE ENTRY. *Crown 8vo.* 2s.
[Commercial Series.

J. A. MacCulloch. COMPARATIVE THEOLOGY. *Crown 8vo.* 6s.
[The Churchman's Library.
'Most carefully executed, readable and informing.'—*Scotsman.*

F. MacCunn. JOHN KNOX. With Portrait. *Crown 8vo.* 3s. 6d.
[Leaders of Religion.

A. M. Mackay. THE CHURCHMAN'S INTRODUCTION TO THE OLD TESTAMENT. *Crown 8vo.* 3s. 6d.
[Churchman's Library.
'The book throughout is frank and courageous.'—*Glasgow Herald.*

Laurie Magnus, M.A. A PRIMER OF WORDSWORTH. *Crown 8vo.* 2s. 6d.

J. P. Mahaffy, Litt.D. A HISTORY OF THE EGYPT OF THE PTOLEMIES. Fully Illustrated. *Crown 8vo.* 6s.

F. W. Maitland, LL.D., Downing Professor of the Laws of England in the University of Cambridge. CANON LAW IN ENGLAND. *Royal 8vo.* 7s. 6d.

H. E. Malden, M.A. ENGLISH RECORDS. A Companion to the History of England. *Crown 8vo.* 3s. 6d.
THE ENGLISH CITIZEN : HIS RIGHTS AND DUTIES. *Crown 8vo.* 1s. 6d.

E. C. Marchant, M.A., Fellow of Peterhouse, Cambridge, and Assistant Master at St. Paul's School. A GREEK ANTHOLOGY. *Second Edition. Crown 8vo.* 3s. 6d.

E. C. Marchant, M.A., and **A. M. Cook,** M.A. PASSAGES FOR UNSEEN TRANSLATION. *Second Edition. Crown 8vo.* 3s. 6d.
'We know no book of this class better fitted for use in the higher forms of schools.' —*Guardian.*

J. E. Marr, F.R.S., Fellow of St. John's College, Cambridge. THE SCIENTIFIC STUDY OF SCENERY. *Second Edition.* Illustrated. *Crown 8vo.* 6s.
'A volume, moderate in size and readable in style, which will be acceptable alike to the student of geology and geography and to the tourist.'—*Athenæum.*

A. J. Mason. THOMAS CRANMER. With Portrait. *Crown 8vo. 3s. 6d.* [Leaders of Religion.

George Massee. THE EVOLUTION OF PLANT LIFE: Lower Forms. With Illustrations. *Crown 8vo. 2s. 6d.* [University Extension Series.

C. F. G. Masterman, M.A. TENNYSON AS A RELIGIOUS TEACHER. *Crown 8vo. 6s.*
'A thoughtful and penetrating appreciation, full of interest and suggestion.'— *World.*

Annie Matheson. See Mrs. Craik.

Emma S. Mellows. A SHORT STORY OF ENGLISH LITERATURE. *Crown 8vo. 3s. 6d.*
'A lucid and well-arranged account of the growth of English literature.'—*Pall Mall Gazette.*

L. C. Miall, F.R.S. See Gilbert White.

E. B. Michell. THE ART AND PRACTICE OF HAWKING. With 3 Photogravures by G. E. LODGE, and other Illustrations. *Demy 8vo. 10s. 6d.*

J. G. Millais. THE LIFE AND LETTERS OF SIR JOHN EVERETT MILLAIS, President of the Royal Academy. With 319 Illustrations, of which 9 are Photogravure. *2 vols. Royal 8vo. 20s. net.*
'This splendid work.'—*World.*
'Of such absorbing interest is it, of such completeness in scope and beauty. Special tribute must be paid to the extraordinary completeness of the illustrations.'—*Graphic.*

J. G. Milne, M.A. A HISTORY OF ROMAN EGYPT. Fully Illustrated. *Crown 8vo. 6s.*

P. Chalmers Mitchell, M.A. OUTLINES OF BIOLOGY. Illustrated. *Second Edition. Crown 8vo. 6s.*
A text-book designed to cover the Schedule issued by the Royal College of Physicians and Surgeons.

D. M. Moir. MANSIE WAUCH. Edited by T. F. HENDERSON. *Pott 8vo. Cloth, 1s. 6d. net; leather, 2s. 6d. net.* [Little Library.

F. C. Montague, M.A. See Macaulay.

H. E. Moore. BACK TO THE LAND: An Inquiry into the cure for Rural Depopulation. *Crown 8vo. 2s. 6d.* [Social Questions Series.

W. R. Morfill, Oriel College, Oxford. A HISTORY OF RUSSIA FROM PETER THE GREAT TO ALEXANDER II. With Maps and Plans. *Crown 8vo. 7s. 6d.*
This history, is founded on a study of original documents, and though necessarily brief, is the most comprehensive narrative in existence. Considerable attention has been paid to the social and literary development of the country, and the recent expansion of Russia in Asia.

R. J. Morich, late of Clifton College. GERMAN EXAMINATION PAPERS IN MISCELLANEOUS GRAMMAR AND IDIOMS. *Sixth Edition. Crown 8vo. 2s. 6d.* [School Examination Series.
A KEY, issued to Tutors and Private Students only, to be had on application to the Publishers. *Second Edition. Crown 8vo. 6s. net.*

Miss Anderson Morton. See Miss Brodrick.

H C. G. Moule, D D., Lord Bishop of Durham. CHARLES SIMEON. With Portrait. *Crown 8vo. 3s. 6d.* [Leaders of Religion.

M. M. Pattison Muir, M.A. THE CHEMISTRY OF FIRE. The Elementary Principles of Chemistry. Illustrated. *Crown 8vo. 2s. 6d.* [University Extension Series.

V. A. Mundella, M.A. See J. T. Dunn.

W. G. Neal. See R. N. Hall.

H. W. Nevinson. LADYSMITH: The Diary of a Siege. With 16 Illustrations and a Plan. *Second Edition. Crown 8vo. 6s.*

J. B. B. Nichols. A LITTLE BOOK OF ENGLISH SONNETS. *Pott 8vo. Cloth, 1s. 6d. net; leather, 2s. 6d. net.* [The Little Library.

James Northcote, R.A., THE CONVERSATIONS OF, WITH JAMES WARD. Edited by ERNEST FLETCHER. With many Portraits. *Demy 8vo. 10s. 6d.*

A. H. Norway, Author of 'Highways and Byways in Devon and Cornwall.' NAPLES: PAST AND PRESENT. With 40 Illustrations by A. G. FERARD. *Crown 8vo. 6s.*

Mrs. Oliphant. THOMAS CHALMERS. With Portrait. *Crown 8vo. 3s. 6d.* [Leaders of Religion.

C. W. Oman, M.A., Fellow of All Souls', Oxford. A HISTORY OF THE ART OF WAR. Vol. II.: The Middle Ages, from the Fourth to the Fourteenth Century. Illustrated. *Demy 8vo. 21s.*
'The whole art of war in its historic evolution has never been treated on such an ample and comprehensive scale, and we question if any recent contribution to the exact history of the world has possessed more enduring value.'—*Daily Chronicle.*

Prince Henri of Orleans. FROM TONKIN TO INDIA. Translated by HAMLEY BENT, M.A. With 100 Illustrations and a Map. *Crown 4to, gilt top. 25s.*

R. L. Ottley, M.A., late Fellow of Magdalen College, Oxon., and Principal of Pusey House. THE DOCTRINE OF THE INCARNATION. *Second and cheaper Edition. Demy 8vo. 12s. 6d.* [Handbooks of Theology.
'A clear and remarkably full account of the main currents of speculation. Scholarly precision . . . genuine tolerance . . . intense interest in his subject—are Mr. Ottley's merits.'—*Guardian.*

LANCELOT ANDREWES. With Portrait. *Crown 8vo.* 3s. 6d.
[Leaders of Religion.

J. H. Overton, M.A. JOHN WESLEY. With Portrait. *Crown 8vo.* 3s. 6d.
[Leaders of Religion.

M. N. Oxford, of Guy's Hospital. A HANDBOOK OF NURSING. *Crown 8vo.* 3s. 6d.
'The most useful work of the kind that we have seen. A most valuable and practical manual.'—*Manchester Guardian.*

W. C. C. Pakes. THE SCIENCE OF HYGIENE. With numerous Illustrations. *Demy 8vo.* 15s.
'A thoroughgoing working text-book of its subject, practical and well-stocked.'—*Scotsman.*

Prof. Léon Parmentier and M. Bidez. EVAGRIUS. Edited by. *Demy 8vo.* 10s. 6d. net. [Byzantine Texts.

Pascal, THE THOUGHTS OF. With Introduction and Notes by C. S. JERRAM. *Pott 8vo.* 2s.; *leather,* 2s. 6d. net.
[Library of Devotion.

George Paston. SIDELIGHTS ON THE GEORGIAN PERIOD. With many Illustrations. *Demy 8vo.* 10s. 6d.
'Touched with lightness and sympathy. We recommend this book to all who are tired with the trash of novels.'—*Spectator.*
'This book is the highly diverting product of research and compilation. It is a magazine of instructive and amusing information.'—*Academy.*

H. W. Paul. See Laurence Sterne.

E. H. Pearce, M.A. THE ANNALS OF CHRIST'S HOSPITAL. With many Illustrations. *Demy 8vo.* 7s. 6d.
'A well-written, copious, authentic history.'—*Times.*

R. E. Peary, Gold Medallist of the Royal Geographical Society. NORTHWARD OVER THE GREAT ICE. With over 800 Illustrations. *2 vols. Royal 8vo.* 32s. net.
'His book will take its place among the permanent literature of Arctic exploration.'—*Times.*

Sidney Peel, late Fellow of Trinity College, Oxford, and Secretary to the Royal Commission on the Licensing Laws. PRACTICAL LICENSING REFORM. *Second Edition. Crown 8vo.* 1s. 6d.

M. Perugini. SELECTIONS FROM WILLIAM BLAKE. *Pott 8vo. Cloth,* 1s. 6d. net; *leather,* 2s. 6d. net.
[Little Library.

J. P. Peters, D.D. THE OLD TESTAMENT AND THE NEW SCHOLARSHIP. *Crown 8vo.* 6s.
[Churchman's Library.

'Every page reveals wide reading, used with sound and scholarly judgment.'
—*Manchester Guardian.*

W. M. Flinders Petrie, D.C.L., LL.D., Professor of Egyptology at University College. A HISTORY OF EGYPT, FROM THE EARLIEST TIMES TO THE PRESENT DAY. Fully Illustrated. *In six volumes. Crown 8vo.* 6s. each.
'A history written in the spirit of scientific precision so worthily represented by Dr. Petrie and his school cannot but promote sound and accurate study, and supply a vacant place in the English literature of Egyptology.'—*Times.*

VOL. I. PREHISTORIC TIMES TO XVITH DYNASTY. *Fifth Edition.*

VOL. II. THE XVIITH AND XVIIITH DYNASTIES. *Third Edition.*

VOL. IV. THE EGYPT OF THE PTOLEMIES. J. P. MAHAFFY, Litt.D.

VOL. V. ROMAN EGYPT. J. G. MILNE, M.A.

VOL. VI. EGYPT IN THE MIDDLE AGES. STANLEY LANE-POOLE, M.A.

RELIGION AND CONSCIENCE IN ANCIENT EGYPT. Fully Illustrated. *Crown 8vo.* 2s. 6d.

SYRIA AND EGYPT, FROM THE TELL EL AMARNA TABLETS. *Crown 8vo.* 2s. 6d.

EGYPTIAN TALES. Illustrated by TRISTRAM ELLIS. *In Two Volumes. Crown 8vo.* 3s. 6d. each.

EGYPTIAN DECORATIVE ART. With 120 Illustrations. *Crown 8vo.* 3s. 6d.
'In these lectures he displays rare skill in elucidating the development of decorative art in Egypt.'—*Times.*

Philip Pienaar. WITH STEYN AND DE WET. *Second Edition. Crown 8vo.* 3s. 6d.
A narrative of the adventures of a Boer telegraphist of the Orange Free State during the war.

Plautus. THE CAPTIVI. Edited, with an Introduction, Textual Notes, and a Commentary, by W. M. LINDSAY, Fellow of Jesus College, Oxford. *Demy 8vo.* 10s. 6d. net.
For this edition all the important MSS. have been re-collated. An appendix deals with the accentual element in early Latin verse. The Commentary is very full.

THE CAPTIVI. Adapted for Lower Forms, by J. H. FREESE, M.A., late Fellow of St. John's, Cambridge. 1s. 6d.

J. T. Plowden-Wardlaw, B.A., King's College, Cambridge. EXAMINATION PAPERS IN ENGLISH HISTORY. *Crown 8vo.* 2s. 6d.
[School Examination Series.

Frank Podmore. MODERN SPIRITUAL-ISM. *Two Volumes. Demy 8vo. 21s. net.*
A History and a Criticism.
'A complete guide to a very complex subject.'—*Academy.*
'Of great scientific value and considerable popular interest.'—*Scotsman.*
'A masterpiece of scientific analysis and exposition. There is no doubt it will hold the field for a long time.'—*Star.*
'The entire book is characterised by the greatest candour and fairness, and affords pleasant reading upon an entrancing theme.'—*Public Opinion.*

A. W. Pollard. OLD PICTURE BOOKS. With many Illustrations. *Demy 8vo. 7s. 6d. net.*

M. C. Potter, M.A., F.L.S. A TEXT-BOOK OF AGRICULTURAL BOTANY. Illustrated. *2nd Edition. Crown 8vo. 4s. 6d.* [University Extension Series.

G. Pradeau. A KEY TO THE TIME ALLUSIONS IN THE DIVINE COMEDY. With a Dial. *Small quarto. 3s. 6d.*

L. L. Price, M.A., Fellow of Oriel College, Oxon. A HISTORY OF ENGLISH POLITICAL ECONOMY. *Fourth Edition. Crown 8vo. 2s. 6d.* [University Extension Series.

"Q." THE GOLDEN POMP. A Procession of English Lyrics. Arranged by A. T. QUILLER COUCH. *Crown 8vo. Buckram. 6s.*

R. B. Rackham, M.A. THE ACTS OF THE APOSTLES. With Introduction and Notes. *Demy 8vo. 12s. 6d.* [Westminster Commentaries.
'A really helpful book. Both introduction and commentary are marked by common sense and adequate knowledge.'—*Guardian.*

B. W. Randolph, D.D., Principal of the Theological College, Ely. THE PSALMS OF DAVID. With an Introduction and Notes. *Pott 8vo. Cloth, 2s.; leather, 2s. 6d. net.* Library of Devotion.
A devotional and practical edition of the Prayer Book version of the Psalms.

Hastings Rashdall, M.A., Fellow and Tutor of New College, Oxford. DOCTRINE AND DEVELOPMENT. *Crown 8vo. 6s.*

W. Reason, M.A. UNIVERSITY AND SOCIAL SETTLEMENTS. *Crown 8vo. 2s. 6d.* [Social Questions Series.

Charles Richardson. THE ENGLISH TURF. With numerous Illustrations and Plans. *Demy 8vo. 15s.*

M. E. Roberts. See C. C. Channer.

A. Robertson, D.D., Bishop of Exeter. REGNUM DEI. The Bampton Lectures of 1901. *Demy 8vo. 12s. 6d. net.*
'A notable volume. Its chief value and interest is in its historic treatment of its great theme.'—*Daily News.*
'It is altogether a solid piece of work and a valuable contribution to the history of Christian thought.'—*Scotsman.*

Sir G. S. Robertson, K.C.S.I. CHITRAL: The Story of a Minor Siege. With numerous Illustrations, Map and Plans. *Second Edition. Demy 8vo. 10s. 6d.*
'A book which the Elizabethans would have thought wonderful. More thrilling, more piquant, and more human than any novel.'—*Newcastle Chronicle.*

J. W. Robertson-Scott. THE PEOPLE OF CHINA. With a Map. *Crown 8vo. 3s. 6d.*

A. W. Robinson, M.A. THE EPISTLE TO THE GALATIANS. Explained. *Fcap. 8vo. 1s. 6d. net.* [Churchman's Bible.
'The most attractive, sensible, and instructive manual for people at large, which we have ever seen.'—*Church Gazette.*

Cecilia Robinson. THE MINISTRY OF DEACONESSES. With an Introduction by the Lord Bishop of Winchester. *Crown 8vo. 3s. 6d.*

G. Rodwell, B.A. NEW TESTAMENT GREEK. A Course for Beginners. With a Preface by WALTER LOCK, D.D., Warden of Keble College. *Fcap. 8vo. 3s. 6d.*

Fred Roe. ANCIENT COFFERS AND CUPBOARDS: Their History and Description. With many Illustrations. *Quarto. £3, 3s. net.*

E. S. Roscoe. ROBERT HARLEY, EARL OF OXFORD. Illustrated. *Demy 8vo. 7s. 6d.*
This is the only life of Harley in existence.

Edward Rose. THE ROSE READER. With numerous Illustrations. *Crown 8vo. 2s. 6d. Also in 4 Parts. Parts I. and II. 6d. each; Part III. 8d.; Part IV. 10d.*
A reader on a new and original plan.
The distinctive feature of this book is the entire avoidance of irregularly-spelt words until the pupil has thoroughly mastered the principle of reading, and learned its enjoyment. The reading of connected sentences begins from the first page, before the entire alphabet is introduced.

E. Denison Ross, M.A. See W. Beckford

A. E. Rubie, M.A., Head Master of the Royal Naval School, Eltham. THE GOSPEL ACCORDING TO ST. MARK. Edited by. With three Maps. *Crown 8vo. 1s. 6d.* [Methuen's Junior School Books.

W. Clark Russell. THE LIFE OF ADMIRAL LORD COLLINGWOOD. With Illustrations by F. BRANGWYN. *Fourth Edition. Crown 8vo. 6s.*
'A book which we should like to see in the hands of every boy in the country.'— *St. James's Gazette.*

St. Anselm, THE DEVOTIONS OF. Edited by C. C. J. WEBB, M.A. *Pott 8vo. Cloth, 2s.; leather, 2s. 6d. net.* [Library of Devotion.

Viscount St. Cyres. THE LIFE OF FRANÇOIS DE FENELON. Illustrated. *Demy 8vo. 10s. 6d.*
'We have in this admirable volume a most valuable addition to our historical portrait gallery.'—*Daily News.*

St. Francis de Sales. ON THE LOVE OF GOD. Edited by W. J. KNOX-LITTLE, M.A. *Pott 8vo. Cloth, 2s.; leather, 2s. 6d. net.* [Library of Devotion.

A. L. Salmon. CORNWALL. Illustrated by B. C. BOULTER. *Pott 8vo. Cloth, 3s.; leather, 3s. 6d. net.* [The Little Guides.

J. Sargeaunt, M.A. ANNALS OF WESTMINSTER SCHOOL. With numerous Illustrations. *Demy 8vo. 7s. 6d.*

C. Sathas. THE HISTORY OF PSELLUS. *Demy 8vo. 15s. net.* [Byzantine Texts.

H. G. Seeley, F.R.S. DRAGONS OF THE AIR. With many Illustrations. *Crown 8vo. 6s.*
A popular history of the most remarkable flying animals which ever lived. Their relations to mammals, birds, and reptiles, living and extinct, are shown by an original series of illustrations.

V. P. Sells, M.A. THE MECHANICS OF DAILY LIFE. Illustrated. *Crown 8vo. 2s. 6d.* [University Extension Series.

Edmund Selous. TOMMY SMITH'S ANIMALS. Illustrated by G. W. ORD. *Second Edition. Fcap. 8vo. 2s. 6d.*
'A quaint, fascinating little book : a nursery classic.'—*Athenæum.*

William Shakespeare.
THE ARDEN EDITION.
Demy 8vo. 3s. 6d. each volume. General Editor, W. J. CRAIG. An Edition of Shakespeare in single Plays. Edited with a full Introduction, Textual Notes, and a Commentary at the foot of the page.
'No edition of Shakespeare is likely to prove more accurate and satisfactory than this one. It is beautifully printed and paged and handsomely and simply bound.'— *St. James's Gazette.*

HAMLET. Edited by EDWARD DOWDEN, Litt.D.

ROMEO AND JULIET. Edited by EDWARD DOWDEN, Litt.D.

KING LEAR. Edited by W. J. CRAIG.

JULIUS CAESAR. Edited by M. MACMILLAN, M.A.

THE TEMPEST. Edited by MORTON LUCE.

A. Sharp. VICTORIAN POETS. *Crown 8vo. 2s. 6d.* [University Extension Series.

J. S. Shedlock. THE PIANOFORTE SONATA: Its Origin and Development. *Crown 8vo. 5s.*

Arthur Sherwell, M.A. LIFE IN WEST LONDON. *Third Edition. Crown 8vo. 2s. 6d.* [Social Questions Series.

Evan Small, M.A. THE EARTH. An Introduction to Physiography. Illustrated. *Crown 8vo. 2s. 6d.* [University Extension Series.

Nowell C. Smith, M.A., Fellow of New College, Oxford. SELECTIONS FROM WORDSWORTH. *Pott 8vo. Cloth, 1s. 6d. net; leather, 2s. 6d. net.* [Little Library.

Sophocles. ELECTRA AND AJAX. Translated by E. D. A. MORSHEAD, M.A., Assistant Master at Winchester. *2s. 6d.* [Classical Translations.

R. Southey. ENGLISH SEAMEN (Howard, Clifford, Hawkins, Drake, Cavendish). Edited, with an Introduction, by DAVID HANNAY. *Second Edition. Crown 8vo. 6s.*
'A brave, inspiriting book.'—*Black and White.*

C. H. Spence, M.A., Clifton College. HISTORY AND GEOGRAPHY EXAMINATION PAPERS. *Second Edition. Crown 8vo. 2s. 6d.* [School Examination Series.

W. A. Spooner, M.A., Warden of New College, Oxford. BISHOP BUTLER. With Portrait. *Crown 8vo. 3s. 6d.* [Leaders of Religion.

J. W. Stanbridge, B.D., Rector of Bainton, Canon of York, and sometime Fellow of St. John's College, Oxford. A BOOK OF DEVOTIONS. *Pott 8vo. Cloth, 2s.; leather, 2s. 6d. net.* [Library of Devotion.
'It is probably the best book of its kind. It deserves high commendation.'—*Church Gazette.*
See also Cardinal Bona.

'Stancliffe.' GOLF DO'S AND DONT'S. *Second Edition. Fcap. 8vo. 1s.*

A. M. M. Stedman, M.A.
INITIA LATINA : Easy Lessons on Elementary Accidence. *Sixth Edition. Fcap. 8vo. 1s.*

FIRST LATIN LESSONS. *Seventh Edition. Crown 8vo. 2s.*

FIRST LATIN READER. With Notes adapted to the Shorter Latin Primer and

Vocabulary. *Sixth Edition revised.* 18mo. 1s. 6d.

EASY SELECTIONS FROM CÆSAR. The Helvetian War. *Second Edition.* 18mo. 1s.

EASY SELECTIONS FROM LIVY. Part I. The Kings of Rome. 18mo. *Second Edition.* 1s. 6d.

EASY LATIN PASSAGES FOR UNSEEN TRANSLATION. *Eighth Edition.* Fcap. 8vo. 1s. 6d.

EXEMPLA LATINA. First Exercises in Latin Accidence. With Vocabulary. *Crown 8vo.* 1s.

EASY LATIN EXERCISES ON THE SYNTAX OF THE SHORTER AND REVISED LATIN PRIMER. With Vocabulary. *Ninth and Cheaper Edition, re-written. Crown 8vo.* 1s. 6d. KEY, 3s. net. *Original Edition.* 2s. 6d.

THE LATIN COMPOUND SENTENCE: Rules and Exercises. *Second Edition. Crown 8vo.* 1s. 6d. With Vocabulary. 2s.

NOTANDA QUAEDAM: Miscellaneous Latin Exercises on Common Rules and Idioms. *Fourth Edition. Fcap. 8vo.* 1s. 6d. With Vocabulary. 2s. Key, 2s. net.

LATIN VOCABULARIES FOR REPETITION: Arranged according to Subjects. *Eleventh Edition. Fcap. 8vo.* 1s. 6d.

A VOCABULARY OF LATIN IDIOMS. 18mo. *Second Edition.* 1s.

STEPS TO GREEK. *Second Edition, revised.* 18mo. 1s.

A SHORTER GREEK PRIMER. *Crown 8vo.* 1s. 6d.

EASY GREEK PASSAGES FOR UNSEEN TRANSLATION. *Third Edition, revised.* Fcap. 8vo. 1s. 6d.

GREEK VOCABULARIES FOR REPETITION. Arranged according to Subjects. *Third Edition. Fcap. 8vo.* 1s. 6d.

GREEK TESTAMENT SELECTIONS. For the use of Schools. With Introduction, Notes, and Vocabulary. *Third Edition.* Fcap. 8vo. 2s. 6d.

STEPS TO FRENCH. *Sixth Edition.* 18mo. 8d.

FIRST FRENCH LESSONS. *Sixth Edition, revised. Crown 8vo.* 1s.

EASY FRENCH PASSAGES FOR UNSEEN TRANSLATION. *Fifth Edition, revised.* Fcap. 8vo. 1s. 6d.

EASY FRENCH EXERCISES ON ELEMENTARY SYNTAX. With Vocabulary. *Second Edition. Crown 8vo.* 2s. 6d. KEY. 3s. net.

FRENCH VOCABULARIES FOR REPETITION: Arranged according to Subjects. *Tenth Edition. Fcap. 8vo.* 1s.

FRENCH EXAMINATION PAPERS IN MISCELLANEOUS GRAMMAR AND IDIOMS. *Twelfth Edition. Crown 8vo.* 2s. 6d. [School Examination Series.

A KEY, issued to Tutors and Private Students only, to be had on application to the Publishers. *Fifth Edition. Crown 8vo.* 6s. net.

GENERAL KNOWLEDGE EXAMINATION PAPERS. *Fourth Edition. Crown 8vo.* 2s. 6d. [School Examination Series. KEY (*Second Edition*) issued as above. 7s. net.

GREEK EXAMINATION PAPERS IN MISCELLANEOUS GRAMMAR AND IDIOMS. *Sixth Edition. Crown 8vo.* 2s. 6d. [School Examination Series. KEY (*Third Edition*) issued as above. 6s. net.

LATIN EXAMINATION PAPERS IN MISCELLANEOUS GRAMMAR AND IDIOMS. *Eleventh Edition. Crown 8vo.* 2s. 6d. [School Examination Series. KEY (*Fourth Edition*) issued as above. 6s. net.

R. Elliott Steel, M.A., F.C.S. THE WORLD OF SCIENCE. Including Chemistry, Heat, Light, Sound, Magnetism, Electricity, Botany, Zoology, Physiology, Astronomy, and Geology. 147 Illustrations. *Second Edition. Crown 8vo.* 2s. 6d.

PHYSICS EXAMINATION PAPERS. *Crown 8vo.* 2s. 6d. [School Examination Series.

C. Stephenson, of the Technical College, Bradford, and **F. Suddards,** of the Yorkshire College, Leeds. ORNAMENTAL DESIGN FOR WOVEN FABRICS. *Demy 8vo. Second Edition.* 7s. 6d.

J. Stephenson, M.A. THE CHIEF TRUTHS OF THE CHRISTIAN FAITH. *Crown 8vo.* 3s. 6d.

An attempt to present in clear and popular form the main truths of the Faith. The book is intended for lay workers in the Church, for educated parents and for teachers generally.

Laurence Sterne. A SENTIMENTAL JOURNEY. Edited by H. W. PAUL. *Pott 8vo. Cloth,* 1s. 6d. *net; leather,* 2s. 6d. *net.* [Little Library.

W. Sterry, M.A. ANNALS OF ETON COLLEGE. With numerous Illustrations. *Demy 8vo.* 7s. 6d.

Katherine Steuart. BY ALLAN WATER. *Second Edition. Crown 8vo.* 6s.

'A delightful mixture of fiction and fact, tradition and history. There is not a page which is not informing and not entertaining.' —*Spectator.*

'A charming book.'—*Glasgow Herald.*

'Has a unique charm.'—*Pilot.*
'A unique series of historical pictures.'—*Manchester Guardian.*

R. L. Stevenson. THE LETTERS OF ROBERT LOUIS STEVENSON TO HIS FAMILY AND FRIENDS. Selected and Edited, with Notes and Introductions, by SIDNEY COLVIN. *Sixth and Cheaper Edition. Crown 8vo.* 12s.
LIBRARY EDITION. *Demy 8vo.* 2 *vols.* 25s. *net.*
'Irresistible in their raciness, their variety, their animation . . . of extraordinary fascination. A delightful inheritance, the truest record of a "richly compounded spirit" that the literature of our time has preserved.'—*Times.*

VAILIMA LETTERS. With an Etched Portrait by WILLIAM STRANG. *Third Edition. Crown 8vo. Buckram.* 6s.

THE LIFE OF R. L. STEVENSON. See G. Balfour.

E. D. Stone, M.A., late Assistant Master at Eton. SELECTIONS FROM THE ODYSSEY. *Fcap. 8vo.* 1s. 6d.

Charles Strachey. See Chesterfield.

A. W. Streane, D.D. ECCLESIASTES. Explained. *Fcap. 8vo.* 1s. 6d. *net.*
[Churchman's Bible.
'Scholarly, suggestive, and particularly interesting.'—*Bookman.*

Clement E. Stretton. A HISTORY OF THE MIDLAND RAILWAY. With numerous Illustrations. *Demy 8vo.* 12s. 6d.

H. Stroud, D.Sc., M.A., Professor of Physics in the Durham College of Science, Newcastle-on-Tyne. PRACTICAL PHYSICS. Fully Illustrated. *Crown 8vo.* 3s. 6d.
[Textbooks of Technology.

Capt. Donald Stuart. THE STRUGGLE FOR PERSIA. With a Map. *Crown 8vo.* 6s.

F. Suddards. See C. Stephenson.

Jonathan Swift. THE JOURNAL TO STELLA. Edited by G. A. AITKEN. *Crown 8vo.* 6s. [Methuen's Standard Library.

J. E. Symes, M.A. THE FRENCH REVOLUTION. *Crown 8vo.* 2s. 6d.
[University Extension Series.

Netta Syrett. A SCHOOL YEAR. Illustrated. *Demy 16mo.* 2s. 6d.
[Little Blue Books.

Tacitus. AGRICOLA. With Introduction, Notes, Map, etc. By R. F. DAVIS, M.A., late Assistant Master at Weymouth College. *Crown 8vo.* 2s.

GERMANIA. By the same Editor. *Crown 8vo.* 2s.

AGRICOLA AND GERMANIA. Translated by R. B. TOWNSHEND, late Scholar of

Trinity College, Cambridge. *Crown 8vo.* 2s. 6d. [Classical Translations.

J. Tauler. THE INNER WAY. Being Thirty-six Sermons for Festivals by JOHN TAULER. Edited, with an Introduction. By A. W. HUTTON, M.A. *Pott 8vo. Cloth,* 2s. ; *leather,* 2s. 6d. *net.*
[Library of Devotion.

E. L. Taunton. A HISTORY OF THE JESUITS IN ENGLAND. With Illustrations. *Demy 8vo.* 21s. *net.*
'A history of permanent value, which covers ground never properly investigated before, and is replete with the results of original research. A most interesting and careful book.'—*Literature.*

F. G. Taylor, M.A. COMMERCIAL ARITHMETIC. *Third Edition. Crown 8vo.* 1s. 6d. [Commercial Series.

Miss I. A. Taylor. SIR WALTER RALEIGH. With 12 Illustrations. *Fcap. 8vo. Cloth,* 3s. 6d. ; *leather* 4s. *net.*
[Little Biographies.

T. M. Taylor, M.A., Fellow of Gonville and Caius College, Cambridge. A CONSTITUTIONAL AND POLITICAL HISTORY OF ROME. *Crown 8vo.* 7s. 6d.
'We fully recognise the value of this carefully written work, and admire especially the fairness and sobriety of his judgment and the human interest with which he has inspired his subject.'—*Athenæum.*

Alfred, Lord Tennyson. THE EARLY POEMS OF. Edited, with Notes and an Introduction, by J. CHURTON COLLINS, M.A. *Crown 8vo.* 6s.
[Methuen's Standard Library.
Also with 10 Illustrations in Photogravure by W. E. F. BRITTEN. *Demy 8vo.* 10s. 6d.
An elaborate edition of the celebrated volume which was published in its final and definitive form in 1853.

IN MEMORIAM, MAUD, AND THE PRINCESS. Edited by J. CHURTON COLLINS, M.A. *Crown 8vo.* 6s.
[Methuen's Standard Library.

MAUD. Edited by ELIZABETH WORDSWORTH. *Pott 8vo. Cloth,* 1s. 6d. *net; leather,* 2s. 6d. *net.* [Little Library.

IN MEMORIAM. Edited, with an Introduction and Notes, by H. C. BEECHING, M.A. *Pott 8vo. Cloth,* 1s. 6d. *net; leather,* 2s. 6d. *net.* [Little Library.

THE EARLY POEMS OF. Edited by J. C. COLLINS, M.A. *Pott 8vo. Cloth,* 1s. 6d. *net; leather,* 2s. *net.* [Little Library.

THE PRINCESS. Edited by ELIZABETH WORDSWORTH. *Pott 8vo. Cloth,* 1s. 6d. *net; leather,* 2s. 6d. *net.* [Little Library.

Alice Terton. LIGHTS AND SHADOWS IN A HOSPITAL. *Crown 8vo.* 3s. 6d.

W. M. Thackeray. VANITY FAIR. With an Introduction by S. GWYNN. *Three*

Volumes. *Pott 8vo. Each volume, cloth,*
1s. 6d. net; leather, 2s. 6d. net.
[Little Library.
PENDENNIS. Edited by S. GWYNN.
Three Volumes. Pott 8vo. Each volume,
cloth, 1s. 6d. net · leather, 2s. 6d. net.
[Little Library.
ESMOND. Edited by STEPHEN GWYNN.
Two volumes. Pott 8vo. Each Volume,
cloth, 1s. 6d. net; leather, 2s. 6d. net.
[Little Library.
F. W. Theobald, M.A. INSECT LIFE.
Illustrated. *Crown 8vo.* 2s. 6d.
[University Extension Series.
A. H. Thompson. CAMBRIDGE AND
ITS COLLEGES. Illustrated by E. H.
NEW. *Pott 8vo. Cloth,* 3s.; *leather,*
3s. 6d. net. [Little Guides.
'It is brightly written and learned, and
is just such a book as a cultured visitor
needs.'—*Scotsman.*
Paget Toynbee, Litt.D., M.A. See Dante.
DANTE STUDIES AND RESEARCHES.
Demy 8vo. 10s. 6d. net.
THE LIFE OF DANTE ALIGHIERI.
With 12 Illustrations. *Second Edition.*
Fcap. 8vo. Cloth, 3s. 6d.; *leather,* 4s.
net. [Little Biographies.
Herbert Trench. DEIRDRE WED: and
Other Poems. *Crown 8vo.* 5s.
G. E. Troutbeck. WESTMINSTER
ABBEY. Illustrated by F. D. BEDFORD.
Pott 8vo. Cloth, 3s.; *leather,* 3s. 6d. net.
[Little Guides.
'In comeliness, and perhaps in complete-
ness, this work must take the first place.'—
Academy.
'A really first-rate guide-book.'—
Literature.
Gertrude Tuckwell. THE STATE AND
ITS CHILDREN. *Crown 8vo.* 2s. 6d.
[Social Questions Series.
Louisa Twining. WORKHOUSES AND
PAUPERISM. *Crown 8vo.* 2s. 6d.
[Social Questions Series.
E. A. Tyler. A JUNIOR CHEMISTRY.
With 73 Diagrams. *Crown 8vo.* 2s. 6d.
[Methuen's Junior School Books.
G. W. Wade, D.D. OLD TESTAMENT
HISTORY. With Maps. *Second Edition.*
Crown 8vo. 6s.
'Careful, scholarly, embodying the best
results of modern criticism, and written
with great lucidity.'—*Examiner.*
Izaak Walton. THE LIVES OF DONNE,
WOTTON, HOOKER, HERBERT AND
SANDERSON. With an Introduction by
VERNON BLACKBURN, and a Portrait. 3s. 6d.
THE COMPLEAT ANGLER. Edited by
J. BUCHAN. *Pott 8vo. Cloth.* 1s. 6d. net;
leather, 2s. 6d. net. [Little Library.
D. S. Van Warmelo. ON COMMANDO.
With Portrait. *Crown 8vo.* 3s. 6d.
'A fighting Boer's simple, straightforward
story of his life on commando. . . . Full of
entertaining incidents.'—*Pall Mall Gazette.*

Grace Warrack. See Lady Julian of Nor-
wich.
Mrs. Alfred Waterhouse. A LITTLE
BOOK OF LIFE AND DEATH. Edited
by. *Second Edition. Pott 8vo. Cloth,* 1s. 6d.
net; *leather,* 2s. 6d. net. [Little Library.
C. C. J. Webb, M.A. See St. Anselm.
F. C. Webber. CARPENTRY AND
JOINERY. With many Illustrations.
Third Edition. Crown 8vo. 3s. 6d.
'An admirable elementary text-book on
the subject.'—*Builder.*
Sidney H. Wells. PRACTICAL ME-
CHANICS. With 75 Illustrations and
Diagrams. *Second Edition. Crown 8vo.*
3s. 6d. [Textbooks of Technology.
J. Wells, M.A., Fellow and Tutor of Wadham
College. OXFORD AND OXFORD
LIFE. By Members of the University.
Third Edition Crown 8vo. 3s. 6d.
A SHORT HISTORY OF ROME. *Fourth*
Edition. With 3 Maps. *Cr. 8vo.* 3s. 6d.
This book is intended for the Middle and
Upper Forms of Public Schools and for
Pass Students at the Universities. It con-
tains copious Tables, etc.
'An original work written on an original
plan, and with uncommon freshness and
vigour.'—*Speaker.*
OXFORD AND ITS COLLEGES. Illus-
trated by E. H. New. *Fifth Edition.*
Pott 8vo. Cloth, 3s.; *leather,* 3s. 6d. net.
[Little Guides.
'An admirable and accurate little treat-
ise, attractively illustrated.'—*World.*
Helen C. Wetmore. THE LAST OF THE
GREAT SCOUTS ('Buffalo Bill'). With
Illustrations. *Second Edition. Demy 8vo.* 6s.
'A narrative of one of the most attractive
figures in the public eye.'—*Daily Chronicle.*
C. Whibley. See Henley and Whibley.
L. Whibley, M.A., Fellow of Pembroke
College, Cambridge. GREEK OLIGAR-
CHIES: THEIR ORGANISATION
AND CHARACTER. *Crown 8vo.* 6s.
G. H. Whitaker, M.A. THE EPISTLE
OF ST. PAUL THE APOSTLE TO
THE EPHESIANS. Edited by. *Fcap.*
8vo. 1s. 6d. net. [Churchman's Bible.
Gilbert White. THE NATURAL HIS-
TORY OF SELBORNE. Edited by
L. C. MIALL, F.R.S., assisted by W.
WARDE FOWLER, M.A. *Crown 8vo.* 6s.
[Methuen's Standard Library.
E. E. Whitfield. PRECIS WRITING
AND OFFICE CORRESPONDENCE.
Second Edition. Crown 8vo. 2s.
[Commercial Series.
COMMERCIAL EDUCATION IN
THEORY AND PRACTICE. *Crown*
8vo. 5s.
An introduction to Methuen's Commercial
Series treating the question of Commercial
Education fully from both the point of view
of the teacher and of the parent.
[Commercial Series.

Miss Whitley. See Lady Dilke.
W. H. Wilkins, B.A. THE ALIEN INVASION. *Crown 8vo. 2s. 6d.*
[Social Questions Series.
W. Williamson. THE BRITISH GAR-DENER. Illustrated. *Demy 8vo. 10s. 6d.*
W. Williamson, B.A. JUNIOR ENGLISH EXAMINATION PAPERS. *Fcap. 8vo. 1s.* [Junior Examination Series.
A JUNIOR ENGLISH GRAMMAR. With numerous passages for parsing and analysis, and a chapter on Essay Writing. *Crown 8vo. 2s.* [Methuen's Junior School Books.
A CLASS-BOOK OF DICTATION PASSAGES. *Seventh Edition. Crown 8vo. 1s. 6d.* [Methuen's Junior School Books.
EASY DICTATION AND SPELLING. *Second Edition. Fcap. 8vo. 1s.*
E. M. Wilmot-Buxton. THE MAKERS OF EUROPE. *Crown 8vo. 3s. 6d.*
A Text-book of European History for Middle Forms.
'A book which will be found extremely useful.'—*Secondary Education.*
Beckles Willson. LORD STRATHCONA: the Story of his Life. Illustrated. *Demy 8vo. 7s. 6d.*
'An admirable biography, telling in the happiest manner the wonderful career of this giant of empire.'—*Black and White.*
'We should be glad to see this work taken as a model for imitation. He has given us an excellent and quite adequate account of the life of the distinguished Scotsman.'—*World.*
Richard Wilton, M.A., Canon of York. LYRA PASTORALIS: Songs of Nature, Church, and Home. *Pott 8vo. 2s. 6d.*
A volume of devotional poems.
S. E. Winbolt, M.A., Assistant Master in Christ's Hospital. EXERCISES IN LATIN ACCIDENCE. *Crown 8vo. 1s.6d.*
An elementary book adapted for Lower Forms to accompany the Shorter Latin Primer.
B. C. A. Windle, F.R.S., D.Sc. SHAKE-SPEARE'S COUNTRY. Illustrated by E. H. NEW. *Second Edition. Pott 8vo. Cloth, 3s.; leather, 3s.6d. net.* [Little Guides.

'One of the most charming guide books. Both for the library and as a travelling companion the book is equally choice and serviceable.'—*Academy.*
THE MALVERN COUNTRY. Illustrated by E. H. NEW. *Pott 8vo. Cloth, 3s.; leather, 3s. net.* [Little Guides.
Canon Winterbotham, M.A., B.Sc., LL.B. THE KINGDOM OF HEAVEN HERE AND HEREAFTER. *Crown 8vo. 3s. 6d.* [Churchman's Library.
J. A. E. Wood. HOW TO MAKE A DRESS. Illustrated. *Second Edition. Crown 8vo. 1s. 6d.* [Text Books of Technology.
Elizabeth Wordsworth. See Tennyson.
Arthur Wright, M.A., Fellow of Queen's College, Cambridge. SOME NEW TESTAMENT PROBLEMS. *Crown 8vo. 6s.* [Churchman's Library.
Sophie Wright. GERMAN VOCABU-LARIES FOR REPETITION. *Fcap. 8vo. 1s. 6d.*
A. B. Wylde. MODERN ABYSSINIA. With a Map and a Portrait. *Demy 8vo. 15s. net.*
G. Wyndham, M.P. THE POEMS OF WILLIAM SHAKESPEARE. With an Introduction and Notes. *Demy 8vo. Buck-ram, gilt top. 10s. 6d.*
'We have no hesitation in describing Mr. George Wyndham's introduction as a masterly piece of criticism, and all who love our Elizabethan literature will find a very garden of delight in it.'—*Spectator.*
W. B. Yeats. AN ANTHOLOGY OF IRISH VERSE. *Revised and Enlarged Edition. Crown 8vo. 3s. 6d.*
T. M. Young. THE AMERICAN COTTON INDUSTRY: A Study of Work and Workers. With an Introduction by ELIJAH HELM, Secretary to the Manchester Chamber of Commerce. *Crown 8vo. Cloth, 2s. 6d.; paper boards, 1s. 6d.*
'Thorough, comprehensive, disconcert-ing.'—*St. James's Gazette.*
'Able and interesting; a really excellent contribution.'—*Pilot.*

Methuen's Standard Library

Crown 8vo.   6s. each Volume.

'A series which, by the beauty and excellence of production as well as by the qualifications of its editors, is one of the best things now to be found in the book market.'—*Manchester Guardian.*

MEMOIRS OF MY LIFE AND WRITINGS. By Edward Gibbon. Edited by G. Birkbeck Hill, LL.D.
THE DECLINE AND FALL OF THE ROMAN EMPIRE. By Edward Gibbon. Edited by J. B. Bury, LL.D. *In Seven Volumes. Also, Demy 8vo. Gilt top. 8s. 6d. each.*
THE NATURAL HISTORY OF SELBORNE. By Gilbert White. Edited by L. C. Miall, F.R.S., Assisted by W. Warde Fowler, M.A.
THE HISTORY OF THE LIFE OF THOMAS ELL-WOOD. Edited by C. G. Crump, M.A.
LA COMMEDIA DI DANTE ALIGHIERI. The Italian Text. Edited by Paget Toynbee, Litt.D., M.A. *Also, Demy 8vo. Gilt top. 8s. 6d.*

THE EARLY POEMS OF ALFRED, LORD TENNYSON. Edited by J. Churton Collins, M.A.
IN MEMORIAM, MAUD, AND THE PRINCESS. By Alfred, Lord Tennyson. Edited by J. Churton Collins, M.A.
THE JOURNAL TO STELLA. By Jonathan Swift. Edited by G. A. Aitken, M.A.
THE LETTERS OF LORD CHESTERFIELD TO HIS SON. Edited by C. Strachey, and Notes by A. Calthrop. *Two Volumes.*
CRITICAL AND HISTORICAL ESSAYS. By Lord Macaulay. Edited by F. C. Montague, M.A. *Three Volumes.*
THE FRENCH REVOLUTION. By Thomas Carlyle. Edited by C. R. L. Fletcher, Fellow of Magdalen College, Oxford. *Three Volumes.*

Byzantine Texts.

Edited by J. B. BURY, M.A., Litt.D.

ZACHARIAH OF MITYLENE. Translated by F. J. Hamilton, D.D., and E. W. Brooks. *Demy 8vo.* 12s. 6d. net.

EVAGRIUS. Edited by Léon Parmentier and M. Bidez. *Demy 8vo.* 10s. 6d. net.

THE HISTORY OF PSELLUS. Edited by C. Sathas. *Demy 8vo.* 15s. net.

ECTHESIS CHRONICA. Edited by Professor Lambros. *Demy 8vo.* 7s. 6d. net.

The Little Library

With Introductions, Notes, and Photogravure Frontispieces.

Pott 8vo. Each Volume, cloth, 1s. 6d. net; leather, 2s. 6d. net.

'Altogether good to look upon, and to handle.'—*Outlook.*
'A perfect series.'—*Pilot.*
'It is difficult to conceive more attractive volumes.'—*St. James's Gazette.*
'Very delicious little books.'—*Literature.*

VANITY FAIR. By W. M. Thackeray. Edited by S. Gwynn. *Three Volumes.*

PENDENNIS. By W. M. Thackeray. Edited by S. Gwynn. *Three Volumes.*

ESMOND. By W. M. Thackeray. Edited by Stephen Gwynn. *Two Volumes.*

JOHN HALIFAX, GENTLEMAN. By Mrs. Craik. Edited by Annie Matheson. *Two Volumes.*

PRIDE AND PREJUDICE. By Jane Austen. Edited by E. V. Lucas. *Two Volumes.*

NORTHANGER ABBEY. By Jane Austen. Edited by E. V. Lucas.

THE PRINCESS. By Alfred, Lord Tennyson. Edited by Elizabeth Wordsworth.

MAUD. By Alfred, Lord Tennyson. Edited by Elizabeth Wordsworth.

IN MEMORIAM. By Alfred, Lord Tennyson. Edited by H. C. Beeching, M.A.

THE EARLY POEMS OF ALFRED, LORD TENNYSON. Edited by J. C. Collins, M.A.

A LITTLE BOOK OF ENGLISH LYRICS. With Notes.

THE INFERNO OF DANTE. Translated by H. F. Cary. Edited by Paget Toynbee, Litt.D., M.A.

THE PURGATORIO OF DANTE. Translated by H. F. Cary. Edited by Paget Toynbee, Litt.D., M.A.

THE PARADISO OF DANTE. Translated by H. F. Cary. Edited by Paget Toynbee, Litt.D., M.A.

A LITTLE BOOK OF SCOTTISH VERSE. Edited by T. F. Henderson.

A LITTLE BOOK OF LIGHT VERSE. Edited by A. C. Deane.

A LITTLE BOOK OF ENGLISH SONNETS. Edited by J. B. B. Nichols.

SELECTIONS FROM WORDSWORTH. Edited by Nowell C. Smith.

SELECTIONS FROM THE EARLY POEMS OF ROBERT BROWNING. Edited by W. Hall Griffin, M.A.

THE ENGLISH POEMS OF RICHARD CRASHAW. Edited by Edward Hutton.

SELECTIONS FROM WILLIAM BLAKE. Edited by M. Perugini.

A LITTLE BOOK OF LIFE AND DEATH. Edited by Mrs. Alfred Waterhouse.

A LITTLE BOOK OF ENGLISH PROSE. Edited by Mrs. P. A. Barnett.

EOTHEN. By A. W. Kinglake. With an Introduction and Notes.

CRANFORD. By Mrs. Gaskell. Edited by E. V. Lucas.

LAVENGRO. By George Borrow. Edited by F. Hindes Groome. *Two Volumes.*

THE HISTORY OF THE CALIPH VATHEK. By William Beckford. Edited by E. Denison Ross.

THE COMPLEAT ANGLER. By Izaak Walton. Edited by J. Buchan.

MARRIAGE. By Susan Ferrier. Edited by Miss Goodrich-Freer and Lord Iddesleigh. *Two Volumes.*

THE INHERITANCE. By Susan Ferrier. Edited by Miss Goodrich-Freer and Lord Iddesleigh. *Two Volumes.*

ELIA, AND THE LAST ESSAYS OF ELIA. By Charles Lamb. Edited by E. V. Lucas.

A SENTIMENTAL JOURNEY. By Laurence Sterne. Edited by H. W. Paul.

MANSIE WAUCH. By D. M. Moir. Edited by T. F. Henderson.

THE INGOLDSBY LEGENDS. By R. H. Barham. Edited by J. B. Atlay. *Two Volumes.*

THE SCARLET LETTER. By Nathaniel Hawthorne.

The Little Guides

Pott 8vo, cloth, 3s.; leather, 3s. 6d. net.

OXFORD AND ITS COLLEGES. By J. Wells, M.A. Illustrated by E. H. New. *Fourth Edition.*

CAMBRIDGE AND ITS COLLEGES. By A. Hamilton Thompson. Illustrated by E. H. New.

THE MALVERN COUNTRY. By B. C. A. Windle, D.Sc., F.R.S. Illustrated by E. H. New.

SHAKESPEARE'S COUNTRY. By B. C. A. Windle, D.Sc., F.R.S. Illustrated by E. H. New. *Second Edition.*

SUSSEX. By F. G. Brabant, M.A. Illustrated by E. H. New.

WESTMINSTER ABBEY. By G. E. Troutbeck. Illustrated by F. D. Bedford.

NORFOLK. By W. A. Dutt. Illustrated by B. C. Boulter.

CORNWALL. By A. L. Salmon. Illustrated by B. C. Boulter.

BRITTANY. By S. Baring-Gould. Illustrated by J. Wylie.

THE ENGLISH LAKES. By F. G. Brabant, M.A. Illustrated by E. H. New. 4s.; leather, 4s. 6d. net.

Little Biographies

Fcap. 8vo. Each volume, cloth, 3s. 6d. ; leather, 4s. net.

DANTE ALIGHIERI. By Paget Toynbee, Litt.D., M.A. With 12 Illustrations. *Second Edition.*

SAVONAROLA. By E. L. S. Horsburgh, M.A. With Portraits and Illustrations. *Second Edition.*

JOHN HOWARD. By E. C. S. Gibson, D.D., Vicar of Leeds. With 12 Illustrations.

TENNYSON. By A. C. Benson, M.A. With 12 Illustrations.

WALTER RALEIGH. By I. A. Taylor. With 12 Illustrations.

ERASMUS. By E. F. H. CAPEY. With 12 Illustrations.

The Little Blue Books

General Editor, E. V. LUCAS.

Illustrated. Demy 16mo. 2s. 6d.

'Very elegant and very interesting volumes.'—*Glasgow Herald.*
'A delightful series of diminutive volumes.'—*World.*
'The series should be a favourite among juveniles.'—*Observer.*

1. THE CASTAWAYS OF MEADOWBANK. By T. COBB.
2. THE BEECHNUT BOOK. By JACOB ABBOTT Edited by E. V. LUCAS.
3. THE AIR GUN. By T. HILBERT.
4. A SCHOOL YEAR. By NETTA SYRETT.
5. THE PEELES AT THE CAPITAL. By T. HILBERT.
6. THE TREASURE OF PRINCEGATE PRIORY. By T. COBB.

The Library of Devotion

With Introductions and (where necessary) Notes.

Pott 8vo, cloth, 2s. ; leather, 2s. 6d. net.

'This series is excellent.'—THE LATE BISHOP OF LONDON.
'Well worth the attention of the Clergy.'—THE BISHOP OF LICHFIELD.
'The new "Library of Devotion" is excellent.'—THE BISHOP OF PETERBOROUGH.
'Charming.'—*Record.*   'Delightful.'—*Church Bells.*

THE CONFESSIONS OF ST. AUGUSTINE. Edited by C. Bigg, D.D. *Third Edition.*

THE CHRISTIAN YEAR. Edited by Walter Lock, D.D. *Second Edition.*

THE IMITATION OF CHRIST. Edited by C. Bigg, D.D. *Second Edition.*

A BOOK OF DEVOTIONS. Edited by J. W. Stanbridge, B.D.

LYRA INNOCENTIUM. Edited by Walter Lock, D.D.

A SERIOUS CALL TO A DEVOUT AND HOLY LIFE. Edited by C. Bigg, D.D. *Second Edition.*

THE TEMPLE. Edited by E. C. S. Gibson, D.D.

A GUIDE TO ETERNITY. Edited by J. W. Stanbridge, B.D.

THE PSALMS OF DAVID. Edited by B. W. Randolph, D.D.

LYRA APOSTOLICA. Edited by Canon Scott Holland and H. C. Beeching, M.A.

THE INNER WAY. Edited by A. W. Hutton, M.A.

THE THOUGHTS OF PASCAL. Edited by C. S. Jerram, M.A.

ON THE LOVE OF GOD. Edited by W. J. Knox-Little, M.A.

A MANUAL OF CONSOLATION FROM THE SAINTS AND FATHERS. Edited by J. H. Burn, B.D.

THE SONG OF SONGS. Edited by B. Blaxland, M.A.

THE DEVOTIONS OF ST. ANSELM. Edited by C. C. J. Webb, M.A.

The Westminster Commentaries

General Editor, WALTER LOCK, D.D., Warden of Keble College,
Dean Ireland's Professor of Exegesis in the University of Oxford.

THE BOOK OF JOB. Edited by E. C. S. Gibson, D.D. *Demy 8vo. 6s.*

THE ACTS OF THE APOSTLES. Edited by R. B Rackham, M.A. *Demy 8vo. 12s. 6d.*

Handbooks of Theology

General Editor, A. ROBERTSON, D.D.

THE XXXIX. ARTICLES OF THE CHURCH OF ENGLAND. Edited by E. C. S. Gibson, D.D. *Third and Cheaper Edition in One Volume. Demy 8vo. 12s. 6d.*

AN INTRODUCTION TO THE HISTORY OF RELIGION. By F. B. Jevons, M.A., Litt.D. *Second Edition. Demy 8vo. 10s. 6d.*

THE DOCTRINE OF THE INCARNATION. By R. L. Ottley, M.A. *Second and Cheaper Edition. Demy 8vo. 12s. 6d.*

AN INTRODUCTION TO THE HISTORY OF THE CREEDS. By A. E. Burn, B.D. *Demy 8vo. 10s. 6d.*

THE PHILOSOPHY OF RELIGION IN ENGLAND AND AMERICA. By Alfred Caldecott, D.D. *Demy 8vo. 10s. 6d.*

The Churchman's Library

General Editor, J. H. BURN, B.D., F.R.S.E., Examining Chaplain to the Bishop of Aberdeen.

THE BEGINNINGS OF ENGLISH CHRISTIANITY. By W. E. Collins, M.A. With Map. *Crown 8vo. 3s. 6d.*

SOME NEW TESTAMENT PROBLEMS. By Arthur Wright, M.A. *Crown 8vo. 6s.*

THE KINGDOM OF HEAVEN HERE AND HERE-AFTER. By Canon Winterbotham, M.A., B.Sc., LL.B. *Crown 8vo. 3s. 6d.*

THE WORKMANSHIP OF THE PRAYER BOOK: Its Literary and Liturgical Aspects. By J. Dowden, D.D. *Second Edition. Crown 8vo. 3s. 6d.*

EVOLUTION. By F. B. Jevons, M.A., Litt.D. *Crown 8vo. 3s. 6d.*

THE OLD TESTAMENT AND THE NEW SCHOLAR-SHIP. By J. W. Peters, D.D. *Crown 8vo. 6s.*

THE CHURCHMAN'S INTRODUCTION TO THE OLD TESTAMENT. Edited by A. M. Mackay, B.A. *Crown 8vo. 3s. 6d.*

THE CHURCH OF CHRIST. By E. T. Green, M.A. *Crown 8vo. 6s.*

COMPARATIVE THEOLOGY. By J. A. MacCulloch. *Crown 8vo. 6s.*

The Churchman's Bible

General Editor, J. H. BURN, B.D., F.R.S.E.

The volumes are practical and devotional, and the text of the Authorised Version is explained in sections, which correspond as far as possible with the Church Lectionary.

THE EPISTLE TO THE GALATIANS. Explained by A. W. Robinson, M.A. *Fcap. 8vo. 1s. 6d. net.*

ECCLESIASTES. Explained by A. W. Streane, D.D. *Fcap. 8vo. 1s. 6d. net.*

THE EPISTLE TO THE PHILIPPIANS. Explained by C. R. D. Biggs, D.D. *Fcap. 8vo. 1s. 6d. net.*

THE EPISTLE OF ST. JAMES. Edited by H. W. Fulford, M.A. *Fcap. 8vo. 1s. 6d. net.*

ISAIAH. Edited by W. E. Barnes, D.D., Hulsaean Professor of Divinity. *Two Volumes. Fcap. 8vo. 2s. net each.* Vol. I. With Map.

THE EPISTLE OF ST. PAUL THE APOSTLE TO THE EPHESIANS. Edited by G. H. Whitaker, M.A. *Fcap. 8vo. 1s. 6d. net.*

Leaders of Religion

Edited by H. C. BEECHING, M.A. *With Portraits. Crown 8vo. 3s. 6d.*

A series of short biographies of the most prominent leaders of religious life and thought of all ages and countries.

CARDINAL NEWMAN. By R. H. Hutton.
JOHN WESLEY. By J. H. Overton, M.A.
BISHOP WILBERFORCE. By G. W. Daniell, M.A.
CARDINAL MANNING. By A. W. Hutton, M.A.
CHARLES SIMEON. By H. C. G. Moule, D.D.
JOHN KEBLE. By Walter Lock, D.D.
THOMAS CHALMERS. By Mrs. Oliphant.
LANCELOT ANDREWES. By R. L. Ottley, M.A.
AUGUSTINE OF CANTERBURY. By E. L. Cutts, D.D.
WILLIAM LAUD. By W. H. Hutton, M.A.

JOHN KNOX. By F. MacCunn.
JOHN HOWE. By R. F. Horton, D.D.
BISHOP KEN. By F. A. Clarke, M.A.
GEORGE FOX, THE QUAKER. By T. Hodgkin. D.C.L.
JOHN DONNE. By Augustus Jessopp, D.D.
THOMAS CRANMER. By A. J. Mason.
BISHOP LATIMER. By R. M. Carlyle and A. J. Carlyle, M.A.
BISHOP BUTLER. By W. A. Spooner, M.A.

Social Questions of To-day

Edited by H. DE B. GIBBINS, Litt.D., M.A.

Crown 8vo. 2s. 6d.

TRADE UNIONISM—NEW AND OLD. By G. Howell. *Third Edition.*
THE CO-OPERATIVE MOVEMENT TO-DAY. By G. J. Holyoake. *Second Edition.*
PROBLEMS OF POVERTY. By J. A. Hobson, M.A. *Fourth Edition.*
THE COMMERCE OF NATIONS. By C. F. Bastable, M.A. *Second Edition.*
THE ALIEN INVASION. By W. H. Wilkins, B.A.
THE RURAL EXODUS. By P. Anderson Graham.
LAND NATIONALIZATION. By Harold Cox, B.A.
A SHORTER WORKING DAY. By H. de B. Gibbins and R. A. Hadfield.
BACK TO THE LAND: An Inquiry into Rural Depopulation. By H. E. Moore.
TRUSTS, POOLS, AND CORNERS. By J. Stephen Jeans.
THE FACTORY SYSTEM. By R. W. Cooke-Taylor.

THE STATE AND ITS CHILDREN. By Gertrude Tuckwell.
WOMEN'S WORK. By Lady Dilke, Miss Bulley, and Miss Whitley.
SOCIALISM AND MODERN THOUGHT. By M. Kauffmann.
THE HOUSING OF THE WORKING CLASSES. By E. Bowmaker.
THE PROBLEM OF THE UNEMPLOYED. By J. A. Hobson, B.A.
LIFE IN WEST LONDON. By Arthur Sherwell, M.A. *Third Edition.*
RAILWAY NATIONALIZATION. By Clement Edwards.
WORKHOUSES AND PAUPERISM. By Louisa Twining.
UNIVERSITY AND SOCIAL SETTLEMENTS. By W. Reason, M.A.

University Extension Series

Edited by J. E. SYMES, M.A.,
Principal of University College, Nottingham.

Crown 8vo.   Price (with some exceptions) 2s. 6d.

A series of books on historical, literary, and scientific subjects, suitable for extension students and home-reading circles. Each volume is complete in itself, and the subjects are treated by competent writers in a broad and philosophic spirit.

THE INDUSTRIAL HISTORY OF ENGLAND. By H. de B. Gibbins, Litt.D., M.A. *Eighth Edition.* Revised. With Maps and Plans. 3s.

A HISTORY OF ENGLISH POLITICAL ECONOMY. By L. L. Price, M.A. *Third Edition.*

PROBLEMS OF POVERTY. By J. A. Hobson, M.A. *Fourth Edition.*

VICTORIAN POETS. By A. Sharp.

THE FRENCH REVOLUTION. By J. E. Symes, M.A.

PSYCHOLOGY. By S. F. Granger, M.A. *Second Edition.*

THE EVOLUTION OF PLANT LIFE: Lower Forms. By G. Massee. Illustrated.

AIR AND WATER. By V. B. Lewes, M.A. Illustrated.

THE CHEMISTRY OF LIFE AND HEALTH. By C. W. Kimmins, M.A. Illustrated.

THE MECHANICS OF DAILY LIFE. By V. P. Sells, M.A. Illustrated.

ENGLISH SOCIAL REFORMERS. By H. de B. Gibbins, Litt.D., M.A. *Second Edition.*

ENGLISH TRADE AND FINANCE IN THE SEVENTEENTH CENTURY. By W. A. S. Hewins, B.A.

THE CHEMISTRY OF FIRE. By M. M. Pattison Muir, M.A. Illustrated.

A TEXT-BOOK OF AGRICULTURAL BOTANY. By M. C. Potter, M.A., F.L.S. Illustrated. *Second Edition.* 4s. 6d.

THE VAULT OF HEAVEN. A Popular Introduction to Astronomy. By R. A. Gregory. With numerous Illustrations.

METEOROLOGY. By H. N. Dickson, F.R.S.E., F.R. Met. Soc. Illustrated.

A MANUAL OF ELECTRICAL SCIENCE. By George J. Burch, M.A., F.R.S. Illustrated. 3s.

THE EARTH. An Introduction to Physiography. By Evan Small, M.A. Illustrated.

INSECT LIFE. By F. W. Theobald, M.A. Illustrated.

ENGLISH POETRY FROM BLAKE TO BROWNING. By W. M. Dixon, M.A. *Second Edition.*

ENGLISH LOCAL GOVERNMENT. By E. Jenks, M.A.

THE GREEK VIEW OF LIFE. By G. L. Dickinson. *Second Edition.*

Methuen's Commercial Series

Edited by H. DE B. GIBBINS, Litt.D., M.A.

COMMERCIAL EDUCATION IN THEORY AND PRACTICE. By E. E. Whitfield, M.A.
An introduction to Methuen's Commercial Series treating the question of Commercial Education fully from both the point of view of the teacher and of the parent.

BRITISH COMMERCE AND COLONIES FROM ELIZABETH TO VICTORIA. By H. de B. Gibbins, Litt.D., M.A. *Third Edition.* 2s.

COMMERCIAL EXAMINATION PAPERS. By H. de B. Gibbins, Litt.D., M.A. 1s. 6d.

THE ECONOMICS OF COMMERCE. By H. de B. Gibbins, Litt.D., M.A. 1s. 6d.

A GERMAN COMMERCIAL READER. By S. E. Bally, With Vocabulary. 2s.

A COMMERCIAL GEOGRAPHY OF THE BRITISH EMPIRE. By L. W. Lyde, M.A. *Third Edition.*

A PRIMER OF BUSINESS. By S. Jackson, M.A. *Third Edition.* 1s. 6d.

COMMERCIAL ARITHMETIC. By F. G. Taylor, M.A. *Third Edition.* 1s. 6d.

FRENCH COMMERCIAL CORRESPONDENCE. By S. E. Bally. With Vocabulary. *Third Edition.* 2s.

GERMAN COMMERCIAL CORRESPONDENCE. By S. E. Bally. With Vocabulary. 2s. 6d.

A FRENCH COMMERCIAL READER. By S. E. Bally. With Vocabulary. *Second Edition.* 2s.

PRECIS WRITING AND OFFICE CORRESPONDENCE. By E. E. Whitfield, M.A. *Second Edition.* 2s.

A GUIDE TO PROFESSIONS AND BUSINESS. By H. Jones. 1s. 6d.

THE PRINCIPLES OF BOOK-KEEPING BY DOUBLE ENTRY. By J. E. B. M'Allen, M.A. 2s.

COMMERCIAL LAW. By W. Douglas Edwards. 2s.

A COMMERCIAL GEOGRAPHY OF FOREIGN NATIONS. By F. C. Boon, B.A. 2s.

Classical Translations

Edited by H. F. FOX, M.A., Fellow and Tutor of Brasenose College, Oxford.

ÆSCHYLUS—Agamemnon, Choephoroe, Eumenides. Translated by Lewis Campbell, LL.D. 5s.

CICERO—De Oratore I. Translated by E. N. P. Moor, M.A. 3s. 6d.

CICERO—Select Orations (Pro Milone, Pro Mureno, Philippic II., in Catilinam). Translated by H. E. D. Blakiston, M.A. 5s.

CICERO—De Natura Deorum. Translated by F. Brooks, M.A. 3s. 6d.

CICERO—De Officiis. Translated by G. B. Gardiner, M.A. 2s. 6d.

HORACE—The Odes and Epodes. Translated by A. Godley, M.A. 2s.

LUCIAN—Six Dialogues (Nigrinus, Icaro-Menippus, The Cock, The Ship, The Parasite, The Lover of Falsehood). Translated by S. T. Irwin, M.A. 3s. 6d.

SOPHOCLES—Electra and Ajax. Translated by E. D. A. Morshead, M.A. 2s.

TACITUS—Agricola and Germania. Translated by R. B. Townshend. 2s. 6d.

Methuen's Junior School=Books

Edited by O. D. INSKIP, LL.D., and W. WILLIAMSON, B.A.

A CLASS-BOOK OF DICTATION PASSAGES. By W. Williamson, B.A. *Seventh Edition. Crown 8vo. 1s. 6d.*

THE GOSPEL ACCORDING TO ST. MARK. Edited by A. E. Rubie, M.A., Headmaster of the Royal Naval School, Eltham. With Three Maps. *Crown 8vo. 1s. 6d.*

A JUNIOR ENGLISH GRAMMAR. By W. Williamson, B.A. With numerous passages for parsing and analysis, and a chapter on Essay Writing. *Crown 8vo. 2s.*

A JUNIOR CHEMISTRY. By E. A. Tyler, B.A., F.C.S., Science Master at Swansea Grammar School. With 73 Diagrams. *Crown 8vo. 2s. 6d.*

School Examination Series

Edited by A. M. M. STEDMAN, M.A. *Crown 8vo. 2s. 6d.*

FRENCH EXAMINATION PAPERS. By A. M. M. Stedman, M.A. *Twelfth Edition.* A KEY, issued to Tutors and Private Students only, to be had on application to the Publishers. *Fifth Edition. Crown 8vo. 6s. net.*

LATIN EXAMINATION PAPERS. By A. M. M. Stedman, M.A. *Eleventh Edition.* KEY (*Fourth Edition*) issued as above. *6s. net.*

GREEK EXAMINATION PAPERS. By A. M. M. Stedman, M.A. *Sixth Edition.* KEY (*Second Edition*) issued as above. *6s. net.*

GERMAN EXAMINATION PAPERS. By R. J. Morich. *Fifth Edition.* KEY (*Second Edition*) issued as above. *6s. net.*

HISTORY AND GEOGRAPHY EXAMINATION PAPERS. By C. H. Spence, M.A., Clifton College. *Second Edition.*

PHYSICS EXAMINATION PAPERS. By R. E. Steel, M.A., F.C.S.

GENERAL KNOWLEDGE EXAMINATION PAPERS. By A. M. M. Stedman, M.A. *Fourth Edition.* KEY (*Second Edition*) issued as above. *7s. net.*

EXAMINATION PAPERS IN ENGLISH HISTORY. By J. Tait Plowden-Wardlaw, B.A. *Crown 8vo. 2s. 6d.*

Junior Examination Series

Edited by A. M. M. STEDMAN, M.A. *Fcap. 8vo. 1s.*

JUNIOR FRENCH EXAMINATION PAPERS. By F. Jacob, B.A.

JUNIOR LATIN EXAMINATION PAPERS. By C. G. BOTTING, M.A.

JUNIOR ENGLISH EXAMINATION PAPERS. By W. Williamson, B.A., Headmaster West Kent Grammar School, Brockley.

JUNIOR ARITHMETIC EXAMINATION PAPERS. By W. S. Beard.

JUNIOR ALGEBRA EXAMINATION PAPERS. By W. S. Finn, M.A., Sandbach School.

Technology—Textbooks of

Edited by W. GARNETT, D.C.L., and PROFESSOR J. WERTHEIMER, F.I.C. *Fully Illustrated.*

HOW TO MAKE A DRESS. By J. A. E Wood. *Second Edition. Crown 8vo. 1s. 6d.*

CARPENTRY AND JOINERY. By F. C. Webber. *Third Edition. Crown 8vo. 3s. 6d.*

PRACTICAL MECHANICS. By Sidney H. Wells. *Second Edition. Crown 8vo. 3s. 6d.*

PRACTICAL PHYSICS. By H. Stroud, D.Sc., M.A. *Crown 8vo. 3s. 6d.*

MILLINERY, THEORETICAL AND PRACTICAL. By Clare Hill. *Crown 8vo. 2s.*

PRACTICAL CHEMISTRY. By W. French, M.A. *Crown 8vo.* Part I. *Second Edition. 1s. 6d.*

PART II.—FICTION

Marie Corelli's Novels.

Crown 8vo. 6s. each.

A ROMANCE OF TWO WORLDS. *Twenty-Fourth Edition.*

VENDETTA. *Nineteenth Edition.*

THELMA. *Twenty-Eighth Edition.*

ARDATH: THE STORY OF A DEAD SELF. *Fourteenth Edition.*

THE SOUL OF LILITH. *Eleventh Edit.*

WORMWOOD. *Twelfth Edition.*

BARABBAS: A DREAM OF THE

WORLD'S TRAGEDY. *Thirty-Eighth Edition.*

'The tender reverence of the treatment and the imaginative beauty of the writing have reconciled us to the daring of the conception. This "Dream of the World's Tragedy" is a lofty and not inadequate paraphrase of the supreme climax of the inspired narrative.'—*Dublin Review.*

THE SORROWS OF SATAN. *Forty-Sixth Edition.*
'A very powerful piece of work. . . . The conception is magnificent, and is likely to win an abiding place within the memory of man. . . . The author has immense command of language, and a limitless audacity. . . . This interesting and remarkable romance will live long after much of the ephemeral literature of the day is forgotten. . . . A literary phenomenon . . . novel, and even sublime.'—W. T. STEAD in the *Review of Reviews.*

THE MASTER CHRISTIAN.
[*165th Thousand.*
'It cannot be denied that "The Master Christian" is a powerful book ; that it is one likely to raise uncomfortable questions in all but the most self-satisfied readers, and that it strikes at the root of the failure of the Churches—the decay of faith—in a manner which shows the inevitable disaster heaping up. . . . The good Cardinal Bonpré is a beautiful figure, fit to stand beside the good Bishop in " Les Misérables." It is a

book with a serious purpose expressed with absolute unconventionality and passion . . . And this is to say it is a book worth reading.'—*Examiner.*

TEMPORAL POWER: A STUDY IN SUPREMACY.
[*150th Thousand.*
'It is impossible to read such a work as "Temporal Power" without becoming convinced that the story is intended to convey certain criticisms on the ways of the world and certain suggestions for the betterment of humanity. . . . The chief characteristics of the book are an attack on conventional prejudices and manners and on certain practices attributed to the Roman Church (the policy of M. Combes makes parts of the novel specially up to date), and the propounding of theories for the improvement of the social and political systems. . . . If the chief intention of the book was to hold the mirror up to shams, injustice, dishonesty, cruelty, and neglect of conscience, nothing but praise can be given to that intention.'—*Morning Post.*

Anthony Hope's Novels.
Crown 8vo. 6s. each.

THE GOD IN THE CAR. *Ninth Edition.*
'A very remarkable book, deserving of critical analysis impossible within our limit ; brilliant, but not superficial ; well considered, but not elaborated ; constructed with the proverbial art that conceals, but yet allows itself to be enjoyed by readers to whom fine literary method is a keen pleasure.'—*The World.*

A CHANGE OF AIR. *Sixth Edition.*
'A graceful, vivacious comedy, true to human nature. The characters are traced with a masterly hand.'—*Times.*

A MAN OF MARK. *Fifth Edition.*
'Of all Mr. Hope's books, "A Man of Mark" is the one which best compares with "The Prisoner of Zenda."'—*National Observer.*

THE CHRONICLES OF COUNT ANTONIO. *Fifth Edition.*
'It is a perfectly enchanting story of love and chivalry, and pure romance. The Count is the most constant, desperate, and

modest and tender of lovers, a peerless gentleman, an intrepid fighter, a faithful friend, and a magnanimous foe.'—*Guardian.*

PHROSO. Illustrated by H. R. MILLAR. *Sixth Edition.*
'The tale is thoroughly fresh, quick with vitality, stirring the blood.'—*St. James's Gazette.*

SIMON DALE. Illustrated. *Sixth Edition.*
'There is searching analysis of human nature, with a most ingeniously constructed plot. Mr. Hope has drawn the contrasts of his women with marvellous subtlety and delicacy.'—*Times.*

THE KING'S MIRROR. *Fourth Edition.*
'In elegance, delicacy, and tact it ranks with the best of his novels, while in the wide range of its portraiture and the subtilty of its analysis it surpasses all his earlier ventures.'—*Spectator.*

QUISANTE. *Third Edition.*
'The book is notable for a very high literary quality, and an impress of power and mastery on every page.'—*Daily Chronicle.*

W. W. Jacobs' Novels.
Crown 8vo. 3s. 6d. each.

MANY CARGOES. *Twenty-Sixth Edition.*
SEA URCHINS. *Ninth Edition.*
A MASTER OF CRAFT. Illustrated. *Fifth Edition.*
'Can be unreservedly recommended to all who have not lost their appetite for wholesome laughter.'—*Spectator.*
'The best humorous book published for many a day.'—*Black and White.*

LIGHT FREIGHTS. Illustrated. *Fourth Edition.*
'His wit and humour are perfectly irresistible. Mr. Jacobs writes of skippers, and mates, and seamen, and his crew are the jolliest lot that ever sailed.'—*Daily News.*
'Laughter in every page.'—*Daily Mail.*

FICTION 33

Lucas Malet's Novels.
Crown 8vo. 6s. each.

COLONEL ENDERBY'S WIFE. *Third Edition.*
A COUNSEL OF PERFECTION. *New Edition.*
LITTLE PETER. *Second Edition.* 3s. 6d.
THE WAGES OF SIN. *Thirteenth Edition.*
THE CARISSIMA. *Fourth Edition.*
THE GATELESS BARRIER. *Fourth Edition.*
'In "The Gateless Barrier" it is at once evident that, whilst Lucas Malet has preserved her birthright of originality, the artistry, the actual writing, is above even the high level of the books that were born before.'—*Westminster Gazette.*

THE HISTORY OF SIR RICHARD CALMADY. *Seventh Edition.* A Limited Edition in Two Volumes. *Crown 8vo.* 12s.
'A picture finely and amply conceived. In the strength and insight in which the story has been conceived, in the wealth of fancy and reflection bestowed upon its execution, and in the moving sincerity of its pathos throughout, "Sir Richard Calmady" must rank as the great novel of a great writer.'—*Literature.*
'The ripest fruit of Lucas Malet's genius. A picture of maternal love by turns tender and terrible.'—*Spectator.*
'A remarkably fine book, with a noble motive and a sound conclusion.'—*Pilot.*

Gilbert Parker's Novels.
Crown 8vo. 6s. each.

PIERRE AND HIS PEOPLE. *Fifth Edition.*
'Stories happily conceived and finely executed. There is strength and genius in Mr. Parker's style.'—*Daily Telegraph.*
MRS. FALCHION. *Fourth Edition.*
'A splendid study of character.'—*Athenæum.*
THE TRANSLATION OF A SAVAGE. *Second Edition.*
THE TRAIL OF THE SWORD. Illustrated. *Seventh Edition.*
'A rousing and dramatic tale. A book like this is a joy inexpressible.'—*Daily Chronicle.*
WHEN VALMOND CAME TO PONTIAC: The Story of a Lost Napoleon. *Fifth Edition.*
'Here we find romance—real, breathing, living romance. The character of Valmond is drawn unerringly.'—*Pall Mall Gazette.*

AN ADVENTURER OF THE NORTH: The Last Adventures of 'Pretty Pierre.' *Third Edition.*
'The present book is full of fine and moving stories of the great North.'—*Glasgow Herald.*
THE SEATS OF THE MIGHTY. Illustrated. *Twelfth Edition.*
'Mr. Parker has produced a really fine historical novel.'—*Athenæum.*
'A great book.'—*Black and White.*
THE BATTLE OF THE STRONG: a Romance of Two Kingdoms. Illustrated. *Fourth Edition.*
'Nothing more vigorous or more human has come from Mr. Gilbert Parker than this novel.'—*Literature.*
THE POMP OF THE LAVILETTES. *Second Edition.* 3s. 6d.
'Unforced pathos, and a deeper knowledge of human nature than he has displayed before.'—*Pall Mall Gazette.*

Arthur Morrison's Novels.
Crown 8vo. 6s. each.

TALES OF MEAN STREETS. *Fifth Edition.*
'A great book. The author's method is amazingly effective, and produces a thrilling sense of reality. The writer lays upon us a master hand. The book is simply appalling and irresistible in its interest. It is humorous also; without humour it would not make the mark it is certain to make.'—*World.*
A CHILD OF THE JAGO. *Fourth Edition.*
'The book is a masterpiece.'—*Pall Mall Gazette.*
TO LONDON TOWN. *Second Edition.*
'This is the new Mr. Arthur Morrison, gracious and tender, sympathetic and human.'—*Daily Telegraph.*

CUNNING MURRELL.
'Admirable. . . . Delightful humorous relief . . . a most artistic and satisfactory achievement.'—*Spectator.*
THE HOLE IN THE WALL. *Third Edition.*
'A masterpiece of artistic realism. It has a finality of touch that only a master may command.'—*Daily Chronicle.*
'An absolute masterpiece, which any novelist might be proud to claim.'—*Graphic.*
'"The Hole in the Wall" is a masterly piece of work. His characters are drawn with amazing skill. Extraordinary power.'—*Daily Telegraph.*

Eden Phillpotts' Novels.

Crown 8vo. 6s. each.

LYING PROPHETS.
CHILDREN OF THE MIST. *Fifth Edition.*
THE HUMAN BOY. With a Frontispiece. *Fourth Edition.*
 'Mr. Phillpotts knows exactly what school-boys do, and can lay bare their inmost thoughts; likewise he shows an all-pervading sense of humour.'—*Academy.*
SONS OF THE MORNING. *Second Edition.*
 'A book of strange power and fascination.'—*Morning Post.*
THE STRIKING HOURS. *Second Edition.*
 'Tragedy and comedy, pathos and humour, are blended to a nicety in this volume.'—*World.*
 'The whole book is redolent of a fresher and ampler air than breathes in the circumscribed life of great towns.'—*Spectator.*

FANCY FREE. Illustrated. *Second Edition.*
 'Of variety and racy humour there is plenty.'—*Daily Graphic.*

THE RIVER. *Third Edition.*
 '"The River" places Mr. Phillpotts in the front rank of living novelists.'—*Punch.*
 'Since "Lorna Doone" we have had nothing so picturesque as this new romance.' *Birmingham Gazette.*
 'Mr. Phillpotts's new book is a masterpiece which brings him indisputably into the front rank of English novelists.'—*Pall Mall Gazette.*
 'This great romance of the River Dart. The finest book Mr. Eden Phillpotts has written.'—*Morning Post.*

S. Baring-Gould's Novels.

Crown 8vo. 6s. each.

ARMINELL. *Fifth Edition.*
URITH. *Fifth Edition.*
IN THE ROAR OF THE SEA. *Seventh Edition.*
MRS. CURGENVEN OF CURGENVEN. *Fourth Edition.*
CHEAP JACK ZITA. *Fourth Edition.*
THE QUEEN OF LOVE. *Fifth Edition.*
MARGERY OF QUETHER. *Third Edition.*
JACQUETTA. *Third Edition.*
KITTY ALONE. *Fifth Edition.*
NOÉMI. Illustrated. *Fourth Edition.*

THE BROOM-SQUIRE. Illustrated. *Fourth Edition.*
THE PENNYCOMEQUICKS. *Third Edition.*
DARTMOOR IDYLLS.
GUAVAS THE TINNER. Illustrated. *Second Edition.*
BLADYS. Illustrated. *Second Edition.*
DOMITIA. Illustrated. *Second Edition.*
PABO THE PRIEST.
WINIFRED. Illustrated. *Second Edition.*
THE FROBISHERS.
ROYAL GEORGIE. Illustrated.
MISS QUILLET. Illustrated.

Robert Barr's Novels.

Crown 8vo. 6s. each.

IN THE MIDST OF ALARMS. *Third Edition.*
 'A book which has abundantly satisfied us by its capital humour.'—*Daily Chronicle.*
THE MUTABLE MANY. *Second Edition.*
 'There is much insight in it, and much excellent humour.'—*Daily Chronicle.*
THE COUNTESS TEKLA. *Third Edition.*
 'Of these mediæval romances, which are now gaining ground "The Countess Tekla" is the very best we have seen.'—*Pall Mall Gazette.*

THE STRONG ARM. Illustrated. *Second Edition.*

THE VICTORS.
 'Mr. Barr has a rich sense of humour.'—*Onlooker.*
 'A very convincing study of American life in its business and political aspects.'—*Pilot.*
 'Good writing, illuminating sketches of character, and constant variety of scene and incident.'—*Times.*

F. Anstey, Author of 'Vice Versa. A BAYARD FROM BENGAL. Illustrated by BERNARD PARTRIDGE. *Third Edition. Crown 8vo. 3s. 6d.*
 'A highly amusing story.'—
                    Pall Mall Gazette.
 'A volume of rollicking irresponsible fun.'—
                    Outlook.

 'This eminently mirthful narrative.'—
                    Globe.
 'Immensely diverting.'—*Glasgow Herald.*
Richard Bagot. A ROMAN MYSTERY. *Third Edition. Crown 8vo. 6s.*
 'An admirable story. The plot is sensational and original, and the book is full of telling situations.'—*St. James's Gazette.*

Andrew Balfour. BY STROKE OF SWORD. Illustrated. *Fourth Edition. Crown 8vo. 6s.*
'A recital of thrilling interest, told with unflagging vigour.'—*Globe.*
VENGEANCE IS MINE. Illustrated. *Crown 8vo. 6s.*
See also Fleur de Lis Novels.

M. C. Balfour. THE FALL OF THE SPARROW. *Crown 8vo. 6s.*

S. Baring Gould. See page 34.

Jane Barlow. THE LAND OF THE SHAMROCK. *Crown 8vo. 6s.*
FROM THE EAST UNTO THE WEST. *Crown 8vo. 6s.*
THE FOUNDING OF FORTUNES. *Crown 8vo. 6s.*
'This interesting and delightful book. Its author has done nothing better, and it is scarcely an exaggeration to say that it would be an injustice to Ireland not to read it.'—*Scotsman.*
See also Fleur de Lis Novels.

Robert Barr. See page 34.

J. A. Barry. IN THE GREAT DEEP. *Crown 8vo. 6s.*

George Bartram, Author of 'The People of Clopton.' THE THIRTEEN EVENINGS. *Crown 8vo. 6s.*

Harold Begbie. THE ADVENTURES OF SIR JOHN SPARROW. *Crown 8vo. 6s.*
'Mr. Begbie often recalls Stevenson's manner and makes "Sir John Sparrow" most diverting writing. Sir John is inspired with the idea that it is his duty to reform the world, and launches into the vortex of faddists. His experiences are traced with spacious and Rabelaisian humour. Every character has the salience of a type. Entertainingly and deftly written.'—
Daily Graphic.

E. F. Benson. DODO : A Detail of the Day. *Crown 8vo. 6s.*
THE CAPSINA. *Crown 8vo. 6s.*
See also Fleur de Lis Novels.

Margaret Benson. SUBJECT TO VANITY. *Crown 8vo. 3s. 6d.*

Sir Walter Besant. A FIVE YEARS' TRYST, and Other Stories. *Crown 8vo. 6s.*

J. Bloundelle Burton, Author of 'The Clash of Arms.' THE YEAR ONE : A Page of the French Revolution. Illustrated. *Crown 8vo. 6s.*
DENOUNCED. *Crown 8vo. 6s.*
THE CLASH OF ARMS. *Crown 8vo. 6s.*
ACROSS THE SALT SEAS. *Crown 8vo. 6s.*
SERVANTS OF SIN. *Crown 8vo. 6s.*
THE FATE OF VALSEC. *Crown 8vo. 6s.*
'The characters are admirably portrayed. The book not only arrests and sustains the attention, but conveys valuable information in the most pleasant guise.'—*Morning Post.*
See also Fleur de Lis Novels.

Ada Cambridge, THE DEVASTATORS. *Crown 8vo. 6s.*
PATH AND GOAL. *Crown 8vo. 6s.*

Bernard Capes, Author of 'The Lake of Wine.' PLOTS. *Crown 8vo. 6s.*
'The stories are excellently fanciful and concentrated and quite worthy of the author's best work.'—*Morning Leader.*

Weatherby Chesney. JOHN TOPP : PIRATE. *Second Edition. Crown 8vo. 6s.*
THE FOUNDERED GALLEON. *Crown 8vo. 6s.*
THE BRANDED PRINCE. *Crown 8vo. 6s.*
'Always highly interesting and surprising.'—*Daily Express.*
'An ingenious, cleverly-contrived story.'—
Outlook.

Mrs. W. K. Clifford. A WOMAN ALONE. *Crown 8vo. 3s. 6d.*
See also Fleur de Lis Novels.

J. Maclaren Cobban. THE KING OF ANDAMAN : A Saviour of Society. *Crown 8vo. 6s.*
WILT THOU HAVE THIS WOMAN? *Crown 8vo. 6s.*
THE ANGEL OF THE COVENANT. *Crown 8vo. 6s.*

E. H. Cooper, Author of 'Mr. Blake of Newmarket.' A FOOL'S YEAR. *Crown 8vo. 6s.*

Julian Corbett. A BUSINESS IN GREAT WATERS. *Crown 8vo. 6s.*

Marie Corelli. See page 31.

L. Cope Cornford. CAPTAIN JACOBUS : A Romance of the Road. *Cr. 8vo. 6s.*
See also Fleur de Lis Novels.

Stephen Crane. WOUNDS IN THE RAIN. *Crown 8vo. 6s.*

S. R. Crockett, Author of 'The Raiders,' etc. LOCHINVAR. Illustrated. *Second Edition. Crown 8vo. 6s.*
'Full of gallantry and pathos, of the clash of arms, and brightened by episodes of humour and love.'—*Westminster Gazette.*
THE STANDARD BEARER. *Cr. 8vo. 6s.*
'Mr. Crockett at his best.'—*Literature.*

B. M. Croker, Author of 'Peggy of the Bartons.' ANGEL. *Third Edition. Crown 8vo. 6s.*
'An excellent story. Clever pictures of Anglo-Indian life abound. The heroine is delightful.'—*Manchester Guardian.*
PEGGY OF THE BARTONS. *Crown 8vo. 6s.*
A STATE SECRET. *Crown 8vo. 3s. 6d.*

Hope Dawlish. A SECRETARY OF LEGATION. *Crown 8vo. 6s.*

C. E. Denny. THE ROMANCE OF UPFOLD MANOR. *Crown 8vo. 6s.*

Evelyn Dickinson. A VICAR'S WIFE. *Crown 8vo. 6s.*
THE SIN OF ANGELS. *Crown 8vo. 3s. 6d.*

Harris Dickson. THE BLACK WOLF'S BREED. Illustrated. *Second Edition. Crown 8vo. 6s.*

A. Conan Doyle, Author of 'Sherlock Holmes,' 'The White Company,' etc. ROUND THE RED LAMP. *Eighth Edition. Crown 8vo. 6s.*

'The book is far and away the best view that has been vouchsafed us behind the scenes of the consulting-room.'—*Illustrated London News.*

Sara Jeannette Duncan (Mrs. Everard Cotes), Author of 'A Voyage of Consolation.' THOSE DELIGHTFUL AMERICANS. Illustrated. *Third Edition. Crown 8vo. 6s.*

'A rattling picture of American life; bright and good-tempered throughout.'—*Scotsman.*

THE PATH OF A STAR. Illustrated. *Second Edition. Crown 8vo. 6s.*

See also Fleur de Lis Novels.

C. F. Embree. A HEART OF FLAME. *Crown 8vo. 6s.*

G. Manville Fenn. AN ELECTRIC SPARK. *Crown 8vo. 6s.*

ELI'S CHILDREN. *Crown 8vo. 2s. 6d.*

A DOUBLE KNOT. *Crown 8vo. 2s. 6d.*

See also Fleur de Lis Novels.

J. H. Findlater. THE GREEN GRAVES OF BALGOWRIE. *Fourth Edition. Crown 8vo. 6s.*

'A powerful and vivid story.'—*Standard.*

'A beautiful story, sad and strange as truth itself.'—*Vanity Fair.*

'A singularly original, clever, and beautiful story.'—*Guardian.*

A DAUGHTER OF STRIFE. *Crown 8vo. 6s.*

See also Fleur de Lis Novels.

Mary Findlater. OVER THE HILLS. *Second Edition. Crown 8vo. 6s.*

BETTY MUSGRAVE. *Second Edition. Crown 8vo. 6s.*

A NARROW WAY. *Third Edition. Crown 8vo. 6s.*

J. S. Fletcher. THE BUILDERS. *Crown 8vo. 6s.*

See also Fleur de Lis Novels.

M. E. Francis. MISS ERIN. *Second Edition. Crown 8vo. 6s.*

Tom Gallon, Author of 'Kiddy.' RICKERBY'S FOLLY. *Crown 8vo. 6s.*

Mary Gaunt. DEADMAN'S. *Crown 8vo. 6s.*

THE MOVING FINGER. *Crown 8vo. 3s. 6d.*

See also Fleur de Lis Novels.

Dorothea Gerard, Author of 'Lady Baby.' THE MILLION. *Crown 8vo. 6s.*

THE CONQUEST OF LONDON. *Second Edition. Crown 8vo. 6s.*

THE SUPREME CRIME. *Cr. 8vo. 6s.*

HOLY MATRIMONY. *Second Edition. Crown 8vo. 6s.*

'The love story which it enshrines is a

very pretty and tender one.'—*Morning Leader.*

'Distinctly interesting.'—*Athenæum.*

THINGS THAT HAVE HAPPENED. *Crown 8vo. 6s.*

R. Murray Gilchrist. WILLOWBRAKE. *Crown 8vo. 6s.*

Algernon Gissing. THE KEYS OF THE HOUSE. *Crown 8vo. 6s.*

George Gissing, Author of 'Demos,' 'In the Year of Jubilee,' etc. THE TOWN TRAVELLER. *Second Edition. Crown 8vo. 6s.*

THE CROWN OF LIFE. *Crown 8vo. 6s.*

Ernest Glanville. THE KLOOF BRIDE. *Crown 8vo. 3s. 6d.*

THE LOST REGIMENT. *Crown 8vo. 3s. 6d.*

THE DESPATCH RIDER. *Crown 8vo. 3s. 6d.*

THE INCA'S TREASURE. Illustrated. *Crown 8vo. 3s. 6d.*

'No lack of exciting incident.'—*Scotsman.*

'Most thrilling and exciting.'—*Glasgow Herald.*

Charles Gleig. BUNTER'S CRUISE. Illustrated. *Crown 8vo. 6s.*

Julien Gordon. MRS. CLYDE. *Crown 8vo. 6s.*

'A clever picture of many phases of feminine and American life.'—*Daily Express.*

'Full of vivacity, with many excruciatingly clever and entertaining scenes.'—*Pilot.*

S. Gordon. A HANDFUL OF EXOTICS. *Crown 8vo. 3s. 6d.*

C. F. Goss. THE REDEMPTION OF DAVID CORSON. *Third Edition. Crown 8vo. 6s.*

E. M'Queen Gray. ELSA. *Crown 8vo. 6s.*

MY STEWARDSHIP. *Crown 8vo. 2s. 6d.*

A. G. Hales. JAIR THE APOSTATE. Illustrated. *Crown 8vo. 6s.*

'An extraordinarily vivid story.'—*World.*

'Mr. Hales has a vivid pen, and the scenes are described with vigour and colour.'—*Morning Post.*

Lord Ernest Hamilton. MARY HAMILTON. *Third Edition. Crown 8vo. 6s.*

Mrs. Burton Harrison. A PRINCESS OF THE HILLS. Illustrated. *Crown 8vo. 6s.*

'Vigorous, swift, exciting.'—*Outlook.*

'A singularly pleasant story of the Tyrol.'—*Morning Post.*

Robert Hichens, Author of 'Flames,' etc. THE PROPHET OF BERKELEY SQUARE. *Second Edition. Crown 8vo. 6s.*

'One continuous sparkle. Mr. Hichens is witty, satirical, caustic, irresistibly humorous.'—*Birmingham Gazette.*

TONGUES OF CONSCIENCE. *Second Edition. Crown 8vo. 6s.*

FELIX. *Fourth Edition. Crown 8vo. 6s.*

'Firm in texture, sane, sincere, and

natural. "Felix" is a clever book, and in many respects a true one.'—*Daily Chronicle.*
'A really powerful book.'—
Morning Leader.
'The story is related with unflagging spirit.'—*World.*
'"Felix" will undoubtedly add to a considerable reputation.'—*Daily Mail.*
See also Fleur de Lis Novels.

John Oliver Hobbes, Author of 'Robert Orange.' THE SERIOUS WOOING. *Crown 8vo. 6s.*
'Mrs. Craigie is as brilliant as she ever has been; her characters are all illuminated with sparkling gems of description, and the conversation scintillates with an almost bewildering blaze.'—*Athenæum.*

Anthony Hope. See page 32.

I. Hooper. THE SINGER OF MARLY. *Crown 8vo. 6s.*

Violet Hunt. THE HUMAN INTEREST. *Crown 8vo. 6s.*

C. J. Cutcliffe Hyne, Author of 'Captain Kettle.' PRINCE RUPERT THE BUCCANEER. With 8 Illustrations. *Second Edition. Crown 8vo. 6s.*
MR. HORROCKS, PURSER. *Crown 8vo. 6s.*

W. W. Jacobs. See page 32.

Henry James, Author of 'What Maisie Knew.' THE SACRED FOUNT. *Crown 8vo. 6s.*
THE SOFT SIDE. *Second Edition. Crown 8vo. 6s.*

C. F. Keary. THE JOURNALIST. *Crown 8vo. 6s.*

Florence Finch Kelly. WITH HOOPS OF STEEL. *Crown 8vo. 6s.*

Hon. Emily Lawless. TRAITS AND CONFIDENCES. *Crown 8vo. 6s.*
WITH ESSEX IN IRELAND. *New Edition. Crown 8vo. 6s.*
See also Fleur de Lis Novels.

Harry Lawson, Author of 'When the Billy Boils.' CHILDREN OF THE BUSH. *Crown 8vo. 6s.*
'Full of human sympathy and the genuine flavour of a wild, untrammelled, unsophisticated life.'—*Morning Leader.*
'The author writes of the wild, picturesque life "out back," with all the affection of a native and the penetrating insight of long observation.'—*Daily Telegraph.*

E. Lynn Linton. THE TRUE HISTORY OF JOSHUA DAVIDSON, Christian and Communist. *Eleventh Edition. Crown 8vo. 1s.*

Norma Lorimer. MIRRY ANN. *Crown 8vo. 6s.*
JOSIAH'S WIFE. *Crown 8vo. 6s.*

Charles K. Lush. THE AUTOCRATS. *Crown 8vo. 6s.*

Edna Lyall. DERRICK VAUGHAN, NOVELIST. *42nd thousand. Crown 8vo. 3s. 6d.*

S. Macnaughtan. THE FORTUNE OF CHRISTINA MACNAB. *Second Edition. Crown 8vo. 6s.*

A. Macdonell. THE STORY OF TERESA. *Crown 8vo. 6s.*

Harold Macgrath. THE PUPPET CROWN. Illustrated. *Crown 8vo. 6s.*

Lucas Malet. See page 33.

Mrs. M. E. Mann. OLIVIA'S SUMMER. *Second Edition. Crown 8vo. 6s.*
'An exceptionally clever book, told with consummate artistry and reticence.'—*Daily Mail.*
'Full of shrewd insight and quiet humour.'—*Academy.*
'Wholly delightful; a very beautiful and refreshing tale.'—*Pall Mall Gazette.*
'The author touches nothing that she does not adorn, so delicate and firm is her hold.'—*Manchester Guardian.*
'A powerful story.'—*Times.*

Richard Marsh. BOTH SIDES OF THE VEIL. *Second Edition. Crown 8vo. 6s.*
THE SEEN AND THE UNSEEN. *Crown 8vo. 6s.*
MARVELS AND MYSTERIES. *Crown 8vo. 6s.*
THE TWICKENHAM PEERAGE. *Second Edition. Crown 8vo. 6s.*
'It is a long time since my Baronite read a novel of such entrancing interest as "The Twickenham Peerage." He recommends the gentle reader to get the book. In addition to its breathless interest, it is full of character and bubbling with fun.'—*Punch.*

A. E. W. Mason, Author of 'The Courtship of Morrice Buckler,' 'Miranda of the Balcony,' etc. CLEMENTINA. Illustrated. *Crown 8vo. 6s.*
'A romance of the most delicate ingenuity and humour . . . the very quintessence of romance.'—*Spectator.*

Helen Mathers, Author of 'Comin' thro' the Rye.' HONEY. *Fourth Edition. Crown 8vo. 6s.*
'Racy, pointed, and entertaining.'—*Vanity Fair.*
'Honey is a splendid girl.'—*Daily Express.*
'A vigorously written story, full of clever things, a piquant blend of sweet and sharp.'—*Daily Telegraph.*

L. T. Meade. DRIFT. *Crown 8vo. 6s.*

Bertram Mitford. THE SIGN OF THE SPIDER. Illustrated. *Fifth Edition. Crown 8vo. 3s. 6d.*

F. F. Montresor, Author of 'Into the Highways and Hedges.' THE ALIEN. *Second Edition. Crown 8vo. 6s.*
'Fresh, unconventional, and instinct with human sympathy.'—*Manchester Guardian.*
'Miss Montresor creates her tragedy out of passions and necessities elementarily human. Perfect art.'—*Spectator.*

Arthur Morrison. See page 33.

W. E. Norris. THE CREDIT OF THE COUNTY. Illustrated. *Second Edition. Crown 8vo. 6s.*
'A capital novel it is, deftly woven together of the comedy and tragedy of life ' *Yorkshire Post.*
'It is excellent—keen, graceful, diverting.' *—Times.*
THE EMBARRASSING ORPHAN. *Crown 8vo. 6s.*
HIS GRACE. *Third Edition. Crown 8vo. 6s.*
THE DESPOTIC LADY. *Crown 8vo. 6s.*
CLARISSA FURIOSA. *Crown 8vo. 6s.*
GILES INGILBY. *Illustrated. Second Edition. Crown 8vo. 6s.*
AN OCTAVE. *Second Edition. Crown 8vo. 6s.*
A DEPLORABLE AFFAIR. *Crown 8vo. 3s. 6d.*
JACK'S FATHER. *Crown 8vo. 2s. 6d.*
See also Fleur de Lis Novels.

Mrs. Oliphant. THE TWO MARYS. *Crown 8vo. 6s.*
THE LADY'S WALK. *Crown 8vo. 6s.*
THE PRODIGALS. *Crown 8vo. 3s. 6d.*
See also Fleur de Lis Novels.

Alfred Ollivant. OWD BOB, THE GREY DOG OF KENMUIR. *Sixth Edition. Crown 8vo. 6s.*
'Weird, thrilling, strikingly graphic.'—*Punch.*
'We admire this book . . . It is one to read with admiration and to praise with enthusiasm.'—*Bookman.*
'It is a fine, open-air, blood-stirring book, to be enjoyed by every man and woman to whom a dog is dear.'—*Literature.*

E. Phillips Oppenheim. MASTER OF MEN. *Second Edition. Crown 8vo. 6s.*

Gilbert Parker. See page 33.

James Blythe Patton. BIJLI, THE DANCER. *Crown 8vo. 6s.*

Max Pemberton. THE FOOTSTEPS OF A THRONE. *Illustrated. Second Edition. Crown 8vo. 6s.*
'A story of pure adventure, with a sensation on every page.'—*Daily Mail.*
I CROWN THEE KING. With Illustrations by Frank Dadd and A. Forrestier. *Crown 8vo. 6s.*
'A romance of high adventure, of love and war.'—*Daily News.*

Mrs. F. E. Penny. A FOREST OFFICER. *Crown 8vo. 6s.*

Eden Phillpotts. See page 34.

'**Q.**' Author of 'Dead Man's Rock.' THE WHITE WOLF. *Second Edition. Crown 8vo. 6s.*
Every story is an accomplished romance in its own way.'—*Scotsman.*
'The poet's vein, the breadth of vision, the touch of mysticism are plain in all.'—*Times.*

R. Orton Prowse. THE POISON OF ASPS. *Crown 8vo. 3s. 6d.*

Richard Pryce. TIME AND THE WOMAN. *Crown 8vo. 6s.*
THE QUIET MRS. FLEMING. *Crown 8vo. 3s. 6d.*

Walter Raymond. Author of 'Love and Quiet Life.' FORTUNE'S DARLING. *Crown 8vo. 6s.*

Edith Rickert. OUT OF THE CYPRESS SWAMP. *Crown 8vo. 6s.*

W. Pett Ridge. LOST PROPERTY. *Second Edition. Crown 8vo. 6s.*
'The story is an interesting and animated picture of the struggle for life in London, with a natural humour and tenderness of its own.'—*Scotsman.*
'A simple, delicate bit of work, which will give pleasure to many. Much study of the masses has made him, not mad, but strong, and—wonder of wonders—cheerful.' *—Times.*
A SON OF THE STATE. *Crown 8vo. 3s. 6d.*
SECRETARY TO BAYNE, M.P. *Crown 8vo. 6s.*

C. G. D. Roberts. THE HEART OF THE ANCIENT WOOD. *Crown 8vo. 3s. 6d.*

Mrs. M. H. Roberton. A GALLANT QUAKER. *Illustrated. Crown 8vo. 6s.*

W. Clark Russell. MY DANISH SWEETHEART. *Illustrated. Fourth Edition. Crown 8vo. 6s.*

Grace Rhys. THE WOOING OF SHEILA. *Second Edition. Crown 8vo. 6s.*
'A really fine book. A book that deserves to live. Sheila is the sweetest heroine who has lived in a novelist's pages for many a day. Every scene and every incident has the impress of truth. It is a masterly romance, and one that should be widely read and appreciated.'—*Morning Leader.*

W. Satchell. THE LAND OF THE LOST. *Crown 8vo. 6s.*

Marshall Saunders. ROSE A CHARLITTE. *Crown 8vo. 6s.*

W. C. Scully. THE WHITE HECATOMB. *Crown 8vo. 6s.*
BETWEEN SUN AND SAND. *Crown 8vo. 6s.*
A VENDETTA OF THE DESERT. *Crown 8vo. 3s. 6d.*

Adeline Sergeant. Author of 'The Story of a Penitent Soul.' A GREAT LADY. *Crown 8vo. 6s.*
THE MASTER OF BEECHWOOD. *Crown 8vo. 6s.*
BARBARA'S MONEY. *Second Edition. Crown 8vo. 6s.*
'Full of life and incident, and Barbara is a delightful heroine.'—*Daily Express.*
'An unusually entertaining story.'—*World.*

W. F. Shannon. THE MESS DECK. *Crown 8vo. 3s. 6d.*
JIM TWELVES. *Second Edition. Crown 8vo. 3s. 6d.*

'Full of quaint humour, wise saws, and deep-sea philosophy.'—*Morning Leader.*
'In "Jim Twelves" Mr. Shannon has created a delightful character.'—*Punch.*
'Bright and lively reading throughout.'—*Telegraph.*

Helen Shipton. THE STRONG GOD CIRCUMSTANCE. *Crown 8vo. 6s.*

R. N. Stephens. A GENTLEMAN PLAYER. *Crown 8vo. 6s.*
See also Fleur de Lis Novels.

E. H. Strain. ELMSLIE'S DRAG-NET. *Crown 8vo. 6s.*

Esmé Stuart. A WOMAN OF FORTY. *Crown 8vo. 3s. 6d.*
CHRISTALLA. *Crown 8vo. 6s.*

Duchess of Sutherland. ONE HOUR AND THE NEXT. *Third Edition. Crown 8vo. 6s.*

Annie Swan. LOVE GROWN COLD. *Second Edition. Crown 8vo. 5s.*

Benjamin Swift. SIREN CITY. *Crown 8vo. 6s.*
SORDON. *Crown 8vo. 6s.*

R. B. Townshend. LONE PINE : A Romance of Mexican Life. *Crown 8vo. 6s.*

Paul Waineman. A HEROINE FROM FINLAND. *Crown 8vo. 6s.*
'A lovely tale.'—*Manchester Guardian.*
'A vivid picture of pastoral life in a beautiful and too little known country.'
—*Pall Mall Gazette.*

Victor Waite. CROSS TRAILS. *Crown 8vo. 6s.*

H. B. Marriott Watson. THE SKIRTS OF HAPPY CHANCE. Illustrated. *Second Edition. Crown 8vo. 6s.*

H. G. Wells. THE STOLEN BACILLUS, and other Stories. *Second Edition. Crown 8vo. 3s. 6d.*
THE PLATTNER STORY AND OTHERS. *Second Edition. Crown 8vo. 3s. 6d.*

THE SEA LADY. *Crown 8vo. 6s.*
'A strange, fantastic tale, a really beautiful idyll.'—*Standard.*
'In literary charm, in inventiveness, in fun and humour, it is equal to the best of Mr. Wells' stories.'—*Daily News.*
'Highly successful farce and plenty of polished satire.'—*Daily Mail.*
TALES OF SPACE AND TIME. *Crown 8vo. 6s.*
WHEN THE SLEEPER WAKES. *Crown 8vo. 6s.*
THE INVISIBLE MAN. *Crown 8vo. 6s.*
LOVE AND MR. LEWISHAM. *Crown 8vo. 6s.*

Stanley Weyman, Author of 'A Gentleman of France.' UNDER THE RED ROBE. With Illustrations by R. C. WOODVILLE. *Seventeenth Edition. Crown 8vo. 6s.*
'Every one who reads books at all must read this thrilling romance, from the first page of which to the last the breathless reader is haled along. An inspiration of manliness and courage.'—*Daily Chronicle.*

Mrs. C. N. Williamson, Author of 'The Barnstormers.' PAPA. *Second Edition. Crown 8vo. 6s.*
'Full of startling adventures and sensational episodes.'—*Daily Graphic.*
THE ADVENTURE OF PRINCESS SLYVIA. *Crown 8vo. 3s. 6d.*

C. N. and A. M. Williamson. THE LIGHTNING CONDUCTOR : Being the Romance of a Motor Car. Illustrated. *Crown 8vo. 6s.*
'A very ingenious and diverting book.'—*Morning Leader.*

Zack, Author of 'Life is Life.' TALES OF DUNSTABLE WEIR. *Crown 8vo. 6s.*

X.L. AUT DIABOLUS AUT NIHIL. *Crown 8vo. 3s. 6d.*

The Fleur de Lis Novels
Crown 8vo. 3s. 6d.

MESSRS. METHUEN are now publishing a cheaper issue of some of their popular Novels in a new and most charming style of binding.

Andrew Balfour.
TO ARMS!

Jane Barlow.
A CREEL OF IRISH STORIES.

E. F. Benson.
THE VINTAGE.

J. Bloundelle-Burton.
IN THE DAY OF ADVERSITY.

Mrs. Caffyn (Iota).
ANNE MAULEVERER.

Mrs. W. K. Clifford.
A FLASH OF SUMMER.

L. Cope Cornford.
SONS OF ADVERSITY

A. J. Dawson.
DANIEL WHYTE.

Menie Muriel Dowie.
THE CROOK OF THE BOUGH.

Mrs. Dudeney.
THE THIRD FLOOR.

Sara Jeannette Duncan.
A VOYAGE OF CONSOLATION.

G. Manville Fenn.
THE STAR GAZERS.

Jane H. Findlater.
RACHEL.

Jane H. and Mary Findlater.
TALES THAT ARE TOLD.

J. S. Fletcher.
THE PATHS OF THE PRUDENT.

Mary Gaunt.
KIRKHAM'S FIND.

Robert Hichens.
BYEWAYS.

Emily Lawless.
HURRISH.
MAELCHO.

W. E. Norris.
MATTHEW AUSTIN.

Mrs. Oliphant.
SIR ROBERT'S FORTUNE.

Mary A. Owen.
THE DAUGHTER OF ALOUETTE.

Mary L. Pendered.
AN ENGLISHMAN.

Morley Roberts.
THE PLUNDERERS.

R. N. Stephens.
AN ENEMY TO THE KING.

Mrs. Walford.
SUCCESSORS TO THE TITLE.

Percy White.
A PASSIONATE PILGRIM.

Books for Boys and Girls
Crown 8vo.   3s. 6d.

THE ICELANDER'S SWORD. By S. Baring-Gould.
TWO LITTLE CHILDREN AND CHING. By Edith E. Cuthell.
TODDLEBEN'S HERO. By M. M. Blake.
ONLY A GUARD-ROOM DOG. By Edith E. Cuthell.
THE DOCTOR OF THE JULIET. By Harry Colling-wood.
MASTER ROCKAFELLAR'S VOYAGE. By W. Clark Russell.

SYD BELTON : Or, the Boy who would not go to Sea. By G. Manville Fenn.
THE RED GRANGE. By Mrs. Molesworth.
THE SECRET OF MADAME DE MONLUC. By the Author of 'Mdle. Mori.'
DUMPS. By Mrs. Parr.
A GIRL OF THE PEOPLE. By L. T. Meade.
HEPSY GIPSY. By L. T. Meade. 2s. 6d.
THE HONOURABLE MISS. By L. T. Meade.

The Novelist

MESSRS. METHUEN are issuing under the above general title a Monthly Series of Novels by popular authors at the price of Sixpence. Each number is as long as the average Six Shilling Novel. The first numbers of 'THE NOVELIST' are as follows :—

I. DEAD MEN TELL NO TALES. By E. W. Hornung.
II. JENNIE BAXTER, JOURNALIST. By Robert Barr.
III. THE INCA'S TREASURE. By Ernest Glanville.
IV. A SON OF THE STATE. By W. Pett Ridge.
V. FURZE BLOOM. By S. Baring-Gould.
VI. BUNTER'S CRUISE. By C. Gleig.
VII. THE GAY DECEIVERS. By Arthur Moore.
VIII. PRISONERS OF WAR. By A. Boyson Weekes.
IX. Out of print.
X. VELDT AND LAAGER : Tales of the Transvaal. By E. S. Valentine.
XI. THE NIGGER KNIGHTS. By F. Norreys Connel.
XII. A MARRIAGE AT SEA. By W. Clark Russell.
XIII. THE POMP OF THE LAVILETTES. By Gilbert Parker.
XIV. A MAN OF MARK. By Anthony Hope.
XV. THE CARISSIMA. By Lucas Malet.
XVI. THE LADY'S WALK. By Mrs. Oliphant.
XVII. DERRICK VAUGHAN. By Edna Lyall.
XVIII. IN THE MIDST OF ALARMS. By Robert Barr.

XIX. HIS GRACE. By W. E. Norris.
XX. DODO. By E. F. Benson.
XXI. CHEAP JACK ZITA. By S. Baring-Gould.
XXII. WHEN VALMOND CAME TO PONTIAC. By Gilbert Parker.
XXIII. THE HUMAN BOY. By Eden Phillpotts.
XXIV. THE CHRONICLES OF COUNT ANTONIO. By Anthony Hope.
XXV. BY STROKE OF SWORD. By Andrew Balfour.
XXVI. KITTY ALONE. By S. Baring-Gould.
XXVII. GILES INGILBY. By W. E. Norris.
XXVIII. URITH. By S. Baring-Gould.
XXIX. THE TOWN TRAVELLER. By George Gissing.
XXX. MR. SMITH. By Mrs. Walford.
XXXI. A CHANGE OF AIR. By Anthony Hope.
XXXII. THE KLOOF BRIDE. By Ernest Glanville.
XXXIII. ANGEL. By B. M. Croker.
XXXIV. A COUNSEL OF PERFECTION. By Lucas Malet.
XXXV. THE BABY'S GRANDMOTHER. By Mrs. L. B. Walford.
XXXVI. THE COUNTESS TEKLA. By Robert Barr.

Methuen's Sixpenny Library

THE MATABELE CAMPAIGN. By Major-General Baden-Powell.
THE DOWNFALL OF PREMPEH. By Major-General Baden-Powell.
MY DANISH SWEETHEART. By W. Clark Russell.
IN THE ROAR OF THE SEA. By S. Baring-Gould.
PEGGY OF THE BARTONS. By B. M. Croker.
THE GREEN GRAVES OF BALGOWRIE. By Jane H. Findlater.
THE STOLEN BACILLUS. By H. G. Wells.
MATTHEW AUSTIN. By W. E. Norris.
THE CONQUEST OF LONDON. By Dorothea Gerard.
A VOYAGE OF CONSOLATION. By Sara J. Duncan.
THE MUTABLE MANY. By Robert Barr.
BEN HUR. By General Lew Wallace.
SIR ROBERT'S FORTUNE. By Mrs. Oliphant.

THE FAIR GOD. By General Lew Wallace.
CLARISSA FURIOSA. By W. E. Norris.
CRANFORD. By Mrs. Gaskell.
NOEMI. By S. Baring-Gould.
THE THRONE OF DAVID. By J. H. Ingraham.
ACROSS THE SALT SEAS. By J. Bloundelle Burton.
THE MILL ON THE FLOSS. By George Eliot.
PETER SIMPLE. By Captain Marryat.
MARY BARTON. By Mrs. Gaskell.
PRIDE AND PREJUDICE. By Jane Austen.
NORTH AND SOUTH. By Mrs. Gaskell.
JACOB FAITHFUL. By Captain Marryat.
SHIRLEY. By Charlotte Bronte.
FAIRY TALES RE-TOLD. By S. Baring Gould.
THE TRUE HISTORY OF JOSHUA DAVIDSON. By Mrs. Lynn Linton.

Printed in Great Britain by
Amazon.co.uk, Ltd.,
Marston Gate.